# ANTI-ISRAELISM

# ANTI-ISRAELISM

## The New Face of Antisemitism

John D. Garr, Ph.D.

*Anti-Israelism: The New Face of Antisemitism*


Published by Golden Key Press
P.O. Box 421218, Atlanta, GA 30342
www.GoldenKeyPress.org



Design and typeset: Resolute Creative, Inc., Houston, TX
Printed in the United States of America

Unless otherwise indicated, Scripture quotations are from the New American Standard Bible.

ISBN: 978-1-940685-35-9

1. Antisemitism. 2. The Nation of Israel. 3. The Land of Israel. 4. Christian-Jewish Relations. 5. Covenants. 6. Antisemitism. 7. Zionism. I. Garr, John D. II. Anti-Judaism

Library of Congress Control Number: 2018900159
BT93–93.6 2017
Religion, Christianity, Judaism, History, Relations

# DEFINITIONS AND ABBREVIATIONS

## WORD DEFINITIONS:

Definitions of English words are derived from www.Dictionary.com. Definitions of words in other languages are taken from either www.Dictionary.com. or www.WordReference.com.

## HEBREW WORD DEFINITIONS:

Unless otherwise noted, all Hebrew word definitions are from one of the following: Wilhelm Gesenius, *Hebrew and Chaldee Lexicon of the Old Testament* (Andover, MA: Flagg and Gould, 1824); Francis Brown, S.R. Driver, and Charles A. Briggs, *Hebrew and English Lexicon* (Peabody, MA: Hendrickson Publishers, 1996); Ludwig Koehler, Walter Baumgartner, and Johann Jakob Stramm, *Hebrew and Aramaic Lexicon of the Old Testament*, tr. M.E.J. Richardson (Leiden: Brill Academic, 1994); William Lee Holladay, *Hebrew and Aramaic Lexicon of the Old Testament* (Leiden, E.J. Brill, 1988); or R. Laird Harris, Gleason L. Archer, Jr., and Bruce K. Waltke, eds., *Theological Wordbook of the Old Testament* (Chicago: Moody Press, 1980).

## GREEK WORD DEFINITIONS:

Unless otherwise noted, all Greek word definitions are from one of the following: Timothy Friberg, Barbara Friberg, and Neva Miller, *Analytical Lexicon of the Greek New Testament* (Grand Rapids, MI: Baker Books, 2000); Barclay M. Newman, *Greek-English Dictionary* (Reading, UK: United Bible Societies, 2006); Walter Bauer and Fredrick William Danker, *Greek-English Lexicon of the New Testament and Other Early Christian Literature* (Chicago: The University of Chicago Press, 2001); H. G. Lidell and Robert Scott, *Abridged Greek-English Lexicon* (New York: Oxford University Press, 1935); Joseph Thayer, *Thayer's Greek-English Lexicon of the New Testament* (Peabody, MA: Hendrickson Publishers, 1996); or Johan Lust, Erik Eynikel, and Katrin Hauspie, *A Greek-English Lexicon of the Septuagint* (Peabody, MA: Hendrickson Publishers, 2008).

## SCRIPTURE VERSIONS:

Unless otherwise noted, quotations of Scripture are taken from the New American Standard Bible (1995).

## SCRIPTURE VERSION ABBREVIATIONS:

ABPE: Aramaic Bible in Plain English (2007)
AJWS: American Jewish World Service (2010)
BBE: The Bible in Basic English (1964)
CEB: Common English Bible (2011)
CEV: Contemporary English Version (1991)
CJB: Complete Jewish Bible (1998)
DBT: Darby Bible Translation (1890)
DRB: Douay-Rheims Bible (1899)
ERV: English Revised Version (1894)
ESV: English Standard Version (2007)
HCSB: Holman Christian Standard Bible (2004)
ISV: International Standard Version (1998)
JPS: Jewish Publication Society Version (1917)
KJV: Authorized King James Version (1611)
NIV: New International Version (1984)
NASB: New American Standard Bible (1995)
NAU: New American Standard Version (Updated) (1995)
NJB: New Jerusalem Bible (1985)
NET: New English Translation Bible (2005)
NHEB: New Heart English Bible (2010)
NKJV: New King James Version (1982)
NLT: New Living Translation (1996)
nRSV: New Revised Standard Version (1989)
TNK: Tanakh, JPS Tanakh (1985)
WBT: Webster's Bible Translation (1833)
WEB: World English Bible (1901)
WNT: Weymouth New Testament (1903)

*In memory of the countless Jews who, for more than three millennia, have been plundered, dispossessed, enslaved, terrorized, and killed simply for being Jewish—especially the six million (including one million children) who were systematically murdered during the Holocaust.*

# Contents

# INTRODUCTION

For well over two thousand years now, antisemitism[1] has been perhaps the greatest scourge of humanity. Rooted in the darkest impulses of the human soul, the hatred of the Jews has corroded the moral fiber of nation after nation across vast stretches of the world landscape. For the past millennium, it has focused itself primarily in Europe; however, it has also infected and infested many other societies as well. With the concerted efforts that the postmodern world has made toward globalism in the last century, the old antisemitism that was localized in godless and secularist societies and in the larger Muslim world has seeped into the consciousness of individuals and communities around the globe.

Antisemitism is diabolical, a pure and utterly irrational evil for which there is seemingly no cure. It singles out one small people group among the billions of people on the Planet Earth for morbid hatred and violent abuse. It is also one of the most subtle and diabolical manifestations of human hatred, eclipsing all other forms of xenophobia and prejudice by light years. Through the centuries, antisemites have always crawled from under their rocks, bared their fangs, and spewed their venom in the air, poisoning everyone and everything around them. Their deceptive disguises have lured others into their lair, where they have been filled with this sociopathic hatred[2] that radicalizes a deep-seated need for prejudice.[3]

[1] Since the Holocaust, many scholars have suggested the replacement of the nineteenth-century form *anti-Semitism* with a more modern form *antisemitism*. Jewish philosopher and Holocaust scholar Emil Fackenheim has argued that "the spelling ought to be antisemitism without the hyphen, dispelling the notion that there is an entity 'Semitism' which 'anti-Semitism' opposes." Emil L. Fackenheim, "Post-Holocaust Anti-Jewishness, Jewish Identity and the Centrality of Israel," in *World Jewry and the State of Israel*, Moshe Davis, ed. (New York: Arno Press, 1976), p. 11, n. 2. In this volume, we have chosen to use Fackenheim's convention for spelling and capitalization of the term *antisemitism* for the reasons he himself stated.

[2] Theodore Isaac Rubin, *Anti-Semitism: A Disease of the Mind* (New York: Skyhorse Publishing, Inc. 2009), p. 130. Also Phillip L. Hammack, *Narrative and the Politics of Identity: The Cultural Psychology of Israeli and Palestinian Youth* (Oxford, UK: Oxford University Press, 2011), p. 255, and Todd D. Nelson, *Handbook of Prejudice, Stereotyping, and Discrimination* (New York: Psychology Press, 2009), p. 33.

[3] Steven J. Bartlett, *The Pathology of Man: A Study of Human Evil* (Springfield, IL: Charles C. Thomas Publisher, 2005), p. 166ff.

The major problem with antisemitism, however, is that it never seems to remain static but is constantly shifting in appearance, message, and application. It is particularly insidious because of its ability to morph, seemingly at will, into new forms and new manifestations. Even a less-than-reasonable person would have thought that the horrific Holocaust, in which six million Jews from many nations were systematically murdered solely because they were Jews, would have ended antisemitism forever. Surely this tragedy would have inoculated humanity against any recurrence of such a horrendous pathology. Tragically, antisemitism appears to be an incurable disease.[4]

Unfortunately, even after the modernist dream that the evolution of the human species would inevitably bring the human race to a secular utopia was utterly shattered by the horrors of the Holocaust, world war, and nuclear weapons, still the "enlightened" nations of the world have remained gullible and vulnerable to repackaged, even glamorized postmodern manifestations of antisemitism. Prophylaxes should have been formulated and employed to guard against possible mutations or new manifestations of the old antisemitism that had forever scarred the face of the civilized world. Regrettably, that has not been the case, for new, subtle, more virulent, and more universal forms of antisemitism are now spreading like a pandemic all across Planet Earth. Virtually the entire world now engages in some form of antisemitism, and much of the world celebrates its antisemitism with impunity.

In a manner similar to the classic Hans Christian Andersen story, "The Emperor's New Clothes," historical antisemitism—embodied and personified in Adolph Hitler, the Führer of the German Third Reich—has clothed itself in new garments of anti-Israelism which have been widely praised throughout the world. However, even a simple child can see right through the royal garments and see the naked truth: antisemitism personified in all its despicable depravity not only lives but also thrives in the postmodern world, attacking Jews with impunity by delegitimizing their rights to peoplehood, nationhood, and land and, in the process, assigning the Jewish people around the world to

---

[4] Moshe L. Lilienblum, "Antisemitism as an Incurable European Disease," in *Glorious, Accursed Europe: An Essay on Jewish Ambivalence*, Jehuda Reinharz and Yaacov Shavit, eds. (Waltham, MA: Brandeis University Press, 2010), p. 86. Also, Marsha L. Rozenblit, "European Jewry: 1800–1933," in *The Cambridge Guide to Jewish History, Religion, and Culture*, Judith R. Baskin and Kenneth Seeskin, eds. (Cambridge, UK: Cambridge University Press, 2010), p. 192. Rozenblit notes Leo Pinsker's 1882 pamphlet, *Autoemancipation (Selbstemanzipation)*, in which he "declared antisemitism an incurable disease, dismissed any hopes for Jewish assimilation and integration in Europe, and called for a Jewish state to solve the problem of Jewish homelessness."

subhuman status. The nations unite to proclaim that the Jews have no right to exist as Jews with complete sovereignty and self-determination.

## The Erosion and Perversion of Memory

Human memory is a delicate thing, easily eroded and corrupted. With much brainwashing, it can even be rewritten. The greatest tragedy of the post-Holocaust era has been the erosion—and, in some cases, the perversion—of its memory from the corporate consciousness of the human race. Sadly, the horrors of history have been gradually receding from human memory. More and more people are either willfully or negligently forgetting what happened when antisemitism was taken to its "logical" conclusion in Nazi Germany. There, the impossible became possible when a small contingent of criminally insane sociopaths enlisted either the active participation or the benign neglect of one of the world's most enlightened societies to support its "Final Solution" to the Jewish problem—the systematic murder of six million Jews, including over one million children.

Clark Freshman makes this sad but very true observation about one of the major reasons for the receding memory of the Holocaust and the consequent diminishing of the denunciation of the evils of antisemitism in much of the world: "Anti-Semitism has faded from our consciousness, in part because theorists began to view anti-Semitism as part of a larger phenomenon of prejudice."[5] Many scholars argue that the Holocaust is just one of many examples—and perhaps not even the worst—in the history of human prejudice and depravity.[6] Making such comparisons, however, diminishes the Holocaust and robs it of its uniqueness, making it all the more easy to let its memory recede into the past. In reality, no event in human history—no civil war, no ethnic cleansing, no slaughter of political rivals—approaches the Holocaust or can even be compared with it. Any attempt to transform the Holocaust into just another atrocity is a "desecration, an obscenity."[7] Martin

[5] Clark Freshman, "Whatever Happened to Anti-Semitism? How Social Science Theories Identify Discrimination and Promote Coalitions between Different Minorities," *Cornell Law Review* 85, pp. 313–442.

[6] Such theorists deny the uniqueness of the Holocaust by comparing it with political purges like those perpetrated by tyrants against their own citizens as with Stalin, who was responsible for the murder of more than 20 million in the Soviet Union, and Pol Pot, who decimated the intellectual community of Cambodia and presided over the death of some 3 million of his citizens. They also compare the Holocaust with ethnic cleansing programs like that of the Ottoman Turks' attempted genocide against the Armenians in which 1.5 million people were murdered or the Rwandan civil war between the Tutsi and Hutu tribes in 1994 in which hundreds of thousands were slaughtered.

[7] Gabriel Motzkin, "The Memory of Crime and the Formation of Identity," in *The Lesser Evil: Moral Approaches to Genocide Practices (Totalitarianism Movements and Political Religions)*, Helmut Dubiel and Gabriel Motzkin, eds. (Abingdon, UK: Routledge, 2004), p. 207.

Norden says, "The Holocaust is paradoxical since no level of technical artifice could adequately portray the evil of the event."[8]

Sadly, says John Roth, "at the beginning of the twenty-first century, nagging doubts remain about the future of Holocaust memories. Those doubts, which include concerns that 'Holocaust fatigue' may diminish interest in the event, shadow the sense that either new discoveries about the Holocaust's history or ongoing efforts to institutionalize Holocaust memory are themselves sufficient to withstand the corrosive effects of time's passage."[9] The effects of memory loss, compounded by the intentional efforts of the Muslim world and the postmodern nihilist West, are conspiring to be a focal point of the new antisemitism of Holocaust denial. The living witnesses to history's greatest atrocity—those who experienced it firsthand and those who were appalled with the horrific sights they saw when they discovered it—have slowly, but surely, disappeared from the scene of action. Despite heroic efforts to preserve the personal memories and the gripping testimonies of Holocaust survivors for posterity,[10] the vivid, conscience-jarring images grow more dim with each passing generation. At the same time, antisemitism has taken on new, even glitzy manifestations.

George Santayana's adage that "those who cannot remember the past are condemned to repeat it"[11] should challenge all humanity—and, in particular, all Christians—to stand in resolute solidarity with the international Jewish community and the nation of Israel in making the declaration, "Never again!" And the way to guard against a recurrence of the Holocaust is to identify and challenge the thinking, situations, and circumstances that unlock and open the gates of hell, which lead inexorably to the abyss of human depravity. Once the gates are ajar and societies start down that flagitious path, it is

[8] Carol Celli, "Comedy and the Holocaust in Roberto Benigni's *Life Is Beautiful / la vita è bella*," in *The Changing Face of Evil in Film and Television: At the Interface, Probing the Boundaries*, Martin F. Norden, ed. (Amsterdam, The Netherlands: Rodopi B. V., 2007), p. 156.

[9] John K. Roth, *Holocaust Politics* (Eugene, OR: Wipf and Stock Publishers, 2001), p. 128.

[10] The Steven Spielberg Film and Video Archive at the US Holocaust Memorial Museum has featured a monumental effort toward archiving and preserving Jewish documentary files and other resources designed to document for future generations eyewitness testimony to the events of the Holocaust. Perhaps Spielberg's greatest personal contribution to Holocaust remembrance has been the effort which he has organized and led and funded to videotape personal accounts by Holocaust survivors of the ordeals they suffered during the Nazi effort to eradicate all the Jews of Germany and the rest of Europe. Spielberg's laudable effort has captured and preserved on video some 10,000 personal accounts of Holocaust survivors, recollections of their own abuse at the hands of the Nazi regime.

[11] George Santayana, *Reason in Common Sense: The Life of Reason Volume 1* (Mineola, NY: Dover Press, 1980), p. 284.

virtually impossible for them to claw their way back up the slippery slope that draws them ever downward toward oblivion.

## Awakening the Sleeping Kingdom of God: A Midnight Cry

In the decades that immediately succeeded the Holocaust, scholars from a wide range of disciplines in various institutions, especially the Christian church, became very active in Holocaust studies. As a matter of fact, for a time, Holocaust studies were very much in vogue. Years ago, my longtime friend and colleague of blessed memory, Rev. Isaac Rottenberg, in an essay entitled, "They Just Don't Get It!"[12], described an invitation that he received to a "Scholars Conference on the Holocaust" which billed its theme as "Confronting the Holocaust: A Mandate for the 21st Century." In his own inimitable way, Rottenberg, confessing his exasperation, remarked, "A mandate indeed!—A divine mandate to be sure, and one of immediate urgency."[13] Then, drawing on his vast experience in Christian–Jewish dialogue, he observed sardonically, "The tongue-in-cheek character in John Updike's novel *Roger's Version*, who is head of the department of 'holocaustics' at the local university, is alive and well at such gatherings."[14] In spite of this utterly accurate description of the motives of many, however, Rottenberg was still able to exult: "But so—thanks be to God!—are the scholars whose conscientious and sometimes soul-tearing research has finally confronted the church with long-suppressed truths."[15]

For Isaac then, as well as for me now, the great tragedy for most of the Christian church is that "they still just don't get it," and primarily so because "the Holocaust is isolated from Christian history."[16] Most Christians think that there has never been such thing as "Christian antisemitism." For them, antisemitism and the Holocaust were something that "they"—people who were not Christians—did. In fact, however, for the past thousand years or more, the most antisemitic actions have had at the very least a Christian root! Most stereotypes and caricatures of Jews have originated in Christian minds or have been extrapolated from comments of pagans. Most acts of intimidation and violence against Jewish men, women, and children have been perpetrated by people who were, at the bare minimum, nominal Christians. In the corporate consciousness of the

[12] Isaac C. Rottenberg, "They Just Don't Get It," *Restore!*, Issue 10, pp. 16–18.

[13] Rottenberg, p. 16.

[14] Rottenberg, p. 16.

[15] Rottenberg, p. 16.

[16] Rottenberg, p. 17.

Jewish community, therefore, though antisemitism is presently a Western secularist and a Muslim problem, it has long been a Christian problem.[17] And the fight against antisemitism "is not a Jewish problem, it is the problem of all men of good will, and it is above all a Christian problem."[18]

## A Summons to Remembrance

During the more than four decades in which I have been involved in Christian-Jewish relations and in researching, writing, and teaching fundamental truths about the Jewish roots of the Christian faith, I have observed a gradual erosion of memory of the Holocaust both in Western society and in the Christian church. Accompanying this loss of memory, a diabolical effort toward redefining historical antisemitism has possessed liberalism, Islamism, global politics, and the secular media in such as way as to clothe it in new politically and socially acceptable—even laudable—garments.

This volume is a summons for Christians to return to the altar of repentance, restoration, and renewal that was opened for the church and the world when the Holocaust confronted humanity in vivid, unmistakable terms with the vile and vicious nature of the human heart that either rejects God or chooses to ignore him and his Word. Christians have a lot to remember and a lot for which to repent. It is also a summons to the world's secular societies to return to the high ideals that once were promised by Enlightenment thinkers wherein all people could live in peace and tranquility without the threat of violence against their persons because of their race, ethnicity, or religion.

Each Christian needs to assume the mindset of the prophet Daniel who prayed this prayer of repentance: "O Lord, we and our kings, our princes and our fathers are covered with shame because we have sinned against you."[19] In order to confess and repent, however, one has to remember. And memory is a real problem for most Christians when it comes to the Jewish people. For some, the Holocaust is a fading memory. For others, it has already been replaced by the vivid images of post-modern nihilist-created Israeli "crimes against humanity" that have come to dominate the very limited space that they have in their memories for unconscionable acts of human depravity.

My primary reason for writing this book is to help Christians remember by presenting the facts of history and of the present that expose the unrelenting antisemitism that has plagued Christianity for centuries and

[17] Stuart E. Rosenberg, *The Christian Problem: A Jewish View* (New York: Hippocrene Books, 1986).

[18] John Mann, *Antisemitism: The Oldest Hatred* (London, UK: Bloomsbury Publishing, 2015), p. 82.

[19] Daniel 9:8.

has consumed most of the world during this time. My second reason for publishing this volume is to shed light on the subtle, even diabolical, way in which antisemitism has morphed into politically correct and socially acceptable forms that make it possible for people of diverse backgrounds to feel that they can engage with impunity in attacks on the prime collective of the Jewish people today, the nation of Israel. This "new, improved" antisemitism is anti-Israelism (a.k.a. anti-Zionism), which often masquerades as a critique of the policies of the nation of Israel but, in reality, is raw, naked antisemitism, plain and simple. The term *anti-Israelism* "does not refer to merely criticizing Israel; almost every Israeli citizen does this on a daily basis," says David Brog.[20]

One cannot escape involvement in the twenty-first century incarnation of antisemitism if one is willingly or even innocently ignorant. Christians must now understand precisely what antisemitism is, how it has been manifest in history, and how it is revealed in today's world. Having observed what was at first a gradual erosion of Christian support for the international Jewish community and the nation of Israel and what is now a rapidly expanding disregard for the well-being of Jews and their ancestral land, I have come to the conclusion that alarm bells need to be sounded to awaken the sleeping and intoxicated Christian world that has either adopted covert, seemingly benign neglect for Christian responsibilities toward the Jewish people or has embraced overt and malignant positions toward Israel and Jews in general. Once and for all, this must stop.

This book, then, is a call to remembrance of the stark images of human depravity displayed in the butchery of the Nazi killing machine. It is a call to remembrance of the silent complicity of those nations and people who chose to ignore history's most heinous crime even as it was unfolding before their very eyes. It is also a call to remembrance of what could have been prevented if societies around the world had been aware of the antisemitism that had either been overtly demonstrated or had simply lain dormant in the hearts of individuals and communities for centuries, just waiting for a sequence of events to trigger its eruption into hatred, violence, and mass murder.

The church of Jesus must forever cease from fighting against the family of Jesus. When Christians fail to stand in solidarity with the Jewish family

[20] David Brog, "The End of Evangelical Support for Israel?" *The Middle East Quarterly,* Vol. 21: No. 2, Spring 2014, posted at http://www.meforum.org/3769/israel-evangelical-support. One can be a critic of policies of the Israeli government without being anti-Zionist. If one is an anti-Zionist, however, he is, *ipso facto*, an antisemite, for denying the Jewish people the right to political self-determination in their ancestral homeland is the essence of Jew hatred.

of Jesus the Jew, they miss the point of their calling. When Christians fail to support the rights of the Jewish people to self-determination, including living in peace and safety in their own nation, they violate the second most important divine instruction in Scripture: "Love your neighbor as yourself." Like Christians in every realm, the Jewish people in their own land have the right of freedom from coercion of every sort, whether it be social, economic, political, or religious.

## Appreciation

I wish to express my thanks to a number of friends, colleagues, and advisers who have shared insights with me and have inspired me with their wisdom. Foremost among these are Dr. Marvin R. Wilson, Dwight A. Pryor (of blessed memory), Rev. Isaac Rottenberg (of blessed memory), Dr. Karl D. Coke, Dr. DeWayne Coxon, Dr. Richard Booker, Dr. Brad H. Young, and Dr. Jacques B. Doukhan. I wish to thank my Hebraic Heritage Christian College colleague Dr. Robert Bleakney for his careful critique of the manuscript of this book. I am also grateful for review and feedback from Dr. Victoria Sarvadi, Judy Grehan, and Kate Miller, not to speak of a number of others who have critiqued the manuscript. Finally, I am grateful for the questions, comments, and suggestions that I continually receive from friends around the world as together we explore ways in which we can stand against Judaeophobia, anti-Judaism, and antisemitism and as we seek to lend loving support to the international Jewish community and the nation of Israel in what continues to be dangerous times.

## A New Day

The encouraging news is that significant things are happening in the advancement of Christian–Jewish relations and in increasing the potential for helping Christians thereby to avoid being beguiled by the subtlety of anti-Jewish, anti-Israelist rhetoric. A transdenominational, multiethnic effort is advancing a cause that has been long overdue. A solid core of balanced scholarship is establishing, expanding, and implementing foundational insight into this work that we hope will produce short- and long-term benefits.

May the Almighty give us all grace that we may understand the truth that will liberate us and empower us to be instruments of his eternal *shalom* in a world of increasing prejudice, hatred, and violence.

John D. Garr, Ph.D.
*Purim*, 2018

CHAPTER 1

# WHAT IS ANTISEMITISM?

## DEFINING HISTORY'S MOST VILE HATRED

Antisemitism specifically means hatred of, hostility toward, or discrimination against Jews as a religious or ethnic group.[1] The *Cambridge English Dictionary* further defines antisemitism as "having or showing a strong dislike of Jewish people, or treating them in a cruel and unfair way."[2] The Anti-Defamation League gives this even more expansive and detailed definition of antisemitism: "The belief or behavior hostile toward Jews just because they are Jewish. It may take the form of religious teachings that proclaim the inferiority of Jews, for instance, or political efforts to isolate, oppress, or otherwise injure them. It may also include prejudiced or stereotyped views about Jews."[3] Antisemitism, then, can be seen as "hatred, discrimination or prejudice which is directed towards Jews on account of their religion, culture or heritage."[4] Technically, the word *Semite* identifies all people who speak Semitic languages, particularly Jews (who speak Hebrew) and Arabs (who speak Arabic). Hyam Maccoby, however, points out that the term was never intended to include all people of Semitic origin. "The word 'antisemitism' . . . never meant anything but 'hatred of Jews.'"[5]

The term *antisemitism* comes from the German word *antisemitisch*, a neologism coined in 1860 by the Austrian Jewish scholar Mortiz Steinschneider and used by him in the phrase *antisemitische*

[1] *Merriam-Webster Dictionary*, posted at https://www.merriam-webster.com/dictionary/anti–Semitism.

[2] *Cambridge English Dictionary*, posted at http://dictionary.cambridge.org/us/dictionary/english/anti-semitic.

[3] See http://archive.adl.org/hate-patrol/antisemitism.html.

[4] Michael Gray, *Teaching the Holocaust: Practical Approaches for Ages 11–18* (Abingdon, UK: Routledge, 2015), p. 90.

[5] Hyam Maccoby, *Antisemitism and Modernity: Innovation and Continuity* (Abingdon, UK: Routledge, 2006), pp. 7–8. Maccoby points out that "Hitler did not hate Arabs and made common cause with the Mufti of Jerusalem in opposing Jews."

*Vorurteile* ("antisemitic prejudices") to attack the French philosopher Ernest Renan and his argument that "Semitic races" were inferior to "Aryan races."[6] In 1879, Wilhelm Marr, who came to be known as the father of modern antisemitism, used the terms *antisemitism* and *antisemite* in his essay, "*Der Weg zum Siege des Germanenthums uber das Judenthum*" ("The Way to Victory of Germanism over Judaism") to describe his conflict with the Jews that was based on "supposed racial characteristics" rather than on "religious differences."[7] In order to fight Jewish influence in Western society, Marr introduced the word *antisemite* "into the political lexicon," established "the first popular political movement based entirely on anti-Jewish beliefs,"[8] and organized the League of Antisemites.[9]

Over the years, various definitions for antisemitism have been advanced. The following, a "Working Definition of Anti-Semitism," was adopted in 2005 by the European Union Agency for Fundamental Rights: "Anti-Semitism is a certain perception of Jews, which may be expressed as hatred toward Jews. Rhetorical and physical manifestations of antisemitism are directed toward Jewish or non-Jewish individuals and/or their property, toward Jewish community institutions and religious facilities."[10] On May 26, 2016, the International Holocaust Remembrance Alliance endorsed this statement, adding the following words to its concluding phrase: "such manifestations could also target the state of Israel, conceived as a Jewish collectivity."[11] The European Parliament Working Group on Antisemitism adopted this definition with more than 80 cross-party members of the European Parliament supporting the statement.[12] On December 12, 2016, the definition was

[6] Alex Bein, *The Jewish Question: Biography of a World Problem* (Madison, NJ: Fairleigh Dickinson University Press, 1990), p. 594. Also, Avner Falk, *Anti-semitism: A History and Psychoanalysis of Contemporary Hatred* (Westport, CT: Greenwood Publishing Group, 2008), p. 21.

[7] Tait Keller, *Apostles of the Alps: Mountaineering and Nation Building in Germany and Austria, 1860–1939* (Chapel Hill, NC: The University of North Carolina Press, 2016), p. 64.

[8] Jerome A. Chanes, *Antisemitism: A Reference Handbook* (Santa Barbara, CA: ABC-CLIO, Inc., 2004), p. 104.

[9] For a detailed discussion of Wilhelm Marr, see Moshe Zimmermann, *Wilhelm Marr: The Patriarch of Anti-Semitism* (Oxford, UK: Oxford University Press, 1986).

[10] Kenneth S. Stern, "Proposal for a Redefinition of Antisemitism," in *Antisemitism Worldwide, 2003/2004* (Tel Aviv, Israel: The Stephen Roth Institute, 2005).

[11] For details, see International Holocaust Remembrance Alliance, Romanian Chairmanship, May 26, 2016, posted at https://www.holocaustremembrance.com/sites/default/files/press_release_document_antisemitism.pdf. This definition was published in 2005 by the European Union Agency for Fundamental Rights.

[12] For details, see "EJC applauds European Parliament decision to endorse IHRA definition of antisemitism," June 2, 2017, European Parliament Working Group on Antisemitism, posted at http://www.antisem.eu/projects/eumc-working-definition-of-antisemitism/.

also confirmed by the United Kingdom.[13]

Amazingly, however, as an example of how antisemitism rapidly changes its forms and manifestations—and, consequently, the definition of the term *antisemitism*—the same European Union's Agency for Fundamental Rights which had created the "Working Definition of Anti-Semitism" in 2005 dropped its own definition on December 5, 2013, concluding, "We are not aware of any official definition [of antisemitism]"[14] and "[We are] unable to define the term [antisemitism]."[15]

In an action that is designed to define antisemitism further and clarify its meaning and manifestations (including examples of anti-Israelist and anti-Zionist antisemitism), the United States Department of State has further defined the term by listing the following examples of antisemitism:

- Calling for, aiding, or justifying the killing or harming of Jews (often in the name of a radical ideology or an extremist view of religion).
- Making mendacious, dehumanizing, demonizing, or stereotypical allegations about Jews as such or the power of Jews as a collective—especially but not exclusively, the myth about a world Jewish conspiracy or of Jews controlling the media, economy, government ore other societal institutions.
- Accusing Jews as a people of being responsible for real or imagined wrongdoing committed by a single Jewish person or group, the state of Israel, or even for acts committed by non-Jews.
- Accusing the Jews as a people, or Israel as a state, of inventing or exaggerating the Holocaust.
- Accusing Jewish citizens of being more loyal to Israel, or to the alleged priorities of Jews worldwide, than to the interest of their own nations.
- Using the symbols and images associated with classic anti-Semitism to characterize Israel or Israelis.
- Drawing comparisons of contemporary Israeli policy to that of the Nazis.

[13] For details see "Working Definition of Antisemitism," International Holocaust Remembrance Alliance, posted at https://holocaustremembrance.com/media-room/stories/working-definition-antisemitism-0.

[14] Kenneth L. Marcus, *The Definition of Anti-Semitism* (Oxford, UK: Oxford University Press, 2015), p. 23.

[15] See "What Is Anti-Semitism? EU Racism Agency Unable to Define Term," *Jerusalem Post*, December 5, 2013, posted at http://www.jpost.com/Jewish-World/Jewish-News/What-is-anti-Semitism-EU-racism-agency-unable-to-define-term-334043. Also, http://www.timesofisrael.com/eu-drops-its-working-definition-of-anti-semitism/.

- Blaming Israel for all inter-religious or political tensions.
- Applying double standards by requiring of [Israel] a behavior not expected or demanded of any other democratic nation.
- Multilateral organizations focusing on Israel only for peace or human rights investigations.
- Denying the Jewish people the right to self-determination, and denying Israel the right to exist.[16]

In spite of all the attempts to "define" antisemitism—and the herculean efforts to do so with political correctness—the task seems virtually impossible in today's world. As Kenneth Marcus says with much irony, "Nowadays virtually everyone is opposed to anti-Semitism although no one agrees about what it means to be anti-Semitic." Indeed, he concludes, "it may be argued that virtually every anti-Semite today is also a professed enemy of anti-Semitism."[17]

## Historical Aberration or Unitary Phenomenon?

"Is anti-Semitism a product of particular sociohistorical conditions or a more persistent condition?" asks Kenneth Marcus. "Some writers," he says, "argue that anti-Semitism has been, by and large, a unitary phenomenon over hundreds or thousands of years. This approach allows them to perceive both continuities and evolution of Jew-hatred over long periods of time."[18] Though strong arguments have been advanced for defining antisemitism as being limited to distinct and highly individualized sociohistorical situations and as such historical aberrations,[19] the evidence of history points to antisemitism as a recurring, enduring, and even unrelenting malady that has asserted itself in a variety of ways throughout the centuries of Jewish existence. Ritchie Robertson recognizes this transgenerational durability of antisemitism, arguing that "anti-Semitism is a durable, not a unitary phenomenon. The persistence

---

[16] US Department of State, "Defining Anti-Semitism" at https://www.state.gov/s/rga/resources/267538.htm.

[17] Marcus, p. 11.

[18] Marcus, p. 31. Marcus maintains that the unitary, transgenerational view of antisemitism is deficient.

[19] Jonathan Friedman, *The Lion and the Star: Gentile-Jewish Relations in Three Hessian Towns, 1919–1945* Lexington, KY: The University of Kentucky Press, 1998), p. 8. Friedman points out that "until the 1960s, most historians viewed the Third Reich (1933–45) as an aberration in Germany's otherwise 'normal' historical development." Susanne Knittel, however, argues that it "is not only misleading to consider the Holocaust as a historical aberration, but actually dangerous since . . . [it] removes the Holocaust from its sociocultural context." Susanne C. Knittel, *The Historical Uncanny: Disability, Ethnicity, and the Politics of Holocaust Memory* (Bronx, NY: Fordham University Press, 2015), p. 17.

of hostility to Jews as such is as remarkable as the variety of justifications given for it."[20] This view of antisemitism actually conforms to the principle of immutability that Solomon described when he declared that "there is no new thing under the sun."[21]

## A Psychopathology?

Many scholars have argued that "anti-Semitism involves a pathological process of displacing or projecting hatred upon a group of people chosen for this purpose because they are perceived to be different. The persecution of the Jews that results from this process of distortion gives to anti-Semities a fortified sense of their own otherwise inadequate personal identity."[22] For these scholars, "anti-Semitism is a true mass social psychosis, a psychosis of hatred that is infectious,"[23] says Steven Bartlett.

Red Bain has observed that "the neurotic anti-Semite is put on the defensive, has to 'excuse' and 'explain' his conduct, has to compensate for his guilt feelings, and is thus driven to more and more violent 'vicious circle' expressions of the neurosis."[24] History is replete with examples of social, economic, and religious events and circumstances for which Jews were blamed by those who were adversely affected by inexplicable events or circumstances or who simply could offer no other explanation for such situations than to "blame the Jews."

Gordon Allport dealt with this mass psychosis by identifying what he

[20] Ritchie Robertson, "Varieties of Anti-Semitism," in *Encyclopedia of the Jewish Diaspora: Origins, Experiences, and Culture*, Mark Avrum Ehrlich, ed. (Santa Barbara, CA: ABC-CLIO, LLC, 2009), vol. 1, p. 103. Also, Nicholas de Lange, *Anti-Semitism in Times of Crisis* (New York: New York University Press, 1991), p. 32, and John M. G. Barclay, *Pauline Churches and Diaspora Jews* (Philadelphia, PA: Coronet Books, Inc., 2011), p. 159. Attempts to define Christian anti-Judaism and antisemitism leading up to and incorporating the Holocaust as an "aberration or deviation" are often used as a means of insulating Christianity from charges that it was not at its core antisemitic. See William Arnal, "The Cipher 'Judaism' in Contemporary Historical Jesus Scholarship," in *Apocalypticism, Anti-Semitism and the Historical Jesus: Subtexts in Criticism*, John S. Kloppenborg and John Marshall, eds. (New York: T&T Clark International, 2005), p. 30.

[21] Ecclesiastes 1:9: "That which has been is that which will be, and that which has been done is that which will be done. So there is nothing new under the sun." When it comes to the works and actions of God, Solomon took this principle even further: "Whatever is has already been, and what will be has been before; and God will call the past to account" (Ecclesiastes 3:15, NIV). This principle of immutability can be applied to both good and evil in the world.

[22] Steven J. Bartlett, *The Pathology of Man: A Study of Human Evil* (Springfield, IL: Charles C. Thomas Publisher, 2005), p. 166. Also, Theodore Isaac Rubin, *Anti-Semitism: A Disease of the Mind* (New York: Skyhorse Publishing, Inc. 2009), p. 130; Phillip L. Hammack, *Narrative and the Politics of Identity: The Cultural Psychology of Israeli and Palestinian Youth* (Oxford, UK: Oxford University Press, 2011), p. 255; and Todd D. Nelson, *Handbook of Prejudice, Stereotyping, and Discrimination* (New York: Psychology Press, 2009), p. 33.

[23] Bartlett, p. 166.

[24] Red Bain, quoted in Elisabeth Young-Bruehl, *The Anatomy of Prejudices* (Cambridge, MA: Harvard University Press, 1996), p. 174.

called "functional prejudice," the psychological benefit derived from scapegoating, which itself is a crutch that gives an insecure person "reassurance of past failures, safe guidance for present conduct, and . . . confidence in the future."[25] This is why Lucy Dawidowicz was able to claim that "generations of anti-Semitism had prepared the Germans to accept Hitler as their redeemer."[26] She maintains that the economic problems of post-World War I Germany and the suffering that they inflicted on the German people "produced an emotional milieu in which irrationality and hysteria became routine and illusions became transformed into delusions."[27] This delusional order then "assumed mass proportions" so that "in modern Germany the mass psychosis of anti-Semitism deranged a whole people."[28] German psychoanalyst Gertrud Hardtmann agreed that German Nazism was a "collective psychosis."[29]

For most Germans, the Jews were to blame for all of the social and economic problems during the time after World War I. Indeed, Hitler deemed "Jewish journalists to be a seminal factor in Germany's interwar malaise."[30] The Nazis carefully orchestrated the libel against the Jews, whom they "blamed for every ill: the loss of the war, the Diktat of Versailles, and the inflation, from which Jews were said to have profiteered."[31] Indeed, the Weimar Republic, which had been instituted in Germany at the end of World War I, came to be known as the "Jew Republic,"[32] says Edward Flannery. At the same time, "the influx of eastern Jews, who were looked on as aliens and suspected of swindling" was "fantastically exaggerated in the anti-Jewish propaganda."[33] Additionally, all of the Jewish people "were suspected of ties with Communism, which was commonly referred to as 'Jewish Bolshevism.'"[34] No matter what the problem may have been, the Jews were responsible for it!

Anything that was perceived to be evil was blamed on the Jewish people. "If capitalism was bad, Jewish capitalism . . . was worse. . . . If

[25] Gordon W. Allport, *The Nature of Prejudice* (New York: Perseus Books Publishing, 1954), p. 396, quoted in Bartlett, p. 166.

[26] Lucy S. Dawidowicz, *The War against the Jews: 1935–1945* (New York: Holt, Rinehart and Winston, 1975), p. 164.

[27] Dawidowicz, p. 164.

[28] Dawidowicz, p. 164.

[29] Gertrud Hardtmann, ed., *Spuren der Verfolgung: Seelische Auswirkungen des Holocaust auf die Opfer und ihre Kinder* (Stuttgart, Germany: Bleicher, 1992), pp. 203–222, noted in Falk, p. 53.

[30] Paul Reitter, *The Anti-Journalist: Karl Kraus and Jewish Self-Fashioning in Fin-de-Siècle Europe* (Chicago, IL: The University of Chicago Press, 2008), p. 32.

[31] Edward Flannery, *The Anguish of the Jews: Twenty-Three Centuries of Antisemitism* (Mahwah, NJ: Paulist Press, 2004), p. 206.

[32] Flannery, p. 207.

[33] Flannery, p. 206.

[34] Flannery, p. 207.

socialism was bad, Jewish-led socialism was infinitely more damnable."[35] Whatever could be warped or twisted to the advantage of the Nazis was used to make Hitler's program for the eradication of the Jewish people more palatable to the German people. As had been the case throughout history, the Jewish people were once again set up as the "default scapegoats" for every ill in society, and they continued to be the victims of "Christian paranoia by proxy."[36]

This disorder was fanned to a frenzy as the Nazis, who used statements of Christian leaders before and during that time to advance their occult, neopagan agenda that was rife with social and racial Darwinism and with radically perverse eugenics philosophy. Without the Jews as scapegoats, Hitler and the Nazi party likely would not have succeeded in gaining control of German society as they did. "How did [Hitler], mediocre in so many ways, so quickly attract to his standard" such a cross section of German society? Flannery concluded that "the one catalyst that above all else enabled him to reconcile oppositions and finally transform Germany from a liberal republic into a totalitarian state in a single decade was his anti-semitism."[37]

A prime example of scapegoating antisemitism as a collective psychosis can be seen in the Blood Libel myth that afflicted Europeans psychopathically for centuries and produced violent actions against Jews. Unrelentingly, Jews were accused of murdering Christian children so they could use their blood in the rites of Judaism, especially the baking of *matzah* for Passover.[38] This legend originated in 1144 with the murder of William of Norwich, an event which was attributed to Jewish treachery because it was inexplicable otherwise.[39] It continued with the rendition of "Sir Hugh" or "The Jew's Daughter,"[40] a child ballad purporting the murder of a young Gentile boy by the daughter of a Jew. It was also

[35] Bruce F. Pauley, *From Prejudice to Persecution: A History of Austrian Anti-Semitism* (Chapel Hill, NC: The University of North Carolina Press, 1992), p. 319.

[36] Daniel Rancour-Laferriere, *The Sign of the Cross: From Golgotha to Genocide* (Piscataway, NJ: Transaction Publishers, 2011), p. 217. Also Frederic C. Jaher, *A Scapegoat in the New Wilderness: The Origins and Rise of Antisemitism in America* (Cambridge, MA: Harvard University Press, 1994).

[37] Flannery, p. 209.

[38] For an overview of the Blood Libel myth, see Alan Dundes, *The Blood Libel Legend: A Casebook in Anti-Semitic Folklore* (Madison, WI: The University of Wisconsin Press, 1991), p. 91.

[39] Stephen Greenspan, *Annals of Gullibility: Why We Get Duped and How to Avoid It* (Westport, CT: ABC–CLIO, 2009), p. 46.

[40] This Anglo-Norman ballad purported that a "Jew's daughter entices a young boy, Sir Hugh, into her house to retrieve a ball he kicked through the window," whereupon, "she stabs him and throws his body into a well." Robert M. Correale, *Sources and Analogues of the Canterbury Tales* (Cambridge, UK: D. S. Brewer, 2005), vol. 2, p. 591.

perpetuated by Geoffrey Chaucer's poem, "The Prioress's Tale."[41] The Blood Libel legend made a significant contribution to the furor that resulted in the imperial edict for the expulsion of Jews from Spain in 1492[42] and in the initiation of the Spanish Inquisition.[43] Shakespeare's Shylock character in *The Merchant of Venice* also perpetuated such anti-Jewish stereotypes well into the seventeenth century.[44] The unbroken chain of Blood-Libel charges from 1144 until the twentieth century supports a strong argument that antisemitism and its many manifestations have been the product of a transgenerational "collective psychosis."[45]

Ernest Rappaport spoke of this same "collective psychosis" as it related to Christian anti-Judaism. Avner Falk discusses Rappaport's preference for the term *anti-Judaism* over *antisemitism* in discussing Christian collective psychoses, including Christianity's promotion of the Wandering Jew myth, the "psychopathology of the ritual-murder libel . . . the medieval persecution and massacres of Jews by Christian monks, popes, and crusaders, and the paranoid Spanish Inquisition" and its *auto da fé* rituals wherein "Christians burned Jews alive in order to prove their faith."[46] This collective psychosis enabled Christians to deal with their own self-doubts by projecting myths on the Jewish people and their religion.

Saul Friedländer also called Christian anti-Semitism a "collective psychosis," pointing out that the Jew, like witches and demons, served the Christian psyche as "the most enduring symbol of Evil known to Christianity."[47] He maintained that the Jew "fulfills a single function from the sociological and the psychological point of view: he allows the society in question to distinguish Good from Evil, the Pure from the Impure. . . . The Jews represent

[41] "The Prioress's Tale" follows "The Shipman's Tale" in Chaucer's *The Canterbury Tales*. Geoffrey Chaucer, *The Prioress's Tale*, Beverly Boyd, ed. (Norman, OK: The University of Oklahoma Press, 1987). For a discussion of Chaucer's antisemitism, see Hannah Johnson and Heather Burton, *The Critics and the Prioress: Antisemitism, Criticism, and Chaucer's Prioress's Tale* (Ann Arbor, MI: The University of Michigan Press, 2017), and Philip S. Alexander, "Madame Eglentyne, Geoffrey Chaucer and the Problem of Medieval Anti-Semitism," *Bulletin of the John Rylands Library* 74 (1992), pp. 119–120. Alexander argues that trying to justify the anti-Jewish texts in the *Canterbury Tales* is "fundamentally dishonest. . . . The only course of action left open is to ensure that when *The Prioress's Tale* is expounded, the basic facts of antisemitism are expounded as well."

[42] Yehuda Cohen, *The Spanish: Shadows of Embarrassment* (Eastbourne, UK: Sussex Academic Press, 2012), p. 49.

[43] Sandra Sider, *Handbook to Life in Renaissance Europe* (Oxford, UK: Oxford University Press, 2005), p. 40.

[44] Kathy Lavezzo, *The Accommodated Jew: English Antisemitism from Bede to Milton* (Ithaca, NY: Cornell University Press, 2016), p. 215.

[45] For a comprehensive discussion of the Blood Libel history and its manifestation of collective psychosis, see Falk, pp. 51–53.

[46] Ernest Rappaport, *Anti-Judaism: A Psychohistory* (Chicago, IL: Perspective Press: 1975), referenced in Falk, p. 145.

[47] Saul Friedländer, *History and Psychoanalysis: An Inquiry into the Possibilities and Limits of Psychohistory*, tr. Susan Suleiman (London, UK: Holmes & Meier Publishers, 1978), p. 92.

above all the deviant group that allows a society to define its own limits."[48] Eve Garrard said it well: "[The] long tradition of appealing to the idea of Jewishness to explain the world's troubles . . . persists today, both in the West and in the East. . . . There's a Jew-shaped space, and not a pleasant one, in Western culture, and placing actual Jews, both inside and outside the Jewish state, into that space seems obvious, familiar and natural—they seem to fit the space so remarkably well, especially once their actual activities have been reconstructed to conform to a deeply hostile picture of them."[49]

Friedrich Nietzsche expanded further on the psychosis of hatred that would reach its nadir in the antisemitism of the Holocaust some forty years after his time. He explained how prejudice can be multiplied into a pathological hatred and then into inflicting pain and suffering on the objects of prejudice and hatred. In fact, he observed that "to behold suffering gives pleasure, but to cause another to suffer affords an even greater pleasure."[50] Those who resort to scapegoating in order to excuse their own inadequacies, whether personal or societal, also usually derive a measure of pleasure from inflicting suffering and pain—even death—upon those whom they have blamed for their perceived loss of dignity, health, or wealth. No wonder Bartlett observes that "as the Holocaust is to genocide, so is anti-Semitism to prejudice."[51] Antisemitism is prejudice and hatred taken to its furthest possible extreme.

## Antisemitism and Manifest Evil: Cosmic Dimensions

Dennis Prager and Joseph Telushkin point out that "hatred for the Jew has been humanity's greatest hatred. While hatred of other groups has always existed, no hatred has been as universal, as deep, or as permanent as antisemitism."[52] Although antisemitism has emerged from various situations and has had many manifestations, its underlying cause has always been the hatred for Israel's God that rests in the pagan heart—an antipathy which has been directed against the Jewish people because

[48] Friedländer, p. 92.

[49] Eve Garrard points to the example of "Baroness Jenny Tonge's claim that Israel only provided a field hospital to Haiti [during the 2010 earthquake disaster] in order to steal human organs for sale on the black market." Charges such as these rise beyond the realm of decency and dignity and are without doubt extremely antisemitic. Eve Garrard, "Anti-Judaism, Anti-Zionism, Antisemitism," *Fathom*, Winter, 2015, posted at http://fathomjournal.org/anti-judaism-anti-zionism-antisemitism/.

[50] Friedrich Nietzsche, *The Birth of Tragedy and the Genealogy of Morals* (Garden City, NY: Doubleday, 1956), p. 198.

[51] Bartlett, p. 166.

[52] Dennis Prager and Joseph Telushkin, *Why the Jews?: The Reason for Antisemitism* (New York: Simon and Schuster, 1983), p. 3.

they represent God in the earth. This pathology seethes in the subconscious recesses of the Gentile mind and is ready to leap forth at any time and in any place, only to be dismissed by a plethora of excuses for its mistrust and hatred of Jews. For this reason alone, Jews for thousands of years have held the opinion that antisemitism is "religious and particularist."[53]

Antisemitism, then, is much more than a psychopathological hatred for Jews. In fact, antisemitism in the Holocaust was "the apotheosis of evil—the epitome of limitless depravity,"[54] as Judith Hughes poignantly observes. Antisemitism is a deep-seated spiritual issue, the ultimate demonstration of manifest evil. "Anti-Semitism is not," as much "a 'social disease'" as it is "a moral aberration; it is a denial of the humanity of other human beings, and the responsibility for it lies with those who are guilty of it,"[55] says Michael Seizer. Antisemitism has long been perhaps the most vile manifestation of evil in the world.[56] Though many scholars have sought to define evil in terms of psychopathology,[57] its root is much deeper than mere human activity. This is why "psychoanalysis cannot reduce the evil acts of the Holocaust to simple psychopathology."[58]

In the final analysis, antisemitism and the excesses it produces—including its "final solutions"—are not comprehensible through psychology or psychoanalysis. Instead, they require understanding the spiritual dimension of human depravity. Though antisemitism requires human agency in order to be manifest, the malevolence that underlies it is a fundamental manifestation of the cosmic evil that predated human creation and continues unabated in today's world. Antisemitism is the human depravity of manifest evil that, when taken to its extreme and ultimate conclusion, inevitably produces holocaust. Recognizing that antisemitism has an underlying cause that predates every manifestation of its depravity is vital to understanding the quintessential malady itself. Antisemitism is the product of spirit both inside humanity and outside humanity. Indeed, antisemitism is "the inevitable false fruit of man's spirit," and it must have existed even before the manifestation of its various

[53] Prager and Telushkin, p. 56.

[54] Judith M. Hughes, *The Holocaust and the Revival of Psychological History* (Cambridge, UK: Cambridge University Press, 2015), p. 2.

[55] Michael Seizer, *"Kike!" A Documentary History of Anti-Semitism in America* (New York: World Publishing, 1972), p. 7.

[56] Bartlett, p. 166ff.

[57] Carole L. Jurkiewicz, *The Foundations of Organizational Evil* (Abingdon, UK: Routledge, 2015), p. 5.

[58] Steven A. Luel and Paul Marcus, eds., *Psychoanalytic Reflections on the Holocaust: Selected Essays* (Denver, CO: Holocaust Awareness Institute, 1984), p. 70.

appearances, "even before Abraham, the first Jew."[59]

Ultimately, the agent of vile antisemitism is *haSatan*, the personification of evil in the universe. The Hebrew word *satan* means "adversary," one who withstands or stands in opposition to God and to human beings.[60] Jewish sages expressed their personal doubts that *haSatan* is actually a being, preferring to view this "adversary" as merely an aspect of the human psyche.[61] In Jewish tradition, therefore, *haSatan* has come to be connected with the inclination toward evil that is present in each human being from birth. As a matter of fact, some sages suggest that "Satan, the *yetzer hara*, and the Angel of Death are one and the same."[62]

In the Hebrew Scriptures, however, *haSatan* is more than an psychological predisposition or an inclination. *Ha-Satan* is given personification. He was the tempter who deceived Eve and overcame Adam in the Garden of Eden at the very genesis of human creation.[63] As a matter of fact, Paul warned Christians to be on guard lest they also be "outwitted by Satan's schemes"[64] and to be careful not to permit the serpent who "deceived Eve by his craftiness" to lead them "astray from sincere and pure devotion."[65] This is what happened when Satan confronted King David and persuaded him to number Israel,[66] thereby incurring God's judgment because he had not followed the procedures that God had established in the Torah for such a census.[67] When the same Satan positioned himself to resist Joshua the high priest, he was rebuked by God himself.[68]

From the Apostolic Scriptures, it is clear that Jesus and the Jewish leaders of the first-century Messianic community believed *haSatan* to be a literal being, a fallen angel. As a matter of fact, Jesus described the primordial fall of Satan that he himself had witnessed in the beginning of time: "I saw Satan fall like lightning from heaven."[69] Jesus also encountered Satan during his forty days of fasting in the Judean desert and rejected

---

[59] Yoram Hazony, *God and Politics in Esther* (Cambridge, UK: Cambridge University Press, 2016), p. 75. Citing Rabbi Levi, Hazony points out the rabbis' contention that, in effect, it was Cain who was the first antisemite, that he was possessed of the same spirit that produced the Holocaust when he hated and then killed his brother Abel.

[60] "Satan" is mentioned in five instances in the Hebrew Scriptures and 34 times in the Apostolic Scriptures.

[61] Stuart Federow, *Judaism and Christianity: A Contrast* (Bloomington, IN: iUniverse, 2012), pp. 11–13.

[62] Talmud, *Bava Basra* 16a.

[63] Genesis 3:13.

[64] 2 Corinthians 2:11.

[65] 2 Corinthians 11:3.

[66] 1 Chronicles 21:1.

[67] Exodus 30:12.

[68] Zechariah 3:2.

[69] Luke 10:18, NIV.

the "adversary's" three major temptations with specific instructions from the Torah.[70] He also declared that the woman who had been bent double for eighteen years was thus afflicted because "Satan [had] bound [her]."[71] Peter warned the early Christians that "your adversary [*haSatan*], the devil, prowls around like a roaring lion, seeking someone to devour."[72] Finally, John the beloved disciple summed up the overarching apostolic perspective on *haSatan* from creation to the final judgment: "I saw an angel come down from heaven, holding the key of the abyss and a great chain in his hand, and he laid hold on the dragon, the serpent of old, who is the devil and Satan, and bound him for a thousand years."[73] Each of these leaders recognized *haSatan* as more than mere conflict within the human psyche: he was the "devil," the "serpent," the "dragon"—evil personified and self-contained in the adversary of God.

In the ongoing conflict with evil, Paul observed that "our struggle is not against flesh and blood, but against the rulers, against the powers, against the world forces of this darkness, against the spiritual forces of wickedness in the heavenly places."[74] As the most vile and vicious form of human hatred and prejudice, antisemitism is rooted in and prompted by the same *haSatan* and powers aligned with him in a spiritual realm. While antisemitism is inspired by insidious forces in the heavenlies that are aligned against the Almighty and his people, however, the struggle against antisemitism works itself out in human agents and human societies where personal and community choices are made which determine "who is on the LORD's side"[75] and who is aligned with *haSatan* in this most wretched demonstration of manifest evil in the earth.

## Antisemitism and Human Inclinations: The Good and Evil

The prophet Jeremiah declared that "the [human] heart is devious above all else; it is perverse—who can understand it?"[76] Whether it is humanist, secularist, or pagan, the heart of godless man despises the God of Scripture and the Scripture of God. And, like it or not, the Jews still represent God, and the Scriptures of the Jews still speak for God. The

[70] Mark 1:13.

[71] Luke 13:11–16. The condition with which this woman was afflicted could hardly have been psychosomatic. The "Satan" that had bound her for 18 years could hardly have been a psychological problem.

[72] 1 Peter 5:8.

[73] Revelation 20:1–2. John brought together all the metaphors and names for manifest evil personified and applied them to one being: the dragon, the serpent of Eden, the Devil, and Satan.

[74] Ephesians 6:12.

[75] Exodus 32:26.

[76] Jeremiah 17:9.

devious and adiamorphic human heart also hates the Jewish people, the Jewish nation, and the Jewish land, because this people, this nation, and this land bear witness to the existence of the one and only true God.[77]

Paul said it well: "The mindset of the flesh is hostile toward God."[78] This hostility toward God can be both mental and visceral. It prompts the conflict which Paul also lamented when he confessed, "I am of flesh, sold into bondage to sin. . . . I know that nothing good dwells in me . . . the good that I want to do I do not do, but the evil I do not want to do, this I keep doing."[79] Paul's description of this existential battle led him to draw this poignant conclusion: "What a wretched man I am!"[80] Even with the best of intentions and determination, humans often find themselves engaged in actions for which they are sorrowful and for which they know they need to make restitution.

The sages of Israel discussed this same dilemma, noting that God created in the first human being and every person since that time two inclinations[81]—an inclination toward good (*yetzer hatov*) and an inclination toward evil (*yetzer hara*)—and that this creation set the stage for the unending struggle between good and evil in every human person. "The *yetzer tov* serves as people's moral conscience, while the *yetzer ra* drives people to satisfy their personal needs and desires. The *yetzer ra* is not intrinsically bad; it becomes bad when it is not countervailed by *yetzer tov* and leads to wrongdoing," explains Alan Dershowitz.[82] The term *yetzer hara* is usually translated as "evil imagination" and is characterized as evil, the enemy, and a stumbling-block.[83]

The sages generally agreed that the *yetzer hara* is inborn, like a genetic trait, and that it is essentially a nature of evil—characterized by pride—that is resident in the human instinct for survival.[84] At the same time, however, they also agreed paradoxically that the evil inclination is the source of the drive for self-improvement and the restoration of the world, prompting

---

[77] Isaiah 43:10; Malachi 3:6.

[78] Romans 8:7, NHEB.

[79] Romans 7:15–19, NASB, NIV.

[80] Romans 7:24–25. When Paul asked the rhetorical question, "Who shall deliver me from this body doomed to death?" he answered his own question with this conclusion: "I thank God through Jesus Christ our Lord!"

[81] The two inclinations can be transliterated from Hebrew into English as 1) *yetzer hatov* (literally "inclination, the good") or as *yetzer ha-tov, yetzer tov,* or *yetzer-tov* and 2) *yetzer hara* (literally "inclination, the evil") or as *yetzer ha-ra, yetzer ra, or yetzer-ra.*

[82] Alan M. Dershowitz, *Rights from Wrongs: A Secular Theory of the Origins of Rights* (New York: Basic Books, 2004), pp. 239–240. Dershowitz references Genesis 6:5, 8:21 from the Hebrew Scriptures and *Berachot* 61a and *Sukkah* 52a from the Talmud.

[83] Solomon Schecter, *Some Aspects of Rabbinic Theology* (New York: The Macmillan Company, 1910), pp. 242–263.

[84] See *Sifre* Deuteronomy, *Ekev* 45 (a rabbinic collection compiled in the third century in Israel). See also Maimonides, *The Guide for the Perplexed* (1190), III:22.

them to conclude, therefore, that "the inclination toward evil in humans has a potential for good as well."[85] One rabbi even suggested to his colleagues that "the *yetzer ha-ra* is very good. How so? Without it, a man would not build a house, marry a woman, have children, and conduct a business," he said.[86] King Solomon actually established this idea when he said, "I have also noted that all labor and skillful enterprise come from men's envy of each other."[87] As Reuven Bulka has noted, "Only with *yetzer hara* is the world complete, free-choice a reality, and human praiseworthiness a possibility."[88] While elements of the *yetzer hara* are positive and necessary for human existence, the potential for the manifestation of the most heinous evil also rests in its paradoxical realm.

Both good and evil are present in the mind and in the heart of every human being. The sages maintained that unlike the *yetzer hara*, which was present in a human being from birth,[89] the *yetzer hatov* was generally acquired at puberty.[90] Scripture does confirm the presence of an inclination toward evil in humanity from birth. God himself said that, in the antediluvian world, "every inclination of the human heart is evil from childhood."[91] King David took the issue further when he was so overwhelmed with remorse over the heinous nature of his own sin that he exclaimed, "I was sinful at birth, sinful from the time my mother conceived me."[92] The *yetzer hara* concept, wherein the evil inclination is believed to be inborn in all human beings, contrasts with and is distinct from the Augustinian concept of "original sin," since it does not suggest that "sin" is transmitted from generation to generation by the physical act of human conjugation.[93]

Contrary to the rabbinic view that the *yetzer hatov* is received around the

---

[85] For a comprehensive discussion of the *yetzer hara*, see Samuel Tobias Lachs, *Humanism in Talmud and Midrash* (Cranbury, NJ: Associated University Press, 1993), pp. 47–49.

[86] Nachman of Breslov made this statement in the name of Rabbi Shmuel, basing his contention on Ecclesiastes 4:4, *Genesis Rabbah* 9:7, and Babylonian Talmud, *Sanhedrin* 38a. See Joel Lurie Grishaver, *Talmud with Training Wheels* (Los Angeles, CA: Torah Aura Productions, 2005), vol. 3, p. 9.

[87] Ecclesiastes 4:4. See also Genesis *Rabbah* 9:7. See Joseph Telushkin, *Jewish Literacy: The Most Important Things to Know about the Jewish Religion* (San Francisco: HarperCollins Publishers, 2001), p. 599.

[88] Reuven P. Bulka, *Jewish Marriage: A Halakhic Ethic* (New York: KTAV Publishing House, 1986), p. 107.

[89] Babylonian Talmud, *Sanhedrin* 91b. Also Aaron Rabinowitz, *Judaism and Psychology: Meeting Points* (New York: Jason Aronson, 1999), p. 25.

[90] Jack J. Cohen, *Jewish Education in Democratic Society* (Tyler, TX: Reconstruction Press, 1964), p. 328. Also Philip S. Berg, *The Power of You: Kabbalistic Wisdom to Create the Movie of Your Life* (New York: Research Centre of Kabbalah, 2004), p. 164.

[91] Genesis 8:21.

[92] Psalm 51:5, NIV.

[93] Tatha Wiley, *Original Sin: Origins, Developments, Contemporary Meanings* (Mahwah, NJ: Paulist Press, 2002), pp. 56–80. Also, Howard Greenstein, Kendra G. Hotz, and John Kaltner, *What Do Our Neighbors Believe?: Questions and Answers on Judaism, Christianity, and Islam* (Louisville, KY: Westminster John Knox Press, 2007), pp. 68–69.

time of puberty, Scripture indicates that it is also inherent in human creation from birth. Paul made it clear that all the non-Jewish people of the earth have resident in their beings the same Torah (Law of God) that was given to the Israelites at Mt. Sinai.[94] It is the Torah that is written on the heart of every human being that the apostle described as the human conscience.[95] Apparently, the Torah was written in the first human being's heart at the time of his vivification, for Scripture declares that God "breathed into [Adam's] nostrils the breath (*neshamah*) of life, and he became a living being."[96] Since Holy Scripture is "God-breathed,"[97] it is likely that the Torah was "written" on the human heart when God "breathed" life into humanity. As Elihu declared to Job, "There is a spirit in a person, the *neshamah* of the Almighty, that gives them understanding."[98] The "breath of the Almighty" is the "spirit" that generates "understanding" in the human heart. The *yetzer hatov* is, therefore, inherent in human life and coexists with the *yetzer hara* from birth so that both good and evil engage in a continuing conflict in the human heart and mind ever thereafter. From the moment that primal humanity acquired the knowledge of good and evil, all human beings have experienced the "conflict between good and evil . . . conflict within the human person, conflict among human beings, [and] conflict between human person and the cosmos,"[99] Anthony Akinwale rightly concludes.

Zvi Yehuda observes that "this metaphor of duality and constant battle between the *yetzer-tov* and *yetzer-ra* dramatizes the complexity and intensity of the human moral dilemma. . . . Metaphorically, the righteous have the *yetzer* under their grip; the wicked are within the grip of their *yetzer*. The virtuous ones rule over their drives; the wicked ones let their drives rule over them."[100] This is the battle that makes it possible for "human corruption and failure" to be manifest through "conflicts

[94] Romans 2:14: "Gentiles who do not have the Law do instinctively the things of the Law."

[95] Romans 2:15: "[Gentiles] show the work of the Law written in their hearts, their conscience bearing witness and their thoughts alternately accusing or else defending them." The human conscience, therefore, is an application or manifestation of the Torah. The Hebrew word *torah* has been almost universally translated as "law"; however, from its etymology, it actually means "instruction." The word *torah* is derived from *yarah*, an archery term that means "to hit the mark." The word *torah* is related to the words *moreh* ("teacher") and *horeh* ("parent"), which come from the same root. The Torah contains law; however, it is much more than "law"; it is the instruction of a wise father to his children.

[96] Genesis 2:7.

[97] 2 Timothy 3:16.

[98] Job 32:8, NIV.

[99] Anthony Akinwale, "Reconciliation," in *The Oxford Handbook of Sacramental Theology*, Hans Boersma and Matthew Levering, eds. (Oxford, UK: Oxford University Press, 2015), p. 549.

[100] Zvi Yehuda, "*Ve-Khof Et Yitzrenu Le-Hishtabed Lakh*—Direct Our Impulses [*Yetzer*]," in *Yom Kippur Readings: Inspiration, Information, Contemplation*, Dov Peretz Elkins, ed. (Woodstock, VT: Jewish Lights Publishing, 2005), p. 42.

and hatred, loneliness, fear, and depression,"[101] says Kallistos Ware.

Even believing upon the Messiah for salvation from sin does not obliterate the human potential for sin. It merely makes one positionally righteous by the imputation and impartation of the righteousness of Christ to the believer and makes it possible for the Lawgiver (the Holy Spirit) to become resident in the heart of the believer, thereby empowering him to overcome evil by doing good.[102] What God intended in the beginning by infusing humanity with his Word, a "Torah written on their hearts," he completed through the impartation of the Holy Spirit to those who would believe upon his Son for justification from their sins.

Since the human instinct for survival is connected with or a part of the inclination toward evil,[103] it presents a major challenge to the human person in that it also is a focal point for perceived threats to one's wellbeing that can trigger the "flight or fight" impulse when, for whatever reason, one feels threatened. A natural impulse of the fear of potential injury to one's person can expand into paranoia which then can produce prejudice and bigotry. This, too, is both a psychological and a spiritual matter, for these issues can rapidly expand into revulsion, contempt, animosity, and violence. The author of the book of Hebrews says that a "root of bitterness" can "spring up" to "trouble" a person, eventually causing him to be "defiled."[104] Controlling anger and paranoia when they arise, therefore, is essential to both mental and spiritual health. As Paul said, "Do not let the sun go down while you are still angry. . . . In your anger do not sin."[105]

This is why Jesus defined the root cause of murder this way: "You have heard that the ancients were told, 'You shall not commit murder,' and 'whoever commits murder shall be liable to the court.' But I say to you that everyone who is angry with his brother shall be guilty before the court; and whoever says to his brother, 'You good-for-nothing,' shall

[101] Kallistos Ware, "'In the Image and Likeness': The Uniqueness of the Human Person," in *Personhood: Orthodox Christianity and the Connection between Body, Mind, and Soul*, John T. Chirban, ed. (Westport, CT: Bergin & Garvey, 1996), p. 11.

[102] To confirm the Holy Spirit as the lawgiver, compare Deuteronomy 9:10 (where Scriptures says that the Torah was written "by the finger of God") with Luke 11:20 (where Jesus said that he cast out demons by "the finger of God") and Matthew 12:28 (where Jesus said he cast out demons by "the Spirit of God"). For establishing the fact that evil is overcome through Holy Spirit empowerment, see Romans 8:2, 3, 9; 12:21. To establish the fact that the purpose of the law as divine instruction is established by faith, see Romans 3:31.

[103] Abraham J. Twerski, *The Enemy Within: Confronting Your Challenges in the 21st Century* (Brooklyn, NY: Shaar Press, 2002), p. 185. Also, Stan Tenen, *The Alphabet that Changed the World: How Genesis Preserves a Science of Consciousness in Geometry and Gesture* (Berkeley, CA: North Atlantic Books, 2011).

[104] Hebrews 12:15. To describe the "bitterness" that can spring up, the author uses the Greek word *pikea*, which means "bitter gall."

[105] Ephesians 4:26, NIV.

be guilty before the supreme court; and whoever says, 'You fool,' shall be guilty enough to go into the fiery hell."[106] Jesus took this matter much further, however, when he said, "Love your enemies and pray for those who persecute you."[107] The murderous spirit that results in homicide is, therefore, first of all, a heart issue. It results from making concessions to the *yetzer hara* and not controlling that inclination by the *yetzer hatov*.

The prophets and sages of Israel maintained that it is vital for every human being to be educated in the truth, the divine instructions codified in the Torah and the rest of Hebrew Scripture. The blessed and righteous person is the one who "delights in the Torah of the LORD" and meditates in it "day and night" finds that "whatever he does prospers."[108] Because the human mechanism is "hypersensitive, delicately balanced," says Kallistos Ware, it all too easily goes wrong; yet, there is "incomparably more" to the "human person,"[109] because every human being is uniquely God's creation and, as such, is possessed of infinite value. Each person is capable of profound and utterly depraved evil, yet, under the influence of the inclination toward good and the indwelling Spirit of God, each person is capable of immeasurable good.

In order to ensure that the *yetzer hatov*, through the agency of the Spirit and the Word of God, overcomes evil when it is presented, a person must be wise to the devices of *haSatan* when, in his profound subtlety, he presents himself as an "angel of light" and seeks to beguile the person by corrupting him from the "simplicity" of divine truth and righteous conduct.[110] Those who fail to educate themselves in respect to *haSatan's* devices inevitably find themselves outwitted and overcome with evil. Only faith in God and his divine Word can empower for victory.

Sadly, rather than ruling their *yetzer hara* through the power of the Word and Spirit of God, so many human beings come to be ruled by the inclination toward evil to such a degree that the inclination toward good is so severely suppressed as to be virtually nonexistent. Paul spoke of such individuals as having had their "conscience [*yetzer hatov*] seared with a branding iron."[111] These are the people who have submitted themselves to evil to such a degree that they have been "given over to a depraved mind."[112] Because they "love not the truth . . . God sends them a powerful delusion so that they will believe

[106] Matthew 5:21–22.
[107] Matthew 5:44.
[108] Psalm 1:1–3.
[109] Ware, in Chirban, p. 11.
[110] 2 Corinthians 11:3.
[111] 1 Timothy 4:2.
[112] Romans 1:28.

the lie and so that all will be condemned."[113] This is what the apostle said occurred with pagans who, rather than worshiping the living God when they came to know him, converted their insight of God into anthropomorphisms and theriomorphisms and engaged in idolatry that prompted God to turn them over to the reprobate mindset that drove them to hedonistic excesses.[114]

Evil that is resident in the human heart can be controlled by engaging in a spiritual warfare wherein one follows the example of Paul who declared, "I discipline my body and make it my slave so that . . . I myself will not be disqualified."[115] To do so, "everyone who competes . . . exercises self-control in all things."[116] Impulses toward prejudice and hatred are best controlled when they arise, not after they are allowed to fester and breed violent intent. Antisemitism is obviated when human beings employ their God-given inclination toward good to constrain their all-too-human inclination toward evil.

## Antisemitism and Deicide

Antisemitism is even more far-reaching than human evil inclinations toward prejudice and bigotry that are directed against the Jewish people. "What makes the Jewish people such a controversial element in the history of the world?" asks Isaac Rottenberg. "Could it be that their very survival and presence in our midst remind us of the God of Israel, the Great Disturber of our pagan souls?" he rightly wonders, with an answer that is all too obvious.[117] What is the reason for this disruption in the pagan heart? "The God of Israel refuses to be absorbed into a pantheon of gods."[118] Jacob Neusner is correct when he concludes that "those who hate Israel hate God, [and] those who hate God hate Israel."[119] It is the God of Israel who demands a conclusion that the pagan heart cannot endure: "See, I have set before you today life and prosperity, death and destruction. . . . I call heaven and earth to record this day . . . that I have set before you life and death, the blessings and curses. Now choose life, so that you and your descendants may live."[120] This God speaks the same word of truth to the pagan heart that he spoke to Israel in ancient

[113] 2 Thessalonians 2:11–12.

[114] Romans 1:20–32.

[115] 1 Corinthians 9:27.

[116] 1 Corinthians 9:25.

[117] Isaac C. Rottenberg, *Judaism, Christianity, Paganism: A Judeo-Christian Worldview and Its Cultural Implications* (Atlanta, GA: Hebraic Heritage Press, 2007), p. 101.

[118] Rottenberg, p. 101.

[119] Jacob Neusner, *The Theology of the Halakhah* (Leiden, The Netherlands: Koninklijke Brill NV, 2001), p. 243.

[120] Deuteronomy 30:15, 19.

times: "The word is very near you; it is in your mouth and in your heart so you may obey it."[121] And the pagan heart can offer no excuse for choosing to walk in the way of death and destruction, for pagans have God's law written in their hearts.[122] The God of Israel still says, "Choose this day whom you will serve, whether the gods your ancestors served in the region beyond the river or the gods of the Amorites in whose land you are living."[123] And the only acceptable answer is that which Joshua gave, "As for me and my household, we will serve the LORD."[124]

Neusner is correct, therefore, when he concludes, "The nations hate Israel because of their remaining loyal to the Torah."[125] David Patterson argues further that "the anti-Semitic determination to erase the People of the Book from the face of the planet is a determination to erase the Book itself; without the People there is no Book; and without the Book there is no People."[126] Antisemitism, therefore, "is inextricably tied to anti-Judaism: the Jews were an evil nation because they had an evil religion."[127] Patterson exposes the real root of the vitriol against the Jewish people and their nation and land: "What the anti-Zionists would obliterate is precisely the voice of the Torah—and with the Torah, God and Israel as well. Because the Torah determines the covenantal relation to the land . . . the Jewish presence in Israel far transcends any political agenda."[128]

Chaim Schloss takes the argument even further by saying that "the world's hatred of the Jews came down from Mount Sinai together with the Torah"[129] by appealing to the fact that the Hebrew word *Sinai* is derived from the word *sinah*, which means "hatred." Schloss maintains, therefore, that "even if the Jews themselves try to forget their origins, *Hashem* sends the Gentiles to remind them of the truth" by means of outbreaks of antisemitism.[130] The people of Israel are detested—and their destruction is sought—because, in the words of Emmanuel Lévinas, the faith of the Jews "stems from the religion which modern political life

[121] Deuteronomy 30:14.

[122] Romans 2:14–15.

[123] Joshua 24:15.

[124] Joshua 24:15.

[125] Jacob Neusner, *A Theological Commentary to the Midrash: Lamentations Rabbah* (Lanham, MD: University Press of America, 2011), pp. 120–121.

[126] David Patterson, *Anti-Semitism and Its Metaphysical Origins* (Cambridge, UK: Cambridge University Press, 2015), p. 200. "The Book referred to here is, of course, the Torah," says Patterson.

[127] Maccoby, p. 10.

[128] Patterson, p. 100.

[129] Chaim Schloss, *2000 Years of Jewish History: From the Destruction of the Second Bais HaMikdash until the Twentieth Century* (Jerusalem, Israel: Feldheim Publishers, 2002), p. 254.

[130] Schloss, p. 254.

supplants,"[131] the religion that Patterson calls the religion "of creation and covenant, of revelation and redemption."[132] Because "the Torah determines the covenantal relation to the land," postmodernism seeks to obliterate "the voice of the Torah—and with the Torah, God and Israel as well," including the Torah's focus "on the land itself."[133] The prayer that is recited in the synagogue whenever the Torah is removed from the *Aaron HaKodesh* (the Holy Ark) confirms this truth: "Arise God, and let your foes be scattered, let those who hate you flee from you, because: from Zion the Torah will come forth and the word of God from Jerusalem."[134] Postmodern secularist efforts to eliminate the Jewish people and their nation and land are, therefore, merely visible symbols of a determination to eradicate the God of the Jews.

This bent toward eradicating both the Scriptures of the Jews and the Jews of Scripture is at the heart of the secularist agenda for deicide, the murder of God. Because such underlying hatred for God, Torah, and Israel exists in the postmodern world, the Israeli struggle for survival is far more than a sociological problem or a contest for control of a land mass.[135] Though some have suggested that all antisemitism would be cured if the Jewish people had a nation where they could be separate from the rest of the world, Derek Prince made this astute observation: "If the problem of anti-Semitism is primarily sociological, you are correct. The state of Israel will solve this problem. But if the primary cause of anti-Semitism is spiritual, then the existence of the State of Israel will bring the greatest onslaught of anti-Semitism that the world has ever seen."[136] Without a doubt, then, antisemitism is a true spiritual problem that only God can solve.

Patterson draws a striking conclusion when he says that "strictly speaking, anti-Semitism is not reducible to Jew hatred, although that is where it finds its most immediate and most venomous expression. Anti-Semitism is God hatred and human hatred."[137] The hatred for God that consumes the pagan heart perpetually drives it to attempt deicide. Elie

---

[131] Emmanuel Lévinas, *Difficult Freedom: Essays on Judaism*, tr. Sean Hand (Baltimore, MD: Johns Hopkins University Press, 1990), p. 12.

[132] Patterson, p. 101.

[133] Patterson, pp. 200–201.

[134] This prayer is composed of the words of Numbers 10:35 followed by the word *because* and the words of Isaiah 2:3. This prayer uses Scripture to affirm that the reason for antisemitism is "hatred of God" which is manifest in hatred for the Torah and its instructions, including the "word of the LORD from Jerusalem." Nicholas Gura, *Divine Wisdom and Warning: Decoded Messages from God* (Lanham, MD: Rowman & Littlefield, 2011), p. 184.

[135] Patterson, p. 201.

[136] Derek Prince, quoted in Daniel C. Juster, "Anti-Semitism Again," in *Jewish Voice Today Magazine*, July/August/September 2015, p. 7.

[137] Patterson, p. 24.

Wiesel correlated such compulsive and murderous hatred with the very first misanthropic human obsession that led to fratricide, concluding that Cain's murder of Abel was fundamentally deicide: "Cain killed to become God. To kill God."[138]

Richard Rubenstein was right when he spoke of the reason for the profound misotheism that resides in the pagan heart: "Had we but the power, we would murder God, for we will never cease to be tempted by Ivan Karamazov's demonic fantasy that if God were dead, all things would be permitted."[139] Since antisemitism is at bottom God hatred and ultimately human hatred, "killing God requires killing the children of Abraham," notes Patterson.[140] No wonder Immanuel Kant suggested that "the euthanasia of Judaism [would produce] the pure moral religion freed from all ancient statutory teachings," and thereby answer the Jewish Question.[141] And make no mistake about it: the "euthanasia of Judaism" requires the "euthanasia" of the Jews, for Judaism will never die as long as the Jews are a living, breathing entity, standing as God's witnesses to the pagan world that YHWH is the one and only God.[142]

This is why antisemitism differs from all other forms of hatred. Robert Wistrich identifies the core issue: "The sacral, quasi-metaphysical quality of anti-Semitism is singularly absent in other cases."[143] Thomas Torrance said it well: "The story of Israel reveals a people hated by other nations because Israel's life bore witness to divine prohibitions among the Gentiles."[144] The apostle Paul summed up this phenomenon when he said, "The mindset of the flesh is hostile toward God; for it does not subject itself to the law of God, for it is not even able to do so."[145] The heart of godless man universally despises

[138] Elie Wiesel, *Messengers of God: Biblical Portraits and Legends*, tr. Marion Wiesel (New York: Simon & Schuster, 2005), p. 58. In his book *Twilight*, Wiesel has Cain say, "When I killed my brother, it was really Him I wanted to kill. And He knows it. Any fool knows that he who kills, kills God." Elie Wiesel, *Twilight: A Novel*, tr. Marion Wiesel (New York: Summit Books, 1998), p. 58.

[139] Richard Rubenstein, *After Auschwitz: History, Theology and Contemporary Judaism* (Baltimore, MD: Johns Hopkins University Press, 1992), p. 23.

[140] Patterson, p. 24.

[141] Immanuel Kant, *Grounding for the Metaphysics of Morals* (New Haven, CT: Yale University Press, 2002), p. 30. Julius Wellhausen followed in Kant's footsteps when he argued that the apostle Paul was "the great pathologist of Judaism"who rendered Judaism as meaningless. Julius Wellhausen, noted in Claude Montefiore, *Judaism and St. Paul: Two Essays* (New York: Arno Press, 1973), p. 21.

[142] Isaiah 43:12.

[143] Robert S. Wistrich, *A Lethal Obsession: Anti-Semitism from Antiquity to the Global Jihad* (New York: Random House, 2010), p. 588.

[144] Thomas Forsyth Torrance, *The Mediation of Christ* (Grand Rapids, MI: Wm. B. Eerdmans Publishing Co., 1984), pp. 7ff.

[145] Romans 8:7.

God. And because it does, it also hates Israel—the one people, the one nation, and the one land that stands for and bears witness to the one and only true God. The absolute ethics that God demands in Scripture and through his Chosen People are an affront to the "freedom" and "self-actualization" of the postmodern humanist today just as they have been for the pagans and secularists of the past. Like it or not, Israel as a whole represents God, and the Scriptures of Israel still speak for God, even when the Jewish people may not faithfully follow the instructions of the Torah.

While scholars offer various secular explanations for antisemitism, such as resentment of the "higher quality of Jewish life," their first and foremost reason for antisemitism is "hatred of Judaism and ethical monotheism, followed closely by 'the Chosen People idea.'"[146] What they point out is true: "[T]oday, Jew-hatred is generally attributed to factors having little to do with Jews and Judaism; rather, its causes are generally held to be economic, political . . . ethnic prejudice, and the psychopathology of hate—all of which dejudaize antisemitism."[147] At bottom, however, an insidious force of the evil inclination in the human heart resents and hates the Jewish people because they represent a God who is foreign to their thinking—or lack thereof. Prager and Telushkin observe that ultimately "the causes of antisemitism are neither ethnic nor racial nor rooted in economic envy or religious bigotry, but that antisemitism is a response to Jews and their way of life, based upon its very foundations—God, Torah, and Peoplehood."[148]

## Utter Ignorance, Superstition, and Prejudice

"The panorama of human history reveals again and again vast multitudes of people swept away by manias, phobias, and hysterias caused by ignorance and fear and culminating in high emotional excitement and violence," says Clyde Miller.[149] Nineteenth-century Christian scholar Alfred Edersheim gave a clearcut analysis of the basic cause of antisemitism when he said, "It is difficult to associate the so-called Anti-Semitic movement with any but the lowest causes: envy, jealousy, and cupidity on the one hand; or, on the other, ignorance, prejudice, bigotry, and hatred of race."[150] Because antisemitism

[146] Prager and Telushkin, p. vi, Contents.

[147] Prager and Telushkin, p. 56.

[148] Prager and Telushkin, p. 8.

[149] Clyde R. Miller, "Prejudice Can Be Prevented," in *The Jewish Veteran*, vol. XIII, no. 4, December, 1943, p. 7.

[150] Alfred Edersheim, *The Life and Times of Jesus the Messiah* (Longmans, Green, and Co., 1899), vol. 1, p. xi.

has been history's greatest mania, phobia, and hysteria, it should have come as no surprise that the ignorance, superstition, and prejudice that prompted it should have led to continuing violence that culminated in the Holocaust.

Generally speaking, antisemites have no coherent idea as to why they hate Jews. "Asked to explain why they hate Jews, anti-Semites contradict themselves," says Paul Johnson. "Jews are always showing off; they are hermetic and secretive. They will not assimilate; they assimilate only too well. They are too religious; they are too materialistic, and a threat to religion. They are uncultured; they have too much culture. They avoid manual work; they work too hard. They are miserly; they are ostentatious spenders. They are inveterate capitalists; they are born Communists. And so on." Johnson concludes that "in all its myriad manifestations, the language of anti-Semitism through the ages is a dictionary of *non sequiturs* and antonyms, a thesaurus of illogic and inconsistency."[151] Anthony Julius agrees: "Anti-Semitism takes on the character of both perverted or 'partial' truths and the sheerest of fantasy. It is evidence of a "blurring" of "perfect knowledge and utter ignorance."[152]

It has been said that "prejudice is being down on something you're not up on."[153] This is particularly true of antisemitism. The Jewish Anti-Defamation League observed in the 1930s before the rise of the Nazi regime in Germany that "there are major contributing factors to this antagonism against the Jew. Underlying most of them is the lack of knowledge of the Jew by the general public. This ignorance makes the Jew somewhat mysterious and creates suspicion, which, in turn, simplifies the propagandist's task. Ignorance of any group makes it an emotional mystery. This causes apprehension, leading easily to dislike and even to hatred."[154] The level of ignorance of Jews and things Jewish in the non-Jewish world is simply breathtaking. And what little most people think they know is drawn from media disinformation and caricature. It is no wonder that ignorance reigns

[151] Paul Johnson, "The Anti-Semitic Disease," *Commentary*, 1 June 2005, p. 34, quoted in Gary A. Tobin, Aryeh Kaufmann Weinberg, and Jenna Ferer, *The UnCivil University: Intolerance on College Campuses* (Lanham, MD: Rowman & Littlefield Publishers, 2009), p. 68. Also John Mann, *Antisemitism: The Oldest Hatred* (London, UK: Bloomsbury Publishing, 2015), p. 7.

[152] Anthony Julius, *Trials of the Diaspora: A History of Anti-Semitism in England* (Oxford, UK: Oxford University Press, 2010), p. 13.

[153] Unknown author, quoted in Gordon W. Allport, *The Nature of Prejudice* (New York: Perseus Books, 1958), p. 7.

[154] Anti-Defamation League statement, quoted in Stuart Svonkin, *Jews against Prejudice: American Jews and the Fight for Civil Liberties* (New York: Columbia University Press, 1997), p. 15.

and fuels antisemitism of every vile sort.

Too many Christians, for that matter, have minimal knowledge about the Hebrew Scriptures (which they have pejoratively called the "Old Testament"), and they have virtually no knowledge of the vast array of Jewish literature which is foundational to Rabbinic Judaism. With such monumental ignorance, it is easy for non-Jewish people—even Christians—to make false assumptions about the Jews. Because their opinions about the Jews are based on what others—including ignorant or biased Christian commentators—have said about the Jews rather on what the most reliable sources, the Jews themselves, have said about themselves, they have only stereotypes which secular and religious Judaeophobes and antisemites have created.

As Wayne Dosick has observed, "while simple ignorance and prejudice do not constitute anti-Semitism, hateful and virulent attacks against Jews—usually just for being Jewish—is an insidious disease that still grips much of the world."[155] Sadly, many mainstream Christian denominations and even some Evangelicals are regularly duped by the subtlety of today's antisemitism that woos them into joining politically fashionable efforts to delegitimize the Jewish people, the Jewish nation, and the Jewish land. In the process, some Christians have even aligned themselves with the most virulent form of antisemitism that has existed since the Holocaust—radical Islamism. They have also chosen to be on the wrong side of history and, worse yet, on the wrong side of the God of the universe who has said unequivocally, "Have you not observed what this people have spoken, saying, 'The two families which the LORD chose [Judah and Israel], he has rejected them'? . . . This is what the LORD says, 'He who appoints the sun to shine by day, who decrees the moon and stars to shine by night, who stirs up the sea so that its waves roar—the LORD Almighty is his name; Only if these decrees vanish from my sight, declares the LORD, will Israel ever cease to be a nation before me, declares the LORD.'"[156] When will Christians—supposedly the most enlightened and spiritually sensitive people in the world—ever learn? The answer may well be found in the refrain of Bob Dylan's anthem about war, peace, and human freedom: "The answer, my friend, is blowin' in the wind."[157]

---

[155] Wayne Dosick, "Anti-Semitism," in *An Introductory Dictionary of Theology and Religious Studies*, Orlando O. Espin and James B. Nickoloff, eds. (Collegeville, MN: Liturgical Press, 2007), p. 65.

[156] Jeremiah 31:35–36, NIV.

[157] Bob Dylan, "Blowin' in the Wind" (Burbank, CA: Warner Bros, Inc: 1963).

CHAPTER 2

# THE BIRTH OF ANTISEMITISM

## THE FIRST EXISTENTIAL THREAT TO JEWISH EXISTENCE

In order to understand antisemitism and its current manifestations in the world, it is important to explore the history of antisemitism and, in particular, the first known instance in which this manifest evil impacted the Jewish community. From the time four thousand years ago when God chose Abraham and entered into a covenant with him, the patriarch and his progeny faced challenges from various Gentile tribes and nations that sought to afflict them, establish hegemony over them, enslave them, and even destroy them. God's predicted reign over the Promised Land would not take place without conflict!

First, just as God had predicted to Abraham,[1] his descendants suffered vicious exploitation in Egypt by pharaohs who forced them to construct some of the architectural marvels of that realm.[2] Then, after God moved to liberate them from Egyptian bondage though Moses, they were attacked by the Amalekites as they journeyed through the Sinai desert on their way to the Promised Land.[3] Finally, after the Israelites settled in the land of Canaan, they were periodically attacked by various tribes from the surrounding area, and they were also brought under the hegemony of various invading Gentile kingdoms, including the Assyrians, the Egyptians, and the Babylonians. While numerous atrocities were perpetrated against them by invading

[1] Genesis 5:13.

[2] John Ashton and David Down, *Unwrapping the Pharaohs: How Egyptian Archaeology Confirms the Biblical Timeline* (Forest Green, AR: New Leaf Publishing Group, 2006), pp. 89–95. Also, James K. Hoffmeier, *Israel in Egypt: The Evidence for the Authenticity of the Exodus Tradition* (Oxford, UK: Oxford University Press,1999).

[3] Martin Sicker, *The Convocation at Sinai: A Study in Biblical Interpretation* (Bloomington, IN: iUniverse, 2008), p. 60. Also, John H. Sailhamer, *Old Testament History* (Grand Rapids, MI: Zondervan Publishing, 1998), p. 42.

foreign armies during the centuries of classical antiquity, however, these events generally were nothing more than struggles between conquerors and those who were conquered. Even Pharaoh's attempt to destroy all the male children born to Israelite women was largely an attempt at population control.[4]

During the first millennium after Abraham's call, therefore, most of the random acts of violence and mayhem against the Hebrews/Israelites were motivated by the perennial human lust for conquest, the desire for power and privilege at the expense of others, not by antisemitism, a vile hatred of the people themselves. What exacerbated the conflict between Abraham's progeny and the nations around them was the fact that the land that God had given to the patriarch and his descendants was, as Scripture itself noted, "the center of the land,"[5] situated at the confluence of three continents as well as at the juncture of the prominent north-south and east-west overland and maritime trade routes of the eastern Mediterranean world. "Wedged between the Arabian Desert and the Mediterranean, [Israel's] narrow sixty miles afforded the only caravan routes for north-south trade between the major nations of the world."[6] This trade route featured commercial traffic between Mesopotamia to the northeast and Egypt to the southwest. The location of the land of Israel made it not only attractive to empire builders but also virtually essential for the exercise of military might, for controlling commerce, and for mitigating against the designs of others who would impinge upon such interests.

The military powers surrounding this vital area, therefore, were more focused on controlling the fulcrum of the Asia-Europe-Africa land mass where the Hebrews/Israelites lived and on extracting taxes from the land's inhabitants than they were on annihilating the people. The geography of Israel, therefore, made its people continually vulnerable to the political and economic ambitions of virtually all of its neighbors. This was the case with the first major military exercise that resulted in the destruction of Israel and the captivity of its people. In 597 BC, Nebuchadnezzar, the king of Babylon, invaded Israel, sacked its capital city of Jerusalem, and enslaved its aristocracy and

[4] Exodus 1:9, 16. Pharaoh said, "The Israelites have become far too numerous for us. . . . When you help Hebrew women give birth . . . if the baby is a boy, kill him; if it is a girl, let her live."

[5] Ezekiel 38:12. See Jonathan Lewis, ed., *World Mission: An Analysis of the World Christian Movement* (Pasadena CA: William Carey Library, 1987), p. 217.

[6] Leon J. Wood, *A Survey of Israel's History* (Grand Rapids, MI: Zondervan Publishing House, 1970), p. 5.

ruling class. In as little as seventy years later, however, the Babylonian kingdom was conquered by the armies of Cyrus the Medo-Persian, who promptly released the Judeans, instructed them to return to their land, and funded the rebuilding of their temple.[7] Less than 15% of the Judeans involved themselves in this challenging task of uprooting themselves from the cultural and economic milieu in which they had found themselves. The 85% majority continued to live in Babylon and among other the Gentile peoples.[8] Those who remained preferred the comforts of the Tigris-Euphrates valley; however, they left themselves vulnerable to shifting sociological tides and changing political fortunes in the non-Jewish world and to increasingly vile and violent reactions against them from the native populations of the lands into which they were dispersed.

Bernard Lazare was essentially correct, therefore, when he observed that "there is no antisemitism until the Jews, having abandoned their native land, settle as immigrants in foreign countries and come into contact with natives or older settlers, whose customs, race and religion are different from those of the Hebrews."[9] As long as the Jewish people were allowed to remain in their own homeland as a separate and distinct people and nation with their own laws and traditions, antisemitism—the hatred of Jews as Jews—did not exist. After the Israelites were dispersed among the nations either through captivity, expulsion, or economic hardship, their laws and customs posed a psychological, social, and, indeed, a religious threat to the nations among whom they lived and the people among whom they refused to integrate and compromise their faith and traditions.

## A New Menace Rising

In the fifth century BC, something insidious was brewing in the Persian Empire of Xerxes the Great. A malady was in the process of emerging that would have continuing and enduring impact upon the Jews for centuries to come. There, in the world's proudest and most powerful kingdom, the first recorded attempt to annihilate the Jewish people through systematic genocide emerged. In the egocentric intrigue of the imperial court, antisemitism, the

[7] Ezra 1:1—6:22.

[8] Frank M. Loewenberg, *From Charity to Social Justice* (New Brunswick, NJ: Transaction Publishers, 2001), p. 59.

[9] Bernard Lazare, *Antisemitism, Its History and Causes* (New York: The International Library Publishing Co., 1903), p. 27.

hatred of Jews—including prejudice, hostility, and discrimination against Jews—was born. And for the twenty-five hundred years that have ensued since that time, the unparalleled[10] sociopathic disease of antisemitism has infected and befouled large portions of the non-Jewish world, wreaking havoc upon the Jewish people through intimidation, violence, mayhem, and murder.

The philosophical foundation for the emergence of this Persian antisemitism had actually been established earlier in Medo-Persia, where jealous bureaucratic administrators in the court of Darius the Mede desperately sought for an excuse that they could use to have the prophet and sage Daniel removed from his position as chief advisor to the king. After a diligent and unproductive search rendered no evidence of malfeasance or unethical conduct with which they could accuse Daniel before the king, they finally reached this conclusion: "We will never find any basis for charges against this man Daniel unless it has something to do with the law of his God."[11] Having made that determination, they immediately began to formulate a plan to depose the prophet. In doing so, they established a foundation for an insidious and enduring phenomenon wherein the Jewish people would be targeted individually and collectively simply because of their faith. This, then, was the root cause of antisemitism: making charges against the Jewish people because of "something to do with God's law." And, the same indictment has continued to resonate across the annals of time.

Not long after Daniel's experience, this same idea was taken to extreme in another generation of the Persian Empire.[12] In the fortress city of Shushan (Susa),[13] the capital city of this realm, Xerxes the Great[14] ruled over the vast domain that stretched from India to Ethiopia and into southern Europe. At this time, Persia dominated the entire Middle East and beyond; therefore, virtually every Jew in the entire world lived in the Persian Empire. This created a unique situation in which every living Jew was vulnerable to decisions that

[10] Alice L. Eckardt and A. Roy Eckardt, *Long Night's Journey into Day: A Revised Retrospective on the Holocaust* (Detroit, MI: Wayne State University Press, 1982), p. 58. The Eckardts said, "The phenomenon of antisemitism is incomparable. There are no parallels to it. There simply is no historical analogue to antisemitism. . . . Whether we speak of space or of time, the two primordial dimensions of human existence, no prejudice comes anywhere near antisemitism. No prejudice can approach antisemitism for either geopolitical pervasiveness or temporal enduringness."

[11] Daniel 6:5, NIV.

[12] Xerxes I was actually the grandson of Cyrus through his daughter Atossa's marriage to Darius the Great.

[13] The term *Shushan* described both the city and the palace of Xerxes (Esther 9:12–15).

[14] In most translations of Scripture, Xerxes is called Ahasuerus, which is a Latinized form of the transliteration of the Hebrew *Akhashverosh*. Both Ahasuerus and Xerxes ultimately are transliterated or approximated forms of the Persian *Xsayarsa*.

issued forth from the Shushan palace and were then enforced by the strong, efficient, and merciless Persian military. This expansive and powerful empire was to become the staging ground for a plot that, if successful, would have resulted in the complete genocide of the Jewish people and the consequent failure of the God's covenant with Abraham. At the same time that the forces of evil were feverishly working to create such a scenario of death and destruction, however, God was at work, orchestrating events that would preserve the lives of his Chosen People in the same way in which he had previously intervened in the politics of Babylon and Medo-Persia.

## A New Queen Is Chosen

Xerxes had conquered a large swath of land and established a dynamic and powerful capital city for his empire. He was, therefore, in a celebratory mood. So, he organized an ostentatious party to showcase Shushan and the monuments to his wealth and power. "For a full 180 days [Xerxes] displayed the vast wealth of his kingdom and the splendor and glory of his majesty."[15] Then, at the conclusion of that time, he staged a seven-day banquet for all the people in Sushan so that they could see the sumptuous magnificence of his palace. Finally, on the last day of that celebration, as if to put an exclamation point on his grandeur, the king summoned his queen Vashti to appear before him so that everyone could see her beauty. When the orders were delivered to the queen, however, she refused to appear.[16] The king was furious and after consulting with his advisors determined that in order to limit confusion throughout the realm, Vashti should be removed and replaced by another queen.[17]

After a long process of evaluation and elimination, a new queen was indeed chosen. The chosen one was Hadassah ("Esther" in Persian), a young Jewish girl of such extraordinary beauty that the biblical account describing her is straightforward and graphic: "The young lady was very attractive and had a beautiful figure."[18] The young woman who was to

---

[15] Esther 1:4, NIV.

[16] There are various interpretations as to why Vashti refused her husband's bidding. Some suggest that it was because she would have been paraded in the nude before the male nobles in the midst of a drunken orgy. Mark Mangano, *The College Press NIV Commentary: Esther & Daniel* (Goshen, IN: College Press Publishing Co., 2001), p. 44. Some commentators have even suggested that she was to wear only her royal crown. Walter A. Elwell and Philip W. Comfort, *Tyndale Bible Dictionary* (Wheaton, IL: Tyndale House Publishers, 2001), vol. 4, p. 800. Others argue that the idea Xerxes demanded that Vashti appear before the nobles in the nude is an interpolation into the text of Esther that has no substance. Howard D. Wilcox, *Divine Providence* (Bloomington, IN: Life Way Publishers, 2011), p. 84.

[17] The reason given for Vashti's deposal was that her refusal would foment the rebellion of women throughout the realm against their husbands.

[18] Esther 2:7, NET.

become the Queen of Persia was, however, more than just a pretty face. She was intelligent, graceful, resourceful, and courageous. She was a master of the etiquette of the imperial court and was able to relate in every way to the king who chose her as his bride. As it turned out, Esther was also amazingly creative, socially adroit, and powerfully resolute. Beyond being a beautiful, perspicacious, and capable young woman, however, Esther was also the example *par excellence* of the proverbial idealized "Woman of Valor" that Solomon had described centuries before that time.[19] The phrase translated "woman of valor" appears in Hebrew as אֵשֶׁת־חַיִל (*eshet chayil*),[20] The word *chayil* is almost always associated in Scripture with the strength of a warrior. As the narrative of the Book of Esther unfolded, Persia's young queen clearly demonstrated that she met all the qualities of Solomon's *eshet chayil* by demonstrating not only her beauty, grace, and resourcefulness, but also her tenacity and bravery.

Esther's emergence as queen of the Persian realm was the result of circumstances and events that were being divinely orchestrated in preparation for what would be needed to ensure the survival of the Chosen People; therefore, on the advice of Mordecai, her cousin and mentor, Esther kept her true identity as a Jewish maiden totally secret. The strategic placement of Esther as the queen of the realm and a favorite of Xerxes could not have been more important in this circumstance. Then, Esther's position was strengthened even more when Mordecai discovered an assassination plot against Xerxes and encouraged Esther to expose the plot to Xerzes. Afterwards, both Esther and Mordecai were honored by the king for their loyalty and integrity, and they both obtained favor in the royal court.

## Treachery Festers

A powerful and insidious evil, however, was lurking in the highest ranks of the Persian government. The realm's newly appointed prime minister, Haman, was a man who suffered from severe egomania. He loved the pomposity and the perquisites of power. He relished seeing the

[19] The "Woman of Valor" declaration was not original to Solomon, for he confessed that it was taught to him by his mother. Rabbinic tradition suggests that it was written by Abraham as a eulogy for his wife, Sarah, centuries before the time of Solomon. Penina Adelman, *Praise Her Works: Conversations with Biblical Women* (Philadelphia, PA: Jewish Publication Society, 2005), p. xiv.

[20] Virtually all English translations fail to capture the quality and nature of the Woman of Valor of Proverbs 31:10, translating the Hebrew as "an excellent wife" (NASB, ESV); "a wife of noble character" (NIV); "a virtuous woman" (KJV); "a capable wife" (NRS). The JPS, however, translates the phrase correctly: "a woman of valor." When associated with men, the Hebrew word *chayil* is translated "valiant men" (Judges 18:2), "valiant warriors" (Judges 20:44, 46, NASB), "men of valor" (Judges 20:44, 46, KJV). When associated with women, however, *chayil* is translated "capable" and "virtuous," while "valiant" is rare.

people bowing themselves to the ground in his presence. Because the Jewish people were under divine instructions not to bow to anyone except their God, Mordecai refused to do obeisance before Haman when he passed by in all of his pomp and glory. This, in turn, infuriated the prime minister and prompted him to devise a way in which he could avenge himself against Mordecai's audacity and assuage the pain that this impudent Jew had inflicted on his ego. Haman's inability to deal with his narcissistic pride prompted the sages of Israel label him as *Haman ha-Rasha* ("Haman the Wicked"), thereby designating him as a living "symbol of absolute evil."[21] The fact that Scripture reported that Haman was an Agagite,[22] a descendant of the Amalekites who had terrorized the Israelites during their wilderness journey, strengthened the sages' understanding of his evil nature, for Amalek was a "symbol of the most unqualified kind of evil, the most dangerous and reviled enemy of the Jews."[23]

It just so happened that the Jew whom Haman loathed was Mordecai. The fury that this petty bureaucrat felt was so excessive that he simply could not be satisfied with personal revenge against Mordecai. So, he "looked for a way to destroy all Mordecai's people, the Jews, throughout the whole kingdom of Xerxes."[24] As Anthony Julius notes, "[T]he refusal of *one* Jew to observe *Haman's* 'law' thus becomes, in a typical anti-Semitic twist, a refusal by *all* Jews to observe the *king's* law. A threat to Haman's self-esteem becomes a threat to the well-being of the kingdom."[25]

## A Damnable Conspiracy Emerges

Instead of dealing directly with Mordecai, Haman approached the king with these scurrilous words of slander: "There is a certain people

[21] Albert S. Lindemann and Richard S. Levy, eds., *Antisemitism: A History* (Oxford, UK: Oxford University Press, 2010), p. 12.

[22] Esther 3:1.

[23] Lindemann and Levy, p. 21.

[24] Esther 3:6, NIV.

[25] Anthony Julius, *Trials of the Diaspora: A History of Anti-Semitism in England* (Oxford, UK: Oxford University Press, 2010), p. 13, Julius' emphasis. Julius compares Haman's position vis-à-vis the Jews as being parallel with that of Amalek, Haman's ancestor, who Scripture says "knew nothing about the Jews" but was also a witness "to miracles and revelation" (Exodus 17:8–16). He notes, therefore, that Haman's irrational hatred of the Jews was similar to that of Amalek in that it was based on "perfect knowledge and utter ignorance" at the same time! Haman, the Agagite, was also a descendant of Agag, the king of the Amalekites at the time when Saul was king of Israel. Ultimately, Haman's ancestry could be traced through Agag to Amalek and thence to Jacob's brother Esau, who Elaine Glickman says "looms in rabbinic literature as a virtual embodiment of evil and Jew-hatred." Elaine Rose Glickman, *Haman and the Jews: A Portrait from Rabbinic Literature* (New York: Jason Aronson, 1999), p. 18. In fact, God declared that the Almighty himself would make war with Amalek "throughout the generations" (Exodus 17:6).

dispersed among the peoples in the provinces of your kingdom who keep themselves separate. Their customs are different from those of all other people, and they do not obey the king's laws; it is not in the king's best interest to tolerate them. If it pleases the king, let a decree be issued to destroy them."[26] Then, he petitioned the king for the enactment of a vicious edict for genocide of the Jews and pledged to remunerate the king for any loss of revenue that might result from his plan to eliminate them: "I will give ten thousand talents of silver to the king's administrators for the royal treasury."[27] To Haman, the lives of "all the Jews" in the Persian Empire would have been worth over $200 million in today's money.[28]

In expressing his personal animus for the Jews in that realm, however, Haman was actually demonstrating his hatred for the God of the Jews. The contempt that seethed in his heart and the political machinations that his anger produced have become hallmarks for countless antisemites across the pages of history who have also sought to delegitimize and destroy the Jews. This people has been singled out for marginalization, persecution, violence, mayhem, and murder simply because they have been "different." And their primary difference from others is manifest in their belief system, for they have worshiped their God alone, and they have refused to syncretize their faith with that of their neighbors or their conquerors.

The declaration, "It is not in the king's best interest to tolerate [this certain people]," was perhaps the first and most succinct description of overt antisemitism ever set forth. Throughout their history, the Jewish people had been—and would continue to be—judged because "their customs are different from those of other people," for they had followed God's instructions to separate themselves from participation in the idolatry of other nations. More often than not, the Jewish people found themselves unable to "keep the king's laws." While they did their best to be loyal subjects of the realms in which they lived, still they were bound by the Torah to keep God's commandments,[29] even if it meant suffering persecution and

[26] Esther 3:8–9. The text literally says, "It is not worthwhile for the king to let them rest."

[27] Esther 3:9, NIV.

[28] Haman's intention was to contribute this sum to the royal treasury from the booty seized from the Jews during their slaughter. Interestingly, this sum was approximately 60% of the annual income of the Persian government at that time. Michael D. Coogan, Marc Z. Brettler, Carol A. Newsom, and Pheme Perkins, eds., *The New Oxford Annotated Bible with Apocrypha: New Revised Standard Edition* (Oxford, UK: Oxford University Press, 2010), p. 1417.

[29] Specific commandments that prompted, if not assured, Israelite separation from the idolatry of the Gentile world included the laws concerning circumcision (Deuteronomy 10:16), Sabbath (Exodus 20:8), hairstyles (Leviticus 19:27), dress (Numbers 15:40), and dietary regulations (Leviticus 11).

martyrdom. Their time in Persia was no different.

Haman's appeal was so effective that Xerxes gave him his own signet ring, told him to keep his money, and ordered him to "do with the people as you please."[30] Immediately, the royal secretaries wrote the decree in Xerxes' name in the languages of every province and sealed them with the king's signet ring. Dispatches were sent by couriers to all the provinces of the Persian Empire with this order: "Destroy, kill, and annihilate all the Jews—young and old, women and children—on . . . the thirteenth day of the twelfth month . . . and plunder their goods."[31] Haman's evil plot had the force of imperial law that was irrevocable. The prospect was simple: all the Jews in Persia—and, therefore, virtually all the Jews in the world—were going to be killed, effecting their complete genocide.

When Mordecai learned of the edict, he, like Jews throughout the realm, tore his clothes, put on sackcloth and ashes, and went about "wailing loudly and bitterly."[32] In short order, he conveyed the information of Haman's plot to Esther. The queen thought her hands were tied because unless she was summoned to appear before Xerxes, she could not do so without risking her own life in the process. Mordecai made this response to her excuse: "Do not think that because you are in the king's house you alone of all the Jews will escape. For if you remain silent at this time, relief and deliverance for the Jews will arise from another place, but you and your father's family will perish."[33] Then he addressed his cousin with these immortal words: "Who knows but that you have come to royal position for such a time as this?"[34]

## Exposing the Conspiracy

Esther immediately demonstrated her profound faith by asking Mordecai to request that all the Jews in Shushan fast and pray for her for three days and nights. Then, with astounding bravery, she said, "I will go to the king, even though it is against the law. And if I perish, I perish."[35] As she had promised, on the third day, Esther put on her royal robes and, fearing the worst, cautiously entered the royal court. When Xerxes saw her, however, he was pleased, so

[30] Esther 3:11.

[31] Esther 3:13, NIV.

[32] Esther 4:1.

[33] Esther 4:13–14a, NIV.

[34] Esther 4:14b, NIV.

[35] Esther 4:16, NIV.

he held out the golden scepter, sparing her life. "What is it, Queen Esther? What is your request? Even up to half of the kingdom, it will be given you," he said.[36] The ever-resourceful Esther had already devised a plan as to how she would approach the king in the context of the court intrigue wherein Haman appeared to have the upper hand. "If it pleases the king," she replied, "let the king, together with Haman, come today to a banquet I have prepared for him." The king agreed, and, in due course, with Haman in tow, he dutifully arrived at Esther's banquet, asking, "Now what is your petition?" The coy Esther replied, "Let the king and Haman come tomorrow" to another banquet, and "then I will answer the king's question."[37]

The biblical text reports that Haman went out that day happy and in high spirits. "I'm the only person Queen Esther invited to accompany the king to the banquet she gave," he boasted. At the same time, however, he moaned to his wife, "All this gives me no satisfaction as long as I see that Jew Mordecai sitting at the king's gate."[38] The devious woman had a solution: "Have a pole set up, reaching to a height of seventy-five feet, and ask the king in the morning to have Mordecai impaled on it."[39] This suggestion delighted Haman, so he had the pole erected on which he just knew he would see Mordecai die the next day.

During the ensuing night, Xerxes could not sleep, so he ordered his servants to read to him from a book that chronicled the events of his reign. This book just happened to open to the records that detailed how Mordecai had exposed the assassination plot against the king. "What honor and recognition has Mordecai received for this?" the king inquired. "Nothing," his servants replied. At that moment, Haman just happened to enter the royal chambers, so the king summoned him and asked, "What should be done for the man the king delights to honor?" he asked. The prime minister, thinking that the king was speaking of him, replied, "Have them bring a royal robe the king has worn and a horse the king has ridden, one with the royal crest placed on its head. . . . Let them robe the man . . . and lead him on the horse through the city streets, proclaiming before him: 'This is what is done for the man the king delights to honor!'"

To Haman's utter shock and dismay, Xerxes immediately gave

---

[36] Esther 5:3, NIV.

[37] Esther 5:8.

[38] Esther 5:12–13, NIV.

[39] Esther 5:14, NIV.

him this order: "Go at once. Get the robe and the horse and do just as you have suggested for Mordecai the Jew, who sits at the king's gate." Now filled with fear and consternation, Haman dutifully fulfilled his king's command and then rushed home only to hear his wife say ominously, "Since Mordecai, before whom your downfall has started, is of Jewish origin, you cannot stand against him—you will surely come to ruin!"[40] Before Haman could do a thing, however, the king's messengers arrived to escort him to the queen's banquet.

After the festivities began, Xerxes again asked Esther, "What is your request?" This time, the queen boldly replied, "If it pleases you, grant me my life—this is my petition. And spare my people—this is my request. For I and my people have been sold to be destroyed, killed, and annihilated."[41] Immediately, the shocked king asked his bride, "Who is . . . the man who has dared to do such a thing?" Unhesitatingly, Esther pointed out the enemy: "This vile Haman!" Upon hearing this news, the king was furious and went out into the palace garden to collect his thoughts. Realizing that the king would certainly decide his fate in a matter of minutes, Haman stayed behind to beg the queen for his life. When Xerxes returned, he found Haman falling on the couch where Esther was reclining and exclaimed, "Will he even molest the queen while she is with me in the house?" The king's judgment was immediate and final: "Impale Haman on the pole by his house," and the sentence was then carried out forthwith.

Esther chose to risk all and make an unannounced appearance before Xerxes. Then, she carefully orchestrated a series of events which would culminate in her opportunity to inform her husband of the insidious plot that Haman had created. In the end, Haman was exposed and was summarily executed by the command of Xerxes on the same device that he had prepared for Mordecai's execution.

## Antisemitism Avenged

That left one important bit of unfinished business. What could be done about the inalterable imperial decree that specified a date for the annihilation of all the Jews in the Persian Empire? As a counter-measure, Xerxes issued another decree giving the Jews in every city the right to assemble and protect themselves against anyone who would attack them. When this decree was published, there was great joy in Persia, especially

[40] Esther 6:13, NIV.

[41] Esther 7:3–4, NIV.

among the Jews, and Mordecai was highly honored. Then, the text of Scripture makes this startling declaration: "Many people of other nationalities became Jews because fear of the Jews had seized them."[42] The text does not explain how this was accomplished, but it does note the turn of events. Finally, on the day appointed, when "the enemies of the Jews had hoped to overpower them, now the tables were turned and the Jews got the upper hand over those who hated them."[43] The victory of the Jews was complete. Genocide was averted. *Am Yisrael chai*!

Among the Jews, the next day was a time of such great rejoicing that a new festival celebrating that day was added to the calendar of Torah festivals outlined in Leviticus 23. This festival, called Purim, thereafter became a prominent fixture in the lives of the Jews.[44] The term *purim* was chosen for the name of this annual memorial in order to remind the Jews of the fact that Haman had cast lots (*purim*) in order to set the date for his planned massacre of the Jews[45] and that this date which Haman had chosen by lots became the date for the great Jewish victory over genocide that had been planned for them. Each year thereafter, Purim was a time to celebrate God's deliverance of the Jews from the certainty of death into abundant life—all because divine providence had positioned a young Jewish girl in the palace of the world's most powerful king and had emboldened her with faith to intercede for the deliverance of her people. Esther was, indeed, elevated by God's hand into royalty "for such a time as this," and she did not fail to accomplish her mission. The genocide of the entire Jewish people was averted, and antisemitism failed.

## Lessons for Confronting Antisemitism

The chronicle of Esther and Mordecai and their brave actions to prevent the genocide of the Jews during the height of the Persian Empire is a lesson not only for Jews but also for all human beings of conscience. Christians especially should take a fresh look at interpreting the Book of Esther with a view toward its parallels with the Holocaust. Drawing on these parallels, Emil Fackenheim identifies the state of Israel as "a new Mordecai for a new age in the history of Judaism, guarding the Jewish remnant."[46] Moshe Aberbach says that "the story of Esther . . . gives the

[42] Esther 8:17.

[43] Esther 9:1, NIV.

[44] Esther 9:20–26.

[45] Jeffrey M. Cohen, *Prayer and Penitence: A Commentary on the High Holy Day Machzor* (Northvale, NJ: Jason Aronson, 1994), p. 136.

[46] Emil L. Fackenheim, *The Jewish Bible after the Holocaust: A Re-reading* (Bloomington, IN: Indiana University Press, 1991), p. 95.

same cathartic message—that Jews can escape genocide" when "in some cases human intervention may be necessary, though the invisible hand of God is in the background."[47] Bruce Zuckerman and Zev Garber maintain that the Book of Esther serves as an example "in which human protagonists must face and overcome a genocidal threat to the future of the Jewish people posed by an irresponsible Gentile government."[48] On a more personal level, Deborah Prescott suggests poignantly that the Book of Esther may well "serve as a paradigm for Shoah autobiographies as a 'new Bible.'"[49]

It should not be considered unusual, therefore, that the sages of Israel have ascribed powerful significance to the Book of Esther in the canon of the Hebrew Scriptures. While sixteenth-century Christian Reformers vilified this book as not worthy of being included in Holy Scripture,[50] while secular Enlightenment philosophers excoriated it for the "execrable cruelty of the sweet Esther,"[51] and while even twentieth-century Protestant scholars maintained it reflected "a low ethical standard [wherein] nothing seems wrong if only it furthers the advancement of the Jews"[52] and was "an exaltation of nationalism at its worst,"[53] Jewish scholar Flavius Josephus listed the Book of Esther among texts considered inspired of God by Jews and Christians of his day,[54] and eleventh-century Talmudist Moses Maimonides ranked it next to the Torah in importance in the Hebrew Scriptures: "When the Messiah comes, only Esther and the Torah will remain."[55]

---

[47] Moshe Aberbach, *Jewish Education and History: Continuity, Crisis and Change* (Abingdon, UK: Routledge, 2009), p. 80.

[48] Bruce Zuckerman and Zev Garber, *The Impact of the Holocaust in America* (West Lafayette, IN: Purdue University Press, 2008), p. 172.

[49] Deborah Lee Prescott, *Imagery from Genesis in Holocaust Memoirs: A Critical Study* (Jefferson, NC: McFarland & Company, Publishers, 2010), p. 25. Prescott's statement was likely made to amplify the importance of Holocaust memories rather than to equate them with Holy Scripture. Holocaust remembrance literature is not, nor can it be, canonical, for only Holy Scripture is the divinely inspired self-disclosure of God to Israel. For an excellent discussion of biblical prophecy and the modern Jewish experience, see Yehoshua Pfeffer, *Prophecies and Providence: A Biblical Approach to Modern Jewish History* (Jerusalem, Israel: Urim Publications, 2015).

[50] Martin Luther, "On the Jews and Their Lies," quoted in Heinrich Bornkamm, *Luther and the Old Testament*, tr. E. W. Gritsch and R. C. Gritsch (Philadelphia, PA: Fortress Press, 1969), pp. 188–189. Luther said, the Jews "love the book of Esther, which so well fits their bloodthirsty, vengeful, murderous greed and hope." Luther also expressed his view that the Book of Esther should not have existed at all because it "judaized too much" and had much "pagan impropriety." Martin Luther, *Table Talk XXIV*, in William Hazlitt, *Table-Talk; or Original Essays* (London, England: John Warren, 1821), p. 11.

[51] Voltaire, quoted in Elias Joseph Bickerman, *Four Strange Books of the Bible: Jonah, Daniel, Koheleth, Esther* (New York: Schocken Books, 1984), p. 215.

[52] Thomas Witton Davies, *Ezra, Nehemiah, and Esther* (Charleston, SC: Nabu Press, 2010), vol. 15, p. 318.

[53] Henry Wheeler Robinson, *The Old Testament: Its Making and Meaning* (London, UK: University of London Press, 1966), p. 74.

[54] Flavius Josephus, *Against Apion*, in Steve Mason, ed., *Flavius Josephus: Against Apion,* tr. John M. G. Barclay (The Netherlands: Koninklijke Brill NV, 2007), pp. 29–30.

[55] Moses Maimonides, *Mishneh Torah, Hilchot Megillah* 2.18.

As Brevard Childs says, "The inclusion of Esther within the Christian canon serves as a check against all attempts to spiritualize the concept of Israel—usually by misinterpreting Paul—and thus removing the ultimate scandal of biblical particularity."[56] Richard Bauckham is right when he argues that in the light of the persecution of the Jews that culminated in the Holocaust, "Christians would do well to read Esther precisely as a Jewish book whose presence in the Christian Bible claims Christian attention. They should read Esther as the book which Jewish inmates of the Nazi death-camps were forbidden to read, but wrote out from memory and read in secret on Purim."[57]

The truth is that the book of Esther "is a story of the *co-operation* between divine providence, manifest in unpredictable events, and the resourceful and courageous actions of Mordecai and Esther."[58] As such, this text confirms God's sovereign faithfulness to his Chosen People. It also affirms the very existence of God as the one who said, "I am YHWH, I change not: therefore you children of Jacob are not consumed,"[59] and who assures Christians that "Jesus Christ is the same yesterday, and today, and forever."[60] In reality, God can be utterly trusted to be faithful to Christians only because he has proven that he is faithful to the Jewish people.

The words of Haman's diabolical indictment of the Jewish people in Persia must continue to echo across the corridors of time so people of conscience can immediately recognize the subtlety of the newest guise of antisemitism and make an unequivocal stand against it. Red lights must flash and sirens must scream whenever and wherever words like these are heard: "There is a certain people dispersed among the peoples in the provinces of your kingdom who keep themselves separate. Their customs are different from those of all other people, and they do not obey the king's laws; it is not in the king's best interest to tolerate them."[61] Ironically, this kind of rhetoric is increasingly featured in postmodern indictments against all those who stand on the authority of the Hebrew Scriptures, whether they be Jews or Christians.

---

[56] Brevard S. Childs, *Introduction to the Old Testament as Scripture* (Philadelphia, PA: Fortress Press, 1979), p. 606.

[57] Richard Bauckham, *The Bible in Politics: How to Read the Bible Politically* (London, UK: Society for Promoting Christian Knowledge, 1989), p. 125.

[58] Bauckham, p. 125.

[59] Malachi 3:6.

[60] Hebrews 13:8.

[61] Esther 3:8.

CHAPTER 3

# ANTISEMITISM IN ANTIQUITY

## THE MANY GUISES OF SHAPESHIFTING ANTISEMITISM

While Haman epitomized antisemitism more than any other person in history except for Adolph Hitler, his maxim, "Never tolerate the Jews," has reverberated across the centuries among various peoples and in diverse circumstances. The deep-seated pathology of utter intolerance toward the Jewish people and their faith has spread like wildfire to most of the societies into which the Jewish people have been scattered, and it has continued to seethe beneath the surface in significant numbers of Gentile nations. Wherever the Jewish people have had to live since they were forcibly removed from their homeland, they have encountered varying degrees of antisemitism—prejudice, hatred, persecution, confiscation, violence, and murder.

This history can be documented at least to the fourth century BC, when Democritus of Thrace made this profoundly libelous indictment against the Jews: "Every seven years the Jews captured a stranger, brought him to the temple in Jerusalem, and sacrificed him, cutting his flesh into bits."[1] This charge of Jewish ritual sacrifice of Gentiles was repeated in various nations and cultures, culminating in the twelfth-century Blood Libel in England that accused Jews of murdering Christian children in order to use the blood for making *matzah* (unleavened bread) for Passover.[2] Sadly, this vicious indictment has continued to survive in some form well into the twenty-first century when it is still being used by antisemites to justify

[1] Democritus, quoted in Joshua Trachtenberg, *The Devil and the Jews: The Medieval Conception of the Jew and Its Relation to Modern Antisemitism* (Philadelphia, PA: Jewish Publication Society, 1983), p. 126. Also, David Matas, *Aftershock: Anti-Zionism and Antisemitism* (Toronto, Canada: Dundurn Press, 2005), pp. 30–31, and Phillis Chesler, *The New Antisemitism: The Current Crisis and What We Must Do About It* (San Francisco, CA: Jossey-Bass, 2003), pp. 158–159, 181.

[2] Alan Dundes, *The Blood Libel Legend: A Casebook in Anti-Semitic Folklore* (Madison, WI: The University of Wisconsin Press, 1991), p. vii. Also, Hannah Johnson, *Blood Libel: The Ritual Murder Accusation at the Limit of Jewish History* (Ann Arbor, MI: The University of Michigan Press, 2012), p. 14.

their unbridled hatred for the Jewish people and to issue unrelenting calls for their annihilation as individuals, as a people, and as a nation.[3]

## Antisemitism in the Hellenistic World

The first instance in which antisemitism was documented by sources outside Jewish literature also took place in the fourth century BC, when another calumny similar to that of Democritus was leveled against the Jews. During the time when Alexander the Great conquered Egypt, significant numbers of Greek and Jewish people immigrated into Alexandria, bringing with them cultures and practices that were significantly different from those of the indigenous Egyptian people. Because both of these immigrant cultures were quite different from their Egyptian culture, there was no sociological reason why the Egyptians should resent and hate the Jews more than the Greeks; however, that is precisely what happened. Why? "The Egyptians found the Jews' religious culture and traditions offensive,"[4] says Dennis Prager. As a matter of fact, the Egyptian priest Manetho was so "annoyed by the Jews' liturgy and Bible with its depictions of the Jews' exodus from Egypt" that he "decided to rewrite that event, saying that the Jews were expelled from Egypt because they were lepers."[5] Because of this charge, Manetho is considered by some to be the source of antisemitism.[6] This historical document offers proof that the underlying cause of antisemitism is hatred for Jews as symbols of God.

Alexander took a novel approach toward the peoples whom he conquered in that he did not seek to destroy their gods and their religions. Instead, he sought to infuse their cultures—and their religions—with Hellenism, the language, culture, philosophy, and religion of the Greek realm that he had learned from his mentor Aristotle. This process of syncretism was profoundly subtle and was usually successful in imbuing the Greek worldview and mindset into many realms into which Alexander took his conquest. In this way, the hegemony that Alexander established over the territories that he conquered was perpetuated long after his own death when those territories incorporated much of Hellenistic thought

[3] Raphael Israeli, *Blood Libel and Its Derivatives: The Scourge of Antisemitism* (New Brunswick, NJ: Transaction Publishers, 2012), pp. 21–23.

[4] Dennis Prager and Joseph Telushkin, *Why the Jews?: The Reason for Antisemitism* (New York: Simon and Schuster, 1983), pp. 68–69.

[5] Prager and Telushkin, pp. 68–69.

[6] Albert S. Lindemann and Richard S. Levy, *Antisemitism: A History* (Oxford, UK: Oxford University Press, 2010), p. 22. Also, Peter Schäfer, *Judeophobia: Attitudes toward the Jews in the Ancient World* (Cambridge, MA: Harvard University Press, 1997), p. 208.

and practice into their own sociological and religious traditions.

In the case of the Jews and the nation of Israel, however, Hellenization largely failed to amalgamate itself with Jews and Judaism, much less to supersede Jewish culture and religion.[7] This was because Hellenism and Judaism could not be fused, amalgamated, or even held in suspension. Because the Jews rejected efforts to syncretize Judaism with Hellenism the Greeks created "Hellenistic antisemitic tracts, which continually harp[ed] on Jewish distinctiveness as a great evil and an offense to the religious-political unity of the polis,"[8] says Michael Fox. The Jewish people "were never quite like the others . . . they had no part in the morals and customs of the people about them, nor in that syncretism that was meant to be so tolerant."[9] This is why "sharp criticism of the Jews because of their ἀμιξία [*amixia*], non-mingling with the Gentiles . . . resounds in a whole scale of tones in the literature of ancient writers."[10] Consequently, Hellenism's inherent anti-Judaism and antisemitism impacted the Jewish people in one way or another from the time of Alexander forward and continue to do so even to the present day.

This is why Leo Strauss maintains that "in order to understand ourselves, we [Jews] must understand Jerusalem and Athens."[11] Strauss explains that whereas Hellenism (Athens) stands for "free inquiry," Judaism (Jerusalem) means "obedient love."[12] Greek philosophy insists that truth "lies in the free inquiry of autonomous reason." This means that "philosophy would first deduce the right path and then take a step"; it "would first hear—first understand—and then do." In contrast, Judaism

[7] Hellenism did impact Judaism from the time of the sages when they drifted from commitment to absolute truth into dialectic exercises. Daniel Boyarin says, "Hellenistic ways of life, thought and expression were integral to Jewish Palestinian culture from at least the mid third century [BC] on, and these tendencies affected Pharisaism and later Rabbinic writings." Concerning interpretation, he adds, "There is testimony . . . for a late Babylonian talmudic understanding of hermeneutics which denies completely the concept of a Logos lying behind and outside the text, limiting and controlling meaning. . . . This understanding of hermeneutics correlates . . . with . . . rabbinic dialectic as dialectic without resolution, without telos, and in itself a representation of the *polynoia* of the divine Word and the divine mind." Daniel Boyarin, *Border Lines: Partition of Judaeo-Christianity* (Philadelphia, PA: The University of Pennsylvania Press, 2004), p. 191. For additional influences of Hellenism in Rabbinic Judaism, see Boyarin, pp. 75, 86, 278

[8] Michael V. Fox, *Character and Ideology in the Book of Esther* (Eugene, OR: Wipf and Stock Publishers, 1991), p. 49. Fox references Jan Nicholaas Sevenster, *The Roots of Pagan Anti-Semitism in the Ancient World* (Leiden, The Netherlands: E. J. Brill, 1975).

[9] Sevenster, p. 89.

[10] Sevenster, p. 89.

[11] Leo Strauss, *Studies in Platonic Political Philosophy* (Chicago, IL: The University of Chicago Press, 2003), p. 147. For an excellent discussion of Hellenism (Athens) vs. Judaism (Jerusalem), including Strauss' observations, see David Patterson, *Anti-Semitism and Its Metaphysical Origins* (Cambridge, UK: Cambridge University Press, 2015), pp.107–114.

[12] Leo Strauss, *The Rebirth of Classical Political Rationalism: An Introduction to the Thought of Leo Strauss* (Chicago, IL: The University of Chicago Press, 1989), p. 71.

(represented by Israel's response when God gave them his Torah at Sinai) says, "All that the Lord has said, we shall do and we shall hear [understand]."[13] Strauss observes this fundamental truth: "By saying that we wish to hear first and then to act, we have already decided in favor of Athens against Jerusalem."[14] When Greek rationalism pervades and subverts pure faith that is manifest in faithfulness to divine imperatives, one has become a disciple of Hellenism and not of biblical faith. Hellenism, therefore, though subtle, is *ipso facto* a form of anti-Judaism and antisemitism. Hyam Maccoby observes that "it was in the first century CE, in Hellenistic intellectual circles, especially in Alexandria, that a coherent historical schema can be seen in its most hostile form,"[15] a "cerebral" antisemitism that denied self-determination to Jews and Judaism in favor of the politically and socially correct Hellenism that subsumed other cultures under its "multiculturalism." Multiculturalism in Hellenistic thought was not "a movement calling for resilience to cultural diversity or endowing immigrants with essential rights. . . . [M]ulticulturalism is described as 'an attempt to subsume plurality of cultures within the framework of . . . national identity.'[16] . . . Multiculturalism *à la grecque* predicates a symbolic transition from social and cultural introversion to universalist scenes and debates.'"[17]

## A Hellenism Devotee and Antisemitism Personified

It should have come as no surprise, therefore, that during the second century BC, the same antisemitic spirit that had possessed Haman in Persia was manifest in a passionate, fanatical devotee to Hellenism, Antiochus IV, grandson of Seleucus Nicator, one of the four generals who succeeded Alexander the Great after his death. Antiochus became yet another incarnation of the demon of antisemitism when he assumed the title *Epiphanes* ("God manifest") and exalted himself against the God and the faith of the Jews. Because

[13] Exodus 24:7. The implication of the word *shema* ("hear") in Hebrew is that of hearing with a view toward doing. It is in doing that "hearing" is completed, and it is in doing that "understanding" is achieved. This is why the apostle James declared that only the person who looks into the Torah and *does it* is "blessed in his deeds" (James 1:25).

[14] Strauss, p. 150.

[15] Hyam Maccoby, *Antisemitism and Modernity: Innovation and Continuity* (Abingdon, UK: Routledge, 2006), p. 10.

[16] Akhil Gupta and James Ferguson, "Beyond 'Culture': Space, Identity, and the Politics of Difference," in *Cultural Anthropology,* 1992, vol. 7, no. 7, quoted in Marina Petronoti, "Disguising the Sense of Insecurity in 'Multicultural' Greece," in *Dangerous Others, Insecure Societies: Fear and Social Division,* Michalis Lianos, ed. (Abingdon, UK: Routledge, 2016), p. 64.

[17] Petronoti, p. 64.

of his vile, manipulative, and vicious nature, Antiochus was labeled by the sages of Israel as *Sinat Yisrael* ("Enemy of Israel"), the closest equivalent in the Hebrew language for the word *antisemite*.[18]

Antiochus approached Israelite society with great subtlety. First, he liberated Israel from the hegemony of the Egyptian Ptolemies. Then he gained support from the aristocracy and intelligentsia of Israelite society, convincing them that blending Jewish culture and religion with Hellenism would be good for their economy. After campaigning unsuccessfully to induce the Jews to syncretize their Judaism with his beloved Hellenism,[19] Antiochus finally resorted to violence against the Jews in order to destroy Judaism and replace it with Hellenism. Antiochus "forbade all peoples in his realm their ancestral practices and laws on the grounds that 'all should become one people, and everyone should give up his particular customs.'"[20]

In 167 BC, Antiochus polluted the Jerusalem temple by introducing the sacrifice of swine on YHWH's altar in homage to Zeus, the king of the Greek gods. He also established cultic prostitution in the temple complex, and tormented and murdered unknown numbers of Jews.[21] He forbade circumcision, kosher diets, and Sabbath observance upon penalty of death.[22] While much of the Jewish aristocracy at least acquiesced to Antiochus, the more religiously fervent common people rebelled against his effort to force Hellenism upon them. Finally, when the Maccabees defeated the armies of Antiochus, they rededicated the temple and restored the cultus of Jewish worship. From this development, the Seleucid rulers produced the first governmental edict that sought the genocide of the Jews. Maccoby points out that in 133 BC, advisers of Antiochus Sidetes "urged this policy on the grounds of the Jews' alleged unsociability and refusal to assimilate to other nations, and of the failure of Antiochus Epiphanes' attempt to force them to conform."[23] Tragically, this official

---

[18] Albert S. Lindemann, *Anti-Semitism before the Holocaust* (Abingdon, UK: Routledge, 2000), p. 20.

[19] The syncretism that Antiochus first promoted was perhaps the most insidious antisemitic attack on the Jewish people in history, for, if it had succeeded, the faith of the Jews would have been corrupted. What could not be destroyed by an outside military action would have been eaten away from the inside.

[20] 1 Maccabees 1:41. See Fox, p. 49.

[21] 2 Maccabees 6:1–2, 4–6 notes that Antiochus sent an Athenian senator to Jerusalem "to compel the Jews to forsake the laws of their ancestors and no longer to live by the laws of God; also to pollute the temple in Jerusalem and to call it the temple of Olympian Zeus. . . . And the temple was filled with debauchery and reveling by the Gentiles, who dallied with prostitutes and had intercourse with women in the sacred precincts. . . ."

[22] Lawrence Schiffman, *Reclaiming the Dead Sea Scrolls* (New Haven, CT: Yale University Press, 1995), pp. 69–70.

[23] Maccoby, p. 10.

governmental policy that was pervasive in the Seleucid empire came to influence the political decisions of other realms that followed it.

## Antisemitism in the Roman World

For a time after Rome conquered the Greek realm during the second century BC, the majority of Roman leaders were at least tolerant of the Jews, with Julius Caesar and a few others actually being pro-Jewish.[24] Because much of the intelligentsia of the Roman realm embraced Hellenism, however, the Hellenic intolerance for any culture that was not fully committed to its worldview, philosophy, sociology, and religion pervaded much of the Roman Empire and gave antisemitism a significant role in Roman thought and practice.

In the first century BC, famed Roman philosopher and statesman Marcus Tullius Cicero virtually repeated the advice that Haman gave King Xerxes regarding the Jews when he said, "Justice demands that the barbaric superstition [the Jew's religion and culture] should be opposed; and it is to the interest of the state not to regard that Jewish mob which at times breaks out in open riots. . . . At one time the Jewish people took up arms against the Romans; but the gods showed how little they care for this people, suffering it to be conquered and made a tributary [of Rome]."[25] While Cicero and other Roman leaders reviled Judaism as a "barbaric superstition," the Roman posture toward the Jews was heavily influenced by the Roman vision of universal conquest and repression of any defiance of its absolute dominance. The final Roman conquest and universal dispersion of the Jewish people in the second century, therefore, involved a politically driven hatred that was primarily focused on the Jews' fierce independence and their belief that their God-appointed status as the Chosen People conveyed to them independent sovereignty over the land of Israel.

From the time when Imperial Rome rose to world domination just before the beginning of the Common Era, this empire was determined never to countenance the expression of such anarchical ideas, which could well have spread like a virus throughout their far-flung dominion, causing both political and economic disaster for Rome itself. Rome was certain

[24] Elsa Laurenzi, *Jewish Catacombs: The Jews of Rome: Funeral Rites and Customs* (Rome, Italy: Gangemi Editore Spa, 2013), pp. 17–18. Also, Moshe Aberbach, *Jewish Education and History: Continuity, Crisis and Change* (Abingdon, UK: Routledge, 2009), p. 8. Auerbach points out that because of Julius Caesar's pro-Jewish stance, he was "uniquely mourned by the Jews after his murder."

[25] Marcus Tullius Cicero, quoted in Arnold James Rudin, *Christians & Jews—Faith to Faith: Tragic History, Promising Present, Fragile Future* (Woodstock, VT: Jewish Lights Publishing, 2011), p. 85.

of its destiny to dominate the world. Its divine right was confirmed by the imperative recorded in the *Rhetorica ad Herennium*, which issued this command to the Romans: "*Imperium orbis terrae*" ("Rule the whole earth").[26] Rome's perceived divine right to world dominance was also ensconced in the Roman poet Virgil's recapitulation of Rome's destiny:

> *Tu regere imperio populos, Romane memento*
> *Hae tibi erunt artes, pacisque imponere morem,*
> *Parcere subiectis et debellare superbos.*[27]
>
> You, Roman, remember to rule the people with power.
> [These will be your arts] and to impose customs on peace,
> To spare the vanquished, and to crush the proud.

The Romans had come to believe that the gods had given the entire earth to them and that they were destined to rule over it. And rule Rome did, extending its power far and wide and bringing millions of people under its crushing dominion. In such universal dominance, the Jewish claim of independence and sovereignty over its own nation and land could never be tolerated.

Rome brought the Holy Land under its hegemony in 63 BC when Pompey invaded Israel and besieged Jerusalem. Thus began the occupation that would eventually result in the complete exile of the Jews from their land. Within less than seventy years of its annexation of Palestine in 4 AD,[28] Rome would utterly destroy Jerusalem and the temple and begin the dispersion of the Jewish people throughout the world. Always on guard against any perceived threat to its domination of its vassal states, imperial Rome would descend upon Judea and systematically destroy every vestige of even suspected Jewish rebellion. This campaign would bring massive loss of life to the Jewish people and threaten the existence of Judaism. Only the hand of God and the resourcefulness of Jewish sages

---

[26] *Rhetorica ad Herennium* 4.9.13. This first-century BC text was attributed to Cicero; however, its authorship is unknown. *Rhetorica ad Herennium* is still important today because it is used as a textbook on structure and rhetoric as yet another gift from Rome to the modern world. Noted in Doron Mendels, *The Rise and Fall of Jewish Nationalism* (Grand Rapids, MI: Wm. B. Eerdmans Publishing Co., 1992), p. 244.

[27] Virgil, *The Aeneid*, VI., 851–853.

[28] The term *Palestine* derives from the Roman designation of the entire Middle East as "*Syria Palaestina.*" The terms *Palestine* and *Palestinian* were first used by the Roman government to refer exclusively to the land of Israel and to the Jewish people. While the name *Syria Palaestina* originally included Syria and Phoenicia, by the end of the second century AD, the Emperor Hadrian had narrowed the term to define the land of Israel, particularly Judea. The word *Palaestina* was actually derived from the Semitic language term that is transliterated as Philistine. This is confirmed by the fact that the Arabic word for Palestine is *Filastin*. Hadrian actually applied the term *Palaestina* to Judea out of his personal animus and derision for the Jews, thereby calling them, in effect, Philistines and Syrians (Israel's great continuing enemies) rather than Jews or Israelites.

prevented such a dreadful outcome from taking place then and there.

The Jews and Judaism were destined to survive what became one of history's most massive paradigm shifts, but it would not be easy, and it would be costly in terms of Jewish life and treasure. Refusing to bow to Roman domination would cost countless Jewish lives. Thousands would be executed by means of crucifixion, the most cruel and unusual instrument of capital punishment that was ever developed in human history.[29] In the process of these violent actions, the Jews would eventually be forced to cease the active efforts to convert the nations to the faith of Abraham to which they had been called.[30]

## Rome's Most Antisemitic Emperor and the Final Diaspora

The final nail in the sarcophagus that Rome had made for any idea of Israelite independence was driven in AD 135 by Hadrian, an apostle of Hellenism and Rome's most antisemitic emperor.[31] "Until the Hadrianic persecutions," says Shlomo Riskin, "Jews attempted to fulfill [their] mission" to be God's light to the nations. After Hadrian's onslaught against them, however, "the Jewish people were forced to leave history. Jews were exiled from the stage of historic actors, and perforce became insularly concerned with ethnic survival."[32] The Roman destruction of the Jewish nation, its dispersion of the Jewish people, and its nullification of the Jewish claim to the land of Israel represented perhaps one of the most cruel—and undeserved—ethnic cleansings in human history.[33]

---

[29] Andreas J. Köstenberger, *John: Baker Exegetical Commentary on the New Testament* (Grand Rapids, MI: Baker Academic, 2004), p. 531. The first-century BC Roman statesman Cicero described crucifixion as "the most cruel and horrifying death." Marcus Tullius Cicero, quoted in Michael Licona, *The Resurrection of Jesus: A New Historiographical Approach* (Downers Grove, IL: InterVarsity Press, 2010), p. 304. William Barclay points out that crucifixion was originated by the Persians as a means of elevating an evildoer's body above the "sacred" earth so as not to defile it. The Persian system was appropriated by the Carthaginians, from whom it was learned by the Romans. William Barclay, *The Gospel of John* (Edinburgh, UK: Saint Andrew Press, 1975), vol. 2, p. 250.

[30] The Israelites had been commissioned by YHWH to be witnesses to the fact he alone is God (Isaiah 43:10). The Almighty also instructed the Jewish people to be his "light for revelation to the nations" and the agents who would take his "salvation to the ends of the earth" (Isaiah 49:6). Because they were determined to fulfill these commissions, the sages instructed their disciples to "make many disciples" by engaging in a missionary endeavor to make proselytes to the faith of Israel. The Mishnah in *Pirkei Avot* 1:1 declares, "Raise up many disciples."

[31] Michael L. Morgan, ed., *The Jewish Thought of Emil Fackenheim: A Reader* (Detroit, MI: Wayne State University Press, 1987), p. 275. Also Maccoby, p. 10.

[32] Shlomo Riskin,"Covenant and Conversion: The United Mission to Redeem the World," in *Covenant and Hope: Christian and Jewish Reflections*, Robert W. Jenson and Eugene B. Korn, eds. (Grand Rapids, MI: Wm. B. Eerdmans Publishing Co., 2012), p. 127.

[33] Ethnic cleansing has been defined as the action that is undertaken "when one group forcibly removes another by violence or deportation." See Harry I. Chemotsky and Heidi H. Hobbs, *Crossing Borders: International Studies for the 21st Century* (Thousand Oaks, CA: SAGE Publications, Inc., 2016), p. 242.

This tragedy occurred because a Jewish general, named Shimon bar Kosiba declared the restoration of the state of Judea and its independence from Rome and subsequently ruled over Judea as *Nasi* ("prince") for a period of three years. In the process, Bar Kosiba was proclaimed to be the Jewish Messiah by no less a luminary than the great Rabbi Akiva, who changed bar Kosiba's name to bar Kokhba ("son of the star"—in reference to the messianic prophecy of Numbers 24:17).[34] As could have been expected, the Romans did not take lightly this affront to their absolute control over all of Israel. The armies of the Emperor Hadrian utterly crushed the rebellion, eventually killing both bar Kokhba and Akiva.

Because they engaged in open defiance of Rome, virtually all of the Judean Jews were methodically hunted down and slaughtered, resulting in the virtual depopulation of Judea that some scholars have described as genocide.[35] Indeed, according to Roman historian and statesman Cassius Dio, at least 580,000 Jewish civilians were massacred, and the rest of the population of Judea was sold into slavery.[36] By the time the smoke had cleared, the emperor Hadrian had utterly destroyed the city of Jerusalem. Subsequently, he built a completely new city directly over the ruins of the Holy City and named it *Aelia Capitolina*[37] in homage to the Roman god Jupiter Capitolinus. The virulently antisemitic Hadrian then forbade the Jews to enter their own capital city upon penalty of death.[38]

In less than two centuries, then, the Roman perception of the Jewish threat to their hegemony over the entire Middle East precipitated the razing of Israel's capital city Jerusalem, the destruction of the temple,

---

[34] Christopher Rimare, *Blinded by Paradise: The Rise and Fall of Hadrian* (Bloomington, IN: iUniverse, 2010), p. 253. Also Oskar Skarsaune, *In the Shadow of the Temple: Jewish Influences on Early Christianity* (Downers Grove, IL: InterVarsity Press, 2002), p. 52.

[35] Samuel Totten, *Teaching about Genocide: Issues, Approaches and Resources* (Charlotte, NC: Information Age Publishing, Inc., 2004), p. 24. Also, Joan E. Taylor, *The Essenes, the Scrolls, and the Dead Sea* (Oxford, UK: Oxford University Press, 2012), p. 243. Taylor observes that "the Bar Kokhba documents indicate that towns, villages, and ports where the Jews lived were busy with industry and activity. Afterwards there is an eerie silence, and the archaeological record testifies to little Jewish presence until the Byzantine era . . . The crucial date for what can only be described as genocide, and the devastation of Jews and Judaism within central Judea, was 135 CE."

[36] Cassius Dio, *Historia* 69, 13. Also noted in Arnold James Rudin, *Christians & Jews Faith to Faith: Tragic History, Promising Present, Fragile Future* (Woodstock, VT: Jewish Lights Publishing, 2011), p. 60. Dio estimated that 50 fortified towns and 985 villages were razed to the ground during the time of Hadrian's invasion and destruction of Judea. Rudin claims that the 580,000 Jews who were killed represented "horrendous numbers not reached again until the Holocaust." He also reports the account in the Jerusalem Talmud (*Ta'anit* 4:5) which said that the Romans "went on killing until their horses were submerged in blood up to their nostrils." Also, Mendels, p. 388. Mendels says that "in the slave market at Hebron at the time a Jew was worth no more than a horse."

[37] The name *Aelia* was a form of Hadrian's nomen gentile, *Aelius.*

[38] Craig A. Evans, *Jesus and His Contemporaries: Comparative Studies* (Leiden, The Netherlands: E. J. Brill, 1995), p. 72. Hadrian also forbade the Jews to teach the Torah.

the symbol of the Jewish religion, the decimation of the Jewish people themselves, and finally the systematic exile of the remaining Jews from their God-given homeland in an act that would redefine the Jewish people as an endlessly wandering, nationless people who were void of political rights and personal and corporate sovereignty.[39] The Jews, of whom God said, "You are my people,"[40] came to be viewed as no people at all. Their nation was destroyed, its capital city razed to the ground. They were banished from their land. They would endure century after century of dispersion, degradation, and death; however, they would ever refuse to recant their faith. Who did these Jews think they were, anyway?

## Continuing Libels and Antisemitism in Antiquity

As the Jewish people made determined efforts to survive these vicious attempts to destroy them, they faced increasingly scurrilous charges. It came as no surprise that when the Roman historian Tacitus wrote what was supposedly an objective account of Jewish history in the late second century AD, he represented the Jews "as a threat to the purity of the Roman Empire and as bringers of degeneracy. The chief thrust of his argument is that the Jews, being antisocial, except within their own community, can never cooperate with the rest of humanity and are therefore always bound to be bad citizens in any overall political system."[41]

In the early first century AD, Apion, a Greek rhetorician of Egyptian extraction, had argued that the tenets of Judaism obliged Jews to hate the rest of humankind. He further charged that once each year the Jews murdered a Gentile, tasted his intestines, and swore during the meal to hate the nation of which the victim was a member, a practice that he said Antiochus Epiphanes "discovered" when he entered the Jerusalem Temple.[42] He also maintained that the Hebrew word *Shabbat* was derived from the ancient Egyptian word for a disease of the groin. Additionally, he argued that the Jews worshipped an ass's head in the Jerusalem temple. Apion's antisemitic arguments were so popular that Josephus wrote his treatises, *Contra Apion I* and *II*, for the express purpose of debunking the Hellenist's libelous antisemitism.

---

[39] Despite the fact that Jews who were believers in Jesus did not support Bar Kokhba's rebellion, they too were banned from Jerusalem in the aftermath of Hadrian's victory. Karen Armstrong, *Jerusalem: One City, Three Faiths* (New York: Random House, 2005), p. 170.

[40] Leviticus 26:12; Isaiah 43:20; Jeremiah 30:22; 32:38; Ezekiel 14:11; 2 Chronicles 7:14.

[41] Maccoby, p. 11.

[42] Jerome A. Chanes, *Anti-Semitism: A Reference Handbook* (Santa Barbara, CA: ABC–CLIO, 2004), p. 131; John G. Gager, *The Origins of Anti-Semitism: Attitudes toward Judaism in Pagan and Christian Antiquity* (Oxford, UK: Oxford University Press, 1983), p. 121.

In the early third century AD, Cassius Dio Cocceianus claimed that Jews "would eat the flesh of their victims, make belts for themselves of their entrails, anoint themselves with their blood, and wear their skins for clothing."[43] Such scurrilous charges provoked preemptive and retributive acts of violence against the Jewish people during the third century and afterward. Sadly, these same antisemitic indictments continued to echo across the centuries in ever "new" forms, as Gentile societies of every sort repeated them *ad nauseam* in order to isolate the Jewish people, consign them to subhuman status, and make them vulnerable to persecution and violence.

## An Increasingly Vulnerable Populace

After the Jewish people were forcibly exiled from their land following the Bar Kokhba rebellion, they became disenfranchised, nationless, and landless. Only in their dreams of the past and in their visions of the future did they have any idea of personal and corporate sovereignty and of connection with their native land. The extent of their dispersion separated them into small groups that had no means of common defense and little means of mutual communication. They were also forcibly evicted from various trades and were straitjacketed into roles that were easily stereotyped and caricatured.[44] Essentially, they became a people without a country. As a result, they rapidly lost everyday connection with their native tongue.[45] Forced to learn the languages of the Diaspora, they neglected Hebrew except for the recitations and prayers of synagogal life whenever and wherever that was possible. Eventually, they came to believe that Hebrew was such a "holy" language that it should be restricted to the synagogue and no longer be used in everyday discourse. Bereft of land and language, the Jews were scattered throughout the world where for centuries they continued to be completely at the mercy of the nations and people among whom they were forced to live their lives. In some situations, those people were tolerant, even hospitable toward the Jews. In others, Judaeophobic and superstitious masses taunted them because of their strange customs and beliefs.

[43] Fergus Miller, *A Study of Cassius Dio* (Oxford, UK: Oxford University Press, 1964), p. 130.

[44] Dean Phillip Bell, *Jews in the Early Modern World* (Lanham, MD: Rowman & Littlefield Publishers, 2008), p. 18. Also, Guido Bolaffi, *Dictionary of Race, Ethnicity, and Culture* (Thousand Oaks, CA: SAGE Publications, 2003), p. 16.

[45] Paul Azous, *In The Plains of the Wilderness* (Jerusalem, Israel: Mazo Publishers, 2006), p. 54. Azous notes that "as Jews became scattered among the nations they adopted either the vernacular of the land or created their own languages, such as Yiddish (a blend of German with Hebrew) or Ladino (a blend of Old Spanish with Hebrew and other languages)."

Vile and vicious religious and political leaders expanded endemic Judaeophobia into ever-new forms of antisemitism that enabled them to scapegoat the Jews as the reason for every societal ill and to promote violence and murder of Jewish men, women, and children. The Jews, however, could never deny who they were as Jews, and even minimal manifestation of their historical self-identity often caused them great suffering.

CHAPTER 4

# CHRISTIAN ANTISEMITISM

## THE HERESY OF SUPERSESSIONISM IN ANTIQUITY

Tragically, antisemitism was not just a pagan phenomenon in antiquity. During that time, Christian leaders who were influenced by Judaeophobia, anti-Judaism, and antisemitism also began a downward spiral into the heresies of Christian triumphalism and supersessionism in respect to Judaism and the Jews.[1] Accordingly, Christian antisemitism most often took the form of this teaching of "replacement theology," which maintained that Christianity had forever replaced Judaism as God's religion, that Christians had forever replaced Jews as God's Chosen People, and that the divine particularity accorded to Israel in Scripture had been replaced by the Christian universality of the kingdom of God on earth.[2]

This heresy, which would continue to define Christianity for nearly twenty centuries, was formulated in the early second century AD by the very first official Christian heretic, Marcion of Sinope, who introduced a theology that subtly infected Christianity with a Gnostic form of pure antisemitism. First, Marcion maintained that Jesus was the good God from heaven who came to replace and destroy the evil God of the Jews, who, he believed, had created the evil material world and the false religion of Judaism. For him, the God of the Jews was a vicious and vengeful character whom he identified with the Demiurge of Platonism, the craftsman who had created the universe and

[1] The definition of heresy as "a deliberate denial of revealed truth coupled with the acceptance of error" is a perfect description of supersessionism or replacement theology. See Walter A. Elwell, ed., *Evangelical Dictionary of Theology* (Grand Rapids, MI: Baker Academic, 2011), p. 508. For a discussion of the heretical nature of supersessionism, see David Zaslow, *Jesus: First-Century Rabbi* (Brewster, MA: Paraclete Press, 2014), p. 218; James H. Charlesworth, *The Historical Jesus: An Essential Guide* (Nashville, TN: Abingdon Press, 2008), p. 57; and Peter Ochs, *Another Reformation: Postliberal Christianity and the Jews* (Grand Rapids, MI: Baker Academic, 2011), pp. 51–52.

[2] Roger E. Olson, *The Mosaic of Christian Belief: Twenty Centuries of Unity & Diversity* (Downers Grove, IL: InterVarsity Press, 2002), p. 353.

in so doing had entrapped higher spiritual realities in evil matter.[3] Marcion openly argued that Jesus destroyed both the Torah and Judaism, even going so far as to pervert the focal point of the Sermon on the Mount in which Jesus declared, "Think not," or, "Do not even begin to think that I have come to destroy the Torah or the prophets; I have not come to destroy but to fulfill."[4] When Marcion created the very first "canon" of Christian Scripture, he rendered the words of Jesus in this manner: "Think ye, that I came to fulfill the law or the prophets? I am come to destroy, not to fulfill."[5] In his canon, Marcion also omitted the entire corpus of the Hebrew Scriptures, which *was* the Bible of Jesus, and he heavily edited the Apostolic Scriptures to make them support his Gnostic, antinomian, supersessionist, and antisemitic ideas.

Through the efforts of such heretics as Marcion, Christianity came to consider Judaism to be "null and void" and to consider itself to be not only "the self-appointed heir to Judaism" but also the religion that replaced "the parent faith altogether."[6] It was in this situation that "contempt [for the Jews] became a 'virtue'" among Christians, says Paul O'Shea.[7] By the time of the Middle Ages, this ancient Gnostic heresy had clothed itself in the ostentatious garments of Christian triumphalism wherein it was continually argued that God had replaced Judaism with Christianity and Jews with Christians in the economy of salvation. In century after century, supersessionism, in various guises, has continued to characterize much, if not most, of the Christian church. Sadly, to this day, a virtual neo-Marcionism, as it were, continues to survive in the teaching and practice of Christian replacement and displacement doctrines. And to this day, an astounding number of scholars and church leaders continue to promote the insidious heresy that is often called "replacement theology" and is thought to be an outworking of "covenant theology,"[8] as well as other Christians traditions.

---

[3] Sebastian Moll, *The Arch-Heretic Marcion* (Tübingen, Germany: Mohr Siebeck Verlag, 2010), p. 60. Also, Samuel H. Moffett, *A History of Christianity in Asia: Beginnings to 1500* (San Francisco: HarperSanFrancisco, 1992), p. 62.

[4] Matthew 5:17, CEB, along with Southwestern Baptist Theological Seminary's "*Preaching Source* rendering with author's edits. The KJV renders this text: "Think not that I have come to destroy the law or the prophets."

[5] Jesus made his intentions regarding the Torah and Judaism perfectly clear when he continued his discourse: "Until heaven and earth pass away, not one *yud* or tittle will pass from the Torah until all has been fulfilled" (Matthew 5:18). Nathaniel Lardner, *The Works of Nathaniel Lardner*, Andrew Kippis, ed. (Whitefish, MT: Kessinger Publishing, 2010), vol. 3, p. 463.

[6] Paul O'Shea, *A Cross Too Heavy: Pope Pius XII and the Jews of Europe* (New York: Palgrave Macmillan, 2011), p. 35.

[7] O'Shea, p. 35.

[8] Paul P. Enns, *The Moody Handbook of Theology* (Chicago, IL: Moody Publishers, 1989), p. 15. Enns notes that the replacement theology which maintains that the church has replaced Israel in God's program is a distinctive of Reformed Theology, which is a development from Calvinistic theology.

Despite the fact that Christian theologians, overseers, pastors, teachers, and laypeople—from Marcion to today's academicians and pulpiteers—have attempted to contort the clear "think-not" command that came from the lips of Jesus in the Sermon on the Mount in order to imply that he was saying just the opposite of what he actually said, the infallible words of the Lord have continued to echo across the corridors of time to this day. Jesus said what he meant, and he meant what he said. Both his own faith and the faith that he established were anchored in the authority of the Hebrew Scriptures.[9]

Marcion was branded a heretic for his radical Gnostic ideas, and he was excommunicated from the church by his own father. Still, his theology, which distorted wide segments of Christianity in his own generation, has continued to influence Christian thought to one degree or another ever since that time. If Marcion's teaching was not the source of Christian antisemitism within the Christian church, it was certainly one of the earliest manifestations of Christian supersessionism. Even in the present day, neo-Marcionism continues to manifest itself in the form of antinomianism,[10] supersessionism, Judaeophobia,[11] anti-Judaism,[12] and antisemitism, not to speak of various ongoing mischaracterizations of the God of Scripture, both subtle and overt, which make every effort to strip God of his identification as the God of Abraham, the God of Isaac, and the God of Jacob—and, therefore, the God of the Jews.

Because most—if not all—of the ante-Nicene, Nicene, and post-Nicene church fathers at least to some degree embraced supersessionist teachings—though not to the degree to which Marcion did—they generally and increasingly rejected the validity of the claim that the Jews were God's Chosen People and the rightful heirs of the Promised Land. Perhaps because of the tide of anti-Judaism in Gentile Christianity, these spiritual giants who correctly thought through many of the most foundational ideas and doctrines of the Christian faith obviously had a significant blind spot when it came to understanding the continuity of

---

[9] Jesus was not a supersessionist; he was a reformer, one who reformed through restoration, not innovation. He did not believe that he was creating a new religion to replace the faith of his ancestors. Instead, he was intent upon fulfilling Judaism by filling it full—bringing it to completion through his life, death, resurrection, and ascension. Jesus was a Jew, his religion was Judaism, and he never changed either his ethnicity or his religion. During his entire life and ministry on earth, he knew full well that "salvation is from the Jews" (John 4:22). He declared that he was "sent only to the lost sheep of the house of Israel" (Matthew 15:4), and he commanded his disciples, "Do not go among the Gentiles" (Matthew 10:5).

[10] Antinomianism literally means "against the Law." It describes those who believe that Christianity has no need for any part of God's law, including the moral law, because faith only is required for salvation.

[11] Judaeophobia is morbid fear of Jews and things Jewish.

[12] Anti-Judaism is opposition to Judaism by those who consider Judaism to be a dead religion that God has abolished or a religion that is inferior to Christianity.

biblical faith that demanded Jewish inclusion in God's election and the maintenance of the historical, sociological, and theological Jewish roots of the Christian faith.

Virtually throughout Christianity, therefore, Jews increasingly became "no people," and they were entitled to no land. Since Christian views of the hereafter had come to be focused on the neo-Platonic philosophy of escaping the evil material earthly realm and inheriting heaven, there was increasingly less room for a this-worldly understanding of God's dealings with humanity wherein the meek would inherit the earth forever as Scripture clearly declares.[13] By embracing the Greek view of the hereafter, the church allegorized and spiritualized the land promises of the Abrahamic covenant so that, for Christians, they became heavenly inheritance. This, in turn, which further voided any expectation of the restoration of Israel, further eliminated the Jewish people from the economy of salvation, and made Christian antisemitism even more possible, if not inevitable.

Many—if not most—of the leaders and constituents of Eastern Christianity had been reared under the influence of Hellenistic thought and its rationalist antisemitism that denied self-determination to the Jewish people in favor of the socially correct Hellenism that had subsumed other cultures under its "multiculturalism."[14] Because Hellenism had long viewed the Jews as separatists and even elitists, they characterized them as antisocial misanthropes[15] who were inimical to the cause of Hellenism.[16] It was easy for patristic Christian leaders who were influenced by such Hellenic stereotypes and caricatures of Jews and Judaism to engage in a form of philosophical and theological supersessionism in which they relegated Judaism to the status of a failed religion that had been replaced by the new Christian faith and consigned the Jews to the status of a rejected people that had been replaced by Christians in the economy of God's salvation.

Even if later Greek scholars, particularly those in the modern and postmodern eras, have attempted to excuse Orthodox antisemitism as being nothing more than an innocuous anti-Judaism—a theological debate over the merits of Christianity as contrasted with Judaism—the truth

[13] Psalm 37:11; Matthew 5:5; 25:34; Daniel 7:18.

[14] Victor Tcherikover, *Hellenistic Civilization and the Jews* (New York: Atheneum Books, 1975), p. 297.

[15] Peter Willem van der Horst, *Philo's Flaccus: The First Pogrom (Philo of Alexandria Commentary Series)* (Leiden, The Netherlands: Koninklijke Brill NV, 2003), vol. 2, p. 31.

[16] John J. Collins, *Between Athens and Jerusalem: Jewish Identity in the Hellenistic Diaspora* (Grand Rapids, MI: Wm. B. Eerdmans Publishing Co., 2000), p. 14. Collins notes that "in the Hellenistic world . . . Jewish mores were denounced as antisocial superstition." This view of Judaism was established on the Hellenistic view that Judaism was "far from ecumenical and strongly discouraged any form of syncretism."

is that in antiquity,[17] the church fathers not only saw Christianity as a replacement for Judaism but also believed that Christians had replaced Jews as God's Chosen People. They also formulated and perpetuated the myth of the evil Jew in the antisemitic schema that Hyam Maccoby succinctly describes in this manner: "The Jews, after a long career of crime, including the murder of prophets, finally forfeited God's grace by their deicide of Jesus. As punishment for this, their Temple was destroyed, and they themselves were exiled. They were doomed to suffer as slaves and exiles until the Second Coming of Christ, when they would finally see the light. Christians should regard the Jews as an accursed nation, and should refrain from friendly intercourse with them."[18]

While the influence of Hellenistic thought was introduced into Christianity by Greek church fathers, anti-Judaism and antisemitism were not unique to Greek Orthodoxy. Across the centuries, writings of Christian leaders and scholars from east to west and north to south evidence varying degrees of supersessionism and triumphalism toward the Jews and Judaism. In the late first century AD, Irenaeus of Lyons basically accepted and became an advocate of an *adversus-Judaeos* theology, placing the Jews outside God with "hands full of blood."[19] In the second century AD, Justin Martyr debated the Jewish scholar Trypho about Christianity's replacement of Judaism as God's religion. While he did not maintain that the Jews had been totally rejected by God for their failure to believe in Jesus as Messiah, he initiated the teaching of supersessionism that became foundational to most subsequent Christian antisemitism.[20] In the fourth century AD, John Chrysostom took anti-Judaism and antisemitism to another level when he produced a series of homilies called "*Adversus Judaeos*" which were filled with vile and vituperative denunciations of both Jews and Judaism. Chrysostom famously described the synagogue as "worse than a brothel . . . a den of scoundrels, the repair of wild beasts, a temple of demons, the refuge of brigands and debauchees, and the cavern of devils, a criminal assembly of the assassins of Christ . . . an abyss

[17] Demetrios J. Constantelos, "The Jews in the Works of the Church Fathers," in *Early Christianity and Judaism*, Everett Ferguson, ed. (New York: Garland Publishing, Inc., 1993), p. 273. Constantelos says, "The cliché is perpetuated that the Greek Fathers were anti-Semitic, intolerant, and narrow-minded. . . . It is an error to accuse the Greek Fathers of being 'anti-Semitic.'" Any objective analysis of the writings of the Greek fathers, however, reveals more than anti-Judaism: they clearly contain antisemitic tropes.

[18] Hyam Maccoby, *Antisemitism and Modernity: Innovation and Continuity* (Abingdon, UK: Routledge, 2006), P. 17.

[19] A. J. Springer, "Proof of Identification: Patristic and Rabbinic Exegesis of the Cain and Abel Narrative," in *Papers Presented at the Fourteenth International Conference on Patristic Studies*, Frances Margaret Young, Mark J. Edwards, and Paul M. Parvis, eds. (Louvain, Belgium: Peeters Publishers, 2006), p. 261.

[20] Michael J. Vlach, *Has the Church Replaced Israel? A Theological Evaluation* (Nashville, TN: B&H Publishing Group, 2010), p. 37.

of perdition."[21] Chrysostom also said, "Brothel and theatre, the synagogue is also a retreat for brigands and a lair for wild beasts . . . living by their stomach, mouth always gaping, the Jews do not act any better than pigs and goats, in their lewd grossness and extremes of their gluttony. They only know how to do one thing: stuff themselves and get drunk."[22] Also in the fourth century AD, Gregory of Nyssa characterized Jews as "murderers of the Lord, assassins of prophets, rebellious and hateful toward God . . . confederates of the devil, race of vipers, informers, calumniators, mentally clouded, pharisaic fermentors, sanhedrin of the devil, curse, execrable, stoners, enemies of all that is beautiful."[23] In the fifth century AD, Cyril of Alexandria made many theological arguments against Judaism, concluding that the Sabbath had been rejected by God, and he engaged in antisemitic polemics and actions against the Jewish people, including leading riots against the Jews that resulted in their expulsion from Alexandria.[24]

Sadly, from the end of the first century of the Christian era, Judaeophobia, anti-Judaism, and antisemitism characterized significant numbers of church fathers. Though it is difficult to measure the level of their displeasure with Judaism and Jews—whether they were merely Judaeophobic or downright antisemitic—there can be no mistaking the fact that much of what they argued in their diatribes against Judaism, the Torah, and the Jews of their time served as foundations for subsequent church-sponsored acts of violence in various regions in the Christian East as well as in the Christian West. It is a simple fact that prejudice will never remain in the realm of the philosophical or theological but will eventually be translated into the realm of physical reality. Theological anti-Judaism and antisemitism will inevitably manifest itself in anthropological and sociological antisemitism and the vile acts that it precipitates.

The Christian heresy of supersessionism also removed from the thoughts and discourse of Christians any serious thought of restoration of the land of Israel to the Jewish people. Though Hebrew and Apostolic Scripture promised such a restoration, the idea that a divine kingdom might be established on earth that might have included Jews and Christians

[21] Walter Laqueur, *The Changing Face of Antisemitism: From Ancient Times to the Present Day* (Oxford, UK: Oxford University Press, 2006), pp. 47–48.

[22] John Chrysostom, quoted in Ervin Straub, *The Roots of Evil: The Origins of Genocide and Other Group Violence* (Cambridge, UK: Cambridge University Press, 1989), p. 101.

[23] Gregory of Nyssa, quoted in Richard L. Rubenstein and John K. Roth, *Approaches to Auschwitz: The Holocaust and Its Legacy* (Louisville, KY: Westminster John Knox Press, 2003), p. 52.

[24] A. Davids, "Cyril of Alexandria's First Episcopal Years," in *The Impact of Scripture in Early Christianity,* Jan den Boeft and M. L. van Poll-van de Lisdonk, eds. (Leiden, The Netherlands: Brill 1999), p. 201. Also, Hans van Loon, *The Dyophysite Christology of Cyril of Alexandria* (Leiden, The Netherlands: Koninklijke Brill NV, 2009), p. 10.

gradually became anathema to most of the church fathers.[25] Gershom Scholem and R. J. Werblowsky note that "the ancient struggle between the heritage of Greek thought—which never inclined to apocalypse—and that of Judaism reached a new climax inside the Christian church with the chiliast controversy. The theological spokesmen of the 'Greek' mentality denounced the concept of chiliasm (from the Greek word *chilias*, meaning 1,000 as in the "thousand-year" reign of Christ predicted in the Apocalypse) as a 'Jewish heresy' and argued that a kingdom that was limited in time (in this case, to a chiliasm or 1,000 years) was devoid of religious value."[26]

Indeed, in the third century, the idea of the existence of such an earthly kingdom—the "millennial reign of Christ" that the apostle John had predicted—was even negatively portrayed as being "sensual" in the writings of Origen Adamantius, as well as those of other church fathers.[27] This emerging emphasis represented a renunciation of the Hebraic apocalypticism of Jesus and the apostles that expected the kingdom *on earth*, a position that was consistent with all of the Hebrew Scriptures.[28] "The Greek Church's philosophic preference for

[25] Largely because the major sources for the idea were Jewish, most church fathers denied the possibility of premillennialism, the coming of the Messiah to establish God's kingdom on earth; therefore, the teaching of chiliasm which spoke of the literal thousand-year reign of Christ as predicted by the apostle John in Revelation 20:6, was renounced as a "Jewish heresy" and was even anathematized at the Council of Ephesus in 431 AD. In other words, these church fathers essentially denied the inspiration of the passages of the Apocalypse that clearly speak of a chiliasm simply because these declarations did not fit their idea that the Christian church would gradually assume control of the earth in an everlasting kingdom not limited to a specific time period.

[26] Gershom G. Scholem and R. J. Zwi Werblowsky, *Sabbatai Sevi: The Mystical Messiah, 1626–1676* (Princeton, NJ: Princeton University Press, 1976), p. 98.

[27] Paul Hughes, *Finishing History Well* (Maitland, FL: Xulon Press, 2012), p. 47. Also Robert H. Mounce, *The Book of Revelation* (Grand Rapids, MI: Wm. B. Eerdmans Publishing Co., 1977), p. 368, and Matthew H. G. Francis, "'Blessed is the One Who Reads Aloud. . .': The Book of Revelation in Orthodox Lectionary Traditions," in *Exegesis and Hermeneutics in the Churches of the East*, Vahan S. Hovhanessian, ed. (New York: Peter Lang Publishing, 2009), p. 71.

[28] One of the supreme ironies of ecclesiastical history is that for centuries the Greek and Latin church fathers utterly rejected the clear teaching of the Hebrew Scriptures that the Messiah would come and establish God's dominion on the earth. Daniel 7:18 stated this truth unequivocally: "But the holy people of the Most High will receive the kingdom and will possess it forever," and Zechariah 14:3, 4, 9: "Then the LORD will go forth and fight . . . his feet will stand on the Mount of Olives. . . . And the *LORD will be king over all the earth*" (emphasis added). The supersessionist, amillennialist church fathers also rejected the apocalyptic teaching of Jesus, who said, "The meek shall *inherit the earth*" (Matthew 5:5 [emphasis added]), and "Then the king will say to those on his right, 'Come, you who are blessed of my Father, *inherit the kingdom* prepared for you from the foundation of the world" (Matthew 25:34 [emphasis added]). They also rejected the chiliastic teachings of the apostles: "You have made them to be a kingdom of priests to our God; and *they will reign upon the earth*" (Revelation 5:10 [emphasis added]). According to both the Hebrew and Apostolic Scriptures, the Messianic Kingdom will be the fulfillment of the Abrahamic promise of dominion over the earth. It will involve the ultimate outworking of the land clause of the Abrahamic covenant that was expanded in the New Covenant: "The promise to Abraham or to his descendants that he would be *heir of the world* was . . . through the righteousness of faith" (Romans 4:13 [emphasis added]). This is the covenant that is made sure to the lineal descendants of Abraham as well as to those who have become heirs of the promises by faith (Galatians 3:29: "If you belong to the Messiah, then you are Abraham's descendants, *heirs according to the promise*" [emphasis added]).

Heaven over a Messianic Kingdom on Earth may have been a concession to Gnosticism,"[29] says Hughes. The church at large essentially rejected the "this-worldly" teachings of biblical and Second-Temple Judaism that were reinforced by Jesus and the apostles.[30]

The Christian abandonment of apocalypticism was certainly a concession to concepts of neo-Platonism that were also present in Gnostic thought in that apocalypticism sanctified the material earthly rather than insisting that it be replaced by the spiritual heavenly. The truth is that many church fathers were highly influenced by the dualism of both neo-Platonism and Gnosticism which posited the holiness of the heavenly and the realm of ideas while excoriating the evil of the earthly and everything related to it.[31] Prominent among these was Augustine, who was trained early in the philosophy of Plotinus and Prophyry,[32] and Origen, who was influenced by Plotinus, and joined Clement in espousing ideas rooted in Gnosticism.[33] In the context of such neo-Platonic and Gnostic otherworldly thought, the concept of an earthly kingdom rather than a heavenly domain was considered to be an utter impossibility.[34] The ideal of belief in the hereafter was transposed from resurrection to life with the Messiah on earth to translation into heaven, a concept that was based more in Platonic thought than in biblically Hebraic understanding.[35]

In the third century AD, Clement of Alexandria also claimed that Israel had "denied the Lord" and thereby had "forfeited the place of the true Israel."[36] Because they believed that God had voided his covenant with the land as well as the people of Israel, Christian scholars increasingly abandoned any connection with the land of Israel. Many notable Christian supersessionists like Augustine, John

---

[29] Hughes, p. 47.

[30] John D. Garr, *God and Israel: Chosen People, Holy Nation, Promised Land* (Atlanta, GA: Golden Key Press, 2016), pp. 201–202.

[31] Vincent P. Branick, *Understanding the New Testament and Its Message: An Introduction* (Mahwah, NJ: Paulist Press, 1998), p. 166. Also Mary Ellen Waithe, ed., *Ancient Women Philosophers: 600 B.C.–500 A.D.* (Dordrecht, The Netherlands: Martinus Nijhoff Publishers, 1987), p. 142.

[32] Gerald P. Boersma, *Augustine's Early Theology of Image: A Study in the Development of Pro-Nicene Theology* (Oxford, UK: Oxford University Press, 2016), pp. 141–144.

[33] Robert Franks, *A History of the Doctrine of the Work of Christ* (Nashville, TN: Thomas Nelson and Sons, 1962), p. 44, n. 5.

[34] Roger E. Olson, *The Mosaic of Christian Belief* (Downers Grove, IL: InterVarsity Press, 2016), p. 385.

[35] Howard A. Snyder and Joel Scandrett, *Salvation Means Creation Healed: The Ecology of Sin and Grace: Overcoming the Divorce between Earth and Heaven* (Eugene, OR: Wipf and Stock Publishers, 2011), pp. 22–23.

[36] Michael J. Vlach, *The People, the Land, and the Future of Israel: Israel and the Jewish People* (Grand Rapids, MI: Kregel Publications, 2014), p. 36.

Chrysostom, and Gregory of Nyssa even discouraged Christians from making pilgrimages to Israel[37] since, for them, geographical Israel had no more importance than any other part of the earth. In fact, the world headquarters for their particular denomination of Christianity had actually become the "new Jerusalem."[38] Sadly, the one place on earth where God chose to "place his name"[39] became "no man's land" for vast parts of the Christian church.

Because he was profoundly influenced by Greek philosophy, Origen was perhaps the strongest Ante-Nicene advocate of hyper-allegorized interpretations of Scripture that promoted supersessionism.[40] Origen's arguments for theological replacement became fodder for expressions of antisemitism that later Orthodox Christians would use to justify acts of repression and violence against the Jewish people for centuries to come. Various scholars have described the positions that Origen posited, including his argument for the "two callings of Israel"—that "the church was called between the two callings of Israel; that is to say, first Israel was called, and afterwards when Israel had stumbled and fallen, the church of the Gentiles was called. 'But when the fullness of the Gentiles has come in, then will all Israel, having been called again, be saved.'"[41] Gerald Bray notes Origen's position that

[37] Augustine: Epistle 78, *Migne Patrologie Latina* XXII, col. 489; Chrysostom: *Ad Populum Antiochenum V, Migne Patrologie Graeca* XLIX, col. 49; Gregory of Nyssa, *Migne Patrologie Graeca* XLIX, col. 49, noted in Walter Zander, *Israel and the Holy Places of Christendom* (London: Weidenfeld & Nicolson, 1991), pp. 6–8. The common discouragement of pilgrimage to Israel in Christian history was sometimes based on the words of Jesus to the Samaritan woman, "The hour is coming when neither on this mountain nor in Jerusalem will you worship the Father" (John 4:21). John Calvin even described pilgrimages to Jerusalem as "counterfeit worship." John Calvin, *The Acts of the Apostles*, tr. Oliver and Boyd, Ltd. (Grand Rapids, MI: Wm. B. Eerdmans Publishing Co., 1965), p. 225. Also, Robert L. Wilken, "Christian Pilgrimage to the Holy Land," in *City of the Great King: Jerusalem from David to the Present*, Nitza Rosovsky, ed. (Cambridge, MA: Harvard University Press, 1996), p. 121. Additionally, the reformers who drafted the Augsburg Confession denounced pilgrimages as "childish and useless works." Hunt Janin, *Four Paths to Jerusalem: Jewish, Christian, Muslim, and Secular Pilgrimages* (Jefferson, NC: McFarland & Company Publishers, 2002), p. 149.

[38] Andrew Wheatcroft, *Infidels: A History of the Conflict between Christendom and Islam* (New York: Random House, 2003), p. 46. Wheatcroft observes that leaders in the Eastern Church, came to view Constantinople as the "holy City" that Revelation 21:21 predicted would come down from God out of heaven. Increasingly, therefore, "Jerusalem was the past. New Jerusalem [Constantinople] was the future."

[39] 2 Chronicles 6:6; 7:16; cf. Exodus 20:24.

[40] Thomas Finan, *Scriptural Interpretations in the Fathers: Letter and Spirit* (Dublin, Ireland: Four Courts Press, 1995), p. 15. Also, Henri de Lubac, *Theological Fragments*, tr. Rebecca Howell Balinski (San Francisco, CA: Ignatius Press, 1989), pp. 129–164. Lubac says that "patristic allegorization of Scripture constituted a uniquely Christian transformation of the Philonic and Greek modes of interpretation." Also Eugen J. Pentiuc, *The Old Testament in Eastern Orthodox Tradition* (Oxford, UK: Oxford University Press, 2014), p. 170. Pentiuc maintains that "the excess of a high allegorization of biblical texts, while underestimating or even eschewing historical and literary contexts, represents probably one of the obvious downsides of patristic interpretation as a whole." This tendency is in context with the traditional Greek predisposition toward hyperallegorization.

[41] Origen, noted in *The Song of Songs,* in *Ancient Christian Writers*, J. Quasten and J. C. Plumpe, eds. (Westminster, MD: Newman Press, 1957), p. 26.

"the people of Israel are still missing from the complete picture. But when the fullness of the Gentiles has come in and Israel comes to salvation at the end of time, then it will be the people which, although it existed long ago, will come at the last and complete the fullness of the Lord's portion and inheritance."[42] Origen, therefore, was ambivalent, wavering between absolute supersessionism and the possibility of a residual restoration of Israel after the church had fulfilled its destiny. He may well have been the first advocate of what would later come to be called the "parenthesis theory of the church," in which the church was viewed as having been inserted parenthetically—and unexpectedly—into salvation history because the Jewish people rejected Jesus as the Messiah.[43] This "parenthesis theory" persists to this day in certain parts of Evangelical Christianity, despite the fact that it absurdly suggests that God either did not know what he was doing when he chose Abraham and his lineal descendants in the first place or that the Omniscient One was surprised when Israel rejected Jesus as Messiah and had to adopt an alternative plan.

Even as Christian supersessionism was gaining traction throughout the church and as allegorical hermeneutics became the standard for biblical interpretation, honest brokers of Christian theology were still expecting the words of the prophets to be literally fulfilled in the restoration of the Jewish people to their land. Christians simply could not take all of the blessings from the Hebrew Scriptures, apply them to the church (as the allegorists did), and then leave all the curses for the Jews.[44] If they had been faithful to the Hebrew-based hermeneutical principles that were employed by Jesus and the apostles, they would have readily concluded that God's gifts and callings relating to the Jews were irrevocable[45] and that, in the end, God would move heaven and earth to fulfill the literal, material, and historical aspects of his covenant, his oath, and his promises to Abraham and his descendants.

---

[42] Origen, "Commentary on the Epistle to the Romans," in *Ancient Christian Commentary on Scripture: New Testament VI: Romans*, Gerald Bray, ed. (Downers Grove, IL: InterVarsity Press, 1998), vol. 6, p. 291.

[43] Stanley J. Grentz, *The Millennial Maze* (Downers Grove, IL: InterVarsity Press, 1992), p. 97. Grentz describes the "parenthesis theory of the church" thus: "The Israel phase, which began with Abraham, was suspended when the Jews rejected Jesus as their Messiah. Consequently, the church phase, which is a parenthesis in God's Israel program, was inaugurated at Pentecost. The advent of the church, however, did not spell the end of God's program for Israel. God neither abrogated the divine promises to his Old Testament people nor enmeshed them into the church."

[44] W. H. Griffith Thomas, "The Lord's Coming and the Supreme Theme of the Bible," in *The Christian Workers Magazine*, vol. XX, no. 1 (September, 1919), p. 96.

[45] Romans 11:29.

CHAPTER 5

# THE RISE OF ISLAM

## A New Vehicle for Supersessionist Antisemitism

In late antiquity, the Jewish people had already been forced from their homeland in successive expulsions that had left them scattered throughout most of the known world, especially in various nations of the Middle East, Northern Africa, Europe, and parts of Asia. For centuries, they lived among the peoples of the Assyrian, Babylonian, Persian, Greek, Roman, Byzantine, Carthaginian, and Ottoman empires. The Jewish people who had once had their own nation and their own land became strangers in the lands to which they had been dispersed, and they were, therefore, vulnerable to the shifting sands of time and chance in an environment dominated by Gentile cultures and religions.

During the seventh century AD, a new religion was developing which would be filled with ambiguities toward the Jewish people and the land of Israel. An Arabian merchant from Mecca[1] named Muhammad began to formulate a religion that would come to be called Islam. Very early in his religious musings, Muhammad had utterly rejected the polytheism of his native Arabian culture and had become a fervent monotheist. When he introduced his newly discovered theology in his native city of Mecca, however, he met with fierce opposition and persecution and was forced to flee with his followers to Medina.[2] Either because of his personal discovery of monotheism or because he had learned of the concept of absolute monotheism from Jewish sources (which is more likely the case), Muhammad attempted to join himself to monotheistic Judaism and to the Jews who had become socially, politically, and economically

[1] Mecca is now the holiest site in Islam.

[2] Daniel Jacobs, *The Rough Guide to Jerusalem* (New Delhi, India: Rough Guides, Ltd., 2009), p. 278.

dominant in Medina.[3] Initially, Muhammad "tried to use Judaism as the basis" for his religion; however, when he was rejected by the Jewish leaders,[4] he turned against them, either "wiping out or sending into exile the Jewish tribes of Mecca and Medina."[5] Then, after he had been rejected by the Jews, Muhammad explored Nestorian (monophysite[6]) Christianity whose adherents in Arabia "had attempted to convert the Arab polytheists by contextualizing Christianity for Arab culture."[7] Muhammad, however, was disenchanted with what he considered to be the polytheism of Christian theology that made Jesus divine and claimed that God had a son,[8] and he again found himself rejected by leaders of Christianity. Try as he would, he could not align himself with the two historical monotheistic faiths that had clearly sprung from Abraham and his descendants. Subsequently, Muhammad claimed that he had been visited by the angel Gabriel, who conveyed to him the true revelation of God and the understanding of his Word and will for his people, the Arabian descendants of Abraham through Ishmael.

## Supersessionism at Its Finest

Muhammad subsequently purloined and expropriated the Hebrew Scriptures from the Jewish people. Then he became a historical revisionist by rewriting biblical history,[9] making Ishmael and the Arabs

---

[3] Ironically, from the end of the fifth century AD to the time of Muhammad in the seventh century AD, Medina was actually a center for Jews who had fled persecution, especially from Persia. Samuel Safrai, "The Lands of the Diaspora," in *A History of the Jewish People*, Haim Hillel Ben-Sasson, ed. (Cambridge, MA: Harvard University Press, 1985), p. 380. In fact, according to Salo Baron, Medina was first settled by Jewish tribes, and Jews were the prominent leaders of virtually every aspect of the city's civic and social life. Salo W. Baron, *A Social and Religious History of the Jews* (New York: Columbia University Press, 1937), vol. 1, p. 308. With the rise of Muhammad and the creation of Islam, the Jews suffered persecution, murder, and, ultimately, expulsion at Muhammad's hand, with their possessions, homes, and businesses expropriated by the Arab followers of the prophet. Alfred Guillaume, *Islam* (London, UK: Penguin Books, 1956), pp. 20–32.

[4] Alexander D. Knysh, Yaron Eliav, and Ralph Williams, *Judaism, Christianity, and Islam: A Source Book* (Atlanta, GA: Kendall Hunt Publishing Co., 2007), p. 366.

[5] Naomi E. Pasachoff and Robert Littman, *A Concise History of the Jewish People* (Lanham, MD: Rowman & Littlefield Publishers, 1995), p. 111.

[6] Monophysitism was a fifth century AD Christian teaching which maintained that Jesus had only one nature, which was either wholly divine or a synthesis of the divine and the human in which the human was so overwhelmed by the divine as to have virtually no meaning.

[7] Gannon Murphy, ed., *American Theological Inquiry*, Vol. 7, Issue 1, p. 50.

[8] *Qur'an* 4:171; 5:73. Steve Bateman, *Brothers, Stand Firm: Seven Things Every Man Should Know, Practice, and Invest in the Next Generation* (Eugene, OR: Wipf & Stock, 2014), p. 58. Also, Donald S. Tingle *Islam & Christianity* (Downers Grove, IL: InterVarsity Press, 1985), p. 7.

[9] Tom Holland, "When I Questioned the History of Muhammad," *The Wall Street Journal*, January 9, 2015, posted at http://www.wsj.com/articles/when-i-questioned-the-history-of-muhammad-1420821462. Holland writes, "Did the Quran, the supposed corpus of Muhammad's revelations, in fact derive from a whole multiplicity of pre-existing sources? . . . The answer to all these questions, I gradually came to conclude, was yes."

the leading characters in the Abrahamic drama,[10] appropriating the Abrahamic blessing exclusively for his own Arabian people, and asserting that his own newly minted religion superseded both Judaism and Christianity.[11] Muhammad's religion claimed Moses as one of its prophets, and it transformed Jesus from Messiah and Lord of Christianity into another of its succession of Islamic prophets. In much the same fashion as Christianity had claimed that it superseded Judaism in the economy of God's salvation, Islam appropriated elements of both Judaism and Christianity to its story and insisted that Muhammad was the final prophet who had superseded both Moses and Jesus and whose religion, Islam, had superseded both Judaism and Christianity.

Islam, therefore, became perhaps the most unique application of supersessionism in that it claimed for its own the history and Scriptures of the Jews— albeit in heavily redacted form—and claimed Jesus, the foundation of Christianity, subordinating him as one of its own prophets who prepared the way for Muhammad, God's final prophet. Without a doubt, Islam has deep Jewish roots;[12] however, those roots were genetically modified to produce a hybrid religion that would eventually challenge the very existence of Judaism and the Jewish people. What was established on a foundation of Hebrew truth from the Jewish Scriptures eventually became a tool for forcing the Jewish people into forms of slavery and setting the stage for violent persecution and death to Jewish men and enslavement of Jewish women and children. Because Islam claimed Jesus as one of its own prophets, it also served as a challenge to Christianity that resulted in the persecution and slaughter of untold numbers of Christians as Islam spread its "religion of peace" on the edge of the sword. And some of these actions against both Jews and Christians occurred in the time of Muhammad and under his personal command.

[10] In order to justify his act of rewriting the history of the Hebrew Scriptures, Muhammad claimed that it was the Jews, not he, who had stolen the Scriptures from the Arabs and had perverted them in order to claim the Abrahamic blessing and faith for themselves. Muhammad also claimed that Christians had also perverted their own Scriptures! In *Qur'an* 4:46 and 5:13, Muhammad claimed that "the Jews distorted Allah's message. . . . [His] view was that the *Qur'an* confirms and corrects the Torah." Dan Cohn-Sherbok, *Judaism: History, Belief and Practice* (Abingdon, UK: Routledge, 2017), p. 134. Also Reuven Firestone, *An Introduction to Islam for Jews* (Philadelphia, PA: Jewish Publications Society, 2008), p. 152; Randall Price, *Unholy War* (Eugene, OR: Harvest House Publishers, 2001), p. 183; and Marteen Elass, *Understanding the Koran: A Quick Christian Guide to the Muslim Holy Book* (Grand Rapids, MI: Zondervan Publishing, 2004), pp. 32–34.

[11] Terence Lovat and Robert Crotty, *Reconciling Islam, Christianity and Judaism: Islam's Special Role in Restoring Convivencia* (New York: Springer, 2015), p. 6.

[12] Mark S. Glickman, *Sacred Treasure—The Cairo Genizah: The Amazing Discoveries of Forgotten Jewish History in an Egyptian Synagogue Attic* (Woodstock, VT: Jewish Lights Publishing, 2012), p. 144. Also, Sander L. Gilman, *Multiculturalism and the Jews* (Abingdon, UK: Routledge, 2006), p. 5.

Muhammad even coopted Israel's God, *YHWH*, renaming him *Allah*, the name that before Muhammad's time had been applied to one member of the pantheon of "deities in Arabian polytheistic tradition."[13] He also expropriated the *Shema*, Israel's first and most important commandment: "*Shema, Yisrael, YHWH eloheinu, YHWH echad*" ("Hear, O Israel, YHWH, our God, is YHWH alone"),[14] and replaced it with the Muslim *Shahada*:[15] "*La 'ilaha 'illa-llah, muhammadur rasulu-llah*" ("There is no God but Allah. Muhammad is the messenger of Allah").[16] Indeed, the *Qur'an* even went so far as to place Abraham with Ishmael at the *Ka'aba* in Mecca "praying that Allah will send Muhammad as a messenger."[17] It is a simple fact, however, that Muhammad could not have "written"—nor could he

[13] John M. Duffey, *Science and Religion: A Contemporary Perspective* (Eugene, OR: Wipf and Stock Publishers, 2013), p. 182. Also, David W. Shenk, *Journeys of the Muslim Nation and the Christian Church: Exploring the Mission of Two Communities* (Nairobi, Kenya: Uzima Publishing House, 2006), p. 22; and Karen Armstrong, *Islam: A Short History* (New York: Random House, 2000), p. 11. Armstrong says that the *Ka'aba*, Islam's holiest site, was originally a shrine to a Nabatean god known as Hubal and that it originally contained 360 images representing deities for each day of the year that were enshrined as tutelary guardians of the Arab year. Patrick Fairbairn, *The Imperial Bible-Dictionary: Historical, Biographical, Geographical, and Doctrinal* (London, England: Blackie and Son, 1866), p. 113. The enshrined gods included images of each of the gods of the various Arabian tribes. In his *Histories of Herodotus*, Book 3: *Thalia*, 3.8, Herodotus noted that Orotal and Aililat (who corresponded to the Greek gods Bacchus and Urania), were the most prominent gods that the ancient Arabians worshipped. Herodotus, *Herodotus: Thalia. Melpomene. Terpsicore.*, tr. William Beloe (London, England: Henry Colburn and Richard Bentley, 1830), p. 7. Also John Ramsay McCulloch, *A Dictionary, Geographical, Statistical, and Historical* (London, England: Longman, Orme, Brown, Green, and Longmans, 1841), vol. 1, p. 139. One of these lesser deities in the Arabian pantheon of gods was named Allah. Apparently by Muhammad's time, says Armstrong, Allah had become "the High God," supplanting Hubal, Urotalt (Orotal), and Ailat (Alilat). Because the *Ka'aba* contained idols dedicated to all of the gods in the Arabian polytheistic pantheon, the structure was dedicated to peace; therefore, when warring Arabian clans sought to make peace, they brought their gods with them to the *Ka'aba* where they found those same gods living in peace inside the shrine. The *Ka'aba*, therefore, became "the centre of a peace zone (*haram*), where tribal hostilities were put aside." See F. Donald Logan, *A History of the Church in the Middle Ages* (New York: Routledge, 2013), p. 36. This fact was thought to have contributed to the making of peace among warring tribes, especially during the month of *Dhu al-Hijja*, which required a cessation of the hostilities that were all too common among the competing, bellicose tribes of Arabia. James Wynbrandt, *A Brief History of Saudi Arabia* (New York: Infobase Publishing, 2004), p. 26. When the sacred site of the *Ka'aba* was taken over by Muhammad and became the central shrine of Islam, the theme of making peace was carried over. This is probably the historical background of the claim that Islam is a "religion of peace," even though the term is essentially more a modern political fabrication used to describe Islam than it is a practical reality. Etymologically, the Arabic word *Islam* is, in fact, cognate with the word *salam* ("peace"), even though technically the word *Islam* means "submission" or "surrender to Allah's will." Norio Suzuki, "The Problem of Peace and World Order in an Islamic Context: The Case of Modern Japan," in *Peace Movements and Pacifism after September 11*, Shin Chiba and Thomas J. Schoenbaum, eds. (Cheltenham, UK: Edward Elgar Publishing, 2008), p. 114.

[14] Deuteronomy 6:4–9. In context with the faith of his Jewish community, Jesus affirmed that the *Shema* was the first and greatest commandment in the Torah (Matthew 22:36–40) and was, therfore, foundationsal to Christianity., Paul affirmed that the "gospel of Christ" was, in fact, still the "gospel of God" (Romans 1:1, 9; 15:16; 2 Corinthians 11:7; 1 Thessalonians 2:2.

[15] The Arabic word *shahada* means "testimony." The *Shema* was, in effect, the "testimony," a declaration of faith, of Judaism.

[16] The *Shahada* was first used in the late seventh century, AD. James E. Lindsay, *Daily Life in the Medieval Islamic World* (Indianapolis, IN: Hackett Publishing Co., 2005), p. 140.

[17] *Qur'an* 2:129. John Kaltner, *Ishmael Instructs Isaac: An Introduction to the Qur'an for Bible Readers* (Collegeville, MN: The Liturgical Press, 1999), p.117. This book provides an excellent discussion of the expropriations and aberrations of the *Qur'an* as they relate to biblical history.

have created—the traditions and principles of the *Qur'an*[18]—especially with many of its concepts and narratives being so closely parallel with those of Judaism and Christianity—if he had not plagiarized[19] the sacred writings and traditions of both faiths.[20]

By far Muhammad's worst perversion of the Hebrew Scriptures, however, occurred when he commandeered the *Akedah*, the binding of Isaac, and misrepresented what was by then a 2600-year-old biblical truth by saying that instead of presenting Isaac as a sacrifice on Mt. Moriah, Abraham offered Ishmael near Mecca. "Since Ishmael went on to become the founding father of the Arabic peoples in the Hebrew Bible as well as the Koran, Muhammad thus expropriated Judaism's foundational sacrifice[21] for his desert tribes and their own ancestral place of pilgrimage near Mecca."[22] Then, in order to lend authenticity to his religion, Muhammad

---

[18] In fact, Muhammad did not write the *Qur'an*; therefore, its opening verse, "This book has been sent down to you," is an inaccurate statement. The teachings and commentary of the *Qur'an* was not compiled into a book until a century after Muhammad's death. Ira M. Lapidus, *A History of Islamic Societies* (Cambridge, UK: Cambridge University Press, 1988), p. 22. Lapidus points out what many scholars believe: "The traditional story of the origins and early history of Islam was a later invention intended to demonstrate, via historical narrative, the mythical, doctrinal, and other beliefs of Muslims and their superiority to religious rivals, including pagan Arabians, Jews, and Christians."

[19] David James Burrell, *The Religions of the World: An Outline of the Great Religious Systems* (Philadelphia, PA: Presbyterian Board of Publication and Sabbath-School Work, 1888), pp. 274–275. Burrell observed that the *Qur'an* is "made up of visions, legends, plagiarized and distorted Bible-stories, apocryphal traditions, dogmas, moral maxims, and civil laws."

[20] An example of Muhammad's plagiarism from Christian Scripture is this: "The Prophet said, "Allah said, 'I have prepared for my righteous slaves [such things] as no eye has ever seen, nor an ear has ever heard, nor a human heart can ever think of" (*Sahih Al-Bukhari*, vol. 9, book 93, no. 589). This is virtually a verbatim expropriation of 1 Corinthians 2:9. Unlike Muhammad, however, Paul rightfully attributed his declaration by saying, "It is written . . ." The apostle's statement appeared in Isaiah 64:4 in the Hebrew Scriptures. Since Paul wrote seven centuries before Muhammad lived and Isaiah wrote eight centuries before Paul, Muhammad's use of this statement can only be seen as plagiarism. Muhammad expropriated other stories of Scripture while mixing them with legends and ideas of his own. In some cases, he actually did give attribution, albeit rather obliquely, to Judaism as when he wrote, "For this we prescribed to the children of Israel that whoever kills a person, unless it be for punishing murder or for violence in the land, it would be as if he had killed all mankind; and if anyone saves a life, it would be as if he saved all mankind" (Sura 5:31–33). This is a quote, not from Scripture, but from the Jerusalem Talmud, *Sanhedrin* 37a, which says, "Whoever destroys a soul, it is considered as if he destroyed an entire world. And whoever saves a life, it is considered as if he saved the entire world." Since the Jerusalem Talmud was compiled from centuries-old oral traditions in the fourth and fifth centuries AD, it predated the time of Muhammad by at least two centuries. The oral tradition which was finally codified in the Talmud, however, predated the first century AD and, according to rabbinic tradition, dated from the time of Moses. It certainly dated from the time of Ezra and from the later *Amoraim* (sages—literally "spokesmen")—who lived in the third through the sixth centuries AD, all of whom preceded the time of Muhammad.

[21] For centuries, Jews viewed the *Akedah* of Isaac as a vicarious atonement and a substitutionary sacrifice for all of Abraham's descendants through Isaac and Jacob. "Rashi restated the classic teaching that when Jews suffer, God remembers Isaac on the altar as if he had been a burnt offering." Rashi noted in David Zaslow, *Jesus: First-Century Rabbi* (Brewster, MA: Paraclete Press, 2014), p. 77. Also, Ivan G. Marcus, "A Jewish-Christian Symbiosis," in *Cultures of the Jews: A New History*, David Biale, ed. (New York: Schocken Books, 2002), p. 466, and Jan N. Bremmer, *Greek Religion and Culture, the Bible, and the Ancient Near East* (Leiden, The Netherlands: Koninklijke Brill NV, 2008), p. 212.

[22] Patrick Tierney, *The Highest Altar: The Story of Human Sacrifice* (New York: Viking Press, 1989), p. 371.

even claimed that Abraham (*Ibrahim* in Arabic) was somehow given the cuboid-shaped black stone[23] which was to become the center of Islamic worship and that the patriarch and Ishmael traveled from Jerusalem to Mecca in order to build the *Ka'aba* and the first mosque to house the black stone.[24] In an effort to establish the ancient nature of monotheism among the Arabs, Muhammad maintained that Abraham and Ishmael also smashed the idols of the pre-Islamic polytheistic tribes that were housed in the *Ka'aba*,[25] in an alleged incident that was designed to parallel the rabbinic *midrash* that described young Abraham as having destroyed the stone idols in his father Terah's workshop in Ur of the Chaldeans.[26]

## Islam and the Jewish People

Having been rejected by both Jews and Christians when he sought to be included among them, Muhammad created his own religion, Islam. Subsequently, this new religion was spread across the Middle East, Northern Africa, and Southern Europe on the edge of the sword.[27] In fact, "the Muslim armies were so powerful that within a hundred years of the Prophet's death, the Islamic empire extended from the edge of China on the east, across the upper part of Africa, to Spain on the west."[28] In 637 AD, the Islamic conquest overwhelmed the land of Palestine and forced the surrender of the city of Jerusalem. Before Islam's military conquest

[23] The black stone in the *Ka'aba* is probably a meteorite. The fact that it became a focal point of Arabian worship was not uncommon in the ancient world, for meteorites were often objects of worship. E. L. Krinov, *Principles of Meteoritics: International Series of Monographs on Earth Sciences* (New York: Pergamon Press, Inc., 1960), p. 1.

[24] *Qur'an* 2:127; 14:39.

[25] *Qur'an* 21:51–73. David R. Topper, *Idolatry and Infinity: Of Art, Math, and God* (Boca Raton, FL: Universal Publishers, 2014), p. 4.

[26] Genesis *Rabbah* 38:13.

[27] Frederick M. Denny, *Islam and the Muslim Community* (Long Grove, IL: Waveland Press, 1987), p. 38.

[28] James A. Beverley, *Islam: An Introduction to Religion, Culture, and History* (Nashville, TN: Thomas Nelson, 2011), p. 37. Also, Abu al-Fazl 'Izzati, *The Spread of Islam: The Contributing Factors* (London, UK: Islamic College for Advanced Studies Press, 2002), p. 383. Many scholars try to discredit the charge that Islam was spread on the edge of the sword, saying that this idea is a myth concocted by Christians to discredit Muhammad and Islam. Gerard Delanty, *Routledge Handbook of Cosmopolitanism Studies* (Abingdon, UK: Routledge, 2012), p. 191; and Betsy Hartmann and James K. Boyce, *A Quiet Violence: View from a Bangladesh Village* (London, UK: Zed Books Ltd., 1983), p. 215. The truth is, however, that no religious idea has ever come to dominate such a wide swath of geography in one century without the exercise of military power. As Brigitte Gabriel says, "Islam did not emerge peacefully from the Arabian Peninsula floating harmlessly on the breeze. Islam was spread across the Middle East and North Africa at the edge of the sword. The only choice offered by Muslim conquerors was conversion or submission to Islam, or death." Brigitte Gabriel, *Because They Hate: A Survivor of Islamic Terror Warns America* (New York: St. Martin's Press, 2006), p. 151. Gerald Leinwand describes the seventh century Muslim conquests far more accurately: "In 633, armies of fierce nomads, carrying the sword of Islam, galloped east toward Persia, north toward the Fertile Crescent, and west toward Egypt." Gerald Leinwand, *Pageant of World History* (Upper Saddle River, NJ: Prentice-Hall, 1990), p. 304.

of Palestine, there had been no Muslims or Arabs in Jerusalem, Judea, or Samaria. Any Muslim claim to the land of Israel, therefore, has always been associated "with a violent attack on the Jews."[29] The Muslims took the land by force. "It is they who established the rules of the game that no matter how long the Jews had lived on the land, no matter if they had been the majority for well more than a thousand years, that those Jews were still subject to be conquered."[30] Notwithstanding, Marvin Wilson observes, "Military conquest may not be used to prove a nation's right to a given land."[31]

Like other pre-Islamic people groups whose ancestors had lived in the geographical area that came to be dominated by Muslim conquest, Jews and Christians were accorded the status of *dhimmi*, citizens who were subjected to taxation that did not apply to Muslims.[32] At the same time, however, despite the fact that they were not followers of Allah and Islam, they were considered by Muhammad and his immediate followers to be of a higher status than the pagans because they were monotheists. Muhammad himself designated Jews and Christians as "People of the Book," saying that they were "privileged above all people"[33] because they both recognized the inspiration and authority of the Hebrew Scriptures, the *Tanakh*. He recognized the Torah as a divine book, a "guidance and light"[34] and a source of "blessing and guidance for the righteous."[35]

---

[29] Lawrence J. Epstein, "The Moral Case of Zionism," in *Israel Opinion*, 04.17.14, p. 1.

[30] Epstein, p. 1.

[31] Marvin R. Wilson, *Our Father Abraham: Jewish Roots of the Christian Faith* (Grand Rapids, MI: Wm. B. Eerdmans Publishing Co., 1989), p. 266.

[32] Bat Ye'or, *The Dhimmi: Jews and Christians under Islam* (Madison, NJ: Fairleigh Dickinson University Press, 1985), p. 45. In Arabic, the word *dhimmi* means "covenant" or "protected person" and originally referred to "a person living in a region overrun by Muslim conquest who was accorded a protected status and allowed to retain his or her original faith." See *Merriam-Webster Dictionary* posted at https://www.merriam-webster.com/dictionary/dhimmi. Also, Avner Falk, *A Psychoanalytic History of the Jews* (Cranbury, NJ: Associated University Presses, 1996), p. 376. Falk notes: "The early Muslim rulers regarded the non-Muslim 'aliens' in their realm as 'protected' people who had to show their submission by paying special taxes. . . . In exchange for paying the *jizyah* (head tax or poll tax) and *kharaj* (land tax), these aliens received *dhimmi* (protection) of their Muslim rulers, were granted freedom of worship, and were allowed to organize themselves into religious communities." The collection of the *jizyah* and *kharaj* taxes was one of Islam's five precepts or "pillars." Ultimately, the term *dhimmi* referred to non-Muslim citizens of Muslim lands who "were granted special status and safety in Islamic law in return for paying the capital tax." Eventually, Islamic law required all adult *dhimmi* males to pay a land tax (*kharaj*), a graduated poll tax (*jizyah*) of five dinars for the wealthy, three dinars for the middle class, and one dinar for the working poor (although not for the totally indigent), and a tax on harvests (*ushr*), which was 10% on irrigated land and 20% on non-irrigated land. Norman A. Stillman, "Dhimma" in *Medieval Islamic Civilization: A–K, Index*, Josef W. Meri and Jere L. Bacharach, eds. (Abingdon, UK: Routledge, 2006), p. 206.

[33] *Qur'an* 45:15.

[34] *Qur'an* 5:44.

[35] *Qur'an* 6:153–154.

As Islam conquered the Middle East, all of Northern Africa, and parts of Southern Europe, then, a significant portion of the Jewish people found themselves living under Muslim hegemony. Because of what at that time was their two-millennia-old entitlement to the land of Israel, significant numbers of the Jewish people continued to live in the land of Israel after the Muslim conquest, just as they had done after their ancestors' defeat at the hands of the Assyrians, the Babylonians, and the Romans. Unlike previous conquering armies, however, the Muslim invaders, at the time of their invasion of Israel, did not try to remove the Jews from the land when they conquered Palestine, nor did they attempt to force them to convert to Islam. Instead, they preferred the economic advantages of enforcing upon their Jewish subjects the Muslim taxes and thereby "permitting" them to live as Jews and to practice Judaism.[36] Even though the Jews were a suppressed and exploited minority, they lived relatively well under Muslim rule compared with what they experienced in the Christian nations of medieval Europe.[37] Whereas in Europe, the stated goal of the rulers was to force Jews to convert to Christianity, Daniel Gavron says that in Muslim lands during this time, Jews were only *encouraged* to convert to Islam.[38]

Gavron maintains that "in Mesopotamia, the Jews flourished under Islam. Although as non-Muslims they were in most ways second-class citizens, they were honored as the 'People of the Book.'"[39] In fact, because of this perspective, early Muslims did not regard the Jews as "nonbelievers, since they shared with them the belief in one God,"[40] though they could not be considered to be "true believers either, because they failed to acknowledge the mission of Muhammad and did not accept the Koran as divine revelation."[41] In the Muslim world of that day, however, many Jewish scholars excelled in Arabic literature and in science, particularly medicine, and Jewish leaders "played an important role in the consolidation of the Muslim civilization."[42]

[36] Nissim Rejwan, *Israel's Place in the Middle East: A Pluralist Perspective* (Gainesville, FL: The University of Florida Press, 1998), p. 36.

[37] Benny Morris, *The Road to Jerusalem: Glubb Pasha, Palestine and the Jews* (London, UK: I.B. Tauris & Co, 2002), p. 28.

[38] Scott A. Merriman, *Religion and the Law in America: An Encyclopedia of Personal Belief and Public Policy* (Santa Barbara, CA: ABC–CLIO, Inc., 2007), p. 87.

[39] Daniel Gavron, *Holy Land Mosaic: Stories of Cooperation and Coexistence between Israelis and Palestinians* (Lanham, MD: Rowman & Littlefield Publishers, 2008), p. 88.

[40] Rejwan, *Israel's Place*, p. 36.

[41] Rejwan, *Israel's Place*, p. 36.

[42] Gavron, p. 88

Léon Poliakov observes that during the early ages of Islam, Jews enjoyed individual privileges and community prosperity, with few laws or social barriers restricting their lives and commercial activities.[43] Mark Cohen reports that the Jewish people also experienced a significant degree of Muslim tolerance during the early Middle Ages.[44] At the same time, however, both in antiquity and during the Middle Ages, Islamic rule was "punctuated by anti-*dhimmi* persecution, some of it quite violent."[45] Still, "for Jews, it was different—less frequent and less brutal than anti-Jewish persecution in Christendom," Cohen notes.[46] In Islamic territories, laws and social barriers did not restrict Jewish commercial activities, and the exclusion from trade and craft guilds did not exist as it did in Europe.[47]

As a result, as Nissim Rejwan notes, the "Jews of Mesopotamia welcomed the change to Muslim rule, mainly because the new masters left them very much to themselves."[48] The rulers of Baghdad even trusted Jewish bankers and gave Jews oversight of international trade. Iranian leaders apparently appointed a Jewish governor for its principal port of Siraf.[49] It was not insignificant, says Rejwan, that during the eighth century AD and thereafter, Baghdad "became the center of gravity not only for the Muslim Empire but also of Babylonian Jewish life and learning."[50]

In the twelfth century AD, one of the greatest Talmudists in Jewish history, Moses Maimonides, lived much of his life in Tunisia and Egypt, where he became the personal physician of Saladin, the Sultan of Egypt and Syria who had cemented Muslim control over Jerusalem and Judea by seizing Palestine from the Crusaders. Maimonides had fled intolerant Muslim regimes that had come to power in his native Spain and Morocco.[51] In similar fashion, during continuing outbreaks of antisemitic Christian violence and persecution in subsequent

---

[43] Léon Poliakov, *The History of Anti-Semitism: Volume 1, From the Time of Christ to the Court of the Jews* (Philadelphia, PA: The University of Pennsylvania Press, 2003), p. 68.

[44] Mark R. Cohen, "The Neo-Lachrymose Conception of Jewish-Arab History," *Tikkun* 6.3 (1991), p. 58.

[45] Mark R. Cohen, *Under Crescent and Cross: The Jews in the Middle Ages* (Princeton, NJ: Princeton University Press, 1994), p. 163.

[46] Cohen, *Under Crescent*, p. 163.

[47] Cohen, "The Neo-Lachrymose," p. 58.

[48] Nissim Rejwan, *The Last Jews in Baghdad: Remembering a Lost Homeland* (Austin, TX: The University of Texas Press, 2004), p. 244.

[49] Cohen, "The Neo-Lachrymose," p. 58.

[50] Rejwan, *The Last Jews*, p. 244.

[51] Reuven Firestone, *An Introduction to Islam for Jews* (Philadelphia, PA: The Jewish Publication Society, 2008), p. 66. Also, Stephen Lock, John M. Last, and George Dunea, eds., *The Oxford Illustrated Companion to Medicine* (Oxford, UK: Oxford University Press, 2001), p. 62.

centuries in medieval Europe, significant numbers of Jews relocated to Muslim-controlled nations.[52]

In fact, Jews who were expelled from Spain and Portugal were even invited to immigrate to territory within the Ottoman Empire. "The greatest influx of Jews into Asia Minor and the Ottoman Empire" occurred in the early sixteenth century when Sultan Bayezid II "issued a formal invitation to the Jews expelled from Spain and Portugal."[53] The "bulk of the nonconverted Jews who were expelled [from Spain and Portugal] went to the Ottoman Empire and settled in commercial centers such as Salonika and Istanbul, where they were allowed to cultivate their Jewish identity and to live in an atmosphere of tolerance," says Sebouh Aslanian.[54] During this time, "the conditions [the Jews] found were ones of linguistic and religious tolerance."[55] Many of the Sephardic Jews who immigrated "achieved high professional and social standing in the Ottoman world."[56]

Merlin Swartz has called this time a new era for Jews when an attitude of tolerance led to Jewish integration into Arab-Islamic society.[57] Some scholars have even referred to this time period as the "Golden Age" for the Jews.[58] Others, however, have argued that the term *Golden Age* is a myth designed to hold forth a historical example of an era of tolerance for Jews and Judaism that never really existed.[59] Some scholars maintain that the "Golden Age" idea was actually developed by European Jewish activists to encourage Jews to emigrate from Europe to predominantly Muslim Palestine in order to take over the land from rightful owners, the Muslim Arabs.[60] Firestone suggests that the "Golden Age" concept was adopted by Muslim Arab intellectuals to

---

[52] Bernard Lewis, *The Jews of Islam* (Princeton, NJ: Princeton University Press, 1984), p. 62.

[53] Farid Adel, *The Champions of the True Faith* (Bloomington, IN: Xlibris Corp., 2016), p. 192.

[54] Sebouh David Aslanian, *From the Indian Ocean to the Mediterranean: The Global Trade Networks of Armenian Merchants from New Julfa* (Berkeley, CA: The University of California Press, 2011), p. 226.

[55] Ralph J. Penny, *Variation and Change in Spanish* (Cambridge, UK: Cambridge University Press, 2000), p. 176.

[56] Penny, p. 176.

[57] Cohen, "The Neo-Lachrymose," p. 56.

[58] Cohen, "The Neo-Lachrymose," p. 55.

[59] Mark R. Cohen, "Islam and the Jews: Myth, Counter-Myth, History," in *Jews among Muslims: Communities in the Precolonial Middle East*, Shlomo Deshen and Walter P. Zenner, eds. (London, UK: Macmillan Press, 1996), pp. 50ff; Marvin Perry and Frederick M. Schweitzer, *Antisemitism: Myth and Hate from Antiquity to the Present* (New York: Palgrave Macmillan 2002), p. 267; Mark Avrum Ehrlich, *Encyclopedia of the Jewish Diaspora: Origins, Experiences, and Culture* (Santa Barbara, CA: ABC–CLIO, LLC, 2009), p. 306; and Dario Fernandez-Morera, *The Myth of the Andalusian Paradise: Muslims, Christians and Jews under Islamic Rule in Medieval Spain* (Wilmington, DE: Intercollegiate Studies Institute, 2016).

[60] Firestone, p. 69.

blame Zionists for "ruining what they claimed was the near-utopian generosity and tolerance of the Muslim world toward the Jews."[61] They also deny that antisemitism is a "Muslim phenomenon."[62] To this day, Arab Muslims in the Middle East advance this patently false argument that if the nation of Israel were to be dismantled, "Jews and Arabs would return to the halcyon days of tolerant interfaith relations as in the Golden Age, with Jews living peacefully in Palestine under Arab-Muslim rule."[63] In response to these arguments, others have sought to prove that the historical Muslim treatment of Jews was continually intolerant and violent. Scholarly literature created before the time of postmodern politically correct muticulturalism declares unequivocally that "in Arabia . . . the first home of Muhammadanism, the Jews have always been subject to persecution."[64]

The truth of this matter probably lies between the extremes that argue on the one hand that "in the Islamic world . . . Jews have always . . . been treated with respect"[65] and on the other hand that there is "clear historical evidence of specific Islamic antisemitism, from the time of Geniza record" to the present day.[66] Although Jewish life under Islamic rule represented an improvement over their treatment in Europe, the interfaith Utopia that some scholars have said existed under ancient and medieval Muslim rule in the Middle East simply did not exist, does not exist, and never can or ever will exist.[67] One fact remains that, in spite of claims to the contrary, Jews still experienced persecution and various levels of violence throughout the Islamic era from its inception to the present day.

[61] Firestone, p. 69.

[62] Mark R. Cohen, "Muslim Anti-Semitism: Old or New?" in *A History of Jewish-Muslim Relations: From the Origins to the Present Day*, Abdelwahab Meddeb and Benjamin Stora, eds. (Princeton, NJ: Princeton University Press, 2013), p. 547.

[63] Mark R. Cohen, "Medieval Jewry in the World of Islam," in *The Oxford Handbook of Jewish Studies*, Martin Goodman, Jeremy Cohen, and David Jan Sorkin, eds. (Oxford, UK: Oxford University Press, 2002), p. 194.

[64] A. M. Hyamson, "Jews in Islam," in *Encyclopaedia of Religion and Ethics*, James Hastings, ed. (New York: Charles Scribner's Sons, 1915), vol. VII, pp. 560–562. Hyamson gives a balanced account of the way Jews were treated in various parts of the Muslim-dominated world; however, he notes the various forms of oppression that Jews endured in virtually every place where they lived under Muslim rule. His discussion of the enforcement of the Ordinances of Khalif Omar in various Muslim societies—including requirements that Jews not build new synagogues, never enter a mosque, always wear distinctive dress—is excellent.

[65] Philip Spencer and Sara Valentina Di Palma, "Antisemitism and the Politics of Holocaust Memorial Day in the UK and Italy," in *Perceptions of the Holocaust in Europe and Muslim Communities: Sources, Comparisons, and Educational Challenges*, Günther Jikeli and Joëll Alouche-Benayoun, eds. (Dordrecht, The Netherlands: Springer Science+Business Media, 2013), p. 77.

[66] Andrew G. Bostom, *The Legacy of Islamic Antisemitism: From Sacred Texts to Solemn History* (Amherst, NY: Prometheus Books, 2008), pp. 32ff.

[67] Cohen, "The Neo-Lachrymose," p. 58.

Whatever the case may have actually been, one thing is certain: Jewish dominion over all of Israel—from the Mediterranean Sea to the Jordan River and from Eilat to Mt. Hermon, including the Golan Heights—has always ensured and continues to ensure freedom of religion for all the inhabitants of the Promised Land whereas Muslim dominance of the same land has historically guaranteed and will always guarantee denial of rights of access to holy sites for Jews and Christians—and for other religious groups as well—and will guarantee political, social, and religious prejudice, persecution, and violence to all the non-Muslim inhabitants of the Holy Land.[68]

## A Seedbed for a New Antisemitism

Without a doubt, the theological and philosophical seeds for unfolding Muslim antisemitism and violence against the Jewish people were sown by Muhammad himself[69] when he revised and edited the Hebrew Scriptures so as to coopt the history and genealogy of the Jewish people in order to "prove" that "Abraham was not a Jew nor yet a Christian; but he was true in Faith, and bowed his will to Allah's [Islam]"[70] and that Abraham was the founder of the *Ka'aba* in Mecca.[71] After initially affirming the inspiration of the Torah, he later argued that it had become perverted by the Jews.[72] After saying the Jews were "privileged above all people," he proclaimed that they were "those who show the greatest hostility to the [Muslims]."[73] After his stunning victory at Quarysh at Badr in 624 AD, Muhammad's future intentions toward the Jews were made very clear when "he assembled the Banu Qaynuqa Jews at their market-place and ominously warned: 'O Jews, beware lest God bring upon you the vengeance that He brought upon Quraysh (at Badr) and become Muslims. You know that I am a Prophet who was sent (by God)!"[74]

[68] W. Eugene March, *Israel and the Politics of Land: A Theological Case Study* (Louisville, KY: Westminster/John Knox Press, 1994), p. 21. March points out how the initial Muslim conquest of the Holy Land resulted in the destruction of the Church of the Holy Sepulchre in 1009 and the denial of Christian access to the Holy Land. These were the major factors that produced the Crusades. Also Ron E. Hassner, *War on Sacred Grounds* (Ithaca, NY: Cornell University Press, 2009), p. 114, and Yitzhak Reiter, *Contested Holy Places in Israel-Palestine: Sharing and Conflict Resolution* (Abingdon, UK: Routledge, 2017), p. 319.

[69] M. A. Khan, *Islamic Jihad: A Legacy of Forced Conversion, Imperialism, and Slavery* (Bloomington, IN: iUniverse, 2009), pp. 45ff.

[70] *Qur'an* 3:67.

[71] *Qur'an* 2:126–130.

[72] *Qur'an* 2:70.

[73] *Qur'an* 5:82.

[74] Muhammad, quoted in Ibn Ishaq, *The Life of Muhammad*, tr. Alfred Guillame (Karachi, Pakistan: Oxford University Press, 2004), p. 363, noted in Khan, p. 45.

As is usually the case, prejudice and antisemitism rarely remain in the realm of theology or philosophy but are soon translated into the worlds of anthropology and sociology. It was not strange, therefore, that Muhammad's theology was manifest in various acts of violence, most notably his expulsion and massacre of the Jewish tribes of Medina in which he ordered the beheading of the men and pubescent boys and the enslavement of the women and children.[75] In another act attributed to Muhammad, the *Qur'an* describes Jews with a dehumanizing calumny, saying that Allah turned them into "pigs and apes."[76] Finally, even on his deathbed, Muhammad manifest his antisemitism by forbidding the coexistence of Islam and Judaism in Arabia[77] and ordering the execution of Jewish poet Ka'b Ibn al-Ashraf on the grounds that his erotic poems had defamed Muslim women.[78]

In the times following Muhammad's death, Jews were subjected to continuing prejudice, intolerance, oppression, and violence. From the eleventh century AD forward, significant instances of Muslim pograms against Jews were actually orchestrated and carried out by Islamic leaders and their communities. A prime example was the Granada massacre in 1066 when the Jewish quarter of the city was completely razed.[79] A massive Muslim slaughter of Jews occurred in 1391 throughout the Iberian Peninsula.[80] Numerous instances of violence against Jews in Northern Africa during the Middle Ages have also been documented.[81] In 1465, only eleven Jews survived when Arab mobs in Fez slaughtered thousands of Jews in an action that incited similar massacres throughout Morocco.[82] And the list goes on and on!

[75] Richard A. Gabriel, *Muhammad: Islam's First Great General* (Norman, OK: The University of Oklahoma Press, 2007), p. 142, and Robert Spencer, *The Truth about Muhammad: Founder of the World's Most Intolerant Religion* (Washington, DC: Regnery Publishing, Inc., 2006), p. 131.

[76] *Qur'an,* Suras 2:65; 5:59–60; 7:166. Melvin Ember, Carol R. Ember, and Ian Skoggard, eds., *Encyclopedia of Diasporas: Immigrant and Refugee Cultures around the World* (New York: Springer Science+Media, 2005), p. 183.

[77] Shabbir Akhtar, *Islam as Political Religion: The Future of an Imperial Faith* (Abingdon, UK: Routledge, 2011), p. 23.

[78] Uri Rubin, "The Assassination of Ka'b Ibn al-Ashraf," in *Oriens: Journal of Philosophy, Theology and Science in Islamic Societies*, vol. 32 (1990), pp. 65–71.

[79] Richard Gottheil and Meyer Kayserling, "Granada," in *The Jewish Encyclopedia* (New York: Funk & Wagnalls, 1906), posted at http://jewishencyclopedia.com/articles/6855-granada.

[80] Jarbel Rodriguez, *Muslim and Christian Contact in the Middle Ages: A Reader* (Toronto, Canada: Toronto University Press, 2015), p. 348.

[81] Florin Curta and Andrew Holt, eds., *Great Events in Religion: An Encyclopedia of Pivotal Events in Religious History, Volume 1: Prehistory to AD 60* (Santa Barbara, CA: ABC-CLIO, LLC, 2017), p. 915.

[82] David A. Gerber, ed., *Anti-Semitism in American History* (Urbana, IL: The University of Illinois Press, 1986), p. 84.

Long before the unfolding of Muslim violence against the Jewish people in the twentieth century, an incipient antisemitism had existed in the Islamic world that was present in the teachings and actions of Muhammad himself and was continued for generations thereafter. The more fanatical the Muslim regime has been, the more antisemitic its leaders and its citizens have been. Among the interpreters of the *Qur'an*, the *Hadith*, and other sacred Muslim texts, Islamic literalists have found adequate material over the centuries to justify—even demand—acts of terrorism, violence, mayhem, and murder against the Jewish people. One can only conclude that historical reports of Muslim tolerance for Jews must have been practical compromises that were made for the sake of material and financial benefits through commerce and taxation rather than for the sake of religious or ethnic tenderheartedness. The idea that Islam has always been a religion of peace is entirely spurious.

CHAPTER 6

# A MILLENNIUM OF VIOLENCE

## UNRELENTING ANTISEMITISM AND DEATH

For a short time after the Roman dispersion, the Diaspora Jews found a degree of mercy and tranquility in Europe and elsewhere. Rodney Stark maintains that the five centuries from 500–1000 AD were relatively tranquil times for the Jews with only one confirmed instance of Christian anti-Jewish violence occurring in 554 in Clermont, France, where many Jews were killed, and five hundred accepted forced baptism.[1] Léon Poliakov notes that, generally speaking, during this time, "kings, nobles, and bishops granted Jews a broad autonomy. . . . Talmudic scholarship flowered again on the banks of the Rhine and the Seine at the very period when it was falling into decay in Babylonia. . . . [The Jews] continued to mix freely with the Christian populations and to live on excellent terms with them."[2]

The five centuries of Christian tolerance for the Jews of Europe largely resulted from a decree by Pope Gregory the Great in 590 AD in which he declared that Jews "should have no infringement of their rights" and in which he gave this injunction to the church: "We forbid to vilify the Jews. We allow them to . . . have full authority over their possessions."[3]

---

[1] Rodney Stark, *One True God: Historical Consequences of Monotheism* (Princeton, NJ: Princeton University Press, 2001), p. 135.

[2] Léon Poliakov, *The History of Anti-Semitism, Volume 1: From the Time of Christ to the Court Jews*, tr. Richard Howard (Philadelphia, PA: The University of Pennsylvania Press, 2003), p. 35.

[3] Gregory I, quoted in Sam Waagenaar, *The Pope's Jews* (Chicago, IL: Open Court Pub. Co., 1974), p. 71. Twentieth-century Jewish historian Cecil Roth, editor-in-chief of the *Encyclopedia Judaica*, said, "Of all the dynasties in Europe, the papacy not only refused to persecute the Jews . . . but through the ages popes were protectors of the Jews. . . .For this we Jews must have gratitude." Cecil Roth, quoted in David Goldstein, *Jewish Panorama* (Boston, MA: Catholic Campaigners for Christ, 1940), p. 200. Berel Wein also points out that because the Jews of Renaissance Italy were protected by the pope, there were no overt acts of violence against them there, as was commonly the case across the rest of Europe. Berel Wein, *Patterns in Jewish History: Insights into the Past, Present, and Future of the Eternal People* (Jerusalem, Israel: Koren Publishers, 2011), p. 15.

This decree from one of history's most powerful popes certainly had an impact on the clergy and laity of the Western Church. For at least 500 years, therefore, the Jews in Western Europe were able to live in relative peace and tranquility. Unfortunately, as ensuing history would prove, many further papal pronouncements and ecclesiastical declarations regarding the Jews would have ulterior motives, such as promoting forced baptism and conversion to Christianity, and some would not bode well for the physical well-being of the Jewish people.[4] For those Jews who had retreated into Europe in an effort to escape the onslaught of the Roman violence in Palestine, therefore, living in relative peace must have seemed odd, and they must have been wary that such a respite might not continue.

Indeed, security and peace for the Jewish people during the second half of the first millennium AD was to be short lived, for danger and death were lurking on the horizon of an immediate future that would bring to them centuries of misery, trauma, and death. Beginning with the turn of the eleventh century, Jews found that the Gentile people among whom they lived had become increasingly inhospitable and antisemitic. The times were changing. Christians, who for centuries had expended their energies fighting one another and advancing their vision for expanding the City of God,[5] would soon be blindsided by a whirling dervish of political and religious fervor, prejudice, and hate. Militant Islam was rising, and it was taking its prophet's vision for world conquest to radical extremes.[6]

Shortly after the turn of the millennium, a group of radical Muslims led by Fatmid Caliph al-Hakim attacked Jerusalem and destroyed the

[4] The papacy was largely responsible for the ongoing medieval European requirement for Jews to wear distinctive clothing or an emblem or mark on their outer garments to distinguish themselves as Jews. Established by Pope Innocent III in the Fourth Lateran Council in 1215, this requirement set a precedent for the yellow badge or the *Judenstern* ("Jews' star") in Germany, in the 3" x 6" yellow felt image of the Decalogue in thirteenth-century England, in full-length red robes in fourteenth century Rome, and in the cone-shaped hat (*Judenhut*) that was common during most of the Middle Ages. This papal-inspired practice eventuated in Hitler's yellow star decree in 1938. For further discussion, see Frank K. Flinn, *Encyclopedia of Catholicism* (New York: Facts On File, Inc., 2007), p. 37, and Harry J. Cargas, *Holocaust Scholars Write to the Vatican* (Westport, CT: Greenwood Press, 1998), p. 9. Similarly, it was Pope Paul IV who created the Roman Ghetto in 1555, forcing the Jews of Rome to live on the left bank of the Tiber in a walled slum, called "the menagerie of the Jews," where they endured almost unspeakably unsanitary conditions. This practice then became entrenched in Europe, making it possible for horrors like the twentieth-century Warsaw and Krakow Ghettos to exist. For further analysis, see Avner Falk, *A Psychoanalytic History of the Jews* (Madison, NJ: Fairleigh Dickinson University Press, 1996), p. 519; Edward Kessler and Neil Wenborn, eds., *A Dictionary of Jewish-Christian Relations* (Cambridge, UK: Cambridge University Press, 2005), p. 166; and Judith R. Baskin, *The Cambridge Dictionary of Judaism and Jewish Culture* (Cambridge, UK: Cambridge University Press, 2001), p. 202.

[5] Gerard O'Daly, *Augustine's City of God: A Reader's Guide* (Oxford, UK: Oxford University Press, 1999), p. 9.

[6] Though early expressions of Islam were thought to be tolerant, it was not long before disciples of Muhammad adopted violent aspects of his worldview and lifestyle, making Islam arguably the most violent and destructive religion in human history.

Church of the Holy Sepulchre, the very basilica that Constantine, at his mother Helena's request, had erected to enshrine the site of the tomb in which Jesus was interred before his resurrection. Even though a measure of calm had been restored to the Christian and Jewish communities in the Middle East when al-Hakim was subsequently assassinated by his own political rivals, it was not long before a new set of Muslim rulers seized control of the Middle East. Unlike their predecessors, these Turkish Muslims recognized the stream of Christians who continually made pilgrimage to Jerusalem as easily exploitable objects for extortion, torture, and even slavery. Because of the extreme religious fanaticism of the Turkish Muslims, they discounted the general economic benefit to themselves and the inhabitants of Palestine of having thousands of pilgrims visiting the Holy Land and spending their money there in favor of enforcing their radical views of Islamic purity.

When word of the Muslim desecration of the Church of the Holy Sepulchre reached Europe, Christian passions were inflamed to such a high intensity that they turned their fury upon the new "infidels," as the Muslims came to be known.[7] Tragically, this development could mean only one thing: trouble for the Jews. Reports of the restrictions that these Turks had placed on pilgrimages and the atrocities that they regularly carried out against Christians who tried to visit the Holy Land enraged Europeans so much that when Byzantine emperor Comnenus appealed to Western Christians to rescue the Muslim-oppressed Orthodox Christians, the Roman Catholic pope decided that it was time for action.

Sadly, as the passions of Christians were being inflamed against the Muslim infidels for daring to desecrate the holy site of the crucifixion and entombment of Jesus and as calls for retribution against them were echoing across Christian Europe, Christian scholars were engaged in other discussions and reaching conclusions that would not bode well for the Jewish people in a time of such anger and prejudice. In 1090 AD, Anselm of Laon advanced an argument that took to another level the long-held Christian belief that the Jews were responsible for the death of Jesus. R. I. Moore says that Anselm claimed that "the Jews knowingly committed deicide" and thereby set in motion a charge of premeditated malice aforethought that "came to dominate Christian attitudes by the

[7] Andrew Wheatcroft, *Infidels: A History of the Conflict between Christendom and Islam* (New York: Random House, 2005), pp. 3–35. The term *infidel* is a pejorative that literally means "unfaithful." It was applied by medieval Christians to those who did not accept their established orthodoxy for Christian belief, those who followed other religions, and those who were irreligious.

mid-thirteenth century"[8] and continued to do so for at least seven centuries thereafter. The alleged Jewish crime of deicide would further inflame Christian antisemitism against the Jews that would manifest itself in the coming conflict with the Middle East Muslims.

## Onward, Christian Soldiers!

On November 27, 1095, Pope Urban II may have made the most important speech of the Middle Ages when he delivered an impassioned oration to a throng of people who had gathered at the Council of Clermont. The pope made a call for vengeance against the Muslim infidels. He spoke of the atrocities, murders, and rapes that had been inflicted upon Christians by these "Saracens,"[9] and he stressed the fact that by being under Muslim control, Christianity's holiest shrine was continually the object of desecration. Urban ordered both nobles and commoners, both rich and poor, to mount a campaign to liberate Jerusalem from the Turks,[10] promising that "whoever goes from pure devotion and not desire for earthly profit to liberate the Church of God in Jerusalem, his journey will be considered a substitute for all penance."[11] The stage was set. The First Crusade to liberate the Holy Land from the Muslim infidels was launched.[12] In doing so, Urban II set in motion what would become a series of nine "crusades" that would enmesh the Middle East in conflict and violence well into the thirteenth century.[13]

The papal-sponsored campaign against the Muslims did not, however, remain focused solely on the followers of Islam. At that time, many Christians in Europe turned the anger that they had developed toward the Saracens against an even older rival, the Jews. Abbé Pierre of the French monastery at Cluny encapsulated their "reasoning" in this manner: "What is the good

[8] R. I. Moore, "Anti-Semitism and the Birth of Europe," in *Christianity and Judaism*, Diana Wood, ed. (Oxford, UK: Ecclesiastical History Society, 1992), p. 40, noted in Jay Ruud, "Dante and the Jews," in *Jews in Medieval Christendom: Slay Them Not*, Kristine T. Utterback and Merrall L. Price, eds. (Leiden, The Netherlands: Koninklijke Brill NV, 2013), p. 149, n. 3.

[9] The term *Saracen* was used in Greek and Latin writings at the beginning of the Common Era to describe the non-Arab people, including Jews, who lived in the Middle Eastern provinces of the Roman Empire. By the time of the Crusades, the term had come to be associated almost exclusively with the Arab Muslims.

[10] Sylvia Schein, *Gateway to the Heavenly City: Crusader Jerusalem and the Catholic West (1099–1187)* (Burlington, VT: Ashgate Publishing Co., 2005), pp. 9–11.

[11] Robert Somerville, *The Councils of Urban II: Decreta Claromontensia* (Amsterdam, The Netherlands: Adolf M. Hakkert Publishing, 1972), vol. 1, p. 74.

[12] R. N. Swanson, ed., *The Routledge History of Medieval Christianity: 1050–1500* (Abingdon, UK: Routledge, 2015), p. 185.

[13] S. J. Allen and Emilie Amt, eds., *The Crusades: A Reader* (Toronto, Canada: The University of Toronto Press, 2014), pp. 327ff. Also Elizabeth Hallam, ed., *Chronicles of the Crusades: Nine Crusades and Two Hundred Years of Bitter Conflict for the Holy Land* (New York: Weidenfeld and Nicolson, 1989). Of the nine crusades, four were major, four were minor, and the other was the tragic "Children's Crusade."

of going to the end of the world, at great loss of men and money, to fight Saracens, when we permit among us other infidels who are a thousand times more guilty toward Christ than are the Mohammedans?"[14] With clerics like Pierre spouting such vitriolic invective and incitement, Christian extremists launched and maintained a reign of terror upon Jews throughout the Western world, especially in Germany, where violent attacks in cities like Cologne, Würzburg, Mainz, Strasbourg, and Worms resulted in countless deaths, untold suffering, and horrendous destruction of real and personal Jewish property.[15] There was no rational excuse for this rampage of violence against the Jewish people as the inflamed Christians vented their anger against infidels of every sort and description who did not fit their definition of Catholic Christianity. Spearheaded by Christian leaders like Peter the Hermit and Count Emicho,[16] these Rhineland massacres also produced additional violent attacks against Jews in other parts of Europe.[17]

The conduct of these and countless other "Christian soldiers" was reprehensible at best and downright abominable at worst. Together, they pillaged, raped, and murdered their way across virtually all of Europe, and from there through Constantinople, on to the Holy Land, and finally into Jerusalem. In short, the First Crusade was "a hideous chronicle of human suffering, fanaticism, and cruelty,"[18] and the Jews in its path were among the victims who suffered the most from the mob violence that Christians inflicted upon them. No Jew was safe, and few were spared at least some degree of suffering.

No one was safe from the Crusaders' blood lust and greed. They were simply not satisfied with fulfilling their quest to liberate Jerusalem from the Muslims. Their fury was carried out on virtually everyone and everything in their path. Over the course of all the crusades, these Western Church Christians destroyed and plundered so much of the Eastern Church's treasure that Orthodox Christianity remained impoverished

---

[14] Abbé Pierre quoted in Poliakov, p. 48.

[15] Rodney Stark, *One True God: Historical Consequences of Monotheism* (Princeton, NJ: Princeton University Press, 2001), p. 143. Also, Christopher Tyerman, *God's War: A New History of the Crusades* (Cambridge, UK: Belknap Press, 2006), pp. 103–106.

[16] Robert Chazan, *European Jewry and the First Crusade: Hebrew Chronicles of the First and Second Crusades* (Berkeley, CA: University of California Press, 1996), pp. 55–60.

[17] David Nirenberg, "The Rhineland Massacres of Jews in the First Crusade, Memories Medieval and Modern," in *Medieval Concepts of the Past: Ritual, Memory, and Historiography*, Gerd Althoff, Johannes Fried, and Patrick J. Geary, eds. (Cambridge, UK: Cambridge University Press, 2002), pp. 279–310. Also Robert Chazan, *In the Year 1096: The First Crusade and the Jews* (New York: The Jewish Publication Society of America, 1996), p. 125; and Shlomo Eidelberg, *The Jews and the Crusaders: The Hebrew Chronicles of the First and Second Crusades* (Jersey City, NJ: KTAV Publishing,1996), p. 192.

[18] Karen Armstrong, *The Spiral Staircase: My Climb Out of Darkness* (New York: Random House, 2004), p. 258.

for centuries thereafter.[19] Such fratricidal carnage was but a further manifestation of the internecine conflicts within Christendom in which theological debates often degenerated into political infighting that sometimes became violent.

The toll on the Jews was no less devastating, if not exponentially more so. As they traversed along the way to Jerusalem, the Christian soldiers regularly pillaged, tortured, raped, and murdered Jews and others. Then, when the Crusaders finally took Jerusalem in 1099, all the surviving Jewish men, women, and children of the city were herded together into the Great Synagogue, the doors were locked, and the building was torched. The entire Jewish population of Jerusalem was immolated while the Christian Crusaders held their crosses high[20] and marched around the burning synagogue, drowning out the agonized screams of Jewish martyrs by chanting the *a cappella* Christian anthem, "Christ, We Adore Thee."[21] No wonder the nineteenth-century Roman Catholic historian Lord Acton described the extreme irony of the horrific actions of the Crusaders in this manner: "The men who took the cross, after receiving communion, heartily devoted the day to the extermination of the Jews."[22] Sadly, the same mixing of religious "piety" with godless murder would be repeated nearly five centuries later by German Christians. As Richard Cohen observes, "The multitudes of Nazis and their collaborators who carried out the Holocaust . . . to a person (excepting only a limited number of Muslim collaborators) had been a baptized Christian."[23]

After it was determined that over 5,000 Jews had been slaughtered in Europe during the First Crusade and after the news of Crusader atrocities

[19] Frank N. Magill, *The Middle Ages: Dictionary of World Biography* (New York: Routledge, 1998), vol. 2, p. 899.

[20] David Rausch, *Legacy of Hatred: Why Christians Must Not Forget the Holocaust* (Grand Rapids, MI: Baker Publishing Group, 1990), p. 27.

[21] Dagobert D. Runes, *The War against the Jew* (New York: Philosophical Library, 1968), p. 37. Also, Arthur Blech, *The Causes of Anti-Semitism: A Critique of the Bible* (Amherst, NY: Prometheus Books, 2006), p. 360; Hillel Halkin, *Yehuda Halevi* (New York: Random House, 2010), p. 111; and Michael Brown, *What Do Jewish People Think about Jesus? And Other Questions Christians Ask about Jewish Beliefs, Practices, and History*. Grand Rapids, MI: Baker Publishing Group, 2007, p. 126.

[22] Lord Acton, quoted in Bettina Liebowitz Knapp, *Céline, Man of Hate* (Tuscaloosa, AL: The University of Alabama Press, 1974), p. 94.

[23] Richard A. Cohen, "The Holocaust Is a Christian Issue: Christology Revisited," in *The Philosopher as Witness: Fackenheim and Responses to the Holocaust*, Michael L. Morgan, and Benjamin Pollock, eds. (Albany, NY: State University of New York Press, 2008), p. 119. Harry J. Cargas even more graphically observed that "every Jew killed in the Holocaust was murdered by a baptized Christian." Henry R. Huttenbach, "In Memoriam: Harry James Cargas," *Journal of Genocide Research*, 1 (3), p. 311. Cargas also posed this rhetorical question: "Can one be a Christian today, given the death camps that, in major part, were conceived, built, and operated by a people who called themselves Christians?" Harry James Cargas, *Shadows of Auschwitz: A Christian Response to the Holocaust* (New York: Crossroad Press, 1990), p. 1.

against the Jews in Israel had reached Europe, Pope Calixtus II was so moved by the perversity of the Christian atrocities against the Jews that he issued a bull entitled *Sicut Judaeis* (the "Constitution for the Jews"). The pope's official proclamation was designed to protect the Jewish people by restricting Christians—on pain of excommunication—from coercing Jews to convert to Christianity, from taking their property, from interfering in their festivals, and from harming them in any way.[24] The pope's injunction, however,—as well as similar declarations by later popes and bishops—went largely unheeded, for the seeds of antisemitism had already become deeply rooted in the Christian heart. The antipathy and utter contempt for Jews that had been reinforced in Christianity by charges of Jewish complicity in the death of Jesus inflamed the passions of these Christians against the Jews of their time and prompted them to continue their vengeful violence against them.

The Second Crusade (1146–1149) was a miserable failure that resulted in the defeat of the armies of both Louis VII of France and Conrad III of Germany by the Seljuq Turks. It also led to the fall of Jerusalem to the Muslims and set the stage for the Third Crusade (1188–1192), the King's Crusade, that featured the European rulers' attempt to reconquer the Holy Land from the powerful Turkish Muslim Sultan Saladin. Though the kings' combined forces conquered most of Palestine, their efforts to retake Jerusalem were thwarted by Saladin's armies. Ultimately, King Richard the Lionheart negotiated a treaty with Saladin that left Jerusalem in Muslim control but allowed Christian pilgrims and merchants to visit the city. The second and third crusades produced enormous suffering and death, including that of countless Jews.

A decade later, in 1202, a fourth Crusade was then launched, again with the goal of retaking Jerusalem; however, the focus of this quest was quickly diverted to Constantinople, the center of Orthodox Christianity. There, after Christian soldiers of the West had breached the walls of the city, they were given three days in which to rage through the streets, raping, killing, and pillaging the Eastern Orthodox Christians and other inhabitants of the city.[25] This preoccupation with Constantinople was prompted by the rising conflict over theology and polity between Eastern Orthodoxy and Roman Catholicism. Dean Eyerly notes that when this crusade reached its climax in the destruction of Constantinople,

[24] Herbert Thurston, "History of Toleration," in *The Catholic Encyclopedia* (New York: Robert Appleton Company, 1913), vol. 14, p. 761.

[25] Rex Lentz, *An Abridged History of World Religions* (Lincoln, NE: iUniverse, Inc., 2002), p. 71.

the Roman Catholic Pope Innocent III "could not conceal his satisfaction when he contemplated this victory over the Eastern Orthodox Church, which had refused to submit to the Western Pope."[26] In fact, the destruction of Constantinople was one of the final acts of the Great Schism that divided Eastern Orthodoxy from Roman Catholicism and so severely weakened the Christian presence the East that once-dominant Christianity became a virtual footnote in the history of the Middle East.

Finally, the Shepherds' Crusade, launched in 1320, was led by a teenage shepherd who, with his brigands, marched through southern France, attacking everything in sight but focusing on Jews, including the 300 who were killed at Montclus. Hundreds of other Jews suffered violence or perished in the utter madness that was masked as righteous indignation of Christians against the Jewish people for their perceived impiety, opposition to the cross of Christ, and deicide.

Sadly, although the Crusades have long been glamorized in Western Christian lore, they were examples of some of the most vile and contemptible unchristian conduct in all of ecclesiastical history. With the complicity and downright encouragement of popes, bishops, and priests, "Christian soldiers" launched unbridled campaigns of violence and mayhem, torturing and murdering countless Muslims, Jews, and other Christians. The violence that was so specifically targeted against the Jews was a prime example of antisemitism at its worst. In a detailed—but chilling—account, Rodney Stark presents a documentation of the acts of Crusader violence against the Jewish people from the eleventh through the fourteenth centuries that every Christian should read.[27] Karen Armstrong is right when she says that "crusading made anti-Semitism an incurable disease in Europe"; however, her contention that the Crusades "would indelibly scar relations between Islam and the West"[28] fails to take into account the fact that the Crusades, though vicious and heartless in the extreme, were largely retributive for the Muslim violence against Christians that had preceded and prompted the Christian action and perhaps were also even self-defensive and preemptive efforts to prevent future Muslim aggression against Christians.

The real scar that was indelibly placed upon the face of Western Christianity was the utterly gratuitous violence that European Christians exacted against fellow Christians in the East and even more so the

[26] Dean R. Eyerly, *Between Heaven and Hell: The Historical Jesus* (Mustang, OK, Tate Publishing, 2009), p. 312.

[27] Stark, pp. 129–133.

[28] Karen Armstrong, *The Case for God* (New York: Alfred A. Knopf Publishing, 2009), p. 140.

despicable mayhem and murder that they inflicted on totally defenseless and utterly undeserving Jews—from the neighbors in their own cities, to Jews along the path, to the Holy Land, and ultimately to the rightful inhabitants of the only Holy City that God recognizes.[29] Post-Crusade Christianity has been indelibly disfigured, and no amount of plastic surgery can remove or hide this hideous scar. This record of history is ineradicable. The decidedly unchristian actions of the Crusaders have left Christianity forever marred. Consequently, the cry, "Never again!" must forever echo through the ivy-covered halls of Christian academic institutions and through the hallowed basilicas and cathedrals of the Christian ecclesiastical community. Christians must ever be vigilant against the rise of ever more subtle forms of antisemitism that could easily arouse deep-seated human prejudices and anger and produce similar acts of violence and mayhem—all in the name of Jesus!

## Black Death for Europe; Even More Suffering for Jews

No sooner had the Crusades and their dreadful toll on Jewish life ended than another specter arose and swept across the face of Europe, again bringing death and destruction to the Jews. The cause of this outbreak of a new form of antisemitism was the Black Death, one of the most devastating pandemics in human history. In the seven years from 1346–1353 AD, 60% of the entire population of Europe—as many as 50 million people[30]—perished from bubonic plague.[31] The proper name of this plague is derived the Greek word *boubon*, which means "groin," the principal physical part of the human body where the bacterial infection from the *Yersinia pestis* enterobacteriaceae attacks the lymph nodes.[32] The bubonic plague is highly aggressive and extremely painful, for the lymph nodes rapidly become necrotic, leading to the decomposition of the human body, particularly the skin, while the victim is still alive. Death is almost inevitable, and it follows in very short order after a person has been infected with the bacteria.

In 1347, the disease, which had originated in Mongolia, made its way

[29] Psalm 2:6: "Yet have I set my king on my holy hill of Zion, my holy mountain." Joel 3:17: "Then you will know that I, the LORD your God, dwell in Zion, my holy hill . . . and Jerusalem shall be holy."

[30] Ole J. Benedictow, "The Black Death: The Greatest Catastrophe Ever," *History Today*, Vol. 55, Issue 3, March 2005. In this article, Benedictow explains how he calculated the death toll from Black Death at 50 million people.

[31] William Duiker and Jackson J. Spielvogel, *The Essential World History, Seventh Edition* (Wadsworth Cengage Learning, 2012), p. 341.

[32] *Yersinia pestis* also attacks the lymph nodes in the armpits; however, the major concentration of the disease is in the groin.

to Europe, carried there by fleas that infested rats which were ubiquitous on merchant ships in that day.[33] Because sanitation was not a particularly important issue at that time, people were easily infected by bites from plague-carrying fleas. With healthy people contracting the plague and dying in agony within days, terror and confusion swept across Europe, and people began to look everywhere for someone or something to blame. "The horrors of the pestilence . . . unleashed humanity's darkest impulses."[34] And it was not long before the long, dark finger of death pointed directly at the greatest scapegoat in human history, the Jewish people, marking them for violence and murder. Antisemitism began to reveal itself in a new form yet with the same old results that had brought suffering to the Jews for centuries.

Almost immediately after the plague arrived in European cities, many civil and religious leaders declared that it was not the product of natural causes but was of "human artifice," and they quickly affixed the blame for the malady on those "evil men, sons of the Devil," a popular Christian designation for the Jews at that time.[35] One German Franciscan monk, Hermann Gigas, reported in 1349: "Some say . . . the Jews planned to wipe out all the Christians with poison and had poisoned wells and springs everywhere."[36] Christian political and religious leaders also alleged that in order for the Jews to complete their conspiracy against Christians to destroy all the Christians of Europe, they had also "used black magic to concoct the plague-causing poison from such ingredients as frogs, lizards, spiders, the hearts of murdered Christians, and the skin of a basilisk, a mythical and highly deadly snake."[37]

Another factor that contributed to the Christian leaders' conclusion that Jews were the agents of the Black Death was the fact that because the Jewish people generally "did not use water from the common wells of towns and villages,"[38] they must have been poisoning those wells. Additionally, the fact that most, if not all, medieval cities were

[33] The Black Death did not represent the appearance of a new disease. Bubonic plague is also estimated to have killed another 50 million people in the Roman Empire during the sixth century AD. Lester K. Little, "Life and Afterlife of the First Plague Pandemic," in *Plague and the End of Antiquity: The Pandemic of 541–750*, Lester K. Little, ed. (Cambridge, UK: Cambridge University Press, 2007), pp. 8–15. It also caused the deaths of millions of other people in various locations around the world at various times in history.

[34] Joseph P. Byrne, *The Black Death* (Westport, CT: Greenwood Publishing, 2004), pp. 83–84.

[35] Byrne, p. 82.

[36] J. G. Meuschen, ed., *Hermanni Gygantis, ordinis fratrum minorum, Flores Temporum seu Chronicon Universale ab Orbe condito ad annum Christi MCCCXLIX* (Leiden, The Netherlands, 1750), pp. 138–139. See Rosemary Horrox, *The Black Death* (Manchester, UK: Manchester University Press, 1994), p. 207.

[37] Louise Chipley Slavicek, *The Black Death* (New York: Infobase Publishing, 2008), p. 60.

[38] Diane Zahler, *The Black Death* (Minneapolis, MN: Lerner Publishing Group, 2009), p. 55.

filthy places without sewers or garbage collection made them perfect environments for rats and other vermin that were allowed to live in close proximity to and contact with humans.[39] Louise Slavicek points out that this was also a time when most of the population of Europe, including the wealthy and powerful, "viewed bathing as unnecessary and even unhealthy" so that they "rarely washed their bodies, clothes, or bedding."[40] This general absence of concern with matters of cleanliness and personal hygiene[41] also made the general populace ready hosts for the fleas that carried the bubonic plague.

While the general citizenry of Europe lived in squalor, the Jewish people followed the commandment that Jacob had given to his household, "Be clean, and change your garments,"[42] and they knew that rats were "unclean" animals with which they were not to have contact according to the laws of the Torah. Jews, therefore, were able to limit their exposure to the plague. The fact that a smaller percentage of the Jewish population contracted the Black Death came to be seen, therefore, as incontrovertible evidence that the Jews were poisoning public and Christian wells or that it was their working of black magic that was causing Christian suffering and death. The contempt that medieval Christians had long had for the Jews and the separation that their piety and obedience to the Torah demanded of them became an excuse for their persecution and murder by the non-Jewish population of Europe.

For the next three years, as the Black Death swept across the land, Jews were targeted for violence and death. In southern France, they were dragged from their homes by angry mobs and burned alive. In Basel, Switzerland, "the city's entire Jewish population were taken to a nearby island, locked in a specially constructed wooden building, and incinerated."[43] In Mainz, 6,000 Jews were murdered in a single day in 1349. In Strasbourg, 2,000 Jews were publicly immolated on a wooden platform.[44] By 1351, "more than sixty major Jewish communities in Germany had been completely exterminated."[45] The violence and death that were directed against Jews was systematically orchestrated by civil authorities and was supported

[39] Jordan Rubin, *The Great Physician's Rx for Health and Wellness* (Nashville, TN: Thomas Nelson, Inc., 2005), p. xxvii.

[40] Slavicek, p. 33.

[41] John Haywood, *Medieval Europe* (Chicago, IL: Reed Elsevier, Inc., 2008), p. 45.

[42] Genesis 35:2, KJV.

[43] Slavicek, pp. 61–62.

[44] Jackson J. Spielvogel, *Western Civilization: Alternate Volume: Since 1300* (Boston, MA: Wadsworth, Cengage Learning, 2006), p. 312.

[45] Spielvogel, p. 311.

by ecclesiastical leaders and was but a new manifestation of the same antisemitism that had brought untold suffering to their ancestors in other ages.[46] At the same time, however, yet another "new, improved," and different manifestation of antisemitism was being developed that would result in more torture and death for even more Jews.

## Inquisitions

Beginning in twelfth-century France, institutions were initiated within the judicial system of the Roman Catholic Church that were designed to combat heresies by suppressing Christian groups that dared to challenge canon law and official church doctrine. This was the Inquisition, a program led primarily by the Dominican *Ordo Praedicatorum* (Order of Preachers) to bring officially church-sponsored violence first to Christians and then to Jews. The Inquisition was greatly expanded in reaction to the Protestant Reformation of the sixteenth century. Its purpose was explained in a 1578 handbook for inquisitors: "Punishment does not take place primarily and *per se* for the correction and good of the person punished, but for the public good in order that others may become terrified and weaned away from the evils they would commit."[47]

The Inquisition followed the principles laid down in 1252 by Pope Innocent IV in his papal bull *Ad extirpanda,* which authorized agents of the Roman Catholic Church to employ torture as a means of extracting confessions from heretics.[48] Thinking to absolve the church of responsibility for these acts of violence that were perpetrated upon such heretics, the church decided that those who were convicted of heresy by the Dominican Inquisition tribunals should be remanded to custody of civil authorities for the imposition of penalties for their religious crimes upon the miscreants.[49] These verdicts could include life imprisonment, banishment, and death by burning.

Superstition ruled the day in medieval Europe. When what came to be

[46] Marshall D. Isaacson, *Children of the Covenant: What Christians Should Know about Jews* (Bountiful, UT: Horizon Publishers, 1998), p. 48.

[47] *Directorium Inquisitorum*, Book 3, p. 137, edition of 1578 (Cornell University Collection), quoted in Janis Lander, *Spiritual Art and Art Education* (Abingdon, UK: Routledge, 2014), p. 178.

[48] Jordan Bishop, "Aquinas on Torture," in *New Blackfriars*, Vol. 87, Issue 1009, May 2006, p. 229.

[49] This action was taken on the basis of a misinterpretation of 1 Corinthians 5:4–5 where Paul gave instructions for judgment within the context of the Christian assembly: "So . . . hand this man over to Satan for the destruction of the flesh, so that his spirit may be saved on the day of the Lord." The church remanded miscreants to the state (rather than to Satan as Paul instructed). The state then supervised the "destruction of their flesh" with the "hope" that their immortal soul could be saved in the day of final judgment.

called the Little Ice Age[50] began to affect Europe in 1350, ecclesiastical and civil leaders became convinced that the freezing weather and the mass starvation it prompted had been produced by magicians and witches in Germany.[51] Pope Innocent VIII, therefore, issued a papal bull, *Summis Desiderantes*, in which he authorized inquisitors Heinrich Kramer and Jacobus Sprenger to engage in a campaign for eradicating witches from the German populace.[52] As evidenced by their 1486 manual for witch hunts, *Malleus Maleficarum* ("Hammer of Witches"), these Dominican friars were inveterate misogynists—and doubtless gynophobic, as well. It has been estimated that in this part of the Inquisition, as many as 100,000 people, most of them women, were systematically tortured in order to extract "confessions" from their own lips. Then, they were convicted of being witches and were summarily burned at the stake.[53] Some of the implements of torture that the inquisitors used to inflict pain on women—along with the descriptions of how they were employed—are hideous beyond the imagination of sane and civilized people.

In 1478, the Roman Catholic monarchs Ferdinand II and Isabella I replaced the medieval Inquisition in Spain with the Tribunal of the Holy Office of the Inquisition. This Inquisition was intended largely to ensure that those who had converted to Christianity from Judaism and Islam were adhering to official Catholic Christian belief and practice. This was especially true after 1492 when the royal Spanish edict of expulsion had ordered Jews and Muslims to convert to Christianity or be expelled from Spain. The major purpose of this Inquisition was to discover and punish crypto-Jews, the so-called *Conversos*, *Anusim*,[54] or, more pejoratively, *Marranos*[55] who had officially con-

[50] The term *Little Ice Age* was first used in 1939 in scientific literature by François E. Matthes to describe what occurred in Europe in 1350 when an entire summer was lost as temperatures plummeted precipitously, causing widespread crop failures and consequent famine. See Bryan Fagan, *The Little Ice Age: How Climate Made History* (New York: Basic Books, 2000), pp. 47–48. Some scientists have suggested that the Little Ice Age resulted from a volcanic explosion on the Indonesian Lombok Island. "Scientists pinpoint a 13th Century volcanic explosion [that was] eight times bigger than Krakatoa that devastated globe" in 1883. Ellie Zolfagharifard, *The Daily Mail*, 1 October 2013, posted at http://www.dailymail.co.uk/sciencetech/article-2440039/The-13th-Century-volcanic-explosion-triggered-Little-Ice-Age-created-Far-Eastern-Pompeii-just-waiting-discovered.html.

[51] The ever-superstitious populace of Europe was totally convinced that these conditions could not be natural; therefore, they looked everywhere for someone to blame. And, of course, the Jews were always the default scapegoats of choice.

[52] Brian P. Levack, *The Witch-Hunt in Early Modern Europe* (Abingdon, UK: Routledge, 2006), p. 5.

[53] Sandra Sider, *Handbook to Life in Renaissance Europe* (Oxford, UK: Oxford University Press, 2005), p. 40.

[54] *Anusim* is the Hebrew word for "forced," indicating that the Jews were "converted" in "forced" baptisms.

[55] The term *marrano* is derived from the Arabic word *muharram*, which means "forbidden." In Spanish the word came to mean "pig," originally because of Jewish and Muslim abstinence from eating pork. The word *marrano* still means "pig" or "dirty" in Spanish.

verted to Christianity but continued to practice Judaism in secret. Of the 80,000 Jews in Spain at the time, half had chosen emigration over conversion. Those who did choose conversion were to be hounded, examined, and tortured by the worst of all the inquisitors, the Segovian Dominican friar Tomás de Torquemada. From 1480 until 1530, over 2,000 Jews were convicted of being crypto-Jews and were executed in what had come to be called "*autos-da-fé*"[56] wherein the condemned were burned at the stake.[57] That the Spanish Inquisition specifically targeted Jews is confirmed by the fact that 90% of all those who were executed in that inquisition were Jewish.[58] The monarchs and church leaders of Spain, therefore, wreaked havoc on countless Jewish communities all across the land, torturing and killing Jews at will.

Parallel and contemporaneous with the Spanish Inquisition was the Portuguese Inquisition. The motive for both was the same: rooting out those who had converted to Christianity from other faiths who did not abide by Catholic orthodoxy or who secretly engaged in practices of their pre-conversion religions. The 40,000 Jews who had emigrated to Portugal after they had been expelled from Spain were immediately suspect and were pursued vigorously. In the end, over 31,000 people, most of them Jews, were subjected to the punishments of the Portuguese Inquisition. This number included the more than the 2,000 Jews who were publicly executed. Almost half of these Jews suffered death in the agonizing flames of *autos da fé* while the Christian citizens of the executing Portuguese cities viewed the haunting scenes of human suffering and jeered at the tormented, taunting the hapless victims of the violence heaped upon them by their church and state.

## Confiscations and Expulsions

Jewish wealth and property were constant targets for confiscation in medieval Europe. Often, expulsions from nations were used as a means of seizing Jewish assets. "In addition to confiscatory taxes on Jews during the Middle Ages by kings and princes, there were attacks on, and

[56] The term *auto-da-fé* means "act of faith," which refers to the repentance (penance) that was exacted upon the miscreant before the punishment of death by immolation was inflicted.

[57] António José Saraiva, Herman P. Salomon, and Isaac S. D. Sasson, trs. and eds., *The Marrano Factory: The Portuguese Inquisition and Its New Christians, 1536–1765* (Leiden, The Netherlands: Koninklijke Brill NV, 2001), p. 20.

[58] Henry Kamen, *The Spanish Inquisition: A Historical Revision* (New Haven, CT: Yale University Press, 1998), p. 20.

confiscations of, synagogues" which were, in fact, "often instigated by the local bishop" to benefit the church.[59] To aid confiscations, monarchs frequently issued edicts of expulsion, ordering all the Jews to leave their nation. Such was the case in 1290 when King Edward I expelled all Jews from England. After being the first among the European nations to require Jews to wear an identifying badge,[60] this English monarch proceeded to seize all Jewish property and then decreed that all outstanding debts that were owed to Jews were from that time on payable to the king's treasury instead of to the Jews. In this case, Jews and their assets were easy targets for the absolute and avaricious English monarchs who obviously lacked any sense of true Christian conscience.

The rulers of Spain and Portugal also issued edicts of expulsion; however, their orders were based on demands for Jews either to convert to Christianity or to leave those nations. While the primary motive was religious, a secondary—and pecuniary—motive was not lost on the monarchs. Both Spain and Portugal profited greatly from the seizure of Jewish assets. As a matter of fact, the Spanish Queen Isabella is said to have used a large part of assets confiscated from Jews to finance the voyages of Columbus.[61] Such confiscations were nothing new, however, for across Europe for centuries before and after,[62] it was common for rulers to seize Jewish property and other assets to enrich the royal treasuries and to support their own ambitions while reducing the Jews to poverty and deprivation.

As history stretched into the sixteenth century, matters only became worse for the Jewish people. "Jews were depicted as avaricious, cheating, treacherous, and sadistic; they were impure and displayed repulsive physical abnormalities; they were heretical and sacrilegious, and they conspired against Christians and Christianity."[63]

---

[59] Robert Michael and Philip Rose, *Dictionary of Antisemitism from the Earliest Times to the Present* (Lanham, MD: Roman & Littlefield Publishing, 2007), p. 104.

[60] Peter Brown, *A Companion to Medieval English Literature and Culture* (Chichester, UK: Wiley Blackwell Publishing, 2009), p. 251.

[61] Seymour Fiedler, *The Orphans Among God's Children: The History of Anti-Semitism* (Bloomington, IN: AuthorHouse, 2003), p. 57. Also, Simon Wiesenthal, *Sails of Hope: The Secret Mission of Christopher Columbus*, Richard Winston and Clara Winston, trs. (New York: MacMillan Publishing Co, 1979).

[62] The first known confiscation of Jewish assets by a Christian monarch occurred in Spain in 586. Jacob Marcus notes that Reccared, "the first Visigothic king to become a Catholic, was the first to pursue an active anti-Jewish policy." He and his successors established the Visigothic Code, under which Jews were given the alternative of baptism or exile. Many Jews "became unwilling converts and secretly practiced Judaism" in order to survive these ordeals. Jacob Rader Marcus, *The Jew in the Medieval World: A Source Book*, 315–1791 (Cincinnati, OH: Hebrew Union College Press, 1938), p. 22.

[63] Susan Sarah Cohen, *Antisemitism: An Annotated Bibliography* (Munich, Germany: Walter de Gruyter, 2007), vol. 19, p. 366.

With such evil caricatures ingrained in the very corporate psyche of Western society, the Jewish people continued to be easy targets for persecution, violence, theft, and murder by Christians of virtually every sort. The Christian reign of terror on the Jews was systematic and unrelenting because contempt for the Jews had become enshrined in both secular society and in the Christian church at large.

## Pogroms

By the time of the Middle Ages, Eastern Christianity had long since engaged in antisemitism that was focused in anti-Judaism and supersessionism. This was particularly true in the Russian Orthodox Church, where antisemitism was more virulent than in most other Orthodox traditions.[64] In the eleventh century AD, an anti-Judaic treatise by Metropolitan Hillarion of Kiev entitled, "Sermon on Law and Grace," became a classic example of antisemitism in Russian literature.[65] The Russian Orthodox Church also focused on apocalyptic works in which its particular Christian denomination was designated as the "New Israel," with Moscow as the "Third Rome" and the ancient capital of Kiev as the "Second Jerusalem."[66] In post-Communist Russia, Metropolitan Ioann still maintained this supersessionist antisemitism, claiming that the "Jewish" God is actually a demon, the Jews are "God-killer people," and Judaism is the "religion of hate."[67] In this context, he also propounded Russian history as a "two-thousand-year war" between Christianity and Judaism.[68]

Concurrent with the persecutions of the Jews in Western Europe, waves of anti-Jewish violence swept across Eastern Europe in the form of pogroms. A pogrom is a violent riot focused on the persecution and massacre of an ethnic or religious group. The English term *pogrom* is taken directly from the Russian word *pogróm*, which is derived from *pogromít*, which literally means "destruction." For centuries, pogroms have been the Russian and Eastern European version of organized massacres of the

[64] Sherwin T. Wine, *A Provocative People: A Secular History of the Jews* (Farmington Hills, MI: International Institute for Secular Humanistic Judaism, 2012), p. 314. Also, Alan L. Berger and David Patterson, *Jewish-Christian Dialogue: Drawing Honey from the Rock* (St. Paul, MN: Paragon House, 2008), p. 99. Berger and Patterson note that the form of antisemitism found in Russian orthodoxy has been "even more insidious than the traditional, frank, and open Jew hatred of the Roman Catholic [Church]."

[65] Richard S. Levy, *Antisemitism: A Historical Encyclopedia of Prejudice and Persecution, Volume 1* (Santa Barbara, CA: ABC-CLIO, Inc., 2005), p. 637.

[66] H. Leeming and K. Leeming, eds., *Josephus' Jewish War and Its Slavonic Version: A Synoptic Comparison* (Leiden, The Netherlands: Koninklijke Brill NV, 2003), p. 101. Also Vadim Joseph Rossman, *Russian Intellectual Antisemitism in the Post-Communist Era* (Lincoln, NE: The University of Nebraska Press, 2002), p. 199.

[67] Levy, p. 637.

[68] Levy, p. 637.

Jews, particularly during the nineteenth- and twentieth-century Russian Empire. A large portion of the pogroms took place within the Pale of Settlement, the area staked out[69] in 1791 by Empress Catherine the Great as a space for confining Jews in order to keep them out of Russia.[70] The land mass for the Pale included what is now Ukraine, Moldova, Lithuania, Poland, and Belarus. Catherine's predecessor Elizabeth had tried to expel all the Jews from Russia who would not convert to Russian Orthodox Christianity, so Catherine merely undertook the task of completing what Elizabeth had begun. When all the Jews in Russia had been summarily forced to relocate within the Pale, this region's Jewish population reached a height of five million, which at that time represented 40% of the worldwide Jewish population.

The geographical, political, and economic restrictions of the Pale were onerous for the Jewish people. Living in *shtetls* ("small towns"), they experienced extreme poverty and isolation. Additionally, they were easy targets for the irrational religious fervor and hatred of the non-Jews around them. With the support of the Russian Orthodox Church and the Russian government, the organized mob violence of pogroms was continually staged against the Jews for as long as the Pale existed. As it was throughout Europe, the days on the Jewish calendar that were most dreaded in the Pale were the Christian holy days, especially Good Friday and Easter when "Christians" regularly vented their anger against the Jewish people for being "Christ-killers." In this situation, Christian "Holy Days" became literal hell days for the Jewish people.

The most devastating of all the pogroms took place between 1881 and 1883 and then later between 1903 and 1906. During these vicious attacks, hundreds of Jewish communities were utterly overrun by antisemites in violence that produced extensive property damage and the murder of thousands of Jews. These included the particularly devastating pogroms of Warsaw in 1881; Kishinev in 1903 when 2,000 Jews were killed on Easter Sunday with Orthodox priests leading crowds that chanted, "Kill the Jews"; Kiev and 660 other towns in 1905; and Białystok in 1906.[71] Even beyond that time, pogroms in Lwów in 1918 and Kiev in 1919 resulted in great loss of Jewish life. Violent mob actions against the Jews like these continued well into the twentieth century, as evidenced in the 1941 pogrom in the

[69] The word *pale* literally means "stake."

[70] The Pale of Settlement encompassed roughly 20% of European Russia.

[71] Sara Bender, *The Jews of Białystok during World War II and the Holocaust*, Yaffa Murciano, tr. (Boston, MA: Brandeis University Press, 2008), pp. 91–92.

Romanian city of Iasi, where over 13,000 Jews were murdered.

The pogroms in Russia and other Eastern European nations were organized by governmental authorities and were often encouraged by leaders and priests of the Russian Orthodox Church, which for centuries has continued to be a major hotbed and bastion for antisemitism. Jews who were regularly targeted by such mob violence continually faced the threat of bodily harm and even death on a regular basis. Such action was yet another example of the way in which the cross became a sword in the hands of utterly intolerant, hate-filled "Christians" who were determined to exterminate the "Christ-killing" Jews whom for centuries they had blamed for all the ills and maladies of societies throughout the entire continent of Europe.

## The Age of Reason's Irrationality; The Enlightenment's Darkness

The Renaissance that had begun to make great strides in moving Europe out of the Dark Ages by restoring elements of classical culture did virtually nothing to diminish the vile hatred that European Christians had for the Jews. The focus on reviving Greek and Latin literature and philosophy was not extended to the even more ancient Hebrew culture and literature. The Renaissance, therefore, did not represent a "rebirth"[72] of civil attitudes and relationships toward the Jews. Indeed, one of the greatest scholars of the Renaissance, sixteenth-century Dutch theologian Desiderius Erasmus, had utter contempt for the Jewish people and their literature. Though subsequent scholarship described Erasmus as the "Prince of Humanists" and "the crowning glory of Christian humanism,"[73] he did not extend his "humanism" to the Jews by arguing for even their basic human rights. Instead, he summed up the prevailing attitude of virtually all Renaissance scholarship toward the Jews when he said, "Is there any one among us who can be accused of lukewarmness in cursing that unhappy race [the Jews]? If it is the mark of a Christian to hate the Jews, we are all of us the very best of Christians in this quarter."[74]

Ironically, in the seventeenth century, it was a Jew, Baruch Spinoza,

---

[72] The word *renaissance* is translated from French into English as "rebirth."

[73] Kenneth Scott Latourette, *A History of Christianity* (New York: Harper & Brothers, 1953), p. 661.

[74] Desidereus Erasmus, quoted in Robert B. Drummond, *Erasmus, His Life and Character* (London, England: Smith, Elder & Co., 1873), p. 30. Erasmus was particularly exercised against the legal defense that Christian Hebraist Johannes Reuchlin had mounted before Maximilian, emperor of the Holy Roman Empire, against efforts to destroy all Jewish books, including the Talmud, *Kabbalah*, *Midrash*, and *Sefarim*. It seems that Erasmus despised the literature of the Jews more than he detested the Jews themselves. Johannes Reuchlin, *Recommendation Whether to Confiscate, Destroy, and Burn All Jewish Books*, Peter Wortsman, tr. and ed. (Mahwah, NJ: Paulist Press, 2000), pp. 31–51.

one of the greatest of the scholars of the Age of Reason and the builder of the foundation for the later Enlightenment, who did much damage to the Jewish people in what was to become an increasingly secularized society. Spinoza was the first scholar to analyze the Hebrew Scriptures from a purely secular perspective when he began the work of demythologizing the Scriptures that reached fruition in the works of nineteenth- and twentieth-century German theologians. Spinoza's writings provided a foundation of contempt for the Jews of Scripture, one which would serve later Enlightenment scholars with ammunition to fight against the movement to restore the Jewish roots of the Christian faith. Frederic Raphael observes that "Spinoza's break with Judaism has been taken to be an emancipatory element" in "the radical Enlightenment."[75]

The nineteenth-century Enlightenment, with its emphasis on the scientific method, secularization of learning, reason, and religious tolerance, did very little to improve either religious or secular perspectives on Jews and Judaism, nor did it diminish the endemic antisemitism that had pervaded European society for more than a millennium.[76] In fact, during this time, "religious antisemitism took on a new leitmotif, emanating from the attacks leveled on the Jewish religion by such eminent secularists as Voltaire, Diderot, Montesquieu, von Dohm, and d'Holbach," who "condemned Judaism for remaining a fossilized religion, persisting in a self-image of its special 'election,' and upholding anti-progressive beliefs."[77] In this way, the Enlightenment probably contributed to the "modernizing and secularizing [of] antisemitism."[78]

The French philosopher François-Marie Arouet who wrote under the nom-de-plume of Voltaire was profoundly antisemitic. Though he was an advocate for freedom of speech and religion and for separation of church and state, he was "notoriously hostile [in his] pronouncements on Jews,"[79] calling them in his *Treatise on Toleration* "the most detestable [nation] ever to have sullied the earth,"[80] and in his *Dictionary*,

[75] Frederic Raphael, *Anti-Semitism* (London, UK: Biteback Publishing, Ltd., 2015), p. 212.

[76] Adam Sutcliffe, *Judaism and Enlightenment* (Cambridge, UK: Cambridge University Press, 2003); Léon Poliakov, *The History of Anti-Semitism, Volume 3: From Voltaire to Wagner* (Philadelphia, PA: The University of Pennsylvania Press, 2003); and Walter Laqueur, *The Changing Face of Anti-Semitism: From Ancient Times to the Present Day* (Oxford, UK: Oxford University Press, 2006).

[77] William Brustein, "European Antisemitism before the Holocaust and the Roots of Nazism," in *The Routledge History of the Holocaust*, Jonathan C. Friedman, ed. (Abingdon, UK: Routledge, 2011), p. 19.

[78] Brustein, p. 19.

[79] Sutcliffe, p. 7.

[80] Voltaire, *Treatise on Toleration*, 1763, quoted in David Turner, "From anti-Judaism to antisemitism: The Enlightement," *The Jerusalem Post*, 11/08/2012, posted at http://www.jpost.com/Blogs/The-Jewish-Problem---From-anti-Judaism-to-anti-Semitism/From-anti-Judaism-to-antisemitism-The-Enlightenment-365181.

"the most imbecile people on the face of the earth . . . ignorant and barbarous,"[81] and elsewhere as "enemies of mankind," and "obtuse, cruel, and absurd."[82] Arthur Hertzberg observes that Voltaire was "the 'vital link' between medieval and modern antisemitism."[83] In fact, Voltaire even "blamed the Jews for inventing Christianity."[84] Ironically, Voltaire and other French Enlightenment philosophers can be credited with helping to transform antisemitism from being largely an exercise in anti-Judaism into a secular, social, and racial practice. Voltaire stood between Montesquieu[85] who, though largely antisemitic, did argue for full Jewish emancipation and Denis Diderot who was strongly antisemitic, arguing that Jews possessed "all the defects indicative of an ignorant and superstitious nation."[86] Adam Sutcliffe echoes Herzberg's argument that "Jew-hatred . . . was not a deformation of Enlightenment reason, but was deeply ingrained within its spirit, which, in this respect at least, merely coated ancient prejudices with a fresh veneer of secularism."[87] Voltaire and his contemporary secularists, therefore, merely painted a new face on ancient and medieval antisemitism to make it socially acceptable, which is not unlike what has been accomplished by radical secularists in the twentieth and twenty-first centuries when they have made anti-Israelism the "new, improved" and politically correct antisemitism. Most of the Enlightenment scholars would have agreed with Voltaire when he said, "I would not be in the least surprised if these people would not some day become deadly to the human race."[88]

## The Unreformed in the Reformation

Even the Protestant Reformation did little to stem the tide of contempt for the Jews. This was ironic because the Reformation was actually birthed from the matrix of scholarship produced by self-styled Christian Hebraists,

[81] Voltaire, *Dictionary*, quoted in Turner, "From anti-Judaism."

[82] Voltaire, quoted in Edward H. Flannery, *The Anguish of the Jews: Twenty-three Centuries of Antisemitism* (Mahwah, NJ: Paulist Press, 1985), p. 176.

[83] Arthur Hertzberg, *The French Enlightenment and the Jews: The Origins of Modern Anti-Semitism* (New York: Columbia University Press, 1990), p. 313, noted in Sutcliffe, p. 7.

[84] Jeffrey Goldberg, "Is It Time for the Jews to Leave Europe?" *The Atlantic*, April 2015, posted at https://www.theatlantic.com/magazine/archive/2015/04/is-it-time-for-the-jews-to-leave-europe/386279/. This may have been one of the few times Voltaire was right, for if there had been no Jews, there would have been no Jesus and no Christianity, for "salvation is from the Jews" (John 4:22).

[85] Montesquieu was Charles-Louis de Secondat, Baron de La Brède et de Montesquieu.

[86] Diderot, quoted in Arthur Wilson, *Diderot* (Oxford, UK: Oxford University Press, 1972), p. 237.

[87] Sutcliffe, p. 7.

[88] Voltaire, quoted in Laqueur, p. 71.

who had insisted that no one could understand true Christian faith unless 1) he was immersed in the Hebrew text of what had come to be called almost pejoratively the "Old Testament" and in the Hebrew thought and Hebraisms that permeate the text of the Apostolic Scriptures (commonly called the "New Testament") and 2) he was familiar with the history and culture of the Jewish people, to whom, through whom, and for whom Holy Scripture had been given in the first place. Because the Christian Hebraists espoused *veritas Hebraica* (Hebraic truth), they knew that they had to establish interpersonal relationships with Jewish scholars and rabbis who understood the Hebrew language and could give them an accurate understanding of the biblical texts from the Jewish milieu from which those text emerged.

These Christian Hebraists laid the foundation for the Protestant Reformation and for the establishment of the grammatico-historical method of biblical interpretation that came to be known as the Reformation Hermeneutic. If the Reformation had pursued the Hebraic emphases that birthed it, the new movement could have changed the tide of history and saved millions of Jewish lives. Tragically, this was not to be the case, for the antisemitism that was embedded in the European psyche could not be eradicated by the logic and passion of the few radical Christian Hebraist scholars who were honest brokers of Hebrew truth of the prophets, sages, apostles, and, indeed, the Messiah of the Hebrew and Apostolic Scriptures.

Probably through the influence of Christian Hebraists, Martin Luther, the founder of the Reformation, was strongly philosemitic in the early years of his career as a reformer. During this time, he published a tract entitled, "That Jesus Christ was born a Jew," which he had written a year after he had translated the New Testament into German. In this document, Deanna Thompson reports that Luther "pointed to Jesus' scandalous particularity as a Jewish man, and he urged humility and Christian love when relating to the Jews, reminding Christians that Jews are blood relatives of Christ and that 'God committed Holy Scripture to no nation but the Jews.'"[89] Later in his life, however, Luther became virulently antisemitic[90] when it became clear to him that the "obdurate Jews" would never convert

[89] Deanna A. Thompson, *Crossing the Divide: Luther, Feminism, and the Cross* (Minneapolis, MN: Augsburg Fortress Press, 2004), p. 121.

[90] Mortimer Ostow, *Myth and Madness: The Psychodynamics of Antisemitism* (New Brunswick, NJ: Transaction Publishing, 1995), p. 14.

to Christianity as his eschatology required.[91] At that time, he wrote his treatise *On the Jews and Their Lies,* in which he advocated the burning of Jewish synagogues and schools, the razing of houses owned by Jews, the forcing of Jews to live in agricultural outbuildings, the execution of rabbis who refused to abide by an edict that forbade them to teach, the confinement of the Jewish population to the role of agricultural slave laborers, and not allowing them to live.[92]

## The Chosen People Designated as "No People"

It was during the second millennium of the Common Era that the Jews whom God had designated as *Ammi B'chiri* ("my People, my Chosen")[93] for all intents and purposes became "no people" to virtually all the inhabitants of the earth. Pope Alexander II wrote to the bishops of Spain around 1060 AD, "In the same manner Saint Gregory also admonished those [who] agitated for annihilating [the Jews], indicating that it is impious to wish to annihilate those who are protected by the mercy of God, so that, with homeland and liberty lost, in everlasting penitence, damned by the guilt of their ancestors for spilling the blood of the Savior, they live dispersed throughout the various areas of the world."[94] Later, during the Reformation, German Protestant scholars assigned the Jews to the *Unheilsgeschichte* (disaster or damnation history) that was contrasted with the *Heilsgeschichte* (salvation or redemption history) of God's acts in biblical history that continued in and through the church.[95] In fact, in order to personify the notion of the Jewish *Unheilsgeschichte*, one of Martin Luther's students, Paul von Eitzen, created the myth of Ahasverus,[96] the "eternal Jew" (or the "wandering Jew"), who had been condemned to wander the earth forever with no home and no opportunity to escape his suffering even through death because he had scoffed at Jesus as the Lord carried his cross to Golgotha.[97] This mythical

[91] Luther's "love" for the Jews was predicated on whether or not they would be willing to act out the role that he had devised for them in his eschatological scenario. Luther believed that Jesus would return in his day, and he was certain, therefore, that all the Jews would convert to Christianity—particularly to Protestant Christianity—as a precondition of the Messiah's return.

[92] Martin Luther, *On the Jews and Their Lies*, in *Luther's Works*, tr. Martin H. Bertram (Philadelphia: Fortress Press, 1971).

[93] Isaiah 43:20.

[94] Alexander II, quoted in Robert Chazan, ed., *Church, State, and Jew in the Middle Ages* (New York: Behrman House, 1980), pp. 99–100.

[95] The German term *Heilsgeschichte* was devised by German scholars to contrast with *Weltgeschichte* (world history) in order to point to "salvation history" as distinct from "universal history."

[96] Ahasverus is sometimes written as Ahasver or Ahasuerus.

[97] Richard Eldemann, "Ahasuerus, the Wandering Jew: Origin and Background," in *The Wandering Jew: Essays in the Interpretation of a Christian Legend*, G. Hasan-Roken and A. Dundes, eds., (Bloomington, IN: Indiana University Press, 1986), pp. 1–10.

character came to be identified with the entire Jewish population[98] which, even from Nicene Christianity, was thought to be doomed to wander forever with no homeland and to be afflicted with terrible poverty and deprivation as a living witness to the judgment that they believed God has pronounced upon anyone who rejects Jesus. The peoplehood of the Jews was reduced to a caricature of deprecation and denigration that made them easy prey for Judaeophobes and antisemites.

This concept had already gained solid credibility in the church in the fifth century AD when Augustine, in his "Reply to Faustus the Manichean," drew a shocking parallel between Cain, the murderer of Abel, and the Jews, the "murderers of Jesus."[99] Just as Cain was to be kept from being executed for his crime by bearing a mark that would distinguish him from the rest of humanity and wandering the earth thereafter,[100] so the Jews were not to be executed for their crime of killing Jesus but were to be marked and separated from others so that they would "wander the earth as vagabonds.[101] As Clark Williamson explains, Augustine believed that the Jews should "groan and tremble on the earth, witnessing to the fate of those who reject Christ." In so doing, he says, "the 'wandering Jew' makes the strange witness of unbelief in dispersion from the land of promise."[102] Later, at the Fourth Lateran Council in 1215 AD, the church drew from Augustine's spurious Cain analogy to require the Jews to wear a "mark of separation."[103] Even as late as the 1930s when the Nazi Party was ascending to power, German bishop Michael von Faulhaber was still making the same argument: "After the death of Christ, Israel was dismissed from the service of Revelation . . . and from that time forth Ahasuerus wanders, forever restless, over the face of the earth."[104] Their theory of the dispersion

---

[98] Paul Lawrence Rose, *Revolutionary Antisemitism in Germany from Kant to Wagner* (Princeton, NJ: Princeton University Press, 1990), pp. 23–43.

[99] Augustine, *Contra Faustum*, Book XII, Sections 10–13.

[100] Genesis 4:12–15. God cursed Cain, saying, "A fugitive and a vagabond you will be on the earth."

[101] Salo Wittmayer Baron, *Social and Religious History of the Jews* (New York: Columbia University Press, 1974), vol. 12, pp. 177–182.

[102] Clark M. Williamson, *A Guest in the House of Israel: Post-Holocaust Church Theology* (Louisville, KY: Westminster John Knox Press, 1993), pp. 115–116. For a more favorable view of Augustine, see Paula Fredricksen, *From Jesus to Christ: The Origins of the New Testament Images of Christ* (New Haven, CT: Yale University Press, 1988).

[103] John Byron, *Cain and Abel in Text and Tradition: Jewish and Christian Interpretations of the First Sibling Rivalry* (Leiden, The Netherlands: Koninklijke Brill NV, 2011), pp. 239–244.

[104] Michael von Faulhaber, quoted in George Mosse, *Nazi Culture: A Documentary History* (New York: Random House, 1966), p. 239.

of the Jews and their wandering was the only "logical" reason that church theologians and leaders, afflicted as they were with rampant antisemitism, could give for what, to them, was the inexplicable anomaly of continuing Jewish existence. In their eyes, the Jews who were God's People became no people.

## All-Pervasive Judaeophobia, Anti-Judaism, and Antisemitism

Across all of Christian Europe, then, the second millennium of the Common Era was a time of unrelenting violent attacks on Jews, featuring pillage, rape, violence, and murder. Some of the tragic events arose spontaneously from the superstitious and prejudiced populace; however, most instances of antisemitism were well-organized, government-sponsored, and church-endorsed efforts to eradicate the Jews from Christian kingdoms. Jews who had fled the onslaught of the Roman Empire and had settled across Europe where they had enjoyed a time of tranquility during the second half of the first millennium were then subjected to systematic efforts to bring about their genocide for virtually all of the second millennium. While many popes and other church leaders urged Christians to be merciful to the Jews,[105] more often than not church leaders were either silent in the face of atrocities against the Jews or they were active sponsors of and participants in those acts.[106] Richard Rubenstein may well be right when he says that "the more one studies the classical utterances of Christianity on Jews and Judaism while at the same time reviewing the terrible history of the Nazi period, the more one is prompted to ask whether there is something in the Christian philosophy of history, when pushed to a metaphysical extreme, that ends in the justification of, if not the incitement to, the extermination of the Jews."[107]

The Christian church should have served the Jewish people under

[105] The papal tradition of tolerance for and protection of the Jews is traceable to the sixth century AD from the time of Gregory the Great; however, though other popes followed suit with official pronouncements of support for the Jews, delegated institutional leaders in the hierarchy of the Western Church often condoned and were sometimes complicit in the atrocities that were perpetrated against the Jews by civil authorities. This organizational ambivalence continued to manifest itself even during the time of the Holocaust wherein Pope Pius XII never "made it explicit that it was a sin for a Catholic priest to cooperate in delivering Jews to the Nazis." Richard L. Rubenstein and John K. Roth, *Approaches to Auschwitz: The Holocaust and Its Legacy* (Louisville, KY: Westminster John Knox Press, 2003), p. 274.

[106] Mordecai Paldiel, *Churches and the Holocaust: Unholy Teaching, Good Samaritans and Reconciliation* (Jersey City, NJ: KTAV Publishing House, 2006), pp. 26–23.

[107] Richard L. Rubenstein, *Wrestling with God: Jewish Theological Responses during and after the Holocaust* (Oxford, UK: Oxford University Press, 2007), p. 410.

the humility of the cross. Instead it took up the cross as a sword with which to inflict unimaginable suffering on countless Jewish men, women, and children. The movement that was designed by Jesus to be an instrument of life became the foremost mechanism of death for Jewish people. The details of the complicity of Christian church leaders and civil authorities in the ongoing Jewish suffering can never be expunged from ecclesiastical and secular history, and it certainly cannot be eradicated from the corporate memory of the Jewish people. Christianity itself has been forever disfigured by this evil.

## Unrelenting Efforts to Obliterate the Jewish People

A veritable parade of Gentile empires has marched across the pages of history, trying in every way possible to obliterate Israel and the Jews from the face of the earth. The Assyrians destroyed the cities of the Northern Kingdom of Israel and forcefully removed its inhabitants, replacing them with Gentile pagans. The Babylonians destroyed Jerusalem and the temple and took the inhabitants of Judah into captivity. The Greeks tried to destroy Judaism first through syncretism and then on the edge of the sword. The Romans obliterated Jerusalem and scattered the Jews throughout the world.[108] Erik Peterson said it well, however: "No power in the world will be able to extirpate Judaism. Indeed not even the Jews themselves will be able to extirpate themselves so long as God's long-suffering endures."[109] Against all the laws of history concerning the assimilation of conquered peoples, the Jews have maintained their separate identity as God instructed them to do.[110] Right in the face of death, they have confessed their faith in the one who is Lord of death and life. For countless Jewish martyrs, the last words that escaped their lips were, "*Shema, Yisrael, Adonai Elohenu, Adonai Echad*" ("Hear, O Israel, the LORD our God, the LORD is One"). Even in death, the Jewish people have remained triumphant, for they have known that

[108] Richard Bell, *The Irrevocable Call of God: An Inquiry into Paul's Theology of Israel* (Tübingen, Germany: Mohr Siebeck Verlag, 2005), p. 347.

[109] Erik Peterson, *Die Kirche aus Juden und Heiden* (Salzburg, Germany: Anton Pustet Verlag, 1933), p. 18, quoted in Karl Barth, *Church Dogmatics, II/2: The Election of God; the Command of God* (New York: Bloomsbury Academic, 2004), p. 226.

[110] Steven Beller, *Vienna and the Jews, 1867–1938: A Cultural History* (Cambridge, UK: Cambridge University Press, 1989), p. 74. As an example of how the Jewish people defied total assimilation, Beller noted that in nineteenth- and twentieth-century Vienna, Jews "had some idea of what being Jewish entailed. Full assimilation would have meant that this sense of a Jewish identity would have disappeared. . . . This is not what happened."The Jewish self-identity as Jews could never be obliterated."

their God is the one who is always faithful, even—and especially—to those who sleep in the dust of the earth.

Contemporary Christians can only repent in sackcloth and ashes for the "sins of the fathers" and vow in their hearts that they will never allow the same atrocities to be repeated. Eternal vigilance is essential, for, as Daniel Goldhagen says, antisemitism and the "antisemite's eliminationist" plans are "the devil that never dies."[111] The only way to avoid repeating history is to study it and learn from it, for as George Santayana said, "Those who cannot remember the past are condemned to repeat it."[112] It is vital, therefore, for every Christian to undertake a personal study of readily available historical research in order to know personally the extent of Christian-sponsored violence against the Jewish people. One of the best texts for such a review is Máttis Kantor's *Codex Judaica*, an exhaustive listing of the suffering and loss of life that the Jewish people have experienced through history. In this text, hundreds of entries listed in short, succinct statements of historical fact that document the horrible suffering of the Jewish people in the second millennium of the Common Era.[113] These statements cover 89 pages of condensed text that should be read by every Christian in the world. It is a chilling account of the senseless and ceaseless terror and cruelty that were continually imposed upon Jewish men, women, and children by nominal Christians from the turn of the eleventh century until well into the twentieth century.

[111] Daniel J. Goldhagen, *The Devil that Never Dies: The Rise and Threat of Global Antisemitism* (New York: Little, Brown and Co., 2013), p. 142.

[112] George Santayana, *Reason in Common Sense, Vol. 1: The Life of Reason* (Mineola, NY: Dover Publications, 1980). p. 221.

[113] Máttis Kantor, *Codex Judaica: Chronological Index of Jewish History* (New York: Zichron Press, 2005), pp. 185–274.

CHAPTER 7

# CHALLENGING ANTISEMITISM

## Philosemites, Restorationists, Zionists, and Hope

For two millennia, a long line of Judaeophobes and antisemites paraded triumphalistically across the pages of secular and religious history, afflicting and terrorizing the Jewish people in generation after generation, denying them access to their ancestral homeland, and condemning them to miserable lives in the Diaspora.[1] The Jewish people were transformed from being a happy, prosperous people living in the land that God had ceded to their father Abraham some 2,000 years before the time of Jesus to being a pariah among the nations to which they had fled in order to escape suffering and death. In the eyes of the Gentile world, they had been transmogrified from being God's Chosen People to being no people.[2]

From the second century AD, when the virulently antisemitic Roman Emperor Hadrian slaughtered untold thousands of Jews and exiled the remnant of the Jewish population from their own Holy City, until the twenty-first century, the Jewish people have endured unrelenting suffering and death. From the third through the fifth centuries, Greek and Latin Christian leaders were often Judaeophobic, antisemitic, and triumphalistic vis-à-vis the Jewish people and their faith. Later, during the religious conflicts of the Crusades, Jews were viewed as "infidels" and as such were targeted for persecution and death. Later, the Jews were blamed for the appearance of the Black Death in Europe and were randomly murdered. Even during the Age of Reason and the Enlightenment, the Jewish people continued

[1] Lionel B. Steiman, *Paths to Genocide: Antisemitism in Western History* (New York: Palgrave Macmillan, 1998), p. 6. Also, Frank E. Eakin, *What Price Prejudice?: Christian Antisemitism in America* (Mahwah, NJ: Paulist Press, 1998), p. 15; Yehuda Bauer, *The Jews: A Contrary People* (Zürich, Switzerland, LIT Verlag GmbH & Co., 2014), p. 87; and Gabriel Wilensky, *Six Million Crucifixions: How Christian Teachings about Jews Paved the Road to the Holocaust* (San Diego, CA: Qwerty Publishers, 2010), p. 393.

[2] Robert Michael, *Holy Hatred: Christianity, Antisemitism, and the Holocaust* (New York: Palgrave Macmillan, 2006), p. 21.

to be victimized by prejudice and antisemitism. Finally, as modernity and postmodern secularism unfolded, the Jews continued to be subjected to mayhem and death. For over 18 centuries, virtually every place where the Jewish people lived was all too often infested with Judaeophobes and antisemites. Terror and death were lurking around every corner, and safe havens for the Jews were few and far between.

Still, the hope of return to the land of Israel never faded from the individual or corporate Jewish consciousness. Every time a Jew unrolled the scrolls of the Torah and opened the texts of Hebrew Scriptures, the covenant of the Promised Land leapt from parchments, causing faith to rise in their hearts that one day God would restore the people, the nation, and the land of Israel. Many, if not most, of the Jews connected this expectation with the hope of the coming Messiah, and over the centuries, they prayed the following *Kaddish* hymn of praise: "Exalted and hallowed be God's great Name in this world of His creation. (Amen.) May His will be fulfilled by the revelation of His sovereignty and the flowering of His salvation. (Amen.) May He hasten the coming of his anointed Messiah in your lifetime and in the life of the whole House of Israel, speedily and soon, and let us say, Amen."[3]

As the Diaspora unfolded, realistic prospects for the restoration of the Jewish people to their ancestral homeland must have seemed increasingly remote, if not impossible. Still the God-intoxicated heart of the Torah-observant Jew[4] refused to relinquish the hope (*ha-tikvah*) that the Eternal would move to fulfill his promises to Abraham and his lineal descendants. Many Jews, however, for their own safety and survival, chose to sublimate this hope and to make every reasonable effort to assimilate into the nations where their journeyings had brought them. Through the most difficult of times in the two millennia following the destruction of the Jerusalem Temple, however, the Jewish people were not always utterly alone with no one to plead their cause either to God, to civil magistrates, or to the Gentile peoples of nations into which they had been dispersed. Not all Christians were Judaeophobes and antisemites. As a matter of fact,

[3] Shmuel Kaplan, *Beneath the Sheltering Wings* (Bloomington, IN: ExLibris Press, 2011), p. 119.

[4] Samuel Umen, *Jewish Concepts and Reflections* (New York: Philosophical Library, 1962), p. 32. Umen has said, "Jewish history is the record of a god-intoxicated, god-thirsty people." Also, Murray J. Kohn, *Is the Holocaust Vanishing?: A Survivor's Reflections on the Academic Waning of Memory and Jewish Identity in the Post-Auschwitz Era* (Lanham, MD: Hamilton Books, 2005), p. 141. Kohn declares that the theophany at Mt. Sinai "became profoundly imbedded in the memory of Israel, which rendered it forever a God-intoxicated people," and he maintains that Israel's uniqueness and open-endedness "allows anyone to share its monotheistic ecstasy with the Commanding Voice of Sinai."

though they sometimes represented but a small smattering of support in many of the darkest days of the Diaspora, philosemites and supporters of the Jewish people did arise to defend the Chosen People and their rights to political and religious self-determination in the land that Scripture had deeded to them. Lonesome, forlorn, and often ignored, they persisted in their advocacy for the Jewish people and their right to the land of promise. These few voices stood out as a conscience for a civilization and a church that rushed headlong toward history's greatest manifestation of abject evil, the Holocaust.

## Apostolic and Patristic Support for Israel and the Jewish People

Many leaders in the church before and after Titus' destruction of Jerusalem in 70 AD and the Hadrian exile of the Jews in 135 AD had shared the same expectation that the Jews themselves had long held for the restoration and renewal of their nation and land. Those early Gentile leaders of the Christian church found that the eschatological resurrection of the dead at the end of days which was at the core of their faith was specifically associated in the biblical texts with the restoration of the Jewish people to their ancestral home in the land of Israel. In fact, they came to understand that the two events—resurrection and restoration—were inextricably connected in the pages of Scripture. Beginning with Paul's magisterial argument in Romans 11 for Gentile inclusion without Jewish exclusion,[5] recognition of God's parallel dealings with Israel and the church—though mystifying at best[6]—became part of the ongoing evaluation of what God was doing

[5] Jeffrey S. Siker, *Disinheriting the Jews: Abraham in Early Christian Controversy* (Louisville, KY: Westminster John Knox Press, 1991), p. 197. Siker notes that "Paul did not equate Jewish rejection of the gospel with God's rejection of the Jews. Nor would he allow such an equation to be inferred. Rather, Jewish rejection of the gospel served God's purpose of Gentile inclusion within the gospel. . . . Paul would not affirm the theological doctrine that became entrenched among later generations of Christians, namely, that Gentile inclusion necessitates Jewish exclusion." For Paul, the unequivocal, eternal, and irrevocable covenant that God made with Abraham had provisions for both Jew and Gentile, even as God himself said when he commissioned Abraham: "I will bless you, and through your descendants all the nations of the earth be blessed" (Genesis 18:18; 22:18). For a detailed excursus on the Abrahamic covenant as the one and only covenant that God has made with his "Chosen People" and how that covenant was expanded to include both the Israelite Sinai covenant and the New ("Renewed") Covenant prophesied by Jeremiah (31:31–34) and applied to the Christian community in Hebrews 8:7–12, see John D. Garr, *Christian Fruit, Jewish Root: Theology of Hebraic Restoration* (Atlanta, GA: Golden Key Press, 2016), pp. 281–344.

[6] Paul specifically used the word *mystery* to describe Israel's "hardness in part" (Romans 11:25). His use of this term indicated that what was unfolding in sacred history was not completely understood and ultimately had to be entrusted to the wisdom of God. His level of insight into God's actions regarding both Israel and the Christian community prompted him to exclaim his amazement at God's mysterious actions in this moving doxology: "O, the depth of the riches both of the wisdom and knowledge of God! How unsearchable are his judgments and unfathomable his ways!" (Romans 11:33).

and how he might accomplish his "plan of salvation."[7] Karl Barth encapsulated the nature of God's act of including Gentiles without voiding his covenant with Israel and excluding Jews: "Without a doubt the Jews are to this very day the chosen people of God in the same sense as they have been so from the beginning. . . . They have the promise of God; and if we Christians from among the gentiles have it too, then it is only as those chosen with them; as guests in their house, as new wood grafted onto their old tree."[8]

In subsequent church history, however, many Christian scholars proceeded to reverse the clear intentions of both Jesus and Paul by arguing that the Jews were required to come under the domain of the church in order to continue to be included in the covenant. In contrast, Paul understood that even the branches of God's family tree that were broken off because of unbelief could be regrafted into their own tree,[9] an expectation that was based on his assurance from Scripture that the "calling of God is irrevocable."[10] Perhaps Paul himself wondered how and when this would take place, but, then, less than twenty years before that time, who would have even remotely suspected that Gentiles would come to faith in the God of Israel *en masse*?[11] No wonder the apostle considered the inclusion of the Gentiles to be a mystery.[12]

Brad Young, in effect, gives a very simple answer to the paradox of God's hardening of Israel while maintaining their election when he poses this rhetorical question: "Does God break covenant with one to fulfill a promise with another?"[13] The answer to this question is Paul's graphic, "God forbid!" or "May it never be!"[14] Pope John Paul II expanded upon this answer with these observations: "The permanence

[7] Brian J. Abasciano, *Paul's Use of the Old Testament in Romans 9.1–18: An Intertextual and Theological Exegesis* (New York: T & T Clark International, 2011), p. 68. Abasciano says that the parallels between Jews and Gentile Christians in Paul's teaching run deeper. "Not only is God presented as sovereign over both Israel and the Gentiles, but he also declares that his sovereign dealings with the Gentiles will glorify him and move Israel to acknowledge his greatness and covenant faithfulness."

[8] Karl Barth, *Against the Stream: Shorter Post-War Writings, 1946–1952*, Ronald Gregor Smith, ed. (London, UK: SCM Press, 1954), p. 200.

[9] Romans 11:23.

[10] Romans 11:29. For an excellent discussion of Jewish perspectives on Romans 9–11, see Mark D. Nanos, *The Mystery of Romans: The Jewish Context of Paul's Letters* (Minneapolis, MN: Augsburg Fortress Press, 1996).

[11] Matthew 10:5–6; Ephesians 3:5; Acts 15:15.

[12] Ephesians 3:1–6.

[13] Brad H. Young, *Paul the Jewish Theologian* (Peabody, MA: Hendrickson Publishing, 1997), p. 139.

[14] Romans 11:11. The KJV renders the Greek phrase *Me genoito*, "God forbid!" The NASB translates it "May it never be!"

of Israel (while so many ancient peoples have disappeared without a trace) is a historic fact and a sign to be interpreted within God's design. We must in any case rid ourselves of the traditional idea of a people *punished*, preserved as a *living argument* for Christian apologetic. It remains a chosen people, 'the pure olive' on which were grafted the branches of the wild olive which are the gentiles."[15]

Paul's understanding of the "mystery" of Gentile inclusion[16] prompted him to issue this warning to those to whom he had been commissioned with the church's apostolate to the Gentiles:[17] "Do not be arrogant toward the [natural] branches."[18] It was not long after Paul's death, however, that church leaders began to surmise that Gentile inclusion must, in some way, have required Jewish exclusion. By the middle of the second century AD, Justin Martyr still affirmed his belief in a future restoration of Israel and in an eschatological earthly kingdom that would be established in Israel with its capital in Jerusalem despite the fact that he had become the first church father to identify the church as Israel and, by doing so, had added credibility to teachings that would grow into Christian triumphalism and supersessionism vis-à-vis the Jews. Justin said: "And what the people of the Jews shall say and do, when they see Him coming in glory, has been thus predicted by Zechariah the prophet."[19] Shortly thereafter, other church fathers further connected the restoration of Israel directly with the Christian expectation of the resurrection at the end of days. Kevin Madigan and Jon Levenson note that these "ancient Christian writers were well aware of both potential meanings" in the texts of the Hebrew Scriptures. Indeed, "they could be remarkably sensitive to the interwoven meanings—restoration and resurrection—in the original text."[20]

In the second century AD, Irenaeus, a church apologist from Gaul, "expected that Jerusalem would be rebuilt"[21] and restored to the Jews. To support his teaching, he quoted "the prophecies of the

[15] John Paul II, quoted in *Selected Works of Joseph Cardinal Bernardin*, Alphonse P. Spilly, ed. (Collegeville, MN: The Liturgical Press, 2000), p. 291.

[16] Ephesians 3:1–6.

[17] Galatians 2:9; Romans 11:13; 2 Timothy 1:11.

[18] Romans 11:18.

[19] Justin, *First Apology* 52. A. Cleveland Coxe, James Donaldson, and Alexander Roberts, eds., *The Ante-Nicene Fathers* (Edinburgh, Scotland: T & T Clark, 1885), vol. 1, p. 180.

[20] Kevin J. Madigan and Jon D. Levenson, *Resurrection: The Power of God for Christians and Jews* (New Haven, CT: Yale University Press, 2009), pp. 227–228.

[21] Irenaeus, *Against Heresies* 5.25.4, 28.2, 30.2–4.

restoration of the children of Israel."[22] Irenaeus' views were shared by the third-century Roman theologian Hippolytus, who argued for the return of the Jewish people from the lands into which they had been dispersed by the Assyrians, Babylonians, and Romans.[23] Irenaeus maintained that this restoration would take place despite the fact that the vast majority of the Jews did not believe in Jesus as Messiah. Because a number of other church fathers—among them, the second-century Apostolic Father Papias, bishop of Hierapolis,[24] and the fourth-century Epiphanius, bishop of Salamis,[25]—interpreted the prophecies of the Hebrew Scriptures literally, they believed "in a rather worldly millennium involving a far-reaching, miraculous transformation of the natural world,"[26] says Carey Newman. Similarly, from the second to the sixth centuries, the Montanist movement, which was widespread with many adherents, also believed in the restoration of Israel.[27]

As late as the third century AD, the North African polemicist Tertullian argued for the restoration of the Jewish state by interpreting texts like Ezekiel 37 as speaking first about Israel's restoration and then about the eschatological resurrection. "For Tertullian, it is obvious," Madigan and Levenson note, "the reincorporation and recompacting of bones symbolizes the 'restoration of the Jewish state,' 'tribe to tribe, people to people'—for the text itself supplies its own interpretation."[28] Tertullian also made this argument: "[God] will favour with his acceptance and blessing the circumcision, even the race of Abraham, which by and by is to acknowledge him."[29] On another occasion, he also observed, "It will be fitting for the Christian

[22] T. L. Frazier, *A Second Look at the Second Coming: Sorting Through the Speculations* (Ben Lomond, CA: Conciliar Press, 1999), p. 91. Also, Carole Monica Burnett, "Eastern Orthodox Perspectives on Zionism and Christian Zionism," in *Zionism and the Quest for Justice in the Holy Land*, Donald E. Wagner and Walter T. Davis, eds. (Cambridge, UK: The Lutterworth Press, 2014), p. 98.

[23] Romanus Hippolytus, *Treatise on Christ and the Anti-Christ,* Sn. 54, tr. Philip Schaff, in *The Ante-Nicene Fathers*, A. Cleveland Coxe, James Donaldson, and Alexander Roberts, eds. (Edinburgh, Scotland: T & T Clark, 1885), vol. 5, pp. 522, 527–528.

[24] Papias, noted in Eusebius, *Ecclesiastical History,* 3.39.12.

[25] Epiphanius, *Against Heresies*, 49.1.2–3.

[26] Carey C. Newman, *Jesus & the Restoration of Israel: A Critical Assessment of N. T. Wright's* Jesus and the Victory of God (Downers Grove, IL: InterVarsity Press, 1999), p. 130.

[27] The Montanists were widely considered to be a heretical group because they were thought to take matters of Scripture too literally, emphasizing ecstatic and prophetic experiences and disregarding ecclesiastical authorities. Their understanding and teachings relating to the restoration of Israel were included among their literalist views of the beliefs and experiences of those in pre-Christian Israel and then within the earliest Christian church.

[28] Madigan and Levenson, p. 228.

[29] Tertullian, *Against Marcion*, 5.9, in Coxe, Donaldson, and Roberts, eds., vol. 3, p. 448.

to rejoice, and not to grieve, at the restoration of Israel, if it is to be true (as it is) that the whole of our hope is intimately united with the remaining expectation of Israel."[30] Other third-century church fathers who believed in and taught the restoration of Israel included Lactantius[31] and Commodian,[32] who even predicted that the ten "lost"[33] tribes of Israel would return to the land of Israel.

## Philosemitic Christians and the Vision for Israel's Restoration

Long before the time when the nation of Israel would be resurrected from the ashes of the Holocaust, Christians had begun to join their Jewish brothers and sisters in praying for the peace of Jerusalem and for the restoration of the nation of Israel. As a matter of fact, early Christian belief in the rebirth of Israel was actually called "Restorationism"[34] because it focused on a renewal of the ancient faith and practices of both the Jews and earliest Christianity. Restorationism developed three centuries before largely secular Jewish leaders coined the term *Zionism* to describe their vision for the reestablishment of Jewish sovereignty over the land of Israel. Christian Restorationism originated at the turn of the seventeenth century, long before the time in the mid-twentieth century when Christians began to employ the term *Christian Zionism* to show their support for the Jewish people and for the restoration of Israel.

Restorationists saw "the Jews as continuers of the biblical children of Israel, heirs to the covenant between God and Abraham, and the object of biblical prophecies about a restored Davidic kingdom in the land of Israel."[35] Goran Gunner points out that "in restorationism, the relation of Christianity to the Jews remains one of universalism to particularism. But instead of negating Jewish particularism and demanding that it obliterate itself into Christian universalism, it seeks to restore Jews to

---

[30] Tertullian, *On Modesty* 8, in Coxe, Donaldson, and Roberts, eds., vol. 4, p. 82.

[31] Lactantius, *Divine Institutes* 7.24–26.

[32] Commodian, *Carmen Apologeticum*, 941–946.

[33] Garr, *Christian Fruit*, p. 290, n. 59.

[34] Stephen R. Haynes, *Reluctant Witnesses: Jews and the Christian Imagination* (Louisville, KY: Westminster/John Knox Press, 1995), p. 51. Hayes observes that "Restorationism denotes the Christian belief that Jews will be restored to their homeland in biblical Israel as a sign of God's impending millennial reign, usually just before, after or during a mass conversion of Jews to Christianity." He points out that Restorationist thought was a feature of all the various millenarian movements in the sixteenth through the eighteenth centuries and that Restorationism was also central to Puritan theology in Holland, Britain, and America during that time. Also, Yohanna Katanacho, *The Land of Christ: A Palestinian Cry* (Eugene, OR: Wipf and Stock Publishers, 2013), p. 9.

[35] Jonathan Rynhold, *The Arab-Israeli Conflict in American Political Culture* (Cambridge, UK: Cambridge University Press, 2015), p. 98.

their status as a nation in their national land under Christian imperial patronage."[36] While this Christian position was not without many different ulterior motives, at least it was a step in the right direction toward enlisting Christian support for restored Jewish sovereignty over their own nation and their ancestral homeland.

It is not inconsequential that the greatest Christian advocacy for the restoration of the Jewish state arose during the birth and development of the Protestant Reformation which emerged from sixteenth-century Christian teachings called *veritas Hebraica*[37] that were promoted by Christian Hebraists.[38] With their emphasis on the importance of returning to Hebrew texts of Holy Scripture and recovering the Hebraic foundations of the Christian faith, these Christian Hebraists created the matrix which produced the Reformation.[39] They certainly provided the intellectual foundation for the Reformers' focus on faith and Scripture alone, and they provided a platform for Restorationism.

Reformation Christians, especially those who espoused the restoration of Israel, were often persecuted by the Roman Catholic Church. Some of them were even expelled from their own homelands because of their views on Israel and the Jews. As Heiko Oberman has observed, "Once the homeless, fugitive Christians were compelled to share the destiny of the Jews, expulsion no longer bore the unambiguous marks of a God-sent punishment. The destiny of worldwide diaspora, formerly the proof of the obstinate Jew's guilt, was

[36] Goran Gunner and Robert O. Smith, *Comprehending Christian Zionism: Perspectives in Comparison* (Minneapolis, MN: Augsburg Fortress Press, 2014), p. 178.

[37] The term *veritas Hebraica* was probably coined in the early fifth century AD by Jerome as a description of his desire to go *ad fontes* ("[back] to the sources") for accurate translation of Holy Scripture. Jerome espoused studying both Hebrew and Greek in his efforts to translate the Scriptures into Latin. The result was his Latin Vulgate, which was *the* "Bible" of the Western Church for centuries. By the turn of the sixteenth century, however, the Christian Hebraists had concluded that they could no longer trust either Jerome's Vulgate or church tradition, so they advocated a return to studying the Hebrew texts of the "Old Testament," along with analyzing the Hebraic thought and the innumerable Hebraicisms that are found to be underlying the Greek text of the "New Testament."

[38] Through the centuries, the term *Christian Hebraist* has been given to scholars who have believed that the study of Hebrew is necessary for proper exegesis of Holy Scripture. Though it can be applied to scholars who lived from 450 AD to 1800 AD, it is generally used to describe scholars who lived and worked from the sixteenth century forward. Stephen G. Burnett, *Christian Hebraism in the Reformation Era (1500–1660)* (Leiden, The Netherlands: Koninklijke Brill NV, 2012), p. 139. Burnett notes, "By the end of the sixteenth century Christian Hebraists of all confessions had developed both a rationale for studying the Hebrew language and Jewish texts and the necessary expertise to do so." Garr, *Christian Fruit*, pp. 379–380, and John D. Garr, *Life from the Dead: The Dynamic Saga of the Chosen People* (Atlanta, GA: Golden Key Press, 2014), pp. 293–294.

[39] Both Huldrych Zwingli, in the Reformed tradition, and Philip Melanchthon, the premier sixteenth-century Lutheran theologian, were Christian Hebraists. See Robert J. Wilkinson, *Tetragrammaton: Western Christians and the Hebrew Name of God* (Leiden, The Netherlands: Koninklijke Brill NV, 2015), p. 399, and Hans-Martin Kirn, "Traces of Targum Reception in the Work of Martin Luther," in *A Jewish Targum in a Christian World*, Alberdina Houtman, E. van Staalduine-Sulman, and Hans-Martin Kirn, eds. (Leiden, The Netherlands: Koninklijke Brill NV, 2014), p. 270.

now the badge of faith of the avowed Christian."[40]

It is obvious that as reformed and reforming Christians reconnected with the authority of Holy Scripture—evidenced by their motto *Sola Scriptura*[41]—they began to understand the power and perdurability of God's promises to Abraham and his descendants. They could no longer subscribe to the tradition of the Western Church which, from the time of Augustine, had promoted an entrenched amillennialism that was focused on maintaining the politico-ecclesiastical power and privilege of the church. Because they endured persecution and violence from the church, the Protestant Christians more readily empathized with the plight of the Jewish people and the suffering that they had endured at the hand of those "Christian" civil authorities whose actions were either overtly or tacitly condoned and were often endorsed, if not outright promoted, by the same church that was harassing them. Protestants' own experiences opened their eyes to see the bigger picture of what was actually happening in the church.

For scholars at the time, "analogies between the persecution of the Jews and of the French Protestants and the rational and balanced historical description of Jews as having both positive and negative characteristics led to . . . 'a sympathetic history, full of understanding for the Jews.'"[42] As a result, "Protestants were more likely to *see* Jews clearly as a people with a real history in time and place" and to "identify profoundly with the Israelites" with a "more sympathetic perception of Jewish history."[43] In fact, "the religious wars that emerged after the early sixteenth century between Protestantism and Catholicism reoriented religious hostility away from the Jews," says Hans Hillerbrand.[44] In subsequent centuries—perhaps as a result of the empathy that Protestants gained from the personal experience during this time—"the situation of Jews in largely Protestant countries, especially in the

[40] Heiko Oberman, *The Origins of Anti-Semitism in the Age of Renaissance and Reformation*, tr. James I. Porter (Philadelphia, PA: Fortress Press, 1984), p. 140.

[41] *Sola Scriptura* means "Scripture Alone" or "Scripture Only." It was accompanied by other Reformation slogans, including *Sola Fide* ("Faith Alone") and *Sola Gratia* ("Grace Alone").

[42] Imanuel Clemens Schmidt, "Revealing the Absurdity of Jewish Hopes: From Polemical Ethnography to Basnage's *L'Histoire des Juifs*," in *Revealing the Secrets of the Jews: Johannes Pfefferkorn and Christian Writings about Jewish Life and Literature in Early Modern Europe*, Jonathan Adams and Cordelia Heß, eds. (Berlin, Germany: Walter de Gruyter, 2017), quoting from Myriam Yardeni, "New Concepts of Post-Commonwealth Jewish History in the Early Enlightenment: Bayle and Basnage," *European Studies Review* 7.3 (1977), no. 90, p. 251.

[43] Jonathan Elukin, "Post-Biblical Jewish History Through Christian Eyes: Josephus and the Miracle of Jewish History in English Protestantism," in *The Jew as Legitimation: Jewish-Gentile Relations beyond Antisemitism and Philosemitism*, David J. Wertheim, ed. (Cham, Switzerland: Palgrave Macmillan, 2017) p. 105.

[44] Hans J. Hillerbrand, *Encyclopedia of Protestantism* (Abingdon, UK: Routledge, 2004), vol.1-4, p. 1762.

English-speaking world, was categorically better than in other parts of the European world."[45]

## The Restorationist Awakening

For centuries, Christians lost sight of the purposes of God toward Israel and haughtily displayed contempt for the Jews, a malady that continues even to this day to one degree or another in most of the Christian church.[46] Before and during the time of restoration, however, increasing numbers came forward to support the restoration of the nation of Israel.[47] In the thirteenth century, Thomas Aquinas confessed that he expected a future salvation of the Jews: "It is possible to designate a terminus, because it seems that the blindness of the Jews will endure until all the pagans chosen for salvation have accepted the faith."[48] During that same time in France, Gerardo di Borgo San Donnino displayed grace that had no ulterior motive or expectation by teaching that "some Jews would be blessed as Jews in the end time and would return to their ancient homeland."[49] In the fourteenth century, Johannes of Rupescissa believed that "the converted Jews would become God's new imperial nation and Jerusalem would be completely rebuilt to become the center of the purified faith."[50] Though some, if not most, Christian leaders did have ulterior motives for their support of Israel—*e.g.*, eliciting conversion of the Jews to Christianity or believing Jewish conversion to be a prerequisite to the second coming of Jesus—at least they did voice their faith in the restoration of the people and the land.

While the French took the lead in promoting pre-millennialism on the

[45] Hillerbrand, p. 1762.

[46] Recently, the Latin Patriarchate of Jerusalem even argued that Christian use of Hebrew liturgy was only a modern phenomenon and complained about Christian use of "Jewish customs" when, in fact, the most ancient Christian church maintained continuity with the synagogal model of fellowship, study, and worship by employing Hebrew liturgy and prayers. Acts 2:42 makes this clear, noting that the earliest Christians "continued faithful . . . in *the* prayers" (emphasis added), obviously connecting the "prayers" of the church with the prayers of the synagogue by employing the Greek definite article, *pais "the,"* with the word *proseuchais "prayers."* This passage is frequently mistranslated as "in prayer"; however, the Greek text is explicit: They continued "in *the prayers*" (emphasis added).

[47] Michael J. Vlach, *Has the Church Replaced Israel? A Theological Evaluation* (Nashville, TN: B & H Publishing Group, 2010).

[48] Thomas Aquinas, quoted in John Y. B. Hood, *Aquinas and the Jews* (Philadelphia, PA: The University of Pennsylvania Press, 1995), p. 77.

[49] Carl F. Ehle, Jr., "Prolegomena to Christian Zionism in America: The Views of Increase Mather and William E. Blackstone Concerning the Doctrine of the Restoration of Israel," Ph.D. Dissertation for New York University, 1977, pp. 41–42. Ehle notes that because Gerardo supported millenarian eschatology, he was sentenced to life in prison by Pope Alexander IV.

[50] Robert E. Lerner, "Millennialism," in *The Encyclopedia of Apocalypticism*, John J. Collins, Bernard McGinn, and Stephen J. Stein, eds. (New York: Continuum Press, 2000), vol. 2, p. 353.

European continent, perhaps the strongest movement of Restorationism developed in England, where it emerged from the ranks of pietistic Protestants. Stephen Spector points out that there were "Christian proto-Zionists in England 300 years before modern Jewish Zionism emerged."[51] One of the first of these Restorationists was Francis Kett who, in 1585, called for the Jewish people to return to Palestine. Because of his views on theology and on eschatology and Israel, Kett was declared a heretic by the Church of England,[52] and he was burned at the stake by civil authorities.[53] The death of a martyr, however, did not stop the march toward the restoration of Israel. Amazingly—and only thirty years later—Thomas Brightman fathered what would be the British restorationist perspective on "the Restoration of the Jews."[54] His views were rapidly expanded by men like Sir Henry Finch, a member of the British Parliament, who made this distinct argument regarding what Scripture meant when it spoke of the restoration of Israel: "Where Israel, Judah, Zion, and Jerusalem are named, the Holy Ghost meant not the spiritual Israel, or the church of God collected of the Gentiles or of the Jews and Gentiles both . . . but Israel properly descended out of Jacob's loynes."[55]

By the mid-seventeenth century, Restorationism had become well entrenched in England, especially among the Puritans, who believed that the Abrahamic covenant still applied to Abraham's physical descendants even though they also viewed themselves as a reembodied Israel.[56] In all likelihood, the strong interest that the Puritans maintained in the restoration of Israel

---

[51] Stephen Spector, *Evangelicals and Israel: The Story of American Christian Zionism* (Oxford, UK: Oxford University Press, 2009), p. 16.

[52] Kett's conviction for heresy was largely on the basis of his profession of a form of Arianism in which he denied the deity of Jesus. Additionally, Kett's views on the return of the Jewish people to Palestine were connected with his own eschatological millenarian scenario which anticipated the second coming of Jesus in the late seventeenth century, with the Jews being sent "to divers countries to publish the new covenant" in the year 1588. In a 1589 message entitled "Sermon Preached at Paules Crosse, Richard Bancroft singled out "the late obstinate heretike *Francis Ket*," for taking biblical references to "the spiritual kingdom of Christ" and applying "them to the materiall restauration of the earthly Jerusalem" and arguing that Christ was then gathering the true church into Judea by "affirming that as manie as woulde be saved must go and dwell there in the land of Canaan." Francis Kett, quoted in Richard Bancroft, *Sermon Preached at Paules Crosse*, noted in David Loewenstein, *Treacherous Faith: The Specter of Heresy in Early Modern English Literature and Culture* (Oxford, UK: Oxford University Press, 2013), p. 160.

[53] Spector, p. 16.

[54] Regina Sharif, *Non-Jewish Zionism: Its Roots in Western History* (London, UK: Zed Books, 1983), p. 25.

[55] Finch made these and other insightful arguments in his book, *The World's Great Restoration or the Calling of the Jews, and of all the Nations and Kingdoms of the Earth, to the Faith of Christ.* Michael J. Vlach, "Israel in Church History," in *The People, the Land, and the Future of Israel: Israel and the Jewish People*, Darrell L. Bock and Mitch Glaser, eds. (Grand Rapids, MI: Kregel Publications, 2014), p. 206. Also, Mayir Verete, "The Restoration of the Jews in English Protestant Thought, 1790–1840," in *Middle Eastern Studies*, vol. 8, no. 1 (1972), p. 14.

[56] Iain Murray, *The Puritan Hope* (Edinburgh, Scotland: Banner of Truth Publishers, 1971), p. 326.

resulted primarily from the fact that they placed much greater emphasis on the Hebrew Bible than other dissenters[57] of their time did.[58] It was the Puritans who were also largely responsible for bringing Restorationism to the New World when they emigrated from England in search of religious freedom.[59]

In the eighteenth century—particularly in its second half—Christian support for the restoration of the nation of Israel in the land of Israel was widespread and growing, especially in England. "It was during these years that the *social* and *political* foundations of a Jewish homeland converged with the centuries-old *biblical* and *theological* foundations," says Timothy Demy.[60] What was developing in late eighteenth-century Christianity provided the foundation for nineteenth-century events that would allow the restoration of the Jews to their ancient land to be worked out practically through Jewish resettlement of the land and the building of a social order that would eventuate in the reestablishment of the long-dormant nation of Israel. "The coalescing of history, politics, and theology in the events of the era reassured Christians of God's continued divine plan for the Jewish people,"[61] and increasing numbers of them made bold and public demonstrations of their support for both the Jewish people wherever they were and for what they perceived to be a prophetic movement that God was orchestrating to bring about the restoration of the nation and the land of Israel.

One of the many prominent eighteenth-century Restorationism activists was Thomas Newton, Bishop of Bristol in England, who supported the return of the Jews to their land while condemning anti-Jewish prejudice in his own country.[62] During this time, Joseph Priestly, a clergyman who, as a polymath, had attained fame as the co-discover of oxygen, believed and taught that the Jews would be restored to "Canaan."[63] The passion that many Christians had for the restoration of Israel as a people, a nation, and

[57] Christians who separated from the Church of England in the sixteenth, seventeenth, and eighteenth centuries were called "dissenters." The dissenters opposed the interference of the state in religious and educational matters and simply wanted to have freedom to worship God according to the dictates of their own consciences rather than according to the doctrine and polity of the Church of England.

[58] Rynhold, p. 98.

[59] Gerhard Falk, *The Restoration of Israel: Christian Zionism in Religion, Literature, and Politics* (New York: Peter Lang Publishing, 2006), pp. 81–82. Falk points out that the Puritans believed the Jews would be restored to their land, "but only after they became Christians."

[60] Timothy Demy, *Marching to Zion: Social and Political Foundations of Nineteenth-Century Christian Zionism* (author's emphasis), posted at www.pre-trib.org/articles/view/marching-to-zion-social-and-political-foundations-of-nineteenth-century-christian-zionism.

[61] Demy, *Marching.*

[62] Verete, p. 3.

[63] Spector, p. 18.

a land was reflected in a Charles Wesley hymn entitled "Almighty God of Love" which he published in 1762. This work enshrined the vision that God would regather the Jewish people to a restored Israel and then employ them to proclaim the gospel to all the nations. John Wesley considered this theme so important that he selected it for *A Collection of Hymns for the Use of the People Called Methodists*, a hymnal published in 1789.

The influence that the Christian Restorationists had at that time and the impact that they made upon governments was considerable. When Napoleon Bonaparte invaded Palestine in 1799, the French Restorationist movement petitioned him to approve the restoration of the Jewish homeland in Palestine. In response to this request, Napoleon issued a "Proclamation to the Jewish Nation," in which he emphatically encouraged the Jewish people to begin work on restoring their ancient nation: "Hasten!" he exclaimed, "Now is the moment that may not return for thousands of years, to claim the restoration of your rights among the population of the universe that had been shamefully withheld from you for thousands of years, your political existence as a nation among the nations, and the unlimited natural right to worship Yehovah in accordance with your faith, publicly and in likelihood for ever."[64]

Whatever Napoleon's political or religious motives may have been for making this proclamation,[65] when he urged the Jewish people to reclaim their long-denied right to nationhood, their right to self-determination, and their right to worship as they chose, he set forth a powerful and positive position that was free from traditional underlying Christian motives for supporting the Jews. This official recognition of the fundamental human rights of the Jewish people, including their legal right to possess their ancestral homeland, represented a profound shift from the positions that had been taken by the leaders of all European and Middle Eastern governments before that time. Tragically, the window of opportunity that this Proclamation clearly opened would prove to be short lived. The dispersed and oppressed Jewish populace was simply not prepared at that time to take advantage

[64] Napoleon Bonaparte, quoted in Lawrence J. Epstein, *A Treasury of Jewish Inspirational Stories* (Northvale, NJ: Jason Aronson, 1993), p. 180.

[65] Napoleon may well have been more focused on what he considered best for France rather than the Jewish people, for in another situation, he had, in fact, "attempted to force the Sanhedrin he convoked to accept as a requirement that a third of all Jewish marriages be mixed marriages, so that the Jews' blood will lose its particular character, since a mass of vitiated blood can be improved only through time." See Irving Massey, *Philo-Semitism in Nineteenth-Century German Literature* (Tübingen, Germany: Max Niemeyer Verlag GmbH, 2000), p. 102.

of the emperor's largesse. What could well have been a *kairos*[66] moment of opportunity for the Jewish people vanished into thin air with the unfolding vicissitudes of European political and military engagements.

## Mixed Emotions, Ulterior Motives

"With the rise of philosemitism in the seventeenth century, Protestant interpreters . . . boldly announced the return of the Jewish people to the land of Israel as a prelude to the Millennium."[67] Generally speaking, the Restorationist belief that the Jewish people would be restored to their nation in the land of Israel was accompanied, if not driven, by their eschatological projections regarding the return of Jesus. Most Restorationists believed that immediately prior to that event, the Jewish people would accept Jesus as Messiah and Lord. It was at least partially for this reason that they adopted philosemitic feelings and visions toward the Jewish people. The danger of basing support for the return of the Jewish people to the land of Israel upon the view that such action was necessary to ensure the fulfillment of the Christian hope of the *parousia* of Jesus could not have been more tragically manifest than in the case of Martin Luther.

Early in his career, Luther expressed great love and admiration for the Jewish people; however, because he had also created his own personal eschatological scenario in which the Jews would be converted *en masse* to Protestantism and because he did not witness the fulfillment of that vision, Luther's initial philosemitism was transformed into virulent antisemitism which prompted him to produce some of the most vile pronouncements against the Jewish people in all of Christian literature. Mark Levene observes that Luther's "briefly moderated tone" toward the Jews was based on "his own eschatological wish-fulfillment that imminent mass Jewish conversion would prove him right in the face of his papal detractors."[68] When he was "disabused of this notion by leading German rabbis," however, Luther

[66] The Greek word *kairos* refers to an opportune moment in time. Literally, it speaks of two metaphorical images: 1) the "moment in which an arrow may be fired with sufficient force to penetrate the target" and 2) "the moment in which the shuttle could be passed through the threads on the loom." For more details, see Hunter W. Stephenson, *Forecasting Opportunity: Kairos, Production, and Writing* (Lanham, MD: University Press of America, 2005), p. 4. In the Apostolic Scriptures, the word *kairos* is used some 80 times, often signifying "God's appointed time" as in Mark 1:15: "The *kairos* is fulfilled, and the kingdom of God is at hand." Success in divine initiatives is achieved when preparation meets the *kairos* moment that allows for their fulfillment.

[67] David Brown, *The Restoration of the Jews* (Charleston, SC: BiblioLife, 2008), pp. 38–64. Also David S. Katz, *Philo-Semitism and the Readmission of the Jews to England 1603–1655* (Oxford, UK: Clarendon Press, 1982), pp. 94, 98, 123, and Shalom Goldman, *Zeal for Zion: Christians, Jews, & the Idea of the Promised Land* (Chapel Hill, NC: The University of North Carolina Press, 2009), p. 7.

[68] Mark Levene, *Genocide in the Age of the Nation State, Volume 2: The Rise of the West and the Coming of Genocide* (New York: I.B. Tauris & Co., 2005), p. 135.

embarked on "diatribes against the Jews" that "were couched in language as vitriolic and ugly as anything in the annals of anti-Semitism."[69]

Thankfully, most Restorationists did not follow Luther's example and allow themselves to drift into antisemitism as a result of their unfulfilled expectations. Still, their primary interest in the restored people, nation, and land of Israel was not always purely for the sake the Jewish people themselves but was significantly motivated by their beliefs about Christianity itself. It was not surprising, therefore, that many Restorationists had varying degrees of ambivalence toward the Jewish people. While they supported the creation of the state of Israel and the return of the Jewish people to their own land, they often did not support equal rights for Jews in their own lands, nor did they welcome Jewish immigration into their own societies. Eventually, this ambivalence was to foster some of the greatest tragedies in human history.

One of many prime examples of this paradox of ambivalence was mid-nineteenth-century Englishman Anthony Ashley-Cooper, Earl of Shaftesbury, a prime mover in the London Society for Promoting Christianity Amongst the Jews, an organization which considered the promotion of the "restoration of the Jews to their national existence in Palestine" as being integral to its purpose.[70] While Ashley-Cooper was a vocal proponent of a restored nation of Israel,[71] at the same time, he also "opposed the Emancipation Bill that would have removed disabilities from Jews to full participation in English political and cultural life."[72] The irony was that for the Earl of Shaftesbury, Jews could be fully Jewish with self-determination as long as they would do so in some location besides Britain.

Yet another example of such ambivalence—and perhaps surprisingly so—was the case of British Foreign Secretary Arthur James Balfour, who openly promoted the restoration of the Jewish homeland in Palestine and ultimately formalized such a proposal in his 1917 Balfour Declaration.

---

[69] Levene, p. 135.

[70] Rosemary Radford Ruether, "The Quest for Peace with Justice in the Middle East: Christian Zionist and Palestinian Theologies," in *Theologies of Liberation in Palestine-Israel: Indigenous, Contextual, and Postscolonial Perspectives*, Nur Masalha and Lisa Isherwood, eds. (Eugene, OR: Wipf and Stock Publishers, 2014), p. 129.

[71] Ashley-Cooper also promoted the establishment of the first Anglican bishopric in Jerusalem. Gunner and Smith report that he "envisioned a vast redemptive project in which unconverted Jews would return to Palestine" and become Christians. Like many Christians before, during, and after that time, Ashley-Cooper probably believed that the return of the Jewish people to Israel and their conversion to Christianity were two of the major events that would prepare the way for the second coming of Jesus. See Gunner and Smith, p. 181.

[72] Ruether, p. 129.

When he became prime minister of Britain, however, Balfour supported the Alien Immigration Act of 1905,[73] and he "worked tirelessly for the enactment of stringent anti-immigration legislation meant primarily to prevent Jewish immigrants who were fleeing the pogroms of Eastern Europe from entering Britain."[74] Balfour, to say the least, was inconsistent in his approach to the plight of the Jewish people.

Prior to the Balfour Declaration, there were even proposals to create a Jewish homeland in Argentina, Cyprus, and Uganda.[75] It seems that many British people were willing to consider a "Jewish homeland" if it were not on European soil. Some Zionists, who were dubbed "politicals" (including Theodore Herzl, Max Nordau, and their followers) even "accepted" the Uganda proposal[76] at the sixth Zionist Congress in Basel in 1903; however, the "practicals" (the Eastern European delegates) rejected the proposal and exited *en masse* from the Congress because they insisted that any idea of a Jewish homeland outside of the land of Palestine was unthinkable and untenable.[77] Indeed, the idea of placing the Jewish people in a remote place anywhere in the world was incongruous with the centuries-old Jewish vision of being restored to the Promised Land.

Some Christian leaders, however, actually had entirely pure motives for their support of the Jews and of the restoration of Israel wherein there was no inherent Christian self-interest. Mirroring the thirteenth-century views of Gerardo di Borgo San Donnino, James Cicheno concluded in 1800 that the restoration of the Jews to their ancient homeland "was not conditional on conversion to Christianity."[78] Cicheno was accurate in his assessment because the terms of the Abrahamic covenant: "I will give to you and to your offspring after you . . . all the land of Canaan, for an everlasting possession,"[79] were not predicated on whether or not Jews would accept Jesus as Messiah

[73] Andrew Prescott and Elizabeth M. Hallam, eds., *The British Inheritance: A Treasury of Historic Documents* (Berkeley, CA: The University of California Press, 1999), p. 125.

[74] Brian Klug, *Being Jewish and Doing Justice* (London, UK: Vallentine Mitchell, 2011), pp. 199–299.

[75] Julie Cole, Sarah Snyder, and Teresa Garlake, *Making Peace: Teaching About Conflict and Reconciliation*, Teresa Garlake and Rose Welshman, eds. (Oxford, UK: Oxfam, 2002), section 6, p. 52.

[76] It is likely that Herzl and his colleagues were simply moving the process of the very idea of a "Jewish homeland" along by acceding to the proposal.

[77] Norbert M. Samuelson, *An Introduction to Modern Jewish Philosophy* (Albany, NY: State University of New York Press, 1989), p. 51. The Eastern European delegates were dubbed "practicals" because their insistence on having the ancestral Jewish homeland restored to the Jewish people was the only "practical" solution to Zionist aspirations. The "politicals" were so called because they were trying to work out a political compromise that would perhaps lay a foundation for later considerations but may well not have come to fruition.

[78] Derek Prince, *The Key to the Middle East: Discovering the Future of Israel in Biblical Prophecy* (Bloomington, MN: Chosen Books, 1982), p. 35.

[79] Genesis 17:8.

four millennia later. The unilateral nature of God's particularist covenant with Abraham placed no performance demands upon the patriarch or upon his descendants. The fulfillment of the covenant's land grant was contingent upon one thing and one thing only: the immutable faithfulness of the Almighty to fulfill his covenant oath and promise to the patriarch of faith and to his lineal progeny. Those Christians who would be faithful to the "heavenly vision" would support the cause of restoration as God had designed it and had described it in Scripture rather than clouding the issue with their own expectations, no matter how noble those expectations may have been.

## Increasing Philosemitism and Intensified Support for Israel

As the nineteenth century continued to unfold, Christians in even greater numbers joined the ranks of the Restorationists. Derek Prince suggests that "the names of nineteenth-century Christians who embraced the concept of a restored Jewish state read like a section of Who's Who."[80] One of the greatest preachers of that time, Charles H. Spurgeon, was a leading supporter of Restorationism.[81] Another stream of Evangelical belief, which would come to be called Dispensationalism, developed in this time frame and was also highly supportive of Restorationism. Early leaders of this movement included John Nelson Darby in Britain and later Cyrus Scofield in the United States. As time progressed, Dispensationalists would be among the most ardent Restorationists and Christian Zionists.

Many authors and poets joined in the rising chorus of support for the Jewish people, lending their voices to affirm the rights of the Jewish people to return to and reclaim the land of their ancestors. Herman Melville penned this poignant statement in his *Clarel: A Poem and Pilgrimage in the Holy Land*:

> The Hebrew seers announce in time
> The return of Judah to her prime;
> Some Christians deemed it then at hand
> Here was an object. Up and On.
> With Seed and tillage help renew–
> Help reinstate the Holy Land.[82]

[80] Prince, p. 35.

[81] Clifford A. Kiracofe, *Dark Crusade: Christian Zionism and US Foreign Policy* (New York: I.B. Tauris & Co., 2009), p. 55. Spurgeon followed in the tradition of American Calvinism's Jonathan Edwards, who in his eighteenth-century, posthumously published book, *The History of the Work of Redemption*, affirmed his support for "the restoration of the Jews as a nation." Also Falk, p. 82.

[82] Herman Melville, *Clarel, I.17: Nathan*, lines 259–264. Herman Melville, *Clarel: A Poem and Pilgrimage in the Holy Land* (Evanston, IL: Northwestern University Press, 1991), p. 62.

During this time, however, "Palestine" was seen and represented as "empty, wretched, and desolate."[83] At the beginning of the twentieth century, "Palestine was indeed sparsely populated outside the interior hill and mountain range."[84] In his book *The Innocents Abroad*, Mark Twain confirmed this description of Palestine and its inhabitants in personal accounts of his own visit to the Holy Land in 1867. After generally depicting Palestine as a "blistering, naked, treeless land,"[85] he continued to say, "There is not a solitary village [in Galilee]. . . . There are two or three small clusters of Bedouin tents, but not a single permanent habitation. One may ride ten miles, hereabouts, and not see ten human beings."[86] In describing ancient Samaria, he observed, "There was hardly a tree or a shrub anywhere." As he continued his trek through the land, what he observed prompted him to conclude, "No landscape exists that is more tiresome to the eye than that which bounds the approaches to Jerusalem.[87]

Though Twain also described areas like Shechem (Nablus) as "under high cultivation" and "well watered,"[88] and though he found isolated spots between Jerusalem and the Elah Valley where there were "luxuriant orchards of figs, apricots, pomegranates," he also observed that these scenes contrasted with the vast majority of the land, which was "rugged, mountainous, verdureless, and forbidding."[89] He also remarked that "in the flush of spring," there were "small shreds" of "very beautiful" spaces near Jaffa that were "all the more beautiful by contrast with the far-reaching desolation that surrounds them on every side."[90] Twain's descriptions of such isolated pockets of verdant, productive land were confirmed by Bayard Taylor who in 1852 described the Jezreel Valley as "one of the richest districts in the world" where the soil "produces annually superb crops of wheat and barley."[91] Also in 1886, Laurence Oliphant identified the same area as "a huge green lake of waving wheat . . . one of the most striking pictures of luxuriant fertility which is possible to conceive."[92] Despite these few and far-between examples of verdurous

[83] Gudrun Krämer and Graham Harman, *A History of Palestine: From the Ottoman Conquest to the Founding of the State of Israel* (Princeton, NJ: Princeton University Press, 2008), p. 128.

[84] Krämer and Harman, p. 128.

[85] Mark Twain, *The Innocents Abroad: The New Pilgrims' Progress* (Hartford, CT: The American Publishing Co., 1869), p. 482.

[86] Twain, p. 485.

[87] Twain, p. 555.

[88] Twain, p. 551.

[89] Twain, p. 604.

[90] Twain, p. 607.

[91] Bayard Taylor, *The Lands of the Saracen* (Alexandria, Egypt: The Library of Alexandria, 1854), p. 32.

[92] Laurence Oliphant, *Haifa: Life in Modern Palestine* (London, England: William Blackwood, 1887), p. 96. Oliphant was a Christian who was an advocate for the Jewish resettlement of Palestine.

landscapes in Palestine, the general consensus of the status of the Promised Land was summed up in Twain's conclusion: "It truly is monotonous and uninviting. . . . It is a hopeless, dreary, heart-broken land. . . . Palestine sits in sackcloth and ashes . . . and why should it be otherwise? Can the curse of the Deity beautify a land?"[93]

The sad state of affairs in what at one time had been described as a "land flowing with milk and honey" with abundant agricultural produce could be traced to the fact that few of those who inhabited the land at that time had any significant value for agriculture. The Bedouin Arabs were a largely nomadic people, dependent upon flocks for their livelihood. Additionally, a cruel form of taxation that had been imposed on the land by the Ottoman Empire wherein taxes were levied upon trees,[94] prompted the residents to engage in a virtual deforestation of the land, including the removal of untold numbers of fruit trees.[95] "When trees died they were never replanted because of the Turkish law taxing fruit-bearing, or indeed any tree from time of planting."[96] J. V. Thirgood pointed out that in order to "escape the tree tax, the men from a village in Hebron district one winter cut down some five hundred trees."[97] In another incident, apricot trees on the Mount of Olives that were destroyed by locusts in 1864 "were never replanted because of the severity of the Turkish law."[98] Though indirect, the Ottoman assault on the flora of Israel produced an environmental disaster that literally changed the climate of Palestine with rain patterns of the land altered to such a degree that desertification of the land became even more intense.[99]

The tragically barren condition of the land of Palestine did not discourage or deter the Christian Restorationists. They used the sad condition of the land that had resulted from the neglect of its non-Jewish inhabitants as an argument for the return of the Jews to their ancient homeland not only to reestablish their own sovereignty but also to save and restore the land itself.

---

[93] Twain, pp. 606–608.

[94] Alon Tal, *Pollution in a Promised Land: An Environmental History of Israel* (Berkeley, CA: The University of California Press, 2002), p. 39.

[95] Shaul Ephraim Cohen, *The Politics of Planting: Israeli-Palestinian Competition for Control of Land in the Jerusalem Periphery* (Chicago, IL: The University of Chicago Press, 1993), p. 45.

[96] J. V. Thirgood, *Man and the Mediterranean Forest* (London, UK: Academic Publishers, 1981), p. 113, cited in Cohen, p. 45.

[97] Thirgood, p. 113.

[98] Thirgood, p. 113.

[99] This situation was not reversed until the Israeli Jews engaged in a massive tree-planting exercise that eventually restored the climate of Israel to what it had been before the Ottoman occupation. One of the greatest of these efforts was Theodore Herzl's call for the planting of 10 million trees. See Cohen, pp. 46–51. Also, Alon Tal, "Combating Desertification: Evolving Perceptions and Strategies," in *Between Ruin and Restoration: An Environmental History of Israel*, Daniel E. Orenstein, Alon Tal, and Char Miller, eds. (Pittsburgh, PA: The University of Pittsburgh Press, 2013), pp. 106–127.

In the 1890's, Restorationists joined the early Zionists in repeating Israel Zangwill's sardonic aphorism: "Palestine is a land without a people for a people without a land."[100] To the Restorationists and Zionists who followed, there was no logical reason why the desolate land of the Bible should not be restored to the Jewish people. A land that had been largely neglected for centuries was surely the very place where the restored Jewish nation would bring about the fulfillment of Isaiah's prediction that the "desert [land] would bloom like a crocus."[101] In the Restorationists' vision, though the Jewish people had been landless for nearly two millennia, they would become landed again, they would do so in the same Promised Land that God had ceded to their father Abraham, and they would again make that land flow with milk and honey as it had done at the time of the Exodus from Egypt.[102]

## Christian Zionists and the Vision for Jewish Restoration

"Covenantal restorationism helped to prepare the public mood for the later, more sharply defined Christian Zionism that was to follow,"[103] says Clifford Kirakofe. By the late nineteenth century, the Restorationist movement had taken on the title of Christian Zionists, and they had become involved in pro-Zionist lobbying efforts in the United States.[104] Perhaps the most prominent Restorationist supporter of the early Zionist movement was American real estate tycoon William E. Blackstone who took up the Restorationist cause by publishing a book entitled *Jesus Is Coming*, which was translated into 48 languages and sold millions of copies worldwide. Although Blackstone was an evangelical Methodist, he maintained that the Jewish people were not required to convert to Christianity either before or after the return of the Messiah. Avi Beker reports that "before promoting the political restoration of the Jews in their Promised Land, Blackstone had to recognize their Chosen role and reject the prejudices of traditional Christianity toward the Jews and absolve them from the need to convert."[105] With positions such as this, Blackstone's book was published

[100] Beverley Milton-Edwards, *The Israeli-Palestinian Conflict: A People's War* (New York: Routledge, 2009), p. 16. Zangwill coined the dictum that was to become a mantra for the early Jewish and Christian Zionist movements. This saying was quite true, for, with the exception of enclaves of Jews and Arabs in the more arable areas of the land, Palestine was, indeed, a barren, uncultivated land.

[101] Isaiah 35:1.

[102] Exodus 33:3.

[103] Kiracofe, p. 55.

[104] Rynhold, pp. 98–99.

[105] Avi Beker, *The Chosen: The History of an Idea, and the Anatomy of an Obsession* (New York: Palgrave Macmillan, 2008), p. 143.

in Yiddish, which allowed it to have considerable impact on the Jewish community of Europe. Paul Boyer points out that late in his career, Blackstone even warned European and American Jews, almost vatically, that "[Jewish] assimilationists [who] wish[ed] to remain in the various nations enjoying their social, political, and commercial advantages" would suffer difficult consequences for not having embraced Zionism.[106]

Then, in 1890, Blackstone organized the Conference on the Past, Present, and Future of Israel at the First Methodist Episcopal Church in Chicago. While this conference produced strong resolutions of sympathy for the oppressed Jews living in Russia, Blackstone remained unconvinced that simple resolutions were adequate, so he began to promote resettlement of Jewish people, especially those from Russia, in Palestine. In 1891, in what came to be known as the Blackstone Memorial,[107] he developed a petition that was to be presented to US President Benjamin Harrison asking him to "consider the situation of the Israelites and their claims to Palestine as their ancient home."[108] When this petition was signed by over 400 of the most prominent Americans of the day—including an impressive list of legislators, Supreme Court justices, industrialists, newspaper editors, and religious leaders—Blackstone was able to lobby President Harrison to begin to promote the migration of American Jews to Palestine, thereby laying foundations for the restoration of Israel.[109]

Blackstone was one of the first to argue that the "law of dereliction" did not apply to the Jews and their relationship to the land of Israel. "They never abandoned the land," he said. "They made no treaty; they did not even surrender. They simply succumbed, after months of conflict, to the overwhelming power of the Romans."[110] Eventually, his viewpoints were resurrected by Supreme Court Justice Louis D. Brandeis, who asserted that Blackstone could be called the "Father of Zionism"

---

[106] Paul Boyer, *When Time Shall Be No More: Prophecy Belief in Modern American Culture* (Cambridge, MA: Harvard University Press, 1992), p. 219.

[107] Rosemary Radford Ruether and Herman J. Ruether, *The Wrath of Jonah: The Crisis of Religious Nationalism in the Israeli-Palestinian Conflict* (Minneapolis, MN: Augsburg Fortress Press, 2002), p. 83. Ruether points out that Blackstone and others suggested "that President Harrison might be the modern-day Cyrus who would return the Jews from exile." The astounding way in which world leaders were seemingly sovereignly positioned in order to effect God's restoration purposes toward Israel is certainly unique.

[108] Ruether and Ruether, p. 83.

[109] Naim S. Ateek, "Foreword," in *Zionism through Christian Lenses: Ecumenical Perspectives on the Promised Land*, Carole Monica Burnett, ed. (Eugene, OR: Wipf and Stock Publishers, 2013), p. xiv.

[110] William E. Blackstone, "May the United States Intercede for the Jews?" in *Our Day* VIII, October, 1891, p. 46.

because his work predated that of Herzl. Brandeis, in turn, championed the Restorationist cause to US President Woodrow Wilson, who, as a devout Presbyterian and the son of a minister, was probably "the last President of the United States who was disposed to be persuaded by the arguments of the Blackstone Memorial."[111] Before his death, Wilson marveled, "To think that I, a son of the manse, should be able to help restore the Holy Land to its people."[112] Though much of this action took place in private, it served to assure the British that there was American support for the Balfour Declaration.[113] It was also strongly instrumental in the unanimous drafting of the League of Nations Covenant for Palestine of 1922, which became the foundation for the 1947 United Nations Resolution which recommended the partitioning of Palestine.[114] It is also likely that this action also had a positive influence on the thinking of later US Presidents Warren Harding, Calvin Coolidge, and Herbert Hoover, all of whom were supportive of the establishment of a Jewish homeland in Palestine. The concern that high-ranking members

[111] Paul C. Merkley, *The Politics of Christian Zionism 1891–1948* (New York: Routledge, 1998), p. 93. Merkley says that "while it would be reckless to claim that we can trace a clear line of cause and effect from Blackstone's Memorial of 1891 to the Creation of the State of Israel in 1948, it is not at all far-fetched to say that the Memorial is the place to go to find the clearest expression of the motivation that won President Woodrow Wilson, and which would continue to be the surest, the most constant course of American Christian Zionism." Merkley also succinctly noted the political and religious situation that succeeded Wilson: "The Presidents of the 1920s were not men of the same intellectual and mental and moral type. . . . The 1920s was the decade when the hegemony of American Protestantism was finally broken up—in the realms of thought and learning and in the realm of politics, and within the increasingly beleaguered house of Protestantism itself, Fundamentalism, though it won many battles, finally lost the war for control of thought and policy in all the major denominations."

[112] Woodrow Wilson, quoted by Stephen S. Wise in Levi Soshuk and Azriel Louis Eisenberg, eds., *Momentous Century: Personal and Eyewitness Accounts of the Rise of the Jewish Homeland and State 1875–1878* (Cranbury, NJ: Cornwall Books, 1984), p. 118.

[113] Isaiah L. Kenen, *Near East Report—Volumes 18–20* (Washington, DC: Near East Report, 1974), p. 41.

[114] When the League of Nations was disbanded following World War II, the United Nations Organization which was established in its place "inherited all the agreements made by its predecessor, including the Mandate for Palestine." Cynthia D. Wallace, *Foundations of the International Legal Rights of the Jewish People and the State of Israel and Implications for the Proposed Palestinian State* (Lake Mary, FL: Creation House, 2012), p. 19. Wallace observes that even though Britain notified the United Nations of its intention to terminate its stewardship of the Mandate of the League of Nations Covenant for Palestine in 1947, "*the Mandate itself was not terminated*" (author's emphasis). Eli Hertz notes that "the 'Mandate for Palestine' was not a naive vision briefly embraced by the international community in blissful unawareness of Arab opposition to the very notion of Jewish historical rights in Palestine." The Mandate was created in 1920 and modified in 1922. The League of Nations Mandate for Palestine was a Trust, and the British Mandate was the Trustee. Then on April 18, 1946, when the League of Nations "was dissolved and its assets and duties transferred to the United Nations, the international community, in essence, reaffirmed the validity of this international accord and reconfirmed that the terms for a Jewish National Home were the will of the international community, a 'sacred trust,'" says Hertz. The League of Nations Mandate for Palestine established "Jewish legal rights in Palestine. Then, the League of Nations commissioned the British government with the mandate of "responsibility to administrate the area delineated by the League's 'Mandate for Palestine.'" For a comprehensive discussion of the history and legal rights of the Jewish people to the land of Israel, maps of the land designated for the Jewish state in the League of Nations Covenant for Palestine and its Mandate to Britain, see Eli E. Hertz, "'Mandate for Palestine': The Legal Aspects of Jewish Rights," posted at http://www.mythsandfacts.org/conflict/mandate_for_palestine/mandate_for_palestine.htm#top.

of the United States government had for the plight of the Jewish people created a climate in which events could emerge that would eventuate in the restoration of the ancient homeland of the Jewish people in the land of Israel. Though the actual outworking of the visions of those who lobbied for US government support for the restoration would unfold over more than five decades, the seeds that had been planted centuries earlier were sprouting and beginning to bear fruit.

In the twentieth century, a significant part of Evangelical Christianity continued the rich tradition of the nineteenth-century Restorationists by maintaining some degree of support for the Jewish people and for the eventual establishment of a Jewish state.[115] Though Evangelicalism's influence in United States politics waned as the nation became increasingly influenced by secular humanism, still a significant force of Christian support for the Jewish people and continuing prayer for the restoration of the nation of Israel placed public pressure on secular leaders to maintain at least some degree of sensitivity toward the plight of the Jews. This Christian influence helped prepare the way for the Jewish restoration of Israel.

## Zionism: A New Jewish Movement for the Restoration

When the Jews began a revival of their rightful claim to their nation and their land, the verve and vigor of the young Jews who coalesced into the Zionist movement were certainly the motivating force behind their efforts. It is a simple fact of history, however, that "the rise of Christian Zionism prepared the ground for the emergence of European Jewish Zionism in the late nineteenth century," and "Political (Jewish) Zionism . . . was inspired and directly influenced by its contemporary, Christian Zionism."[116] Perhaps in the sovereignty of God, the seeds of the divine plan for restoring the Jewish nation had ironically been planted in the world's corporate consciousness by Christians who had forsaken the sins of their fathers that had brought so much pain to the larger Jewish community and who had embraced varying degrees of philosemitism and love for Israel. For the first time in nearly two thousand years, these Christians had heard the

[115] Not all Evangelicals were strong supporters of the Jewish people's right to restore their nation in the land of Israel. Before, during, and after the establishment of the nation of Israel, some segments of Evangelicalism had either antipathy for or ambivalence toward Restorationism and Zionism. Gilbert S. Rosenthal, *A Jubilee for All Time: The Copernican Revolution in Jewish-Christian Relations* (Eugene, OR: Wipf and Stock Publishers, 2014), p. 118. Rosenthal points out that at the time of the restoration of Israel, "nonmillennial evangelicals were not at all certain that [Israel] had any prophetic significance, and some even were opposed and called the developments an 'unjust restoration.'" Also Dwight Wilson, *Armageddon Now: The Premillenarian Response to Russia and Israel since 1917* (Grand Rapids, MI: Baker Book House, 1977), p. 169.

[116] Merkley, pp. 15–21.

plain and simple words that God spoke to the patriarchs and prophets of Israel: "I will give you this land."[117] For four centuries before the rise of Jewish political Zionism, Christian Restorationists had been proclaiming what could only be seen as the clear word of the Lord: "Let my people go. . . . I will plant them in their land never to be uprooted again."[118] And, more importantly, they had been working in the halls of governments to sound the alarm against antisemitism and to promote means by which the security of self-sovereignty could be restored to the Jewish people.

David Novak notes the supreme irony of the history of Zionism: "In fact, it is sometimes embarrassing for Jewish Zionists to learn that there are Christian Zionists who have better biblically based arguments for their Zionism than many Jews have for their own Zionism."[119] Anita Shapira, a contemporary Israeli historian, suggests that Evangelical Christian Zionists of the 1840s "passed this notion on to Jewish circles."[120] This fact rests on the 500-year continuing quest by Restorationists and Christian Zionists to pray for, support, and work to effect the restoration of the land of Israel to the sovereignty of the Jewish people. What may be even more ironic, however, is the fact that a few early Jewish Zionists took their argument for the importance of the restored Jewish state in Israel even further by maintaining that "a Jewish state would be 'a light unto the nations.'"[121] While Christian Restorationists had exercised significant influence on the birth of Zionism, the work of the Zionists would have a much more powerful impact on the church because the restoration of Israel would force the church to come face to face with the fallacy of its supersessionist triumphalism vis-à-vis the Jews. There can be no doubt that restored Eretz Yisrael has radically influenced the theology of virtually all Christian denominations![122] Perhaps the greatest

[117] Genesis 13:15; Exodus 6:8; Deuteronomy 1:8.

[118] Exodus 5:1; Amos 9:15.

[119] David Novak, *Zionism and Judaism* (Cambridge, UK: Cambridge University Press, 2015), p. 21.

[120] Anita Shapira, *Israel: A History*, tr. Anthony Berris (London, UK: Weidenfeld and Nicolson, 2014), p. 15.

[121] Robert O. Freedman, "Introduction," in *Contemporary Israel: Domestic Politics, Foreign Policy, and Security Challenges*, Robert O. Freedman, ed. (Boulder, CO: Westview Press, 2009), p. 2.

[122] Eva Fleischner, *Judaism in German Christian Theology Since 1945* (Lanham, MD: Scarecrow Press, 1975), p. 27. Fleischner says that "the concrete fact of Israel's existence is effecting a major change in Christianity's view of Judaism." Also, Herman N. Ridderbos, "The Future of Israel," in *Prophecy in the Making: Messages Prepared for Jerusalem Conference on Biblical Prophecy*, Carl F. H. Henry, ed. (Carol Stream, IL: Creation House, 1971), p. 316. Ridderbos notes the dilemma that Israel's restoration has presented to Christian theology: "The existence of Israel once again becomes a bone of contention, this time in a theoretical and theological sense. Do the misery and suffering of Israel in the past and in the present prove that God's doom has rested and will rest upon her, as has been alleged time and again in so-called Christian theology? Or is Israel's lasting existence and, in a way, her invincibility, God's finger in history, that Israel is the object of His special providence (*providential specialissima*) and the proof of her glorious future, the future that has been beheld and foretold by Israel's own seers and prophets?"

light that Restored Israel has brought and will bring to Christianity is the restoration of the inherent Jewish roots of the Christian faith that will enable Christianity to recognize its supreme debt to Judaism and to the Jewish people.

## Zionism: Transforming Hope into Reality

Restorationism had to be transformed, however, from a Christian eschatological hope into a physical reality, and only the Jewish people themselves could accomplish this seemingly impossible task. Fortunately, the God of history had the power to transform into material substance a dream to which Christians, after centuries of blindness, had come to share with their Jewish brothers: the vision of a restored Zion. What some Christians had come to believe and to act upon in the spheres of their influence, Jews would labor intensely and incessantly to bring into reality with all the vigor and determination steeled into the very fiber of their being by centuries of fire and pressure. The Zionist Movement was ready to emerge on the human scene and effect one of history's most amazing miracles, the full restoration of the long-dormant nation and land of Israel. It would not be an easy task, however, for "most of the Jewish world at the beginning of the twentieth century was non-Zionist or anti-Zionist."[123]

Even before the Zionist movement came to prominence, however, another advocate of what would come to be known as Zionism received a vision that would have a powerful impact upon the emergence of the restored nation. This man was Eliezer Ben-Yehuda, a Lithuanian Jewish linguist, who "came to believe that the Jewish people could also revive the Jewish nation on its ancient national soil."[124] In 1880, Ben-Yehuda reached a conclusion that stunned even him: "I have decided that a national revival of the Jewish people could only be successfully accomplished if it were accompanied by a revival of the Jews' ancient language, Hebrew."[125]

After he immigrated to Palestine in 1881 and saw the social and political realities there, Ben-Yehuda reached the conclusion that "just as the Jews cannot really become a living nation other than through their returning to their ancestral land, so too, they are not able to become a

[123] Chaya Herman, *Prophets and Profits: Managerialism and the Restructuring of Jewish Schools* (Cape Town, South Africa, HSRC Press, 2006), p. 84.

[124] Sara E. Karesh and Michael M. Hurvitz, *Encyclopedia of Judaism* (New York: Infobase Publishing, 2006), p. 52.

[125] Lawrence Jeffrey Epstein, *A Treasury of Jewish Anecdotes* (Northvale, NJ: Jason Aronson, Inc., 1989), p. 35.

living nation other than through their returning to their ancestral language."[126] Ben-Yehuda came to believe that a conjunctive symbiosis existed between Zionism and the Hebrew language. His agenda was simple: "The Hebrew language can live only if we revive the nation and return it to the fatherland."[127] He also understood that the long-term success of the nation would depend to a large degree upon whether or not it would adopt a common language—in this case, Hebrew, the language common to the ancient ancestors of the Jewish people.

Ben-Yehuda's task was daunting. His undertaking was profoundly stressful not only because of the incredible amount of work that had to be done in order to transform the 8,000-word vocabulary of biblical Hebrew into a modern language but also because he was confronted with significant opposition from traditionalists of the Jewish society of Palestine who objected to his "profaning" the sacred language of Scripture by promoting it for everyday use. With Ben-Yehuda's work, however, Hebrew became the unifying language of the Jewish people and the nation of Israel. Regardless as to what nation and language the Jewish people left when they made *aliyah* to the Promised Land, when they arrived in Israel, they found a polyglot people speaking one universal language, Hebrew. They did so largely because Ben-Yehuda labored tirelessly, despite his ongoing battle with tuberculosis, to complete the work that he knew he had been called to do on behalf of his people. His works culminated in a seventeen-volume *Complete Dictionary of Ancient and Modern Hebrew*. One month before Ben-Yehuda died in December, 1922, the British Mandate for Palestine declared Hebrew to be the official language of the Jewish community in Palestine.[128]

In reality, Eliezer Ben-Yehuda was a prophet,[129] though a prophet of a different sort.[130] He was not an ecstatic voice bubbling up with

[126] Eliezer Ben-Yehuda, quoted in Anton La Guardia, *War Without End: Israelis, Palestinians, and the Struggle for a Promised Land* (New York: St. Martin's Press, 2001), p. 81.

[127] Eliezer Ben-Yehuda, quoted in William M. Schniedewind, *A Social History of Hebrew: Its Origins through the Rabbinic Period* (New Haven, CT: Yale University Press, 2013), p. 206.

[128] The declaration of the British Mandate said, "English, Arabic, and Hebrew shall be the official languages of Palestine." Anat Stavans, "Challenges Faced by a Medium-Sized Language Community in the 21st Century: The Case of Hebrew," in *Survival and Development of Language Communities: Prospects and Challenges*, F. Xavier Vila, ed. (Bristol, UK: Multilingual Matters, 2013), p. 82.

[129] For an excellent personal account of the life of Eliezer Ben-Yehuda written by his grandson, Rabbi Eliezer Ben-Yehuda, see Eliezer Ben-Yehuda, *Fulfillment of Prophecy: The Life Story of Eliezer Ben-Yehuda, 1858–1922* (Charleston, SC: BookSurge Publishing, 2009).

[130] Kenneth Katzner, *The Languages of the World* (New York: Taylor & Francis Group, 2002); Robert St. John, *Tongue of the Prophets: The Fascinating Biography of Eliezer Ben-Yehuda, the Father of Modern Hebrew* (Beverly Hills, CA: Wilshire Book Co., 1972).

spiritual insight; however, he was a prophet of restoration. He even spoke of his mission in life in highly mystical terms: "During this time, suddenly—it was as if the heavens opened and a light shone forth—a pure and gleaming ray flashed before my eyes, and a mighty inner voice called in my ears. Israel's Rebirth on the Soil of the Fathers!"[131] Cecil Roth encapsulated Ben-Yehuda's mission well when he said, "Before Ben-Yehuda, Jews could speak Hebrew, after him, they did."[132] Ben-Yehuda truly revolutionized Israeli life and culture.

By far the most important leader of the Zionist movement that emerged in the late nineteenth century was Theodore Herzl, a Jewish journalist with a doctorate in law who was both a thinker and an organizer. During this time, as writer for the liberal Viennese newspaper, Herzl had encouraged Jews to assimilate in the various nations where they lived.[133] "In 1896, after witnessing the anti-Jewish rioting in France that was connected to the Dreyfus affair, in which a French Jewish army officer was falsely accused of giving military secrets to the Germans," however, "Herzl concluded that there was no safe place for the Jews of Europe and that assimilation was not possible."[134] It was at this time that Herzl wrote his defining work *Der Judenstaat* (*The Jewish State*), in which he made two seminal arguments: 1) the Jews throughout the world were "one people" and 2) the only solution to the Jewish plight was "the establishment of their own nation.[135] At first, Herzl suggested "that any tract of land big enough to accommodate the Jews would suffice,"[136] and he even suggested that a part of Uganda could serve that purpose. When this matter was considered during the Sixth Zionist Congress (also known as the Uganda Congress), however, Franz Oppenheimer argued poignantly and correctly: "Allocating [the Jewish people] the most magnificent expanses of farm land in Canada or Argentina will not enhance the strength of the wandering Jew as much as settling on the lowly Plain through which the Jordan flows and upon which the

[131] Eliezer Ben-Yehuda, quoted in La Guardia, p. 80.

[132] Cecil Roth, "Was Hebrew Ever a Dead Language?" in *Personalities and Events in Jewish History* (Philadelphia, PA: Jewish Publication Society of America, 1953), pp. 136–142.

[133] Richard D. Bank, *The Everything Jewish History and Heritage Book* (Avon, MA: F+W Publications, 2003), p. 256.

[134] Freedman, p 2.

[135] Bank, p. 256.

[136] Bank, p. 256. Bank points out that some of the first ideas for a location for the Jewish state included land in Argentina where Baron de Hirsch had funded the settlement of 6,000 Jews in an agricultural colony. Also included was Rothschild's work of funding Jewish settlements in Palestine. Ultimately, with the Balfour Declaration, even Uganda was considered as a possibility for a new Jewish homeland.

Lebanon looks out."[137] Ultimately, however, Herzl came to believe that a Jewish state in Palestine was necessary for the security and survival of the Jewish people. Herzl envisioned a new Jewish nation as a "socialist utopia" which he described in his novel, *Altneuland* (*The Old New Land*),[138] as "a secular, socialist, and peace-loving society, a vision not entirely detached from Torah and the message of Israel's prophets."[139] As Isaac Rottenberg said, however, "Rare, indeed, is the Jewish soul so secular that all remnants of Israel's spiritual heritage have been erased."[140]

In 1897, Herzl organized the First Zionist Congress in Basel, Switzerland,[141] a meeting with 200 participants from seventeen nations. On the second day of the meeting, the congress established the goal of the emerging Zionist movement in what became known as The Basel Program: "Zionism aims at establishing for the Jewish people a publicly and legally assured home in Palestine. For the attainment of this purpose, the Congress considers the following means serviceable: 1) the promotion of the settlement of Jewish agriculturists, artisans, and tradesmen in Palestine; 2) the federation of all Jews into local or general groups, according to the last of the various countries; 3) the strengthening of the Jewish feeling and consciousness; 4) preparatory steps for the attainment of those governmental grants which are necessary to the achievement of the Zionist purpose."[142] The Zionists called for the restoration of "the Jewish national home in Palestine, where Jews could find sanctuary and self-determination, and work for the renascence of their civilization and culture."[143]

Shortly after the Congress, Herzl summed up the significance of the three-day meeting as he wrote in his diary, "At Basel I founded the Jewish state. If I said this out loud today I would be greeted by universal

---

[137] Franz Oppenheimer, quoted in Shmuel Almog, *Zionism and History: The Rise of a New Jewish Consciousness* (New York: St. Martin's Press, 1987), p. 259. Also, Chaim Gans, *A Just Zionism: On the Morality of the Jewish State* (Oxford, UK: Oxford University Press, 2008), p. 33.

[138] Bank, p. 256.

[139] Isaac C. Rottenberg, "Israelic Christians," *Restore!*, Issue 52, p. 32.

[140] Isaac C. Rottenberg, *Christian-Jewish Dialogue: Exploring Our Commonalities and Our Differences* (Atlanta, GA: Hebraic Heritage Press, 2005), and Isaac C. Rottenberg, *Judaism, Christianity, Paganism: A Judeo-Christian Worldview and Its Cultural Implications* (Atlanta, GA: Hebraic Heritage Press, 2007), p. 108. Rottenberg maintained and promoted balance in the Christian support of Israel's right to exist with complete self-determination while at the same time avoiding the extremes of political party endorsements that have impacted many Christians.

[141] Freedman, p. 2.

[142] Isidore Singer, Cyrus Adler, *et. al.*, eds. "The Basel Program," in *The Jewish Encyclopedia* (New York: Funk and Wagnalls Company, 1906), vol. II, pp. 570–571.

[143] Leonard J. Davis, *Myths and Facts: A Concise Record of the Arab-Israeli Conflict*, Eric Rozenman and Jeff Rubin, eds. (Washington, DC: Near East Report, 1989), p. 3.

laughter. In five years perhaps, and certainly in fifty years, everyone will perceive it."[144] What may have seemed presumptuous at that time was to become a reality as history progressed toward the establishment of the nation of Israel, proving that Herzl had perhaps even been prescient in his claim. "What began as an evanescent movement whose most ardent supporters never believed that the objective of Jewish sovereignty in Palestine would be achieved in their lifetime became a real national movement that shaped a society and nation and built a state."[145]

Exhausted from his supreme devotion to the Zionist cause Herzl died an untimely death at the age of 44 only seven years after that historical event. Significantly, however, the death of Zionism's founder "marked the beginning of the Second Aliyah (1904–1914)," which brought to Palestine over forty thousand Jews. These socialist Jews, who came primarily from Russia, founded the enduring Israeli institution of *kibbutzim* (national farms)[146] that did wonders in reclaiming the barren land for agriculture. At the same time, with their philosophy of egalitarianism, they helped foster the first democratic nation in the Middle East. The principles outlined by the early Zionists established a solid basis not only for the dream of a Jewish nation but also for the practical principles through which that dream could be achieved. John Judis points out that "the outward logic of Zionism was impeccable," for "the nations of Europe, where Jews had dwelt for hundreds of years, were treating them as a nation in their midst," and "nationalist politicians and intellectuals in central and Eastern Europe called for purging their countries of this alien nation."[147] Who could argue, then, with the Zionist leaders' call for the establishment of a genuine Jewish state where "they could be secure from persecution and oppression"?[148]

## Making *Aliyah*: "Going Up" to the Promised Land

From its inception, the Zionist movement began to encourage Jewish migration into Ottoman-controlled Palestine,[149] confirming the

---

[144] Theodor Herzl, quoted in Naomi E. Pasachoff, *Great Jewish Thinkers: Their Lives and Work* (Springfield, NJ: Behrman House, 1992), p. 98.

[145] Shipira, p. 3.

[146] Bank, p. 257.

[147] John B. Judis, *Genesis: Truman, American Jews, and the Origins of the Arab/Israeli Conflict* (New York: Macmillan, 2014), p. 15.

[148] Judis, p. 15.

[149] Robin Cohen, *The Cambridge Survey of World Migration* (Cambridge, UK: Cambridge University Press, 1995), p. 504. Also, James Gelvin, *The Israel-Palestine Conflict: One Hundred Years of War* (Cambridge, UK: Cambridge University Press, 2007), p. 51.

long-standing view of the Jewish community, as well as that of significant parts of the Christian community, that the restoration of the Jewish people to their ancestral homeland was absolutely essential for Jewish survival in an increasingly hostile world filled with Judaeophobia and antisemitism. The bravery that individual Jews and Jewish families manifest by enduring the inhospitable conditions of a long-neglected land and overcoming the constant dangers of violence against their persons that were lurking in the shadows was key to the restoration of the land and nation of Israel. These brave and determined Jews were merely following in the footsteps of others before them who, despite the exile of the vast majority of the Jewish people from Israel, had continued to cling tenaciously to the land of their ancestors.

The Zionist movement merely strengthened and expanded what had been maintained in some form throughout all the centuries of the history of Israel. The Zionists purposed to add to those numbers the millions of Jews who still suffered oppression across Europe and in other parts of the world. All the advocates of Zionism, Jewish and Christian, have had one common agenda: the repatriation of the Jewish people to the homeland from which their ancestors were dispersed millennia earlier.[150] Michael Brown states the truth well: "At no time was Palestine considered an independent Arab nation, and throughout the millennia, only one group claimed this land as its ancestral homeland: the Jews!"[151] For more than a century, Zionism's one common denominator has been what is succinctly noted by Gideon Shimoni: "At the heart of the Zionist ideology was the claim to Eretz Israel, or Zion, as the national homeland of the Jews, hence, as the legitimate locus for the national self-determination of the Jews."[152]

During the second half of the nineteenth century, a growing realization of the dangers that threatened the persecuted Jewish population of most of Europe began to foster insight in the hearts of avant-garde Jews into the need for creating an independent, modern Jewish nation.[153] Some believed that this emerging viewpoint was a contrived, illegitimate

[150] Ran Aronson, "Settlement in Eretz Israel—A Colonialist Enterprise? 'Critical' Scholarship and Historical Geography," in *Israel Studies*, Indiana University Press, vol. 2, no. 2, (1997) pp. 214–229. Also, Michael J. Cohen, "Zionism and British Imperialism II: Imperial Financing in Palestine" in *Journal of Israeli History: Politics, Society, Culture*, vol. 30, no. 2 (2011), pp. 115–139.

[151] Michael L. Brown, *What Do Jewish People Think about Jesus? And Other Questions Christians Ask about Jewish Beliefs, Practices, and History* (Grand Rapids, MI: Baker Publishing Group, 2007), p. 32.

[152] Gideon Shimoni, *The Zionist Ideology* (Boston, MA: Brandeis University Press, 1995), p. 333.

[153] *Jewish Quarterly*, (Braintree, UK: Jewish Literary Trust, 1977), vol. 25–27, p. 7.

idea based on a myth of the "ancient site from which the 'ethnic' tribe [of Israel] had ostensibly sprouted."[154] Creating a modern state of Israel in the land of Israel as a vision for the survival of the Jewish people was, in fact, more than simply a good idea: it was a prophetic vision, the accuracy of which would be shockingly confirmed a century later in Nazi Germany. This national territorialization birthed from religious philosophies may well have been "one of Zionism's most important, even if not completely original, achievements,"[155] but in reality, it was the outworking of the Jewish soul's longing for restoration to the matrix from which it had been birthed some four millennia earlier.

This phenomenon of return to the land came to be called *aliyah*. The Hebrew word *'aliyah*, meaning "ascent," comes from the verb *'alah*, which means "to go up." The word *'aliyah* refers to the Psalm of Ascents (Psalm 122) in which the ancients said, "Let us *go up* to the house of the LORD. . . . Jerusalem is a city that is bound firmly together, to which the tribes *go up* . . . to give thanks to the name of the LORD."[156] The "origin of the term *'aliyah*" is, therefore, "purely sacred, or religious" in that "it initially referred to the pilgrimage made three times a year during the Second Jewish Commonwealth period, when, on the three major holidays, Jews were obliged to ascend to the Jerusalem Temple and to bring tributes and sacrifices to God and his holy servants, the priests of the Temple."[157]

After the destruction of the temple and the dispersion of the Jewish people, the word *'aliyah* came to describe "making *aliyah* to the Torah," the act of being called up to the *bema* of the synagogue to read the Torah.[158] The term *'aliyah* was also used to describe immigration to Israel, primarily for burial purposes. It was from this background of figurative applications that the literal application of "making *aliyah*" as the act of moving to the land of Israel in order to take up residence there was born. This was the meaning of the word *'aliyah* that the early Zionists adopted to describe their

[154] Shlomo Sand, *The Invention of the Land of Israel: From Holy Land to Homeland*, tr. Jeremy Forman (London, UK: Verso Books, 2012), p. 256.

[155] Sand, p. 256.

[156] Isaiah 2:3.

[157] Baruch Kimmerling, "Academic History Caught in the Cross-Fire," in *Postzionism: A Reader*, Laurence J. Silberstein, ed. (New Brunswick, NJ: Rutgers, the State University Press, 2008), p. 108.

[158] Rich Cohen, *Israel Is Real: An Obsessive Quest to Understand the Jewish Nation and Its History* (New York: Farrar, Straus and Giroux, 2009), p. 58. Cohen points out that in each synagogue, the *Aron Kodesh* that contains the Torah is elevated on a *bema* (platform), which represents Mt. Sinai. Those who are called upon to read the Torah make *aliyah* by ascending to the *bema*.

intentions for the Jews regarding the land of Israel, and it became a focal point for encouraging Jews to immigrate into Israel following the establishment of the State of Israel.

In addition to the small percentage of world Jewry who insisted on remaining connected with the land of their ancestors, virtually all of the Jews who have lived outside the land of Israel (because of the evictions and exiles) have continually "referred to themselves as living in the 'Diaspora,'" and have "never abandoned their claim to return to the land from which so many of their ancestors had been forcibly driven."[159] Throughout the Diaspora, therefore, the Jewish hope of reclaiming the land of Israel continued to be encapsulated in the concept of "making *aliyah,*" of "going up" to the land of their forefathers. Though "the center of gravity of the Jews and Judaism had moved from the Middle East to Europe,"[160] still a Jewish presence remained in the land of Israel. The passion of the Jewish people for the land could not be quenched, and, at incredible risk to their lives, Jews insisted on remaining in the land of their ancestors because they understood that this was the Holy Land that was consecrated by God himself and given to them, as he himself said, "forever."[161] This understanding was so ingrained on the individual and corporate consciousness of the Jewish people that it was ineradicable. Abba Eban argued that the prayers in Jewish memory had the effect of infusing "Jewish life with a peculiar nostalgia, strong enough to prevent any sentiment of finality or permanence in any other land." Consequently, he said, "The physical link was never broken."[162]

It is not insignificant that the word *'aliyah* is the very last word in the *Tanakh*, appearing in the record of the decree of Cyrus, King of Medo-Persia, when he recounted the fact that God had instructed him to sponsor the reconstruction of the Temple in Jerusalem. This is what Cyrus decreed: "The LORD . . . has charged me to build him a house at Jerusalem, which is in Judah. Whoever is among you of all his people, may the LORD his God be with him. Let him go up

[159] Alan M. Dershowitz, "Countering Challenges to Israel's Legitimacy," in *Israel's Rights as a Nation-State in International Diplomacy*, Alan Baker, ed. (Jerusalem, Israel: Jerusalem Center for Public Affairs, 2011), p. 160.

[160] Gavin I. Langmuir, "Continuities, Discontinuities and Contingencies of the Holocaust," in *Studies in Contemporary Jewry: Volume XIII: The Fate of the European Jews*, Jonathan Frankel, ed. (Oxford, UK: Oxford University Press, 1997), p. 10.

[161] Genesis 13:15; 17:8; 48:4; 2 Chronicles 20:7; Jeremiah 7:7

[162] Abba Eban, *Heritage: Civilization and the Jews* (New York: Simon & Schuster, 1984), p. 244.

(*'alah*)."[163] Since the commandment for the restoration of the temple and the rebuilding of Jerusalem concluded with the word *'alah*, it is altogether appropriate that the same term, in the form *'aliyah*, should be used to describe the work of the Jewish people to "go up" to the land of Israel and there to do the work of restoring Israel, the Chosen People; Israel, the Jewish nation; and Israel, the Holy Land. Just as it was a sacred quest for the Israelites to "go up" to Jerusalem to worship their God three times each year during the pilgrimage festivals, and just as it has been a sacred responsibility for Jews to "go up" to read the Torah in their synagogues around the world, it has also been a sacred opportunity for Jews from the nations of the world—east, west, north, and south—to hear the voice of God beckoning them to "go up" from the nations of their dispersion to the land of their ancestors. Answering the call for *aliyah* is the fundamental key to restoring the people of Israel to the land, restoring the land of Israel to the people of Israel, and restoring the people of Israel to their God. Perhaps the imperative of Cyrus to the post-exilic Judean community will be seen to have been God's prophetic word to his Chosen People in this day: "Go up!"

In the early nineteenth century, only a few Jews lived in Palestine, concentrated primarily in the Jewish Quarter of what is now called the Old City of Jerusalem in what Bank describes as "a dismal ghetto where scholars and other observant Jews subsisted on charitable contributions sent by their European brethren."[164] In the 1870s, however, a new approach to settlement in Israel was initiated by Yehudi Shlomo Hai Alkali, who became one of the first Jewish leaders to promote "taking active measures towards Jewish resettlement in *Eretz-Yisrael*."[165] The idea was to encourage Jewish people around the world to return to Israel to reclaim the land by purchasing individual plots of ground and settling there.

[163] 2 Chronicles 36:23, ESV. This verse is the last statement in the Hebrew Scriptures because the *Tanakh* is organized in a different order from that of the Christian canon of the Hebrew Scriptures ("Old Testament"). The word *Tanakh* (sometimes written *TaNaKh*) is an acronym for Torah, *Nevi'im*, and *Ketuvim* (Law, Prophets, and Writings, respectively). The *Ketuvim* begins with the Book of Psalms, and it includes all the poetic and historical books of the Hebrew Scriptures. These books conclude with 2 Chronicles, the last word of which is *'alah*, the root of *'aliyah*. Interestingly, then, the Hebrew Scriptures begin with the word *b'reshit* ("In the beginning"), and they end with the command *'alah* ("Go up"). The Hebrew word עֲלִיָּה (*'aliyah*) appears in the Hebrew Scriptures only in 2 Chronicles 9:4: "[Solomon's] ascent (*'aliyah—'aliyato*) by which he went up into the house of the LORD" (KJV). The final imperative of King Cyrus is one word in Hebrew: וְיַעַל (*v'ya'al*), "And go up!"

[164] Bank, p. 254.

[165] Efraim Karsh, ed., *Israel: The First Hundred Years, Volume I: Israel's Transition from Community to State* (London, UK: Frank Cass Publishers, 2000), p. 99. The Hebrew phrase *Eretz Yisrael* means the "land of Israel."

Shortly after Alkali's effort to promote such resettlement efforts, Baron Edmund James de Rothschild began to take an active interest in Jewish resettlement of Palestine by supporting significant land purchases and assisting Jewish reclamation of the land by means of agricultural settlements. With Rothschild's help, Jews who immigrated to Palestine were able to secure rights to property through long-term leases which made it practical for them to invest enormous energies in reclaiming the land and making it agriculturally productive. Rothschild's interest and extensive financial support began to change the odds for Jewish reclamation of the ancient land of their ancestors from the status of "slim to none" as had been the case for centuries and moving them into the realm of possibility.

This small group of immigrants was soon joined by those of the "first wave of Jewish immigration" of 1882–1903 which was prompted by "the Russian pogroms of 1881–1882."[166] Because of harsh conditions in the land and onerous Turkish taxation, coupled with growing hostility from the Arabs, fully half of the 35,000 settlers who made up the First Aliyah[167] eventually returned to Europe.[168] Those who remained, however, were steeled in their determination to reclaim their right to the land of Israel. Additionally, a steady stream of new immigrants added to the total Jewish population in Palestine. These early resettlement efforts produced a Jewish majority in the population of Jerusalem by the end of the nineteenth century.[169] The 1918 census confirmed that Jews "formed the largest community in Jerusalem."[170] The increasing numbers of Jews who had immigrated to the Holy Land set the stage for the restoration of the nation of Israel in the land of Israel.

## From Ephemeral Vision to Concrete Substance

The intense work of both Christian Restorationists and the original Zionists had not only visionary aspects but practical applications as well. This was especially true of those who lobbied in the halls of

166 Bank, p. 99.

167 Bank, p. 99. Bank notes that there were five *Aliyahs* in total that occurred as the Jewish settlement of Palestine unfolded.

168 Bank, p. 99.

169 Arthur Lourie, "Palestine Under the British Mandate (1918–1948)" in *A History of Israel and the Holy Land*, Michael Avi-Yonan, ed. (New York: The Continuum International Publishing Group, 2003), p. 322.

170 Roberto Mazza, *Jerusalem: From the Ottomans to the British* (New York: I.B. Tauris & Co., 2009), p. 40.

government in both Britain and the United States. One such meeting that was to have profound impact on establishing the cause of Jewish national restoration as something that could reasonably be accomplished occurred when Chaim Weizmann met with Arthur James Balfour, the foreign secretary of the United Kingdom. When Balfour suggested that the Jews settle for a state in Uganda, Weizmann responded, "Mr. Balfour, supposing I was to offer you Paris instead of London, would you take it?" Balfour said, "But Dr. Weizmann, we have London," to which Weizmann responded, "That is true, but we had Jerusalem when London was a marsh." This exchange prompted Balfour to ask, "Are there many Jews who think like you?" Weizmann assured the Foreign Secretary, "I believe I speak the mind of millions of Jews," prompting Balfour to exclaim, "If that is so, you will one day be a force."[171]

Weizmann's relationship with Balfour had begun much earlier in 1905, and their interactions continued for years. It was propitious for Weizmann that, as a chemist, he had invented a new process for producing acetone, one of the key ingredients in cordite, an important military propellant that facilitated the British army's execution of World War I.[172] This fact alone had opened doors for Weizmann to then British minister of munitions, David Lloyd George, who later became Britain's prime minister. Lloyd George recalled a meeting he had had with Weizmann in 1916 wherein the Jewish inventor and Zionist "explained his aspirations as to the repatriation of the Jews to the sacred land they had made famous." Their conversation was to be "the fount and origin of the famous declaration about the National Home for the Jews in Palestine," said Lloyd George, for "as soon as I became Prime Minister, I talked the whole matter over with Mr. Balfour."[173]

These and other behind-the-scenes activities eventually elicited the issuance of what came to be called the Balfour Declaration, which was actually a letter written by James Balfour to Walter Rothschild on November 2, 1917, for transmission to the Zionist Federation of Great

---

[171] Chaim Weizmann, *Trial and Error: The Autobiography of Chaim Weizmann* (Westport, CT: Greenwood Publishing Group, 1972), p. 111.

[172] James Wei, *Great Inventions that Changed the World* (Hoboken, NJ: John Wiley & Sons, 2012), p. 177. Weitzmann developed a process for "producing acetone through bacterial fermentation of starch."

[173] David Lloyd George, *Memoirs of the Peace Conference* (New Haven, CT: Yale University Press, 1939), vol. II, pp. 724–734.

Britain and Ireland. This document made the following momentous statement: "His Majesty's government view with favour the establishment in Palestine of a national home for the Jewish people, and will use their best endeavours to facilitate the achievement of this object, it being clearly understood that nothing shall be done which may prejudice the civil and religious rights of existing non-Jewish communities in Palestine, or the rights and political status enjoyed by Jews in any other country."[174] The Balfour Declaration of 1917 became the foundation for the 1922 League of Nations Covenant for Palestine and its Mandate to Britain, which, in turn, was the basis for the November 29, 1947, United Nations Resolution 181 that called for the establishment of the Jewish state in Palestine and set the stage for the Declaration of the Statehood of Israel on May 14, 1948.[175]

In reality, however, neither the United Nations Resolution, the League of Nations Covenant for Palestine, the British Mandate, the Balfour Declaration, nor any other document or action by individuals, nations, or groups of nations created the nation of Israel. This action had been accomplished by the hand of God over three millennia before that time when the Almighty summoned the Israelites from the land of Egypt and joined with them in a covenant that formed the people of Israel into the nation of Israel. Then, it was the God of Israel who brought the people and nation of Israel to the land that he had promised to Abraham, Isaac, and Jacob where he established his "holy nation" on irrevocable promises. The growing Jewish *aliyah* and the emergence of a new nation of Jews, therefore, were not to be the result of international altruism. It was not the product of political or military machinations. What had happened and what would happen was to be solely the work of the Almighty to fulfill the divine destiny of his Chosen People! God himself, the God of Israel, had been and would be the architect of the amazing, the author of the impossible. He alone had orchestrated and would continue to orchestrate the interactions of millions of characters and the intersection of thousands of incidents that would produce what was completely unattainable but utterly inevitable. The Restorationist and Zionist dream was gradually

---

[174] Alex Bein, *The Jewish Question: Biography of a World Problem* (Madison, NJ: Fairleigh Dickinson University Press, 1990), p. 692.

[175] Howard Grief, *The Legal Foundation and Borders of Israel Under International Law: A Treatise on Jewish Sovereignty over the Land of Israel* (Jerusalem, Israel: Mazo Publishers, 2008), pp. 136–147. May 14, 1948, was chosen as the date for the Israeli Declaration of Independence because the League of Nations Covenant for Palestine and its Mandate to the British expired at midnight on on the previous day.

moving toward ultimate reality as God used human instruments to fulfill divine purposes, but it was the hand of God that was doing what was impossible for humans to achieve.

## Ultimate Tragedy Looming Ahead

Amazing and even miraculous events had occurred in the international Jewish community for most of the nineteenth and early twentieth centuries. Four centuries of enlightened Christian support for the resurrection of the Jewish nation had begun to bear practical fruit. The spirit of *aliyah* had seized upon growing numbers of the Jewish people in what was more than a desperate attempt to escape persecution. For them, restored Israel was more than an escape mechanism. It was a rebirth, a resurrection, a renewal of ancient promises. In fact, what is called the First Aliyah was defined by the goal of "the political, national, and spiritual resurrection of the Jewish people in Palestine."[176] What Christians could only dream about, Jews accomplished by returning to the land of their ancestors and beginning the arduous tasks of reclaiming and renewing that land. In this milieu, "the image of the romantic pioneer, the hard-working agricultural colonist, the brawny Jewish farmer" answered the long-standing Gentile caricature of the Jews as "mere parasites, racially incapable of 'productive' labor."[177] Operating within the parameters of a renewed concern for the welfare of the Jewish people in ecclesiastical and political circles, there was hope for good things to come. Surely visions of Jewish restoration to their native land were about to be fulfilled.

By the time of the rise of the Nazi Party in Germany, however, Judaeophobia and antisemitism had come to cloud the vision and sensitivities of far too many in world governments as well as in far too many parts of the Christian church. This did not bode well for the Jewish people anywhere in the world and in particular for those who were trapped in Germany and Europe when the doors for immigration into Britain and America were finally slammed shut. What had been on track for nearly four centuries was suddenly derailed. Conspiracy after conspiracy was launched in the halls of Western governments to close every avenue of escape for the Jewish people from the confines of

[176] Mitchell Geoffrey Bard and Moshe Schwartz, *One Thousand and One Facts Everyone Should Know about Israel* (Lanham, MD: Rowman & Littlefield Publishers, 2005), p. 14.

[177] Allon Gal, ed., *Envisioning Israel: The Changing Ideals and Images of North American Jews* (Jerusalem: The Magnes Press, 1996), p. 41.

Europe where the cruelest, most diabolical tragedy in human history awaited them.

Lawrence Epstein described the situation both accurately and succinctly: "The Zionists were completely and presciently correct about the principal moral reasons why a state for the Jews was needed. There was a deadly 'racial' hatred of the Jews charging through history and aiming right at them. The Zionists were frighteningly correct in their assessment of the dangers the Jews faced. Not only was hatred of the Jews loose in the world, but soon there would be no escape from it. After the 1924 immigration act in the United States, there would be no remaining haven for Jews in trouble."[178] The voices of conscience that had sounded the alarm of impending doom for the Jewish people were soon drowned out in vociferous promotions of nationalism and isolationism, based on economic despair, fear, and impending manifest evil. The ultimate catastrophe was on the horizon.

[178] Lawrence J. Epstein, "The Moral Case of Zionism: If Both Jews and Palestinian Arabs Start Their Historical Narrative with Beginning of Zionism, Jews Have Deeper Moral Claim to Land of Israel," in *Israel Opinion*, April 17, 2014, p. 1, posted at http://www.ynetnews.com/articles/0,7340,L-4509231,00.html.

CHAPTER 8

# THE HOLOCAUST

## ANTISEMITISM'S "FINAL SOLUTION"

Judaeophobia, anti-Judaism, and antisemitism were first documented in history in the diabolical schemes of Haman, the prime minister of the Persian kingdom of Xerxes the Great. Then, all of these pathologies were manifest in the remnants of the Grecian Empire by Antiochus IV Epiphanes, who sought to stamp out Judaism by imposing Hellenism upon the Jews.[1] Later, they influenced the Roman Empire to react violently against the inextinguishable yearning of the Jewish heart for liberty and self-determination. Finally, they came to characterize much of the Christian church,[2] the organism which had emerged from the matrix of biblical and Second Temple Judaism but then all too quickly had lost its bearings and had turned against the Jewish people in a psychosis of fratricidal carnage wherein the church of Jesus despised and abused the family of Jesus.

Sadly, the Haman spirit sprayed its venom far and wide, especially throughout Christian Europe so that, for a thousand years, Europeans engaged in religiously excused, even religiously endorsed, persecution and violence against the Jews. In decade after decade and in nation after nation across the European continent, the Jewish people were subjected to decidedly

[1] The antisemitic actions of Antiochus were perhaps more insidious than other overt and frontal attacks on Judaism and the Jewish people, for initially his efforts were designed to create a syncretism between Hellenism and Judaism. When this failed, however, he viciously sought to impose Hellenism upon the Jewish people, polluting the temple by offering swine on its altar in homage to Zeus and killing significant numbers of the Jews. See Mark Adam Elliott, *The Survivors of Israel: A Reconsideration of the Theology of Pre-Christian Judaism* (Grand Rapids, MI: Wm. B. Eerdmans Publishing Co., 2000), p. 192.

[2] These three dynamics of disdain for the Jews and their faith gradually gained control of much, if not most, of Christianity. The first to be manifest was *Judaeophobia*, wherein early leaders of the church feared debate with the more learned Jewish rabbis and sought to ingrain an almost morbid fear of legalism in the hearts of their constituents in order to combat the perceived threat that the rabbis would somehow convert them to Judaism. Second, an ever-increasing *anti-Judaism* began to invade Christianity, with church leaders attacking the Jewish faith as being antiquated and superseded by Christian faith. Ultimately, full-blown *antisemitism* appeared when Christians began to hate Jews themselves and to seek to do them emotional and physical harm.

unchristian attitudes and actions that kept them under constant fear of the next spark that would ignite another mob action. Violence, mayhem, and murder against Jews were systematic and unrelenting as "Christian" nations, often encouraged by "Christian" clerics, incited the masses to rain down terror upon the Jewish communities among them. Sadly, Christian holy days came to be the most terrifying times of the year for the Jewish people!

This millennium-long, Christian-endorsed persecution of the Jews would not reach its nadir until the twentieth century. Ironically, this was the century when the long-anticipated utopia of modernity had been expected to manifest itself and bring a seismic change in the human situation.[3] This was to be the age when the evolution of the human species would finally produce the peace and prosperity that philosophers thought the essential nature of humanity would unquestionably produce. Secular humanists were convinced that the evolving physical, intellectual, emotional, and social makeup of humankind could not help but actualize the utopian dream.[4] It was inevitable, and it was close at hand!

Whereas in the Middle Ages antisemitism had been based largely on religion, it took on a new and even more treacherous form in the post-Enlightenment era, basing itself in "science" or, more accurately, in two pseudosciences. First was the "scientific study of race," which drew support from anthropology and a philosophy of racial difference. Jonathan Sacks explains: "Different races had different civilisational attributes and these could be traced by physical markers, such as the color of a person's skin or shape of the nose."[5] At the same time, "the other pseudo-science was the curious hybrid of biology and sociology known as social Darwinism" which argued that "the evolution of society followed the same laws as the evolution of species."[6] In this schema, "Nature is a battleground in which the ruthless survive and the weak perish. So is human history. The strong prevail; the weak die and disappear. There is nothing moral or immoral about this process. It

[3] James K. Dew, *Science and Theology: An Assessment of Alister McGrath's Critical Realist Perspective* (Eugene, OR: Wipf and Stock Publishers, 2011), p. ix.

[4] Modernity was based on the idea that the human race was constantly evolving, ever improving in and of itself, and moving inexorably toward a utopia of universal peace. The foundations of modernity came crashing down in the twentieth century with two world wars, the development of nuclear weapons of mass destruction, and the unthinkable Holocaust. Over 68 million soldiers and civilians were killed in the two world wars, and over 6 million Jews, including over one million children, were murdered in the Holocaust. These horrific events proved that humanity had not evolved either physically, mentally, emotionally, or socially. If anything, it seemed to be devolving! In reality, nothing had changed in the nature of human beings. Only technology had made possible more massive manifestations of human depravity.

[5] Jonathan Sacks, *Future Tense: Jews, Judaism, and Israel in the Twenty-first Century* (New York: Schocken Books, 2009), p. 100.

[6] Sacks, p. 100.

is simply how things are."[7] This climate of irrational Enlightenment "rationalism" and "scientific" pseudoscience stripped antisemitism of its inherent religious element (at least in the minds of secularists, agnostics, and atheists) and transmogrified it into an even more insidious form. While some elements of the German church openly supported the Nazis or acquiesced to them, and while the church in general (including Roman Catholicism) raised little protest against the Third Reich, the antisemitism that resulted in the Holocaust was not a Christian invention. Instead, it was "carried out for the purpose of a Neopagan, modernist, progressive, racial Darwinist agenda." Though Christians participated to varying degrees in the Holocaust, "this agenda was not itself defined primarily in theological terms."[8] In the end, United Nations Secretary General Antonio Guterres said it well when he concluded that "it would be a dangerous error to think of the Holocaust as simply the result of the insanity of a group of criminal Nazis. On the contrary, the Holocaust was the culmination of millennia of hatred and discrimination targeting the Jews—what we now call anti-Semitism."[9]

At the turn of the twentieth century, Europe was embroiled in the constant warfare that had characterized its entire recorded history. The Europeans were a bellicose people. Across the landscape of time, the bloodletting between competing the European nations and factions was incessant. Nothing could seem to prevent them from attacking one another. Since the first century AD, at least 417 wars had been fought on European soil. Then, by 1914, ten more wars had been fought in the twentieth century. Finally, the war came that everyone believed would be the "war to end all wars," the Great War,[10] which drew into its conflict not only most European nations but also other countries from around the world. Because of new military inventions such as machine guns, grenades, tanks, aircraft, and chemical weapons, this conflict resulted in the loss of more than 20 million lives. Death from warfare swept across Europe on a scale that had never been seen before as the Western Entente Powers of France, Britain, and Russia met the Triple Alliance made up of Germany, Austria-Hungary, and Italy in a fight to the finish. In the end, the defeated and dispirited German people bore

[7] Sacks, p. 100.

[8] Robert W. Bleakney, personal communication. Bleakney notes Cuthbert Carson Mann, *Hitler's Three Struggles: The Neo-Pagan Revenge* (Chicago, IL: Chicago Spectrum Pr., 1995).

[9] Antonio Guterres, United Nations Secretary-General, "Secretary-General's Remarks at Observance of the International Day of Commemoration in Memory of the Victims of the Holocaust," 27 January 2017, posted at https://www.un.org/sg/en/content/sg/statement/2017-01-27/secretary-generals-remarks-observance-international-day. Guterres has spoken kindly in support of Israel; however, as leader of the UN, his positions and actions vis-à-vis Israel are often ambivalent at best.

[10] With the advent of World War II, the Great War came to be called World War I.

the brunt of blame for the conflict, and they were severely punished by enforced disarmament, demands for reparations and other economic strictures. In 1933, after years of ever deepening economic hardships, the German people were fully ripe for the ascent of Adolf Hitler and the great tragedy that was to follow.[11]

## Blame the Jews

In order to advance his autocratic agenda, Hitler needed a scapegoat on which to blame the woes of post-war Germany, and an easy target was readily available, one that had been blamed for virtually every malady in the last ten centuries of European history. Hitler used the same scapegoat that he had already attacked in *Mein Kampf*, his personal memoir: he targeted the Jews.[12] This tactic had been used repeatedly throughout the Middle Ages and beyond, so it was very simple to employ it again.[13] Hitler, however, took antisemitism to extremes never imagined by anyone in the history of the world.[14] He planned, plotted, and began the implementation of his *Endlösung der Judenfrage* (Final Solution to the Jewish Question)[15] which, if it had been completely successful, would have resulted in the total annihilation of the entire Jewish population of Europe and perhaps of the world. Inspired by an idiosyncratic reinterpretation of plays by Ibsen, Hitler "decreed a war against the Jews to override all else"[16] in an effort to fulfill his

[11] Samuel Totten and Stephen Feinberg, eds., "Teaching and Studying the Holocaust: Curricular Issues, Teaching Strategies, and Learning Activities," in *Essentials of Holocaust Education: Fundamental Issues and Approaches*, (Abingdon, UK: Routledge, 2016), p. 68, n. 1. Totten and Feinberg note that "in the 19th century . . . religious antisemitism evolved, in many quarters, into political antisemitism, which ultimately influenced Adolf Hitler. Over time, traditional religious antisemitism and political antisemitism morphed, at least in the hands of the Nazis and their collaborators, into racial antisemitism." For an exhaustive history of the manner in which antisemitism evolved into the Holocaust, see also Lucy S. Dawidowicz, *The War Against the Jews: 1933–1945* (New York: Open Road Integrated Media, 1975).

[12] Sarah Ann Gordon, *Hitler, Germans, and the "Jewish Question"* (Princeton, NJ: Princeton University Press, 1984), p. 134.

[13] Martin Collier, Bill Marriott, and Rosemary Rees, *Colonisation and Conflict 1750–1990* (Oxford, UK: Heinemann Educational Publishers, 2002), p. 176.

[14] Richard Weikart, *Hitler's Ethic: The Nazi Pursuit of Evolutionary Progress* (New York: Palgrave Macmillan, 2009); Richard Weikart, *From Darwin to Hitler: Evolutionary Ethics, Eugenics, and Racism in Germany* (New York: Palgrave Macmillan, 2004); and Lukman Harees, *The Mirage of Dignity on the Highways of Human 'Progress': The Bystanders' Perspective* (Bloomington, IN: AuthorHouse, 2012), p. 296.

[15] The German phrase *Endlösung der Judenfrage* was actually a euphemism designed to disguise the true nature of the Third Reich's intention, which was simply the genocide through systematic extermination of the entire Jewish population of Europe. Donald Bloxham, *The Final Solution: A Genocide* (Oxford, UK: Oxford University Press, 2009).

[16] Steven F. Sage, *Ibsen and Hitler: The Plagiarist, the Poet, and the Plot for the Third Reich* (New York: Carroll & Graf Publishers, 2006), p. 317. Sage does a brilliant job of demonstrating that Hitler drew upon Henrik Ibsen's plays, *Emperor and Galilean, The Masterbuilder, and An Enemy of the People*, for his lifelong obsession with the quest for the genocide of the Jews. Also Robert W. Bleakney, "Hitler's Mindset for Mass Murder: A Review of Books by Steven F. Sage and Richard Weikart," *Restore!*, vol. 17, no. 4, Issue 62.

longstanding obsession with the genocide of the Jews.

The Führer argued that everything that had occurred in Germany after World War I had been the fault of the Jews. He deemed "Jewish journalists to be a seminal factor in Germany's interwar malaise."[17] The Nazis carefully orchestrated the libel against the Jews, whom they "blamed for every ill: the loss of the war, the *Diktat* of Versailles, and the inflation, from which Jews were said to have profiteered."[18] Indeed, the Weimar Republic, which had been instituted in Germany at the end of World War I, had come to be known as the "Jew Republic."[19] At the same time, "the influx of eastern Jews, who were looked on as aliens and suspected of swindling" was "fantastically exaggerated in the anti-Jewish propaganda."[20]

All of the Jewish people "were suspected of ties with Communism, which was commonly referred to as 'Jewish Bolshevism.'"[21] No matter what the problem may have been, the Jews were its cause, and they were responsible for it! Anything that was perceived to be evil was blamed on the Jewish people. "If capitalism was bad, Jewish capitalism . . . was worse. . . . If socialism was bad, Jewish-led socialism was infinitely more damnable."[22] Whatever could be warped or twisted to the advantage of the Nazis was used to make Hitler's program for the eradication of the Jewish people more palatable to the German people. As had been the case throughout history, the Jewish people were once again set up as the "default scapegoats" for every ill in society, and they continued to be the victims of "Christian paranoia by proxy."[23] This disorder was being fanned to a frenzy as the Nazis used Christians to advance an occult, neopagan agenda that was rife with racial Darwinism and radically perverse eugenics philosophy.

If Hitler and the Nazi party had not used the Jews as scapegoats, they likely would never have succeeded in gaining control of German society. "How did [Hitler], mediocre in so many ways, so quickly attract to his standard" such a cross section of German society? Edward Flannery concluded that "the one catalyst that above all else enabled him to reconcile

[17] Paul Reitter, *The Anti-Journalist: Karl Kraus and Jewish Self-Fashioning* in *Fin-de-Siècle Europe* (Chicago, IL: The University of Chicago Press, 2008), p. 32.

[18] Edward Flannery, *The Anguish of the Jews: Twenty-Three Centuries of Antisemitism* (Mahwah, NJ: Paulist Press, 2004), p. 206.

[19] Flannery, p. 207.

[20] Flannery, p. 206.

[21] Flannery, p. 207.

[22] Bruce F. Pauley, *From Prejudice to Persecution: A History of Austrian Anti-Semitism* (Chapel Hill, NC: The University of North Carolina Press, 1992), p. 319.

[23] Daniel Rancour-Laferriere, *The Sign of the Cross: From Golgotha to Genocide* (Piscataway, NJ: Transaction Publishers, 2011), p. 217.

oppositions and finally transform Germany from a liberal republic into a totalitarian state in a single decade was his anti-semitism."[24] Indeed, in Nazi Germany, the "ultimate limit of antisemitism—as an *ersatz* religion—was reached."[25] Daniel Goldhagen confirmed this fact: "The German people were more dangerously oriented towards Jews than they had been during any other time since the dawn of modernity," and this orientation was easily transformed by the Nazis into "eliminationist antisemitism."[26] Because antisemitism was much more intense in Germany than it was elsewhere in Europe, when the Nazis came to power, Germans, "equipped with little more than the cultural notions current in their country, would easily become genocidal executioners."[27]

## At All Cost, Kill the Jews!

Transforming Jews into caricatures was the order of the day as the Nazi party rose to power in Germany. Their Final Solution to the Jewish Question, however, was not just caricature or social isolation: it was extermination, the complete genocide of the people group that had been derogated, derided, despised, and persecuted in Europe for nearly a thousand years. Christopher Browning observes that "Nazi Jewish policy escalated rapidly from the pre-war policy of forced emigration to the Final Solution . . . the systematic attempt to murder every last Jew within the German grasp."[28] In the end, the Nazis considered Jews to be vermin, subhuman creatures that deserved to be exterminated for the public good.[29] So Hitler and his cohorts launched a well-planned, well-organized, and systematically implemented program that was designed to ensure the complete liquidation of all the Jewish people—men,

[24] Flannery, p. 209.

[25] Flannery, p. 211.

[26] Daniel J. Goldhagen, *Hitler's Willing Executioners: Ordinary Germans and the Holocaust* (New York: Random House, 1996), pp. 463–466.

[27] Goldhagen, p. 185.

[28] Christopher Browning, *The Origins of the Final Solution: The Evolution of Nazi Jewish Policy, September 1939–March 1942* (Lincoln, NE: The University of Nebraska Press, 2007), p. x.

[29] Christopher R. Browning, "The German Bureaucracy and the Holocaust," in *Genocide, Critical Issues of the Holocaust: A Companion Volume to the Film "Genocide,"* Alex Grobman and Daniel Landes, eds. (West Orange, NJ: Behrman House, 1983), p. 148. Also Caroline Alice Wiedmer, *The Claims of Memory: Representations of the Holocaust in Contemporary Germany and France* (Ithaca, NY: Cornell University Press, 1999), p. 3. Wiedmer notes that "vermin such as spiders and rats were the common figures for Jews in Nazi propaganda, and the German populace was supposed to define the Jews as inhuman and parasitic, as vermin to be feared and ultimately destroyed—robbed of all personal belongings and put into gas chambers to be exterminated with pesticide." Referencing Hans J. Massaquoi, *Destined to Witness: Growing Up Black in Nazi Germany* (New York: William Morrow and Company, 2001), Bleakney notes that Nazis also "considered dark Africans to be more like horses—racial inferiors who should be subjugated but who did not represent a threat to Aryan survival as long as racial intermixing was avoided."

women, and children—in Europe. The ultimate goal was a *Judenrein*[30] Europe, with the Jewish population entirely eradicated.

On November 9, 1938, this Nazi plan for the extermination of the Jews was launched in a four-day pogrom that came to be called *Kristallnacht* ("Crystal Night" or the "Night of Broken Glass").[31] In this and the ensuing days, a hundred Jews were killed, and 30,000 were arrested and placed in concentration camps, while over 1,000 synagogues were burned and over 7,000 Jewish businesses were damaged or destroyed.[32] On the last day of the *Kristallnacht* riots, Joseph Goebbels, the Nazi Reich Minister of Propaganda, attributed the events to the German people's "healthy instincts," noting that "the German people are anti-Semitic. It has no desire to have its rights restricted or to be provoked in the future by parasites of the Jewish race."[33] Dehumanizing language such as this was designed to make the Nazis' program for the genocide of the Jews more acceptable to the German people. And it worked.

In organized and well-coordinated efforts, the German *Schutzstaffel* (SS) and the *Gestapo* raided Jewish homes in Germany and Austria and imprisoned the Jews in German concentration camps in Dachau, Buchenwald, and Sachsenhausen. Then, in Lithuania, Russia, Ukraine, and Poland, they herded Jewish families into killing zones where they were shot and dumped into long, trench-like mass graves.[34] This liquidation process was begun several years before the infamous crematoria were ever built.[35] During this operation, mobile firing squads called *Einsatzgruppen* killed an estimated 1.3 million Jews.[36] When Heinrich Himmler, *Reichsführer* of the SS,[37] heard of complaints from firing-squad executioners who were being repulsed

[30] The German word *Judenrein* means "clean of Jews." Another German word which was used to describe the actions of the Nazis against the Jews was *Judenfrei*, meaning "free of Jews."

[31] *Kristallnacht* was also called *Pogromnacht* ("Pogrom Night"). The term *Kristallnacht* was applied to this event because of the millions of shards of broken glass that littered the streets in German and Austrian cities after the windows of Jewish stores, buildings, and synagogues were smashed in that night of terror produced by Nazi-led paramilitary forces and civilians.

[32] Michael Berenbaum and Arnold Kramer, *The World Must Know* (Washington, DC: United States Holocaust Memorial Museum, 1993), p. 49.

[33] Joseph Goebbels, quoted in *The Daily Telegraph,* November 12, 1938, cited in Martin Gilbert, *Kristallnacht: Prelude to Destruction* (New York: Harper Collins, 2006), p. 142.

[34] James R. Norton, *The Holocaust: Jews, Germany, and the National Socialists* (New York: The Rosen Publishing Group, 2008), p. 33. Also, Patrick Desbois, *The Holocaust by Bullets: A Priest's Journey to Uncover the Truth Behind the Murder of 1.5 Million Jews* (New York: Palgrave Macmillan, 2008). Desbois documents the murder of Jews by firing squads in virtually every village across Eastern Europe.

[35] Avraham Burg, *The Holocaust Is Over; We Must Rise from Its Ashes* (New York: Palgrave Macmillan, 2008), p. 15.

[36] Norton, p. 33.

[37] The German term *Schutzstaffel* meant "Protective Squadron." At first,the SS served as Hitler's personal bodyguards. In time, however, it grew to one of the most powerful and feared organizations in Nazi Germany.

by the fact that they were required to murder unarmed men, women, and children, he decided that other, more efficient means had to be developed for killing Jews.[38] In 1941, the Nazis experimented with loading Jews into rear compartments of mobile vans, driving them to places prepared for their execution, then introducing carbon monoxide gas from engine exhaust into those compartments in order to asphyxiate the Jews, and finally throwing the Jewish bodies into mass graves and burying them with bulldozers.

It became increasingly clear to the SS, however, that an even more efficient killing system was needed if the goal of exterminating all of Europe's Jews was to be realized. In order to implement their Final Solution, the Nazis built concentration camps in Poland and equipped them with gas chambers and crematoria designed for mass murder. The first opened at Chelmno in December, 1941, followed by others in Belzec, Sobidor, Treblinka, Auschwitz, and Birkenau. All of these death camps became infamous for their killing efficiency. In Birkenau alone, up to 6,000 Jews were murdered daily. The Nazis also made use of Europe's rail systems, herding the Jews whom they had arrested in France, Belgium, Italy, the Netherlands, and other nations into cattle cars and transporting them to the killing centers.[39]

Hitler and the leading Nazis were utterly consumed by a maniacal obsession for ridding Europe of all Jews. Daniel Goldhagen notes that during this period of time, "the exterminationist option of the eliminationist anti-Jewish program was given priority over other German goals."[40] Hannah Arendt has observed that "Hitler could rejoice even in the midst of military setbacks over the extermination of the Jews and the establishment of death factories."[41] Even when it was clear that the Nazis had lost the war, they continued to service the killing centers in their determined march toward the genocide of all European Jews. Trains transporting troops to the front lines were shunted onto sidings to avoid delaying other trains that were delivering Jews to the death camps. Then, when transportation systems became scarce, Jewish victims were force-marched to the killing centers.[42] The Nazis considered the Final Solution to be more important than winning the war. This strategy reflected

---

[38] Yitzhak Arad, *Belzec, Sobidor, Treblinka: The Operation Reinhard Death Camps* (Bloomington, IN: Indiana University Press, 1987), p. 379.

[39] Paul Azous, *In the Plains of the Wilderness* (Jerusalem, Israel: Mazo Publishers, 2006), p. 146.

[40] Goldhagen, p. 158.

[41] Hannah Arendt, *The Origins of Totalitarianism* (Orlando, FL: Harcourt-Brace, Inc., 1968), p. 442.

[42] Suzette Cotte, *Criminological Theories: Bridging the Past to the Future* (Thousand Oaks, CA: Sage Publications, 2002), p. 37. Cotte notes that "the forced marches of camp inhabitants over hundreds of miles in the last days of the war were meant to kill Jews, even though the guards knew that the German war effort was lost." Also, see the website: http://www.scetv.org/education/holocaust_forum/contents/lesson_6.cfm.

not only the ultimate insanity of the leaders of the Third Reich but also that of thousands of ordinary German citizens who supported and manned the death camps.[43] The Nazi sociopaths orchestrated the death of six million Jews, including more than one million children. This was the Holocaust[44] of staggering and unprecedented proportions, the *Shoah*[45] that came very close to the total annihilation of European Jewry. Raul Hilberg succinctly summed up the unfolding of this awful tragedy of antisemitism: "The missionaries of Christianity had said in effect: You have no right to live among us as Jews. The secular rulers who followed had proclaimed: You have no right to live among us. The German Nazis at last decreed: You have no right to live."[46] As Goldhagen has observed, the eliminationist antisemitism that had been endemic in German society since the nineteenth century evolved into the exterminationist antisemitism of the twentieth century.[47]

## Blood-Stained Hands in Britain and the United States

While Nazi Germany bears full responsibility for the Holocaust and its atrocities, antisemitism in Great Britain and the United States played significant roles first in not preventing the Holocaust altogether and then in not saving millions of Jewish lives by facilitating their emigration from Germany and Eastern Europe to the West. In a very real way, rampant antisemitism in both the British Foreign Secretary's Office and the US State Department conspired against those Jews who found themselves in the path of the Nazi *blitzkrieg* by making it virtually impossible for them to escape the Holocaust.

[43] Even when leaders of the Third Reich ordered local commanders to desist from the brutality against the Jews in an effort to achieve better surrender terms from the allied armies, those commanders continued with the atrocities. See Cotte, p. 47. With this in mind, Cotte observed that "the destruction of the Jews did not derive from structures of higher authority but from the close and cruel handiwork of thousands of ordinary Germans operating within an exterminationist anti-Semitic culture."

[44] The word *Holocaust* is from the Greek word *holókaustos*, meaning "burnt whole." The Greek term originally was a translation of the Hebrew word *'olah*, the "whole burnt offering" (*korban 'olah* in the Hebrew Scriptures), which was an animal sacrifice that was completely burned.

[45] The Hebrew word *sho'ah* means "the catastrophe" or "devastation." In Scripture the word is translated "waste" (Job 30:3). Many Jewish scholars have maintained the term *Shoah* is to be preferred over the word *Holocaust* as a description of the Nazis' genocide of the Jews because the Hebrew word *holocaust* implies a "burnt offering to God" and in no way can the six million who died be considered to be a "burnt offering to God." Walter Laqueur rightly argued, "It was not the intention of the Nazis to make a sacrifice of this kind and the position of the Jews was not that of a ritual victim." Walter Laqueur, quoted in Richard Evans, *In Hitler's Shadow: West German Historians and the Attempt to Escape from the Nazi Past* (New York: Pantheon Books, 1989), p. 142. Also Richard L. Rubenstein and John K. Roth, *Approaches to Auschwitz: The Holocaust and Its Legacy* (Louisville, KY: Westminster John Knox Press, 2003), p. 5.

[46] Raul Hilberg, *The Destruction of the European Jews* (New Haven, CT: Yale University Press, 1961), vol. 3, pp. 3ff.

[47] Goldhagen, p. 420.

Some voices in the West were raised against the persecution of the Jewish people during the time of the Holocaust; however, those raised by Christians and others were drowned out by the cacophony of self-serving arguments that were at bottom merely reiterations of ancient antisemitism. Hubert Locke is correct when he notes that "those who spoke out in the United States" against the Nazis and antisemitism "did so in a national climate of isolationism, racism, and antisemitism that made their views not only unpopular but, in many circles, unpatriotic."[48] Even the outcry of some British churches against the unfolding atrocities of the time "ended in futility," he adds. Voices raised against the antisemitism and Judaeophobia of both Britain and the United States were either silenced or ignored.

The US State Department and the British Foreign Secretariat were simply not nearly as concerned about the genocide of Europe's Jews as they were with winning the war with Germany; therefore, they were unwilling to allocate resources for addressing what was becoming a more and more obvious fact: that the Nazis were presiding over the systematic genocide of European Jews.[49] Allied aircraft that could have at least destroyed the railways leading to the death camps and perhaps even disabled their gas chambers and crematoria flew directly over those sites on their way to attacking military and industrial sites in German controlled territory.[50] When the Allies military units finally reached the death camps, they viewed firsthand the horrors; however, for millions of Jews, it was simply too late.

Decades before the time of Nazism, however, antisemitism in Western politics not only forestalled developments that could have mitigated against the Holocaust or perhaps have prevented it altogether but even nurtured the environment in which it emerged. Long before the rise of the Nazis, the League of Nations had promised the Jewish people a state in Palestine. In an action unanimously viewed as a sacred duty by the 51 nations that comprised

---

[48] Hubert G. Locke, *Learning from History: A Black Christian's Perspective on the Holocaust* (Westport, CT: Greenwood Press, 2000), p. 115.

[49] Richard Breitman and Allan J. Lichtman, *FDR and the Jews* (Cambridge, MA: Belknap Press, 2013), p. 2.

[50] George R. Lee, *Holocaust, Grades 5–8* (Quincy, IL: Mark Twain Media, 1998), p. 65. Lee notes that as early as 1942, "the Polish resistance sent reports about the genocide" of the Jews, urging "that railroads, gas chambers, and crematoria be bombed." Instead, he says, "the US military refused because it would divert aircraft from bombing military targets, and they thought the best way to help concentration camp inmates was quick victory in the war." Then, in 1944, after a very real problem of the difficulty of reaching targets in Poland had been solved, "the bombing was always postponed" despite "pleas from the World Jewish Congress." The excuses given for the Allies' inaction included that "such an attack would require great air support" and that "it might provoke even more vindictive action by the Germans" Actually, in August, 1944, "American bombers with fighter escorts flew over the railway to Auschwitz and bombed the synthetic rubber factory at Buna, five miles away. No bombs came near Auschwitz or its rail connections." At the same time, The British Royal Air Force "was more concerned about relations with Arab oil producers than the inmates of the camps."

the League of Nations, a Covenant for Palestine was created, and Britain was given this Mandate: "The Mandatory shall be responsible for placing the country [Palestine] under such political, administrative, and economic conditions as will secure the establishment of the Jewish National Home."[51] In its first draft in 1920, this Covenant was to have given Palestine[52] and the Transjordan, to the Jews.[53] In its final form in 1922, the Covenant prescribed that all of the land west of the Jordan River and the Golan Heights were to comprise "Jewish Palestine,"[54] while the eastern portion of the land, the Transjordan, would be designated as "Arab Palestine."

If the British had fulfilled the League of Nations Mandate between 1922 and 1933, virtually all of the Jews who died in the Holocaust could have immigrated into Palestine and escaped the killing machines of Eastern Europe.[55] Sabina Citron notes that "twenty years were wasted while the British played up to the Arabs. Even after the 1939 outbreak of World War II, there were still many possibilities to save the Jews of Europe. But even those ships with refugees from Europe were mercilessly turned away practically from the very shores of the Land! British perfidy knew no bounds!"[56] Additionally, for the first half of the twentieth century, antisemitism in both the British Foreign Secretariat and the United States State Department[57] was demonstrated in their refusal to

[51] Article 2 of the League of Nations Covenant for Palestine.

[52] Before 1948, the term *Palestinian* referred exclusively to Jews. Virtually all of the Muslims living in Palestine considered being called "Palestinian" an insult. They preferred to be called simply "Arabs."

[53] Charles River Editors, *Decoding the Conflict between Israel and the Palestinians: The History and Terms of the Middle East Peace Process* (Cambridge, MA: Create Space, 2013), p. 1970. This ebook notes that "The British Mandate for Palestine gave the British control over the lands that have since become Jordan, Israel, the West Bank, and the Gaza Strip. The terms of the British Mandate incorporated the language of the Balfour Declaration, recognizing the 'historical connection of the Jewish people with Palestine.' The British were also tasked by the League of Nations with creating a Jewish state, an action which the United States Congress also endorsed in 1922." It is ironic—yet absurd—that the British were somehow able to create the nations of Jordan and Iraq as homelands for Palestinian Arabs and yet, at the same time, were totally unable to create the Jewish homeland that the Covenant and Mandate required. It is also ironic that after 26 years of British dithering and Machiavellian manipulation failed to fulfill the mandate of the Covenant, the nation of Israel was born on the very next day after the British Mandate expired and still exists some seventy years since that time!

[54] Ze'ev Shemer, *Israel and the Palestinian Nightmare* (Bloomington, IN: iUniverse, 2010), p. 25. In 1923, the Golan Heights was ceded to Syria by the British even though it was part of the League of Nations Mandate.

[55] Alexander Zephyr, *State of Israel: Its Friends and Enemies: Prophetic Future* (Bloomington, IN: iUniverse, 2013), p. 58. Zephyr points out that "the State of Israel was not created because of the Holocaust." This conclusion is true because most of the 1948 Jewish population of Palestine had arrived there before the Holocaust and World War II began.

[56] Sabina Citron, *The Indictment* (Jerusalem: Gefen Publishing House, 2006), p. 149.

[57] Alan M. Kraut and Richard D. Breitman, "Anti-Semitism in the State Department, 1933–44: Four Case Studies," in *Anti-Semitism in American History*, David A. Gerber, ed. (Urbana, IL: The University of Illinois Press, 1986), pp. 150–174, and David S. Wyman, *The Abandonment of the Jews: America and the Holocaust*, 1941–1945 (New York: The New Press, 1998).

allow immigration of Jews into Britain and the United States respectively from Germany and Eastern Europe.

Alan Dershowitz says, "Even in the United States—historically among the least anti-Semitic nations in the world—the State Department was rife with anti-Semitism in the 1930s and the 1940s."[58] Regarding Britain, Dershowitz adds, "Great Britain was even worse, as evidenced by its active suppression during the war of documented information about the Holocaust and its adamant refusal to open Palestine to Jewish immigration."[59] Thomas Adam notes that "the late 1930s marked a high point in American antisemitism, and many US State Department officials, themselves antisemitic, refused to make full use of the quota allotments available to Germans. Notable among these antisemitic officials was Assistant Secretary of State Breckenridge Long, who ordered US consulates to hinder Jewish immigration as far as possible and who personally acted illegally to do so."[60] When World War II began, "Britain banned all emigration [including Jews] from Nazi-controlled territories." Then, in 1939, in order to pacify their Arab "allies,"[61] the British banned Jewish immigration into Palestine,[62] a policy they enforced rigorously.

That same year, the US State Department also forced 937 Jews, who were fleeing from the German Reich on the German transatlantic liner *St. Louis,* to return to Europe after they had landed in Cuba and awaited transfer to the US.[63] In 1942, after being refused entry into Palestine, all but two of the Jewish refugees from Romania who were on the ship *Struma* drowned when it sank in the Black Sea.[64] Even after the war ended, the British denied Holocaust survivors aboard the SS *Exodus 1947* entry into Palestine, only to change their minds when "the world

[58] Alan M. Dershowitz, *The Vanishing American Jew: In Search of Jewish Identity for the Next Century* (New York: Touchstone, 1997), p. 83.

[59] Dershowitz, p. 83.

[60] Thomas Adam, ed., *Germany and the Americas: Culture, Politics, and History* (Santa Barbara, CA: ABC-CLIO, Inc., 2005), p. 88.

[61] David M. Keithly, *The USA and the World* (Lanham, MD: Rowman & Littlefield Publishers, 2007), p. 101. Also, Irwin M. Berent, *Norfolk, Virginia: A Jewish History of the 20th Century* (Norfolk, VA: United Jewish Federation of Tidewater, 2001), p. 168.

[62] Robert Rozett and Shmuel Spector, eds., *Encyclopedia of the Holocaust* (Jerusalem, Israel: The Jerusalem Publishing House, 2000), p. 249. Also Patrick J. Hearden, *Architects of Globalism: Building a New World Order during World War Two* (Fayetteville, AR: The University of Arkansas Press, 2002), p. 136; Rebecca Boehling and Uta Larkey, *Life and Loss in the Shadow of the Holocaust: A Jewish Family's Untold Story* (Cambridge, UK: Cambridge University Press, 2011), p. 166; and Mati Alon, *Holocaust and Redemption* (Victoria, Canada: Trafford Publishing, 2003), p. 198.

[63] "U. S. Policy during the Holocaust: The Tragedy of the SS *St. Louis:* May 13–June 20, 1939," *Jewish Virtual Library*, posted at http://www.jewishvirtuallibrary.org/the-tragedy-of-s-s-st-louis.

[64] Edgar S. Marshall, *Israel: Current Issues and Historical Background* (Hauppauge, NY: Nova Science Publishers, 2002), p. 113.

saw that the Jews of the *Exodus* would rather die than be denied entry to their homeland."[65]

From 1941 onward, then, a "sudden reversal of US refugee policy during World War II had catastrophic consequences for Europe's Jews," for, until that time, "the Nazis had emphasized a policy of forcing Jews to emigrate, initially through social and economic pressures and later through widespread use of violence and terror."[66] James Ciment and John Radzilowski point to scholars who have argued that "Hitler turned to the 'Final Solution' of genocide after the continued failure of the forced emigration policy, due in large part to the international community's refusal to provide sanctuary to Jewish refugees."[67] If antisemitism had not been so pervasive in the West, especially in Britain and the United States, significant numbers of the six million Jews who died in the Holocaust might well have escaped the clutches of the Third Reich. If, however, Britain and the United States had not fought and defeated the Nazis, the complete genocide of European Jews might well have occurred.

Tragically, even with the League of Nations Covenant and Mandate[68] and the decisions of the United Nations to endorse the creation of the Jewish State of Israel, backhanded dealings prevented the implementation of those plans and created the regional and territorial circumstances that continue to plague the land of Israel to this day. First, the territory east of the Jordan

---

[65] Eugene Korn, *The Jewish Connection to Israel, the Promised Land: A Brief Introduction for Christians* (Woodstock, VT: Jewish Lights Publishing, 2008), p. 88.

[66] James Ciment and John Radzilowski, eds., *American Immigration: An Encyclopedia of Political, Social, and Cultural Change* (New York: Routledge, 2014), p. 217.

[67] Ciment and Radzilowski, p. 217.

[68] The League of Nations Covenant and Mandate of July 24, 1922, made this declaration: "Whereas recognition has thereby been given to the historical connection of the Jewish people with Palestine and to the grounds for reconstituting their national home in that country. . . . The Mandatory [Britain] shall be responsible for placing the country under such political, administrative, and economic conditions as will secure the establishment of the Jewish national home . . . and also for safeguarding the civil and religious rights of all the inhabitants of Palestine, irrespective of race and religion." Alan Baker, ed., *Israel's Rights as a Nation-State in International Diplomacy* (Jerusalem, Israel: Jerusalem Center for Public Affairs, 2011), p. 76. Also, see maps and commentary in the Appendices, pp. 423–42 of this volume. The original League of Nations Covenant for Palestine on April 24, 1920, had set aside all the land west of the Jordan River from Lebanon to Eilat and all the land of Transjordan east of the Jordan River (along with the Golan Heights) for a Jewish National Homeland. Then, on September 16, 1922, with the collusion of the British, the Mandatory was further modified by the Transjordan Memorandum, which annulled the articles of the original Covenant regarding the Jewish National Homeland in the territory east of the Jordan River, ceding control of Transjordan (modern Jordan) to Abdullah bin al-Hussein and the land further east to his brother, Faisal bin al-Hussein, as part of the newly created Iraq. In effect, the British carved away 77% of the land originally mandated for the Jewish National Homeland and created two emirates, one for Abdullah and the other for Faisal, to reward them for their support for the British against the remnants of the Ottoman Empire in World War I. Finally, December 23, 1923, the Paulet-Newcombe Agreement carved out the Golan Heights from the original Covenant and ceded it to Syria under the French Mandate. Ira M. Lapidus, *A History of Islamic Societies* (Cambridge, UK: Cambridge University Press, 1988), pp. 587–597.

River— Transjordan—was taken over by Abdullah Ibin al-Hussein and eventually became the Hashemite Kingdom of Jordan. Then, after Abdullah's forces killed unknown numbers of "Palestinian"[69] residents of Transjordan, many of the ones who remained in the East Bank were expelled to the West Bank. In the years to follow, this forced relocation set the stage for continuing political and social problems for the Israeli government and precipitated much suffering from terrorist actions against innocent Jewish civilians. The British Empire was bent on protecting its own interests in the Middle East and, as a result, it miserably failed in fulfilling the Mandate for Palestine that had been entrusted to it by the League of Nations Covenant for Palestine.

Except for the political machinations designed to further British colonialism, the entire land of Israel, including the West Bank that was later illegitimately annexed by Abdullah in 1949,[70] could well have been a place of refuge for millions of Jews who wished to escape the Nazi reign of terror. If even a small concession to the fulfillment of the Mandate had been made, most, if not all, of the Holocaust could have been avoided, and untold numbers of Jewish lives could have been spared. Israeli Prime Minister Benjamin Netanyahu stated a powerful truth when he retorted to the erroneous idea that the Holocaust somehow "produced" the nation of Israel by saying, "There are those who say that if the Holocaust had not occurred, the State of Israel would never have been established. But I say that if the State of Israel would have been established earlier, the Holocaust would not have occurred."[71]

The Western nations that were complicit in exercises to postpone the restoration of the nation of Israel and to restrict the emigration of Jews from Europe bear a significant responsibility for the extent of the Holocaust. When the British Foreign Secretary's office demonstrated its inherent antisemitism by closing Britain's doors to Jewish immigration and then manipulated the political scene in the Middle East to preclude Jewish emigration to that area, they effectively slammed the door shut on Germany and Eastern Europe and, whether knowingly

[69] Masses of Arabs, natives of Transjordan, would later be called "Palestinians" after they were expelled from Jordan in order to consolidate the "Hashemite Kingdom" that was created through Abdullah's complicity with Great Britain.

[70] Interestingly, when Abdullah annexed the West Bank, the only nations in the world that approved his actions were Great Britain and Pakistan.

[71] Benjamin Netanyahu, Foreign Policy Speech in June, 2009, quoted in Pieter Vermeulen, "The Novel Form and the Timing of the Nation," in *See Under: Shoah: Imagining the Holocaust with David Grossman*, Marc De Kesel, Bettine Siertsmea, and Katarzyna Szurmiak, eds. (Leiden, The Netherlands: Koninklijke Brill NV, 2014), p. 155.

or unknowingly, ensured that the killing machines would operate without any restraint. The United States Department of State also bears considerable responsibility because it denied Jewish immigration into the "Land of the Free." The Canadian government likewise considered calls from church leaders to facilitate Jewish immigration into that nation "an exercise in impractical idealism"[72] and refused to permit it. Endemic antisemitism in Western governments, therefore, kept the "Free World" from being free when it came to Jews.

## The Antisemitic Torahphobia of Stalinist Russia

While the actions of the British Foreign Secretariat and the US State Department that systematically prevented the emigration of Jews from Germany to either of those nations or to other nations, including Palestine, where they could have escaped the Holocaust were in most cases clearly antisemitic in nature, their actions did not come close to the level of antisemitism exhibited by Russia before, during, and after World War II. The antisemitism that had been inherent in the Russian Orthodox Church and in the Tsarist Regime for centuries was still evident during the Bolshevik revolution when, as Helen Fien points out, it was manifest in the battle cry of the White Russian army during its effort to destroy Bolshevism: "Beat the Jews and Save Russia."[73] Perhaps as a social reaction to the overt antisemitism in the Tzarist regime, antisemitism was officially outlawed in Bolshevik Russia. Though Jews had represented only 1.6% of the Bolshevik party in the 1917 Revolution that toppled the Czarist regime, apparently the Russian history of cultural and institutional antisemitism that had created the Pale of Settlement and supported the continuing pogroms against the Jewish people warranted the Bolshevik prohibition of antisemitism. This prohibition apparently worked to a significant degree in that it prompted pro-Bolshevik declarations from Jews like the Yiddish-American poet Abraham Liessin (who was not a Communist): "While in all the countries surrounding Bolshevik Russia anti-Semitism is fanned with increasingly infernal power . . . Bolshevik Russia presents an example of humaneness and justice, the like of

[72] Alan Davies and Marilyn F. Nefsky, *How Silent Were the Churches?: Canadian Protestantism and the Jewish Plight during the Nazi Era* (Waterloo, Canada: Wilfrid Laurier University Press, 1997), p. 129.

[73] Helen Fein, ed., *The Persisting Question: Sociological Perspectives and Social Contexts of Modern Antisemitism* (Berlin, Germany: Walter de Gruyter & Co, 1987), p. 385.

which the history of the Jewish Diaspora has never seen before."[74]

German philosopher and social scientist Friedrich Engels joined with Prussian-born philosopher, economist, and political theorist Karl Marx to develop and publish *The Communist Manifesto* in 1848.[75] Marx was of Jewish ancestry, even though he was converted to Christianity when he was six years old.[76] Following in Marxist theory was another man of Jewish ancestry, Vladimir Ilyich Ulyanov (Vladimir Lenin), who became the leader of the Bolshevik revolution and head of the Russian Republic in 1917 and the Soviet Union in 1922.[77] As a result of the involvement of Jews in the formation of Communism, the entire movement was vulnerable to the German antisemitic canard of "Judeo-Bolshevism."[78]

Dennis Prager points out an important aspect of the political and social theories of both Marx and Lenin: "It was a basic tenet of Marxism and Leninism that the Jews should disappear through assimilation."[79] Assimilation, whether voluntary or forced, has long been a technique employed by those who would see the Jewish people and Jewishness disappear. It is subtle; however, the end result is the same. If the Jews and Judaism had simply disappeared as Marx and Lenin had hoped, the Bolsheviks would have been pleased; however, the insistence of the Jewish people on faithfulness to their ethnicity and to their Torah did not sit well with the Communist agenda of establishing a totally godless society.

Though antisemitism was officially forbidden in Bolshevik and Communist Russia, it was not obliterated: it merely moved underground and changed form. Robert Bleakney observes that "racial antisemitism may have been outlawed; however, Marxism's materialism remained antithetical to Jewish faithfulness to the supernaturalism of the Torah."[80] In this case, the Communist regime's stance against antisemitism was similar to that of Napoleonic France: it was merely a nominal position

[74] Abraham Liessin, in *Di Tsukunft*, January 1920, p. 1, quoted in Fein, ed., p. 385.

[75] Karl Marx and Friedrich Engels, *The Communist Manifesto* (Portland, OR: The Floating Press, 2008, reproduction of an 1888 edition).

[76] S. L. Gilman, "Karl Marx and the Secret Language of Jews," in *Karl Marx's Social and Political Thought: Critical Assessments*, Bob Jessop and Russell Wheatley, eds. (London, UK: Routledge, 1999), p. 22.

[77] Lenin's grandfather, like Marx's father, converted to Christianity. It is possible that he did not know about his Jewish ancestry; however, it is certain that he did not advertise it. Robert Service, *Lenin: A Political Life: Volume 3: The Iron Ring* (Blasingstoke, UK: MacMillan Press Ltd., 1995), p. 131.

[78] Michael Berkowitz, *The Crime of My Very Existence: Nazism and the Myth of Jewish Criminality* (Berkeley, CA: The University of California Press, 2007), p. 221.

[79] Dennis Prager and Joseph Telushkin, *Why the Jews?: The Reason for Antisemitism* (New York: Simon & Schuster, Inc., 2003), p. 45.

[80] Bleakney, personal communication.

that did not destroy antisemitism but allowed it to reconstitute itself in later political philosophies that its avowed atheism would impose upon the Jewish people for their unwillingness to concede their faith. The overt secularism of the Communist regime opened the door for the rise of Joseph Stalin who became one of history's greatest tyrants and genocidists. As a matter of fact, Stalin's forced starvation of six million Ukrainians may well have been a source of encouragement for Hitler's crimes against humanity.[81] The cynical materialism of the Russian regime made it possible for the Jewish plight during the Holocaust to be ignored in similar fashion as the neglect demonstrated by the United States and Britain. It would later lead to profound abuses of the Jewish people, including forbidding Jews from learning Hebrew and studying Judaism and the enforcement of such strict limitations on Jewish emigration from the Soviet Union that for decades made the Jews virtual prisoners in one massive gulag called the Union of Soviet Socialist Republics.

## Righteous Gentiles

Even in the midst of history's most heinous genocide which was supported and carried out by those who claimed to be Christians, there were numerous Christians—"Righteous Gentiles"[82] as the Jewish community came to call them—who not only stood up for the Jewish people in the face of the Nazi onslaught but also put their own lives on the line to hide, protect, and help Jews escape the clutches of the Nazis during World War II. Many Christians died at the hands of the crazed Third Reich in its genocidal determination to exterminate the Jewish people and make Europe *Judenrein* (cleansed of Jews). Over 26,000 of these righteous Gentiles (nearly 7,000 of them Polish) have been honored at Yad Vashem Holocaust Museum in Jerusalem. Some 130 of these Righteous Gentiles actually chose to settle in Israel, where they were granted citizenship by the Israeli authorities. While 26,000 is a small number compared to the millions of Christians in Europe during World War II, it still speaks to the fact that men and women of conscience were willing

[81] For an extensive analysis of Stalin's mass violence including his starvation of 14.5 million Russians and Ukrainians between 1930 and 1937, see Robert Conquest, *The Great Terror: Stalinist Purge of the Thirties* (Oxford, UK: Oxford University Press, 1990); Robert Conquest, *The Harvest of Sorrow: Soviet Collectivization and the Terror-famine* (Oxford, UK: Oxford University Press, 1986); and Anne Applebaum, *Gulag: A History* (New York: Doubleday, 2003). For an exposé of Stalin's role in World War II, including the influence of his agents in high places in both the US and German governments, see Diana West, *American Betrayal: The Secret Assault on Our Nation's Character* (New York: St. Martin's Press, 2013), and Louis C. Kilzer, *Hitler's Traitor: Martin Bormann and the Defeat of the Reich* (New York: Presidio Press, 2000).

[82] Some of those whom the Jewish people honored as "Righteous Gentiles" were Muslims, e.g. those from Albania.

to risk all, including their own lives in order to save Jewish lives during the Holocaust and thereby do their part in preventing the genocide of the Jews.

## The Holocaust: Beyond Any Comparison

Steven Bartlett rightly observes that "the Holocaust stands as the most horrifying obscene eruption of human evil in man's history. It is as different from other genocides as a devastating disease pandemic is to localized and more limited infections."[83] Indeed, Dan Gillerman was totally right when he said, "The Holocaust constituted a systematic and barbarous attempt to annihilate an entire people in a manner and magnitude that have no parallel in human history."[84] While historians, sociologists, and politicians of various backgrounds make every attempt to compare the Holocaust with other historical genocidal efforts by tyrants of all sorts, the fact remains that such comparisons are utterly impossible and profoundly inaccurate, for, with the exception of the Jews, no one people has been targeted transnationally for mass murder simply because of their ethnicity, culture, and religion. Wars that have been fought throughout history have seen the decimation of populations as millions have been murdered by empire builders. Likewise, despots have slaughtered untold numbers of their own citizens in order to seize and maintain power.[85] No other atrocity in history, however, has targeted an entire multinational people group for utter extermination everywhere in the world solely because of the uniqueness of its ethnic self-identity and its religion.[86]

Because of its nature and substance, David Ben-Gurion said that "the Holocaust . . . is not like other atrocities . . . [of] the Nazis . . . but a unique

[83] Steven J. Bartlett, *The Pathology of Man: A Study of Human Evil* (Springfield, IL: Charles C. Thomas, Publisher, 2005), p. 165.

[84] Dan Gillerman, Statement to the United Nations General Assembly 31 October 2005. See http://mfa.gov.il/MFA/InternatlOrgs/Speeches/Pages/Israel%20submits%20draft%20UN%20resolution%20on%20Holocaust%20remembrance%2031-Oct-2005.aspx.

[85] The prime example of such despots in history is Mao Tse-tung who was responsible for the deaths of 40 to 70 million people. Jonathan Fenby, *Modern China: The Fall and Rise of a Great Power, 1850 to the Present* (New York: Ecco Press, 2008), p. 351. Another is Joseph Stalin, who, from 1927 to 1953, was responsible for the murder of more than 20 million and the displacement of an additional 20 million of his own Russian people. Richard Alan Schwartz, *Eyewitness History: The 1990s* (New York: Infobase Publishing, 2006), p. 32. Another example is Pol Pot who was responsible for the murder of upwards of three million citizens of his native Cambodia. René Provost and Payam Akhavan, eds., *Confronting Genocide* (Dordrecht, The Netherlands: Springer Science+Business Media B.V., 2011), p. 85.

[86] Robert Bleakney makes a succinct summation: "The Holocaust was the only case of an international, indeed intercontinental, campaign of mass murder of an entire people group as defined by the religious affiliation of grandparents (thus victims were targeted both religiously and genetically), with a goal of complete destruction of that group wherever in the world its members might be found" (Robert W. Bleakney, personal communication). Bleakney cites Emil L. Fackenheim, *The Jewish Bible after the Holocaust: A Re-reading* (Bloomington, IN: Indiana University Press, 1991).

episode that has no equal, an attempt to totally destroy the Jewish people."[87] Elie Wiesel was correct, therefore, when he said that the Holocaust "transcends history."[88] Claude Lanzmann argues that it is impossible, therefore, to "engender the Holocaust" because "there is an unbreachable discrepancy" between "the gassing of three thousand persons, men, women, children, in a gas chamber" and any conditions that might be construed to have been causes of those atrocities.[89] "There is no solution of continuity between the two; there is rather a gap, an abyss, and this *abyss* will never be bridged."[90] The Holocaust stands alone as a singular event in human history for which there can be no explanation.[91] Louise Vasvári sums up this truth well: "The Holocaust is essentially different from any other historical events; it is unexplainable because the extension and dreadfulness of the Holocaust are beyond human reason."[92] While many have tried to explain it—or explain it away—the Holocaust is simply The Holocaust, and it is incomparable and inexplicable.

Many Jews have wondered, "Where was God during the Holocaust?" Elie Wiesel gave an account of a group of religious Jewish inmates at Auschwitz who had experienced the horrors committed in the concentration camp. They decided to put God on trial, with a judge, a jury, and counsel for both prosecution and defense. When the time came to pronounce judgment, there was unanimity: God was guilty as charged. Then, with the announcement that it was time for evening prayers, the "court" adjourned, and the court officers went off to worship the God whom they had just found guilty,[93] pausing to recite the *Shema* and the *Amidah*, thereby expressing their continuing faith in God.[94] Although they could never understand the apparent silence of God in the face

[87] David Ben-Gurion, quoted in Tom Segev, *The Seventh Million: The Israelis and the Holocaust* (New York: Hill and Wang, 1993), p. 329.

[88] Elie Wiesel, "Trivializing the Holocaust: Semi-Fact and Semi-Fiction," *The New York Times*, April 16, 1978, § 2, p. 29. Wiesel prefaced his conclusion, "the Holocaust transcends history," with the declaration that "Auschwitz cannot be explained." Then, he somberly added these poignant words: "The dead are in possession of a secret that we, the living, are neither worthy of nor capable of recovering."

[89] Claude Lanzmann, "The Obscenity of Understanding: An Evening with Claude Lanzmann," in *American Imago*, vol. 48, no. 4 (Winter 1991), pp. 473–495.

[90] Lanzmann, p. 481.

[91] For a comprehensive discussion of the uniqueness of the Holocaust, see Eliezer Schweid, "Is the *Shoah* a Unique Event?" in *Wrestling with God: Jewish Theological Responses during and after the Holocaust*, Steven T. Katz, Shlomo Biderman, and Gershon Greenberg, eds. (Oxford, UK: Oxford University Press, 2007), pp. 219–229.

[92] Tamás Kistanal, "The Holocaust as a Paradigm for Ethical Thinking and Representation," in *Comparative Central European Holocaust Studies*, Louise O. Vasvári and Steven Tötösy de Zepetnek, eds. (West Lafayette, IN: Purdue University Press, 2009), p. 19.

[93] Anne Geldart, *Judaism, Second Edition* (Portsmouth, NH: Heinemann Library, 2001), p. 58.

[94] Elie Wiesel, paraphrased in Stefan Einhorn, *A Concealed God: Religion, Science and the Search for Truth* (Radnor, PA: Templeton Foundation Press, 1998), p. 3.

of evil unparalleled in human history, perhaps they had hope that God could deliver them from their circumstances and that even if they were not physically delivered, God would keep faith with them while they slept in the dust of the earth.[95]

These Jewish men arrived at the conclusion that Issachar Jacobsohn made when he said, "We must give up the idea of arriving at a rational explanation of the Holocaust in order to remain believers."[96] Death for the Jews in the gas chambers and crematoria was not the end: it was only the beginning, the door to a resurrection of the people, the nation, and the land of Israel. Two dynamic post-Holocaust truths, therefore, remain. The first truth is that the Jewish people survived the insidious force of manifest evil. "Without entering into a discussion of the metaphysics of history, let this point just stand for further reflection, i.e., that the Jews survived Hitler and Jewish history did not end at Auschwitz," says Steven Katz. The second and perhaps more significant truth is that the Jews not only survived the Holocaust but also thrived by recreating the long-destroyed Jewish commonwealth in the land of Israel. "This event, too, is remarkable in the course of Jewish existence," says Katz. "Logic and conceptual adequacy require that if in our discussion of the relation of God and history we want to give theological weight to the Holocaust, then we *must* also be willing to attribute *theological* significance to the state of Israel."[97] The poignant words of Michael Wyschogrod sum up the Holocaust and its impact upon Israel, the Chosen People, the Holy Nation, and the Promised Land: "If there is hope after the Holocaust, it is because, to those who believe, the voices of the Prophets speak more loudly than did Hitler, and because the divine promise sweeps over the crematoria and silences the voice of Auschwitz."[98]

---

[95] Eliezer Berkovits, *With God in Hell: Judaism in the Ghettos and Deathcamps* (Brooklyn, NY: Hebrew Publishing Co., 1969).

[96] Adele Berlin, ed., *The Oxford Dictionary of the Jewish Religion* (Oxford, UK: Oxford University Press, 2011), p. 356. For excellent examples of positive and uplifting testimonies of Holocaust survivors, see also Itta Halberstan and Judith Leventhal, *Small Miracles of the Holocaust: Extraordinary Coincidences of Faith, Hope, and Survival* (Guilford, CT: The Globe Pequot Press, 2010).

[97] Steven T. Katz, "The Issue of Confirmation and Disconfirmation in Jewish Thought after the Shoah," in *The Impact of the Holocaust on Jewish Theology*, Steven T. Katz, ed. (New York: New York University Press, 2005), pp. 15–16.

[98] Michael Wyschogrod, "Faith and the Holocaust," *Judaism* 20 (1971), quoted in Michael L. Morgan, ed., *A Holocaust Reader: Responses to the Nazi Extermination* (Oxford, UK: Oxford University Press, 2000), p. 171.

CHAPTER 9

# A NATION REBORN

## DIVINE RESPONSE TO TWO MILLENNIA OF ANTISEMITISM

The God of Israel, asked two different Hebrew prophets these seemingly unanswerable questions: "Can a nation be born in a single day?"[1] and, "Can these [dry] bones live?"[2] The obvious and logical answer to both questions would have been, *No!* But, the obvious answer was not the correct one. God was not looking for a logical answer—or even for an illogical answer, for that matter. In his infinite wisdom and foreknowledge, the Almighty knew that there was a supralogical answer, one that would transcend human reasoning and tap into his own infinite logic and power. The restorative action that God had planned for the Jewish nation was, in fact, "not simply *super*natural; it [was] *contra*natural,"[3] in that it defied all the known laws of nature and of history. God was planning to do something that no one could have reasonably expected. He was going to do the impossible.

Can a nation, indeed, be born in a day? While it might have seemed impossible in the twentieth century, there was every reason for the Jewish people to believe that such a miracle could—and would—occur, for the nation of Israel had already been born in one day over three millennia before that time. God had summoned the descendants of Abraham, Isaac, and Jacob out of Egyptian slavery and had brought them to Mt. Sinai for the express purpose of celebrating his festival.[4] Then, in one day, on *Shavuot* (the Day of Pentecost), when the Israelites had assembled before the smoking, quaking mountain, God constituted them as a "holy nation," a "kingdom of priests,"[5]

---

[1] Isaiah 66:8.

[2] Ezekiel 37:3.

[3] Jon D. Levenson, *The Death and Resurrection of the Beloved Son: The Transformation of Child Sacrifice in Judaism and Christianity* (New Haven, CT: Yale University Press, 1993), p. 155.

[4] Exodus 9:1.

[5] Exodus 19:6.

and gave them his Torah as their declaration of independence and their national constitution. In reality, such a thing must have seemed as utterly impossible then as it did when Zionism was birthed at the end of the nineteenth century. Indeed, could an enslaved, abused, rag-tag, motley group of people ever in their wildest dreams have expected to be molded into a nation in years, much less in a day? The answer was, Yes! because, at Sinai, God was birthing his chosen nation, the only nation in history that had been born in one day!

Nearly 3,500 years later, after an experience among the nations of the world that was far more devastating than the Egyptian bondage that their ancestors had encountered, the distant descendants of the ancient Israelites finally reached the appointed time for them to experience an event similar to what had occurred at Sinai. This time, the nation would be reborn. Though it had seemed long dead, Israel would be resurrected from the dust and ashes of the Holocaust through the miraculous power of the Creator,[6] who alone has the power to summon existence from absolute nothingness.[7] Mark Lindsay poignantly described the miracle of Israel's rebirth in this manner: "In religious rather than mythological terms, Israel's re-birth was a 'resurrection', after the 'crucifixion' of the Jews in Auschwitz."[8] What had long seemed like an utterly obliterated nation would rise again after being buried for nearly two thousand years in the dust of history. The dry bones of the long decimated Israelite army would, indeed, live again. God's nation would once more stand as a sovereign dominion among the diverse nations of the world. This was to be an event far greater than what Paul Johnson described as Israel's slipping "into existence through a fortuitous window of history."[9] It was more, far more: this was a divinely orchestrated miracle.

When God asked the prophet, "Can a nation be born in a day?" he continued with the exclamatory rhetorical question: "Who has ever

[6] Eliezer Berkovits, *Faith After the Holocaust* (New York: KTAV Publishing House, 1973), p. 156. Berkovits connected the Holocaust spiritually with the resurrection of Israel: "If at Auschwitz . . . we have witnessed 'The Hiding Face of God,' in the rebirth of the State of Israel and its success 'we have seen a smile on the face of God.'" Eliezer Berkovits cited in Mark R. Lindsay, *Barth, Israel, and Jesus: Karl Barth's Theology of Israel* (Burlington, VT: Ashgate Publishing Co., 2007), p. 60.

[7] Genesis 1:1. The Genesis narrative says that God "created" the heavens and the earth. In this case, the word *bara* is used, which means "to create something out of nothing." In Romans 4:17, Paul expanded upon this divine power: "God . . . summons into existence the things that do not exist" (author's translation).

[8] Lindsay, p. 60. Lindsay reports Richard Rubenstein's observation that if the Holocaust and the establishment of Israel are not kept independent of each other, "one runs the risk of retrospectively infusing the Holocaust with positive significance." The Holocaust was not a *quid pro quo* for the birth of Israel. Israel was God's divine solution to the Holocaust of human depravity, confirming the words of Paul, "Where sin increased, grace abounded all the more" (Romans 5:20, ESV). The imagery of the "crucifixion of the Jews" was expanded upon by Franklin Littell in Franklin H. Littell, *The Crucifixion of the Jews* (Macon, GA: Mercer University Press, 1986).

[9] Paul Johnson, *A History of the Jews* (London, UK: Orion Press, 1993), p. 526.

heard of such a thing?" The answer to these questions, however, was obvious, for the Lord God immediately said, "As soon as Zion travailed, she also brought forth her sons."[10] Israel's rebirth was not, however, to be predicated solely on the ingenuity or strength of the Jewish people. This work of the *Ruach HaKodesh*[11] was an outworking of the utter faithfulness of Israel's God: "'Shall I bring to the point of birth and not cause to bring forth?' says the LORD. . . . 'Rejoice with Jerusalem, and be glad for her.' . . . For thus says the LORD, 'Behold, I will extend peace to her like a river, and the glory of the nations like an overflowing stream.'"[12] God himself was the one who signed Israel's birth certificate, guaranteeing the right of the Jewish people to corporate and national sovereignty, and God has never signed—nor will he ever sign—Israel's death certificate! He who was the midwife who birthed Israel has been her constant protector and sustainer, and he will continue to be so forever.

After appearing to be in the grave of history for almost two millennia, Israel would be reborn in a resurrection, just as Ezekiel had witnessed in his prophetic vision concerning the revivified dry bones. Most of the Jewish people had surely concluded what the prophet had predicted, "Our bones are dried up and our hope is gone; we are cut off."[13] What looked like a hopeless bone yard, the remnants of a long-since defeated army, was to become the site of a miracle of resurrection and restoration. God promised, "Behold, I will open your graves and cause you to come up out of your graves, my people; and I will bring you into the land of Israel."[14] God would summon his people from the four corners of the earth and bring them again out of exile to their own land: "I will say to the north, 'Give them up!' And to the south, 'Do not hold them back.' Bring my sons from afar and my daughters from the ends of the earth."[15] Yes, the dead bones would live again, and they would "stand up a mighty army."[16] As Jon Levenson has pointed out, "The revitalization of the downtrodden and despondent people is clearly patterned on the old legends of their having come into being against all odds, historical and natural."[17]

---

[10] Isaiah 66:8, NIV, ESV, NASB paraphrased.

[11] The Hebrew term *Ruach HaKodesh* means "the Holy Spirit."

[12] Isaiah 66:9, 10, 12, ESV.

[13] Ezekiel 37:11, NIV.

[14] Ezekiel 37:12.

[15] Isaiah 43:6.

[16] Ezekiel 37:10.

[17] Levenson, p. 145.

## Declarations and Independence

John Stuart Mill summed up basic principles of sociology and politics: "A portion of mankind may be said to constitute a Nationality, if they are united among themselves by common sympathies, which do not exist between them and any others which make them co-operate with each other more willingly than with other people, desire to be under the same government, and desire that it should be government by themselves or a portion of themselves, exclusively."[18] These principles were certainly descriptive of the ancient Israelites and their descendants through the centuries, and they also defined the Jewish people in the twentieth century. The long-delayed League of Nations Covenant for Palestine, which had been enacted on July 24, 1922, and entrusted as a Mandate to the British government for its fulfillment, was coming to a point of fulfillment. As Howard Grief points out, "The Jewish People were ripe for independence because, unlike the situation that existed at the start of the Mandate, it was now able to stand alone and exercise the powers of self-government . . . which was the only requirement for terminating the Mandate under Article 22 of the Covenant of the League of Nations that was an integral part of the Mandate for Palestine."[19] The excuse that Britain had used to continue its control of all of Palestine and to deny the Jewish people the right of self-determination had become a moot issue,[20] for at that time, "the consent of the League of Nations or the British Mandatory was not formally needed because declaring independence was not a 'modification' of the terms of the Mandate but the realization or fulfillment of its purpose for which it existed."[21]

It should have come as no surprise that something powerfully spiritual and prophetic was taking place in the Holy Land. The British Mandate over Palestine had expired after Britain had notified the United Nations in 1947 of its intention to terminate its stewardship of the Mandate from the League of Nations Covenant for Palestine. On November 29, 1947, the United Nations passed Resolution 181 which included its plan to partition the territory of the Covenant for Palestine in its final form into two independent countries, an Arab state in the Transjordan and a

[18] John Stuart Mill, *Considerations on Representative Government* (Chicago, IL: Gateway Publishing, 1962), p. 303.

[19] Howard Grief, *The Legal Foundation and Borders of Israel under International Law: A Treatise on Jewish Sovereignty over the Land of Israel* (Jerusalem, Israel: Mazo Publishers, 2008), p. 167.

[20] Charles River Editors, *Decoding the Conflict between Israel and the Palestinians: The History and Terms of the Middle East Peace Process* (Cambridge, MA: Create Space, 2013), p. 1970.

[21] Grief, p. 167.

Jewish state in Judea, Samaria, and Galilee.[22] On the very next day after the United Nations had passed its resolution, the Arabs launched an uprising in an effort to obviate and negate the United Nations action. Although the Jews defeated this uprising, it was unable to repel the Jordanian army counterattack and its illegal occupation of land west of the Jordan River, including areas in and around Jerusalem. After he had consolidated this control of the West Bank, Jordanian King Abdullah brought 2,000 Arabs loyal to Jordan into the West Bank[23] and thereby initiated the birth of what was to become the myth of a "West-Bank" Palestinian Arab people. Abdullah was intent upon maintaining control of his own kingdom by precluding the formation of a Palestinian Arab state on the east side of the Jordan River,[24] where its existence had already been mandated by the League of Nations for some 26 years.

Despite the bellicosity of its neighbors, however, the state of Israel was finally emerging. Finally, on May 14, 1948, the next day after the British Mandate for the League of Nations Covenant with Palestine had expired at midnight, David Ben-Gurion became the first person to sign the Israeli Declaration of Independence, and then he formally proclaimed *The Declaration of the Establishment of the State of Israel*, which said, in part:

> ERETZ-ISRAEL was the birthplace of the Jewish people. Here their spiritual, religious and political identity was shaped. Here they first attained statehood, created cultural values of national and universal significance and gave to the world the Book of Books.

[22] In 1922, the second iteration of the original League of Nations Mandate for Palestine had assigned all the land west of the Jordan River to the Jewish state and the land east of the Jordan to the Arab state.

[23] With the help of the British, Abdullah circumvented the allotment to the Arab (Palestinian) state and formed the "Hashemite" kingdom of Jordan, for which there was no prior history or legitimacy. Abdullah, an Arabian born in Mecca, was not a "Jordanian"; however, he exploited his support for the British during World War I in order to create his own "kingdom" out of thin air. This, in turn, produced the "West Bank" and the "Palestinian" controversies that continue to this day. Abdullah had absolutely no right to control of any land west of the Jordan River; therefore, his occupation of the "West Bank" was entirely illegal and illegitimate. Mary C. Wilson thoroughly documents these facts of history and exposes the fallacy of the "Palestinian" Arab state west of the Jordan River. Mary Christian Wilson, *King Abdullah, Britain and the Making of Jordan* (Cambridge, UK: Cambridge University Press, 1987), pp. 179–181, 195.

[24] William W. Haddad and Mary M. Hardy, "Jordan's Alliance with Israel and its Effects on Jordanian-Arab Relations" in *Israel, the Hashemites, and the Palestinians: The Fateful Triangle,* Efraim Karsh and P. R. Kumaraswam, eds. (London, UK: Frank Cass Publishers, 2003), pp. 31–48. Haddad and Hardy point out that when Israel retook the West Bank in 1967 nearly twenty years after Abdullah's invasion, "they did not conquer the Palestinians; they made war with Jordan. Jordan had occupied the territory in 1948, and it was not their territory to begin with." In reality, Israel was the liberator, not the occupier of the West Bank. This territory had been "occupied" by Jordan for nineteen years before it was liberated by the Israeli army in the 1967 Six-Day War. The West Bank, therefore, has not been "occupied territory" since the time when it was controlled by Jordan from 1948 until 1967. It has been, and continues to be, a part of the nation of Israel.

> After being forcibly exiled from their land, the people kept faith with it throughout their Dispersion and never ceased to pray and hope for their return to it and for the restoration in it of their political freedom.
>
> Impelled by this historical and traditional attachment, Jews strove in every successive generation to re-establish themselves in their ancient homeland. In recent decades they returned in their masses. Pioneers, *ma'pilim*, [immigrants coming to Eretz-Israel in defiance of restrictive legislation] and defenders, they made deserts bloom, revived the Hebrew language, built villages and towns, and created a thriving community controlling its own economy and culture, loving peace but knowing how to defend itself, bringing the blessings of progress to all the country's inhabitants, and aspiring towards independent nationhood. . . .
>
> We, members of the People's Council, representatives of the Jewish community of Eretz-Israel and of the Zionist movement, are here assembled on the day of the termination of the British Mandate over Eretz-Israel and, by virtue of our natural and historic right and on the strength of the resolution of the United Nations General Assembly, hereby declare the establishment of a Jewish state in Eretz-Israel, to be known as the State of Israel. . . . Placing our trust in the "Rock of Israel", we affix our signatures to this proclamation at the session of the Provisional Council of State, on the soil of the homeland, in the city of Tel-Aviv, on this Sabbath eve, the 5th day of Iyar, 5708 (14th May, 1948).[25]

Within minutes of Ben-Gurion's historic proclamation of the statehood of Israel, United States President Harry Truman "rejected the advice of his State Department and made the United States the first nation to recognize the new country."[26] This was another example of divine orchestration of world events, for Truman was a Baptist who "believed that the Jewish people and the Holy Land had distinct roles in God's plan." Also, "because of the great suffering that they had endured over two millennia as a dispersed people," Truman "strongly identified with Jews' quest for a homeland, especially in

[25] The *Official Gazette*, No. 1 of the 5th, Iyar, 5708 (14th May, 1948).

[26] Michael Nelson, *Guide to the Presidency* (New York: Routledge, 2015), p. 611.

the aftermath of the Holocaust."[27] The fact that Truman was able to withstand the vociferous objections of his clearly antisemitic US State Department is testimony to the strength of his personal convictions, but it is also testimony to divine providence that positioned the right person in the right place at the right time to do the right thing in recognizing Israel, for when the US recognized Israel, worldwide acceptance of Israel's existence was a *fait accompli*.

What had been in the making for more than fifty years since the earliest Zionists[28] were moved by their passion for the holy land to begin working toward recreating a Jewish nation came to fruition on that day. The centuries-long struggle of individual Jews to make *aliyah* by "going up" to the land of Israel—living there, purchasing land there, and praying there that God would one day completely fulfill his promise to their ancestors—was finally realized. Against all odds, Jews had begun to return to the land of the Bible. At first, it had been a mere trickle, then a stream, then a torrent. After nineteen centuries in exile, the Jews were finding their way back home again. The legendary stereotypical "wandering Jew" would wander no more: the Jews were going home. They were not to be in a remote and alien plot of ground assigned to them by other nations; they were home in the land contracted to them by their God, the God of the universe, in the eternal, irrevocable covenant that he had made with Abraham four millennia earlier!

Immediately after its rebirth, however, Israel was attacked by Muslim and Arab nations that had done everything possible to abort the Jewish nation before it could be born and were then intent on inflicting infanticide on the newly born nation. They were utterly determined to destroy forever what had suddenly and spontaneously come to life in their midst. Consequently, on the very next day after the Israeli Declaration of Independence had been signed and the proclamation of the formation of the State of Israel had been made, seven Arab nations—Egypt, Transjordan (now Jordan), Syria, Iraq, Yemen, Saudi Arabia, and Lebanon—along with the Arab Liberation Army, invaded Israel with what appeared to be an overwhelming force that would simply crush the newly born Jewish nation and eradicate the Jews once and for all from the land of Israel.[29] The Arab forces sprang into action to fulfill the pre-World War II promise of the Arab Higher Committee: "Whenever the English remove their hands from this land, we will throw and chase all the

---

[27] Mark R. Amstutz, *Evangelicals and American Foreign Policy* (Oxford, UK: Oxford University Press, 2014), p. 130.

[28] Over fifty years before this time, in 1897, Theodor Herzl, the father of the movement that would eventually produce the Jewish State, convened the First Zionist Congress which proclaimed the right of the Jewish people to a national rebirth in their own country.

[29] Alex Wolf, *The Arab-Israeli War since 1948* (Chicago, IL: Capstone Global Library, 2012), p. 14.

Jews in a stampede into the sea!"[30] As the Arab nations discovered, however, Israel was not nearly as easy a foe to defeat as they had thought. Finally, after ten months of intense warfare, the Israelis prevailed against their invaders, the Islamist nations were repelled,[31] and an armistice agreement was signed between Israel and Egypt,[32] ending the hostilities—at least for the moment.

## The Holocaust and the Resurrected Jewish State

There can be no direct connection either materially or spiritually between the Holocaust and the rebirth of the nation of Israel. The Holocaust was not a cosmic price that the Jews had to pay for the birth of Israel. Abraham Heschel declared, "The State of Israel is not an atonement. It would be blasphemy to regard it as a compensation."[33] The Holocaust was not a penalty exacted upon the Jewish people for some perceived evil or sin on their part. The evil—grotesque and unprecedented—emerged entirely from the hearts of the Nazis and their antisemitic collaborators in Europe. The Holocaust was a wholly undeserved monstrosity imposed upon the Jews by evil personified in Hitler and his henchmen. In reality, the Holocaust did not precipitate the creation of the Nation of Israel, for the stage had already been set politically and practically for the formation of Israel by the continuing *aliyah* of the Jewish people that had begun in earnest in the nineteenth century and by the Balfour Declaration and the League of Nations Covenant for Palestine of the early twentieth century.

The miracle of post-Holocaust Jewish existence stands, therefore, as a memorial to the indomitable will of the Jewish people not only to survive but also to thrive. This is why Elie Wiesel has argued that any attempt to link the Holocaust and reborn Israel diminishes both because they are two different mysteries.[34] At the same time, however, for Jews in the land of Israel, "the 'Holocaust-Israel' motif of 'death/rebirth' became a central dogma of Jewish civil religion,"[35]

---

[30] Klaus-Michael Mallmann and Martin Cüppers, *Nazi Palestine: The Plans for the Extermination of the Jews in Palestine*, tr. Krista Smith (New York: Enigma Books, 2010), p. 18.

[31] Israel expelled all the Arab invaders except the forces of Abdullah from the Transjordan who continued to occupy the "West Bank" for 19 years after the 1948 war.

[32] Moshe Naor, *Social Mobilization in the Arab/Israeli War of 1948: On the Israeli Home Front* (Abingdon, UK: Routledge, 2013), p. 87.

[33] Abraham Joshua Heschel, *Israel: An Echo of Eternity* (New York: Farrar, Straus and Giroux, 1969), p. 113.

[34] Elie Wiesel noted in Adele Berlin, ed., *The Oxford Dictionary of the Jewish Religion* (Oxford, UK: Oxford University Press, 2011), p. 356.

[35] Byron L. Sherwin, *Faith Finding Meaning: A Theology of Judaism* (Oxford, UK: Oxford University Press, 2009), p. 26.

says Byron Sherwin. He also argued that, quite amazingly, "this blatantly Christian motif of death and resurrection, death and salvation, proclaimed an indisputable nexus between the Holocaust and the State of Israel."[36] Irving Greenberg has rightly argued that "the lesson of the Holocaust is that powerlessness is immoral, because it is not compatible with survival."[37] He also has pointed out that "the existence of the State of Israel validates continuing faith in God and constitutes a redeeming act, which matches the great catastrophe."[38]

After the incredible numbers of deaths that were experienced by the Jewish people during the Holocaust, the rebirth of the nation of Israel has to be seen as a profound act of divine resurrection, the restoration of the nation and its people to the ancient land. Emmanuel Lévinas was entirely correct to assert that "the Shoah re-establishes the link—which up until then had been incomprehensibly hidden—between present-day Israel and the Israel of the Bible."[39] Abraham Heschel even saw the act of restoring the Nation of Israel as making the Holy Land even more holy: "No act is as holy as the act of saving human life. The Holy Land, having offered haven to more than two million Jews . . . has attained a new sanctity."[40]

The corporate consciences of the nations of Western Europe and the United States were awakened by the Holocaust from an abyss of dark contempt for the Jewish people and of utter disdain for their right to their own Jewish state in the land of their ancestors. The Christian

[36] Sherwin, p. 26. Sherwin apparently did not understand that the death and resurrection motif has never been blatantly or exclusively "Christian." As a matter of fact, Christians inherited the entire resurrection idea and theme from the Jews and Judaism, particularly from the Pharisees, the progenitors of Rabbinic Judaism. Paul made this clear: "I am a Pharisee, a son of Pharisees; I am on trial for the hope and resurrection of the dead" (Acts 23:6).

[37] Irving Greenberg, paraphrased in Berlin, p. 356.

[38] Greenberg, in Berlin, p. 356. Greenberg also observed that the "embrace of modernity was a profound blunder, and Jews must learn to resist the absoluteness of the secular." Indeed, it was the absolute secularity of modernity that altogether denied the spiritual and created the climate for the Holocaust. The utter denial of the supernatural in German theology, wherein Christian scholars systematically sought to "demythologize" the Scriptures, so elevated the material and secular while diminishing the spiritual in Christian life that German Christians willingly participated in the horrors of the Holocaust. The "social" issues of the secular modernist state overwhelmed the spiritual issues of true Christianity and rendered them inoperative. For a comprehensive discussion of Christian complicity in the Holocaust, see Robert P. Ericksen, *Complicity in the Holocaust: Churches and Universities in Nazi Germany* (Cambridge, UK: Cambridge University Press, 2012). Also, Robert P. Ericksen and Susannah Heschel, *Betrayal: German Churches and the Holocaust* (Minneapolis, MN: Augsburg Fortress Publishers, 1999), and Mary M. Solberg, tr., *A Church Undone: Documents from the German Christian Faith Movement 1932–1940* (Minneapolis, MN: Fortress Press, 2015).

[39] Emmanuel Lévinas, *Difficult Freedom: Essays on Judaism,* tr. Sean Hand (Baltimore, MD: Johns Hopkins University Press, 1990), p. 12.

[40] Heschel, p. 113.

church likewise felt the imprint of nails driven by the Holy Spirit into its corporate consciousness that made eternal truth undeniable.[41] For centuries, the church had been overwhelmed by the darkness of abject evil in its evaluation of and attitude toward the Jewish people and their inalienable right to their homeland. In reality, all Christians in history should have been deeply distressed by the condition in which Jewish believers in the same God that the church worshipped were subjected to unrelenting and systematic persecution, torture, and death. Instead, the vast majority of Christians had fully experienced the condition that Paul had observed in the lives of many people who had far less evil intentions than many in later generations had against the Jewish people: "Such teachings come through hypocritical liars whose consciences have been seared as with a hot [branding] iron."[42]

The branding iron of abject evil and perversion had for centuries left a deep and wide scar on Christianity's conscience, so much so that, for all intents and purposes, it had very little conscience at all when it came to the Jewish people and their plight. Occasionally, isolated Christian voices did arise in history to condemn efforts to harm the Jews, to encourage Christian commiseration with the plight of the Jews, and to support the rights of Jews to life and liberty. Generally speaking, however, both official Christianity and individual Christians were so blinded by centuries of the heresies of supersessionism and contempt for the Jews that they either engaged in actions that were utterly non-Christian or they remained silent in the face of such evil,[43] neither of which was acceptable conduct for anyone who had taken the teachings of Jesus seriously.

## Long-Established Jewish Rights to the Nation and Land

World reaction to the Holocaust may have been the catalyst that advanced and reified the right of the Jewish people to live in their ancestral homeland and to have a nation of their own that would guarantee to them the basic human rights that all people deserve. The political actions of the United Nations on November 29, 1947,

---

[41] Ecclesiastes 12:11.

[42] 1 Timothy 4:2, NIV.

[43] One of the things that troubled post-Holocaust Jewish and Christian children in the United States and in Germany was the Christian silence in the face of the atrocities of the Holocaust. Björn Krondorfer, *Remembrance and Reconciliation: Encounters between Young Jews and Germans* (New Haven, CT: Yale University Press, 1995), p. 105. In an analysis of the lack of German response to the Holocaust, Krondorfer notes that "the American Jewish and Christian students were astounded by the ubiquity of the conspiracy of silence their German peers had experienced in their families; and the East and West German students came to realize how deeply they themselves were invested in that conspiracy."

and of the Israeli Declaration of Independence on May 14, 1948, however, were not the events that established the rights of the Jewish people to the nation and the land. These rights were established in antiquity, and they were reasserted in century after century of Jewish presence in the land that their Scriptures called "Israel." Many factors had already established and reaffirmed those rights for some four millennia, including the following:

**1) Continuity in the Land for Millennia:** From 2000 BC, when Abraham received the divine covenant and its irrevocable land contract which secured the land of Canaan as an everlasting inheritance to his descendants, there was never a time when Hebrews/Israelites/Jews did not live in the land of Israel. Both the Jewish Scriptures and secular history[44] confirm the existence of Israel at least to the twelfth century BC or to 3,200 years ago. Though their numbers were at times decimated by occupying foreign powers, still they managed to cling to *Eretz Yisrael* as the inheritance conveyed to them by the Eternal God of Scripture, an inheritance renewed in perpetuity to every generation of Abraham's descendants. As Edwin Black observes, significant numbers of Jews "always lived" in this land: "Jews had always lived throughout the nearly barren land of Palestine in such cities as Gaza, Ashkelon, Jaffa, Caesarea, and Tsfat. Indeed, Jews lived in great numbers throughout the Ottoman Empire's Middle East, from Syria to the Persian Gulf."[45]

As a matter of fact, large communities were present in Jerusalem and Tiberias in the ninth century,[46] and in the eleventh century, Jews grew and prospered in Ashkelon, Jaffa, Caesarea, and Rafah.[47] This inherent Jewish bravery was indubitably confirmed when, after the disastrous slaughter of all the Jews in Jerusalem during the Crusades,

[44] The Egyptian Memeptah Stele documented the name *Israel* around 1200 BC. Kenton L. Sparks, *Ethnicity and Identity in Ancient Israel: Prolegomena to the Study of Ethnic Sentiments and Their Expression in the Hebrew Bible* (Winona Lake, IN: Eisenbrauns, Inc., 1998), pp. 96ff. In lines 26–28, the stele records, "The Canaan has been plundered into every sort of woe . . . Israel is laid waste and his seed is not. . . ." For greater detail on archaeological evidence for the historicity of the Exodus and the existence of the Israeli people and state, see David Rohl, *Exodus: Myth or History* (Minneapolis, MN: Thinking Man Media, 2015), David Rohl, *From Eden to Exile: The Five-Thousand-Year History of the Bible* (Lebanon, TN: Greenleaf Press, 2002), and Joan Peters, *From Time Immemorial: The Origins of the Arab-Jewish Conflict over Palestine* (New York: Harper & Row Publishers, 1984).

[45] Edwin Black, *Banking on Baghdad: Inside Iraq's 7,000-Year History of War, Profit, and Conflict* (Hoboken, NJ: John Wiley & Sons, Inc., 2004), pp. 234–235.

[46] Danny Danon, *Israel: The Will to Prevail* (New York: Macmillan, 2013), p. 141.

[47] Michael Medved, "Does Israel Have a Right to Exist? Does the U.S.?, *Townhall*, July 26, 2006, posted at https://townhall.com/columnists/michaelmedved/2006/07/26/does-israel-have-a-right-to-exist-does-the-us-n757024.

"Jews reestablished centers of Jewish learning and commerce in the Land of Israel. From this time on, Palestine was never without a significant and well-documented Jewish presence," says Alan Dershowitz.[48] After the Crusades, significant immigrant rabbis and Jewish pilgrims also established major religious communities in Tzfat and Jerusalem.[49]

The Jewish families that made possible the eventual establishment of the Jewish state in Israel were the ones who made the trek to the Holy Land and then purchased and developed property. Shaul Bartal notes that "Jews throughout the generations have always lived in the land of Israel and were, already in the nineteenth century, a majority in certain areas, including Jerusalem."[50] Sandra Teplinksy points out that during the time of Ottoman rule, "About 50,000 Jews lived on legally purchased or inherited real estate that would eventually become Israel."[51] By the early nineteenth century, more than 10,000 Jews lived throughout what is today Israel.[52]

The solid history of Jewish presence in Palestine prompted Abba Eban to observe, "A thin but crucial line of continuity had been maintained by small Jewish communities and academies in Jerusalem, Safed, Jaffa, and Hebron."[53] Abraham Heschel pointed out just one of the many continuously surviving Jewish communities in Israel: "In the mountain village of Peki'in in Galilee a flawless line of descent can be traced from the Hebrews of yore to the present-day inhabitants."[54] And this is but one example of the incredible tenacity of the Jewish people to maintain their claim on the land of the Bible as its legitimate occupants.

These long-standing historical facts are important to current circumstances in Israel because they further confirm the unbroken history of Jewish settlement in Palestine and establish the fact that those Jews were not the object of the intense genocidal antipathy that had come to characterize world Islam since the restoration of Israel in the twentieth century. Such simple continuing Jewish ownership of land in Israel maintained the right of the Jewish people to continue to live in

[48] Alan M. Dershowitz, "Countering Challenges to Israel's Legitimacy," in *Israel's Rights as a Nation-State in International Diplomacy,* Alan Baker, ed. (Jerusalem, Israel: World Jewish Congress, 2011), p. 160.

[49] Simon Federbusch, *World Jewry Today* (New York: Thomas Yoseloff, 1959), p. 75.

[50] Shaul Bartal, *Jihad in Palestine: Political Islam and the Israeli-Palestinian Conflict* (Abingdon, UK: Routledge, 2016), p. 68. Also Bernard Reitsma, *The God of My Enemy: The Middle East and the Nature of God* (Eugene, OR: Wipf and Stock Publishers, 2014), p. 17.

[51] Sandra Teplinsky, *Why Care about Israel? How the Jewish Nation Is Key to Unleashing God's Blessings in the 21st Century* (Grand Rapids, MI: Baker Publishing Group, 2004), p. 190.

[52] Dan Bahat, ed., *Twenty Centuries of Jewish Life in the Holy Land* (Jerusalem: *The Israel Economist,* 1976), pp. 61–63.

[53] Abba Eban, *Heritage: Civilization and the Jews* (New York: Simon & Schuster, 1984), p. 244.

[54] Abraham Joshua Heschel, *Israel: An Echo of Eternity* (New York: Macmillan, 1967), p. 71.

the homeland of their ancient ancestors.[55] The unbroken line of Jewish patriots who loved the land given by God to Abraham, Isaac, and Jacob so much that they were willing to suffer constant hardship and risk their lives to maintain residence in that land ensured the right of the Jewish people for reclaiming their land and their nation.[56]

**2) Reclamation of the Land for Generations:** Jews made *aliyah* to Israel for centuries before the Israeli Declaration of Independence by purchasing and cultivating land under extreme hardship. During the eighteenth and nineteenth centuries, significant numbers of Jews returned to the land of their ancestors. Then, in the nineteenth century, many Jews from various parts of the world began to trickle into Palestine to join those Jews whose ancestors had somehow managed to remain in the land or had made *aliyah* to the land through the centuries. During this time, Laurence Oliphant wrote of his encounter with an enclave of Jews in Bukeia (Peki'in) who were believed to be lineal descendants of ancestors who had lived uninterruptedly in the Holy Land from the time of the Second Temple: "There were the Jews—the only group of Jews existing in the world whose ancestors have clung to the soil" ever since the time of Jesus, representing "the faith which was the repository of the highest moral teaching prior to Christianity, prior to Mohammedanism."[57] From a sweep of history, it is clear that Jews have lived continuously as Jews in the land of Israel since they inherited the land in the time of Joshua. One needs only examine the history of Jews who were persecuted and murdered in Jerusalem through the centuries to confirm this fact. Every effort to obliterate the Jews so as to make Jerusalem either a Christian or a Muslim city failed to eradicate the Jewish people, who, despite indescribable suffering continued to cling to their native land with an undying love and unquenchable passion. Together with them, they began in earnest the formidable task of reclaiming

[55] Dennis Prager and Joseph Telushkin maintain that "Jews have lived continuously as a community in Palestine since approximately 1200 B.C.E." Dennis Prager and Joseph Telushkin, *Why the Jews?: The Reason for Antisemitism* (New York: Simon and Schuster, 1983), p. 105. Also, Michael Bard, *The Complete Idiot's Guide to the Middle East Conflict* (New York: Penguin Books, 2008), p. 288, and Shalom Goldman, *Zeal for Zion: Christians, Jews, & the Idea of the Promised Land* (Chapel Hill, NC: The University of North Carolina Press, 2009), p. 69. Many conservative Christian scholars date the Jewish presence in Palestine from as early as the beginning of the fifteenth century BC. Eugene H. Merrill, Mark F. Rooker, and Michael A. Grisanti, *The World and the Word: An Introduction to the Old Testament* (Nashville, TN: B &H Academic, 2011), p. 277. Israel Finkelstein and Neil Silberman, however, place the conquest of Canaan as between 1230 and 1220 BCE. Israel Finkelstein and Neil Asher Silberman, *The Bible Unearthed: Archaeology's New Vision of Ancient Israel and the Origin of Its Sacred Texts* (New York: Simon & Schuster, 2001), p. 76.

[56] The continuing presence of Jews in Palestine is confirmed by the fact that significant numbers of Jews were slaughtered by the Crusaders in the invasion of Israel and Jerusalem in 1099. If Palestine were an exclusively Arab (*qua* "Palestinian") land at that time—as some stridently claim—how is it that there was a Great Synagogue into which the Jewish population of Jerusalem was herded and then immolated by the Christian crusaders?

[57] Laurence Oliphant, *Haifa: Life in Modern Palestine* (London, England: William Blackwood, 1887), p. 111.

the desolate, barren landscape—of restoring the land that had been violently commandeered from their ancestors by violent Gentile nations and peoples.

**3) Legal Heirs to the Land:** The dwelling of the Hebrews/Israelites/Jews in the land of Canaan for over two millennia from the time of Abraham and the political control of the land from the time of Joshua until the Roman occupation are more than adequate to demonstrate the historicity of the Jewish legal right to the land of Israel. The continual occupation of that land by Jews for the ensuing 1800 years despite expulsions by foreign powers and despite organized and spontaneous acts of violence against those Jewish inhabitants is also irrefutable evidence of Jewish right to the land of their ancestors. The *aliyah* of thousands of Jews to the land prior to the twentieth century is also evidence of the Jewish reclamation of the land. These Jews were not squatters, using the law of adverse possession to claim their land. They were legitimate heirs of the land with title transferring from generation to generation through the laws of inheritance. Then, if these points of fact were not enough to establish the Jewish right to their land, the unanimous action of the League of Nations in 1923 confirmed that right unequivocally.

On July 24, 1922, the Council of the League of Nations unanimously confirmed the draft of the Covenant for Palestine to create a homeland for the Jewish people which was to include all of the land that is currently Israel and Jordan and a significant part of what is now Iraq. Then, following the ratification of the Treaty of Lausanne and the Transjordan Memorandum, the League of Nations Covenant for Palestine was finalized on September 29, 1923, reserving territory for a Jewish homeland that included all the land from the Mediterranean Sea on the west to the Jordan River on the east (in addition to the Golan Heights on the east and north of the Sea of Galilee) and all the land from Eilat on the south to Lebanon and Mt. Hermon on the north. This League of Nations Covenant that was then mandated to the British Empire for fulfillment in the creation of the state of Israel "weathered the test of time," for "on April 18, 1946, when the League of Nations was dissolved and its assets and duties [were] transferred to the United Nations, the international community, in essence, reaffirmed the validity of this international accord and reconfirmed that the terms for a Jewish National Home were the will of the international community, a 'sacred trust.'"[58]

[58] Eli E. Hertz, "'Mandate for Palestine,' The Legal Aspects of Jewish Rights," posted at http://www.mythsandfacts.org/conflict/mandate_for_palestine/mandate_for_palestine.htm. Hertz documents in great detail the nature and scope of the League of Nations Covenant and Mandate for Palestine which "laid down the Jewish legal right to settle anywhere in western Palestine" in the area "between the Jordan River and the Mediterranean Sea." The evidence that Hertz presents is incontrovertible proof that the "West Bank" is part of Israel, as it has always been.

When the United Nations was formed on October 24, 1945, it was legally responsible to assume all the obligations of the League of Nations, which would have included the Covenant for the Jewish Homeland. Based on the United Nations Charter, Chapter XII, Article 80 UN Trusteeship Agreement, of November 29, 1947, the United Nations assumed responsibility for all decisions and commitments of the League of Nations. This action involved the mandate for Britain to create the national homeland for the Jewish people, including this declaration: "The mandatory shall be responsible for placing the country [Palestine] under such political, administrative and economic conditions as will secure the establishment of the *Jewish National Home*."[59]

Sadly, glorified self-interest consumed a largely antisemitic British Foreign Secretariat to such a degree that the land mass that was originally confirmed by the League of Nations Covenant for Palestine was pared down first when Britain ceded the Golan Heights to Syria on February 3, 1922, and then carved off sections of the original League of Nations Covenant for Palestine to form what is now Iraq and the Hashemite Kingdom of Jordan.[60] Amazingly, the British easily formed a homeland for the Arabs by creating Iraq and Jordan; however, it was never "able" to create the "Jewish National Home" in the land west of the Jordan River!

## From Holocaust to Nationhood

After some nineteen centuries of dispersion, disparagement, and despair, the Jews who made *aliyah* to the newly reconstituted nation of Israel were simply overjoyed when they finally witnessed the reestablishment of their nation in the land of their ancestors. These relatively new citizens of Israel were determined to continue the tradition that had been established for over a century by settlers who had braved the deserts, the swamps, and the hostile environs of Palestine; therefore, they continued to accept the challenge of making the desert bloom by establishing agricultural marvels, of building modern, bustling cities like Tel Aviv to replace the swamps that those before them had drained, and of living day-to-day life with the stress of dwelling in close proximity to neighbors who were so often inhospitable and violent.

"With great love," the Sabras—those Jews who had been born in the land—"received the uprooted Jews from many lands, taught them Hebrew, helped them adjust, and transformed them into proud and productive

[59] Hertz, "'Mandate for Palestine'" (emphasis added)

[60] Wilson, pp. 179–181, 195.

citizens."[61] Like the established Israelis, the new citizens of the renewed state of Israel often found themselves stressed, but they were at the same time blessed. Their lives were filled with hard work and struggle, but they knew that they had been blessed to experience realities about which their ancestors could only have dreamed. In spite of all the challenges, they both survived and thrived, transforming a backwater and largely barren land into an agricultural, industrial, and technological wonder. "Today, Israel is a modern agricultural and industrial state, her desert serrated by fertile fields, her swamps drained . . . her cities growing, bustling with health."[62]

Stuart Eisenstat said it well when he discussed the incredible perseverance of the Jewish people. Through the Babylonian captivity, the Roman destruction and dispersion, the pogroms, the expulsions, the *Shoah*, and the continuing state of war by the Arab world against the restored nation—"through all of this, the Jewish people have survived and thrived, while the empires that conquered, dispersed, or threatened us are in the dustbin of history."[63] Lawrence Epstein accurately described the circumstances, contrasting the manner in which Muslims had come to dominate not only Palestine but also the entire Middle East and the high moral approach that the Jews had taken when they reclaimed the land of Israel: "The modern Palestinian Arabs couldn't then morally complain if the Jews wished to reclaim the land, even by force. However, the Jews were not doing it by force the way the Muslims did. The Jews did it by building homes, reclaiming swamps, and by employing Arab labor. They didn't conquer the land. They moved back to their old neighborhood and were willing to live beside their new neighbors."[64]

Employing the words of the Talmud in which the Jews swore that they would neither resist their persecutors nor prematurely "climb the wall" to return to Jerusalem,[65] Emil Fackenheim graphically and poignantly discussed the real walls over which they had to climb in their struggle to reclaim the land of their ancestors, the title of which land they neither corporately nor individually had ever surrendered. David Patterson elaborated on Fackenheim's theme in this manner: "Which wall have the Jews climbed?" he asked. "It is not the wall surrounding Jerusalem but the electrified fence surrounding

[61] Leo Trepp, *Judaism: Development and Life* (Belmont, CA: Dickenson Publishing Co., 1966), p. 62.

[62] Max I. Dimont, *The American Zionist* (1971), vol. 62, p. 18.

[63] Stuart E. Eisenstat, *The Future of the Jews: How Global Forces Are Impacting the Jewish People, Israel, and Its Relationship with the United States* (Lanham, MD: Rowman & Littlefield Publishers, 2012), p. 317.

[64] Lawrence J. Epstein, "The Moral Case of Zionism: If Both Jews and Palestinian Arabs Start Their Historical Narrative with Beginning of Zionism, Jews Have Deeper Moral Claim to the Land of Israel," in *Israel Opinion*, April 17, 2014, p. 1, posted at http://www.ynetnews.com/articles/0,7340,L-4509231,00.html.

[65] Babylonian Talmud, *Ketuvot* 111a.

Auschwitz, the wall whose only gate is embossed with the words *Arbeit Macht Frei*, the wall that would wall the Jews out from the world and into a graveyard without a single grave: the Jewish return to Jerusalem is nothing less than a resurrection."[66] It was not, however, merely the historical and physical walls of the death camps that the Jews figuratively "climbed over" in order to escape death itself. "The walls that the Jews have climbed in their return to Jerusalem are the walls that the Holocaust deniers would deconstruct and that the anti-Zionists would reconstruct."[67] It is these walls that "all who oppose the existence of the Jewish state—from the 'benign' left-wing liberal to the murderous fanatic Jihadist—erect which even now threaten the annihilation of the resurrection of the Jews and Israel."[68]

Despite the fact that their neighbors were largely inhospitable and often bellicose, the Jews who reclaimed their ancestral land over the centuries were not deterred or limited by fear and the threat of violence. Instead, they persevered with such determination—and, indeed, faith—that as a result of their efforts, the Jewish state of Israel "has become a major player on the world scene, raising its head unashamedly high among the nations,"[69] says Stuart Eisenstat. Consequently, "the modern State of Israel has enabled the Jewish people to emerge from the shadows of history, to cast aside centuries of living at the caprice of rulers and hostile populations; to serve as an example of democratic nation building; to become a center of the technologies that will be the keys to the twenty-first century's prosperity and security."[70] Considering the amazing successes of the Jewish people in the land of Israel in the midst of such ongoing conflict, one can only wonder what they might have accomplished had the history of Israel always been one of peace, tranquility, and mutual respect among all of the diverse inhabitants of the Middle East. Doubtless, the entire area would have been an economic powerhouse serving the three continents that are contiguous with it.

## Replacing Death and Deprivation with Life and Prosperity

For centuries, the corporate consciences of the nations of Europe and, for that matter, of the United States, were, indeed, seared with a branding iron, making them utterly insensitive to the enduring plight of the Jewish people

---

[66] David Patterson, *Emil L. Fackenheim: A Jewish Philosopher's Response to the Holocaust* (Syracuse, NY: Syracuse University Press, 2008), p. 143.

[67] David Patterson, *Anti-Semitism and Its Metaphysical Origins* (Cambridge, UK: Cambridge University Press, 2015), p. 206.

[68] David Patterson, *Anti-Semitism*, p. 206.

[69] Eisenstat, p. 317.

[70] Eisenstat, p. 317.

not only in their forced exile from their ancestral home but also in their being subjected to cruel and unrelenting persecution, mayhem, and murder in virtually all the lands into which they had been forcibly dispersed. Perhaps it took something of the magnitude of the Holocaust to convict those nations of their arrogance and contempt toward the Jews and of their need to make restitution to the Chosen People by recognizing their right to their homeland.

The Holocaust was not inflicted upon the Jewish people for what some Christians viewed as the obduracy and unbelief of either their ancestors or themselves, nor was it a *quid pro quo* for the establishment of the nation of Israel. "There is no salvation to be extracted from the Holocaust," says Michael Wyschogrod.[71] The Holocaust was not an act of God. It was entirely the product of pure evil incarnated in the hearts of utterly conscienceless human beings.

God, however, who created life from nothing and who summons things that are not into reality, did the impossible for the Jewish people. He took the evil that centuries of despots had inflicted upon the Jewish people, the evil that culminated in history's most horrific manifestation of utter human depravity, and, in its place, orchestrated the events before and after the Holocaust to bring about the rebirth of the nation of Israel in the Promised Land. The Almighty turned the tables on manifest evil by taking what others had planned for evil to the Jewish people and turning it into his own good—the means of fulfilling his own prophetic promise to establish the Jewish people in Israel, a secure nation, a land from which they will never be removed again[72] and in Jerusalem, a capital city "that will never again be uprooted or demolished."[73]

By producing this prophetic miracle, the Almighty not only foiled the Nazi's planned genocide of the Jewish people but also forged in them an undying determination to fulfill what Emil Fackenheim called the 614th commandment:[74] Never give Hitler any posthumous victories.[75] Since that time, the cry, "Never again!" has unceasingly resounded across the landscape of Israel and has echoed in the hearts of the Jewish people around the world.

---

[71] Michael Wyschogrod, *Abraham's Promise: Judaism and Jewish-Christian Relations* (Grand Rapids, MI: Wm. B. Eerdmans Publishing Co., 2004), p. 120.

[72] Amos 9:15.

[73] Jeremiah 31:40.

[74] The sages have calculated that there are 613 commandments in the Torah.

[75] Emil L. Fackenheim, *To Mend the World: Foundations of Post-Holocaust Jewish Thought* (Bloomington, IN: Indiana University Press, 1982), pp. xix–xx.

CHAPTER 10

# ISRAEL'S CONTINUING DILEMMA

## Hostile, Bellicose Muslim Neighbors

Compared to the unrelenting persecution and violence that the Jewish people experienced in Europe in the millennium that preceded the twentieth century, there was relative peace for those Jews who lived in Palestine and various other Middle Eastern and North African Arab Muslim nations, as well as in Spain in the centuries between the Muslim Umayyad conquest of Spain in the eighth century until the Spanish expulsion of the Jews in 1492. The Jewish experience in these lands was, however, far from the idyllic utopia of religious tolerance and mutuality that some historians have claimed as normative in Muslim societies of that time.[1] Indeed, the Islamic faith of those communities in which the Jews lived consigned them to the indignity of *dhimmi*, a form of second-class citizenship that was imposed by those dominions upon non-Muslims that subjected them to legal restrictions and taxation that were not imposed on Muslim citizens. Still, the circumstances for Jews were generally better than the constant dangers and threats of violence that confronted them in most of Christian Europe.

Bernard Harrison reports that "prior to the nineteenth century, a Jewish population had been immemorially present in Palestine, augmented over the centuries by a steady trickle of Jews immigrating either for religious reasons or to escape European persecutions."[2] During the

[1] For perspectives on Muslim religious tolerance, see María Rosa Menocal, *The Ornament of the World: How Muslims, Jews, and Christians Created a Culture of Tolerance in Medieval Spain* (New York: Little, Brown and Co., 2002). Menocal writes in glowing terms about the supposed utopian coexistence of the three monotheistic religions in medieval Spain. Robert Spencer, however, explodes Menocal's utopia myth, injecting a balanced analysis of the truth regarding Muslim tolerance. Robert Spencer, *The Myth of Islamic Tolerance: How Islamic Law Treats Non-Muslims* (Amherst, NY: Prometheus Books, 2005).

[2] Bernard Harrison, *The Resurgence of Anti-Semitism: Jews, Israel, and Liberal Opinion* (Lanham, MD: Rowman & Littlefield Publishers), p. 82.

nineteenth century, however, when Jewish immigration to Palestine began to increase significantly, the Arab and Muslim hosts became increasingly suspicious of Jewish intent and less tolerant of their presence. Then, as the twentieth century unfolded, especially before, during, and after World War II, the Muslim nations surrounding the land of Israel gradually became hotbeds of antisemitism,[3] and the Arab citizens of Palestine began to resort to violence against the Jewish people. The followers of Islam increasingly ignored Muhammad's designation of the Jews as "People of the Book" and his observations that they were "privileged above all people"[4] and adopted their prophet's later posture of intolerance toward the Jews, including calling them descendants of pigs and apes and the archenemies of Islam.[5] Even these caricatures, however, did not sink to the level of some in the Latin West which maintained that the "Jews were endowed with Satanic qualities"[6] and that they were vermin that should be exterminated for the health and well-being of Christian societies.

## Western Colonialism and Antisemitism

Muslim nations and communities around the world, particularly the Arab nations and communities in the Middle East, began to see a marked increase in antisemitism. In time, the majority of Muslims—particularly Arab Muslims—became extreme antisemites. Many scholars attribute this change in Muslim attitudes toward Jews to endemic antisemitism that Europeans brought with them when they colonized much of the Muslim world of the Middle East and Northern Africa. In fact, Western incursion into Muslim-dominated lands produced a "frenzied and irrational *new* Muslim anti-Semitism" which Mark Cohen maintains was not "indigenous to Islam."[7] Cohen says that this shift in Muslim views toward the Jews actually began during the Ottoman period[8] "when the

[3] George M. Fredrickson, *Diverse Nations: Explorations in the History of Racial and Ethnic Pluralism* (Abingdon, UK: Routledge, 2016), p. 182. Also, Avi Beker, *Jewish Communities of the World* (Minneapolis, MN: Lerner Publishing Group, 1998), p. 190.

[4] *Qur'an* 45:15.

[5] Andrew Bostom, *The Legacy of Islamic Antisemitism: From Sacred Texts to Solemn History* (Amherst NY: Prometheus Books, 2008), pp. 165–167.

[6] Marvin Perry and Howard E. Negrin, eds., *The Theory and Practice of Islamic Terrorism: An Anthology* (New York: Palgrave Macmillan, 2008), p. 201.

[7] Mark R. Cohen, "Muslim Anti-Semitism: Old or New?" in *A History of Jewish-Muslim Relations: From the Origins to the Present Day*, Abdelwahab Meddeb and Benjamin Stora, eds. (Princeton, NJ: Princeton University Press, 2013), p. 549.

[8] The Ottoman Empire was founded in the thirteenth century and continued to function well into the twentieth century when it finally was defeated during World War I and subsequently occupied by the European Allied Powers.

Islamic world absorbed new Christian populations" and "Muslims first came into contact with European-style anti-Semitism."[9]

Sara Cardaun maintains that European colonialism in the late nineteenth century further exacerbated this situation by importing "Western antisemitism into the Arab and Muslim world."[10] Erich Goode notes that "until the twentieth century, for the most part, Jews in Muslim lands were not persecuted, nor, with only a few exceptions, were they expelled or forced to convert."[11] It was only "with the rise of colonialism and the infusion of European anti-Semitism into Arab lands" that "Muslims began to see the Jews through Western eyes and treat them accordingly."[12] Robert Wistrich notes that the circumstances of Jews in Palestine became more perilous when they "found themselves caught between anti-Semitic European colonial rulers and the hostile indigenous Arab population."[13]

At first, many Jews in Muslim territories had "welcomed European colonialism in North Africa and the Middle East, because the Europeans promised to curtail the worst effects of discriminatory legal and social systems,"[14] says Michael Lerner. As Andrew Bostom points out, "The Jews of Arab lands had no vested interest in the old social and political order of their traditional Muslim overlords. Therefore, they welcomed European political domination that began with the French conquest of Algeria in the 1830s and culminated in the carving up of the Ottoman Empire at the end of World War I."[15] Sadly, the Jews had the misfortune of discovering that "the hopes they placed in their British, French, and Italian masters would be disappointed again and again."[16]

Tudor Parfitt observes that by the middle of the nineteenth century, "European influence in North Africa and the Middle East had serious repercussions for Jewish communities [as] doctrinaire Christian anti-Semitism increasingly started to find its way into the

---

[9] Cohen, p. 549.

[10] Sarah K. Cardaun, *Countering Contemporary Antisemitism in Britain: Government and Civil Society Responses between Universalism and Particularism* (Leiden, The Netherlands: Koninklijke Brill NV, 2015), p. 74.

[11] Erich Goode, *Deviant Behavior* (Abingdon, UK: Routledge, 2016), p. 327.

[12] Goode, p. 327.

[13] Robert S. Wistrich, *A Lethal Obsession: Anti-Semitism from Antiquity to the Global Jihad* (New York: Random House, 2010), p. 242.

[14] Michael Lerner, *The Socialism of Fools: Anti-Semitism on the Left* (Berkeley, CA: Tikkun Books, 1992), p. 44.

[15] Bostom, p. 156.

[16] Bostom, p. 156.

Islamic lands."[17] Indeed, "Jews had to face continual and periodic violent antisemitic outbursts from the European colonial population."[18] Tragically, says Micha Bar-Am, "many Jewish autonomous institutions ceased to exist as a direct result of European colonial legislation."[19]

Taoufik Djebali and Lee Whitfield maintain that the "European settlers exported their anti-Semitism to the Maghreb"[20] and that they expressed "their bigotry against the Maghrebi Jews in political and economic discrimination . . . and in violent forms," encouraging the "Muslim population to emulate their structured and aggressive anti-Semitism behavior."[21] Goode cites one of the glaring example of European antisemitism that began to afflict Arab Muslim societies: "Perhaps one of the strangest manifestations of the insidious trail of anti-Semitism is the contemporary credibility and popularity of the scurrilous *The Protocols of the Elders of Zion* in so much of the Muslim world."[22] As a matter of fact, this complete forgery, which was produced by the Russian secret service Okhrana in 1903,[23] has been used extensively by Middle Eastern Muslims and is "still widely reproduced by state-owned printing houses and circulated *en masse* in Islamic lands,"[24] often with Arab government subsidies.[25] This

[17] Tudor Parfitt, *The Jews of Africa and Asia: Contemporary Anti-Semitism and Other Pressures* (Budapest, Hungary: Minority Rights Group, 1987), p. 6.

[18] Micha Bar-Am, *Jews in Arab Lands Today* (Tel Aviv, Israel: Beit Hatfutsot, The Nahum Goldmann Museum of the Jewish Diaspora, 1996), p. 16.

[19] Mircea Eliade and Charles J. Adams, *The Encyclopedia of Religion* (London: UK: Macmillan Library Reference, 1987), vol. 8, p. 163.

[20] The Maghreb is comprised of the nations of Northern Africa, including Libya, Tunisia, Algeria, and Morocco.

[21] Taoufik Djebali and Lee Whitfield, "The Ethnic Mosaic in the Maghreb: Cultures in Crisis," in *North African Mosaic: A Cultural Reappraisal of Ethnic and Religious Minorities* (Newcastle, UK: Cambridge Scholars Publishing, 2007), p. 78.

[22] The *Protocols of the Elders of Zion* is purported to have been the minutes of a meeting of Jewish leaders in which plans were discussed for subverting the morality of the Gentile world so that the Jews could accomplish their plan for global domination. While the entire forged document is utterly spurious; it has been used for more than a century to lend "support" to the outrageous charges of antisemites around the world that the Jewish people have an evil agenda to rule the world. The *Protocols of the Elders of Zion* was responsible for virulent antisemitism that spread across Russia and Europe and has extended unchecked into Muslim societies around the world and to many other nations as well. In the early twentieth century, Henry Ford sponsored the production and dissemination of 500,000 copies of this book so that it gained a foothold in the United States and other countries. Neil Baldwin, *Henry Ford and the Jews: The Mass Production of Hate* (New York: PublicAffairs, 2001), pp. 141–143, 160.

[23] Riaz Hassan, *Islam and Society: Sociological Explorations* (Melbourne, Australia: Melbourne University Publishing, 2014), p. 182, n. 1.

[24] Robert S. Wistrich, *Anti-Zionism and Antisemitism in the Contemporary World* (Basingstoke, UK: Macmillan Press, Ltd., 1990), p. 103.

[25] Kenneth Levin, *The Oslo Syndrome: Delusions of a People Under Siege* (Hanover, NH: Smith and Kraus Publishers, 2005), p. 168.

spurious book in which the worst elements of European antisemitism's caricature and libel of Jews was codified, has become—and remains to this day—a textbook that is used in Arab educational institutions.

## Nazi Propaganda and Arab Antisemitism

Riaz Hassan maintains that the leading causes for the explosion of antisemitism in the Arab-Muslim world of the twentieth century were twofold: 1) "the rise of the Nazi ideology that elevated the exterminations of the Jews and anti-Semitism to a national goal of the Nazi state," and 2) "success of the Nazi propaganda effort to export it to the Arab Muslim lands by successfully exploiting their resentments."[26] With the crossbreeding of Christian and Islamic antisemitism in the nineteenth century and the rising influence of Nazi antisemitism in the greater Muslim world in the twentieth century, it was no wonder that "Nazi and fascist antisemitic agitation and legislation was an inspiration for Muslim antisemitic pogroms in Algeria, Turkey, Iraq, Morocco, Libya, Egypt . . . and Muslim antisemitic legislation in Egypt and Turkey."[27] A new, more virulent strain of antisemitism was produced as history's oldest and most pernicious psychological and spiritual pathology found a fertile environment for explosive growth among Arab Muslim peoples.[28]

The Third Reich's ideology was advanced in the wider Arab world through Nazi collaboration with "key religious figures like the Grand Mufti [of Jerusalem] Haj Amin el-Husseini with the Nazi regime."[29] This, too, confirms the fact that Arab antisemitism was at least augmented, if not induced, by foreign influences.[30] Before, during, and after the rise of Nazism, El-Husseini was one of the greatest promoters of antisemitism in Palestine.[31] He became such an ardent supporter of the causes of Nazi

[26] Hassan, p. 181. Also, Klaus Gensicke, *The Mufti of Jerusalem and the Nazis: The Berlin Years*, tr. Alexander Gunn (Middlesex, UK: Middlesex House, 2011), and Klaus-Michael Mallmann and Martin Cüppers, *Nazi Palestine: The Plans for the Extermination of the Jews in Palestine* (New York: Enigma Books, 2010).

[27] Michel Gurfinkiel, "France, Antisemitism, and the Prognosis for European Jewry," in *Anti-Judaism, Antisemitism, and Delegitimizing Israel*, Robert S. Wistrich, ed. (Lincoln, NE: The University of Nebraska Press, 2016), p. 185.

[28] *E.g.*, Saudi Arabian Wahhabist extremism, which claims to the most authentic form of Islam.

[29] Cardaun, p. 75.

[30] Cardaun, p. 75.

[31] Joseph B. Schechtman, *The Mufti and the Fuhrer: The Rise and Fall of Haj Amin el-Husseini* (New York: Thomas Youseloff, 1965). Also, Lukasz Hirszowicz, *The Third Reich and the Arab East* (London, UK: Routledge & Kegan Paul, 1966); John F. Rothmann, *Icon of Evil: Hitler's Mufti and the Rise of Radical Islam* (New Brunswick, NJ: Transaction Books, 2009); and Gensicke, *The Mufti*.

Germany, especially its determination to eradicate the Jewish population from the face of the earth, that he has been called "Hitler's henchman."[32] His fixation on preventing Jewish emigration from Europe to Palestine has been blamed for making the Holocaust inevitable.[33] El-Husseini came to believe that "Islam was an inherently anti-Jewish doctrine,"[34] and he blamed the Jews for being "the driving forces of the destruction of the regime of the Islamic Caliphate" in the Middle East. El-Husseini's views on Jews and Judaism made him totally vulnerable to the charge of Nazi propaganda that World War II was a "Jewish war."[35] He certainly shared the Third Reich's claims that the "aim of international Jewry and its Allied stooges was the creation of a Jewish state in Palestine that would expand and threaten the entire Middle East and the Islamic world."[36] Additionally, he believed the Nazi charge that "the Jews were intent on exterminating the Arabs and Muslims in Palestine and even on seeking to 'destroy' Islam."[37] El-Husseini also argued that "wicked American intentions toward the Arabs are now clearer, and there remain no doubts that they are endeavoring to establish a Jewish empire in the Arab world."[38] With this in mind, he urged his fellow Muslims: "Rise as one and fight for your sacred rights. Kill the Jews wherever you find them."[39] Rich Cohen gives a chilling description of the Grand Mufti's passion for ridding Palestine of the Jews when he described the scene of a British engagement against rioting in the Holy City on August 8, 1929: "In Jerusalem, the crowds chanted: Death! Death! Death! Behind the rioters were the Bearded Sheiks . . . and the Grand Mufti, whose face drifted, laughing across the Jerusalem sky."[40]

## Terrorism: Reviving Antisemitism's Ancient Strategy

For nearly seven decades since the establishment of the nation of Israel, the Jewish people have continually sought peace with their Arab

[32] Menahem Kaufman, *An Ambiguous Partnership: Non-Zionists and Zionists in America 1939–1948* (Jerusalem, Israel: Magnes Press, 1991), pp. 306-307.

[33] Wolfgang G. Schwanitz and Barry Rubin, *Nazis, Islamists, and the Making of the Modern Middle East* (New Haven, CT: Yale University Press, 2014), p. 160.

[34] Jeffrey Herf, "Nazi Propaganda to the Arab World during World War II," in *Antisemitism Before and Since the Holocaust: Altered Contexts and Recent Perspectives*, Anthony McElligott and Jeffrey Herf, eds. (Cham, Switzerland: Palgrave Macmillan, 2017), p. 195.

[35] Jeffrey Herf, *Nazi Propaganda for the Arab World* (New Haven, CT: Yale University Press, 2009), p. 263.

[36] Herf, p. 263.

[37] Herf, p. 263.

[38] Herf, p. 263.

[39] Haj Amin el-Husseini, quoted in Herf, p. 195. The Mufti's instructions echoed the command of *Qur'an* 9:5: "Kill the idolaters wherever you find them."

[40] Rich Cohen, *Israel Is Real: An Obsessive Quest to Understand the Jewish Nation and Its History* (New York: Farrar, Straus and Giroux, 2009), p. 192.

neighbors. For the same seven decades, however, the Arab nations and even some Arabs living in religiously tolerant Israel—especially the part of Israel called the "West Bank"—have seized every opportunity to inflict violence on the Jewish people by maiming and murdering innocent civilians—men, women, and children. The pages of restored Israel's short history have been littered with armed insurgencies, suicide bombings of Israeli restaurants, holy sites, and buses, indiscriminate Scud missile attacks, and almost innumerable mortar, rocket, and missile barrages—all of which have been aimed specifically (to the greatest degree possible, given the technical inefficiencies of Arab weaponry) at Israeli civilian population centers. Except for the 1948 Arab war against Israel, the 1967 Six-Day War, and the 1973 Yom Kippur War (all of which were waged against both Israeli military facilities and Jewish civilian centers), virtually all of the Arab violence directed against Israel has taken the form of terrorist acts specifically designed to inflict horrific suffering and death upon Jewish civilians. This strategy has been part of the Muslim grand design to weaken the resolve of the rest of the entire Israeli populace.

In the years immediately after the restoration of the nation of Israel, therefore, those Jewish people who had boldly accepted the challenge to return to the land of their ancestors found themselves constantly "vulnerable to terrorist attacks."[41] The borders of Israel were porous, and the nation was not well equipped to defend incursions from those who were intent on murder and mayhem. The violence that the Arabs had regularly fomented in Palestine since the days of British rule was merely escalated and redirected from the British to the Israelis.[42] Then, in the 1950s, outright terrorism against Israel began in earnest "with cross-border attacks launched from neighboring states, particularly Egypt and Jordan, both of which were known as 'sanctuary states.'"[43] Palestinian *fedayeen*[44] "crossed the Israeli border and attacked Israeli civilians and targets of strategic importance such as irrigation systems, electric supplies, agricultural equipment, and buses,"[45] while at all cost avoiding military installations

[41] Benjamin Pogrund, *Drawing Fire: Investigating the Accusations of Apartheid in Israel* (Lanham, MD: Rowman & Littlefield, 2014), p. 49.

[42] Gary A. Tobin and Dennis R. Ybarra, *The Trouble with Textbooks: Distorting History and Religion* (Lanham, MD: Rowman & Littlefield Publishers, 2008), p. 135.

[43] James Ciment, *World Terrorism: An Encyclopedia of Political Violence from Ancient Times to the Post-9/11 Era* (Armonk, NY: M. E. Sharpe Publishing, 2011), p. 295.

[44] The Arabic word *fedayeen* means "fighters."

[45] Ciment, p. 295.

and posted Israel Defense Forces personnel. The cynical cowardice of the Arab Muslim population and its jihadist terrorists knew no bounds.

The Arab Muslims employed the same strategy for attacking the Israelis that the ancient Amalekites used when they became the first people to oppose God's plan to bring his Chosen People into the Promised Land.[46] The Amalekites "always operated as terrorists, particularly in their attacks against Israel,"[47] says Paul Williams. Here is how God himself described the Amalekite strategy: "Remember what the Amalekites did to you along the way when you came out of Egypt. When you were weary and worn out, they met you on your journey and cut off all who were lagging behind; they had no fear of God."[48] Williams maintains that "the Amalekite strategy was one of terrorism, avoiding the heart of the Israelite military and attacking the weak and weary, the innocent and undefended."[49] The Amalekite plan was simple: launch surprise attacks on the perimeters and prey on the weak and defenseless. The devious warfare strategy that Agag, the king of the Amalekites, employed was certainly manifest in one of his direct descendants: Haman, the Agagite prime minister of Persia, who planned and orchestrated the devious stratagem for the first attempted genocide of the Jewish people.[50]

Some scholars have suggested that Islam's prophet, Muhammad, may also have been a descendant of Amalek.[51] Others have argued that Adolph Hitler was either an Amalekite or, at the very least, operated in the spirit of Amalek.[52] Perhaps this history of terror-

[46] Exodus 17:8.

[47] Paul R. Williams, "The Spirit of Amalek," *Restore!*, Issue 25, pp. 16–18.

[48] Deuteronomy 25:17–18, NIV.

[49] Williams, pp. 16–18. Williams argues that "the spirit of Amalek is still manifest today in world terrorism, particularly that of the Muslim Arabs whose hatred for Israel and the Jewish people knows no bounds. . . . The spirit of terrorism is . . . clearly manifest in those who will 'die to the last man' in order to drive Israel into the Mediterranean."

[50] Esther 3:8.

[51] Irving M. Zeitlin, *The Historical Muhammad* (Cambridge, UK: Polity Press, 2007), p. 27. Zeitlin quotes William Muir's observation: "We learn from the Muslim tradition that the earliest inhabitants of Mecca, Medina, and the deserts of Syria, were Amalekites." Also, William Muir, *The Life of Mahomet and History of Islam* (London, England: Smith, Elder, and Co., 1858), vol. II, p. 207.

[52] Konrad Kwiet and Jürgen Matthaus, *Contemporary Responses to the Holocaust* (Westport, CT: Greenwood Publishing Group, 2004), p. 9. Also Gershon Greenberg, "Ultra-Orthodox Jewish Thought about the Holocaust since World War II," in *The Impact of the Holocaust on Jewish Theology*, Steven T. Katz, ed. (New York: New York University Press, 2005), pp. 143–147; Aaron Rakeffet-Rothkoff and Joseph Epstein, *The Rav: The Word of Rabbi Joseph B. Soloveitchik* (Hoboken, NJ: KTAV Publishing House, 1999), vol. 2, p. 152; and Reuven Firestone, *Holy War in Judaism: The Fall and Rise of a Controversial Idea* (Oxford, UK: Oxford University Press, 2012), pp. 99–107. Firestone is of the opinion that "the Amalekite line was finally destroyed in Persia" when Haman was executed (Firestone, p. 102); however, others say that it continued to be manifest in Adolph Hitler and that it is now demonstrated in Arab Muslim terrorists.

ism proves the truth of the declaration that God made to Moses immediately after the Israelite's first battlefield engagement with the Amalekites: "Write this on a scroll as something to be remembered. . . . The LORD will be at war against the Amalekites from generation to generation."[53] Even if the ancestry of the Palestinian Arabs cannot traced be directly to the Amalekites, the strategy of terrorism that they have employed has certainly mirrored the one that King Agag used. Whenever modern Israel has been vulnerable, the Arab Muslims have not hesitated to launch horrendous terrorist attacks against the Israelis. Plenty of Arab Muslim volunteers have always been ready and willing to launch suicide attacks in hopes of gaining a heavenly reward for their despicable jihadist atrocities.

## Preemptive Warfare: Suppressing Terrorism

The overall scene of violence against Israel changed dramatically, however, with the Six-Day War in 1967, when Israel responded to increasing threats from its Arab neighbors by launching an invasion of Egypt and following it up with attacks on Jordan and Syria. In the bellicosity that led up to and precipitated this war, Egyptian President Gamal Abdel Nasser had blocked the Straits of Tiran, thereby closing Israel's access to the Red Sea through the port of Eilat. Then, on May 27, Nasser boasted, "We intend to open a general assault against Israel. This will be total war. Our basic aim will be to destroy Israel."[54] Syrian defense minister Hafez al-Assad had also declared, "I, as a military man, believe that the time has come to enter into a battle of annihilation."[55] Then, on May 31, Iraqi president Abdul Rahman Aref had arrogantly proclaimed, "This is our opportunity to wipe out the ignominy which has been with us since 1948. Our goal is clear—to wipe Israel off the map."[56] King Faisal bin Abdulaziz Al Saud of Saudi Arabia had also warned, "Every Arab who does not participate in this conflict will seal his fate. He will not be worthy of being called an Arab."[57] Earlier, in 1954, the Saudi king had summed

[53] Exodus 17:14–16, NIV.

[54] Gamal Abdel Nasser, quoted in Pogrund, p. 49.

[55] Hafez al-Assad, quoted in Joseph Telushkin, *A Code of Jewish Ethics, Volume 2: Love Your Neighbor as Yourself* (New York: Bell Tower, 2009), p. 352.

[56] Abdul Rahman Aref, quoted in Mark A. Tessler, *A History of the Israeli-Palestinian Conflict* (Bloomington, IN: Indiana University Press, 1994), p. 393.

[57] King Faisal, quoted in Steven Pressfield, *The Lion's Gate: On the Front Lines of the Six Day War* (New York: Penguin Group, 2014), p. 128.

up the seriousness with which he viewed the necessity of annihilating Israel: "The Arab nations should sacrifice up to 10 million of their 50 million people, if necessary to wipe out Israel. . . . Israel to the Arab world is like a cancer to the human body, and the only way to remedy is to uproot it, just like a cancer."[58]

Believing that the leaders of the Arab nations meant precisely what they had said, Israel wisely initiated a preemptive attack on Egypt on June 5, 1967, in which the Israeli Air Force destroyed more than three hundred Egyptian airplanes on the ground, and the Israeli Defense Force subsequently routed the Egyptian army of 100,000 in the Sinai Peninsula.[59] At the same time, Jordan's King Hussein chose to ignore the message sent to him by the Israeli forces in which they assured the Jordanians that they had no intentions of attacking them. Hussein ordered his troops to begin hurling an estimated 6,000 shells into Jewish Jerusalem's city center and suburbs in the then-partitioned Jerusalem.[60] This action, in turn, prompted the Israeli Defense Force to undertake a counterattack that routed Jordan's vaunted Arab Legion, chasing them out of Jerusalem, out of the West Bank, and across the Jordan River.[61] During this battle, Israel reclaimed the Temple Mount, Judaism's holiest shrine, from which all Jews had been denied access since the time of King Abdullah's invasion of Israel in 1948 and his occupation of East Jerusalem and the West Bank.[62] Finally, as the Six-Day War was winding down, when Israelis were also attacked by Syria, the Israeli army defeated the Syrian forces and secured the Golan Heights. This action removed Arab armies from the plateau of high ground situated above the east side of Sea of Galilee and its surrounding area and brought an end to the periodic and indiscriminate Arab shelling of the greater Galilee.

David Rodman observes that "the outcome of the 1967 Six-Day War radically altered the geographical status quo in the Arab-Israeli

[58] King Faisal, quoted in Alan M. Dershowitz, *Chutzpah* (New York: Simon & Schuster, 1991), p. 214.

[59] Pogrund, p. 50.

[60] Robert O. Freedman, *Contemporary Israel: Domestic Politics, Foreign Policy, and Security Challenges* (Bolder, CO: Westview Press, 2009), p. 8. Hussein later claimed that the shelling "had happened in contravention of his orders." Tom Segev, *1967: Israel, the War, and the Year that Transformed the Middle East* (New York: Metropolitan Books, 2005), p. 510.

[61] Pogrund, p. 50.

[62] During their two decades of control of East Jerusalem and other parts of Israel, the Jordanians denied the Jews access to their shrines and holy places in the Jordanian-occupied territory. This Muslim strategy should be strongly contrasted with the Israeli posture of permitting Muslims free access to their shrines and allowing Arabs to control the Mosque of Omar (the Dome of the Rock) and the Al-Aqsa Mosque, which are situated on the plateau where of the ancient Jewish Temple was located. Israel paid a high price for allowing Arab control of the Temple Mount, however, when the Palestinian Authority destroyed priceless treasures that they had excavated while tunneling under the Temple Mount in a perverse attempt to negate Israeli claims that Jerusalem was the site of the Temples of Solomon and Herod.

conflict. Not only had Israel completely pulverized the Egyptian, Jordanian, and Syrian armies, but it had also captured large tracts of Egyptian, Jordanian, and Syrian territory."[63] These acquisitions "provided [Israel] with a measure of strategic depth for the first time in its history, particularly vis-à-vis Egypt in the south and Jordan in the east. Israel's major population centers, industrial assets, and military bases no longer remained within easy reach of Arab armies and terrorist organizations."[64] Amazingly, however, despite one of the most resounding, rapid, and total defeats in the history of warfare, the Arab nations and the Palestinian Arabs continued to persist with their demands for the destruction of Israel. As Abba Eban, the Israeli Foreign Minister of that time, wryly observed, "This is the first war in history that on the morrow the victors sued for peace and the vanquished called for unconditional surrender."[65]

## Continuing and Unrelenting Hostility

In every conflict between the Arab nations and the Jewish state, the Israelis had won handily. As former Israeli Prime Minister Golda Meir said, "We don't thrive on military acts. We do them because we have to, and thank God we are efficient."[66] Still, the Arab nations have simply refused to recognize the right of the Jews to live in their ancestral land with complete self-determination. From 1969–1970, Israel fought a war of attrition with Egypt, in which the Arab nation was backed by the Soviet Union. This conflict ended in a stalemate. Then, in 1973, the Yom Kippur War took place when Egypt, Syria, Jordan, Iraq, Algeria, Morocco, and Tunisia, supported by Cuba and North Korea, invaded Israel on the highest and holiest day of the Jewish year: *Yom Kippur* (the Day of Atonement). After Israel repelled the invasion, Egypt negotiated a peace treaty with Israel, and Syria agreed to a disengagement.

Then in 1978, Israel forced the withdrawal of the Palestine Liberation Organization, the epitome of terrorist organizations, from Southern Lebanon. In 1982, a mere four years after that event, Israel's action in the First Lebanon War forced the complete expulsion of the

[63] David Rodman, *Sword and Shield of Zion: The Israel Air Force in the Arab-Israeli Conflict* (Eastbourne, UK: Sussex Academic Press, 2014), p. 3.

[64] Rodman, p. 3.

[65] Abba Eban, quoted in Jack Bloom, *Out of Step: Life-Story of a Politician: Politics and Religion in a World at War* (Bloomington, IN: The Indiana University Press, 2005), p. 302.

[66] Golda Meir, quoted in *Vogue* (July 1969).

PLO from Lebanon. Only five years later in 1987, the Palestinian Arabs initiated the First Intifada,[67] a terrorist action that continued for six years, ending only with the Oslo I Accords. This peace, like every other "peace" initiative with the Arabs,[68] did not last, for in 2000, the Palestinian Arabs launched the Second Intifada, a conflict that continued for five years and ended with Israel's victory and the construction of the Israeli West Bank barrier. One year later, in response to missile and mortar attacks from Hezbollah in southern Lebanon, Israel launched the Second Lebanon War, which ended in a stalemate.

In 2005, a "land-for-peace" experiment was undertaken by Israeli Prime Minister Ariel Sharon with Israel's unilateral disengagement from Gaza. This action, however, merely resulted in the establishment of an "independent Palestinian State" in Gaza.[69] Almost immediately, the Israeli territory in Gaza that had been ceded to the Palestinian Authority was coopted by the inveterate terrorist organization Hamas and turned into little more than a launching pad for the missiles and rockets that the terrorists would thereafter hurl indiscriminately toward Israeli population centers. Two years after that, in 2008, Israel was forced to initiate Operation Cast Lead, a three-week engagement against Hamas in order to stop terrorists from launching rocket attacks.[70] Shortly after that time, Operation Pillar of Defense became a necessary measure in order for the Israeli military to ensure the cessation of Hamas rocket fire from Gaza into Israel, at least temporarily.[71] Then again, in 2014, in response to continuing Hamas missile and rocket fire into southern Israel, the Israeli army was forced to launch Operation Protective Edge in order to destroy additional

[67] The Arabic word *intifada* means "uprising," "insurrection," "revolt," or "rebellion." It is an organized opposition to authority in which one faction attempts to wrest control from another. It describes the campaign of protest and violent resistance that the Palestinian Arabs directed at Israel in protest against Israel's so-called "occupation" of the "Palestinian" territories.

[68] The Arabic word for "truce" or "ceasefire," is *hudna*, which does not mean "peace treaty," but actually means a "negotiated halt to fighting intended to be used for rearming" or "a pause until a better fighting opportunity arises." Joshua Spurlock, "Analysis: Hate and Hudna—The True Face of Hamas' Approach to 'Ceasefires,'" posted at www.themideastupdate.com, July 27, 2014.

[69] Paul Eidelberg, *An American Political Scientist in Israel: From Athens to Jerusalem* (Lanham, MD: Rowman and Littlefield Publishers, Inc., 2010), p. 78. Eidelberg gives an excellent analysis of the "land-for-peace" strategy that he says has been "the icon of Israel's ruling elites." It was this strategy that transformed Gaza from "flourishing Jewish land" into a "haven for terrorist organizations" from which Israel has been struck "with thousands of missiles" that have left "women and children traumatized."

[70] Igor Primoratz and David W. Lovell, *Protecting Civilians during Violent Conflict: Theoretical and Practical Issues for the 21st Century* (Abingdon, UK: Routledge, 2012), p. 257.

[71] Amir Lupovici, *The Power of Deterrence* (Cambridge, UK: Cambridge University Press, 2016), p. 174.

Hamas rocket launchers. In the process, the Israeli forces discovered an elaborate system of tunnels that the terrorist organization had surreptitiously designed, constructed, and fortified under Israel's border with Gaza in order to make the Israeli civilian population even more vulnerable to attacks by its jihadists.[72] These tunnels were destroyed; however, their existence proved once again that the Palestinian land-for-peace gambit in Gaza was nothing but a ruse.

The unending litany of violence perpetrated by the Palestinian Arabs has been equipped and funded by terror-sponsoring states that at one time or another have included virtually all of the Arab nations as well as other Muslim-dominated nations such as Iran and Pakistan. This systematic and unrelenting terrorism has continually exposed the Israeli population to mayhem and murder. The international Muslim population has directed an overwhelming and irrational hatred toward the Jewish state for virtually all of its near seven decades of existence. The Israelis have had to live their lives in constant fear of terrorist attacks, listening for the ubiquitous sound of sirens directing them to bomb shelters and reviewing the all-too-frequent reports of murdered and maimed Israeli citizens, virtually all of whom have been civilians, mostly women and children.

The construction of the West Bank barrier has limited the access of suicide bombers to Israel;[73] however, depraved Muslim individuals have continued to launch individual attacks against Jews, shooting them from motorcycles, driving vehicles into crowds waiting at city bus stops, slashing and stabbing them with knives, and generally continuing the Muslim reign of terror by almost exclusively targeting innocent civilians. "Some historical and political context reveals that it is actually the Palestinian leaders who routinely incite and train their people towards the desired goal of the annihilation of the Jews."[74] And it is an undeniable fact that virtually all the terrorism employed by the Palestinian Arabs against Israel is funded by those Muslim nations that are intent on Israel's destruction or by Western

[72] Michal Shavit, *Media Strategy and Military Operations in the 21st Century: Mediatizing the Israel Defense Forces* (Abingdon, UK: Routledge, 2017), pp. 152–154.

[73] The installation of the West Bank barrier has reduced Palestinian Arab terrorist attacks on Israel by an estimated 90%. Elgin F. Hunt and David C. Colander, *Social Science: An Introduction to the Study of Society* (Boston, MA: Pearson, 2006), p. 388. Also, Mitchell Bard, "West Bank Security Fence: Background & Overview," Jewish Virtual Library, posted at www.jewishvirtuallibrary.org.

[74] Tricia Aven and Tricia Miller, *Jews and Anti-Judaism in Esther and the Church* (Cambridge, UK: James Clark & Co., 2015), p. 176.

nations that give billions of dollars to fund Palestinian so-called "humanitarian relief" that is instead funneled into terrorist programs.

## Violence in Muslim Cultures

Such acts of Muslim violence against the Jews, however, certainly come as no surprise because some thirteen centuries have been littered with the impact of Muslim-on-Muslim violence, principally in the ongoing conflicts between Shia and Sunni Muslims.[75] Daily news in electronic and print media is punctuated with reports either of violent attacks launched by one of these prominent denominations of Islam against the other or of brutal barrages from Muslim splinter groups against other Muslim communities. Then, groups of Islamist terrorists also initiate continuing guerrilla actions against various governments and religious groups—Christian, Buddhist, Hindu, Sikh, and others. Every people group that is not Muslim and every religion that is not Islam is fair game, and every day is open season for the slaughter of innocents among them. It has been estimated that for decades, fully 90% of all terrorist incidents in the world have been sponsored, led, and perpetrated by Muslims.[76]

James Gauss observes that the ancient "pattern of Islamic barbarity continues into the modern era and the 21st century."[77] Steve Koehane reports that from 1970–2000, "there were 43,721 terrorist attacks worldwide; 113,425 people were killed; over 82,126 were injured," and he notes that "over 90% of these barbaric acts were committed by Muslims."[78] Listing some 14 nations "where the plague of Islamic aggression is bearing [*sic*] its vicious fangs and encroaching upon others with its marauding tentacles," Ahamkaari says that today, "over three fourths of the world's armed conflicts involve Muslim 'issues' and individuals,"[79] a fact that prompts him to draw the following conclusion: "For a community that accounts for one fifth of the human head count, their hogging such a disproportionate share

[75] The Shia vs. Sunni Muslim conflict, in which both sects vie for the control of Islam, has been raging since the death of Muhammad. For a comprehensive study of this conflict, see Lesley Hazleton, *After the Prophet: The Epic Story of the Shia-Sunni Split in Islam* (New York: Knopf Doubleday Publishing Group, 2009).

[76] Ryszard Stemplowski, *Transnational Terrorism in the World System Perspective* (Warsaw, Poland: Polish Institute of International Affairs, 2002), p. 176.

[77] James F. Gauss, *Islam & Christianity: A Revealing Contrast* (Alachua, FL: Bridge-Logos Publishing, 2009), p. 275.

[78] Steve Keohane, "Muhammad: Terrorist or Prophet?", posted at http://bibleprobe.com/muhammad.htm.

[79] Ahamkaari Ahamkaari, *Will I Be Killed? (for writing the following contents. . .)* (Lincoln, NE: iUniverse, 2003), p. 151.

of troubles cannot be deemed purely coincidental."[80] In virtually every conflict in which Muslim extremists are involved anywhere in the world, they employ the standard *jihadi* terrorist tactic that Islamists always use by targeting civilian populations rather than engaging military or law enforcement personnel. The obsession of Muslim extremists with the spread of Islam on the edge of the sword is legendary, reaching back in history to the seventh-century founding of Islam, and it continues unabated to this day. The facts speak for themselves: a significant portion of the Muslim population of the world engages in extremist interpretations of the *Qur'an*, and they act on their interpretations by seeking to spread Islam through violence and warfare. According to surveys, fully 10% of the Muslim population of the world believes that terrorism is justified at least some of the time.[81] Since there are 1.8 billion Muslims in the world, this means that 180 million Muslims—certainly not an insignificant number—confess that they support terrorism.

A cursory review of the unspeakable atrocities of ISIS, another incarnation of Islamist evil and the latest Muslim "caliphate," serves to underscore the extent to which extremist and fanatical interpreters of the *Qur'an* can stoop in their depraved determination to spread their own version of Islam on the edge of the sword. These include staging mass executions of Yazidis, Druze, and Muslims of different sects, and slaughter of Babylonian and Syrian Christians even by crucifixion, organizing public mass beheadings (with the decapitations sometimes posted live on social media), burning prisoners of war alive, carrying out mass drownings, burying people alive *en masse*, staging firing-squad executions of large numbers of children whose only "sin" was not "properly" celebrating Ramadan. They also engage in vicious child rape, force girls and young women to submit to "circumcision" (a euphemism for excision of the clitoris and the labia of the vagina and sewing it almost completely shut) to "ensure" their virginity, offer women as sex-slave prizes in contests for the best observance of Islam, engage in the gang rape of women of other religions including those of other Muslim sects, slave trade of women and children, and a long, virtually interminable, list of

[80] Ahamkaari, p. 151.

[81] The results of a 2007 Pew Research Foundation poll surveying beliefs of Muslims around the world are staggering. "Muslim Americans: Middle Class and Mostly Mainstream," *Pew Research*, May 22, 2007, p. 97.

other atrocities. ISIS glories in its barbarism, releasing slick pamphlets justifying child rape and sex slavery as well as promoting and glamorizing its atrocities and crimes against humanity in well-crafted propaganda videos designed for distribution on social media.[82]

Considering the brutal, barbaric tactics that ISIS has proudly employed against civilian populations, it should be easy for anyone to understand the continuing danger that Israel faces from Hamas, which is simply another incarnation of the same Islamist evil that ISIS represents. In fact, the same philosophy that ISIS espouses also undergirds Hamas as well as other Islamist organizations like the Muslim Brotherhood.[83] Under this philosophy, Hamas brutalizes the citizens of Gaza, routinely and summarily executes suspected Israeli collaborators without trial or due process, uses women and children as human shields both to protect its military assets and to stand between its militants and the Israeli Defense Forces, and launches missiles against Israeli population centers from its own civilian centers, including hospitals, libraries, schools, hospitals, and even United Nations facilities.[84]

Muhammad himself set the precedent and established this course of action for unfolding world events that would involve his disciples when he boasted, "I, last of the Prophets, am sent with a sword. The sword is the key to heaven and hell. All who draw it in the name of the faith will be rewarded."[85] The ensuing history also clearly speaks for itself: "Within less than 100 years after Islam's appearance, Arab Muslim warriors had swept out of Arabia into the Middle East and North Africa, bringing about the downfall of Byzantium and Persia and inaugurating a succession of Islamic states that would rule a large part of the known world until the collapse of the Ottoman dynasty

---

[82] For greater detail on the atrocities perpetrated by ISIS in the name of Islam, see Erick Stakelbeck, *ISIS Exposed: Beheadings, Slavery, and the Hellish Reality of Radical Islam* (Washington DC: Regnery Publishing, 2015); Johnnie Moore, *Defying ISIS: Preserving Christianity in the Place of Its Birth and in Your Own Backyard* (Nashville, TN: Thomas Nelson, Inc., 2015); and Sami Moubayed, *Under the Black Flag: At the Frontier of the New Jihad* (London, UK: I.B. Tauris & Co., 2015).

[83] The slogan of the Muslim Brotherhood is "*Allah* is our goal. The Prophet is our Leader. The *Qur'an* is our law. *Jihad* is our way. Death in the way of Allah is our exalted hope." Shaul Bartal, *Jihad in Palestine: Political Islam and the Israeli-Palestinian Conflict* (Abingdon, UK: Routledge, 2016), p. 44.

[84] Orde F. Kittrie, *Lawfare: Law as a Weapon of War* (Oxford, UK: Oxford University Press, 2016), p. 305. Also Alan Dershowitz, *The Case Against the Iran Deal: How Can We Now Stop Iran from Getting Nukes?* (New York: Rosetta Books, 2015), p. 151, and Malcolm Russell, *The Middle East and South Asia 2015–2016* (Lanham, MD: Rowman & Littlefield, 2015), p. 102.

[85] Morris Katz, *The Journey: A Trip to Eternity* (Victoria, Canada: Trafford Publishing, 2004), p. 139.

after World War I," writes Juan Campo.[86]

Despite the fact that strong tendencies toward antisemitism exist in the very core religious documents of Islam which support Muslim hatred for Jews and things Jewish, the conclusion that antisemitism is endemic in Muslim societies cannot be made. Such a conclusion is belied by the relatively peaceful coexistence of 1.5 million Arab Israelis and their Jewish neighbors in the land of Israel.[87] These Arabs represent 20% of the population of Israel and are Israeli citizens.[88] They are represented in the Knesset, Israel's parliament,[89] and they join Christian, Druze, and Bahá'í citizens in freely practicing their religion. In 2014, Israel gave formal recognition to Christians in Upper Nazareth who are Arameans, not Arabs, as distinctly Israeli-Arameans.[90] Muslim scholar Muqtedar Khan makes a significant statement when he says, "I must remind you that Israel treats its 1 million Arab citizens with greater respect and dignity than most Arab nations treat their own citizens."[91] Israel allows both Arabic and Hebrew language options, and it "respects Islamic religious laws in marital and family affairs."[92] While the relationship between Muslims and Jews in Israel is far from utopian, it certainly is not always a reflection of the rabid antisemitism that is manifest in the Middle Eastern Muslim world, despite the fact that Arab Muslim Israeli citizens are sometimes involved in acts of terrorism against their Jewish neighbors.

---

[86] Juan Eduardo Campo, *Encyclopedia of Islam* (New York: Infobase Publishing, 2009), p. xxix. Campo says, "On the basis of the success of the Muslim conquests, it has become commonplace to assert that Islam is a violent religion that was spread by the sword." At the same time, however, he argues that "scholars specializing in the early history of Islam and its transregional expansion have found that the historical factors involved were much more varied and complex than the 'conquest by the sword' thesis would suggest.

[87] For perspectives on relations between Arabic and Jewish citizens of Israel, see Ilan Pappé, *The Forgotten Palestinians: A History of the Palestinians in Israel* (New Haven, CT: Yale University Press, 2011); Azar Ajaj, Duane A. Miller, and Philp Sumpter, *Arab Evangelicals in Israel* (Eugene, OR: Wipf and Stock Publishers, 2016); and Raphael Israeli, *Fundamentalist Islam and Israel: Essays in Interpretation* (Lanham, MD: University Press of America, Inc., 1993).

[88] This number includes 122,000 Palestinian Christians living in Israel, who represent 1.6 percent of the total Israeli population. Una McGahern, *Palestinian Christians in Israel: State Attitudes towards Non-Muslims in a Jewish State* (Abingdon, UK: Routledge, 2011), pp. 40–45.

[89] The number of Muslim members of the Knesset varies. Ido Shahar, "A Contextual Analysis of a Legal Circular," in *Law, Custom, and Statute in the Muslim World: Studies in Honor of Ahron Layish*, Ron Shaham, ed. (Leiden, The Netherlands: Koninklijke Brill NV, 2007), p. 210, and Yüksel Sezgin, *Human Rights under State-Enforced Religious Family Laws in Israel, Egypt and India* (Cambridge, UK: Cambridge University Press, 2013), p. 86.

[90] Aryeh Tepper, "Christians in the Holy Land: Don't Call Us Arabs," in *The Tower*, Issue 22, January 2015. These Israeli Arameans are working toward reviving the colloquial use of their ancient tongue, Aramaic, which they have maintained as their language of prayer through the centuries.

[91] Muqtedar Khan, quoted in Raphael Israeli, *Blood Libel and Its Derivatives: The Scourge of Anti-Semitism* (New Brunswick, NJ: Transaction Publishers, 2012), p. 222.

[92] Michael Anbar, *Israel and Its Future: Analysis and Suggestions* (Lincoln, NE: iUniverse, Inc., 2004), p. 203.

Concluding that antisemitism and violence are endemic in all Muslim societies is also belied by the relative pacifistic posture of such Muslim nations as Indonesia where the Ahmadiyah "reject the notion of physical jihad in favour of a Holy War waged by the pen."[93] Even though antisemitism has increased in Indonesia since the establishment of the nation of Israel and though Jewish Indonesians who practice their Jewish faith openly sometimes face hostility,[94] "Indonesia is probably, as a country, less anti-Semitic than any other Muslim nation."[95] Perhaps Muslim nations like Indonesia can set an example of relative tolerance for other Muslim nations and peoples; however, with the idea of *Dar al-Islam* solidly and irreversibly entrenched within the Muslim religion, which insists that no geographical area that has ever been controlled by Islam can ever be permanently ceded to another people or religion,[96] such an effort is at best an uphill struggle. This is especially true in the case of the flash point of Israel which was under Muslim dominance for centuries before it was fully liberated in 1948.

## The Ancient and Enduring Struggle for the Land of Israel

The controversy over Israel can actually be traced to the time of Abraham, for Scripture declares that the patriarch "had two sons."[97] Hagar, the Egyptian bondservant gave birth to Ishmael, the patriarch's first son, when Abraham's wife Sarah despaired of ever having a child herself and invoked the ancient custom of surrogate motherhood. Ishmael was not, however, the answer to God's promise to Abraham. As a matter of fact, when the Almighty gave the command for the *Akedah* ("binding") of Isaac, Abraham and Sarah's son, he instructed the patriarch with these words: "Take now your son, *your only son*,

---

[93] Elizabeth Pisani, *Indonesia, Etc.: Exploring the Improbable Nation* (New York: W. W. Norton & Company, 2014), p. 319.

[94] Olivia Rondonuwu, "In Muslim Indonesia, Tiny Jewish Community Keeps Its Head Down: Worshiping in Secret and Facing Growing Faith-based Intolerance, Jewish Minority Insists It Is Integral Part of Country," *The Times of Israel*, April 27, 2017, posted at http://www.timesofisrael.com/in-muslim-indonesia-tiny-jewish-community-keeps-its-head-down/.

[95] Jason F. Isaacson and Colin L. Rubenstein, *Islam in Asia: Changing Political Realities* (New Brunswick, NJ: Transaction Publishers, 2002), p. 56.

[96] Tom Doyle, *Two Nations Under God: Why You Should Care about Israel* (Nashville, TN: B&H Publishing Group, 2004), p. 35. Doyle points out an undeniable truth: "Islam teaches that no land under the control of Muslims can ever again be ruled by 'infidels." Also, Roberta Green, *Blind Spot: When Journalists Don't Get Religion* (Oxford, UK: Oxford University Press, 2009), p. 34. Green quotes Osama bin Laden's Declaration of War as saying that "jihad will remain an individual obligation until all other lands that were Muslim are returned to us so that Islam will reign again: before us lie Palestine, Bokhara, Lebanon, Chad, Eritrea, Somalia, the Philippines, Burma, Southern Yemen, Tashkent, and Andalusia [Spain]."

[97] Galatians 4:22.

whom you love, Isaac, and go to the land of Moriah, and offer him there as a burnt offering on one of the mountains of which I will tell you."[98] It was specifically through the lineage of Isaac, not Ishmael, that God's covenant was to be perpetuated just as God himself said: ". . . through Isaac your descendants shall be named."[99]

Rivalry for the inherited blessing of Abraham may well have been the underlying cause of the contention that arose between Sarah and Hagar[100] after Ishmael's birth and later between Ishmael and Isaac after Sarah's son was born.[101] Certainly, Ishmael was not inclined to follow the divine instructions that God had given to Abraham. In fact, as God so accurately predicted to Abraham, "He will be a wild ass of a man: he will be hostile to everyone, and everyone will be hostile to him."[102] This graphic prophetic description is certainly an apropos description for many of Ishmael's descendants to this day. Despite the fact that Abraham prayed for Ishmael, imploring God with these words: "O that Ishmael might live before you [the LORD],"[103] and despite the fact that God responded by promising Abraham, "I will bless [Ishmael],"[104] it was unclear whether the descendants of the son of the Egyptian bondwoman would have or maintain allegiance to the faith of Abraham so that they could inherit the blessing of the Abrahamic covenant, including its promise of real estate.

The conflict over the land of Israel that developed between Ishmael's descendants and those of Isaac became one of the most enduring and intractable struggles in history. In Genesis *Rabbah*, an account is given of just such a controversy that occurred during the time of Alexander the Great when

[98] Genesis 22:2 (emphasis added).

[99] Genesis 21:12.

[100] Genesis 16:4–5. Having borne a son to Abraham by means of surrogate motherhood, Hagar may well have thought she had the upper hand over the childless Sarah and that her son would eventually inherit Abraham's estate as his "firstborn."

[101] Genesis 21:9. Ishmael may very well have "mocked" Isaac because he thought that he, Abraham's firstborn, should and would receive the patriarch's inheritance, including the Abrahamic covenant and blessing. Some Jewish scholars have suggested that there may well have been even deeper and far more nefarious elements at play in Ishmael's mocking of Isaac. Robert Alter, *Genesis: Translation and Commentary* (New York: W. W. Norton, 1996), p. 133. Lori Hope Lefkovitz, *In Scripture: The First Stories of Jewish Sexual Identities* (Lanham, MD: Rowman & Littlefield Publishers, 2010), p. 51. Christian scholars agree. Claus Westermann, *Genesis 12–36: A Continental Commentary* (Minneapolis, MN: Fortress Press, 1995), p. 339; Samuel R. Driver, *The Book of Genesis* (London, England: Methurn & Co., Ltd., 1916), pp. 210–211; and Herman Gunkel and Mark E. Biddle, *Commentary on Genesis* (Macon, GA: Mercer University Press, 1997), p. 226.

[102] Genesis 16:12a, TNK; 16:12b, NET. The TNK translates the Hebrew literally with its "He will be a wild ass of a man." The NET captures the essence of the literal Hebrew text: "his hand will be against everyone, and everyone's hand will be against him."

[103] Genesis 17:18.

[104] Genesis 17:20.

certain Ishmaelites, joined by Canaanites and Egyptians, initiated a challenge to Israel's right to the Promised Land and appeared before Alexander to pursue their claim.[105] "Who is laying claim against whom?" Alexander asked. The Ishmaelites responded, "We are the claimants, and we base our claim on [the Jews'] Torah, for it is written, 'But he shall acknowledge the first born, the son of the hated, and Ishmael was the firstborn.'"[106] Israel's respondent, Gebia of Qosem, countered the Ishmaelites' argument by asking Alexander, "My lord, the king, cannot a man do as he likes with his sons?" When Alexander responded in the affirmative, Gebia continued his argument in this manner: "Thus it is written, 'Abraham gave all that he had to Isaac.'"[107] Then the sage asked rhetorically, "Where is the deed of gift to the other sons?" and then proceeded to answer his own question by reading the rest of the text: "But unto the sons of the concubines that Abraham had, Abraham gave gifts."[108] With that Gebia rested his case, and the Ishmaelite, Canaanite, and Egyptian claimants withdrew in embarrassment.[109] This rabbinic *midrash* simply recounts yet another of the continuing efforts that have been put forth by the Arabian descendants of Ishmael to claim title to the land of Israel.

This same conflict over the land of Israel has continued over the centuries from the time of Muhammad until the present day. Initially, there was no question as to Jewish rights to their ancient homeland. Muhammad "even called the Jews God's chosen people and acknowledged that God had given them the Promised Land,"[110] says Richard Booker, who also notes that Muhammad decreed that "the Jews and Christians should not be forced to accept Islam."[111] The *Qur'an* specifically said, "We [Allah] said to the Israelites: 'Dwell in this land [Israel]. When the promise of the hereafter comes to be fulfilled, We [Allah] shall assemble you [the Israelites] all together [in the land of Israel]."[112] When the Jews did not accept Muhammad "as a true prophet of Abraham, he turned against them."[113] Jacob Pressman further explained Muhammad's reaction to Jewish and Christian rejection of Islam

---

[105] For an in-depth study of the history of the Ishmaelite ancestry and heritage of the Arabian people, see Carol Bakhos, *Ishmael on the Border: Rabbinic Portrayals of the First Arab* (Albany, NY: The State University of New York Press, 2006), pp. 77–78.

[106] Deuteronomy 21:17.

[107] Genesis 25:2.

[108] Genesis 25:6. The complete text says, "But to the sons of his concubines, Abraham gave gifts while he was still living, and sent them away from his son Isaac eastward, to the land of the east."

[109] This account is found in Genesis *Rabbah* 61:7.

[110] Richard Booker, *Radical Islam's War Against Israel, Christianity, and the West* (Shippensburg, PA: Destiny Image Publishing, 2008), p. 70.

[111] Booker, p. 70.

[112] *Qur'an* 17:100–104.

[113] Booker, p. 70.

and its prophet: "The Jews in Arabia, from whom Muhammad learned the biblical tradition, refused to recognize him as God's chosen prophet. . . . Enraged and frustrated, Muhammad turned against the Jews and there ensued a series of massacres . . . [for] there was no one left against whom the spirit of intolerance could be exercised—no one but the Jews."[114]

Islam originally did not consider Jews and Christians to be "infidels"[115] as it did polytheists, pagans, and idolaters, who had the option of accepting Islam or being killed. Muhammad even said that "if they submitted peaceably to Islamic authority, they would be permitted the freedom . . . to practice their own faiths."[116] If, however, Jews and Christians refused to convert to Islam or pay the poll tax, they were to be killed.[117] Finally, at the end of his career, Muhammad issued a general decree approving—even commanding—the killing of Jews: "Kill any Jew that falls into your power."[118] Immediately after this decree was issued, when one of Muhammad's zealots killed a Jewish merchant and was rebuked by his younger brother for the cruelty of his act, he replied, "Had the one [Muhammad] who ordered me to kill him ordered me to kill you, I would have cut your head off."[119]

Though some apologists make excuses for Islamic terrorism and insist that "Islam is a religion of compassion and love, as much as any religion like Buddhism or Christianity is,"[120] the fact remains that, by continuing acts of warfare and terrorism, a significant percentage of Muslims cause every reasonable person—with the possible exception of those who are driven by postmodernist multiculturalism and political correctness—to view their religion as the most violent in the world.[121] When the *Qur'an* specifically says,

---

[114] Jacob Pressman, *Dear Friends: A Prophetic Journey through Great Events of the 20th Century* (Jersey City, NJ: KTAV Publishing House, 2002), p. 71.

[115] Muhammad Shafiq and Mohammed Abu-Nimer, *Interfaith Dialogue: A Guide for Muslims* (Herndon, VA: The International Institute of Islamic Thought, 2011), p. 51.

[116] Letty M. Russell, *Hagar, Sarah, and Their Children* (Louisville, KY: Westminster John Knox Press, 2006), p. 12.

[117] *Qur'an* 9:30.

[118] Ibn Ishaq, *The Life of Muhammad*, tr. Alfred Guillaume (Oxford, UK: Oxford University Press, 1955), p. 369.

[119] Ishaq, p. 369.

[120] Asghar Ali Engineer, *Islam in Contemporary World* (Elgin, IL: New Dawn Press Group, 2007), p. xi.

[121] Peter Berger, "Religion and Global Civil Society," in *Religion in Global Civil Society*, Mark Juergensmeyer, ed. (Oxford, UK: Oxford University Press, 2005), p. 18. Berger says, "We have been urged not to identify Islam as such with its most violent element . . . but it seems to me that Islam, even in its moderate forms, has certain characteristics that are unfavorable to the development of civil society. I would particularly emphasize two aspects—the understanding of religious law and the role of women." He continues to note that "despite all of the useful cautions to the effect that the term *jihad* and its applications can also be understood in nonviolent ways," the term itself "has been used throughout Muslim history mainly to describe the extension of Islamic sovereignty through warfare. It hardly needs emphasizing that this is an understanding inimical to civility."

"I will cast terror into the hearts of those who disbelieved," and commands, "Therefore strike off their heads and strike off every fingertip of them,"[122] viewing Islam as a religion of violence cannot be judged as a radically unfair judgment. In fact, as Katerina Dalacoura notes, "Many observers of Islamist terrorism see its causes as primarily ideational. Islamist terrorism is driven by the ideas of Islam as a religion—and occasionally as culture—or Islamism as a political ideology. . . . Their argument is that the precepts of Islam, including the Koran, contain an intolerant view which enables or encourages terrorism's emergence; that the core principles of Islam as a religion or Islamism as a political ideology are *inherently* prone to terrorism; and that the causes of Islamism and Islamist terrorism overlap."[123] Walter Laqueur further develops this premise: "Radical Muslims exhibit hostility toward all those who are different, a free-floating rage, and a tradition of violence that favors the appearance of terrorism. Popular Western perception equates radical Islam with terrorism. While many Muslim purists do not support terrorism, the perception is still more accurate than the apologist's claim that Western fears are 'mythical' in character, based on unfounded apprehensions, prejudices, and insufficient knowledge about Islam."[124]

The simple truth is that Muslims consider the establishment of the state of Israel to be an unlawful intrusion into the *Dar al-Islam*,[125] for "all of historical Palestine [was] conquered by jihad in the fourth decade of the seventh century,"[126] because it must remain "a permanent part of the *Dar al-Islam*, where Islamic law must forever prevail." In Muslim tradition, the land "occupied" by the state of Israel must be returned to Muslim suzerainty[127] and can be rightfully ruled only by Muslims. The foundational covenant[128] of the terrorist

[122] *Qur'an* 8:12.

[123] Katerina Dalacoura, *Islamist Terrorism and Democracy in the Middle East* (Cambridge, UK: Cambridge University Press, 2011), p. 32.

[124] Walter Laqueur, *The New Terrorism: Fanaticism and the Arms of Mass Destruction* (Oxford, UK: Oxford University Press, 1999), p. 129.

[125] *Dar al-Islam* is a classical Muslim legal term used to designate the places in which Islam and *Sharia* law dominates. The *Dar al-Islam* includes any territory that has ever been conquered by the armies of Islam or has come under the aegis of Islam through proselytization. Once a portion of land or a people has come under Islamist control, it is thereafter sacred to Islam and must forever be controlled by Muslims and ruled by *Sharia* law.

[126] Bostom, p. 52.

[127] Jacob Neusner, *Comparing Religions Through Law: Judaism and Islam* (Routledge, 1999), p. 201. Also Paul Charles Merkley, *Christian Attitudes Towards the State of Israel* (Kingston, Canada: McGill-Queen's University Press, 2001), p. 122.

[128] The Hamas covenant is officially called "The Covenant of the Islamic Resistance Movement." Its motto, which is very similar to that of the Muslim Brotherhood, says, "Allah is its goal, the Prophet its model to be followed, the Koran its constitution, Jihad its way, and death for the sake of Allah its loftiest desire."

organization Hamas, which rules Gaza with an iron fist, asserts its right to all of the land of Israel, declaring, "The land of Palestine is an Islamic *Waqf* consecrated for future Muslim generations until Judgment Day. Neither it nor any part of it may be squandered or given up. The law governing the land of Palestine is to be in accordance with the Islamic Sharia (law) . . . because during the times of (Islamic) conquests the Muslims consecrated these lands to Muslim generations until the day of Judgment."[129]

## A Never-Ending Battle?

The ancient conflict over the sacred space that God promised to Abraham and his descendants through Isaac and Jacob has continued to be the object of contention from the descendants of Ishmael and other distant relatives of the ancient Israelites. From the time of Abraham until the present day, the controversy has continued. As has been the case for Muslims since the time of Muhammad, most of the Arab and Muslim nations and a significant portion of the Muslim people remain intractable, refusing to recognize the right of the Jewish people to exist in their own nation and in their own land with complete self-determination, free from all coercion, whether political, economic, or religious.[130]

Shlomo Sharan and Dawid Bûqay pose this pertinent question: "From whence comes the seeming importance of the Land of Israel for Arabs/or Muslims?"[131] for simple antisemitism "does not purport to explain the Arab's 'attachment' to Judea and Samaria and parts of [the] present day State of Israel."[132] They conclude that "given the overwhelming significance of Arabia in the history of Islam, plus early Islam's explicit recognition of Jewry's divine right to the Land of Israel," the only explanation for Arab intransigence toward the Jewish state and the land of Israel must be viewed in this light: "The

[129] Jamal Khader, "Opportunities and Threats for Religions in Conflict and Violence: How (Not) to Use the Name of God," in *Postcolonial Europe in the Crucible of Cultures: Reckoning with God in a World of Conflicts,* Jacques Haers, Norbert Hintersteiner, and Georges De Schrijver, eds. (Amsterdam, The Netherlands: Editions Rodopi B.V., 2007), p. 145.

[130] Of all the Muslim nations, only two, Egypt and Jordan, recognize Israel's right to exist. See Stephen K. Baum, *Antisemitism Explained,* (Lanham, MD: University Press of America, 2012), p. 213. This recognition, however, "can be seen as more of an act of convenience." Moorthy S. Muthuswamy, *Defeating Political Islam: The New Cold War* (Amherst, NY: Prometheus Books, 2009), p. 754.

[131] Shlomo Sharan and Dawid Bûqay, *Crossovers: Anti-Zionism and Anti-Semitism* (Piscataway, NJ: Transaction Publishers, 2010), p. 7.

[132] Sharan and Bûqay, p. 7.

Palestinian objective is to transfer the historic rights of Jewish people to the Land of Israel accrued over four thousand years of existence to the Palestinians who have no history and who emerged only recently. The Palestinian Arabs are trying to implement a policy that aims to appropriate the identity and legitimacy of the Jews for themselves. They demand that the world recognize them as the sole legitimate owner of Palestine."[133]

Amazingly, at the same time when many Muslim nations loudly boast of their intentions to destroy the "cancer of Zionism" and Palestinian Arabs engage in wave after wave of violence against Israel with the avowed motive of driving the Jews into the Mediterranean, the state of Israel is urged by the international community to show restraint even while missiles and mortar shells rain down on its population centers. The question that demands to be asked is this: What other nation in the world would be "tolerant" and then fail to respond in kind if its neighbor were to launch even one missile into its sovereign territory? The answer is, not one![134] Yet, the Israelis are constantly urged to show restraint[135] while missiles and mortar shells land indiscriminately in Israel from Hamas-dominated Gaza and from Hezbollah-controlled southern Lebanon. There seems to be no end to the demands that the Islamists and their allies around the world can make for Israel to absorb attacks on its citizenry without retaliating in kind so as to discourage further jihadist violence. Militant Muslims have free course to inflict acts of terror, mayhem, and murder upon Israeli citizens while being justified in their actions by the Western press on the grounds of "Israeli oppression." At the same time, Israel is warned that if it responds by fighting fire with fire, it is engaging in "crimes against humanity" and "genocide."

When Israel does respond to such terrorist attacks, it announces its intentions to the civilian populations in advance of its response and then attempts to destroy missiles and rocket launchers with almost surgical precision. Inevitably, however, it is accused of

---

[133] Sharan and Bûqay, p. 7.

[134] What would Russia do if Poland suddenly started firing missiles at Moscow? What would the US do if Cuba launched a barrage of missiles at Miami? What would England do if France began shelling London? The answers to all of these questions is purely academic: all of them would counterattack with overwhelming force!

[135] Katarina Engberg, *The EU and Military Operations: A Comparative Analysis* (New York: Routledge, 2014), p. 63. Engberg reported the observations of the G8 Summit in St. Petersburg in July, 2006, "The G8 group stated that Israel had the right to exist, but called for restraint. . . . The French President . . . called for 'a show of moderation' in the Middle East."

"disproportionate response" and "war crimes" because the terrorist entities hide their missiles in hospitals and schools[136] and even use women and children of their own populations as human shields[137] to discourage Israeli response. They even go so far as to launch missiles and shells that fall either accidentally or purposefully on their own population centers and then blame Israel for the atrocities.[138] These facts prompted Israeli Prime Minister Benjamin Netanyahu to observe, "The difference between us is that we're using missile defense to protect our civilians and they're using their civilians to protect their missiles."[139]

Ironically, the one time when Israel was persuaded to show restraint and not react in kind to attacks on its populace occurred when the United States launched a war to expel Saddam Hussein's Iraqi forces from Kuwait. When thirty-nine Iraqi scud missiles rained down upon Tel Aviv and other population centers in Israel in 1991, the Israeli governments acquiesced to requests from the United States government that they not respond in kind. Immediately after the war was concluded, however, the United States betrayed Israel when President George H. W. Bush refused to grant Israel loan guarantees to help it absorb recent Jewish immigrants from the Soviet Union.[140] So much for Israel's cooperation with others, including the US!

Hamas also argues that Israel's responses to its military actions are not "proportional" and "reciprocal" because Israel has bomb shelters whereas Gaza has none. "Has anyone thought to ask the talking heads on TV . . . why there are no bomb shelters in Gaza?" Jonathan Tobin

---

[136] Terrence McCoy, "Why Hamas Stores Its Weapons Inside Hospitals, Mosques and Schools," *The Washington Post*, July 31, 2014, posted at http://www.washingtonpost.com/news/morning-mix/wp/2014/07/31/why-hamas-stores-its-weapons-inside-hospitals-mosques-and-schools/.

[137] Yaakov Katz, "Hamas Used Kids as Human Shields," in *The Jerusalem Post*, 03/15/2010, posted at http://www.jpost.com/Israel/Hamas-used-kids-as-human-shields. Also, Ellen Lust, *The Middle East, 13th Edition* (Thousand Oaks, CA: SAGE Publications, 2014), p. 361.

[138] Yair Lapid, "Gaza Conflict: Hamas Chooses to Let Children Die for Its Own Crazy Ends," *The Telegraph*, July 23, 2014, posted at http://www.telegraph.co.uk/news/worldnews/middleeast/israel/10987095/Gaza-conflict-Hamas-chooses-to-let-children-die-for-its-own-crazy-ends.html. Lapid made this startling observation: "Islamic terror is absolutely cynical, it always was and always will be, and its greatest specialty is taking advantage of every democracy's main weakness—the fact that we sanctify life. . . . Hamas intentionally builds its missile factories and bunkers underneath civilian homes, stores its ammunition in schools and kindergartens (including United Nations schools), launches its rockets surrounded by civilian families, despite knowing beyond any doubt that it will lead to innocent casualties. . . . The absurd result is that Israel does much more to protect Palestinian children than Hamas [does] and yet many Europeans and many Britons accuse us of being responsible for their deaths."

[139] Benjamin Netanyahu in an interview on CBS television's *Face the Nation*, July 12, 2014.

[140] Meron Medzini, *Israel's Foreign Relations: Selected Documents* (Jerusalem, Israel: Israel Ministry for Foreign Affairs, 1988), p. 720.

wonders.[141] The answer is simple: the labyrinth of underground tunnels that honeycomb virtually all of the Gaza Strip are reserved exclusively for military personnel and are closed to civilians! Tobin then poses an amazingly simple question that the worldwide media also ignores: "What if, instead of devoting all of their resources and cash in an effort to turn Gaza into an armed fortress, bristling with thousands of rockets and honeycombed with tunnels and shelters where only Hamas members and their dangerous toys are allowed, the people of Gaza had leaders who had devoted their efforts to improving the lot of the Palestinian people since they took over the strip after Israel's complete withdrawal in 2005?"[142] The answer should be obvious to any thoughtful, fair-minded person. Since the Palestinians through Hamas already control a "Palestinian State" called Gaza, the only reason for their continued acts of violence against Israel is intractable and deep-seated antisemitism and their commitment to the philosophy of *jihad*. Instead of working to improve Gaza's economy, the leaders of Hamas spend millions of dollars—most of which have been donated to them by the West as "humanitarian" relief—to smuggle arms into its territory, conceal them in population centers, and then use them to launch terrorist attacks on hapless Jews.

"Despite the frightening religious bigotry, homophobia, misogyny, violent persecution of Christians in the Middle East, and the chilling Judeophobia," says Robert Wistrich, "Islamists have garnered considerable sympathy in the West as authentic representatives of the Palestinian cause."[143] At the same time, however, "Israel—despite being the region's only free, tolerant, and open society—has been continually vilified by much of the mainstream Western media and by large sectors of public opinion. While Israel is denounced for a purely fictional 'genocide,' the lethal character of Hamas' Jew-hatred has been largely ignored."[144] In its rush toward political correctness, tolerance, and inclusivity, the West utterly ignores the root cause of radical Islamist violence that is solidly anchored in Islamic apocalypticism and its vision for genocide of the Jewish people. "For Islamists today, it is the Prophet himself who points them forward to

[141] Jonathan S. Tobin, "Why Gaza Doesn't Have Bomb Shelters," in *Commentary*, 07.12.2014, posted at https://www.commentarymagazine.com/2014/07/12/why-gaza-doesnt-have-bomb-shelters-hamas-israel-terrorism/.

[142] Tobin, "Why Gaza."

[143] Robert S. Wistrich, "Gaza, Hamas, and the Return of Antisemitism," in *Israel Journal of Foreign Affairs*, VIII:3, July, 2014, p. 38.

[144] Wistrich, "Gaza."

an apocalyptic genocidal resolution of the conflict with the Jews."[145]

The conflict in the Middle East, therefore, "is not a war between Palestinians and Zionists or between the Arab States and Israel, but strictly between Muslims and Jews in which no compromise is possible."[146] This religious dimension to the conflict makes it virtually unsolvable by any normal means of peaceful negotiation, for religious zealotry is based on a reported *hadith* from Muhammad himself: "The Day of Judgment will not come until Muslims fight the Jews, when the Jew will hide between stones and trees. The stones and trees will say, O Muslims, O Abdullah, there is a Jew behind me, come and kill him."[147] Physical attacks upon Israel and the Jewish community, therefore, are not merely political matters for the most violent of radical Islamists. Instead, they are founded in a deeply held religious conviction which produces actions that transcend reason (despite the fact that apologists make every effort to justify such actions in the name of "freedom fighting," struggles against "oppression," and the like). Raphael Israeli concludes, therefore, that "in spite of Israel's readiness to offer concessions, the rhetoric for destroying Israel 'remains much more ubiquitous than the gospel of co-existence' in the Arab world."[148]

Muslim anti-Israelism and the terrorism associated with it are nothing more than today's politically correct—and even socially glamorized—form of the ancient antisemitism of Haman and Hadrian and the modern antisemitism of Adolph Hitler and his Nazi regime. In reality, Western tolerance for—and even promotion of—Islamic terror against Israel is nothing more than a clever disguise for the old antisemitism that has never been purged from the heart of liberal Western societies and their propaganda arms, the mainstream Western media.

## Jewish Resiliency and Divine Faithfulness

Despite every effort by the Palestinian Arabs and their cohorts in Arab and other Muslim nations to terrorize the Israelis, the Jews have refused to be intimidated.[149] Today, as in every day in the nearly seven

[145] Wistrich, "Gaza."

[146] Wistrich, "Gaza."

[147] Daniel J. Goldhagen, *The Devil That Never Dies: The Rise and Threat of Global Antisemitism* (New York: Little, Brown, and Co., 2013), p. 221.

[148] Raphael Israeli, *Islamikaze: Manifestations of Islamic Martyrology* (London: UK: Frank Cass Publishers, 2003), p. 363.

[149] Eugene B. Borowitz, *Reform Judaism Today* (Springfield, NJ: Behrman House, Inc., 1983), p. 65.

decades of life in their restored nation and ancestral land, the Jews boldly go about their everyday lives, refusing to cower in fear in the face of a cloak-and-dagger enemy that hides its face behind masks, launches "lone-wolf" attacks on urban streets, digs cross-border tunnels in order to launch terrorist attacks on civilian population centers, and fires rockets and missiles indiscriminately into schools and other civilian sites.[150] These Jews "are teaching the world how to 'love life more than they fear death.'"[151] They have refused to give Hitler even the smallest posthumous victory either by denying their Jewishness and their faith in the God of Scripture[152] or by shrinking into the shadows and living in fear. They have also refused to have their visions for personal and corporate existence diminished by the terrorist attacks of a shameless and cowardly enemy. They refuse to be terrorized by the terrorists! They boldly go on with their lives and achieve the highest levels of success—all the while living in perhaps the most dangerous part of the world. As former Israeli Prime Minister Golda Meir said, "Above all this country is our own. Nobody has to get up in the morning and worry what his neighbors

---

[150] Contrast the Israeli posture toward terrorism with that of the Western world which Rabbi Eric Carlson says "remains silent, cowering in fear of upsetting Muslims while they torture and abuse women, forbid freedom of speech, behead Jews and Christians, and murder innocent people in the name of Islam. . . . The majority of American News and Press agencies refuse to report the danger and truth of Radical Islam!" Eric Carlson, *Is God Done with America?* (New York: Morgan James Publishing, 2011), p. 16. In fact, the West cannot bring itself to acknowledge that terrorism actually exists! Randall Marshall says that as a consequence, "we cannot develop ways to reduce the impact of fear of terrorism, in its entire spectrum, if we don't acknowledge that it exists." Randall Marshall, "Learning from 9/11: Implications for Disaster Research and Public Health," in *9/11: Mental Health in the Wake of Terrorist Attacks*, Yuval Neria, Raz Gross, and Randall Marshall, eds. (Cambridge, UK: Cambridge University Press, 2012), p. 625. In Europe today, too many politicians and pundits conclude that terrorism is simply an inescapable part of the new world order, and they excuse Muslim theft, rape, and murder of their fellow citizens as "cultural differences" for which the Muslims cannot be judged. See Bruce Bower, *While Europe Slept: How Radical Islam Is Destroying the West from Within* (New York: Broadway Books, 2006), p. 55, and Erich Kolig, "Conclusion," in *Muslim Integration: Pluralism and Multiculturalism in New Zealand*, Erich Kolig and Malcom Voyce, eds. (Lanham, MD: Rowman & Littlefield, Inc., 2016), p. 259, nn. 2, 9.

[151] Phyllis Chesler, *Living History: On the Front Lines for Israel and the Jews 2003–2015* (Jerusalem, Israel: Gefen Publishing House, 2015), p. 180.

[152] Steven T. Katz, "The Issue of Confirmation and Disconfirmation in Jewish Thought after the Shoah," in *The Impact of the Holocaust on Jewish Theology*, Steven T. Katz, ed. (New York: New York University Press, 2005), pp. 22–24. Katz discusses the implications of Emil Fackenheim's famous 614th commandment: "Jews are forbidden to hand Hitler posthumous victories!" by explaining Fackenheim's philosophy: "After Auschwitz, Jews are under a sacred obligation to survive; Jewish existence is itself a holy act; Jews are under a duty to remember the martyrs; Jews are, as Jews, forbidden to despair of redemption, or to become cynical about the world and humanity, for to submit to cynicism is to abdicate responsibility for the here and now and to deliver the future into the hands of the forces of evil. Above all, Jews are 'forbidden to despair of the God of Israel, lest Judaism perish.' Hitler's demonic passion was to eradicate Israel from history. For the Jew to despair of the God of Israel as a result of Hitler's monstrous actions would be, ironically, to do Hitler's work and to aid in the accomplishments of Hitler's goal. . . . To say no to Hitler is to say yes to the God of Sinai; to say no to the God of Sinai is to say yes to Hitler."

think of him. Being a Jew is no problem here."[153]

The Jews in Israel continually seek peace, simply asking their Muslim neighbors and the constantly meddling world powers to allow them to live their lives in peace and security. They would like to have the peoples of the rest of the world—including moralizing, self-righteous Christians—to keep its hands off their children. They have no innate hostility toward their neighbors, no designs on aggression, and no intentions of expanding their domain.[154] Golda Meir spoke for virtually all Jews when she said, "We hate war. We do not rejoice in victories. We rejoice when a new kind of cotton is grown, and when strawberries bloom in Israel."[155] Still, Israel has no choice but to be vigilant in the face of the existential threats of mass destruction that surround and threaten them. With the constant acts of violence that are directed against them, the Israelis would be foolish not to expend every effort to protect and defend themselves. Meir summed up the reason for the Israeli vigilance this way: "We have always said that in our war with the Arabs we had a secret weapon—no alternative. The Egyptians could run to Egypt, the Syrians into Syria. The only place we could run was into the sea, and before we did that we might as well fight."[156]

Though the Israelis have never sought war, they also have never shied away from confrontation because they have a horrible reminder of what can—and will—happen when a people or a nation does not stand up against intimidation, terrorism, and aggression by others. The Holocaust is that utterly unforgettable reminder, the event unparalleled in human history in which the Nazi regime systematically, relentlessly, and unmercifully murdered over six million Jews[157] while the rest of the world either did not know what was occurring or

[153] Golda Meir, quoted in Ashton Applewhite, William R. Evans III, and Andrew Frothingham, eds., *And I Quote: The Definitive Collection of Quotes, Sayings, and Jokes for the Contemporary Speech-Maker* (New York: Macmillan, 1992), p. 437.

[154] There have been times when Israel has expanded the territory that it possessed; however, even its acquisition of the Golan Heights and what has been called the "West Bank" was done with the primary motive of providing security for its citizens in the face of Arab rockets and mortars and various terrorist attacks. Then, the acquisition of both the Golan Heights and the West Bank only restored to Israel the land that was reserved for the Jewish homeland by the original League of Nations 1920 Covenant for Palestine and, more importantly, by the unilateral and irrevocable Abrahamic covenant of the Holy Scriptures.

[155] Golda Meir, quoted in Israel Shenker and Mary Shenker, eds., *As Good as Golda: The Warmth and Wisdom of Israel's Prime Minister* (New York: McCall Publishing Co., 1970), p. 28.

[156] Golda Meir, quoted in *Life*, October 3, 1969, p. 32.

[157] Timothy W. Ryback, "The First Killings of the Holocaust," in *The New York Times*, Jan. 3, 2012, posted at http://www.nytimes.com/2012/01/04/opinion/the-first-killings-of-the-holocaust.html?_r=0. Ryback says that the Holocaust actually began on Wednesday, April 12, 1933, when four Jews, Arthur Kahn, Ernst Godmann, Rudolf Benario, and Erwin Kahn, "were executed in the obscure Bavarian hamlet of Prittlbach." The Holocaust was concluded on May 8, 1945, when World War II officially ended in Europe.

turned a blind eye to the unimaginable genocide of European Jewry. Israel, therefore, does not seek a fight; however, it does not back down from one, and it usually finishes one when it arises. The Israelis, however, do not live in fear. Instead, they live their lives to the fullest, trusting and believing that no matter what comes their way, their incredible resolve and trust in their God will ensure their survival. While for many Jews the memory of the Holocaust and questions about the seeming absence of divine action during that horrific time may lead to misgivings about what the future may hold,[158] still the resolve of the Israeli people never to give posthumous victories to the Nazis steels their will to survive and thrive in the face of all challenges to their individual and corporate well-being.

Israel continues to exist in the midst of profound saber rattling and chest thumping that would cause a less resolute people to cower in fear. The Middle East playbook that the Arab nations have used for a hundred years or more has never changed. The bellicose rhetoric echoes across years and years of ongoing threats. "Right from the start," says Zeev Maoz, "the Arab leaders knew that destroying Israel was an unrealistic dream. At the same time, they could not afford to change the anti-Israel rhetoric from an extremely hostile one to a peaceful one; many of those who tried paid with their lives."[159] So, the news never changes. Iran's self-styled "Supreme Leader," Ayatollah Seyyed Ali Khamenei, continually refers to Israel as "a cancerous tumor that should be cut and will be cut."[160] Hassan Nasrallah, leader of Hezbollah in southern Lebanon says, "The only solution is to destroy [Israel] without giving it the opportunity to surrender."[161] Khaled Mashaal, a political leader of Hamas, the terrorist organization which controls Gaza, has boasted, "We are not giving up any inch of Palestine. . . . Jihad and armed resistance is the only way."[162]

---

[158] Reve Robert Brenner, *The Faith and Doubt of the Holocaust Survivors* (Abingdon, UK: Routledge, 2017).

[159] Zeev Maoz, *Defending the Holy Land* (Ann Arbor, MI: The University of Michigan Press, 2009), p. 576. A prime example of those who have paid with their lives was Egyptian President Anwar Sadat, who was assassinated by Muslim Brotherhood terrorists shortly after he concluded a peace agreement with Israel.

[160] Seyyed Ali Khamenei, quoted in "Khamenei: Israel Is a Cancerous Tumor," *Jerusalem World News,* February 3, 2011, posted at http://jerusalemworldnews.com/2012/02/03/khamenei-israel-is-a-cancerous-tumor/.

[161] Hassan Nasrallah, quoted in "Nasrallah, in Vicious Public Address, Calls for the Destruction of Israel," *The Times of Israel*, August 2, 2015, posted at http://www.timesofisrael.com/hezbollah-leader-rallies-shiites-with-highly-sectarian-speech/.

[162] Khaled Mashaal, quoted in Aaron Kalman, "Abbas Condemns Hamas Head's Statements," *The Times of Israel*, December, 2012, posted at http://www.timesofisrael.com/abbas-condemns-hamas-leaders-call-for-the-destruction-of-israel/.

So, the verbal threats remain the same; however, the physical means of achieving them continue to improve as technology advances. Perhaps in order to conceal his regime's real goal of annihilating Israel with nuclear weapons, Ayatollah Khamenei has unveiled another strategy which advocates "a long period of low-intensity warfare designed to make life unpleasant if not impossible for a majority of Israeli Jews so that they leave the country."[163] He assumes that dual-citizenship Jews "would prefer to live in the US or Europe as opposed to facing death threats on a regular basis" and that "Israel fatigue" will cost the nation support from its allies.[164]

Israel, therefore, lives daily with the threat of religion-inspired acts of barbarity. When small instances of what occurs with regularity in Israel take place in the West, shock, amazement, and consternation arise only to be tamped down by postmodernist politicians and media, all in the name of manifesting their self-righteous "tolerance" and "understanding" and avoiding the career-destroying charge of being Islamophobic. If what has been everyday life for Israeli citizens for decades were constantly manifest on a regular basis in virtually any other nation of the world, postmodern tolerance would give way to unconditional war. This, then, is the level of hypocrisy in the West. Israel is expected to bear with patience and non-retaliation levels of violence against its citizenry that no other government would tolerate. Since the Jewish people have been expendable in the minds of non-Jewish nations and peoples for centuries, they are still expected to sacrifice themselves—even their lives—on the altar of expediency to accommodate for the psychotic impulses of others. The world says through the United Nations that the Jewish citizens of Israel do not deserve protection; therefore, as Ellen Willis notes, "No matter whose side history is on, Jews have always been expendable. As long as we are expendable, to talk of 'Jewish power' is obscene."[165]

The Jewish people in Israel have an iron will to survive and thrive because they are assured by four thousand years of history that they have been chosen to endure even the greatest hardship and to emerge

---

[163] Seyyed Ali Khamenei, *Palestine*, reported in "Iran's Khamenei Reportedly Publishes Book on How to Destroy Israel," *Haaretz*, Aug. 02, 2015, posted at http://www.haaretz.com/news/middle-east/1.669241.

[164] Seyyed Ali Khamenei, reported in Vincent Funaro, "Iran's Supreme Leader Ayatollah Ali Khamenei Pens Book With Plan to Destroy Israel," in *Christian Post*, August 5, 2015, posted at http://www.christianpost.com/news/irans-supreme-leader-ayatollah-ali-khamenei-pens-book-with-plan-to-destroy-israel-142301/.

[165] Ellen Willis, *Beginning to See the Light: Sex, Hope, and Rock-and-Roll* (Minneapolis, MN: The University of Minnesota Press, 2013), p. 244.

victorious. For most Jews, this is much more than mere self-confidence. It is a simple, deep-seated assurance that God, the God of Israel, is with them and that he ensures not only their survival but also their blessing. Michael Wyschogrod encapsulates this history of the Jewish people and their expectation not only to survive but also to thrive in these poignant words: "[Israel] survives the mightiest nation-states, many of which have long disappeared from history, while Israel, against all human calculation, endures. Israel is thus a living witness that the God who chose it is the Lord of history and that his purpose will be achieved."[166] The ongoing and never-ending drama of the continued and continuing presence of the Jewish people in the world as an identifiable entity is testimony to the fact that "the God of Israel is a redeeming God." And, Wyschogrod says, "This is the only message we are authorized to proclaim, however much it may not seem so to the eyes of nonbelief."[167]

---

[166] Michael Wyschogrod, *Abraham's Promise: Judaism and Jewish-Christian Relations* (Grand Rapids, MI: Wm. B. Eerdmans Publishing Co., 2004), p. 182.

[167] Michael Wyschogrod, "Faith and the Holocaust," *Judaism* 20 (1971), pp. 286–294.

CHAPTER 11

# ANTISEMITISM REDUX

## ANTI-ZIONISM: THE RESURRECTION OF AN OLD DEMON

With the Allied victory in World War II, the complete genocide of European Jewry was averted, despite the fact that some two-thirds of European Jews were murdered by the Nazi regime.[1] The overt antisemitism of the Third Reich, however, was not destroyed with the German unconditional surrender. Antisemitism was not even destroyed when it was officially outlawed in Germany[2] or when it was proscribed in many other Eastern European nations—most of which had abused, terrorized, and murdered Jews for centuries before the rise of Hitler and his henchmen.[3]

Antisemitism merely crawled back under its rock, retreating into the underground and awaiting a new birth in a new day. To be sure, it shed its skin; however, it retained its fangs and its venom glands. A new day would enable antisemitism to emerge from the darkness clothed in new, shiny skin so that it could again rear its head and deceive arrogant, self-centered nihilists and the ignorant masses they would influence, including those in nominal Christianity. Without a doubt, antisemitism has been and continues to be the demon that never dies, the evil that constantly reconstitutes itself and clothes

[1] Since a full 60% of all world Jewry lived in Europe, the fact that two-thirds of those were victims of the Holocaust is all the more appalling. Theodore S. Hamerow, *Why We Watched: Europe, America, and the Holocaust* (New York: W. W. Norton & Co., 2008), pp. 325–327.

[2] In the early 1950s, Germany virtually outlawed antisemitism. The Socialist Reich Party was outlawed by the Constitutional Court in 1952. Even in East Germany, right-wing organizations were totally banned. As a result, "Anti-Semitism was thus no longer socially acceptable, and could only be insinuated, indirectly and weakly." Werner Bergmann and Rainer Erb, *Anti-Semitism in Germany: The Post-Nazi Epoch from 1945 to 1995*, tr. Belinda Cooper and Allison Brown (New Brunswick, NJ: Transaction Publishers, 1997), p. 276.

[3] David Robertson, *The Routledge Dictionary of Politics* (Abingdon, UK: Routledge, 2004), p. 19. Robertson observes that "most European nations practised some form of discrimination against Jews . . . for centuries before . . . the National Socialist party changed the emphasis of anti-Semitism from religious to racial hatred." The lone exception was Poland, which for several centuries "was the safest place in Europe for Jews," accommodating "80 percent of the world's Jews" during the late Middle Ages. Michael Kort, *The Handbook of the New Eastern Europe* (Brookfield, CT: Twenty-First Century Books, 2001), p. 211.

itself with the garments of deception that allow it to creep among the masses and perpetrate its monstrous depravity again and again.[4]

Through the centuries, antisemitism has constantly refined itself, morphing from one form to another in order to accommodate public perceptions and changes in living conditions imposed upon the Jewish people. This has resulted in a continually emerging "new antisemitism," which is really nothing new at all.[5] As a matter of fact, as Keith Kahn-Harris and Ben Gidley observe, the term *new antisemitism* was probably first used in 1921 to describe the "twin threat of Nazism in Germany and [Sir Oswald Emald] Mosley's fascism [in Britain]." This "newness" pointed out the "predominance of pseudo-scientific racial themes" that "qualitatively differed from older social prejudices and religious themes."[6]

Sarah Cardaun confirms this truth, noting that "current antisemitic manifestations ... employ many traditional anti-Jewish themes such as conspiracy theories, the belief in malicious Jewish influence in the world, or the blood libel." She reports that while motivations for and sources of antisemitism have changed over time, "there have always been certain tropes and ideas which survived the transformation of anti-Jewish prejudice and were rearticulated in new contexts at later stages."[7] David Nirenberg says that "habits of thought" based on "inherited cultural forms" have always been present in the history of antisemitism.[8] In reality, as antisemitism has continually morphed to accommodate societal perceptions, it has remained constant in its perverse and paranoid hatred for the Jewish people. "History keeps moving forward," says UN Secretary-General Antonio Guterres, "but anti-Semitism keeps coming back."[9] Sadly, antisemitism's "transmission is viral and though the virus stays the same, it mutates into several strains,"[10] and as Phyllis

[4] Daniel J. Goldhagen, *The Devil that Never Dies: The Rise and Threat of Global Antisemitism* (New York: Little, Brown and Co., 2013), p. 142.

[5] Sarah K. Cardaun, *Countering Contemporary Antisemitism in Britain: Government and Civil Society Responses between Universalism and Particularism* (Leiden, The Netherlands: Koninklijke Brill NV, 2015), p. 78. Cardaun notes that "more moderate observers raise the objection that the actual expression 'new antisemitism' is misleading not because anti-Jewish attitudes no longer pose a problem, but because in their view there is nothing particularly new about it."

[6] Keith Kahn-Harris and Ben Gidley, *Turbulent Times: The British Jewish Community Today* (London, UK: Continuum International Publishing Group, 2010), p. 138.

[7] Cardaun, p. 78.

[8] David Nirenberg, *Anti-Judaism: The Western Tradition* (New York: W. W. Norton & Co., 2013), pp. 438–439.

[9] Antonio Guterres, United Nations Secretary-General, "Secretary-General's remarks at Observance of the International Day of Commemoration in Memory of the Victims of the Holocaust," 27 January 2017, posted at https://www.un.org/sg/en/content/sg/statement/2017-01-27/secretary-generals-remarks-observance-international-day.

[10] Steven K. Baum, Antisemitism Explained (Lanham, MD: University Press of America, 2012), p. 2.

Chesler observes, it is all the more dangerous because of the "speed and frequency" with which it can be spread in the world today.[11]

## The "New, Improved" Antisemitism

Antisemitism in the West was forced underground by the atrocities of the Holocaust which were well documented and publicly exposed with graphic visual evidence in the form of photographs and films created by both the German Nazis themselves and the Allied Forces who conquered them. The Nazis had fully expected that they would inevitably triumph in World War II and that their victory would result in the eradication of the disease of Jewishness from the body politic of Germany, Europe, and the world. They had, therefore, carefully documented the work of the death camps that they had established in Eastern Europe and other systems that they had instituted and carefully operated to fulfill their goal of making Germany, Europe and the world *judenrein*, "clean" or "free" of Jews.[12] In most cases, they counted victims and in some cases photographed them as well.[13] When the Allied Forces finally conquered the German army and swept through the concentration camps, freeing the remaining captives who awaited the gas chambers and the crematoria, they were so appalled at the sights they saw that they also carefully documented everything.[14] This photographic evidence was displayed in countless pages of print media, and this video evidence appeared in newsreels for theaters and then on television in the United States and in Western Europe; however, the antisemitism that had been endemic in European societies for centuries—and in parts of the United States government and populace as well—was never eradicated. It merely lurked in the shadows, waiting for an occasion when it could again manifest and vaunt itself.

The antisemitism that had remained dormant in Europe for the twenty years following the end of World War II sprang to life again in 1968 when French president Charles de Gaulle "gave a speech in which he castigated the

---

[11] Phyllis Chesler, *The New Anti-Semitism: The Current Crisis and What We Must Do About It* (Jerusalem, Israel: Gefen Publishing House, 2015), p. 88.

[12] Margaret L. King, *Western Civilization: A Social and Cultural History* (Upper Saddle River, NJ: Prentice Hall, 2000), vol. 3, p. 863. Also Richard Panchyk, *World War II for Kids* (Chicago, IL: Chicago Review Press, 2002), p. 115, and Donald L. Niewyk, "The Holocaust: Jews, Gypsies, and the Handicapped," in *Centuries of Genocide: Essays and Eyewitness Accounts*, Samuel Totten and William S. Parsons, eds. (Abingdon, UK: Routledge, 2013), p. 211.

[13] Lucjan Dobroszycki, "Captured Nazi Documents on the Destruction of Jews in the Soviet Union," in *The Holocaust in the Soviet Union: Studies and Sources on the Destruction of the Jews in the Nazi-Occupied Territories of the USSR, 1941–1945*, Lucjan Dobroszycki and Jeffery S. Gurock, eds. (Abingdon, UK: Routledge, 1993), p. 215.

[14] Jeffrey Shandler, *While America Watches: Televising the Holocaust* (Oxford, UK: Oxford University Press, 1999), pp. 5–24,

Jews as 'an elite people, self-assured and domineering'"[15] and thereby opened the door to a new and improved antisemitism that would be reborn out of the detritus of the old antisemitism. French philosopher Raymond Aron declared that with this statement antisemites "received solemn authorization from the Head of State to make themselves heard again and to employ the same languages as before the Final Solution."[16] As a result, says Aron, "National anti-semitism had once again become *salonfähig*,[17] as the Germans put it."[18] In fact, from that time forward, France subsequently took the lead in the resurrection of the old European antisemitism and became the breeding ground for antisemitism's manifestation in various new and insidious forms, a role that it fulfills—perhaps even relishes—to this day.[19]

The pre-World War II antisemitism in France that "transformed anti-Jewish sentiment into official state-sponsored persecution and assistance to the Nazis in implementing the Final Solution, or Holocaust"[20] has clearly emerged from its banishment to the underground in a new form that has made France among the most anti-Zionist and antisemitic nations in the Western world.[21] In fact, French liberalism has led most of Europe to adopt anti-Israel sentiments and to leave their significant Muslim populations that have immigrated from Northern Africa and elsewhere to those nations virtually unchecked in the expression of the new anti-Israelism,[22] today's socially

---

[15] Caroline B. Glick, *The Israeli Solution: A One-State Plan for Peace in the Middle East* (New York: Crown Forum, 2014), p. 89.

[16] Raymond Aron, *De Gaulle, Israel and the Jews*, tr. John Sturrock (New Brunswick, NJ: Transaction Publishers, 2009), p. 24., referenced in Glick, p. 89.

[17] The German word *salonfähig* means "socially acceptable" or "presentable."

[18] Aron, p. 89.

[19] Richard J. Golson, "Antisemitism in Modern France" in *Antisemitism: A History*, Albert S. Lindemann and Richard S. Levy, eds. (Oxford, UK: Oxford University Press, 2010), pp. 136–149.

[20] James Ciment, "Anti-Semitism in France," in *Social Issues in America: An Encyclopedia*, James Ciment, ed. (Abingdon, UK: Routledge, 2015), p. 155.

[21] Jeffrey Ian Ross, *Religion and Violence: An Encyclopedia of Faith and Conflict from Antiquity to the Present* (Abingdon, UK: Routledge, 2011), p. 284. Ross notes that "among European countries, Austria and Hungary have the highest anti-Semitic sentiment throughout the population"; however, he also observes that "the primary country [in Europe] afflicted with anti-Semitic violence has been France." Ross notes that "the French government reports that approximately two-thirds of racist incidents in France are anti-Semitic," this despite the fact that "France has the highest Jewish population in Europe, approximately 600,000." Joseph McGonagle, *Representing Ethnicity in Contemporary French Visual Culture* (Oxford, UK: Oxford University Press, 2017), p. 129. While much of current antisemitism in France springs from the large population of Muslim immigrants from Northern Africa, antisemitism has long been indigenous in France and continues to be present in its indigenous population. Anthony Julius points out that even "without direct German prompting," the "roots of Vichy anti-Semitism lay deep in nineteenth-century French history." Anthony Julius, *T. S. Eliot, Anti-Semitism, and Literary Form* (Cambridge, UK: Cambridge University Press, 1995), p. 172. Thomas Laub also confirms this indigenous and incipient antisemitism in France. Thomas J. Laub, *After the Fall: Germany Policy in Occupied France, 1940–1944* (Oxford, UK: Oxford University Press, 2010), p. 89.

[22] "Anti-Zionism" is the term of choice among the proponents of the new antisemitism because its use enables them to mask their virulent antisemitism in a more antiseptic form than the term *anti-Israelism* permits.

acceptable antisemitism. French efforts to accommodate Islamist seditions that are undermining French secularist society and the few remaining vestiges of French Christianity have even prompted some to argue that the Islamization of French culture could well be a boon to the French people. This mindset has led to the proposal of the utterly absurd argument that Islam could "be a cure to fragmented, atomized, selfish, and individualistic postmodernity," a means of fighting "the new antisemitism, French and European metaphysical anxiety, and the existential emptiness of zombie Catholic France."[23] But, he wonders, is "Islam lite a solution to antisemitism?"[24] The answer to that question should be for any reasonable person a resounding, "No!" Islamization is neither an answer to Western decadence and nihilism, nor is it an answer to the scourge of Western-inspired antisemitism.

It should come as no surprise, therefore, that the "new and improved" version of the ancient antisemitism that has plagued the Jewish community for centuries has thrived in the postmodern world of consequentialism and multiculturalism. "The Devil, with us for two thousand years, is back," declares Daniel Goldhagen. "[A]fter a period of relative quiescence, [he] has reappeared, flexes his muscles again, and stalks the world, with ever more confidence, power, and followers. The devil is not a he but an it. The devil is antisemitism."[25] The old, despicable antisemitism that was once almost universally deplored is now being marketed in an acceptable—even glitzy—package called anti-Zionism, or, more accurately, anti-Israelism.[26] In fact, "the linchpin [of today's antisemitism] is hostility to Zionism and Israel."[27] After lying low for a time, the ugly and abominable spirit that produced history's greatest and most heinous genocidal effort has now emerged from the shadows in Europe, the Middle East, and in a shocking number of nations around the world. Yehuda Blum had rightly observed that "'anti-Israel' and 'anti-Zionist' slogans are being used by closet and crypto-anti-Semites to disguise their true intentions."[28]

[23] Bruno Chaouat, *Is Theory Good for the Jews: French Thought* (Liverpool, UK: Liverpool University Press, 2016), pp. 242–243. Chaouat discusses ideas advanced by Emmanuel Todd in Emmanuel Todd, *Who Is Charlie? Xenophobia and the New Middle Class* (Cambridge, UK: Plity Press, 2015).

[24] Chaouat, p. 243.

[25] Daniel J. Goldhagen, *The Rise and Threat of Global Antisemitism* (New York: Little, Brown and Company, 2013), p. xv.

[26] Jonathan Freedland, "Is Anti-Zionism Antisemitism?" in *A New Antisemitism? Debating Judeophobia in 21st-Century Britain*, Paul Iganski and Barry Kosmin, eds. (London, UK: Profile Books, 2003).

[27] Brian Klug, "Interrogating 'New Anti-Semitism,'" in *Radicalization and Religion: Race, Culture and Difference in the Study of Antisemitism and Islamophobia*, Nasar Meer, ed. (Abingdon, UK: Routledge, 2014), p. 85.

[28] Yehuda Z. Blum, *For Zion's Sake* (New York: Herzl Press, 1987), p. 34.

Far and wide, antisemitism has become fashionable. Sporting the garments of this new, socially acceptable antisemitism, ultraliberal politicians and the extreme leftist secular press even self-righteously vaunt an increasingly rabid anti-Zionism. Like the old emperor in Hans Christian Andersen's *The Emperor's New Clothes*, they think that the dream weavers of postmodernity have crafted magical garments that are invisible to those who are stupid and incompetent.[29] By clothing themselves in the newest styles of this anti-Israel *haute couture*, they boldly wear their insidious antisemitism with pride and hauteur. This has been especially true in the elite, rarefied air of avant-garde leftist media, entertainment, academia, and politics. The worshipers of the reclothed Führer are so entranced with this illusion that, like the sycophants in Andersen's tale, none of them "would let it appear that he could see nothing, for then he would not be fit for his post, or else he was a fool." In truth, however, even the least discerning could look at the Führer's new clothes, see that they are neither opaque nor even diaphanous but utterly transparent, and exclaim with Andersen's child, "But he has got nothing on!" The selective blindness of the new antisemitism has become an increasingly virulent religious and social obsession among most of the Islamic peoples of the Middle East and in the rest of the world.

In much of Western Europe, the delegitimization of Israel has become a cottage industry,[30] and anti-Zionism has become "a 'respectable' anti-Semitism."[31] While most Western nations still endeavor to mask their not-so-subtle antisemitism, ancient Eastern European hotbeds of antisemitism that had flourished for centuries only to be driven underground by post-World-War-II civility have now begun to erupt with the intensity and regularity of Old Faithful.[32] The antisemitism of their anti-Israelism is bold and apparent. The same libels that were hurled against the Jews during the Middle Ages by these nations have exploded again. Like the pent-up magma

[29] Hans Christian Andersen, *Fairy Tales from Hans Christian Andersen* (London, UK: J. M. Dent & Co., 1906), p. 219.

[30] Jerold S. Auerbach, *Jewish State, Pariah Nation: Israel and the Dilemmas of Legitimacy* (New Orleans, LA: Quid Pro Books, 2014). Auerbach points to British-produced books that have promoted anti-Israelist antisemitism. These include Uri Davis, *Israel: An Apartheid State* (London, UK: Zed Books, 1987) and many of the tomes published by the anti-Zionist Pluto Press, including John Rose, *The Myths of Zionism* (London, UK: Pluto Press, 2004); Jonathan Cook, *Blood and Religion: The Unmasking of the Jewish and Democratic State* (London, UK: Pluto Press, 2006); Joel Kovel, *Overcoming Zionism* (London, UK: Pluto Press, 2007) and Ben White, *Israeli Apartheid: A Beginners Guide* (London, UK: Pluto Press, 2009).

[31] Alvin H. Rosenfeld, *Anti-Zionism in Great Britain and Beyond: A 'Respectable' Anti-Semitism?* (New York: American Jewish Committee, 2004).

[32] Stephan M. Horak and Richard Blanke, *Eastern European National Minorities, 1919–1980: A Handbook* (Santa Barbara, CA: Libraries Unlimited, 1985), p. 56. In Eastern Europe, it was during "the aftermath of the Arab-Israeli war of 1967" that "official anti-Semitism came to the fore again in the form of anti-Zionism."

of long-dormant volcanoes their antisemitism has produced eruptions of hate and violence against the few remaining Jewish citizens among them and in vile condemnation of the six million Jews who live in Israel. Since antisemitism "established itself earlier and with greater intensity"[33] in Eastern Europe than in the West, it should surprise no one that the nations in this bloc should lead the non-Muslim world in anti-Israel vilification and slander.

Now, the old, pustule-infested Nazi emperor thinks he has a gleaming new wardrobe of politically correct garments! The naked truth, however, is that, when clothed with the garments of anti-Zionism, the old antisemitism, though subtle and politically correct, is even perhaps—because of its subtlety—more insidious than its source, the evil Haman, and its most recent incarnation, the Führer himself. As Avner Falk observes, "the 'anti-Semitism' of our own time, that of the twenty-first century, does not seem to care whether the Jews are a religion, a people, a nation, a race, or an ethnic group."[34] Most new antisemites hate all Jews because many believe all Jews are inherently Zionists.

Ironically, it was Hitler who set the stage for clothing antisemitism in the garments of anti-Zionism: "While the Zionists try to make the rest of the world believe that the national consciousness of the Jew finds its satisfaction in the creation of a Palestinian state, the Jews again slyly dupe the dumb *Goyim*. It doesn't even enter their heads to build up a Jewish state in Palestine for the purpose of living there; all they want is a central organization for their international world swindle."[35] Interestingly, when Hitler referenced the "creation of a Palestinian state" in this declaration, he was talking about the *Jewish* state of *Palestine*—Israel. Even the Führer knew that at that time, all the "Palestinians" were Jews, not Arabs! Sadly, the ideas that Hitler projected have continued to thrive through the twentieth century and into today, as is evidenced by 1998 Nobel Prize winner José Saramago's[36] depiction of Israel as a "racist state by virtue of Judaism's monstrous doctrines—racist not just against the Palestinians, but against the entire world, which it seeks to manipulate and abuse."[37]

[33] Hans-Christian Petersen, *Antisemitism in Eastern Europe: History and Present in Comparison* (New York: Peter Lang Publishing, 2010), pp. 53, 91, 183, 191.

[34] Avner Falk, *Anti-Semitism: A History and Psychoanalysis of Contemporary Hatred* (Westport, CT: Praeger Publishers, 2008), p. 97.

[35] Adolf Hitler, *Mein Kampf*, tr. Ralph Manheim (Boston: Houghton Mifflin, 1971), p. 56.

[36] Portugal's Saramago was awarded the Nobel Prize in Literature in 1998. His depiction of Israel deserves the opposite of a Nobel Prize.

[37] José Saramago, quoted in Robert S. Wistrich, *A Lethal Obsession: Anti-Semitism from Antiquity to the Global Jihad* (New York: Random House, 2010), p. 7.

## Repackaging Antisemitism as Anti-Zionism

Robert Wistrich graphically and accurately describes the morphing of older forms of antisemitism into the new politically correct antisemitic anti-Israelism: "[The] radical agitation [of continental leftists and Palestinians] is no longer directed at the 'Christ-killers,' the 'Jewish usurers' of the Middle Ages, the Bourse Jews, or an inferior race of Untermenschen but against the so-called perpetrators of a (fictional) 'genocide' against the Palestinians. Never mind that this grotesque libel is contradicted by all available empirical evidence, never mind that Israel is increasingly threatened by the genocidal antisemitism promoted by Iran, the Muslim Brotherhood, Hamas, Hezbollah, and the global jihad. Such minor details do not for one moment disturb the sleep of left-wing activists (including the Jews among them) whose 'humanist' posture evidently does not extend to the idea that Israelis might also be victims."[38] In fact, adds Eve Garrard, "the deep anti-Judaism embedded in the culture generates an interpretation of Israel which construes it, in the teeth of the evidence, as a uniquely criminal political entity."[39] It is this hostility toward Israel that "provides an alibi for the antisemitism of people who might otherwise have been embarrassed and ashamed to display this ancient and blood-soaked form of racism."[40]

Very subtly, anti-Zionists have concealed the foundation of eugenics, race, and social Darwinism that the Third Reich employed for its antisemitism and have adopted a new, politically correct foundation for their perverse hatred of Jews, which they self-righteously trumpet as "human rights."[41] Recognizing this transition from racial to socio-political antisemitism, Anthony Chase said, "The twentieth century brought with it anti-Zionist and anticolonialist movements in the Arab world, some currents of which looked to human rights as a basis of support."[42] The Arabs were joined immediately by Europeans, Latin Americans, and others who had discovered the new and universally approved means of vaunting their inherent and long-held antisemitism. The banner of "human rights" can mean whatever the banner bearer wants it to

---

[38] Robert S. Wistrich, *From Ambivalence to Betrayal: The Left, the Jews, and Israel* (Lincoln, NE: The University of Nebraska Press, 2012), p. xiv.

[39] Eve Garrard, "Anti-Judaism, Anti-Zionism, Antisemitism," *Fathom*, Winter, 2015, posted at http://fathomjournal.org/anti-judaism-anti-zionism-antisemitism/.

[40] Garrard, "Anti-Judaism."

[41] Fiamma Nirenstein, "How I Became an 'Unconscious Fascist'," in *Those Who Forget the Past: The Question of Antisemitism*, Ron Rosenbaum, ed. (New York: Random House Publishing, 2004), p. 292. Nirenstein says that at the United Nations summit in Durban, South Africa, in 2001, anti-Israel antisemitism "officially became the banner of the new secular religion of human rights, and Israel and Jews became its official enemy."

[42] Anthony Tirado Chase, "Nongovernmental Organizations: Arab NGOs," in *Encyclopedia of Human Rights*, David P. Forsythe, ed. (Oxford, UK: Oxford University Press, 2009), vol. 1, p. 98.

mean. The "human rights" of the preferred group render the "human rights" of the targeted group meaningless—a clear example of the fascist intolerance of multiculturalist dogmatists and the situational ethics of their consequentialism.

Wistrich described the emergence of the new, socially acceptable antisemitism that is marketed as anti-Zionism: "Anti-Semitism did not dissolve or significantly diminish, let alone disappear, after the establishment of Israel in 1948. Instead, Israel itself would gradually be identified as the new 'Jewish question.'"[43] This new antisemitism is even so inane as to maintain that "Jews benefited from exploiting their suffering during the Holocaust."[44] Anti-Zionism, therefore, has become a socially acceptable way to advocate for the elimination of the state of Israel and, in effect, for the elimination of all Jews.[45] Amy Elman declares that "the key elements of 'new" antisemitism . . . [have] moved from *Judenrein* to *Judenstaatrein.*"[46] This new antisemitism is different from historical antisemitism in that "it is no longer directed against Jews as individuals. It is primarily directed against Jews as a nation with their own state in their own land. It is a mutant form of anti-Zionism."[47] In view of the diabolical and convoluted arguments that are continually advanced to support the anti-Israelism of the new antisemites, it should be obvious that anti-Israelism and antisemitism are now virtually indistinguishable.

Jonathan Sacks says it well: "The new antisemitism is clearly continuous with the old. It has recycled all the old myths, from the Blood Libel to The Protocols of the Elders of Zion.[48] Yet it is different. It is not Christian anti-Judaism, nor is it the racial antisemitism of Nazi Germany. It is . . . focused not on Jews as individuals but on Jews as a nation in their land."[49] As David Blumenthal says, "Jew-haters in the West who feel uneasy labeling themselves 'antisemites' find in 'anti-Zionism' an easy way to sustain their Jew-hatred under a socially acceptable label."[50] Despite all the elaborate efforts of Western

[43] Wistrich, *A Lethal Obsession*, p. 22.

[44] Andreas Zick, "Anti-Semitism," in *Encyclopedia of Group Processes and Intergroup Relations*, John M. Levine and Michael A. Hogg, eds. (Thousand Oaks, CA: SAGE Publications, Inc., 2010), p. 24.

[45] Bernard Harrison, "Anti-Zionism, Antisemitism, and the Rhetorical Manipulation of Reality," in *Resurgent Antisemitism: Global Perspectives*, Alvin H. Rosenfeld, ed. (Bloomington, IN: Indiana University Press, 2013), p. 11.

[46] R. Amy Elman, "The EU's Responses to Contemporary Antisemitism," in *Deciphering the New Antisemitism*, Alvin H. Rosenfeld, ed. (Bloomington, IN: The Indiana University Press, 2015), p. 414.

[47] Jonathan Sacks, *Future Tense: Jews, Judaism, and Israel in the Twenty-first Century* (New York: Schocken Books, 2009), pp. 97–98.

[48] Hadassa Ben-Itto, *The Lie That Wouldn't Die: The Protocols of the Elders of Zion* (Estree, UK: Vallentine Mitchell Publishers, 2005).

[49] Sacks, p. 99.

[50] David Blumenthal, "Antisemitism," in *A Dictionary of the Jewish-Christian Dialogue*, Leon Klenicki and Geoffrey Wigoder, eds. (Mahwah, NJ: Paulist Press, 1984), p. 11.

antisemities to disguise their rabid antisemitism, it is clear that "anti-Israelism and anti-Zionism are . . . only thin veneers that mask anti-Semitic sentiments, statements, and actions"[51] and that "antisemitic bigotry is no less morally deplorable when camouflaged as anti-Israelism or anti-Zionism."[52]

Today, old underlying currents of history's despicable antisemitism try to hide behind what is euphemistically called a "critique" of Israel. "This new expression of anti-Semitism is found in right wing populism, Islamist propaganda, and . . . left wing ideologies," says Andreas Zick. Then, in many cases, "Israeli policies against Palestinians are sometimes defined as 'Jewish'[53] and thus attributed to religious rather than nationalistic causes. This anti-Semitic critique is linked to two other themes: first, a comparison of Israeli policies to the crimes of the Nazis; and second, a separatist ideology categorizing Jews as a strange community that is not part of society."[54] No matter how it is disguised, however, "anti-Zionism contains anti-Semitism like a cloud contains a storm,"[55] says Auschwitz survivor Jean Amery. And regardless as to how it is presented, "the antisemitism that is anti-Zionism has permeated respectable public discourse, incorporating the hoary antisemitic stereotypes of Jews as vindictive and bloodthirsty."[56] Even though anti-Zionists have tried desperately to mask their antisemitism with a thick layer of politically correct cosmetics, the hideous, pock-marked ugliness remains. The underlying reality is what Emmanuel Lévinas described: "Do we not smell here . . . beyond all violence which still submits to will and reason, the odor of the camps? Violence is no longer a political phenomenon of war and peace, beyond all morality. It is the abyss of Auschwitz or the world at war."[57]

Sacks speaks of three degrees of anti-Zionism: 1) "Jews are not entitled

---

[51] Gary A. Tobin, Aryeh K. Weinberg, and Jenna Ferer, *The UnCivil University: Intolerance on College Campuses* (Lanham, MD: Rowman & Littlefield Publishers, 2009), p. 214.

[52] US Commission on Civil Rights, Findings and Recommendations Regarding Campus Anti-Semitism, April 3, 2006, quoted in Michael Berenbaum, *Not Your Father's Antisemitism: Hatred of the Jews in the 21st Century* (St. Paul, MN: Paragon House, 2008), p. 282.

[53] It is ironic that anti-Zionists describe Israeli policies as "Jewish" but they could never define the nation of Israel as a "Jewish state."

[54] Zick, p. 24.

[55] Jean Amery, quoted in Benjamin Weinthal, "Why Europe Blames Israel for the Holocaust: Post-1945 Anti-Semitism," in *The Jerusalem Post*, 01/28/2014, posted at http://www.jpost.com/Jewish-World/Jewish-Features/Why-Europe-blames-Israel-for-the-Holocaust-Post-1945-anti-Semitism-339571. Accusations that Jews are "separatists" and a "strange community that is not part of society" clearly echo from the fifth-century-BC antisemitic diatribe that Haman delivered in the court of Xerxes when he sought the genocide of the Jews: "There is a certain people dispersed among the peoples in the provinces of your kingdom who keep themselves separate" (Esther 3:9).

[56] David Matas, *Aftershock: Anti-Zionism & Anti-Semitism* (Toronto, Canada: Dundurn Press, 2005), p. 218.

[57] Emmanuel Lévinas, *Nine Talmudic Readings*, tr. Annette Aronowicz (Bloomington, IN: Indiana University Press, 1990), p. 190, quoted in David Patterson, *Open Wounds: The Crisis of Jewish Thought in the Aftermath of the Holocaust* (Seattle, WA: The University of Washington Press, 2006), p. 102.

to a nation-state of their own," which is, in effect, a denial "of the right of Israel to exist"; 2) "the existence of Israel is merely an aberration" which "is responsible for all the evils of the world"; and 3) "all Jews are Zionists; therefore all Jews are responsible for the sufferings caused by Israel; therefore all Jews are legitimate targets of attack."[58] This third degree, says Sacks, is the "bridge from anti-Zionism to anti-Semitism."[59] This is why, as Walter Laqueur has argued, "There is no clear borderline" between antisemitism and anti-Zionism.[60] Whatever the case, Rosemary Ruether hit the nail on the head when she said, "There is no doubt that anti-Zionism has become a way of reviving the myth of the 'perennial evil nature of the Jews.'"[61] Clearly, in today's world, the "enemies of the Jews nearly always use the word 'Zionist' when they mean Jews."[62] In fact, as time moves on, antisemitism's new garments are becoming less and less subtle and more and more crude and vulgar.

## Collectivizing Antisemitism

Whether in the rarefied air of liberal postmodern think tanks, in the smug, supercilious propaganda of nihilist Western media, or in the psychopathic imaginations of Muslim jihadists, the new antisemitism that is manifest as rabid anti-Zionism represents nothing more than a means of collectivizing the old antisemitism of history and directing it toward the corporate Jewish people by making the modern nation of Israel a pariah among the civilized world. The historical pathological hatred of individual Jews and small Jewish communities has been refocused on the larger entity of Israel, the Jewish state. It is now possible, antisemites evidently think, to hate the Jewish nation and to seek its dissolution and utter destruction while appearing not to hate and seek the destruction of individual Jews. This fabrication is absurd in that it attempts to make Israel a non-Jewish entity—as though the nation of Israel were not somehow comprised of over six million individual Jews.

Rather than recognizing the right of individual Jews to form a collective and to do so in the land of their ancestors, the anti-Israelists of the world

[58] Sacks, pp. 97–98.

[59] Sacks, pp. 97–98.

[60] Walter Laqueur, *The Changing Face of Antisemitism: From Ancient Times to the Present Day* (Oxford, UK: Oxford University Press, 2006), p. 7.

[61] Rosemary Radford Ruether, *Faith and Fratricide: The Theological Roots of Anti-Semitism* (New York: Seabury Press, 1974), p. 227. While Ruether has pointed out this aspect of anti-Zionism, her joint work with her husband Herman J. Ruether has also argued that Israel has betrayed "its own original mandate." Rosemary Radford Ruether and Herman J. Ruether, *The Wrath of Jonah: Crisis of Religious Nationalism in the Israeli-Palestinian Conflict* (Minneapolis, MN: Fortress Press, 2002).

[62] Dennis Prager and Joseph Teluskin, *Why the Jews? The Reason for Antisemitism* (New York: Simon & Schuster, 2003), p. 157.

insist on a non-Jewish Israel (or, better yet, Palestine). In this view, Jews can exist as long as they do not assert their own corporate self-identity, "the one that was molded by Zionism, the Jewish form of nationalism, before and after the establishment of the State of Israel in 1948."[63] This argument, however, has been totally debunked by history wherein individuals and small groups of Jews have been easy targets for acts of violence. In reality, as Elhanan Yakira has observed, "the denial of 'legitimacy' of the political incarnation of the Jew or of Jewishness—the 'Jewish State' or Israel—is . . . as antisemitism has always been, a license to kill," for "saying of something that it is *illegitimate* . . . implies that the law would not have allowed its original coming into existence and now commends its demise."[64] Anti-Israelism, therefore, is an insidious form of antisemitism in that it legitimizes the rights of the nations—Islamists in particular—to destroy the Jewish nation and, with it, most of the Jewish population. This is, in fact, the declared intention of the Iranian ayatollahs: to destroy the people of Israel in one fell swoop of nuclear annihilation.

## The Nations Gather to Vaunt Their Antisemitism

Since the emergence of the new anti-Zionist antisemitism, its major supporter and promulgator has been the United Nations, which has not hesitated to accuse Israel of "racism, apartheid, ethnic cleansing, crimes against humanity, and attempted genocide"[65] and to enact and employ various antisemitic policies that blatantly attack the nation of Israel and its citizens. In perhaps its worst incursion into the abyss of antisemitism, the United Nations General Assembly passed Resolution 3329 in 1975, declaring, "Zionism is a form of racism and racial discrimination." This resolution was so clearly antisemitic in its design and application that anyone with a modicum of morality and human decency should have been revolted by it. Sadly, many Western nations which did not actively promote this new form of antisemitism tacitly endorsed its broad-based indictment of the Jews by their silence in the face of the proposition and by their acquiescence to it.[66] With such absurdly antisemitic pronouncements, it is no wonder that scholars like

[63] Raffaella A. Del Sarto, *Israel under Siege: The Politics of Insecurity and the Rise of the Israeli Neo-Revisionist Right* (Washington, DC: Georgetown University Press, 2017), p. 150.

[64] Elhanan Yakira, "Antisemitism and Anti-Zionism as a Moral Question," in *Resurgent Antisemitism: Global Perspectives*, Alvin H. Rosenfeld, ed. (Bloomington, IN: Indiana University Press, 2013), p. 61.

[65] Sacks, p. 101.

[66] In 1991, Israel forced the passage of Resolution 46/86, which revoked Resolution 3379's charge that Zionism is a form of racism, by making Resolution 46/86 a precondition for its participation in the Madrid Peace Conference. Otherwise, Resolution 3379 would still be in force, and Israel would still be condemned by its vile indictments.

Anne Bayefsky have declared that the United Nations has become "the leading purveyor of anti-Semitism, intolerance and inequity against the Jewish people and its state."[67] Robert Wolfe agrees, saying that "today the United Nations that arose out of the defeat of the Nazis is consumed with hatred of the nation of Israel."[68]

## The Naked Truth: Exposing Anti-Israel Antisemitism

Shalem Coulibaly argues correctly that "culturally, politically, and theologically, antisemitism is reprehensible and must be combated."[69] At the same time, he notes the stark reality of today's growing antisemitism masquerading as anti-Israelism: "Economic globalization, which goes hand in hand with global shrinkage as a result of new information and communication technologies, will give rise not only to a new antisemitism but also to the continuous adaptation and adoption of anti-Zionism by other peoples."[70] David Patterson confirms the ultimate target of this adapting antisemitism: "Like all anti-Semites, the anti-Zionists oppose the Jewish state *not for any action* [that it has committed] but for its *presence.*"[71] "Whatever the current evil might be—racism, colonialism, imperialism, apartheid, ethnic cleansing, crimes against humanity, or genocide—one can be sure that the anti-Zionists will hang the label on the Jewish state. Like the religious and secular anti-Semites of the nineteenth century, the religious and secular anti-Zionists, from rabid jihadists to radical liberals, share a self-righteous indignation over the very existence of the Jewish state precisely because they themselves would be the moral measure of humanity."[72]

What is amazing about such anti-Zionist moralizing is that many—if not most—of those who make such judgments against Israel are generally amoral agnostics who have arrogated to themselves the right to adjudicate morality and "fairness" while living lives of complete hypocrisy often void of constraint and lacking any true ethical boundaries! In reality, many are

[67] Anne Bayefsky, "One Small Step: Is the U.N. Finally Ready to Get Serious About Anti-Semitism?" in a speech at the UN Conference on Anti-Semitism, June 21, 2004, quoted in Robert L. Beir, *Roosevelt and the Holocaust: How FDR Saved the Jews and Brought Hope to a Nation* (New York: Skyhorse Publishing, 2006), p. 230. For an opposing perspective, see Rafael Medoff, *FDR & the Holocaust: A Breach of Faith* (Washington DC: The David S. Wyman Institute for Holocaust Studies, 2013).

[68] Robert Wolfe, *From Habiru to Hebrews and Other Essays* (Minneapolis, MN: Mill City Press, Inc., 2011), p. 47.

[69] Shalem Coulibaly, "Equations in Contemporary Anti-Zionism," in *Global Antisemitism: A Crisis of Modernity*, Charles Asher Small, ed. (New York: Institute for the Study of Global Antisemitism and Policy [ISGAP], 2014), p. 44.

[70] Coulibaly, p. 44.

[71] Patterson, p. 199 (author's emphasis).

[72] Patterson, p. 199.

postmodern nihilists who ultimately believe in nothing—even denying the possibility of objective truth—and accept no moral restrictions except what they in their narcissistic subjectivity wish to impose on others.[73] This is why antisemitism disguised as anti-Israelism is so insidious to the Jewish people. As Sarah Cardaun notes: "Antisemitic anti-Zionism plays a much greater role than any of the other forms that were dominant in previous times. Muslim antisemitism thus highlights the complexity and controversy surrounding the new antisemitism, but also the clearly existing link between anti-Israelism and antisemitism, and the fact that they are very difficult to disentangle."[74]

Like the reptilian shapeshifters of science fiction lore that could change their physical appearance at will,[75] antisemitism has manifest itself in myriads of ways and to varying degrees. Regardless of the form or guise that antisemitism has employed, the common thread that has characterized all manifestations of antisemitism is the extreme prejudice and antipathy that has bred utter intolerance for the Jewish people. From antiquity to the present day, it has unrelentingly manifest itself in increasingly novel and subtle manners. Antisemitism, therefore, has been—and continues to be—utterly insidious because of its ability to morph from one image to another. The root cause, however, remains the same: perverse, even diabolical, hatred for the Jewish people and an undying commitment to their genocide. Now, the undead, pustule-infested Führer struts around, himself to be bedecked in a gleaming new wardrobe of politically correct garments, even thinking that he has gained a posthumous victory![76] The naked truth is apparent, however,

---

[73] Ken Wilber, *The Eye of Spirit: An Integral Vision for a World Gone Slightly Mad* (Boston, MA: Shambhala Publications, Inc., 2001), p. 132. Wilber, an American philosopher who is strongly influenced by Buddhism, says that increasingly in today's world, "truth is whatever you want, which leaves us nothing at all, except that shell of nihilism filled with the thickest of narcissism, a postmodern pastry from hell."

[74] Sarah K. Cardaun, *Countering Contemporary Antisemitism in Britain: Government and Civil Society Responses between Universalism and Particularism* (Leiden, The Netherlands: Koninklijke Brill NV, 2015), pp. 76–77.

[75] Reptilian shapeshifters are imaginary creatures of science fiction that are reptilian but are able to shift their appearance at will so as to appear human. British author David Icke took the idea to the extreme of insisting that many world political leaders are actually reptilian aliens who are working to gain control of earth. Tyson Lewis and Richard Kahn, "The Reptoid Hypothesis: Utopian and Dystopian Representational Motifs in David Icke's Alien Conspiracy Theory" in *Utopian Studies*, vol. 16, no. 1 (Winter, 2005), pp. 45–70.

[76] Emil Fackenheim postulated a "614th commandment" for Jews to be added to the 613 commandments of the Torah. "We are, first, commanded to survive as Jews, lest the people of Israel perish. We are commanded, second, to remember in our guts and bones the martyrs of the Holocaust, lest their memory perish. We are forbidden, thirdly, to deny or despair of God, however much we may have to contend with Him or with belief in Him, lest Judaism perish. We are forbidden, finally, to despair of the world as the place which is to become the kingdom of God lest we help make it a meaningless place in which God is dead or irrelevant and everything is permitted. To abandon any of these imperatives, in response to Hitler's victory at Auschwitz, would be to hand him yet other posthumous victories." Emil Fackenheim, quoted in Richard Rubenstein, *After Auschwitz: History, Theology, and Contemporary Judaism* (Baltimore, MD: Johns Hopkins University Press, 1992), p. 180.

to all who have eyes to see. When the ancient antisemitism that produced the Holocaust is clothed in the subtle, glitzy, and socially acceptable garments of anti-Zionism, it is just as heinous and insidious as its predecessor: the evil Haman and the Führer themselves.

## Anti-Zionism and the Resurrection of Ancient Antisemitism

Perhaps one of the most tragic residual effects of the rise of politically and socially acceptable anti-Zionist antisemitism is the fact that it has opened the door for the resurrection of the vile and virulent antisemitism of antiquity, the Middle Ages, the Enlightenment, and Modernity.[77] Just when most Western societies thought that coarse and base antisemitism had been banished from the public square and perhaps even destroyed in the public outcry and backlash against the atrocities of the German Third Reich, ancient forms of antisemitism have been resurrected from the dust of the earth, ascending from decades of hibernation in the darkest recesses of human depravity to vaunt themselves openly in societies around the world. Jews who have chosen to remain in the societies where their families have lived for decades, even centuries, have increasingly become targets of antisemitic violence. Those who have not been inclined, for whatever reason, to make *aliyah* to Israel, the only Jewish-controlled state in the world, have found themselves living in fear for their well-being and even for their lives.

Tamara Cohen reports on a recent poll in Britain which found that fully 17% of British Jews feel unwelcome there while 80% are concerned that the Labour Party "is too tolerant of anti-Semitism" and just 65% believe that their government is "doing enough to protect them."[78] Consequently, 37% confess that they "need to conceal their Judaism in public," and 31% say that they have "considered moving abroad.[79] The situation is becoming so serious that Mandy Blumenthal, a Jewish commercial property company owner whose father was Lord Mayor of Birmingham, says, "I think within the next ten years it will not be tolerable for Jews here."[80]

Dan Bilefsky reports that in France, Jews who feel "under siege by anti-Semitism" say that terrorist attacks on Jewish communities have left them "unsure of their future in France and increasingly willing to consider

[77] Bernard Harrison, *The Resurgence of Anti-Semitism: Jews, Israel, and Liberal Opinion* (Lanham, MD: Rowman & Littlefield Publishers, 2006), pp. 201, 226.

[78] Tamara Cohen, "More British Jews Considering Move Abroad as Anti-Semitism Fears Grow," *Sky News*, Sunday, 20 August, 2017, posted at http://news.sky.com/story/more-british-jews-considering-move-abroad-as-anti-semitism-fears-grow-poll-10997052.

[79] Cohen, "More British Jews."

[80] Mandy Blumenthal, quoted in Cohen, "More British Jews."

conflict-torn Israel as a safer refuge."[81] Jacqueline Cohen, a Paris art and Judaica store owner in Paris said, "We feel safer in the center of Tel Aviv than we do here in the heart of Paris. . . . We are afraid to send our children to school."[82] Oren Liebermann notes that in 2016, "nearly 8,000 French Jews moved to Israel," an increase from 3,300 in 2013.[83] Sadly, "a total of 59 per cent of French people think members of the Jewish community are at least partially responsible for anti-Semitism," a survey declares.[84] Could anything be more classic antisemitism than this: the Jews who have been blamed for almost everything imaginable by antisemites of all kinds over the past two thousand years are now even blamed for being the cause of antisemitism!

In Spain, antisemitic acts on the part of Palestinian Arab sympathizers have escalated to the point that the chief Rabbi of Barcelona, Meir Bar-Hen, has openly declared, "I tell my congregants: Don't think we're here for good, and I encourage them to buy property in Israel. This place is lost. . . . Better to [get out] early than late. Europe is lost." Of the large and increasing Muslim community in Europe, Ben-Hen says that once they are "living among you, it's very difficult to get rid of them. They only get stronger."[85]

Even in Scandinavia, which prizes itself as being the epitome of "moral innocence and best intentions," antisemitism has become a rising specter of violence against the Jews, especially with the new antisemitism: anti-Zionism. Though Denmark succeeded in "saving nearly the whole of its Jewish population from deportation and extermination" and Sweden protected Jews by the thousands during World War II, "across Scandinavia, anti-Semitism has merged with anti-Zionism" to create an even more insidious monster than ancient antisemitism.[86] Norway has become "perhaps the most extreme European example of anti-Zionism as government policy," mixing sympathy and support for Palestinian Arab causes with a reluctance "to control

[81] Dan Bilefsky, "Fear on Rise, Jews in France Weigh an Exit, *The New York Times*, Jan. 12, 2015, posted at https://www.nytimes.com/2015/01/13/world/europe/fear-on-rise-jews-in-france-weigh-an-exit.html.

[82] Jacqueline Cohen, quoted in Bilefsky, "Fear on Rise."

[83] Oren Liebermann, "Au Revoir and Shalom: Jews Leave France in Record Numbers," *CNN News*, January 25, 2016, posted at http://www.cnn.com/2016/01/22/middleeast/france-israel-jews-immigration/index.html.

[84] Elsa Vulliamy, "6 in 10 French People Think Jews Are Responsible for Anti-Semitism, Survey Finds," *The Independent*, 3 February 2016, posted at http://www.independent.co.uk/news/world/europe/6-in-10-french-people-think-jews-are-responsible-for-anti-semitism-survey-finds-a6848911.html.

[85] Meir Bar-Hen, quoted in Simon Kent, "'This Place Is Lost': Barcelona Chief Rabbi Tells Spain's Jews to Head for Israel," *Breitbart News*, 20 Aug 2017, posted at http://www.breitbart.com/jerusalem/2017/08/20/place-lost-barcelona-chief-rabbi-tells-spains-jews-head-israel/.

[86] Liam Hoare, "The Scandal of Scandinavia: Despite their image of moral innocence and best intentions, the lands of the north have become home to a scary, new form of anti-Semitism," *The Tower Magazine*, April 2013, posted at http://www.thetower.org/article/the-scandal-of-scandinavia/.

domestic anti-Semitic and anti-Zionist violence."[87] In Sweden, the left-wing media demonstrate their solid support for Palestinian Arabs by "associating Israelis with the Nazis, depicting Jews and the Jewish state as copies of their historical persecutors" and by making "explicit or implicit allegations of 'Israel genocides' and modern-day versions of the Holocaust or Nazi war crimes."[88] Though much has changed in the new forms of antisemitism, "for the Jews of Copenhagen and all over Scandinavia, the threat is thus a very real one."[89]

Even in Germany, antisemitism is on the rise again. "Many people were actually surprised to hear that Jews in Germany are still being attacked on a daily basis," says Miki Hermer in an article by Polina Garaev with the ironic—but revealing—title: "Anti-Semitism on the Rise in Germany, But No Anti-Semites To Be Found." Hermer says that Germans "think anti-Semitism is a problem that ended in 1945, that they don't need to worry about that anymore, but we are here to show them that's not true."[90] Some 2,083 cases of antisemitism were documented by the Justice Ministry in 2015, and the total continues to rise each year.

Much of Europe's increasing antisemitism can be laid at the doorstep of the burgeoning Muslim presence in virtually every part of the continent. What the Saracens could not accomplish by the edge of the scimitar is increasingly being fulfilled by militant Muslim immigration in Europe. And these North African and sub-Saharan African Muslims are bringing with them the inherent antisemitism of their Islamist philosophies. Dave Rich says, "Those British Muslims who verbally abuse British Jews on the street are more likely to shout 'Heil Hitler' than '*Allahu akbar*' when they do so."[91] The slogans of antisemites are flexible and cross national, ethnic, and language lines, but, make no mistake, they are the same antisemitic vitriol of the past two thousand years that pollute and poison the air. Abraham Foxman is right on target when he titles an article "Rising Anti-Semitism in Europe: History Repeating Once Again" and reports that 55% of Western European Muslims harbor antisemitic attitudes. Foxman reports that "the anti-Semitism news from Europe . . . has been terrible: Jews murdered in Paris and Copenhagen, synagogues attacked by mobs and firebombed, and

[87] Hoare, "The Scandal."

[88] Mathan Ravid, *Jewish Political Studies Review*, quoted in Hoare, "The Scandal."

[89] Hoare, "The Scandal."

[90] Miki Hermer, quoted in Polina Garaev, "Anti-Semitism on the Rise in Germany, But No Anti-Semites to be Found," *i24 News*, 12/30/2016, posted at https://www.i24news.tv/en/news/international/europe/133894-161230-anti-semitism-on-the-rise-in-germany-but-no-anti-semites-to-be-found.

[91] Dave Rich, "Book Review: Some of My Best Friends: A Journey through Twenty-First Century Antisemitism," *Fathom*, Autumn/2014, posted at http://fathomjournal.org/book-review-some-of-my-best-friends-a-journey-through-twenty-first-century-antisemitism/.

increasing Jewish emigration attributed to fear of more attacks."[92]

This rising tide of coarse and vulgarian antisemitism from Europe's distant past has prompted questions like the one posed in *The Atlantic* magazine in an article entitled, "Is It Time for the Jews to Leave Europe?" in which Jeffrey Goldberg notes that "for half a century, memories of the Holocaust limited anti-Semitism on the Continent. That period has ended" as "renewed vitriol among right-wing fascists and new threats from radicalized Islamists have created a crisis, confronting Jewish with an agonizing choice."[93] Goldberg notes that "in 2014, Jews in Europe were murdered, raped, beaten, stalked, chased, harassed, spat on, and insulted for being Jewish. *Sale Juif*—"dirty Jew"—rang in the streets, as did "Death to the Jews,'" and "Jews to the gas."[94] And the situation across virtually all of Europe has only worsened since that time.[95] In reality, anti-Zionism, the new antisemitism, has produced a globalization of antisemitism.[96]

Anti-Zionism has become such a popular vehicle for the spread of a sanitized, non-toxic version of the ancient and continuing antisemitism that has always sought the destruction of the Jewish people that it has captivated the minds of people not only in Europe but also around the world.[97] Anti-Zionism has made it possible for hatred of the Jews to be packaged as a form of social justice by those whose self-righteous arrogance knows no end. By transforming Jews from victims to victimizers, people from across political, social, ethnic, and religious boundaries have found a way to transform ancient antisemitism into a "righteous cause," thereby willingly or unwittingly committing the most vile and mendacious act of calling good evil and evil good, light darkness light and darkness light, and sweet bitter and bitter sweet. These are they who are "clever in their own sight" and "justify the wicked for a bribe and take away the rights of the ones who are in the right!" In the process, they incur for themselves the judgment of the Almighty.[98]

---

[92] Abraham Foxman, "Rising Anti-Semitism in Europe: History Repeating Once Again," *The WorldPost*, posted at http://www.huffingtonpost.com/abraham-h-foxman/rising-anti-semitism-in-e_b_7835610.html.

[93] Jeffrey Goldberg, "Is It Time for the Jews to Leave Europe?" *The Atlantic*, April 2015 Issue, posted at https://www.theatlantic.com/magazine/archive/2015/04/is-it-time-for-the-jews-to-leave-europe/386279/.

[94] Goldberg, "Is It Time."

[95] Jeffrey M. Peck, "Afterword," in *The New German Jewry and the European Context: The Return of the European Jewish Diaspora*, Y. Michal Bodemann, ed. (Basingstoke, UK: Palgrave Macmillan, 2008), p. 81.

[96] Denis MacShane, *Globalising Hatred: The New Antisemitism* (London, UK: Weidenfeld & Nicolson, 2008).

[97] Jerome A. Chanes, *Antisemitism: A Reference Handbook* (Santa Barbara, CA: ABC-CLIO, Inc., 2004), p. 15.

[98] Isaiah 5:21–23.

CHAPTER 12

# NEW BLOOD LIBELS

## Scurrilous Repackaged Antisemitic Indictments

Through the centuries, every accusation imaginable—and some that are utterly unimaginable—has been hurled at the Jewish people by antisemites of every sort and description. Perhaps the most damnable of these was the unrelenting Christian charge that all Jews were guilty of deicide because they alone were responsible for the crucifixion of Jesus.[1] Of almost equal magnitude to this diabolical charge was the evil Blood Libel—the medieval Christian myth that accused Jews of kidnapping and murdering Christian children in order to use their blood in the religious rituals of Jewish holy days.[2] A third despicable medieval Christian fabrication charged the Jews with "desecration of the host"—the act of "stealing the bread of the Eucharist and then breaking it, torturing it, transfixing it, even causing it to bleed"[3]—so that they could reenact the crucifixion of Jesus by torturing the bread of communion of which Jesus said, "This is my body,"[4] when he introduced the rite to his disciples.

What had been all too common among history's superstitious and

[1] Hyam Maccoby, *Antisemitism and Modernity: Innovation and Continuity* (Abingdon, UK: Routledge, 2006), p. 18. Also, Todd D. Baker, *Matthew 27:25: "His Blood Be on Us.": Are the Jewish People Racially Condemned for the Death of Christ?* (Bloomington, IN: iUniverse, 2008), p. 38; and Eliezer Berkovits, "European and American Responses during and following the War," in *Wrestling with God: Jewish Theological Responses during and after the Holocaust*, Steven T. Katz, Shlomo Biderman, and Gershon Greenberg, eds. (Oxford, UK: Oxford University Press, 2007), p. 480.

[2] For a comprehensive analysis of the Blood Libel charge, see Alan Dundes, *The Blood Libel Legend: A Casebook in Anti-Semitic Folklore* (Madison, WI: The University of Wisconsin Press, 1991).

[3] Dean Phillip Bell, "Host Desecration," in *Antisemitism: A Historical Encyclopedia of Prejudice and Persecution*, Richard S. Levy, ed. (Santa Barbara, CA: ABC-CLIO, Inc., 2005), vol. 1, p. 325. This idea is based on the Roman Catholic doctrine of transubstantiation, which maintains that the bread of the Eucharist experiences a change of substance during Holy Communion so that it becomes the actual body of Christ during Holy Communion. If such were the case, then what might appear to be nonsensical acts of torture or abuse against the bread would actually be acts against the Eucharist's underlying reality of the body of Christ.

[4] Luke 22:19.

ignorant masses, however, has continued to be maintained during humanity's most sophisticated and knowledgeable eras, the times of modernity and postmodernity. In fact, during the time of modernity, Nazi Germany raised the Blood Libel and deicide charges virtually to a religious level, and the record of postmodernity has been just as vile, if not more so. Eric Sundquist claims that "although the Holocaust was a German, not specifically a Christian, act of genocide, the racial mysticism of Nazism turned the traditional anti-Semitic charges of Blood Libel and deicide into a biological principle of human stratification in which the Holy Ghost might be worshipped through murder."[5] In this manner of thinking, "the Reich would be made racially pure, and those who purportedly killed Christ and supped the blood of Christian children would be eliminated in a war of holy purpose," he adds.[6] In reality, however, "as a pantheist neopagan who admired Julian the Apostate, Hitler had nothing but contempt for Catholic teaching in general, including its teaching on transubstantiation."[7]

Even in the post-Holocaust world, fabrications as specious as the Blood Libel[8] and the deicide indictment have been continually leveled against the international Jewish community and more specifically against the nation and people of Israel. These centuries-old charges are demonstrably false, have long been totally discredited, and should be utterly unacceptable to anyone—including the intelligentsia of postmodernity—and yet they continue to be used to inflame the passions of undereducated, superstitious, and impulsive people groups around the world. What is even more insidious, however, is the constant invention of ever new libelous charges that incite anger and violence against the Jewish people.

The false accusations hurled against Israel in particular—and Jews in general—take many forms, commonly stretching to the patently absurd and often to the insane, a fact which only marginalizes any legitimate claims that the Palestinian Arabs may have against Israeli government policies or practices. "[T]oday's most virulent antisemitism is expressed less through

[5] Eric J. Sundquist, *Strangers in the Land: Blacks, Jews, Post-Holocaust America* (Cambridge, MA: Harvard University Press, 2005), p. 471.

[6] Sundquist, p. 471.

[7] Robert W. Bleakney, personal communication.

[8] Amazingly, the medieval Blood Libel myth has transmogrified into twentieth-century Muslim charges that Israel engages in "organ trafficking (of dead Palestinian children)"! Rusi Jaspal, *Antisemitism and Anti-Zionism: Representation, Cognition and Everyday Talk* (Farnham, UK: Ashgate Publishing Limited, 2014), p. 52. Also Robert S. Wistrich, "Gaza, Hamas, and the Return of Antisemitism," in *The Israel Journal of Foreign Affairs*, VIII:3, July, 2014, p. 38. Wistrich points to a racist Muslim movie called Valley of the Wolves, which contains "scenes that show an American Jewish doctor removing organs from injured civilian prisoners to be sold to his wealthy clients in New York, London, and Tel Aviv."

denying the Holocaust than in accusing Jews of perpetrating crimes similar to it," says R. Amy Elman. Because of Europe's "misleading branding, altered research, or the renunciation of its explicit definition, antisemitism is a swiftly moving object on the European agenda. It is addressed and rarely grasped, concealed by the bluster of seemingly sensitive but nonetheless contradictory discourse."[9] The list of outrageous indictments that have been leveled against Israel is long and include the following:

## Charging Israel with Maintaining an Apartheid State

In 2006, in his book, *Palestine: Peace Not Apartheid*, former US President Jimmy Carter famously made the accusation that Israel is an apartheid state, though when his hand was called on the matter, he walked back his blanket statements by saying they applied to the "West Bank" and not to all of Israel.[10] Alan Dershowitz said, "One thing is certain: [Carter's] book has fed the anti-Israel hatred that helps keep the conflict going. He has granted undue legitimacy to the claims of a once-marginal group of extremists that has sought for years to equate Israel with apartheid South Africa."[11] Leftist luminaries like Anglican Archbishop Desmond Tutu have supported such insidious and ridiculous claims, even accusing Israelis of "fighting against God"[12] and comparing the Jews with Hitler and other mass murderers. "The Jewish lobby is powerful—very powerful," said Tutu. "The apartheid government was very powerful, but today it no longer exists. Hitler, Mussolini, Stalin, Pinochet, Milosevec, and Idi Amin were all powerful, but in the end they bit the dust,"[13] he continued, absurdly comparing the leadership of democratic Israel with the most vile, autocratic, and murderous dictators of the twentieth century and perhaps even trying, by implication, to prophesy the future demise of Israel.

Indictments of Israel for "apartheid" policies gained ascendancy in 2001 when the United Nations World Conference against Racism, Racial Discrimination, Xenophobia, and Related Intolerance focused primarily on Israeli treatment of Palestinians and only secondarily, and then minimally, on human-rights violations and attempts at genocide in the rest of the world.

[9] R. Amy Elman, "The EU's Responses to Contemporary Antisemitism," in *Deciphering the New Antisemitism*, Alvin H. Rosenfeld, ed. (Bloomington, IN: The Indiana University Press, 2015), p. 422.

[10] Jimmy Carter, *Palestine: Peace Not Apartheid* (New York: Simon & Schuster, 2006).

[11] Alan Dershowitz, *The Case for Israel* (Somerset, NJ: John Wiley & Sons, Inc., 2004), p. 44.

[12] Desmond Tutu, quoted in Dershowitz, p. 45.

[13] Desmond Tutu, "Apartheid in the Holy Land," in *The Guardian*, April 28, 2002, posted at https://www.theguardian.com/world/2002/apr/29/comment, quoted in Jay Nordlinger, *Peace, They Say: A History of the Nobel Peace Prize, the Most Famous and Controversial Prize in the World* (New York: Encounter Books, 2012), p. 255.

Using the backdrop of Durban, South Africa, where this conference was convened, the UN leaders attempted to reify the charge of apartheid against Israel. The draft of its resolutions included "statements equating Zionism with racism, and alleging that it is an 'apartheid' state guilty of 'genocide' and 'ethnic cleansing' designed to ensure a Jewish state."[14] Journalist Benjamin Pogrund, himself of South African heritage, was shocked—"gobsmacked," as he called it—to see these draft resolutions. "I knew apartheid and had already learned enough about Israel to know that the draft was a concoction of lies and distortions," he said.[15] "The actual text accused Israel of 'a new kind of apartheid, a crime against humanity'; it singled out Israel for alleged 'ethnic cleansing of the Arab population of historic Palestine'; it said Zionism was 'based on racial superiority.'"[16]

The charges that purported Israel to be an apartheid state have always been designed to undercut the right of existence for both the people and the nation of Israel. In fact, it was the Palestinian Liberation Organization, one of history's most mendacious and vicious terrorist movements, which "invented the apartheid canard in the mid-1960s, years before Israel's occupation of the West Bank and Gaza."[17] As Yehuda Bauer says, "Israel is being accused of being an apartheid state, with the obvious conclusion that as an apartheid state, it has no legitimacy of any kind and has to be destroyed, and the same genocidal and antisemitic attitude is propagated as with the antisemitic liberals."[18] Victor Sharpe makes a strong but true rebuttal of such claims: "The Left refuses to admit that it is the Arab-Muslim culture that actively engages in the very evil practices that they falsely hurl at Israel. And where do you find apartheid, racism, repression and torture? Why, in the very Arab-Muslim world the Left supports and embraces."[19] Instead

[14] Anne Bayefsky, "Human Rights Watch Coverup," in *The Jerusalem Post*, April 13, 2004, posted at http://ngo-monitor.org/archives/op-eds/041304-1.htm.

[15] Benjamin Pogrund, *Drawing Fire: Investigating the Accusations of Apartheid in Israel* (Lanham, MD: Rowman & Littlefield, 2014), p. xviii.

[16] Pogrund, p. xviii.

[17] Efraim Karsh, "The Middle East's Real Apartheid," in *The Jerusalem Post*, 03/05/2012, posted at http://www.jpost.com/Opinion/Op-Ed-Contributors/The-Middle-Easts-real-apartheid. Some scholars maintain that both the PLO and its "apartheid" and "racism" canards were inventions of Soviet Union propagandists. Emmett Laor, *The Invention of the "Palestinians": 27 Theses They Won't Let You Hear* (Bloomington, IN: Xlibris Corp., 2012), pp. 115, 135. This should come as no surprise since Russia has long been one of the most antisemitic nations on the face of the earth. Theodore S. Hamerow, *Why We Watched: Europe, America, and the Holocaust* (New York: W. W. Norton & Co., 2008), p. 371. Likewise, according to Richard Levy, the Russian Orthodox Church has long been and continues to be one of the world's most antisemitic Christian denominations. Richard S. Levy, *Antisemitism: A Historical Encyclopedia of Prejudice and Persecution* (Santa Barbara, CA: ABC-CLIO, Inc., 2005), vol. 1, p. 637.

[18] Yehuda Bauer, *The Jews: A Contrary People* (Zürich, Switzerland: Lit Verlag GmbH & Co., 2014), p. 114.

[19] Victor Sharpe, *Politicide: The Relentless Attempts by the Arab and Muslim World to Destroy the State of Israel* (Raleigh, NC: Lulu Press, Inc., 2011), p. 45.

of exposing Arab-Muslim hypocrisy, however, the leftist apologists always retreat "to the tawdry defense of hurling charges of Islamophobia and racism at all who attempt to correct it."[20]

The charge of *apartheid* Israel is demonstrably false. "There is no Israeli ideology, policy or plan to segregate, persecute or mistreat the Arab population. . . . Arab citizens of Israel enjoy the full range of civil and political rights, including the right to organize politically, the right to vote and the right to speak and publish freely. Israeli Arabs and other non-Jewish Israelis serve as members of Israel's security forces, are elected to parliament and appointed to the country's highest courts. . . . These facts serve as a counter to the apartheid argument and demonstrate that Israel is committed to democratic principles and equal rights for all its citizens."[21] In truth, as Efraim Karsh observes, "Israel actually is the only apartheid-free state in the Middle East."[22] If Israel were, indeed, an apartheid state, how could *Haaretz* correspondent Anshal Pfeffer have reported that he was stunned to hear from demonstrators in both Tunis and Cairo—neither of whom knew he represented an Israeli newspaper—that they wanted "a democracy like in Israel."[23] Indeed, at the same time, "the Middle East Media Research Institute published excerpts from articles in the Arab press over the last year that held up Israel as a model Arab states should learn from—in some cases, because of its economic, scientific, and democratic achievements, but in others, because of its democracy and even its morality."[24]

The truth is that Israel is just the opposite of an apartheid state, for it promotes and lives by values that are diametrically opposed to those of the prototypical apartheid regime in South African. "Israel has not since its inception taken away vested Israeli citizenship of even one Palestinian for the sole reason that the person is ethnic Palestinian. Israel has not created designated territories within its border to which it has forcibly removed its own citizens who are ethnic Palestinian. Indeed, when one starts to look at what apartheid really was, any comparison between Israel today and South Africa at the time of apartheid becomes ludicrous."[25] It is for

[20] Sharpe, p. 45.

[21] Response to the charge that Israel is an apartheid state by the Anti-Defamation League posted at http://www.adl.org/israel-international/israel-middle-east/content/AG/inaccuracy-israel-apartheid-state.html.

[22] Efraim Karsh, "The Middle East's Real Apartheid."

[23] Anshel Pfeffer, quoted in Evelyn Gordon, "Israeli Apartheid? To Arabs, It's a Model Democracy," in *Commentary*, 05.09.2014, posted at https://www.commentarymagazine.com/2014/05/09/israeli-apartheid-to-arabs-its-a-model-democracy/.

[24] Gordon in *Commentary*.

[25] David Matas, *Aftershock: Anti-Zionism and Anti-Semitism* (Toronto, Canada: Dundurn Press, 2005), p. 54.

this reason that Jean-Christophe Rufin recommended that the charge of apartheid against Israel should itself be criminalized because is so ridiculously opprobrious. "What should be penalised," he said, "is the perverse and defamatory use of the charge of racism against those very people who were victims of racism to an unparalleled degree. The accusations of racism, of apartheid, of Nazism carry extremely grave moral implications. These accusations have, in the situation in which we find ourselves today, major consequences which can, by contagion, put in danger the lives of our Jewish citizens."[26] Sadly, as Alan Dershowitz points out, "The slander that portrays Israel as a 'racist colonialist apartheid state' is already so widespread as to be part of the international community's ordinary parlance."[27] The rush to make moral equivalencies based on imagined parallels between one set of circumstances and another has not helped anyone except the smugly self-righteous, antisemitic hypocrites who perpetrate such nonsense.

In truth, among virtually all the nations of the Middle East, Israel is the only society that does not engage in systemic political and social discrimination that could be compared with the now-deposed apartheid regime of South Africa. Karsh confirms the longstanding nature of this truth: "Apartheid has been an integral part of the Middle East for over a millennium, and its Arab and Muslim nations continue to legally, politically, and socially enforce this discriminatory practice against their hapless minorities."[28] This is true in Saudi Arabia, where there is no Jewish or Christian admission to the Kaaba in Mecca or the shrines in Medina and in all of the Gulf Coast Muslim states where no churches or synagogues can be constructed and where the religious freedom of foreign workers is severely curtailed. A prime example is the "religious apartheid" of which Pakistan is guilty, wherein Muslims are "a separate—and privileged—class from others." In reality, the very origin of Pakistan is "traceable to religious apartheid," says India's *Foreign Affairs Record*.[29] What can be said of the social and religious practices of Pakistan can also be said of many other Muslim nations whose radical interpretations of the *Qur'an* and Islam in general establish and reinforce institutions of discrimination that are the essence of apartheid against minority religious populations.

[26] Jean-Christophe Rufin, "Chantier sur la lutte contre le racisme et l'antisémitisme," in *La Monde*, October 19, 2004, cited in Matas, pp. 54, 243.

[27] Dershowitz, p. 136.

[28] Karsh, "The Middle East's Real Apartheid."

[29] *Foreign Affairs Record* (New Delhi, India: Ministry of External Affairs, 1964), vols. 10–11, p. 141. Interestingly, despite overwhelming evidence to the contrary in Pakistani society, Pakistan's Foreign Minister Zulfikar Bhutto maintained that "Pakistan is truly founded on Islam which admits of no apartheid, racial or religious." Zulfikar Ali Bhutto, *A South Asian View: A Collection of Speeches and Excerpts* (Information Division, Embassy of Pakistan, 1964), p. 79.

The charge leveled by Muslim Arab nations and other Islamic societies that Israel maintains an apartheid state is particularly pernicious when one considers the fact that the very essence of apartheid is enshrined in the *Qur'an* and has been entrenched in virtually all Muslim nations from the time of Muhammad until this day. In fact, one of the core teachings of Islam is apartheid *par excellence*. In this religion and its application in communities and nations, non-Muslims are assigned an inferior social, political, and religious status that deprives them of social rank and assigns them to economic and political inferiority. Non-Muslims have three options in the nations where Islam dominates: 1) convert to Islam, 2) agree to live in the apartheid *dhimmi* state, or 3) be executed. When one observes the pitiful social and economic status of Christians in Pakistan, the ongoing apartheid in Azerbaijan which makes that nation the world focal point for Islamic-authorized slave trade, and the enslavement of Christian children in Sudan for sale to Muslim masters in the Middle East and elsewhere, one can only conclude that Islam, not Judaism, is a religion of apartheid and that Muslim nations, not Israel, are societies that epitomize apartheid.

## Comparing Zionism with Nazism

Increasingly, in both Arab nations and in other parts of the world, Zionism is being compared with Nazism in what may be one of the most psychotic accusations in world history. This despicable tactic of anti-Zionists simply carries forward and expands the false indictment that Communists made in the 1930s when they said that "Zionism and Nazism were collaborating to produce mass hysteria, a situation most favorable to Zionist plans of mass immigration into Palestine."[30] One of the prominent Middle Eastern agents of Communist International (Comintern)[31] even suggested that "Hitler should be elected honorary president of the Zionist movement."[32] These arguments are mirrored in the rhetoric of Palestinian Arabs: "In general, academic Palestinian historical discourse does not deny the Holocaust, but there is an attempt to describe its 'instrumental' aspects, especially when certain aspects of cooperation between Zionism and Nazism are emphasized."[33] In

[30] Jacob Hen-Tov, *Communism and Zionism in Palestine: The Comintern and the Political Unrest in the 1920's* (Cambridge, MA: Schenkman Publishing Co., 1974), p. 83.

[31] Founded in 1915, the Comintern (an abbreviation for Communist International) was the official advocate and propaganda mouthpiece for world communism.

[32] Hen-Tov, p. 83. This quote is attributed to Avigdor, a likely pseudonym for Egyptian communist Constantine Weiss.

[33] Meir Litvak, *Palestinian Collective Memory and National Identity* (New York: Palgrave Macmillan, 2009), p. 159.

fact, in the larger Muslim world, "Zionism is actually considered to be a far more heinous crime than Nazism."[34] In the words of the so-called "moderate" Muslim prime minister of Turkey, Recep Erdogan, "[The Israelis] curse Hitler morning and night; however, now their barbarism has surpassed even Hitler's."[35] To say that Erdogan's accusation is absurd is a gross understatement, especially when one considers Turkey's attempted genocide of the Armenians in 1915 and its ongoing efforts toward completing the genocide of the Kurdish people in Turkey, Iraq, and Syria!

The very idea of comparing the movement that has labored for more than a century to establish the Jewish people in the safety and security of their own ancestral land with Adolph Hitler and the German Reich, whose goal it was to preside over the genocide of the Jewish people, is so repugnant that it is unclear how anyone with a scintilla of conscience or knowledge of the Holocaust could conceive of such a comparison. In case politicians, autocrats, and media people of the Muslim world have not noticed, Israel has not murdered even one Palestinian Arab with cyanide gas or firing squads, and until recently there has never been a single crematorium in Israel.[36] Yet, it seems that there is no depth to which Muslim anti-Zionists will not stoop in order to stigmatize the Jewish state of Israel, and, sadly, Western media generally march in lockstep with Muslim polemicists and libelists.

Bernard Harrison says, "Coupling the Star of David with the swastika, and Israel with the Nazis . . . is not to engage in 'criticism of Israel'; it is rather to engage in political anti-Semitism in its most traditional form."[37] Alan Dershowitz agrees, "Comparing Israel to Nazi Germany is anti-Semitism, pure and simple. There is no other explanation for it, especially

[34] Robert Satloff, *Among the Righteous: Lost Stories from the Holocaust's Long Reach Into Arab Lands* (Philadelphia, PA: Perseus Books Group, 2006), p. 167. Satloff reports that when al-Jazeera television polled the Muslim world and posed this question: "What Is Worse: Zionism or Nazism?" 84.6 percent of the respondents said that Zionism is worse than Nazism, 11.1 percent said that Zionism is equal to Nazism, and just 2.7 percent said that Nazism is worse than Zionism. These findings represent either mass illiteracy and prejudice in the Muslim world or the lack of a moral compass in the hearts and minds of 97.3 percent of Muslims.

[35] Recep Tayyip Erdogan, quoted in Richard M. Cohen, "With Israel, the World Is Blaming the Victims," in *The Washington Post*, July 28, 2014, posted at http://www.washingtonpost.com/opinions/richard-cohen-with-israel-the-world-is-blaming-the-victims/2014/07/28/104bcc4c-1680-11e4-9349-84d4a85be981_story.html.

[36] Eva Etzioni-Halevy, *The Divided People: Can Israel's Breakup Be Stopped?* (Lanham, MD: Lexington Books, 2002), p. 95. When a crematorium was opened in Israel in 2007 for the use of private Israeli citizens, its existence was roundly condemned. The obvious reason for this reaction was the association of such an operation with the crematoria of the Nazi death camps of Europe. Even now, any Israelis who choose cremation are not entitled to state funding for the procedure. For details, see Matthew Wagner, "Israel's Only Crematorium To Re-open," *The Jerusalem Post*, 10/28/2007, posted at http://www.jpost.com/Israel/Israels-only-crematorium-to-re-open.

[37] Bernard Harrison, *The Resurgence of Anti-Semitism: Jews, Israel, and Liberal Opinion* (Lanham, MD: Rowman & Littlefield Publishers, 2006), p. x.

in light of the reality that there is no actual similarity between Hitler's systematic genocide against the Jews and Israel's efforts to defend itself from genocidal threats against its Jewish population."[38] When people in Germany, of all places, have the audacity to equate Zionism with Nazism, they manifest the pathology that Israeli psychiatrist Zvi Rex described in these terms: "The Germans will never forgive the Jews for Auschwitz."[39] Vladimir Jankelevitch is said to have remarked that the Germans would not be alone in this regard, for the Holocaust was an immense crime for which the Germans were chiefly responsible but for which the list of co-conspirators is long.[40]

## Alleging that Zionism Is Racism

The opponents of the Jewish state of Israel "claim that in pursuing their aims Zionists have actually created a *new* oppressed and homeless people. Moreover, they charge, the sources of Zionism are the same ones that bred western colonialism and racism, meaning that its ideas must be rejected by all right-thinking human beings."[41] This was the theme of the infamous 2001 United Nations Conference Against Racism, Racial Discrimination, Xenophobia, and Related Intolerance, which specifically labeled Zionism as racism. A study of what prefaced this absurd accusation is revealing: while speaking before the 1985 session of the United Nations Special Political Committee, the Representative of Syria summed up the recurring and unending anti-Zionist Muslim charges of Nazism and racism against Israel: "Palestinians are the victims of Zionism, the real heir of Nazism, which not only professes its racism but to this day also exploits the painful memory of the victims of Nazism to justify its crimes and atrocities against the Arab citizens suffering under the yoke of Zionist occupation."[42] Unfortunately for Israel, says Thomas Idinopulos, "the charge that Zionism is racist revives old obfuscations that have bedeviled Zionists for the past 50 years."[43] It extrapolates principles from real cases of racism around the world and then maliciously and mendaciously applies them to the Jewish people.

The lies that have been fabricated against the Jews for more than a millennium simply will not die: they are merely reincarnated in new circumstances

[38] Dershowitz, p. 136.

[39] Zvi Rex, quoted in Richard M. Cohen, *Israel: Is It Good for the Jews?* (New York: Simon & Schuster, 2014), p. 100.

[40] Cohen, pp. 100–101.

[41] David Engel, *Zionism* (New York: Routledge, 2013), p. xii.

[42] Toufic Abouchaer, quoted in Yoram Dinstein and Mala Tabory, eds., *Israel Yearbook on Human Rights 1987* (Dordrecht, The Netherlands: Kluwer Academic Publishers Group, 1988), p. 69.

[43] Thomas A. Idinopulos, "Zionism and Racism," in *Christian Attitudes on Jews and Judaism*, Issues 40–54 (New York: Institute of Jewish Affairs, 1975), pp. 7–8.

and new venues by those antisemites around the world, including those who camouflage their real pathological hatred for the Jews under the banner of anti-Zionism. The 2001 formulation of Zionism as racism merely continued the parade of such charges. Is it any wonder that US Ambassador Daniel Moynihan called the Zionism-racism resolution "obscene" and thundered to the UN's Thirtieth General Assembly, "Today we have drained the word 'racism' of its meaning"?[44] Likewise, who could have been surprised when Yale University political scientist Charles H. Fairbanks wrote, "To call Zionism a form of racism makes a mockery of the struggle against racism as the emperor Caligula made a mockery of the Roman Senate when he appointed to it his horse"? Indeed, Fairbanks was even more incisive when he charged that the UN General Assembly's majority had inflicted "the most crippling blow yet dealt in the irreversible decline of concern with human rights as we know it."[45]

The racism charges that have been made against Israel are "not a constructive call for change in Israeli policies," says Yosef Mazur. Instead, they are "meant to strike at the very foundations of Israel's legitimacy as a nation" by associating "the Jewish state with a system declared a 'crime against humanity.'"[46] Mazur also points out the utter fallacy of the "racism" charge: "The Jews of Israel themselves comprise multiple racial and ethnic groups. Jewish Israelis comprise Europeans, Africans, Ethiopians, Georgians, Persians and other groups. Race, therefore, cannot form the basis for alleged institutionalized discrimination in Israel because the alleged discriminators (Jewish Israelis) are multiracial themselves."[47] Moreover, many Druze, Bahá'ís, Circassians, Bedouins, and Christians are also citizens of Israel even though they certainly come from different ethnic backgrounds.[48]

Even in the United States, where an overwhelming percentage of the population is supportive of Israel, some politicians have "used the chimerical Zionism-racism charge to cast the Palestinians as blacks and the Israelis as rednecks," a feeble attempt to parallel the Israeli-Palestinian conflict with the history of slavery, segregation, and racism in the United States. Although US President Barack Obama protested, "We will always reject the notion that

[44] Daniel Moynihan, quoted in Thomas M. Franck, *Nation Against Nation: What Happened to the U.N. Dream and What the U.S. Can Do About It* (Oxford, UK: Oxford University Press, 1985), p. 209.

[45] Charles H. Fairbanks, quoted in Franck, p. 209.

[46] Yosef Mazur, *Zionism, Post-Zionism & the Arab Problem: A Compendium of Opinions About the Jewish State*, Mike Cohen, ed. (Bloomington, IN: WestBow Press, 2012), p. 217.

[47] Mazur, p. 217.

[48] The Druze highly support the Israeli government and serve in the Israel Defense Forces. While Israel has often encouraged the Bedouins to give up their nomadic lifestyles and integrate more fully into Israeli society, it still respects their lifestyle preferences and does not attempt to force them to make changes with which they are not comfortable.

Zionism is racism," Gil Troy says that this analogy has "reduced the story [of the Israeli-Palestinian conflict] to one of racial oppression, rather than what it is—national conflict."[49] By finding a way to equate Zionism with racism, the antisemites have successfully leveled the ultimate charge that renders one a pariah in US society. The truth is that some multiculturalists are among the most intolerant racists on earth, even advocating the genocide of the Caucasian race as a means of solving all the world's perceived problems.[50]

Apparently, those who attack Israel as being a racist nation do not know the difference between nationalism and racism.[51] If nationalism is racism, then virtually every nation in the world is racist. In reality, however, while some nations do consider their citizens to be racially superior to other nationalities,[52] most nations simply take pride in their own cultures in what can be described as patriotism. Christopher Wellman notes that "we are right to distinguish between racism and patriotism. . . . We not only confirm that patriotism is benign and racism malignant" and "we [also] see better why (and in what forms) patriotism is healthy and why racism is so deplorable."[53] The German Catholic philosopher Dietrich von Hildebrand argued that "genuine patriotism and nationalism are as different from each other as the true, divinely ordained love of self is from egotistical self-love." One commits idolatry, however, by making "the nation the highest criterion for the whole of life and . . . the ultimate goal and highest good"—in essence, "deifying a nation."[54]

From its inception, Zionism has simply sought to restore the Jewish nation of Israel that was destroyed nearly two millennia ago, when the Jewish people were forced into worldwide dispersion. Regardless as to the extent of

[49] Gil Troy, *Moynihan's Moment: America's Fight against Zionism as Racism* (Oxford, UK: Oxford University Press, 2013), p. 12.

[50] Drexel University professor George Ciccariello-Maher has advocated for the abolition of the "White Race" and has said, "All I want for Christmas is White Genocide," while repeating the Nation of Islam's theology that says "Yacub" was a black scientist who created the white race to be a "race of devils." Alex Pfeiffer, "Drexel Professor Has a History of Hating White People and Wishing for Their Genocide," *The Daily Caller*, 12/25/2016, posted at http://dailycaller.com/2016/12/25/drexel-professor-has-a-history-of-hating-white-people-and-wishing-for-their-genocide/.

[51] George L. Mosse, "Racism and Nationalism," in *Nationalism: Critical Concepts in Political Science*, John Hutchinson and Anthony D. Smith, eds. (New York: Routledge, 2000), pp. 1382–1393. Also, Guntram H. Herb and David H. Kaplan, *Nations and Nationalism: A Global Historical Overview* (Santa Barbara, CA: ABC-CLIO, Inc., 2008), p. 1425.

[52] For example, most Japanese people have long considered themselves to be superior to other cultures. Chin-ning Chu, *Asian Mind Game* (New York: Rawson Associates Scribner, 1991), p. 102. Chu points out that "the Japanese consider the 'pure blood' of the Japanese people to be the wellspring of their superiority."

[53] Christopher Heath Wellman, *Liberal Rights and Responsibilities: Essays on Citizenship and Sovereignty* (Oxford, UK: Oxford University Press, 2014), p. 48.

[54] Dietrich von Hildebrand, *My Battle against Hitler: Defiance in the Shadow of the Third Reich*, John H. Crosby and John F. Crosby, trs. and eds. (New York: Random House, 2014), p. 248.

their dispersion and persecution, the Jewish people were able to cling to their sense of corporate—even national—identity; consequently, the restoration of the people, the nation, and the land was transformed from a hope to an expectation and finally to a reality. There is every reason, therefore, for the Israeli people to be patriotic about their nation and their land, considering the fact that for so many centuries their ancestors were involuntarily nationless and landless and were condemned to the status of being Wandering Jews, stripped of human rights and dignity and without any means of protecting themselves and their families from the unending violence of thieves, rapists, and murderers that nearly effected their genocide. The truth is that Jewish nationalism and ethnic pride are far more removed from racism than the patriotism of most European nations and certainly of virtually all Muslim nations.

## Accusing Israel of War Crimes and Genocide

Palestinian Arab propaganda mills constantly churn out indictments against Israel, accusing the Jews of war crimes and attempted genocide. William Cook argues that "the Palestinian people are defending themselves and their land and their homes against Israeli war crimes and Israeli war criminals, both military and civilian."[55] Once again, the United Nations endlessly supports these specious indictments through a complicit and accommodating Western press. With furrowed brow, the UN Commission on Human Rights expressed its grave concern about atrocities inflicted upon the Palestinian people, calling them "war crimes, flagrant violations of international humanitarian law and crimes against humanity."[56] Such oft-repeated diatribes have even affected some Israeli Arabs, as is evidenced by the pronouncement of a Committee for Arab Citizens of Israel that the nation was "committing genocidal actions, war crimes, and crimes against humanity" in its military responses to Hamas missile attacks from Gaza.[57] Needless to say, plenty of hyperventilated charges, filled with extremist rhetoric, have been launched and continue to be hurled against Israel for initiating exercises to protect its people and their land from indiscriminate violence and terrorism. For simply providing for the common defense of its citizens—one of the most basic

[55] William A. Cook, *The Plight of the Palestinians: A Long History of Destruction* (New York: Palgrave Macmillan, 2010), p. 260.

[56] UNHCR, quoted by Cook, p. 260. Ironically, the term *crime against humanity* comes directly from the Nuremberg trials where it was used to describe the atrocities perpetrated against the Jewish people by the leaders of the Nazi regime who were then being prosecuted for their crimes. Alexander Mikaberidze, *Atrocities, Massacres, and War Crimes: An Encyclopedia* (Santa Barbara, CA: ABC-CLIO, 2013), p. 322.

[57] Ilan Peleg and Dov Waxman, *Israel's Palestinians: The Conflict Within* (Cambridge, UK: Cambridge University Press, 2011), p. 88, n. 36.

responsibilities of any nation—Israel is continually charged with racism, war crimes, attempted genocide, and crimes against humanity. For example, when a Muslim Arab recently murdered an Israeli policewoman, the Palestinian Authority immediately proclaimed that the Israelis who neutralized the terrorist before he could murder others were guilty of war crimes![58]

Canadian philosophy professor Michael Neumann may have summed up all the new incarnations of the old Blood Libel against the Jews when he charged Israel with engaging in a "race war" against Palestinians and "specifically accused Jews of pure racism" simply for suggesting that "any shedding of Jewish blood is a world-shattering calamity."[59] As if to lay a capstone on his litany of libels, he also inculpated Israel for "genocide" against Palestinians and of "crimes worse than that of the German people in World War II." Because Newmann is an academic and apparently because he knew that his preposterous charges were so patently irrational and absurd, he appended his diatribe by making the equally absurd argument that "it can be reasonable to be anti-Semitic"![60]

## Behind the Mask of Humanitarianism and Human Rights

Much of the new antisemitism that is manifest in muticulturalism might, in fact, be called humanitarian racism, which "attributes intrinsically reduced responsibility for their acts to people of certain ethnic or national groups."[61] Daniel Farber and Suzanna Sherry observe that "although anti-Semitism was traditionally based on religious aversion, modern anti-Semitism more often takes the form of rejection of Jewish success, and radical multiculturalism falls into this latter category."[62] As humanitarianism and emphasis on "human rights" advanced in liberal circles in Western Europe and elsewhere, they were accompanied by the explosive growth of "obsessional

[58] Daniel J. Roth and Eytan Halon, "Border Police Officer Killed in Jerusalem Terror Attack," *The Jerusalem Post*, June 17, 2017, posted at http://www.jpost.com/Arab-Israeli-Conflict/Report-Suspected-terrorist-shot-wounded-following-attack-in-Jerusalem-497070.

[59] Robert S. Wistrich, *From Ambivalence to Betrayal: The Left, the Jews, and Israel* (Lincoln, NE: The University of Nebraska Press, 2012), p. 64.

[60] Michael Neumann, quoted in Wistrich, p. 64. The problem with rationalism is that it can be used to rationalize virtually anything, including the utterly irrational! See Alasdair C. MacIntyre, *Whose Justice? Which Rationality?* (South Bend, IN: The University of Notre Dame Press, 1989).

[61] Manfred Gerstenfeld, ed., *Behind the Humanitarian Mask: The Nordic Countries, Israel and the Jews*, (Jerusalem, Israel: Jerusalem Center for Public Affairs and Friends of Simon Wiesenthal Center for Holocaust Studies, 2008), pp. 20–22.

[62] Daniel Farber and Suzanna Sherry, *Beyond All Reason: The Radical Assault on Truth in American Law* (Oxford, UK: Oxford University Press, 1997), p. 9. Farber and Sherry argue that radical multiculturalism, which maintains that all people groups are completely equal, cannot account for the disproportionate success of Jewish people except to revert to arguments of "racism and anti-Semitism," asserting historical stereotypes of Jewish power and control.

interest in every violation of human rights that Israel could be thought to have committed."[63] Racists who hide behind humanitarianism use an "inversion of perpetrator and victim" so that victims can be held accountable for the offenses of perpetrators of violence.[64] This is especially true in liberal humanists' views of Muslims. Jihadists are simply not responsible for their acts of terrorism. Instead, it is always the Jews' fault. The Western nations which excuse violent Muslim behavior "keep up a humanitarian mask behind which they hide the greatly divergent standards by which they measure Israelis and Palestinians."[65]

Manfred Gerestenfeld expands on the influence of so-called humanitarians on the increase of anti-Zionist antisemitism: "In the past decades many pioneering efforts to demonize Israel have come from elites of the Nordic countries. The motifs of this anti-Israelism are similar to those of classic anti-Semitism of which it is a new mutation. Such highly discriminatory prejudices are particularly expressed in Norway and Sweden by leading socialist and extreme leftist politicians as well as journalists, clergy, and so-called humanitarians. Behind the Nordic countries' appearance and oft-proclaimed concern for human rights lurk darker attitudes. . . . This disguise hides many ugly characteristics such as false morality, a pretense of superiority, as well as profound humanitarian racism."[66] Suppressed peoples are not responsible for controlling antisocial impulses; therefore, acts of violence and sexual predation that would result in extended incarceration for ordinary citizens are excused if perpetrated by Muslim "refugees."[67] Such examples of utter *social injustice* in the name of "social justice" enacted on postmodernity's consequentialism of situational ethics, its sliding scale of right and wrong are continuing examples of the inability of the liberal left to deal with inconvenient facts about Muslim peoples.

---

[63] Eve Garrard, "Anti-Judaism, Anti-Zionism, Antisemitism," *Fathom,* Winter, 2015, posted at http://fathomjournal.org/anti-judaism-anti-zionism-antisemitism/.

[64] Gerstenfeld, pp. 23–25.

[65] Gerstenfeld, pp. 24–25.

[66] Gerstenfeld, cover.

[67] One Muslim refugee who claimed he was from Syria but was actually from Iraq argued in court that his reason for raping a ten-year-old boy was that he could not help himself: he had experienced a "sexual emergency." His conviction in Austrian court was overturned because judges said prosecutors did not "prove he realised the boy was saying no." Gareth Davies, "Iraqi refugee who raped a 10-year-old boy at a swimming pool in a 'sexual emergency' has his conviction overturned because the Austrian court 'didn't prove he realised the boy was saying no,'" *The Daily Mail*, October 21, 2016, posted at http://www.dailymail.co.uk/news/article-3860168/Iraqi-refugee-raped-10-year-old-boy-Theresienbad-swimming-pool-sexual-emergency-conviction-overturned-Austrian-court-didn-t-prove-realised-boy-saying-no-incident-Austria-December-2015.html. Also, "Denmark, Rapes Reported by National Origin," posted at https://fuhrerious88blog.files.wordpress.com/2016/09/img_3663-0.jpg?w=640.

CHAPTER 13

# INCONVENIENT FACTS

## Truths about Muslim Traditions and Practices

There are many inconvenient truths about Islam, Islamists, and Muslim societies that are troubling at best and downright frightening at worst, despite efforts by both Muslim apologists and propagandists as well as their sympathizers and collaborators in Western media, academia, and governments to disguise, cover up, and excuse them. These characteristics manifest a clear distinction between Muslim societies and the Jewish community and nation which they attempt to delegitimize and render a pariah in the larger community of nations. A clear case of role inversion is manifest when Arab and Muslim nations create invectives and hurl them against the Jewish people and their nation, Israel. Muslims have, in fact, become experts at projecting their own flaws onto Jews and Judaism—and without cause. Muslim views on situational ethics even permit and encourage the "inversion of the perpetrator and victim"[1] so that Muslim perpetrators of terror and violence represent themselves as victims while they charge their Jewish victims with being the perpetrators of such acts! This kind of inversion that has long been applied by Middle Eastern Muslims to Israeli Jews has also become clear in Scandinavia and other parts of Europe,[2] where Muslim sexual perverts

[1] Manfred Gerstenfeld, ed., *Behind the Humanitarian Mask: The Nordic Countries, Israel and the Jews* (Jerusalem, Israel: Jerusalem Center for Public Affairs and Friends of Simon Wiesenthal Center for Holocaust Studies, 2008), pp. 23–25.

[2] William Kilpatrick, *Christianity, Islam, and Atheism: The Struggle for the Soul of the West* (San Francisco, CA: Ignatius Press, 2012), p. 176. Kilpatrick reports that "in 2001, when it was reported that the majority of rapes in Norway were committed by members of the small Muslim minority, a prominent Norwegian academic opined that 'Norwegian women must take their share of responsibility for these rapes. . . . Norwegian women must realize that we live in a multicultural society and adapt to it.'" In fact, Muslim immigrants do not view the rape of Western women as criminal because the *Qur'an* 23:1–7 permits Muslims to take from non-Muslims whatever "right hand possesses," including women," leaving them "free from blame."

are excused for sexual harassment and rape of European women while their victims are assigned responsibility for Muslim crimes by both the Muslim immigrants themselves and by their liberal European apologists who insist that such behavior is "cultural" for the immigrants. In Sweden, "rapes, robberies, school-burnings, 'honor' killings, and anti-Semitic agitation" became so extreme that "the government blamed [the] problems instead on Swedish racism."[3]

## Systematic Muslim Religious Intolerance

While many scholars endeavor to project Islam as having always been a religion of religious tolerance,[4] the truth is that from the time of Muhammad, Islam has been one of the most—if not the most—intolerant of all world religions.[5] Efraim Karsh reports that "Muslims historically viewed themselves as distinct from, and superior to, all others living under Muslim rule, known as 'dhimmis.' . . . Christians, Jews, and Bahá'ís remain second-class citizens throughout the Arab/ Muslim world."[6]

Islam has generally been intolerant of Judaism and of Jews living under their political control, not allowing them self-determination, denying them access to their holy sites, and often calling for their genocide. At the same time, however, Islam has been highly intolerant of any other religion that has stood in its path toward world domination. One need only observe the history of Islam's intolerance for the Hindu and Buddhist religions in the 600-year-long conflict between Pakistan and India over Kashmir—which also involves battles between Shiite Islam and the predominantly Sufi Kashmir[7]—to confirm the level of religious intolerance in Islam.[8]

---

[3] Raphael Israeli, *The Islamic Challenge in Europe* (Abingdon, UK: Routledge, 2008), p. 124.

[4] Sheldon Stoff and Barbara Smith Stoff, *Conscious Evolution: The Dance of Intuition and Intellect* (Bloomington, IN: iUniverse, 2010), p. 81.

[5] Gregory M. Davis, *Religion of Peace? Islam's War Against the World* (Los Angeles, CA: World Ahead Publishing, Inc., 2006); Mark A. Gabriel, *Islam and the Jews: The Unfinished Battle* (Lake Mary, FL: Charisma House Book Group, 2003); and Robert Spencer, *The Truth about Muhammad: Founder of the World's Most Intolerant Religion* (Washington, DC: Regnery Publishing, Inc., 2006).

[6] Efraim Karsh, "The Middle East's Real Apartheid," *The Jerusalem Post*, March 5, 2012, posted at http://www.jpost.com/Opinion/Op-Ed-Contributors/The-Middle-Easts-real-apartheid.

[7] Kashmiri Islam has been influenced by ancient Kashmiri culture's Buddhism and Hinduism and is, therefore, considered to be illegitimate by various sects of Islam.

[8] Anna Ruska, "Kashmir," in *Atrocities, Massacres, and War Crimes: An Encyclopedia*, Alexander Mikaberidze, ed. (Santa Barbara, CA: ABC–CLIO, LLC, 2013), vol. 1, p. 356. Also, Amar Cheerma, *The Crimson Chinar: The Kashmir Conflict: A Politico Military Perspective* (New Dehli, India: Lancer Publishers, 2014), p. 408, and Matthew J. Webb, *Kashmir's Right to Secede: A Critical Examination of Contemporary Theories of Secession* (Abingdon, UK: Routledge, 2012), pp. 21–25.

The violent posture of Muslims against the ancient Coptic Christian Church in Egypt is another prime example of Islamist intolerance for other religions. In this case, a Christian community that predates Islam by at least six centuries is regularly targeted with terrorist attacks that have destroyed churches, murdered prelates, and slaughtered entire communities. In Iraq, the extremist Muslim jihadists that aspired to create a new caliphate under the banner of ISIS virtually destroyed the ancient Yazidi community, murdering thousands of its people because they were "infidels" for being adherents to a centuries-old religion that blended aspects of Zoroastrianism, Christianity, Judaism, and Islam.[9] Penny Nance reports that in this perverse jihadist attempt at genocide, ISIS was "clearly intent on shattering the rich ethnic and religious diversity of Iraq, and had perpetrated appalling crimes on Christians, Kaka'es, Kurds, Sabea-Mandeans, Shi'a, Turkmen and Yazidis, for no other reason than their religious beliefs or ethnic origin."[10]

The Muslim Arab charges of religious intolerance that are hurled against the Jewish people and the nation of Israel are, therefore, all the more patently absurd when Judaism is compared with Islam and when Israel is compared with Muslim nations in the Middle East and elsewhere. The record of the illegal Jordanian occupation of East Jerusalem and the West Bank during the period from 1948 until 1967 is a clear example of Muslim "tolerance," for, in that time, Jews were absolutely forbidden to visit the holy sites, including the Western Wall of the Temple, and Christians were also "allowed only very limited access to Christian holy sites"[11] in Jordan and in occupied East Jerusalem.[12] Since it assumed limited sovereignty over the West Bank, the Palestinian Authority has regularly denied Jews access to the Temple Mount and has limited access of Christians to their holy sites in Bethlehem and elsewhere. Accordingly, since the Palestinian Authority assumed control of Bethlehem in 2002, some "2800 Christians from the Bethlehem area have left the occupied

[9] Adil Rasheed, *ISIS: Race to Armageddon* (Dehli, India: Vij Books India Pvt. Ltd., 2015), p. 61.

[10] Penny Young Nance, *Feisty and Feminine: A Rallying Cry for Conservative Women* (Grand Rapids, MI: Zondervan Publishing, 2016), p. 128.

[11] Silvio Ferrari and Andrea Benzo, *Between Cultural Diversity and Common Heritage: Legal and Religious Perspectives on the Sacred Places of the Mediterranean* (Abingdon, UK: Routledge, 2014), p. 51.

[12] Whereas it used to be a wonderful tourist attraction to Christians, the ancient city of Jericho has been essentially closed to Christians since the Palestinian Authority's occupation of the West Bank, making one of the most ancient of biblical sites inaccessible to most Christian tourists.

territories for other countries"[13] because of the persecution and restriction of rights that they have experienced at the hand of the Muslim Arabs.

In contrast, all the areas which have been controlled and administered by the Israelis since 1948 have been open to people of all religious persuasions. Muslims, Druze, Christians, Bahá'ís,[14] and other groups have been accorded complete religious freedom and access to holy sites. So much for the argument that the Israeli government engages in religious intolerance! Israel's tolerance is virtually unlimited while Muslim intolerance is equally limitless, especially in the Middle East. Eugene Korn is entirely accurate, therefore, when he declares that "democratic and pluralistic Israel remains the one safe haven for Christians and their holy sites in the Middle East."[15]

Robert Spencer argues that the best answer to Islamic intolerance and violence should have been for the West to promote "its own Judeo-Christian heritage, with its emphasis on the dignity of the human person, from which Western freedoms of speech and conscience flow."[16] Instead, Western politicians and media have trumpeted the pseudo-tolerance of multiculturalism in which intolerance is a—if not *the*—fundamental operational principle.

## Muslim Institutionalization of Ethnic Inequality

From its inception, Islam has practiced and enforced ethnic inequality in all the areas where it has dominated politically and militarily. This inequality has been enshrined in the requirements of the *Qur'an* that assign all non-Muslims to the inferior status of *dhimmi* "citizenship." This is not, however, an antiquated practice that has been relegated to history. Karsh reports that "Arabs, Turks and Iranians continue to treat long-converted [to Islam] populations that retained their language, culture and social customs, as inferior."[17] A 2009 report from the Pew

[13] United States Congress House Committee on International Relations, *Annual Report on International Religious Freedom 2005, April 2006, 109–2 Joint Committee Print*, p. 597.

[14] The administrative center for Bahá'ism is in Haifa, Israel, while most of the 5 million Bahá'ís live in Iran and India. Eliz Sanasarian, "The Comparative Dimension of the Baha'i Case and Prospects for Change in the Future," in *Bahá'ís of Iran: Socio-Historical Studies*, Dominic P. Brookshaw and Seena B. Fazel, eds. (Abingdon, UK: Routledge, 2008), p. 166.

[15] Eugene Korn, *The Jewish Connection to Israel, the Promised Land: A Brief Introduction for Christians* (Woodstock, VT: Jewish Lights Publishing, 2008), p. 156.

[16] Spencer, p. 16.

[17] Karsh, "The Middle East's Real Apartheid."

Research Center found that "Muslim-majority nations are marked by inequality, poverty, and conflict. . . . Even in developed economies, or richer countries such as those in the Middle East, the majority of the Muslim populations tend to be poor. Saudi Arabia, for example, has an elite affluent segment and a majority of poor people."[18]

Even in the Turkish Republic, efforts to abolish the "ontological inequality" between Muslims and non-Muslims that were thought to be a model for other Muslim-dominated nations have failed miserably with the rise of the Muslim-dominated government of Recep Erdogan.[19] In Afghanistan, when Muhammad Nadir Shah assumed control of the government in 1929, he "removed all restrictions . . . on the role of mullahs and mawlawis in education, institutionalized the primacy of the Sunni Hanafi school of Shari'a orthodoxy over Shi'a, institutionalized inequality of men and women, curtailed the rights of non-Muslims in the country, closed girls' schools, and reimposed veiling."[20] In doing so, Khan abolished the reforms of his predecessor Amanullah Khan and transformed Afghanistan into a hotbed for Islamist extremism that plagues the world to this day.

Muslim ethnic inequality can be seen very clearly in Pakistan, where all Christians are virtually untouchables, relegated to unrelenting trans-generational poverty and oppression that is continually enforced upon them by the Muslim government of this Islamic nation. A further example can be seen in the colonialist efforts in the eighteenth and nineteenth centuries to unite people of different ethnicities and religions in sub-Saharan Africa. When Muslims and non-Muslims were united in Sudan, Chad, Niger, Mali, Nigeria, and others, "violent and long-lasting civil wars occurred," many of which continue to this day.[21]

## Traditional Muslim Racism and Slavery

One of Islam's ugly little secrets is the historical perspective of the Arabian Islamist on sub-Saharan Africans whom they consider to be an

---

[18] Paul Temporal, *Islamic Branding and Marketing: Creating A Global Islamic Business* (Hoboken, NJ: John Wiley & Sons, 2011), p. 43.

[19] Zana Çitak, Aykan Erdemir, and Tugba Tanyeri-Erdemir,"Differential, Disguised and Deterritorialized: State Funding of Religion in Turkey," in *Public Funding of Religions in Europe*, Francis Messner, ed. (Abingdon, UK: Routledge, 2016), p. 213.

[20] M. Nazif Shahrani, "State Building and Social Fragmentation in Afghanistan: A Historical Perspective," in *The State, Religion, and Ethnic Politics: Afghanistan, Iran, and Pakistan*, Ali Banuazizi and Myron Weiner, eds. (Syracuse, NY: Syracuse University Press, 1986), p. 52.

[21] Max Heller, *Ethnic Stratification and Economic Inequality around the World* (Abingdon, UK: Routledge, 2016), p. 129.

inferior people group.[22] Karsh contends that "Africans of sub-Saharan descent are held in deep contempt, a vestige of the region's historic role as epicenter of the international slave trade."[23] Roman Loimeir reports that "many African Muslims who studied in Saudi Arabia . . . were appalled by many aspects of life in Saudi Arabia, such as Saudi racism toward Africans."[24] Muslims from the Middle East and from Northern Africa have always looked askance upon sub-Saharan Africans. In Libya, "discrimination and racism against migrants was closely linked to their blackness, in spite of the largely African, rather than Arabic or Berber-Arabic, origin of many Libyans," says Antonio Morone.[25] Samuel Aryeetey-Attoh observes that these same historical attitudes which were manifest in incipient Islam continue to this day: "Some of these stereotypes exist today and have been the basis of racist attitudes towards Sub-Saharan Africans and Black people all over the world."[26]

The enslavement of Christian youth by Muslim captors in Sudan has become legendary. Willem Kooman confirms that young Christian boys who are so enslaved are "sold into slavery to Muslim families in Northern Sudan or Libya, where they will be given Muslim names and forced to renounce their Christian faith, say Muslim prayers, are whipped, and given little food. If they try to escape, their Achilles tendons are often severed. . . . Eventually, the young boy will be trained in the army to murder his own people."[27] The fate that young Christian girls who are captured for slavery is even more horrible: "The Islamic Sudanese government has a policy of raping all women and girls who are abducted."[28] All such actions are taken by the Sudanese government that "uses the Quran to justify a mandate of unthinkable cruelty and genocide, and announces it performs the will of Allah."[29] It has been

[22] Ronald Segal, *Islam's Black Slaves: The Other Black Diaspora* (New York: Farrar, Straus & Giroux, 2002). Also, Francis Bok, *Escape from Slavery: The True Story of My Ten Years in Captivity and My Journey to Freedom in America* (New York: St. Martin's Press, 2003). Bok gives a chilling account of his capture by Muslim Arab raiders in southern Sudan when he was seven years old and his subsequent ten years of slavery to wealthy Muslim farmers.

[23] Karsh, "The Middle East's Real Apartheid."

[24] Roman Loimeier, *Between Social Skills and Marketable Skills: The Politics of Islamic Education in 20th Century Zanzibar* (Leiden, The Netherlands: Koninklijke Brill NV, 2009), p. 119, n. 10.

[25] Antonio M. Marone, "The African Migratory Factor in Libyan Transition," in *North African Societies after the Arab Spring: Between Democracy and Islamic Awakening*, Leila El Houssi, Alessia Melcangi, Stefano Torelli, and Massimiliano Cricco, eds. (Newcastle upon Tyne, UK: Cambridge Scholars Publishing, 2016), p. 162.

[26] Samuel Aryeetey-Attoh, *Geography of Sub-Saharan Africa* (New York: Prentice Hall, 2003), p. 86.

[27] Willem Kooman, *Veiled Threat* (Bloomington, IN: AuthorHouse, 2011), p. 62. Also, James A. Beverley, *Christ & Islam: Understanding the Faith of the Muslims* (Joplin, MO: College Press Publishing Co., 1997), p. 27, and Gabriel Andrew Msoka, *Basic Human Rights and the Humanitarian Crises in Sub-Saharan Africa* (Eugene, OR: Wipf & Stock, 2007), p. 19.

[28] Kooman, p. 63.

[29] Kooman, p. 63.

estimated that 2.5 million people, virtually all of them Christians, have died in the Islamic jihad in Sudan since 1983.

K. K. Prah has written extensively on the Arab-led slavery of Africans.[30] In fact, the Arabic word *abeed* means "slave," but it is usually used as an insult to Africans of sub-Saharan, non-Muslim descent. It is no wonder, then, that, as Karsh reports, "the Arabic-speaking countries remain the world's foremost refuge of slavery, from child and sex trafficking in Saudi Arabia and the Gulf states to actual chattel slavery in Sudan and Mauritania." Amazingly, it was not until 1981 that Mauritania—which is ruled by Sunni Muslims—finally became the last nation in the world to abolish slavery.[31] Despite the fact that the Mauritanian government made slaveholders liable to criminal prosecution in 2007,[32] the practice of slavery still continues in Mauritania to this day.[33] It is safe to say that the only remaining true slave traders in the world today are Muslims.[34]

## Entrenched Muslim Gender Discrimination

It is beyond dispute that "legal and social discrimination against women is pervasive throughout the Arab-Islamic world,"[35] as well as in most of the Islamic communities in the world. This condition is well founded in Islamic tradition, for Muhammad himself declared, "We have not been left any calamity more detrimental to mankind than woman."[36]

---

[30] K. K. Prah, ed., *Reflections on Arab-Led Slavery of Africans* (Cape Town, South Africa: Centre for Advanced Studies of African Society, 2005), pp. 2ff.

[31] Alexis Okeowo, "Freedom Fighter: A Slaving Society and an Abolitionist's Crusade," *The New Yorker*, September 8, 2014, posted at https://www.newyorker.com/magazine/2014/09/08/freedom-fighter.

[32] Ibrahima Sylla, "Mauritania's Parliament Passes Law Banning Slavery," Reuters *World News*, August 9, 2007, posted at http://www.reuters.com/article/us-mauritania-slavery/mauritanias-parliament-passes-law-banning-slavery-idUSL0989868220070809.

[33] Johanna Higgs, "It Still Exists: Slavery Drags on in Mauritania Despite Being Illegal," *PassBlue*, February 15, 2017, posted at http://www.passblue.com/2017/02/15/it-still-exists-slavery-drags-on-in-mauritania-despite-being-illegal/.

[34] When radical Islamists announced the establishment of the Islamic State (ISIS), they proclaimed the revival of sex slavery as an institution. Rukmini Callimachi, "ISIS Enshrines a Theology of Rape: Claiming the Quran's Support, the Islamic State Codifies Sex Slavery in Conquered Regions of Iraq and Syria and Uses the Practice as a Recruiting Tool," *The New York Times*, August 13, 2015, posted at https://www.nytimes.com/2015/08/14/world/middleeast/isis-enshrines-a-theology-of-rape.html. Callimachi reports the claims of an Islamic State fighter who raped a 12-year-old girl: In the moments before he raped her, he "took the time to explain that what he was about to do was not a sin. Because the preteen girl practiced a religion other than Islam, the Quran not only gave him the right to rape her—it condoned and encouraged it, he insisted. He bound her hands and gagged her. Then he knelt beside the bed and prostrated himself in prayer before getting on top of her. When it was over, he knelt to pray again, bookending the rape with acts of religious devotion. . . . [The girl said, 'He told me that . . . by raping me, he is drawing closer to God.'"

[35] Karsh, "The Middle East's Real Apartheid."

[36] Mohammed, quoted in Thomas Patrick Hughes, *A Dictionary of Islam: Being a Cyclopaedia of the Doctrines, Rites, and Ceremonies, and Customs, Together with the Technical and Theological Terms, of the Muhammadan Religion* (London: W. H. Allen & Co., 1896), p. 678.

In fact, "gender discrimination is "endemic" to Muslim societies and "becomes an added fertilized substrate upon which the diseased plant of Islamism can grow."[37] Gender discrimination is enshrined in the sacred texts of Islam which say that woman is made from a crooked [rib] bone that cannot be straightened[38] and that men not only can but also *should* beat their wives.[39] Not surprisingly, therefore, the Qur'an has been used to establish, justify, and institutionalize polygamy—but only in the form of polygyny (never polyandry!) wherein a man can have up to four legal wives at a time.[40] In effect, however, in many Muslim societies, men can legally engage in unlimited serial polygyny through a divorce policy that often leaves women victims of male lust and abuse. According to most scholars, any Muslim marriage can be summarily terminated if a husband declares three times to his wife in the presence of male witnesses, "I divorce you."[41] Upon this pronouncement, the man is free to contract another marriage. Likewise, in many Muslim nations, where adultery—particularly that of the offending woman—is often punished by death, marriages of convenience can be legally arranged with predetermined durations of an hour, a day, a week, a month, or a year. These fixed-term "marriages" are called in Arabic *Nikah Mut'ah*, meaning literally "marriage of pleasure" or "marriage of use."[42] While all of these "marriages"

[37] Tsvi Bisk, "The War on Islamism," in *Lone Actors—An Emerging Security Threat*, Aaron Richman and Yair Sharan, eds. (Amsterdam, The Netherlands: IOS Press, 2015), p. 144.

[38] Hughes, p. 671. This characterization is based on the *Qu'ran's* faulty translation of the Hebrew word *tzela* in Genesis 2:22 as "rib" rather than "side" or "arched chamber" as both the Hebrew word and its Greek translation, *pleura*, meant until the second century BC. In the genesis of humanity, woman was not fashioned from expendable male body parts. For details, see John D. Garr, *Coequal and Counterbalanced: God's Blueprint for Women and Men* (Atlanta, GA: Golden Key Press, 2012), pp. 102–123.

[39] Adel Az Abadeer, *Norms and Gender Discrimination in the Arab World* (New York: Palgrave Macmillan, 2015), p. 197. Abadeer notes that "according to widely accepted interpretations of sacred texts such as the *Qur'an*, *hadith*, and *sunna*, husbands can admonish their wives verbally, abandon them in bed, and beat them, respectively, to discipline their wives if husbands fear their wives' disobedience or disloyalty." Gender discrimination is certainly enshrined in the legal and traditional systems of Saudi Arabia.

[40] Islam allows a Muslim man to have four wives at a time; however, if he marries a fifth, the marriage is not void but merely irregular.

[41] Ludwig W. Adamec, *Historical Dictionary of Islam* (Lanham, MD: Rowman & Littlefield Publishing Group, 2009), p. 301. Also Joel A. Nichols, "Multi-Tiered Marriage: Reconsidering the Boundaries of Civil Law and Religion," in *Marriage and Divorce in a Multi-Cultural Context: Multi-Tiered Marriage and the Boundaries of Civil Law and Religion*, Joel A. Nichols, ed. (Cambridge, UK: Cambridge University Press, 2012), p. 40.

[42] The *Nikah Mut'ah* is a time-delimited marriage contract and requires a certain reward paid by the man to the woman. It can be arranged by a woman only every two months. Presumably a man can arrange one as often as he wishes. Though some have argued that *Nikah Mut'ah* is an un-Islamic concept and a circumvention of adultery laws, the practice is established and supported by the Usuli Shia schools of Shari'a (Islamic law). Shahla Haeri, *Law of Desire: Temporary Marriage in Shi'i Iran* (Syracuse, NY: Syracuse University Press, 1989).

terminate automatically upon the passing of the agreed time and the man's payment of the established price to the woman, everyone is assured that this practice is not a form of prostitution, for it fits the parameters of some Islamic views of marriage.

It should come as no surprise that such "inequality enshrined by Islam leads to the institutionalization of structural violence."[43] Much of Islam demands that women be covered from head to toe when they appear in public, while some extreme forms of Islam require women to cover even their faces in public.[44] In Saudi Arabia, women are not allowed to possess birth certificates or passports, and they are required to be accompanied by a male relative chaperone whenever they appear in public.[45] Without rights to passports and with other legal and traditional restrictions imposed upon women in various Muslim societies, women certainly appear to be considered an inferior class either ontologically or socially—or both.

Such inherent and institutionalized concepts of feminine inferiority have led to the imposition of genital mutilation (excision of the clitoris and vaginal labia that is cynically and euphemistically termed "female circumcision"[46]) in order to control female sexuality by "ensuring" the virginity in the unmarried and chastity in the married.[47] Mary Wangila maintains that "Islam draws from the notion of chastity and honor in the pre-Islamic Bedouin Arabs."[48] Sami Abu-Sahlieh reports that in various such cultures, the organs excised in this "circumcision" are believed to be "superfluous excrescence" and their removal cleanses a prepubescent girl from "dirty surpluses that if left would hide the demon."[49] Wangila notes, however, that many Islamic scholars dismiss "arguments about cleanliness, chastity, and aesthetics" and consider female circumcision to be "a crime against

[43] David Ghanim, *Gender and Violence in the Middle East* (Westport, CT: Praeger Publishers, 2009), p. 55.

[44] Theodore Gabriel and Rabiha Hannan, *Islam and the Veil: Theoretical and Regional Contexts* (London, UK: Continuum International Publishing Group, 2011), p. 73.

[45] Kathryn M. Coughlin, ed., *Muslim Cultures Today: A Reference Guide* (Westport, CT: Greenwood Press, 2006), p. 165.

[46] In order for male circumcision to be equivalent to so-called "female circumcision," the entire glans penis, and not just the foreskin, would have to be surgically removed. This is why the term *circumcision* is utterly absurd when applied to female genital mutilation.

[47] Anne Sofie Roald, *Women in Islam: The Western Experience* (London, UK: Routledge, 2001), p. 244.

[48] Mary Nyangwesto Wangila, *Female Circumcision: The Interplay of Religion, Culture and Gender in Kenya* (Maryknoll, NY: Orbis Books, 2007), pp. 122–124

[49] Sami Awad Aldeeb Abu-Sahlieh, *Male & Female Circumcision: Among Jews, Christians and Muslims* (Ithaca, NY: Shangri La Publications, Ltd., 2001), pp. 11, 143, quoted in Wangilla, p. 124.

a girl's body that no one has the right to commit."[50]

Other ancient traditions, coupled with Islamic demands for total submission to its tenets, have also given rise to "honor" killings and other measures of torture in order to "control" female activity in such societies, including some more moderate Muslim communities. A particularly egregious example of the practice of "honor killing" unfolded in the United States when Zein Isa, a Palestinian terrorist who lived in St. Louis, was convicted of killing his daughter Palestina in 1989. Investigators say he was furious because she had a black boyfriend, went to a school dance and got a job at Wendy's. Palestina's mother held her down as Isa plunged a 9-inch knife into his daughter's chest, actions the FBI observed live via wiretap as they investigated Isa for his terrorist ties and exposed the level of his religiously inspired treachery.[51] Could any theology possibly foster a more horrific anthropology when male "honor"—or so-called "family honor"—is valued above the life of a young girl?

Further disregard for half of the human race is also manifest in the practice of some Islamic nations where child brides (with no minimum legal age of consent) are routinely "married" to older men, often in their 60s and 70s in what appears to most of the non-Islamic world as little more than legalized pedophilia.[52] Then, in an appalling outworking of systematized androcentric abuse of women that some Islamists religiously justify, barely pubescent Christian girls are routinely kidnapped by Muslims in the Darfur region of Sudan to be sold into slavery as sex toys for wealthy and self-avowed "devout" Muslim men, subsequently to be discarded like so much expendable refuse when the newness wears off.[53] Amazingly, the Western media—as well as most leaders of the African-American community—choose to ignore this form of enslavement of African children by Arab Muslims.[54]

[50] Muslim opponents of female circumcision "consider narratives that justify female circumcision misinterpretations and corruption of Islamic traditions because they are not part of the Qur'an . . . [and] because it damages a healthy organ in an innocent woman," Wangila says. Wangila, p. 123.

[51] Ellen Francis Harris, *Guarding the Secrets: Palestinian Terrorism and a Father's Murder of His Too-American Daughter* (New York: Charles Scribner's Sons, 2005).

[52] Technically, a girl is not to be handed over to her husband and sexual intercourse is not to be forced upon her until "she is fit for marital congress." Reuben Levy, "The Social Structure of Islam," in *Orientalism: Early Sources, vol. XII* (London: Routledge, 1957), p. 106.

[53] Damien Lewis and Halima Bashir, *Tears of the Desert: A Memoir of Survival in Darfur* (New York: Random House, 2009). Also, Alfred Taban, "Activist Says Child Slavery Exists in Sudan," report by Reuters, July 19, 1997.

[54] Pasha Slatin and Rudolf Von Slatin,"Slavery," in *Historical Dictionary of the Sudan*, Robert S. Kramer, Richard A. Lobban, Jr., and Carolyn Fluehr-Lobban, eds. (Lanham, MD: Rowman & Littlefield Publishing Group, 2013), p. 392.

Without a doubt, then, gender discrimination is strongly enforced in many, if not most, Muslim societies in the world. This is particularly true in parts of the Middle East, including in many of the Muslim Arab societies that surround the nation of Israel. There is simply no comparison between the treatment of women in Israel and those in Muslim nations.

## Ingrained Muslim Political Corruption

The Palestinian Arabs continue to be almost hopelessly bellicose primarily because they are dominated—as they have always been—by shamelessly corrupt political leaders who transfer multiplied millions, if not billions, of dollars of Western "humanitarian aid" into private European bank accounts while keeping their people in abject poverty.[55] If these "foreign aid" and "relief" efforts of Western nations alone had been directed to the Palestinian Arab populace rather than to its political leaders, the people could easily be secure and comfortable. If the oil-rich Arab nations who purport to support the "Palestinians" had given to the Palestinian Arab people the billions of dollars that they have continually distributed to terrorist organizations, the status and situation of those people would have been elevated exponentially, easing a great deal of their frustration and anger and eliminating one of their supposed motivations for terrorism against the Jews. To be sure, Muslim autocrats and Palestinian Arab leaders do not have a monopoly on world political corruption; however, there has been and continues to be a tradition within their ranks that makes too few people profoundly wealthy and powerful and too many others poor and exploited.[56] The very existence of such conditions foment anger and frustration which is unfortunately vented, not against the corrupt Palestinian Arab leaders who deserve

[55] Stuart Arden describes Yasser Arafat's widow Suha's lifestyle: "[S]he wandered about at Gucci, Chanel, Yves St. Laurent, Christian Dior, and other 'thrift(less) shops' she frequents in Paris on the millions of dollars she received from Yasser Arafat's secret Swiss bank accounts. Meanwhile, the PA [Palestinian Authority] bilks European and American donor countries, allowing their leaders to live in luxury while many average citizens live in near squalor." Stuart Arden, *Sense and Nonsense: Everything You Need to Know about the Arab–Israeli Conflict* (Jerusalem, Israel: Gefen Publishing House, 2013), p. 132. Aaron Mannes observes that "reports of corruption have plagued the [Palestinian Authority] since its inception. The Palestinian Legislative Council launched several investigations, finding massive misappropriation of funds. The investigations found that PA money had been embezzled by PA leaders. . . . An independent audit of the 1997 budget could not account for $323 million." Aaron Mannes, *Profiles in Terror: The Guide to Middle East Terrorist Organizations* (Lanham, MD: Rowman & Littlefield Publishers, 2004), p. 294.

[56] The Palestinian Arab leaders have kept the Palestinian Arab people in poverty and squalor in order to foment their hatred for the Jews and to incite them to violence against Israel.

it, but against the easiest target available—in this case, the perennial scapegoat of history, the Jewish people.

## *Qur'an* Teachings and Practices Violate Absolute Torah Ethics

The greatest single ethical document ever produced in human history was actually written by the finger of God himself on tablets of stone.[57] This document is called the Ten Commandments, the outline of God's instructions to human beings for ethical conduct in their relationship with God and with their fellow humans. The Ten Commandments make unequivocal demands of human beings that are absolute, not situational, and deontological, not a maximization of a human-perceived good.[58] When the lineal descendants of Abraham, Isaac, and Jacob were assembled at Mt. Sinai some 3,500 years ago, the one and only God thundered to them this synopsis of his requirements for human beings in the form of ten words of instruction that the Israelites both saw and heard.[59] Then, those same words were inscribed on stone tablets that are generally called the Decalogue. These ten instructions represent the Torah in its most condensed form. All other instructions in the Hebrew Scriptures are merely subsets of the Ten Commandments.[60]

A comparison of teachings in the sacred writings of Judaism with those of Islam produces some amazing contrasts. In the process, it brings to light profound truths that Muslim antisemites and their cohorts in the secularist West attempt to obfuscate and camouflage with politically correct, multicultural dissimulations and prevarications. By examining the Hebrew Scriptures of Judaism—the *Tanakh* (*Torah*, *Nevi'im*, and

---

[57] Exodus 31:18.

[58] *Collins English Dictionary, Complete & Unabridged, 2012 Digital Edition,* posted at http://www.dictionary.com/browse/deontological?s=t.

[59] Exodus 20:18 says that the Israelites "saw the voices and the flames." Philo of Alexandria explained this phenomenon thus: "From the fire . . . there sounded . . . a voice, for the flame became articulate speech . . . so clearly were the words formed . . . that they seemed to see them rather than to hear them." Philo, *De Decalogo* 33; *De Praemiis* 2, quoted in Christopher Forbes, *Prophecy and Inspired Speech in Early Christianity and Its Hellenistic Environment* (Tübingen, Germany: J.C.B. Mohr, Siebeck, 1995), p. 167, n. 43.

[60] Benjamin Blech, *Understanding Judaism: The Basics of Deed and Creed* (Northvale, NJ: Jason Aronson, 1991), p. 29. Blech references *Sefer Azharot* which "shows the link between each one of the 613 mitzvot and its prime category heading. Every one of the 'Ten Sayings' is in fact a major category or principle. Under it may be subsumed countless other laws. For example: Embarrassing someone in public is a sin. But where is it found in the Ten Principles? It is included in the laws forbidding murder, which in Hebrew is called *Shefikhat damim*, the shedding of blood." In reality, the Ten Commandments themselves can also be summarized in one command and in one word from the commandment that Jesus described as the "first" and "most important" of all commandments: "Hear, O Israel, the Lord our God is God alone. And you shall love the Lord your God with all your heart, and with all your soul, and with all your might." This is why Paul concluded that all the commandments of Scripture can be summarized in one word: "love" (Galatians 5:14) and why he said that "love is the fulfillment of the Torah" (Romans 13:10).

*Ketuvim*)—and comparing them with the foundational Scriptures of Islam—the *Qur'an*, *Sunnah*,[61] and *Hadith*[62]—it is relatively easy to see why such a contrast exists between the two religions and between the worldview, mindset, and traditions of Jews and those of Muslims. A few examples of fundamental teachings on basic issues of morality and ethics are particularly revealing.

***Is Murder Ever Permitted?*** For the Jews, the *Torah* stipulates that no human being is ever to commit homicide (murder).[63] This commandment is so important that it is included in the Ten Words that God himself thundered to the Israelites when they were gathered at Sinai to receive their national constitution. This, the sixth commandment of the Decalogue is so simple and unequivocal that it requires only two words in the Hebrew text: "*Lo tirtsach*" ("You shall not [commit] murder"). It is universal and absolute, never situational or provisional. Jack Cohen says, "Both in the prohibition against killing and in that against murder, there is an implicit conception of the human person as sacred and inviolable."[64] In fact, "For Judaism, respect for human life is absolute and sacrosanct. Human life has infinite value because it is a gift of God and because man is made in God's image."[65] Helmut Smith maintains that in Jewish tradition, "the prohibition against murder rests upon the infinite value of the other human being" so that "once the Jewish testimony to the dearness of the other and to the subsequent prohibition against murder is wiped out in the genocide of the Jews, the law against murder is reduced to a matter of political legality."[66] No wonder Rashi even compared the death of a human being with the sight of a Torah scroll being consumed by fire.[67]

In Jewish thought, the commandment proscribing murder is considered to be so utterly inviolable that it cannot be suspended even for the sake of saving one's own life. The Torah's prohibition of murder, therefore, is esteemed as being on a par with the its injunctions against idolatry and adultery. All three of these commandments can never be

[61] *Sunnah* are oral traditions of the practices and teachings of Muhammad.

[62] *Hadith* are sayings attributed to Muhammad.

[63] Exodus 20:13.

[64] Jack J. Cohen, *Democratizing Judaism* (Brighton, MA: Academic Studies Press, 2010), p. 263.

[65] A. Guigui, "Jewish Morality with Respect to Medicine and Biotechnology," in *The Human Rights, Ethical and Moral Dimensions of Health Care* (Strasbourg, France: Council of Europe Publishing, 1998), vol. 434, p. 77.

[66] Helmut W. Smith, *The Holocaust and Other Genocides: History, Representation, Ethics* (Nashville, TN, Vanderbilt University Press, 2002), p. 234.

[67] Rashi, *Moed Qatan* 24a.

suspended even if by doing so one could save his own life.[68] For Jews, then, human life—the life of all human beings—is inviolable, and murder is never acceptable. No wonder Solomon lists "hands that shed innocent blood" among the seven things that the God of Scripture hates.[69]

For Muslims, even though the *Qur'an* also condemns murder,[70] it also says that when Muslims are engaged in *jihad* ("holy war"), they are instructed by the *Qur'an* to "kill [the infidels] whenever you overtake them and expel them from wherever they have expelled you . . . if they fight you, then kill them."[71] Ultimately, radical Islamists and many in mainstream Islam mandate three choices for non-Muslims: conversion to Islam, subjugation to Muslim rule and taxes, or death. These are the only options because the *jihad* ("holy war") must continue until all who resist are killed.[72] The killing in *jihad* is not limited to self-defense: the holy war is a war of aggression against infidels in which even the innocent can be slaughtered with impunity. The holy war is almost never carried out to defend Muslims: it is an offensive action that is designed to expand the realm of Islam. Egyptian Islamic theorist, Sayyid Qutb, made this clear when he "vehemently argued that 'jihad was never defense *in the narrow sense that the term 'defensive war' generally denotes today.*"[73]

The *jihad* also permits the murder of women and children among infidels. "The prophet justified attacking the women and children as they were 'from among them [infidels]."[74] Julie Rajan reports that in order to justify the jihadists' killing of innocents, *Al Qaeda*'s leader, Ayman Mohammed Zawahiri, appealed to an incident in the life of Muhammad when the prophet was unable

[68] With the exception of three of the Ten Commandments, the prohibitions against idolatry, murder, and adultery, Judaism teaches that all of the commandments in the Hebrew Scriptures can be suspended in order to save human life, including one's own life. If one is ordered upon penalty of death to break the commandments against idolatry, murder, or adultery, he must accept martyrdom rather than violate one of those commandments. Barry S. Kogan, *A Time to Be Born and a Time to Die: The Ethics of Choice* (Hawthorne, NY: Aldine De Gruyter, Inc., 1991), p. 123. The principle in Jewish law of *Pikuach Nefesh* (literally "saving of human life") even says that almost any negative commandment of the Torah may become inapplicable when a human life is at stake. This principle is based on Leviticus 18:5 which declares, "You shall keep my laws and ordinances, which if a person does, he shall live by them." This instruction is taken to mean that a person is to live by the laws of the Torah, not die by them. See Joseph Telushkin, *The Book of Jewish Values* (New York: Bell Tower Publishing, 2000), pp. 100–105.

[69] Proverbs 6:17.

[70] *Qur'an* 5:32; 17:33.

[71] *Qur'an* 61:11.

[72] *Qur'an* 9:29.

[73] Irm Haleem, *The Essence of Islamist Extremism: Recognition through Violence, Freedom through Death* (London, UK: Routledge, 2012), p. 124 (author's emphasis).

[74] V. G. Julie Rajan, *Al Qaeda's Global Crisis: The Islamic State, Takfir and the Genocide of Muslims* (Abingdon, UK: Routledge, 2015), p. 303.

to distinguish between "infidels" and "innocents" and, therefore, justified their killing.[75] This position is extended to other Muslims as well when they do not accept the theology or practices of the jihadists and are considered to be apostates.[76] Women and children among such "apostates" can also be murdered at will.[77] In fact, this is the principle applied when Islamist terrorists, including suicide bombers, target even infants in their jihadist attacks.

This same principle applies in Muslim civil societies in which "honor killings" (*ghayra* in Arabic)—in which Muslims sometimes abuse and even kill their own relatives, including wives and children, in order to protect the "honor" of their families against perceived transgressions of Muslim and family traditions—are carried out without fear of retribution.[78] "If a woman appears with a man on the streets who is neither her husband nor a member of her family, [her family must] kill her to avenge Allah's purity," says Charles Miller.[79] Oliver Leaman confirms this practice: "Some Muslim groups will seek to enforce barbaric customs which do involve murder and theft of their own family members when it is thought that dishonor occurs due to the actions of relatives."[80] Islamist scholars also justify murder of political leaders. For example, the assassination of Egyptian President Anwar Sadat was supported and prompted by Abt al-Salem Faraj and his booklet, *Al-Faridah al-Gha'ida* (*The Neglected Duty*). Faraj believed that "there is no Islam without violent jihad, and it is a Muslim's duty never to permit non-Muslim ways of thinking and

---

[75] Rajan, p. 303. Rajan references Zawahiri's essay, "*Jihad*, Martyrdom, and the Killing of Innocents," which is quoted in Raymond Ibrahim, ed. and tr., *The Al Qaeda Reader* (New York: Doubleday, 2007), pp. 137–171. Also, Robert Spencer, *The Complete Infidel's Guide to ISIS* (Washington, DC: Regnery Publishing, 2015), pp. 27–31.

[76] IBP, Inc., *Middle East and Arabic Countries' Environmental Law Handbook* (Washington, DC: International Business Publications, 2015), vol. 1, p. 21, which notes that "in many Muslim countries, the accusation of apostasy is even used against non-conventional interpretations of the Quran. . . . Sunni and Shia Muslims often accuse each other of apostasy."

[77] Jalil Roshandel and Sharon Chadha, *Jihad and International Security* (New York: Palgrave Macmillan, 2006), pp. 73–80.

[78] For a comprehensive study of the Islamic foundations for such internecine violence, see Daniel Akbari and Paul Tetreault, *Honor Killing: A Professional's Guide to Sexual Relations and Ghayra Violence from the Islamic Sources* (Bloomington, IN: AuthorHouse, 2014).

[79] Charles E. Miller, *Fight or Surrender: A Reef of Political Essays* (Bloomington, IN: Trafford Publishing, 2013), p. 552. The *Qur'an* does not explicitly permit "honor killing"; however, its principles are said to encourage the practice. Marianne Kamp, "Femicide as Terrorism: The Case of Uzbekistan's Unveiling Murders," in *Sexual Violence in Conflict Zones: From the Ancient World to the Era of Human Rights*, Elizabeth D. Heineman, ed. (Philadelphia, PA: The University of Pennsylvania Press, 2011), pp. 56–72; p. 272, n. 42.

[80] Oliver Leaman, *Controversies in Contemporary Islam* (Abingdon, UK: Routledge, 2014), p. 136.

acting to enter into Islamic consciousness or society."[81]

The contrast between Judaism and Islam, therefore, is very clear when it comes to the taking of human life. YHWH, the God of the Jews, commands, "Do not murder!" The commandment applies to all humanity with no exceptions. Only actions taken in self-defense are permitted, and they are very limited. Allah, the God of the Muslims, protects Muslim lives; however, he commands his followers to take offensive actions in which non-Muslim infidels, even utterly innocent infants, can be murdered in the course of the advancement of the Muslim cause of world domination.

***Is Lying Ever Acceptable?*** For Jews, the *Torah* commands: "You shall not bear false witness."[82] This, the ninth commandment of the Decalogue, is universal and absolute. It is never situational or conditional. It is "a bulwark . . . against trivial lying but especially against perjury in the court."[83] In fact, the prohibition against lying applies even when "the lie does harm to no one."[84] This rule applies not only to intra-Jewish community communication but also to communication between Jews and non-Jews as well. "If a Jew lies to a non-Jew," says Mordechai Katz, "he not only violates the prohibition against lying, but also is causing a *chilul Hashem* or desecration of G-d's Holy Name."[85] The proscription against lying also includes the act of deceiving another person, for "deceiving someone . . . violates the law against 'stealing a person's consciousness (*gneivat daat*)," an action that "is considered even more blameworthy than stealing someone's possessions."[86] The commandment against prevarication is interpreted by the Jewish sages to extend even to facial expressions that must also be honest and truthful.[87] King Solomon summed up the seriousness with which the Hebrew Scriptures view lying and dissimulation when he listed "a lying tongue" and "a false

---

[81] Abt al-Salem Faraj, quoted in Charles Selengut, *Sacred Fury: Understanding Religious Violence* (Lanham, MD: Rowman & Littlefield Publishing Group, 2017), p. 64.

[82] Exodus 20:16.

[83] W. Sibley Towner, "Exodus 20:1–17, Exegetical Perspective," in *Feasting on the Word: Lent through Eastertide*, David Lyon Bartlett and Barbara Brown Taylor, eds. (Louisville, KY: Westminster John Knox Press, 2008), p. 79.

[84] Aaron Levine, *Moral Issues of the Marketplace in Jewish Law* (New York: Yashar Books, 2005), p. 392.

[85] Babylonian Talmud, *Shabbat* 32. Katz, p. 196.

[86] Steven H. Resnicoff, "Ends and Means in Jewish Law," in *The Jewish Law Annual*, Berachyahu Lifshitz, ed. (London, UK: Routledge, 2004), vol. 15, p. 151.

[87] Talmud *Makkot* 23. Mordechai Katz, *Understanding Judaism: A Basic Guide to Jewish Faith, History, and Practice* (Brooklyn, NY: Mesorah Publications, 2000), p. 196.

witness who pours out lies" in his outline of the seven things that "the LORD hates."[88]

For Muslims, the *Qur'an* specifies not only their right but also their obligation to engage in prevarication and deception if by doing so they can advance the cause of Islam or improve their own material status: "And they [the disbelievers] schemed, and Allah schemed [against them]: and Allah is the best of schemers."[89] The Arabic word for "scheme" (or plot) in this passage is *makara*, which literally means "deceit." If Allah is supremely deceitful toward unbelievers, certainly his followers can employ the same tactics. Indeed, Muhammad himself, through his own conduct, set forth examples of lying and deceit for his disciples to follow. As an example, in 628 AD, the prophet negotiated with the leaders of Mecca a peace agreement, the *Khudaibiya* (or Treaty of Hudaybiya), that gave him and his followers access to the city in return for agreement that both parties of the treaty would abstain from war with the other for ten years. The treaty specifically declared, "Between us evil is to be abstained from and there is to be no raiding or spoilation."[90] All the while, he was clandestinely planning a military action for taking the city by force. Then, two years later, when he conquered the city, he executed the very leaders who had trusted him.[91] In another instance, when Usayr ibn Zarim, leader of the Banu Nadir tribe, prepared for battle against the Muslim forces, Muhammad sent emissaries to ibn Zarim and guaranteed him and his companions safe passage to join Muhammad in Medina for peace negotiations that would include the possibility of his being made ruler of Khaybar. When ibn Zarim accepted the prophet's offer, however, he and his unarmed companions were summarily murdered.[92]

This official policy regarding prevarication that was condoned and even promoted in the *Qur'an* has been featured in the Islamic world

[88] Proverbs 12:22.

[89] *Qur'an* 3:54.

[90] Sumbul Ali-Karamali, *Growing Up Muslim: Understanding the Beliefs and Practices of Islam* (New York: Random House, 2012), p. 131. Also, Bob Sullivan, *Escape the Global Storm* (Maitland, FL: Xulon Press, 2008), p. 123.

[91] This incident is commemorated by Muhammad himself in *Qur'an* Sura 23:26–27. Paul Charles Merkley, *Christian Attitudes towards the State of Israel* (Montreal, Canada: McGill-Queen's University Press, 2001), p. 106. Also, Aaron McDaniels, *Truth Between the Lies* (Bloomington, IN: Ex Libris 2016), p. 164.

[92] Ibn Warraq, *Why I Am Not a Muslim* (Amherst, NY: Prometheus Books, 2003), p. 98. Warraq details a long list of similar instances in which Muhammad lied and deceived others, including fellow Muslims (Warraq, pp. 98–99).

since the time of Muhammad. When the prophet died and a contention arose over who was his rightful successor, the vast majority[93] of his followers maintained that he had named no successor; therefore, by consensus they appointed Abu Bakr al Siddiq to be Caliph of Islam,[94] an action that formed what came to be known as Sunni Islam (from the Arabic *sunnah* ["Muhammad's lifestyle]).[95] At the same time, however, Ali ibn Abi Talib, Muhammad's son-in-law and cousin, claimed to be the legitimate Caliph, saying that Muhammad had appointed him to be his successor. Ali and his followers formed what has come to be called Shia Islam (from the Arabic *Shi'atu 'Ali* ["followers of Ali"]). In the aftermath of the contention between Sunni and Shia Islam, extensive literature called *hadiths*, were created to support the claims of both groups. Ibn Warraq reports that many of those who created these *hadiths* "had no scruples in promoting tendentious lies in a sacred religious form and they were only concerned to find pious authorities who would be prepared to cover such falsifications with their undoubted authority. There was never any lack of these."[96]

Islam teaches that there are three types of deception when a Muslim is dealing with non-believers, *taqiyya* (sacred deception and dissimulation),[97] *kitman* (lying by omission), and *khodeh* (trickery and deceit). In addition, "*adarorah*, meaning 'the ends justify the means,' has become the Sunni version for permitting or commanding deceit in order to protect the faith [of Islam]."[98] If the cause of Islam can be advanced in any way, a Muslim is permitted to lie and is encouraged to do so, especially if he can "gain the trust of

---

[93] The Sunni have maintained their majority through the centuries so that in today's world an estimated 80–90% of Muslims identify themselves as being Sunni.

[94] Heather N. Keaney, "Caliph," in *Encyclopedia of Islam*, Juan Eduardo Campo, ed. (New York: Infobase Publishing, 2009), p. 125.

[95] Masoud Kheirabadi, *Islam* (Philadelphia, PA: Chelsea House Publishers, 2004), p. 39. Kheirabadi gives this clarification: "The sunnah refers to [Muhammad's] lifestyle or example," whereas a *hadith* "is a narration about the life of the Prophet and what he approved."

[96] Ibn Warraq, *The Origins of the Koran: Classic Essays on Islam's Holy Book* (Amherst, NY: Prometheus Books, 1998), p. 21.

[97] The idea that deception and dissimulation could be "sacred" is inimical to both Judaism and Christianity; however, it is built into the Muslim faith and even into the Arabic language. Nonie Darwish, *The Devil We Don't Know: The Dark Side of Revolutions in the Middle East* (Hoboken, NJ: John Wiley & Sons, 2012), p. 60. Darwish says, "For the sake of protecting Mohammed and Islam, practically anything is allowed, and the individual Muslim is taught that protection of Islam is a sacred communal obligation that is more important than family, life, or happiness."

[98] Bill Siegel, *The Control Faction: Our Struggle to See the True Threat* (Lanham, MD: Hamilton Books, 2012), p. 27.

non-believers in order to draw out their vulnerability and defeat them."[99] This is why the *Hadith* reports: "The prophet said, 'War is deceit.'"[100] Abi Hamid Al Gahazali, founder of Sufism, the inner mystical dimension of Islam, goes even further with these arguments by saying, "You can lie if that will keep you from evil or if it will result in prosperity."[101] In similar fashion, it is permissible for a Muslim to lie to other Muslims in order to smooth over a controversy or to make difficult matters better. In other words, lying to advance one's own economic situation is acceptable, even commendable as long as it is being done with a non-Muslim, and lying to a fellow Muslim is permitted if it is for the purpose of someone's good.[102]

The practice of lying in order to advance the cause of Islam and to bring benefits to Muslims, which is supported and recommended in the *Qur'an*, has continued unabated to this day. Zuhdi Jasser argues that this practice has been and remains a false interpretation of Islam: "There was never, ever any mention of *taquiyya*, the previously esoteric but now ubiquitous corrupt idea that a Muslim can lie to non-Muslims if doing so promotes the cause of Islam. The Islamists often practice *taquiyya* in the mistaken belief that their interpretation of God condones lying or deceiving if it serves Muslims' needs over the 'infidel.'"[103] It is a fact, however, that radical Islamists derive their ideas from both the descriptions of Allah and of the actions of his prophet Mohammad that are described in Muslim sacred texts.

With lying not only excused but also promoted when it will advance the cause of Islam or provide material benefit to a Muslim over an infidel, the obvious question that must be asked is: how could anyone trust Muslims to be truthful in any negotiation? Would not the underlying principle of *taqiyya* govern all such situations, making it impossible for

[99] Robert Spencer, *The Politically Incorrect Guide to Islam (and the Crusades)* (Washington, DC: Regnery Publishing, Inc., 2005), pp. 79–81. The context from which this saying was drawn was likely the story of the incident when Muhammad's associates murdered Usayr ibn Zarim and thirty unarmed men with him after Muhammad had "guaranteed" them safe passage. Ibn Ishaq/Hisham, 981.

[100] *Haddith, Bukhari* 42:269.

[101] Abi Hamid Al Gahazali, quoted in Mark A. Gabriel, *Islam and Terrorism* (Lake Mary, FL: Charisma Media, 2002), p. 95. Gahazali maintains that Muslims are encouraged to lie in negotiations with a non-Muslim if it will bring them a profit.

[102] This excuse for lying is the essence of the situational ethics of consequentialism.

[103] Zuhdi Jasser, *A Battle for the Soul of Islam: An American Muslim Patriot's Fight to Save His Faith* (New York: Simon and Schuster, 2012), pp. 42–43. Jasser points out that an excellent example of such dissimulation is the current Muslim claim that "shariah law and US constitutional law are not in conflict with each other," when, in truth, all Muslims know that "shariah law is based on Islamic scriptural exegesis of Muslim legal scholars—religious law for Muslims only—and that alone puts it in conflict with American law, which has a secular basis in reason universal for all citizens equally."

the infidel to know what is true and what is not? If lying and deception are not only permitted but even enshrined as an act of imitating God and, therefore, a religious duty, on what basis could a non-Muslim determine the verity of any declaration or agreement?

When it comes to lying, the contrast between YHWH, the God of the Hebrew Scriptures, and Allah, the God of Islam, is clear and striking. The Hebrew Scriptures declare that "God is not human that he should lie,"[104] that he commands his people, "Do not lie," and that he declares that "a lying tongue" is an abomination in his sight. There are no exceptions to this commandment except in the case of saving a human life. Judaism even takes the simple commandment to be a prohibition against deception, even in body language. The *Qur'an*, on the other hand, says that Allah himself lies and is a deceiver, and Islam maintains that it is not only acceptable for a Muslim to lie in order to advance the cause of Islam or to improve his own economic or social status: it is commendable.

***Is Stealing Ever Allowed?*** For Jews, the *Torah* makes no exceptions when it says, "You shall not steal."[105] This, the eighth commandment of the Decalogue, is universal and absolute. It is never situational or provisional. It is so simple and unequivocal that it occupies only two words in the Hebrew text: *lo tignob* ("you shall not steal"). The rights of each individual to life, liberty, and property are unequivocally protected by this commandment.[106] The prohibition against theft is expanded by Jewish tradition, moreover, to include "overcharging, dishonest weights and measures, kidnapping, shifting a landmark and forcible robbery."[107] The commandment, "You shall not steal," is also extended by the Talmud to include the "prohibition against causing damage to another."[108] It is also understood to forbid deception, for "deception is considered stealing the mind of others, classifying the perpetrator as a thief as it is written, 'And thou hast stolen my heart' (Gen. 31:26)."[109] With the Torah's prohibition against theft, there are no equivocations, no gray areas, no extenuating circumstances, and no restrictive applications. The commandment applies

[104] Numbers 23:19.

[105] Exodus 20:15.

[106] Andrew Knowles, *The Bible Guide: An All-in-One Introduction to the Book of Books* (Oxford, UK: Lion Publishing, 2001), p. 54.

[107] Barbara D. Stephens, "Noah," in *Learn Torah with . . . 1994–1995 Torah Annual: A Collection of the Year's Best Torah*, Joel L. Grishaver and Stuart Kelman, eds. (Los Angeles, CA: Aleph Design Group, 1996), p. 18.

[108] Fred Rosner and Robert Schulman, *Medicine and Jewish Law* (Brooklyn, NY: Yashar Book, 2005), vol. 3, p. 42.

[109] Rosner and Schulman, eds., vol. 3, p. 184.

to all human beings. A Jew is not at liberty to steal from someone outside his own neighborhood, community, or ethnic group.

For Muslims, the *Qur'an* "condemns the act of stealing as one of the worst crimes and punishes it severely."[110] While it prescribes stiff penalties for those who are caught in petty theft, however, the *Qur'an* also permits Muslims to steal from unbelievers who are perceived as warring against Islam. It even gives rules that mandate the manner in which the spoils of war are to be divided.[111] This goes beyond warfare, however, for "forcefully taking the property of unbelievers is not considered stealing under Islam but a legitimate right"[112] that is established in the *Qur'an* declaration: "And He caused you to inherit their land and their houses and their wealth, and the land ye have not trodden. Allah is ever Able to do all things."[113] This ruling easily extends to the positions of Muslim police who do not enforce laws against "thieves who steal from infidels," and it is extrapolated as a means of identifying "infidel business [is a legitimate target] for theft and ransom."[114]

The contrast between Judaism and Islam cannot be clearer when it comes to stealing. The Hebrew Scriptures declare that YHWH, the God of the Jews, unequivocally commands, "You shall not steal!" The *Qur'an*, while prohibiting Muslims from stealing from one another, also condones—even commands—theft from non-Muslims both in war and in peace.

## A Matter of Trust?

Considering the contrast of moral and ethical positions in the *Torah* and the *Qur'an*, one must wonder how anyone—journalist, politician, diplomat, or military commander—could ever trust radical and reactionary Muslims in any matter since their religion not only does not prohibit but also excuses and even commands murder, deception, and theft. Robert Spencer points out: "Islam doesn't have a moral code analogous to the Ten Commandments; the idea that Islam shares the general

[110] *Qur'an* 5:38–39.

[111] *Qur'an* 8:41. Muhammad even promised his followers spoils, which were assets stolen from unbelievers (Qur'an 48:18–20).

[112] Nonie Darwish, *Wholly Different: Why I Chose Biblical Values over Islamic Values* (Washington, DC: Regnery Publishing, 2017), p. 186.

[113] *Qur'an* 33:27.

[114] Marvin W. Heyboer, *Journeys into the Heart and Heartland of Islam* (Pittsburgh, PA: Dorrance Publishing Co., 2009), p. 218.

moral outlook of Judaism and Christianity is another PC myth. In Islam, virtually anything is acceptable if it fosters the growth of Islam."[115]

It is clear that ethics in Islam are situational with the ends always justifying the means: "[K]illing is wrong, but if it is done to promote Islam, it is good. Suicide is prohibited, but suicide bombing that will cause the death of non-Muslims is a holy act. Stealing from fellow Muslims is prohibited, but looting non-believers was prescribed and practiced by Muhammad. Sexual intercourse out of marriage is taboo, but rape of unbelieving women is okay," says Ali Sina.[116] Obviously, such Muslim situational ethics stand in stark contrast to the absolute ethics of Judaism and the Jewish people and of Christianity and Christians, whose ethical system came directly from Judaism; and they do not help foster a relationship of trust wherein progress toward resolution of conflicts and establishment of peace and tranquility can be made.

---

[115] Spencer, p. 79.

[116] Ali Sina, *Understanding Muhammad: A Psychobiography of Allah's Prophet* (LaVergne, TN: Felibri Publications, 2008), p. 173.

CHAPTER 14

# MYTHS AND FANTASIES

## Historical Revisionism by Muslim Antisemites

Among the greatest myth-makers of the twentieth and twenty-first centuries—or any other century, for that matter—are the fabricators of the Führer's new clothes, those who have spun shiny, though diaphanous, illusions that to the trained and honest eye do nothing to cover the naked truth of raw antisemitism. If anything, these fabrications are more insidious than the ancient and Medieval manifestations of Jew-hatred were. Fables woven out of whole cloth are designed to delegitimize the Jewish people and their nation and land, denying them any right of self-determination. Exercises in historical revisionism have been employed to transform the Jews from legal entitlement to the land of Israel into illegitimate "occupiers" of the land to which they and their ancestors have been connected for four thousand years. These fables convey sovereign rights of nationhood and land to people whose ancestors were natives of other nations and who, more often than not, despised the land of Israel. The list of fantasies is long and growing as creators of myth grasp at straws to accomplish their insidious antisemitic anti-Israelist agendas.

### The Myth of the Arab "Palestinian" People

Many Palestinian Arabs, including Yasser Arafat and Faisal Husseini, have claimed that the Palestinians are descendants of ancient autochthonous Canaanite tribes, particularly of the Jebusites.[1] Some have even gone as far as to argue that since Abraham was an "Arab,"[2] the Jews were

[1] Eric H. Cline, *Jerusalem Besieged: From Ancient Canaan to Modern Israel* (Ann Arbor, MI: The University of Michigan Press, 2004), pp. 12, 33.

[2] This allegation is patently untrue, since Abraham was never from Arabia. Instead, he was a Babylonian by birth (Genesis 11:31), then an Assyrian by nationality (Genesis 12:4–5), and finally a Hebrew by divine covenant (Genesis 14:13). For discussion of the origins of ancient people groups spoken of in Genesis, see Bodie Hodge, *The Tower of Babel: The Cultural History of Our Ancestors* (Green Forest, AR: Master Books, 2014).

"descendants of the Arabs [and that] the Arabs, who were Abraham's original offspring . . . possessed prior rights to the land of Palestine."[3] Ted Swedenburg maintains that "by such means [the Palestinian Arabs] meant to affirm that their originary title to the land of Palestine predated and took precedence over rival Israeli Jewish claims."[4] The obvious hope of these Muslim historical revisionists is to place the Palestinian Arabs in Canaan before the arrival of the Jews and thereby to invalidate Israel's claim to the land.

Muslims have even had the nerve to co-opt the Jewish Scriptures in an effort to support their argument since the *Tanakh* says that Jerusalem was a possession of the Jebusites before Israel entered the Promised Land[5] and long before David conquered Jerusalem in the tenth century BC.[6] David Wenkel, who has done an extensive study of the Palestinian Arab claim of historical and genealogical connection with the Jebusites, concludes that "the claim to Jebusite heritage within the Palestinian community is a recent construct."[7] Palestinian activist Rashid Khalidi even confessed that Palestinian nationalists "anachronistically read back into the history of Palestine over the past few centuries, and even millennia, a nationalist consciousness and identity that are in fact relatively modern," and, by doing so, they create a "predilection for seeing in peoples such as the Canaanites, Jebusites, Amorites, and Philistines the lineal ancestors of the modern Palestinians."[8] Randall Price maintains that while some scholars have traced Canaanite artistic traditions to as late as 149 BC, there is simply no evidence in any historical document that indicates any of the Canaanite peoples continued to exist in the land of Israel.[9] On the other hand, says Price, "Arab heritage is traceable in secular history no earlier than references in the Neo-Assyrian annals of the ninth to seventh centuries B.C.," and "even this preserved influence

[3] Ted Swedenburg, *Memories of Revolt: The 1936–1939 Rebellion and the Palestinian National Past* (Fayetteville, AR: The University of Arkansas Press, 2003), p. 80.

[4] Swedenburg, p. 80.

[5] Numbers 13:29; Joshua 11:3.

[6] 2 Samuel 5:6.

[7] David Wenkel, "Palestinians, Jebusites, and Evangelicals," in *Middle East Quarterly*, Summer 2007, pp. 49–56. Wenkel's analysis of this subject is comprehensive, informative, and well documented.

[8] Rashid Khalidi, *Palestinian Identity: The Construction of Modern National Consciousness* (New York: Columbia University Press, 1997), pp. 149, 253, n. 13, quoted in Wenkel, pp. 49–56. Wenkel points out that Khalidi has been accused of failing to give attribution to the original sources on which he based his observations.

[9] Randall Price, *Fast Facts on the Middle East Conflict* (Eugene, OR: Harvest House Publishers, 2003), p. 61.

of Canaanite art still leaves another 1,000 years until the coming of the Arabian nomads of Islam to the Land."[10]

This evidence could well explain the reason why neither the *Qur'an* nor any other Muslim document before, during, or immediately after the Muslim conquest of Israel mentions any "ancestral connection going back to the Canaanites (or to the Philistines or Jebusites)."[11] Even Grand Sharif Hussein bin Ali, Emir of Mecca, King of the Arabs, and guardian of the Islamic Holy Places in Arabia and Jerusalem, said in the early twentieth century that the ancestors of the Palestinian Arabs had only been in the area of the Holy Land for 1,000 years,[12] which, if accurate, would have made their first appearance there around the time of Muhammad. A statement by the British Government also confirms that Palestinians themselves have long acknowledged the fact that their connection with the land reached back in history no further than Muhammad's seventh-century AD conquest of Palestine, which took place more than a millennium after the Israelites/Jews settled the land.[13] Even then, says Eliezer Schweid, "no other separate national entity based on this land alone had come into being in the land of Israel. That is to say, foreign conquest had not turned into the establishment of a new nation. The Arabs who lived in the land belonged, in terms of their national affiliation, to the greater Arab people, for whom the land of Israel was but one of many conquests."[14]

Yehuda Bauer has reached the conclusion that "there was no Palestinian people before the early 20th century, because local Arabs thought of themselves as inhabitants of Southern Syria (*Sooriyah djanoobiyah*)."[15] In fact, for centuries before the founding of the state of Israel until long after that event, the term *Palestinian* was applied exclusively

---

[10] Price, p. 61.

[11] Price, p. 61.

[12] *Al-Qibla* (March 23, 1918), quoted in Samuel Katz, *Battleground—Fact and Fantasy in Palestine* (New York: Bantam Books, 1977), p. 126.

[13] British Government, *Report of the Anglo-American Committee of Enquiry, 1946, Part VI,* (April 20, 1946).

[14] Eliezer Schweid, *The Land of Israel: National Home or Land of Destiny* (Cranbury, NJ: Associated University Presses, 1985), p. 193. The "greater Arab people" included those of Arabian heritage who emigrated from Arabia to other areas, including Israel, during military conquests or economic migrations.

[15] Yehuda Bauer, *The Jews: A Contrary People* (Zürich, Switzerland: Lit Verlag GmbH & Co., 2014), p. 277. During the time of the Roman Emperor Hadrian in the second century AD, Israel was designated as a part of Syria-Palaestina. Because of Hadrian's extreme antisemitism, he appropriated the name of Israel's most detested and long-term enemy, the Philistines, and applied it to Israel in order to denigrate the Jewish people. Roman Syria-Palaestina included all of Israel as well as much of modern Turkey, Syria, Arabia, and Egypt.

to Jews living in Palestine.[16] Since the word *Palestinian* had been used to designate the Jews, none of the Arabs wanted to be associated with the term. As a matter of fact, some of the Arabs even "denounced the term *Palestine* as 'a Zionist invention.'" Daniel Gordis agrees with this assessment: "When Israel was created, there *was* no Palestinian national movement. Palestinian Arabs had long thought of themselves as Southern Syrians, and the term *Palestinian* was actually used to refer to the Jews of Palestine."[17] Interestingly, using the word *Palestinian* to describe both the land of Israel and those Jews who had returned to their ancient homeland was so common in the more than twenty centuries before that time that when the news of Israel's declaration of independence was announced in 1948, it was published in the *Palestine Post*![18]

It is ironic, therefore, that the first time that the term *Palestinian People* was used to describe Arabs in Palestine was when it appeared in the preamble of the 1964 Palestine Liberation Organization (PLO) Charter that was drafted in Moscow. One of Yasser Arafat's military lieutenants, Zuheir Muhsin, made it clear that "the existence of a separate Palestinian identity serves only tactical purposes. The founding of a Palestinian state is a new tool in the continuing battle against Israel."[19] Doubtless, then, Palestinian Arab claims of being related to the Canaanites are a recent phenomenon, and they are contrary to historical evidence. How could the PLO resort to such utterly fallacious arguments to support its agenda? The answer is simple, says Roger Carasso: "The Arabs learned their disinformation tactic from the Nazis: If you repeat the lie long enough, and loud enough, people will actually believe you. As a result, most people now believe there is something called the 'Palestinian' people, a total fabrication, complete with a phony history and a phony culture." Carasso concludes that "there is only one truth here, that there are 1.75 million people, a hodgepodge of Arabs and Turks, intentionally

---

[16] Jews living in Israel and in southern Syria were referred to as "Palestinian Jews" during the time of the Ottoman Empire (AD 1299–1922). Those who lived in two of the provinces of the Byzantine Empire that were called Palaestina Prima (the land east of the Mediterranean from Gaza to Acco stretching to the Dead Sea) and Palaestina Secunda (the land east of a line from Acco to Jericho and stretching to Phoenicia on the north and Arabia on the east) were also called "Palestinian Jews" in the period of time from AD 390–636.

[17] Daniel Gordis, *The Promise of Israel: Why Its Seemingly Greatest Weakness Is Actually Its Greatest Strength* (Hoboken, NJ: John Wiley & Sons, 2012), p. 38 (author's emphasis). Also, Stuart Arden, *Sense and Nonsense: Everything You Need to Know About the Arab-Israeli Conflict* (Jerusalem, Israel: Gefen Publishing House, 2013), p. 10.

[18] *The Palestine Post*, founded in 1932, was not renamed *The Jerusalem Post* until 1950.

[19] Zuheir Muhsin, quoted in the *Dutch Daily Trouw*, March, 1977.

or maybe unwittingly, masquerading as a 'people,' and made into a 'people' by the PLO and many in the world community who relished attacking the Jews in yet another novel way."[20]

Based on these historical facts and arguments, former Israeli Prime Minister Golda Meir said in 1969, "There were no such thing as Palestinians. When was there an independent Palestinian people with a Palestinian state? It was either southern Syria before the First World War, and then it was a Palestine including Jordan. It was not as though there was a Palestinian people in Palestine considering itself as a Palestinian people and we came and threw them out and took their country away from them. They did not exist."[21] Yasser Arafat himself confirmed Meir's argument, proudly boasting in his authorized biography, "If there is any such thing as a Palestinian people, it is I, Yasser Arafat, who created them."[22]

By the terms of the Balfour Declaration and the subsequent League of Nations Covenant for Palestine and its British Mandate, the "occupied territory," then, is not—and has never been—the Israeli-occupied West Bank. Instead, it is the Arab-occupied West Bank and the Hashemite-occupied Transjordan. The "Palestinian People" and the proposed "Palestinian State" are utter fabrications of malicious and mendacious Arabs for whom truth was utterly meaningless. All that mattered to them was their antisemitic struggle to return Israel to the *Dar al-Islam*, to effect the genocide of the Jewish people by driving them into the Mediterranean Sea, and to enrich themselves on the largess of politically amoral Western postmodernists—all the while plundering the heritage of the millions of Jews who had caused the dessicated Palestinian desert to bloom as a crocus and had transformed the Middle Eastern backwater into a thriving, democratic Jewish refuge.

## The Fabrication of the PLO and the Palestinian Authority

Contrary to the specious, melodramatic ways in which it has been promoted, the Palestinian Liberation Organization (PLO) was never an

[20] Roger David Carasso, "What's in a Name: The Western Palestinian Arabs," posted at http://www.carasso.com/israel/palestineterms.html. Yasser Arafat's real name was Rahman Abdel-Raouf Arafat al-Qudwa al-Husseini, and he was born to an Egyptian textile merchant. Then, later in life, he became a member of the Egyptian Muslim Brotherhood. As an Egyptian, his claim to being a "Palestinian" was a total fraud.

[21] Golda Meir, quoted in the *Washington Post* (June 16, 1969).

[22] Yasser Arafat, quoted in Lawrence Solomon, "Playing Make-Believe over Gaza," in *The Financial Post*, August 7, 2014, posted at http://business.financialpost.com/fp-comment/lawrence-solomon-playing-make-believe-over-gaza.

indigenous movement that sprang up among an indigenous "Palestinian" Arab people who were native to the land of Palestine (Israel). Instead, it was created in Jerusalem in 1964 by the Arab League led by Egyptian dictator Gamal Abdul Nasser in the same year that "Yasser Arafat's Fatah terrorists, based in Syria, began murdering Israelis."[23] In reality, "the Palestinians had not been consulted in the establishment of their own liberation organization, and Nasser had imposed a lawyer named Ahmad Shuqayri to lead the PLO."[24] The PLO was ostensibly designed to support "rights" of the "Palestinian" people (Muslim Arabs) to possess a part of the land of Israel in a "two-state solution." In reality, however, its function was to work toward the destruction of the Jewish state of Israel and the expulsion of the Jews from their land. The PLO's purpose was "to destroy the Jewish state of Israel and replace it with an Arab state called Palestine."[25]

When the master Egyptian terrorist Yasser Arafat essentially coopted the PLO for his own purposes by uniting it with al-Fatah,[26] the terrorist organization that he and his Algerian friends had formed in 1965, the PLO's intentions toward Israel became crystal clear: Arafat wanted "to destroy Israel, not negotiate peace with it, and Fatah wanted all the land, not just the West Bank and Gaza."[27] The PLO worldview rested on a "revolutionary doctrine developed among Palestinians in the 1950s and early 1960s [that] blended Islam not only with aspects of Marxism-Leninism but also with Third World radical nationalism" and adopted Mao Zedong and Che Guevara's guerrilla war tactics.[28] The "Palestinian" people were merely a means to an end, and the planned end was to be the destruction of the Jewish state and the return of Israel to Muslim rule.

It should surprise no one that Arafat worked closely with the KGB, the Soviet secret police and spy agency. The KGB created a fraudulent birth certificate for Arafat, expanded his four-page tract called *Falastinua*

---

[23] David G. Dalin, *The Myth of Hitler's Pope: Pope Pius XII and His Secret War against Nazi Germany* (Washington, DC: Regnery Publishing, Inc., 2005), p. 139.

[24] Eugene Rogan, *The Arabs: A History* (New York: Basic Books, 2009), p. 334.

[25] Barry M. Rubin, *Revolution Until Victory?: The Politics and History of the PLO* (Cambridge, MA: Harvard University Press, 1994), p. 1.

[26] The Arabic word *fatah* means "faith"; however, *fatah* is a reverse Arabic acronym for "*Harekat at-Tahrir al-Wataniyyeh al-Falastiniyyeh,*" which means "conquest by means of jihad." Ironically, Al-Fatah was originally opposed to the PLO; however, when Arafat succeeded in coopting the PLO, he gained control of what was at that time the largest terrorist organization in the world. Brian R. Farmer, *Understanding Radical Islam: Medieval Ideology in the Twenty-First Century* (New York: Peter Lang Publishing, 2007), p. 106.

[27] Rubin, p. 15.

[28] Rubin, p. 8.

(*Our Palestine*) into a 48-page monthly magazine for al-Fatah, and formulated for him and his minions an ideology and an image.[29] As a result, Arafat's inextricable link to the KGB was always disguised so as to mask the continuing Soviet influence in the development and ongoing actions of the PLO.[30]

The Palestine Liberation Organization was birthed in rabid antisemitism, then coopted and perverted by antisemitic terrorism incarnate, Yasser Arafat, and finally repackaged and reimaged as the Palestinian Authority under the direction the "fatherly" Mahmoud Abbas. The Palestinian Authority is still a terrorist organization that is hell-bent on the destruction of the nation of Israel and the genocide of the Jewish people. No amount of Madison-Avenue redressing can ever occlude what has always been and will always be under those garments of deception, the Führer's new clothes. Those with eyes to see through the opacity of propaganda and media fraud—and it does not take X-ray vision to do so!—recognize the transparent and naked truth, the repugnant, pock-marked vestiges of the ancient antisemitism that has plagued the Chosen People for millennia. The package is new, but the contents are the same: antisemitism pure and simple, as evil and insidious as it has ever been.

## The Myth of Muhammad's Jerusalem Experience

One of the most spurious of all of Muhammad's phantasmagoria was his tale of flying to heaven from the hills of Jerusalem.[31] The Arabian merchant, who had never set foot in Israel, much less Jerusalem, imagined himself making a night journey to the heart of Judaism's Holy City on his magical horse Al-Buraq, tying his steed to one of the stones of the Jewish Temple's Western Wall, and from thence taking flight to heaven itself.[32] Having coopted the site of the Jewish Temple for his own newly minted religion by perverting the ancient account of the *Akedah* of Isaac and replacing it with his myth of the sacrifice of Ishmael, the prophet proceeded to expropriate the Holy City from the Jews and make it his own. He even had the

[29] Ion Mihai Pacepa, "The KGB's Man," in *The Wall Street Journal*, September 22, 2003, noted in Robert R. Friedmann, *A Diary of Four Years of Terrorism and Anti-Semitism: 2000–2004* (Lincoln, NE: iUniverse, 2005), vol. 2, p. 290. Also, Ion Mihai Pacepa and Ronald Rychlak, *Disinformation: Former Spy Chief Reveals Secret Strategies for Undermining Freedom, Attacking Religion, and Promoting Terrorism* (Washington, DC, WND Books, Inc., 2013).

[30] Herbert Krosney, "The PLO's Moscow Connection," *New York Magazine*, Sep 24, 1979, pp. 64–72.

[31] Jerusalem is never mentioned in the entire *Qur'an*. Instead, the holy city of the Jews is called *Al-Quds*.

[32] Moshe Ma'oz, ed., *The Meeting of Civilizations: Muslim, Christian, and Jewish* (Eastbourne, UK: Sussex Academic Press, 2009), p. 150.

audacity to create a new name, *Al-Quds* ("the Holy One"), for the Holy City, which since at least the time of Abraham and Melchizedek, the priest-king of Salem, had been called Salem or Jerusalem—i.e., for at least 2700 years before Islam's prophet ever lived. Muhammad's fraudulent fable[33] opened the door to the construction of the Dome of the Rock in 691 AD, covering the rock on which Abraham had offered Isaac and the site on which the first and second temples of Judaism (built by Solomon and Nehemiah/Herod respectively). For over 1300 years now, the most sacred site in Judaism has been occupied by a Muslim shrine, and access to the holiest Jewish place on earth was totally denied to Jews until the Temple Mount was liberated by the Israeli Defense Forces in 1967.

The enormity of this evil can be understood only if one were to consider how an occupation of the *Ka'aba* in Mecca by Jews or how an occupation of the Vatican by Hindus would be perceived by virtually everyone in the world. Muslims, however, have been excused when they have occupied and controlled Jewish holy places like the Temple Mount in Jerusalem, Joseph's Tomb in Nablus, Rachel's Tomb in Bethlehem, and the Tomb of Abraham, Isaac, and Jacob in Hebron and have denied Jews access to these sites. Likewise, Muslims have occupied and dominated various Christian holy sites and denied Christians access to them. Such is the case with the Basilica of the Hagia Sophia which was constructed in Constantinople in 537 AD and served the center of Orthodox Christianity for nearly a thousand years until it was seized and ordered to be converted into a mosque by Ottoman Sultan Mehmed the Conqueror during his invasion of Constantinople in 1453 AD. The same is true with the Muslim occupation of the Saint John Church in Damascus in 634 AD when a mosque was built on the site of a razed Orthodox Christian basilica.

As anyone can see with even a cursory view of history, the "peaceful" and "religiously tolerant" religion of Islam has been utterly intolerant of other religions and has literally stolen the holy sites of Jews and Christians and then desecrated them by making them Muslim shrines. But that is only the tip of the iceberg, for through the centuries, frenzied Muslim fanatics have destroyed countless holy sites of a wide range of religions. ISIS, the latest incarnation of militant Islam, has destroyed numerous sites holy to Chaldean

[33] Clinton Bennett, *In Search of Muhammad* (London, UK: Wellington House, 1998), p. 47. Bennett points out that "some *Muslim* scholars have dismissed the whole account [of Muhammad's Jerusalem experience] as a Muslim adaptation of Zoroastrian myth" (emphasis added).

Christians and other religions in its crazed frenzy to defend its radicalized version of Islam.[34]

Unbelievably, the Muslim phantasmal revisionist history and its rapacious coopting of the Jewish Holy City for itself has even been extended by some Muslims to say that "the al-Aqsa mosque in al-Quds was long before Muhammad. The al-Aqsa mosque was built by Adam. There was no temple there, neither by Solomon nor by Herod. . . . These are fictions created by the Jews."[35] So there it is: Muslim mendacity taken to its illogical extreme. And there seems to be no extreme to which Muslim fanatics will not take their chimerical phantasmagoria in order to purloin the sacred elements of Jews and Christians and to destroy those of others. Muslim imaginations and perversions of history know no bounds.

## Temple Denial: Muslim Perversion of History

Muslim Arabs, especially "Palestinians," have concocted a perverse myth out of thin air, one that defies the imagination and utterly perverts history and archaeology. They boldly proclaim the abject lie that the Jewish temple in Jerusalem never existed, and they argue that the idea that such a structure existed is either a figment of the imagination of the Jewish people or an outright falsehood concocted by Zionist leaders in an attempt to give legitimacy to the Jewish claim of sovereignty over Jerusalem and the nation of Israel. If this Muslim "Temple Denial"[36] myth were not so tragic in consequences both for the Jewish people and for their Arab neighbors, it would be utterly laughable. Sadly though, Temple Denial "has become a central tenet of Palestinian nationalism," says Daniel Levin.[37]

[34] Andrew Curry, "Here Are the Ancient Sites ISIS Has Damaged and Destroyed," *National Geographic*, September 2015, posted at http://news.nationalgeographic.com/2015/09/150901-isis-destruction-looting-ancient-sites-iraq-syria-archaeology/. Curry reports that ISIS used pickaxes, bulldozers, and dynamite to destroy sanctuaries and shrines, including the Mar Elian Christian Monastery and the Syriac Catholic Monastery of Mar Behnam in Syria. It also destroyed the St. Elijah's Monastery near Mosul, Iraq, that stood for more than 1,400 years as a monument to Chaldean Christianity. Militant Islamists have also destroyed Buddhist and Hindu shrines because of the Qur'anic prohibitions of images. Chipamong Chowdhury, "Identity and Representation: Marma People in the Chittagong Hill Tracts, Bangladesh," in *Nationalism and Intra-State Conflicts in the Postcolonial World*, Fonkem Achankeng, ed. (Lanham, MD: Lexington Books, 2015), p. 335. Achankeng notes that in a "mechanism of Islamization" in 1986, 54 Buddhist temples and 22 Hindu shrines were destroyed. Also, Irving Chan Johnson, *The Buddha on Mecca's Verandah: Encounters, Mobilities, and Histories Along the Malaysian-Thai Border* (Seattle, WA: The University of Washington Press, 2012), p. 1121.

[35] Gerd Marie Ådna, "The Reception of Islamic Prophet Stories within Muslim Communities," in *Islamic Myths and Memories: Mediators of Globalization*, Itzchak Weismann, Mark Sedgwick, and Ulrika Mårtensson, eds. (Abingdon, UK: Routledge, 2014), p. 222.

[36] The term *Temple Denial* was first used in Dore Gold, *The Fight for Jerusalem: Radical Islam, the West, and the Future of the Holy City* (Washington, DC: Regnery Publishing, Inc., 2007), pp. 10–17.

[37] Daniel Levin, "Denial on the Temple Mount, *Forward*, Oct. 14, 2009, posted at http://forward.com/opinion/116770/denial-on-the-temple-mount/.

Before the Jewish people formed the nation of Israel and recovered the sovereignty over their own land that had been denied them for nearly two thousand years, the city of Jerusalem "was never regarded as particularly important to Muslims when it was under Arab rule."[38] In fact, between 1948 and 1967, "Jordan occupied East Jerusalem and treated the city as did the rest of the Arab world, as a backwater."[39] Strikingly, during the nineteen years that Jordan controlled Jerusalem, only one Arab leader, King Hassan of Morocco, ever visited there,"[40] says Denis Prager.

Temple Denial is a relatively new phenomenon that was created out of thin air by the Palestine Liberation Organization. In 1924, Temple Denial obviously did not exist even among Muslims, for at that time the *Waqf*,[41] the Supreme Moslem Council that controlled the Temple Mount, published a booklet for visitors to the holy site in which it was reported that the substructure of the al-Aqsa Mosque "dates probably as far back as the construction of Solomon's Temple."[42] Later, a 1932 version of this same booklet declared, "The site is one of the oldest in the world. Its sanctity dates from the earliest (perhaps from pre-historic) times. Its identity with the site of Solomon's Temple is beyond dispute."[43] From that time until the statehood of Israel was declared in 1948, there was no question as to the historical accuracy of designating Mount Moriah as the site of the first and second temples, both of which were Jewish shrines to the God of the *Tanakh*. At that time, however, the *Waqf* removed from its tourist guidebooks the correct information about the Temple Mount that it had used for decades. It was not until 1996 that the *Waqf* decided to claim "Solomon's Stables" as a prayer hall for the al-Aqsa Mosque by adding lights and floor tiles to the underground vaulted hall that likely dated to Second-Temple times, if not to the time of Solomon's Temple.

In 2000, Yasser Arafat made another fallacious assertion that Solomon's Temple was actually located near Nablus rather than on Mount Moriah

---

[38] Levin, "Denial."

[39] Levin, "Denial."

[40] Dennis Prager and Joseph Telushkin, *Why the Jews?: The Reason for Antisemitism* (New York: Simon & Schuster, 1983), p. 168.

[41] The *Waqf* or, more specifically, the Jerusalem Islamic Waqf, is the organization that since 1187 has been charged with the responsibility of managing the Islamic shrines on the Temple Mount in Jerusalem, including the Al-Aqsa Mosque and the Dome of the Rock.

[42] *A Brief Guide to al-Haram al-Sharif* (Supreme Muslim Council of Jerusalem, 1924), p. 4. This booklet also declares, "This, too, is the spot, according to universal belief, on which 'David built there an altar unto the LORD, and offered burnt offerings and peace offerings.' (2 Samuel 24:25)."

[43] *A Brief Guide*, p. 16. Steven Carol, *Understanding the Volatile and Dangerous Middle East: A Comprehensive Analysis* (Bloomington, IN: iUniverse, 2015).

in Jerusalem.[44] When Arafat repeated this perverse allegation during the 2000 Camp David Summit meeting with Israeli prime minister Ehud Barak and then argued that the Jewish Temple never existed, his lie "spread across the Middle East like wildfire from the editorial pages of *al-Jazirah* in Saudi Arabia to well-funded international seminars in the United Arab Emirates."[45] It was also in 2000 when the Palestinian Authority's mufti Sheik Ikrama Sabri took the Temple Denial argument much further by famously boasting that "there is not a single stone in Palestine that proves the Jewish existence [in Palestine]."[46] The PA mufti not only denied history; he also refused to hear the voices of the very stones of Israel that cry out continually as archaeology confirms the historical presence of the Jewish people in the Promised Land.

Subsequent to the Camp David Summit, Arafat "set about systematically dismantling the core Jewish claim to the city that had been accepted as axiomatic by Western civilizations for centuries,"[47] Gold says. Within three years, "Arafat's campaign had convinced a leading US weekly[48] to relate the existence of Jerusalem's biblical temples as a debatable matter of religious belief rather than historical fact."[49] Shortly thereafter, Western academia began to embrace the Arafat lie when the University of Chicago Press published a book by Nadi Abu El-Haj in which he deprecatingly described the two Jewish temples as a "national-historical tale."[50]

Arafat's Temple-Denial lies have gradually, but systematically, gained acceptance as fact by the Western media and by what has now become the most institutionalized bastion of antisemitism in history: the United Nations. As a matter of fact, on October 13, 2016, the World Heritage Committee of the United Nations Educational, Scientific and Cultural Organization (UNESCO), the UN body charged with preserving culture and history around the world, passed a resolution that called Israel an "occupying power" of both the

[44] Gold, p. 11.

[45] Gold, p. 12.

[46] Ikrama Sabri, quoted in *Al-Hayat Al-Jadida*, October 15, 2000.

[47] Gold, p. 12.

[48] This was *Time* magazine's October, 2003, issue in which Romesh Ratnesar stated that the Temple Mount was a place "where Jews believe Solomon and Herod built the First and Second Temples."

[49] Gold, p. 12.

[50] Dore Gold, "Defending Israel's Legal Rights to Jerusalem," in *Israel's Rights as a Nation-State in International Diplomacy*, Alan Baker, ed. (Jerusalem, Israel: Jerusalem Center for Public Affairs, 2011), p. 108. Gold refers to Nadi Abu El-Haj, *Facts on the Ground: Archaeological Practice and Territorial Self-Fashioning in Israeli Society* (Chicago, IL: The University of Chicago Press, 2001), p. 207. El-Haj's book, as its title indicates, is an effort to mythologize the history of the people and land of Israel so as to discredit the legitimacy of Jewish claims to the land of Israel.

Temple Mount and the Western Wall and demanded that Israel cease construction and excavation in the Old City of Jerusalem.[51] Then, on November 8, 2016, the UN General Assembly passed two resolutions that referred to the Temple Mount as "Haram al Sharif"—not the Temple Mount—as being one of the "holy places of Jerusalem."[52]

Meanwhile, back at the Temple Mount, the Palestinian Authority (PA), continued the campaign it had begun a decade earlier through Arafat's legacy of lies, deceit, corruption, and terrorism to cover its prevarications and dissimulations by destroying archaeological evidence of the existence of the Jerusalem Temple complex. With very little international condemnation, the PA systematically excavated tons of material from beneath the Temple Mount, using heavy equipment to violate one of the most precious and historically valuable archaeological sites in the world in order to destroy physical evidence which confirms the fact that the Jewish temple was a historical reality. With the reckless abandon that other Muslim jihadists have used to destroy priceless religious monuments in other parts of the world, these Muslim archaeological terrorists—consumed with the lying spirit that demanded cover for the monstrous lies of their master terrorist founder—desecrated and pillaged the world's holiest site. If, as the leaders of the PA claimed, there was no Jewish temple on the Temple Mount, why would they need to go to such great effort and expense to "destroy any archaeological evidence proving otherwise?"[53]

Richard Johnson, former chair of the Antiquities College at Columbia University, denounced the PA's perverse actions with the following fiery statement: "The most infuriating thing is that the Waqf is simply raping the Mount with impunity and destroying irreplaceable artifacts. Again, I believe it is a blatant effort to destroy any evidence of a Jewish temple, and therefore any Jewish claim on the Temple Mount. Do you

---

[51] "Full Text of New UNESCO Resolution on 'Occupied Palestine," *The Times of Israel*, October 13, 2016, posted at http://www.timesofisrael.com/full-text-of-new-unesco-resolution-on-occupied-palestine/. Also, Oren Libermann, "Israel Suspends Ties with UNESCO in Spat over Jerusalem Holy Site," CNN.com, October 14, 2016. Seven of the ten members of this committee represented Muslim-majority nations. Sadly, the perverse actions of UNESCO still continue unabated, for on July 7, 2017, this antisemitic body added the City of Hebron to its World Heritage List as a site in the "State of Palestine," when no such state even exists, and it declared the Tomb of the Patriarchs, Judaism's second holiest site after the Temple Mount, to be a "world heritage site in danger." Aaron Klein, "UNESCO Recognizes Hebron's Tomb of the Patriarchs—Judaism's Second Holiest Place—as Palestinian Heritage Site, *Breitbart News*, 7 Jul 2017, posted at http://www.breitbart.com/jerusalem/2017/07/07/unesco-recognizes-hebrons-tomb-of-the-patriarchs-judaisms-second-holiest-place-as-palestinian-heritage-site/.

[52] Tovah Lazaroff, "UN in New York Votes on Ignoring Jewish Ties to Temple Mount," *The Jerusalem Post*, November 8, 2016. Posted at http://www.jpost.com/Arab-Israeli-Conflict/UN-in-New-York-votes-on-ignoring-Jewish-ties-to-Temple-Mount-472040.

[53] Gold, p. 15.

know that in the last few years, the Waqf has had the audacity to bring bulldozers—*bulldozers*—into the area under the Mount that some have called Solomon's Stables? And the bulldozers have dug out thousands of yards of dirt, poured it into dump trucks, and hauled the dirt to a dump, all without any oversight or supervision from international archaeological agencies."[54]

Why would the PA have undertaken such monumental efforts to deny the existence of the Jewish temple? Presumably, they "reasoned" that if all physical evidence of the Temple Mount could be obliterated, then the Jews' claims to the land of Israel as their ancestral home and to Jerusalem as their capital city would be profoundly diminished, if not altogether destroyed. And, the likelihood that the Third Temple could be built either before or after the coming of the Messiah would be obviated.[55] If the Jews could be shown to have no history, then they would also have no future. Does this not, in effect, represent the fabrication of a new set of garments for the old Führer himself? Is it not just another iteration of the grand design of antisemitism from time immemorial until the present? Does it not mean that once and for all the Jews and their God could finally be destroyed, thereby freeing the earth and its inhabitants from the scourge of Jewish absolute ethics and divine demands on human conduct? Would humanity not finally be free?

In reality, Temple Denial is just as devastating to the claims of Christianity as it is to those of Judaism, for if the Jewish Temple never existed, the Apostolic Scriptures are full of fabricated references to it. If there were no Jewish Temple, how did Jesus walk in its precincts?[56] How did he engage in cleansing the sanctuary by overturning the tables of money-changers and the purveyors of sacrificial animals?[57] If there were no Jewish Temple in Jerusalem, how did Peter and John approach the "Gate Beautiful" and heal the lame beggar?[58] It is clear from Christian Scripture that the disciples of Jesus and the foundational pillars of the

[54] Richard Johnson, quoted in Terry Brennan, *The Sacred Cipher* (Grand Rapids, MI: Kregel Publications, 2009), p. 139.

[55] Temple Denial by the Arab Muslims has a nonsensical precursor. In 1541 AD the Ottoman Sultan Suleiman the Magnificent ordered the sealing of Jerusalem's Eastern Gate (as it remains to this day) in an effort to preclude the possibility of the Jewish hope that the Messiah would enter that gate when he would come to Jerusalem from the Mount of Olives on the east in fulfillment of Ezekiel 44:2 and Zechariah 14:4. Tradition also suggests that Suleiman might have ordered the construction of a cemetery outside that gate in order to prevent the precursor of the Messiah, the prophet Elijah, from entering Jerusalem (since he was a priest and could not enter a cemetery lest he become ceremonially unclean).

[56] Luke 2:41–52.

[57] Matthew 21:12–13.

[58] Acts 3:9–10.

Christian church considered their presence in and participation with the Temple and its order and rituals to be a commonplace part of their existence as Jews who believed Jesus was the Messiah.[59] The Acts of the Apostles documents the continuing interaction of the community of believers in Jesus with the temple, its officers, and its rituals.[60]

For nearly two decades, Muslim Arabs have exhausted themselves and have expended great resources all in an effort to transfer their lie of Temple Denial into "fact," and they have done so with such bravado, volume, and frequency that others actually believe their lies to be the truth. And, just like so many lemmings, Western postmodernist politicians and the perverse Western press follow in lock step with the Arab Muslims to promote the lie of the century so that they can vent their innate antisemitism and call for the ethnic cleansing of all Jewish presence and influence in the land of Israel. These antisemites have their own "final solution" for Palestine, and it is the same as the Nazis' *Endlösung*: once and for all, make Palestine *Judenrein*, cleansed of Jews and Jewish influence. Until then, no lie is too preposterous, no treachery is too insidious, no theft of property and identity is too egregious, and no murderous act of terror is too horrendous not to be used in the quest for "restoring" the Jewish land to its rightful owners, the Arab "Palestinians."

Raymond Apple has wisely observed that the "denial of the facts is an insidious modern sport. . . . We wonder how any sensible person can be so unfeeling, inhuman and insane as to fly in the face of overwhelming evidence. Yet some so-called scholars still persist in saying that black was white and white was black. If truth is no longer sacred, then nothing is safe."[61] Revisionist "history" is a blood sport for postmodernist nihilists who utterly deny the existence of truth and whose only absolute is their absolute certainty that there are absolutely no absolutes. For them, every aspect of history must be rewritten in order to accommodate their own view of the way things should have been, and they radically enforce their denial of historical facts with whatever fascist authoritarianism is needed to achieve their goals.

---

[59] Acts 5:42: "And every day, in the temple and from house to house, they kept right on teaching and preaching Jesus as the Christ."

[60] Acts chapters 2, 3, 5, 21, 22, 24, and 26 give accounts of the apostles' activities in the temple and its precincts. Acts 21:26 specifically says that Paul "went to the temple . . . with the other men" where they "started the purification ritual."

[61] Raymond Apple, *Let's Ask the Rabbi* (Milton Keynes, UK: AuthorHouse UK, Ltd., 2011), p. 141.

CHAPTER 15

# TACTICS OF NEW ANTISEMITISM

## Prevarication, Deception, and Fraud

A stunning array of new strategies has been devised by the proponents of anti-Israelism to accompany the new guises of the old antisemitism.[1] Some, if not most, of these are so utterly absurd that a reasonable person would think they could never gain any traction, much less widespread acceptance. Prominent among these strategies is Holocaust denial,[2] the bold-faced lie that insists that the Holocaust never happened, despite the fact that it and its effects were highly documented by both the Nazis themselves and by the Western nations that conquered them. In addition to that—and perhaps equally insidious—is the program of inversion that the anti-Zionist movements have used wherein they accuse Israel and the Jewish people of employing the tactics that they themselves use while holding the anti-Israelists guiltless or excusing their acts as legitimate "Palestinian" responses to Israeli abuse.

This is a classic example of the human depravity which God excoriated through the prophet Isaiah when he said, "Woe to those who call evil good and good evil, who substitute darkness for light and light for darkness, who substitute bitter for sweet and sweet for bitter."[3] Muslim nations and peoples, Western nations, and other proponents of the new anti-Zionist antisemitism employ a stunning array of tactics in which they engage in political and historical inversion to construct and launch totally fabricated indictments against Israel. Such actors are classical inversionists, those who "habitually write upside down

[1] Manfred Gerstenfeld, *The War of a Million Cuts: The Struggle Against the Delegitimization of Israel and the Jews, and the Growth of New Anti-Semitism* (New York: RVP Press, 2015).

[2] Robert Jan van Pelt, *The Case for Auschwitz: Evidence from the Irving Trial* (Bloomington, IN: Indiana University Press, 2002).

[3] Isaiah 5:20.

and backward"![4] What they say is so utterly the opposite from what is true that their arguments appear as so much gobbledygook, the stuff of gibberish, claptrap, balderdash, and nonsense.

## Denying the Holocaust: Deconstructing History

Holocaust denial has become a centerpiece of the new antisemitism that has been promoted by the Muslim Arab community and supported by many Western ideologues and media organizations for decades now.[5] Robert Wistrich describes this perfidious activity: "Lying about the Holocaust . . . is a postwar phenomenon at whose core lies the rejection of the historical fact that six million Jews were murdered by the Nazis during World War II."[6] It represents the effort of antisemites to cover up the most vile event of human history[7] and thereby further deny the right of the Jewish people to a safe and secure corporate home in the land of their ancestors.

In 1982, in his doctoral dissertation and in a later Arabic book, Mahmoud Abbas, the current president of the Palestinian Authority, argued that "the Zionist movement led to a broad campaign of incitement against the Jews living under Nazi rule to arouse the government's hatred of them, to fuel vengeance against them and to expand the mass extermination."[8] Then, he "described the murder of 6 million Jews as a 'myth' and a 'fantastic lie'" and, quoting the French academic Robert Faurisson's denial of the existence of the Nazi gas chambers, he concluded the events in Germany involved the death of less than a million Jews.[9] Jeremy Havardi exposes the real reason for Holocaust denial in the Muslim Arab world: "Acceptance of the genocide perpetrated against the Jewish would make normalization with the Jewish state much easier. It

[4] This, the *Merriam-Webster Dictionary* definition of the term *inversionist*, is a perfect description of Palestinians and their companions in crime. *Merriam-Webster Dictionary*, posted at https://www.merriam-webster.com/dictionary/inversionist.

[5] Deborah E. Lipstadt, *Denying the Holocaust: The Growing Assault on Truth and Memory* (New York: Simon & Schuster, 1993).

[6] Robert S. Wistrich, ed., *Holocaust Denial: The Politics of Perfidy* (Berlin, Germany: Walter de Gruyter GmbH & Co., 2012), p. 1.

[7] Robert Eaglestone, *Postmodernism and Holocaust Denial* (London, UK: Icon Books, 2001). Also Wistrich, ed., *Holocaust Denial*, and Michael Shermer and Alex Grobman, *Denying History: Who Says the Holocaust Never Happened and Why Do They Say It?* (Berkeley, CA: The University of California Press, 2000).

[8] Mahmoud Abbas, quoted in Jo Roberts, *Contested Land, Contested Memory: Israel's Jews and Arabs and the Ghosts of Catastrophe* (Toronto, Canada: Dundurn Press, 2013), p. 158. Abbas' dissertation was entitled, *The Connection Between the Nazis and the Leaders of the Zionist Movement.*

[9] Jeremy Havardi, *Refuting the Anti-Israel Narrative: A Case for the Historical, Legal and Moral Legitimacy of the Jewish State* (Jefferson, NC: McFarland & Company, Inc., Publishers, 2016), p. 183. Havardi references Mahmoud Abbas, *The Other Side: The Secret Relationship Between Nazism and Zionism* (Amman, Jordan: Dar Ibn Rushd lil-Nashr wal-Tawzi', 1984). Though Abbas claimed to have changed his views on the Holocaust in 2003, it is clear that he still supports the views of Holocaust Denial.

would provide moral justification for a Jewish state and strip away the pretense that Palestinians are the greatest victims of the modern age."[10]

Susan Drummond reports that 40 percent of Palestinians living in Israel claim that the Holocaust never happened, a fact that prompted her to ask this critical question about Palestinian Holocaust denial: "If Palestinian citizens of Israel are increasingly denying the paramount existential *raison d'être* of the state, then how can one hope that Palestinians who want to form a state next to Israel—let alone have the right to flood back into the state in accordance with a Palestinian right of return—would begin to accept this foundational narrative?"[11]

In other parts of the world, the collective memory of the Holocaust seems to have affected different nations in different manners. On the one hand, Poland, which before World War II was one of the focal points of European antisemitism[12] has now made strides in calling for resistance to racism and antisemitism[13] with the result that "philo-Semitism has grown in Poland, even in the absence of Jews."[14] On the other hand, France, which transitioned from being Europe's most tolerant nation toward Jews from the time of Napoleon until well into the twentieth century, actively collaborated with the Nazis during World War II and largely because of its large Muslim population has now become one of the most antisemitic nations in Europe. Similarly, England, which transitioned from centuries of antisemitism under its monarchy to fighting against Nazi Germany and denouncing antisemitism and the Holocaust, has now permitted a resurgence of antisemitism, which is generally promoted by Muslim immigrants but also involves postmodernist multiculturalism.

Could it be that latent antisemitism foments itself when it is not restrained by government and a general populace that recognizes

[10] Havardi, p. 183.

[11] Susan G. Drummond, *Unthinkable Thoughts: Academic Freedom and the One-State Model for Israel* (Vancouver, Canada: The University of British Columbia Press, 2013), p. 59.

[12] Daniel Chirot, "Comparing World War II Memories," in *Confronting Memories of World War II: European and Asian Legacies*, Daniel Chirot, Gi-Wook Shin, and Daniel Sneider, eds. (Seattle, WA: The University of Washington Press, 2014), p. 32.

[13] On the fiftieth anniversary of the liberation of Auschwitz, the Catholic Church in Poland issued a statement that expressed "regret for the complicity of some Polish Christians in [the Holocaust]" and noted that "Auschwitz was set up on occupied Polish territory and held many Poles who were, like Jews, victims of German oppression." At the same time, however, it concluded "with a call to resist racism and anti-Semitism." See Polish Catholic Bishops, "The Victims of Nazi Ideology," *Origins* 24, no. 34 (9 February 1995), pp. 586–588, posted at www.jcrelations.net/en/?item=1034. Also noted in Jeremy M. Bergen, *Ecclesial Repentance: The Churches Confront Their Sinful Pasts* (New York: T & T Clark International, 2011), p. 47.

[14] Elazar Barkan, Elizabeth A. Cole, and Kai Struve, *Shared History, Divided Memory: Jews and Others in Soviet-Occupied Poland 1939–1941* (Leipzig, Germany: Erscheint im Leipziger Universitätsverlag GmbH, 2007), p. 20. Also, Ruth Gruber, *Virtually Jewish: Reinventing Jewish Culture in Europe* (Berkeley, CA: The University of California Press, 2002).

antisemitism for the evil that it is, repents for having manifested it or acquiesced to it, and vows never again to tolerate it under any circumstances? Or could it be that there have never been any gas chambers or crematoria in France and England as, due to the Nazis, there were in Poland to serve as continual reminders of the horror of the Holocaust? Indeed, there are very few physical reminders of the horrors of the Holocaust that confront the daily lives of the French and British.

## The Boycott, Divestment, Sanctions Movement

The Boycott, Divestment, Sanctions Movement (BDS) was begun by the Palestinian BDS National Committee on July 9, 2005, as an effort to create and apply economic and political pressure in order to force Israel to bow to Palestinian Authority demands that Israel surrender control of the West Bank, the Golan Heights, and Jerusalem to the PA, that it allow "Palestinian refugees" to return to Israel, and that it grant "full equality" to Arab citizens of Israel.[15] The ultimate design of the BDS movement is to bring about the political, social, and economic isolation of Israel and to create such financial and social hardships for the Jewish people that they will capitulate to the demands of the Muslim Arab terrorists who control the PA and its subsidiaries. This is nothing more than a twenty-first century antisemitic effort to isolate the Jewish people in yet another ghetto where they can be more easily exploited, abused, and murdered. The BDS movement employs the same strategies that the Nazis used to isolate and destroy the Jews:[16] boycott Jewish businesses and constrict Jewish movement to areas where they are most vulnerable.[17]

The movement enlists the support of willingly ignorant Westerners who support the preposterous propaganda of the PA and feed their own antisemitism with lies about Israel and the Jewish people. Of course,

---

[15] For the pro-BDS argument, see Omar Barghouti, *BDS: Boycott, Divestment, Sanctions: The Global Struggle for Palestinian Rights* (Chicago, IL: Haymarket Books, 2011), and Audrea Lim, *The Case for Sanctions against Israel* (London, UK: Verso, 2012). It should be noted that Omar Barghouti is a cousin of Marwan Barghouti, who is a convicted terrorist. For the anti-BDS argument, see Jed L. Babbin and Herbert I. London, *The BDS War Against Israel: The Orwellian Campaign to Destroy Israel* (New York: The London Center for Policy Research, 2014), and Philip Mendes and Nick Dyrenfurth, *Boycotting Israel Is Wrong: The Progressive Path to Peace between Palestinians and Israelis* (Sydney, Australia: University of New South Wales Press, 2015).

[16] American Zionism, "Comparison of Nazi Policies and BDS" posted at https://americanzionism.wordpress.com/2016/03/13/comparison-of-nazi-policies-and-bds/.

[17] While the BDS movement bills itself as "an inclusive, anti-racist human rights movement that is opposed on principle to all forms of discrimination, including anti-semitism and Islamophobia" (https://bdsmovement.net/what-is-bds) and while many prominent public figures support the movement, BDS actions confirm its inherent antisemitism.

the BDS movement insists that its blatant anti-Zionism is not antisemitism; however, "there are good reasons to think the contrary."[18] Elhanan Yakira says, "What subsumes these allegedly different—antisemitism and anti-Zionism—phenomena under one generic title is not the *content* of the affective or ideological attitudes they manifest but what can be referred to as their common *moral substance*. For in both cases, what is under attack is the legitimacy of a certain concrete form of life, of ways, more precisely, in which Jews have chosen to live their life."[19]

## Boycotts

Organized efforts to promote boycotts against Israel are wide ranging and indiscriminate, essentially targeting anything and everything that can be connected with Israel, including its businesses, universities, and social and political systems. Boycotts are nothing new for Israel, however, for only three years after Israel's war of independence in 1948, the Arab League "formalized its boycott against the state of Israel by broadening it to include non-Israelis who maintained economic relations with Israel or who were perceived to support it."[20] Amazingly, these boycotts have been expanded so that they include the boycotting of Israeli academic institutions.[21] In 2013, an academic boycott was even imposed upon Israeli academia by the American Studies Association, a boycott that just happened to be the only one which that organization had imposed upon anyone in its entire history![22] Additionally, the boycotts have even been extended to include cultural events like musical performances in Israel and performances of Israeli actors and musicians in other nations.

The antisemites who lead the efforts to boycott Israel and Israeli products and institutions have modeled their own efforts on the extensive and successful boycott that was launched in 1959 against South Africa over the

[18] Elhanan Yakira, "Five Reflections on Holocaust Denial, Old and New Forms of Hatred of Jews and the Deligitimation of Israel," in *Antisemitism before and since the Holocaust*, Anthony McElligott and Jeffrey Herf, eds. (New York: Palgrave Macmillan, 2017), p. 338 (author's emphasis).

[19] Yakira, p. 338.

[20] Kenneth L. Marcus & Ilan Troen, "Anti-Jewish Boycotts in History," in *Dreams Deferred: A Concise Guide to the Israeli-Palestinian Conflict & the Movement to Boycott Israel*, Cary Nelson, ed. (Bloomington, IN: Indiana University Press, 2016), p. 30. Nelson gives a broad overview and summary of all the many boycotts that have been directed at Israeli institutions and businesses.

[21] For an overview of arguments in favor of the boycott of Israeli academic institutions, see Ashley Dawson and Bill V. Mullen, *Against Apartheid: The Case for Boycotting Israeli Universities* (Chicago, IL: Haymarket Books, 2015). For views opposing the boycott of Israeli academic institutions, see Cary Nelson and Gabriel Brahm, *The Case Against Academic Boycotts of Israel* (New York: MLA Members for Scholars' Rights, 2014).

[22] Elizabeth Redden, "Backing the Israel Boycott," *Inside Higher Education*, 17 December, 2013.

issue of apartheid. The BDS movement has specifically called for boycotting Israel because of its contention that Israel is an "apartheid" state. The comparison of Israel with South Africa is utterly absurd, for there is simply no semblance of apartheid in Israeli society. In fact, the Muslim Arab nations and the "Palestinian" people that support the boycott are themselves the epitome of apartheid in their nations and in their communities.

The boycott movement operates under the guise of "human rights" while it entirely ignores the "human rights" of the six million Jews who live in Israel. Nations that enforce real apartheid are ignored or excused just as nations that engage in gross human rights violations are ignored or excused as "culturally different" and, therefore, innocent of apartheid. The BDS movement is designed to impact Israel's economy negatively and to make Israel—and its six million Jewish inhabitants—a pariah in world politics and economics. This action differs little from the shattering and shuttering of Jewish businesses in Nazi Germany on *Kristallnacht* on November 9–10, 1938, the Nazi boycott of Jewish businesses, and the ostracization, humiliation, ghettoization, and eventual extermination of the Jewish people in Germany. The motivation of the boycott movement today is the same as it was in Nazi Germany. It is antisemitism, pure and simple, and those who foment the effort are antisemites, pure and simple.

## Demands for Divestment

One of the growing tactics of the radical left against those with whom they disagree has been the call for divestiture of investments in the businesses that support the economies of those nations or people groups that they oppose or that provide resources and equipment for those nations.[23] Divestment efforts are organized to induce individuals and institutions "to withdraw their investments in one or more companies based on political, rather than financial, considerations."[24] The current anti-Israel BDS movement has deployed its tactics against "a variety of civil society arenas, including universities, labor unions, churches, and the socially responsible investing community."[25] For some time now, Palestinian Arabs and their supporters have promoted the use of the same tactic in their ongoing battle against Israel.

[23] This tactic was used effectively in the drive to bring down the apartheid government in South Africa.

[24] Cary Nelson, "Divestment Campaigns," in *Dreams Deferred*, p. 168.

[25] Nelson, p. 168.

Divestment campaigns are designed to restrict investment in Israeli commercial enterprises and in business and industry that does business with Israel. Generally, however, such campaigns have been minimally effective; however, the hope among the anti-Israel antisemites is that they will gain momentum in a way similar to the results of the similar campaign against South Africa, which collapsed the apartheid government. The promoters of the BDS movement against Israel, therefore, try to draw parallels between the circumstances of the black Africans in South Africa and the "Palestinians" in Israel in hopes of producing the same results that were achieved in South Africa.

"The nightmare scenario" of the anti-Israel BDS Movement has the movement "gaining more traction and anti-Israel opinion moving from Western campuses to governments, followed by a lifting of the protective American diplomatic umbrella," says the Jewish Telegraphic Agency news service.[26] Because of Israel's advanced position in global technology, however, such efforts generally fail to produce the desired results.[27] E. J. Clark and Brooks Agnew point out that Israel leads the world in medical equipment patents, ranks second in the world of space sciences, ranks first in the world in usage of solar plants and invented much of the technology, ranks third in the world in scientific institutions, and is ranked number two in the world for venture capital funds (behind the US).[28] The entrepreneurship of the Israeli people severely restricts divestment efforts initiated by Muslim Arabs and their Western accomplices.

## Sanctions

The Palestinian Authority has also sought the imposition of political and economic sanctions upon the nation of Israel from various entities, including the United Nations, the European Union, and individual nations in various parts of the world. The latest such effort took place when the United Nations Security Council, with the abstention of the United States, passed Resolution 2334 on December 23, 2016, condemning

[26] Barghouti, p. 10.

[27] David Singer and Lawrence Grossman, *American Jewish Yearbook 2005* (Atlanta, GA: American Jewish Committee, 2006), p. 170. Also, Joel Benin, "North American Colleges and Universities and BDS," in Lim, ed., p. 74.

[28] E. J. Clark and Brooks A. Agnew, *The Ark of Millions of Years: Book of Updates* (Bloomington, IN: AuthorHouse, 2011), p. 212. Also, Miriyam Aouragh, "Revolutionary Manoeuvrings," in *Media and Political Contestation in the Contemporary Arab World: A Decade of Change*, Lena Jayyusi and Anne Sofie Roald, eds. (New York: Palgrave Macmillan, 2016), p. 143. The stature of Israel and its citizens in the world of science and technology stymies the efforts of the anti-Israel BDS Movement.

Israeli settlements in "Palestinian territories occupied since 1967, including East Jerusalem."[29] In effect, this absurd resolution recognized the "Palestinian" claim to the Temple Mount and denied Israel's right thereto. Of course, this resolution for sanctions came as no surprise, for since 1948, the UN Security Council has passed 226 resolutions relating to Israel, while the UN General Assembly has passed some 400 resolutions relating to sanctions against Israel. With all the violence and open warfare around the world, one can only wonder why the United Nations seems so utterly and obsessively preoccupied with the only democratic state in the Middle East.[30] The answer must be very simple and apparent: the United Nations is essentially an antisemitic organization.

## Collusion with the Perfidious Western "News" Media

Whatever charge is in vogue in the politically correct world of the "tolerant" postmodernism finds easy targets among the Jews and Israel.[31] The Western media are especially devious and corrupt in adopting and promulgating such accusations as "undeniable facts." In fact, when they actually believe the utterly preposterous myths that are fabricated on a regular basis by Palestinian Arabs and Muslims of various backgrounds and then vaunted as "news," some Western journalists demonstrate an incredible level of naïveté. This is especially true when they ignore the simple fact "that the Arab world does not maintain journalistic standards according to western values."[32] When Western media are "exposed to the popular 'Palestinian story' . . . their sympathy for that narrative grows and, eventually, they become dependent on those Palestinian sources" for their information.[33] Then, such deceitful Muslim "media"[34] create totally

[29] Steven Rosefielde, *Trump's Populist America* (Hackensack, NJ: World Scientific Publishing Co., 2017), p. 181.

[30] Margret Müller, *The World According to Israeli Newspapers: Representations of International Involvement in the Israel-Palestinian Conflict* (Berlin, Germany: Herstellung durch Frank & Timme GmbH, 2017), p. 5.

[31] Alan Dershowitz, *The Case Against Israel's Enemies: Exposing Jimmy Carter and Others Who Stand in the Way of Peace* (Hoboken, NJ: John Wiley & Sons, Inc., 2008). Dershowitz methodically counters charges by former US President Jimmy Carter that Israel employs apartheid policies. He also makes a defense against arguments that many have made for boycotting Israeli academic institutions and for divesting from Israeli businesses. Additionally, he builds a strong case against the violent and militant Islamist nation of Iran.

[32] Ron Schleifer and Jessica Snapper, *Advocating Propaganda—Viewpoints from Israel: Social Media, Public Diplomacy, Foreign Affairs, Military Psychology, and Religious Persuasion Perspectives* (Eastbourne, UK: Sussex Academic Press, 2015), p. 58.

[33] Schliefer and Snapper, p. 58.

[34] The reports that follow were taken from comments on the 2001 Holocaust Memorial Day in Israel that were published in the English-language Iran Daily. Meir Litvak, "The Islamic Republic of Iran and the Holocaust: Anti-Semitism and Anti-Zionism," in *Anti-Semitism and Anti-Zionism in Historical Perspective: Convergence and Divergence*, Jeffrey Herf, ed. (Cambridge, UK: Routledge, 2007), p. 260.

unbelievable and outrageous claims like this: "[Palestinian villagers] spoke spontaneously how Nablus, Ramallah, and al-Khalil [Hebron] turned into modern-day Aushwitzes [*sic*], Treblinkas, and Bergen-Belsens," and they make comparisons of the "Nazi holocaust [*sic*] against the Jews" with the "Jewish-perpetuated holocaust [*sic*] against [the Palestinian Arabs]."[35] Such media-generated—or at least media-perpetuated—propaganda is void of reason and is totally lacking in traditional standards for ethical and responsible journalism.

Ultra-hyperbolical propaganda of this sort does not always reach media audiences in the West; however, it does influence naïve and sympathetic Western reporters and writers to such a degree that its vitriol filters down in other accusations against Israel that are equally preposterous, though less sensationalized. As Akbar Ahmed observes, "Hyperbole may be thought appropriate for the mob gathered in the Muslim city—wiping the enemy from the face of the earth, the mother of battles which would claim thousands of lives, and so on—but it translates badly in the international press."[36] On the other hand, some Western media journalists and analysts—particularly television personalities—gleefully report some of the most highly toxic Muslim propaganda as though it were fact, and they report some extreme incidents of supposed Israeli brutality as true when, in reality, they know that those incidents have been deliberately staged by the Palestinian Arabs, sometimes in collusion with those Western reporters themselves.[37] Some Western television crews have even "manipulated

[35] Litvak, p. 260. It is highly unlikely that most, if any, "Palestinian villagers" actually know anything about Treblinka and Bergen-Belsen, including the names of the places themselves!

[36] Akbar S. Ahmed, *Islam Today: A Short Introduction to the Muslim World* (London, UK: I.B. Tauris & Co., 1999), p. 219.

[37] Some incidents of supposed Israeli attacks on Palestinian Arabs have actually been produced and directed by Western television "news" crews. One example is the incident that sparked the Second Intifada in 2001 when, with cameras rolling, France 2's Jerusalem correspondent, Charles Enderlin, reported that twelve-year-old Mohammed al-Dura had been "gunned down in cold blood, even as he cowered for his life." Later, when Ederlin's camera footage was reviewed in a French court, a completely different story emerged. Melanie Phillips reports that "for whatever people think they saw in those 55 seconds, it was not the death of that boy. He was not killed by Israeli bullets; he was not killed at all. At the end of France 2's famous footage, he was still alive and unharmed. The whole thing was staged, a fantastic piece of play-acting, an elaborate fabrication designed to blacken Israel's name and incite the Arab and Muslim mobs to mass murder." Phillips explained that "after Enderlin pronounces the boy dead, the corpse mysteriously assumes four different positions." Then, she says that amazingly, "you see the cameraman's fingers making the "take-two" sign to signal the repeat of a scene," whereupon, "you see the lifeless martyr raise his arm and peep through his fingers—presumably to check whether his thespian services are still required or whether he can now get up and go home." Besides the other widespread bloodshed and destruction of property that this "incident" launched, a "mob of Palestinians shouting, 'Revenge for the blood of Mohammed al-Dura,' lynched two Israeli army reservists and dragged their mutilated bodies through the streets of Ramallah." Melanie Phillips, "Remember This? Palestinian Arab Propaganda Stages Fake Israeli 'Attacks' for Media," in *The Muslim Issue*, September 28, 2012, posted at www.themuslimissue.wordpress.com.

images of Palestinian youth throwing stones to portray them as very skilled fighters,"[38] and others have paid Palestinian Arab youth to add drama to their on-camera reports by engaging in rock-throwing incidents. With such duplicity common in the Muslim media and even not infrequent in the Western media, is it any wonder that the real issues of the Israeli–Palestinian conflict are barely covered and what is reported is more sensationalism that is designed to boost television ratings than it is serious journalism that seeks to discover and report the real issues and events?

## Training and Compensating Terrorists from Cradle to Grave

One of the most deplorable of all the tactics that are being employed by Muslim Arab leaders of anti-Zionist antisemitism is seen in two programs that the Palestinian Authority created. The first trains children from infancy to hate the Jewish people and to plan small lives for entering the glories of jihadism in order to terrorize and murder Jews. The second provides a lifetime stipend that is paid monthly to those who carry out terrorist attacks on Israelis or to their survivors when they either kill themselves in suicide bombings or when they are neutralized by the Israeli police or Defense Forces while carrying out their jihadist attacks on Israeli men, women, and children.

The Palestinian Authority guarantees that the obsessive hatred of the Muslim Arabs is carried on transgenerationally through organized and systematic programs for educating their children from the cradle in the pervasive libels against Israel and the Jewish people around the world. It is not an uncommon sight to see small children chanting anti-Israel and generally antisemitic slogans while they carry fake or real weapons in their small hands. From infancy, Palestinian children have it drilled into their minds that Jews are descendants of pigs and apes and that they are evil to the core, deserving nothing less than death. "On the 'Children's Club,' an educational show the PA sponsors for children, a young boy sings a song that includes these lyrics: 'When I wander into Jerusalem, I will become a suicide bomber.'"[39] In order to facilitate such diabolical exploitation of children by making them actually believe that being a jihadist suicide bomber is a high honor, a noble deed, "groups like Islamic Jihad have operated

[38] Nariman Awwad, *Beleaguered Word: Documentation of Israeli Aggression against the Palestinian Media* (Baghdad, Iraq: Ittihad al-Suhufiyin al-'Arab Press, 2000), p. 21. As Robert Bleakney notes, this is "quite a contrast to Mary Had a Little Lamb." Robert W. Bleakney, personal communication.

[39] Michael V. Uschan, *Terrorism in Today's World: Suicide Bombings in Israel and Palestinian Terrorism* (Milwaukee, WI: World Almanac Library, 2006), p. 18.

summer camps to convince youngsters to become bombers."[40] One such group leader said, "We are teaching the children that suicide bombing is the only thing that makes the Israeli people very frightened [and] that we have the right to do it."[41] As part of children's terrorism classes, "students drew pictures of Israeli victims of suicide attacks or self-portraits depicting themselves as armed and ready to give their lives for the cause."[42] Children are even dressed in fake suicide belts![43] Such groups as Hamas bombard "the general population with posters of martyrs" and teach "children from kindergarten upwards about the desirability of martyrdom" by "according the families of suicide bombers high social status."[44] This vile teaching has produced suicide bombers as young as ten who have sought to destroy Jews by killing themselves.[45] This kind of indoctrination and brainwashing of the most vulnerable members of society takes place in Islamist communities around the world, including the most liberal parts of the United States, where Islamist imams have openly prayed for the destruction of the Jews to the very last person (i.e., complete genocide).[46]

Another stunning aspect of the Palestinian Authority's strategy for terrorism against Israel and the Jewish people is its lifetime compensation package for any jihadist who attacks Jews in any manner, including suicide missions.[47] A significant portion of the budget of Hamas in particular is used to pay lifetime annuities to families of suicide bombers.[48] The practice is actually enshrined in Palestinian Authority "law," which, according to PA Law No. 14, provides that a lifetime monthly stipend be paid either to terrorists themselves (in the event that they survive their attacks) or to their surviving

[40] Uschan, p. 18

[41] Uschan, p. 18.

[42] Robert Greenberger, *Suicide Bombers* (New York: The Rosen Publishing Group, 2007), p. 42.

[43] William C. Banks, Renée de Neveres, and Mitchel B. Wallerstein, *Combating Terrorism: Strategies and Approaches* (Washington, DC: CQ Press, 2008), p. 279.

[44] Jeroen Gunning, "Social Movement Theory and the Study of Terrorism," in *Critical Terrorism Studies: A New Research Agenda*, Richard Jackson, Marie Breen Smyth, and Jeroen Gunning, eds. (Abingdon, UK: Routledge, 2009), p. 170.

[45] Israel W. Charny, *Fighting Suicide Bombing: A Worldwide Campaign for Life* (Westport, CT: Greenwood Publishing, 2007), p. 130.

[46] Egyptian-born American imam Ammar Shahin recently gave a highly antisemitic sermon at the Islamic Center of Davis, California, in which he predicted that "all Muslims would be called upon to kill all the Jews on 'the last day,'" and in which he prayed that Allah would liberate the al-Aqsa Mosque at the Temple Mount from the "filth of the Jews." Lucia I. Suarez. "California Imam Calls on Allah to Annihilate Jews" in *Fox News U.S.*, July 26, 2017, posted at http://www.foxnews.com/us/2017/07/26/california-imam-under-fire-after-asking-allah-to-annihilate-jews-in-sermon.html.

[47] Havardi, p. 182. Harvardi points out that these payments "paid the salaries of Palestinian prisoners held in Israeli jails for terror offenses, as well as 'monthly stipends to the families of suicide bombers.'"

[48] Ian J. Bickerton and Carla L. Klausner, *A History of the Arab-Israeli Conflict* (Abingdon, UK: Routledge, 2016), p. 320.

families. These payments amounted to some $250 million each year.[49] Julie Lenarz notes that while the average monthly wage in the United Kingdom in 2116 was $ 2,973, "under the Palestinian Authority's (PA) "Pay-for-Slay" programme, [in which] terrorists convicted of murder are entitled to monthly lifetime salaries,"[50] one Arab Muslim terrorist who recently murdered three members of an Israeli family while they were sharing their *Shabbat* dinner "will soon enjoy a generous monthly payment" of at least $3,120 per month for life.[51] As a matter of fact, in what can only be viewed as a bounty program, the more Jews that Palestinian terrorists kill, the greater their level of compensation is.[52] This "murder-for-hire" or "pay-for-slay" program encourages and rewards terrorists whose jihad kills and maims Israeli citizens.[53]

Terrorism, including suicide bombings, is, therefore, a central part of the Arab Muslim "Palestinian" civic and social philosophy. Killing Jews is glamorized as a holy act with lifetime compensation for the jihadist and his family and, in the world to come, the promise of living in paradise glorified as a martyr and pleasuring himself with seventy-two "dark-eyed" virgins.[54] Even though civilized nations have demanded that the Palestinian Authority cease and desist from its policy of compensating terrorists on the basis of the degree of their attacks, its leaders refuse to stop the practice that is enshrined in its legal code. There seems to be no end to which the PA will go in order to give vent to its virulent antisemitism and its blood oath to continue their enterprise until every Jew is either killed or driven from their ancestral homeland. And, after all, this is the ultimate goal of every jihadist: Kill the Jews—all of them, in the name of Allah.

[49] Times of Israel Staff, "Palestinians Paid Terrorists $1b in Past 4 Years, Knesset Panel Hears," *The Times of Israel*, May 29, 2017, posted at http://www.timesofisrael.com/palestinians-paid-terrorists-1b-in-4-years-knesset-panel-hears/. Also, Yossi Kuperwasser, "Incentivizing Terrorism: Palestinian Authority Allocations to Terrorists and their Families," *Jerusalem Center for Public Affairs*, posted at http://jcpa.org/paying-salaries-terrorists-contradicts-palestinian-vows-peaceful-intentions/. This stunning report details both the multiplied millions of dollars that the PA receives in "humanitarian aid" from various governments and the payments that the PA makes to terrorists.

[50] Julie Lenarz, "How Can the Palestinian Authority Defend Paying Lifetime Salaries to Terrorists Convicted of Murder?" *International Business Times*, July 27, 2017, posted at http://www.ibtimes.co.uk/how-can-palestinian-authority-defend-paying-lifetime-salaries-terrorists-convicted-murder-1632207.

[51] Lenarz, "How Can the Palestinian . . . " These "Pay-for-Slay" payments represent American and British tax dollars at work!

[52] Kuperwasser, "Incentivizing."

[53] Edwin Black, "How British and American Aid Subsidises Palestinian Terrorism," *The Guardian*, 11 November 2013, posted at https://www.theguardian.com/commentisfree/2013/nov/11/british-american-aid-subsidises-palestinian-terrorism

[54] Merav Nagel, *Addiction Is an Illness We All Share* (Bloomington, IN: XLibris Corporation, 2013), p. 29. Nagel says that Hamas officials have calculated that "2.5 million virgins [are] waiting martyrs." Also, Edna Erez, "Protracted War, Terrorism and Mass Victimization: Exploring Victimological/Criminological Concepts and Theories to Address Victimization in Israel," in *Large-Scale Victimisation as a Potential Source of Terrorist Activities*, U. Ewald and K. Turkoviç, eds. (Amsterdam, The Netherlands: IOS Press, 2006), p. 95.

CHAPTER 16

# DELEGITIMIZING ISRAEL

## The "New, Improved" Corporate Antisemitism

Why are so many people in virtually all of the nations of the world so emotionally distraught about the Jewish people?[1] Why, indeed, is hatred of the Jews—and the violence that is frequently associated with it—so commonplace in so many societies? Why are 18 million Jews so controversial in a world of 7.125 billion people?[2] Why does the nation of Israel, with only 6 million Jews, continue to be a pariah for so many?[3] Why does such a minuscule land mass of less than 11,000 square miles—a mere scintilla of Planet Earth's 24.6 million square miles[4]—continue to be a focal point of world controversy, as it has been century after century, decade after decade, year after year, day after day? Why, indeed, do the most ancient of historical invectives against the Jewish people and their nation and land continue to echo in unending news flashes and pundit commentary in today's print and electronic media? Amazingly, the same things that were spoken and written about Israel and the Jews centuries ago will, without doubt, continue to reverberate in tomorrow's headlines and breaking news bulletins! As Solomon said, "There is nothing new under the sun."[5]

Despite the record and witness of history and the truth that the Hebrew

[1] The United Nations, representing 193 of the world's nations, spends an inordinate amount of its time and funding on efforts to delegitimize Israel, all the while virtually ignoring human rights atrocities in a wide range of nations around the world. Neil J. Kressel, *The Sons of Pigs and Apes: Muslim Antisemitism and the Conspiracy of Silence* (Washington, DC: Potomac Books, Inc., 2012), p. 85, and David A. Harris, *In the Trenches: Selected Speeches and Writings of an American Jewish Activist* (Jersey City, NJ: KTAV Publishing House, 2004), vol. 3, p. 317.

[2] All the Jewish people in the world today (18.4374 million) represent only .25877% of the global population (7.125 billion).

[3] The Jewish citizens of Israel (6 million) represent only .08421% of the world population. The total citizenship of Israel (8.59 million) comprises only .12056% of the world population (7.125 billion).

[4] The present land mass of Israel (10,750 square miles) is .043623% of the inhabitable land mass of the earth (24,642,757 square miles) or .018659% of the total land mass of the earth (57,308,738 square miles).

[5] Ecclesiastes 1:9.

Scriptures confirm, many scholars—among them Christians, Jews, Muslims, and secularists—openly question the historicity of the people, the nation, and the land of Israel.[6] Nothing about the Jews, it seems, can be accorded a modicum of legitimacy. Though stories about the "perfidious Jews" have long endured,[7] for centuries Jews have consistently been denied definition as a "people." As a matter of fact, nearly 1800 years ago in the middle of the third century AD, Cyprian, the Christian bishop of Carthage, said, "Now the peoplehood of the Jews has been canceled; the destruction of Jerusalem was a judgement upon them; the gentiles rather than the Jews inherit the kingdom."[8] From that time forward, Susan Nowak notes, Christians came to support the specious argument which says "the crime of the Jewish people is so great that it annuls, repeals, rescinds the very identity of the Jewish people: to be *Klal Yisrael*, the Chosen People of God, a light to the nations sent to bring all peoples to the Covenant." Additionally, she says, this argument maintains that "without appeal, without reconsideration, the Jews are placed *outside the norms of human relationship.*"[9] As Harry Cargas has noted, Cyprian's statement was "used to justify the intimidation and even slaughter of Jews for seventeen centuries."[10]

When any people group can be viewed as being essentially subhuman, it becomes only a matter of time before calls for their eradication are raised. "The only possible meaning the so-called delegitimation of Israel can have is that the law (or some fanciful idea of law or of legality) not only forbids the existence of the 'Jewish State' but also actually and

---

[6] The effort to delegitimize the history of Israel as a people began with the Enlightenment and became a feature of eighteenth- and nineteenth-century German scholarship, including that of German Christians.

[7] For centuries, until Pope John XXIII decreed otherwise, the Good Friday services of the Catholic Church, prayer was offered for "the perfidious Jews." The Latin word *perfideles*, from which the term *perfidious* is derived, actually means "unfaithful" or "half-believers," as contrasted with the *fideles*, "believers." Eugene Fisher and Dennis McManus point out that "the theological polemics of Christian teaching against Judaism gradually drew out of the Latin word *perfidii* its modern connotations of treachery" and that the term *perfidious Jews* was subsequently used to reinforce the notion that the Jewish people were inherently evil. Eugene J. Fisher and Dennis D. McManus, "Good Friday Prayer for the Perfidious Jews," in *A Dictionary of Jewish-Christian Relations*, Edward Kessler and Neil Wenborn, eds. (Cambridge, UK: Cambridge University Press, 2005), p. 171. For expansive insight into the extremes to which the idea of the "Perfidious Jews" was taken in history, see Mary C. Boys, *Redeeming Our Sacred Story: The Death of Jesus and Relations between Jews and Christians* (Mahwah, NJ: Paulist Press, 2013).

[8] Cyprian, quoted in Franklin Littell, *The Crucifixion of the Jews* (Macon, GA: Mercer University Press, 1986), pp. 27–28. For further analysis, see Leonard P. Zakim, *Confronting Anti-Semitism: A Practical Guide* (Hoboken, NJ: KTAV Publishing House, 2000), p. 97, and Padraic O'Hare, *The Enduring Covenant: The Education of Christians and the End of Antisemitism* (Valley Forge, PA: Trinity Press International, 1997), p. 20.

[9] See Susan Nowak, *Christianity's Original Sin: Anti-Judaism,* posted at www.holocaustroad.org (author's emphasis).

[10] Harry J. Cargas, *Holocaust Scholars Write to the Vatican* (Westport, CT: Greenwood Publishing Group, 1998), p. 6.

positively commands its annihilation."[11] In today's world, the odds have been stacked against the establishment of a legitimate people called Israel, a legitimate nation called Israel, and a legitimate land called Israel. A world that increasingly has no absolutes, no moral standards, and little, if any, notion of absolute ethics, a world that is driven by glorified self-interest and, ultimately, by utter selfishness has no place for a people, a nation, and a land that rests on absolutes and particularity, especially those granted by the only sovereign of the universe: the God of Scripture.

## Delegitimizing Israel: The Jewish People

Scholars, politicians, and pundits have often argued that the biblical stories of Abraham, Isaac, Jacob, Moses, David, and Solomon are nothing more than myths that were created by sages in post-exilic Judea in order to establish at least a modicum of legitimacy to the Jewish claim to nationhood and to the land of Israel.[12] As Robert Bleakney observes, "even 'mainstream' biblical criticism effectively rejects the Bible's own metanarrative as not being historically reliable."[13] Among such critics is Jewish historian Shlomo Sand who, though he does not deny the right of modern Israelis "to live in a democratic, open, and inclusive state of Israel that belongs to all its citizens,"[14] argues that there was no such thing as "a Jewish people scattered across the world," any more than "five hundred years ago, there was no French people, no more than there was an Italian or Vietnamese people."[15] Sand even counters the argument of many scholars that a "Jewish people" actually came to exist in the second-century BC by saying that the Hasmonean Kingdom of that time "in no way amounted to a nation, and we can seriously question

[11] Elhanan Yakira, "Antisemitism and Anti-Zionism as a Moral Question," in *Resurgent Antisemitism: Global Perspectives*, Alvin H. Rosenfeld, ed. (Bloomington, IN: Indiana University Press, 2013), p. 61.

[12] Baruch Kimmerling, *The Invention and Decline of Israeliness: State, Society, and the Military* (Berkeley, CA: The University of California Press, 2001); David Ohana, *The Origins of Israeli Mythology: Neither Canaanites Nor Crusaders* (Cambridge, UK: The Cambridge University Press, 2012); Virginia Tilley, *The One-State Solution: A Breakthrough for Peace in the Israeli-Palestinian Deadlock* (Ann Arbor, MI: The University of Michigan Press, 2005); Raphael Patai and Jennifer Patai, *The Myth of the Jewish Race* (Detroit, MI: The Wayne State University Press, 1975); Nachman Ben-Yehudi, *Masada Myth: Collective Memory and Mythmaking in Israel* (Madison, WI: The University of Wisconsin Press, 1995); and S. Daniel Breslauer, *The Seductiveness of Jewish Myth: Challenge or Response?* (Albany, NY: The State University of New York Press,1997).

[13] Robert W. Bleakney, personal communication.

[14] Shlomo Sand, *The Invention of the Land of Israel: From Holy Land to Homeland*, tr. Jeremy Forman (London, UK: Verso Books, 2012), p.17.

[15] Shlomo Sand, *The Invention of the Jewish People*, tr. Yale Lotan (London, UK: Verso Books, 2009), p. 316.

whether it can be defined as a people."[16] Sand joins a chorus of scholars who trumpet the claim that Jewish attribution of a centuries-old history to the people of Israel is utterly illegitimate nonsense, a contrived effort by Zionists to establish and maintain power in the Middle East.

The truth is that Jews have been a "people" for some 4,000 years since the time of Abraham, but certainly for more than 2,000 years since the Hasmonean Dynasty. Their distinctiveness—and, indeed, their separation—has been well established from history and Scripture. The right of this distinct people group has established for them the legitimate claim to peoplehood, nationhood, and land. Sadly, as Tricia Miller observes, the Arab-Israeli conflict demonizes and delegitimizes the "Jewish Israelis as a people group."[17] In this way, "just as anti-Judaism is the seedbed of anti-Semitism, so too it and anti-Semitism provide the necessary fertile seedbed for anti-Zionism," which is "synonymous with anti-Judaism in that the right of Jews to exist in terms of their own self-understanding—in this case, the right to have a Jewish State in their ancient homeland—is denied them."[18] Ultimately, efforts toward "the delegitimization of Israel today amounts to delegitimizing Jewish existence per se."[19]

## Delegitimizing Israel: The Jewish Nation

Other scholars have sought to delegitimize Jewish claims to recognition of a "Jewish state" based on a historical nationhood dating from the beginning of the unified Davidic Kingdom in the tenth century BC until the Roman Diaspora after the Bar Kokhba revolt in the second century AD.[20] Niels Lemche says, "The Israelite nation . . . is a highly ideological construct created by ancient scholars of Jewish tradition in order to legitimize their own religious community and its religio-political claims on land and religious exclusivity."[21] Sand

---

[16] Sand, p. 317.

[17] Tricia Miller, *Jews and Anti-Judaism in Esther and the Church* (Cambridge, UK: James Clarke & Co., 2015), p. 198.

[18] Miller, p. 198.

[19] Michael Melchior, *Ma'ariv*, June 29, 2001, quoted in Uriel Abulof, *The Mortality and Morality of Nations* (Cambridge, UK: Cambridge University Press, 2015), p. 159.

[20] Keith Whitelam, *The Invention of Ancient Israel* (Abingdon, UK: Routledge, 1996); Gösta W. Ahlström, *History of Ancient Palestine* (Sheffield, UK: Sheffield Academic Press, 1993); Thomas L. Thompson, *Early History of the Israelite People* (Leiden, The Netherlands: Koninklijke Brill NV, 1992); Thomas L. Thompson, *The Mythic Past: Biblical Archaeology and the Myth of Israel* (New York: Basic Books, 1999); John Van Seters, *Prologue to History* (New Haven, CT: The Yale University Press, 1992); and Philip R. Davies, *In Search of Ancient Israel* (Sheffield, UK: Sheffield Academic Press,1992).

[21] Niels Peter Lemche, *The Israelites in History and Tradition* (Louisville, KY: Westminster John Knox Press, 1998), pp. 165–166.

agrees, maintaining that Zionist "historians" in the early twentieth century created the myth that "the people of Israel . . . became a nation issuing from the seed of Abraham" and that they did so because "Zionist colonization could certainly not have been undertaken without an ideological preparation that gave rise to the blossoming and crystallization of myths."[22] Sand, therefore, applauds the science of modern archaeology for what he calls the debunking of claimed historicity for an "Exodus from Egypt" and for proving that "the great, unified monarchy of David and Solomon never existed."[23]

Interestingly, scholars who had long endeavored to disprove biblical stories about the Israelite monarchy based on what they perceived as an absence of archaeological evidence for its existence recoiled in shock when Israeli archaeologists digging at Tel Dan near the northern border of Israel in 1993-94 uncovered a ninth-century BC stele inscribed with the Hebrew words בית דוד (*Beit David*). Since steles were tall stone monuments that were erected for commemorative purposes in the ancient world,[24] this discovery established unmistakable physical evidence for the existence of a "House of David" in the ninth century BC. Immediately after this discovery, however, the coterie of minimalist[25] scholars who had boldly trumpeted their conclusion that the Davidic Kingdom never actually existed immediately launched themselves into extraordinary contortions in order to try to explain away this discovery. Some suggested that the stele was a forgery or that it had been "salted in the tel by some desperate biblical literalist."[26] A frantic Philip Davies even resorted to the argument

[22] Sand, *Invention of the Jewish People,* p. 314.

[23] Sand, *Invention of the Jewish People,* p. 316. For details of this and other arguments against the historical revisionists, see Baruch Halpern, "Erasing History: The Minimalist Assault on Ancient Israel," in V. Phillips Long, ed., *Israel's Past in Present Research: Essays on Ancient Israelite Historiography* (Winona Lake, IN: Eisenbrauns, Inc., 1999), pp. 415–426.

[24] Steles were used in various parts of the ancient world for government proclamations or to mark borders. These monuments set aside space and established rules for conduct within territorial boundaries. The word *stele* comes directly from the Greek word *stele.* Sometimes the Latin *stela* is also used to describe these monuments.

[25] Megan Bishop Moore and Brad E. Keele, *Biblical History and Israel's Past: The Changing Study of the Bible and History* (Grand Rapids, MI: Wm. B. Eerdmans Publishing Co., 2011), p. 33. Biblical minimalism is a label given to a trend that was developed in the 1990s by scholars Niels Peter Lemche and Thomas L. Thompson from the University of Copenhagen who made arguments on biblical history based on their view that the biblical record is not reliable evidence for what actually happened in ancient Israel and that it is very problematic to consider Israel for historical study. Other scholars who shared this perspective included Philip R. Davies and Keith Whitelam. Thomas L. Thompson, *The Historicity of the Patriarchal Narratives* (London: T & T Clark, 2002) and John Van Seters, *Abraham in History and Tradition* (Brattleboro, VT: Echo Point Books & Media, 2014). For a comparison of mimimalism and maximalism, see Christopher D. Stanley, *The Hebrew Bible: A Comparative Approach* (Minneapolis, MN: Fortress Press, 2010), pp. 120–125.

[26] F. H. Creyer, "On the Recently Discovered 'House of David' Inscription," *Scandinavian Journal of the Old Testament* 8 (1994), pp. 14–15, referenced by Halpern in Long, p. 415.

that the Hebrew letters that formed David's name on the stele actually meant "uncle" or "kettle" so that the stele was actually a celebration of the "Kettle House"![27]

Apparently it is easier to argue from the *absence* of archaeological evidence than it is to accept the *presence* of archaeological evidence. Fortunately for the science of biblical studies, the ranks of scholars who recognize and affirm archaeological support for biblical narratives regarding the people, the nation, and the land of Israel is growing,[28] even though their findings are not without controversy. As more and more of the land of Israel is subjected to archaeological exploration, ancient mysteries continue to be unearthed, and evidence mounts for the historical accuracy of biblical narratives concerning the lives of patriarchs, kings, and prophets.[29]

## Delegitimizing Israel: the Jewish Land

Numerous scholars have also questioned the validity of the Jewish claims to the Land of Israel based on the historical entitlement to or control of the land by their ancestors.[30] The most strident of these are the producers or distributors of Arab propaganda who claim that the Jewish people have no right to any of the Land of Israel because there is "no evidence" that their ancestors ever lived there. Unfortunately, there are many Christian scholars who have joined the ranks of the Arab propagandists either out of sympathy for the "plight" of the Palestinian people[31] or out of their own personal animus for the Jewish

[27] Philip R. Davies, "'House of David' Built on Sand," *Biblical Archaeology Review,* July/August, 1994.

[28] For more balanced perspectives on archaeology and biblical studies, Israel Finkelstein and Amihai Mazar, *The Quest for the Historical Israel: Debating Archaeology and the History of Early Israel* (Atlanta, GA: The Society of Biblical Literature Press, 2007), and Neil Asher Silberman and Israel Finkelstein, *The Bible Unearthed: Archaeology's New Vision of Ancient Israel and the Origin of Its Sacred Texts* (New York: Touchstone, 2001). Perhaps the most objective study of biblical archaeology is David M. Rohl, *Pharaohs and Kings: A Biblical Quest* (New York: Crown Publishers, 1995). Rohl's work is especially balanced and pragmatic, lacking any ideological or theological agenda.

[29] James K. Hoffmeier, *Israel in Sinai: The Evidence for the Authenticity of the Wilderness Tradition* (Oxford, UK: Oxford University Press, 2005); Israel Finkelstein and Neil Asher Silberman, *David and Solomon: In Search of the Bible's Sacred Kings and the Roots of the Western Tradition* (New York: Simon & Schuster, 2006); John H. Sailhamer, *Biblical Archaeology* (Grand Rapids, MI: Zondervan Publishing, 1998).

[30] Uri Davis, *Apartheid Israel: Possibilities for the Struggle Within* (London, UK: Zed Books, 2003), p. 65. Davis takes arguments beyond the disputed "West Bank" by asserting that "Israeli claims to West Jerusalem, Safad or Jaffa, occupied in 1948–49, are as thoroughly invalid as Israeli claims to East Jerusalem, Hebron or Gaza, occupied in 1967." Davies believes that Jewish claim to any part of the land of Israel (Palestine) is illegitimate.

[31] Many Evangelical Christians have been recently swayed by inaccurate portrayals of the "suffering" of Palestinian Christians under Israeli "oppression." David Brog, "The End of Evangelical Support for Israel?" *The Middle East Quarterly,* Vol. 21, No. 2, Spring 2014, posted at http://www.meforum.org/3769/israel-evangelical-support. Also Stephen Sizer, *Christian Zionism: Road Map to Armageddon* (Downers Grove, IL: InterVarsity Press, 2004), p. 23.

people in general and Zionists in particular. Others have mistakenly followed the positions established by centuries of scholars who have smugly "proven" to their own satisfaction that the people described in the Hebrew Scriptures simply never existed and the events described there never occurred. They argue that both the characters and the events recorded in the sacred texts were part of an elaborate myth created by later people in an effort to legitimize their claims to the land and the power associated with it.

Davies has taken the lead in some circles, arguing against the notion that "Israel was the natural or rightful owner of this piece of land."[32] He blames the "sad state of affairs" of the Jewish State in the land of "Palestine" on the influence of the Bible in the West where "inherited Christian culture supports the notion that the territory west of the Jordan is and has always been somehow essentially 'the land of Israel.'"[33] Davies laments the fact that "biblical scholarship inevitably focuses on the Israelite identity of a land that has actually been non-Jewish in terms of its indigenous population for the larger part of its recorded history."[34] Such Christian scholarship joins with and adds strength to the pervasive secularist view regarding the land of Israel which maintains that any Jewish claim to the covenantal significance of such a land is not only a mere cultural construct but also worthy of general repudiation.[35]

Such pretensions and fabrications are patently false, for, despite all of the Gentile conquests, captivities, and diasporas, some direct descendants of Abraham, Isaac, and Jacob have lived in the Promised Land in an unbroken chain from the time of Abraham to the present. Though nobles and aristocrats were taken into captivity and though invading armies imposed their citizens upon the land, still not all of the Jews were ever removed. As Joan Peters says, "The Jewish presence in 'The Holy Land'—at times tenuous—persisted through its bloody history. . . . Buried beneath the propaganda—which has it that Jews 'returned' to the Holy Land after two thousand years of separation, where they found crowds of 'indigenous Palestinian Arabs'—is the bald fact that the Jews are

[32] Philip R. Davies, "Minimalism, 'Ancient Israel,' and Anti-Semitism," quoted in Diane Banks, *Writing the History of Israel* (London, UK: T & T Clark International, 2006), p. 217.

[33] Davies in Banks, p. 217.

[34] Davies in Banks, p. 217.

[35] A prime example of the secularist animus toward Israel was seen in the recent case of mega-publisher HarperCollins' creation of a "Middle East Atlas" in which the word *Israel* was purposefully omitted from a map of the Middle East while the words *Gaza* and *West Bank* were clearly identified. This was more than a Freudian slip. It was representative of the liberal secularist view that Israel should be "wiped off the map."

indigenous people on that land who never left, but who have continuously stayed on their 'Holy Land.'"[36] Israeli Prime Minister Benjamin Netanyahu said it well: "There is a Jewish people here, it has been here for close to 4,000 years, we recognize this people, we recognize their historic bond with this land and this city."[37]

It is of great importance, therefore, to note that, unlike Arab or Muslim claims to the land of Israel, the title of the Jewish people to the land was not appropriated by force of armed conquest. It was by divine gift wherein God himself drove out the previous inhabitants from the land. Marvin Wilson is right when he asserts that "military conquest may not be used to prove a nation's right to a given land."[38] Something more—much more—is required. In the case of Israel, it is a historically documented 4,000-year attachment to the land of Canaan, the real estate deeded unequivocally, eternally, and irrevocably to Abraham and to his lineal descendants in perpetuity by the God of the universe. This is an attachment in which Hebrews/Israelites/Jews have lived perpetually—even if in minuscule numbers—in their ancestral homeland despite the efforts of tyrants to evict them and turn their land into an inhospitable no-man's land. The indomitable Jewish will to remain in the land of their ancestors against all odds has further guaranteed their legitimacy as a people and their right as individuals and a collective to remain in that land regardless as to who or what may object to their presence or attempt to obviate the word of the God who said, "I am YHWH, I do not change; therefore, you children of Jacob are not consumed."[39] Israel is not a conquering nation; however, it is an obedient people who heeded the instruction of the Eternal to "go in and take possession of the land the LORD swore he would give to your fathers—to Abraham, Isaac, and Jacob—and to their descendants after them."[40]

## The Antisemites' Ultimate Goal: Denying the Jews Existence

For thousands of years, concerted efforts have been made to marginalize the Jews and to delegitimize their right to exist as a people or a

[36] Joan Peters, *From Time Immemorial: The Origins of the Arab-Jewish Conflict Over Palestine* (London, UK: Michael Joseph Publishers, 1985), p. 83.

[37] Benjamin Netanyahu, quoted in Jerome R. Verlin and Lee S. Bender, *Pressing Israel: Media Bias Exposed from A–Z* (Philadelphia, PA: Pavilion Press, 2012), p. 148.

[38] Marvin R. Wilson, *Our Father Abraham: Jewish Roots of the Christian Faith* (Grand Rapids, MI: Wm. B. Eerdmans Publishing Co., 1989), p. 266. Wilson rightfully warns of the dangers of "real estate theology" which even to this day can inflame passions and move people of various religious persuasions to acts that violate and preclude social justice.

[39] Malachi 3:6.

[40] Deuteronomy 1:8, NIV.

nation—and in their own land. When peoplehood is denied to any group of human beings, they come to be viewed as essentially subhuman, and it is only a matter of time before calls for their eradication are issued and then brutally enforced. This, of course, has been the greatest goal of antisemites throughout history. Whether they are Arab Muslims or Western postmodernists, anti-Zionists today hold the same passionate antisemitic agenda that all antisemites of history have espoused: to deny the Jews peoplehood, national sovereignty, and connection to and ownership of their own land. Shalem Coulibaly confirms the nature of this ongoing connection between anti-Israelists and their forebears, the antisemites of history: "It is worth noting that contemporary anti-Zionism is etched into Western civilization as it is in other human cultures. It is the typical Western way of approaching the Jewish 'being,' who has thus been turned into a global scapegoat."[41]

It is no wonder, then, that despite the fact that historical documentation confirms the existence of the Jewish nation,[42] the Jews have long been—and continue to be—denied acknowledgment as having been a historical nation, and their claim to nationhood today is considered by many—if not most—of the world's nations to be illegitimate.[43] And although undeniable physical and historical evidence supports the Jewish right to their ancestral homeland,[44] Jewish claims to the "Jewish state" in the land of Israel are considered illegitimate. For anti-Zionists, the land of Israel is, in the words of Yehoshafat Harkabi, an "aberration," an "anomaly," and an "artificial state"[45] that was nefariously produced by the evil machinations of Jews who wished to escape their rightful heritage as the forever-doomed

---

[41] Shalem Coulibaly, "Equations in Contemporary Anti-Zionism," in *Global Antisemitism: A Crisis of Modernity*, Charles Asher Small, ed. (New York: Institute for the Study of Global Antisemitism and Policy [ISGAP], 2014), p. 44.

[42] A thirteenth-century BC Egyptian stele makes this proclamation: ". . . carried off is Askelon; seized upon is Gezer; Yanoam is made as that which does not exist; Israel is laid waste, his seed is not. . . ." Archaeological evidence, therefore, supports the fact that shortly after the biblical account of the Israelite conquest of the land of Israel, Israel experienced an invasion by Egypt. Naomi E. Pasachoff and Robert Pittman, *A Concise History of the Jewish People* (Lanham, MD: Rowman & Littlefield Publishers, 1995), p. 14.

[43] Alan M. Dershowitz, "Countering Challenges to Israel's Legitimacy," in *Israel's Rights as a Nation-State in International Diplomacy*, Alan Baker, ed. (Jerusalem, Israel: World Jewish Congress, 2011), pp. 159–167.

[44] Haim Hillel Ben-Sasson, *A History of the Jewish People* (Cambridge, MA: Harvard University Press, 1976), pp. 315–316. Also Rachel Hachlili, *Ancient Jewish Art and Archaeology in the Land of Israel* (Leiden, The Netherlands: E. J. Brill, 1988), pp. 234–235; K. L. Noll, *Canaan and Israel in Antiquity: An Introduction* (New York: Sheffield Academic Press, 2001), p. 312; David Biale, *Power & Powerlessness in Jewish History* (New York: Schocken Books, 1986), p. 11; and Gordon K. Oeste, *Legitimacy, Illegitimacy, and the Right to Rule: Windows on Abimelech's Rise and Demise in Judges 9* (London, UK: T & T Clark International, 2011), pp. 215–217.

[45] Yehoshafat Harkabi, *Arab Attitudes to Israel* (Jerusalem, Israel: Keter Publishing House, 1972), p. 72. Harkabi notes that "Israel is only an anomaly and an aberration [that] is dubbed 'an artificial state' or 'an exceptional situation'."

wanderers of the earth[46] who deserved no sovereignty, no fixed dwelling place, no land of their own.[47]

In the midst of anti-Israelists, therefore, the Jewish people have been totally disenfranchised, judged unworthy of the basic human rights that all people require and deserve. These antisemites have denied Jews the right to be recognized as a people; they have disavowed the Jewish right to establish their own nation; and they have disavowed the right of the Jews to possess the land of their ancestors. The Jews, then, have been viewed by too many as no people, with no political commonwealth and no legal title to a land. In the view of their non-Jewish counterparts, Jews have been nobody and have been entitled to nothing. Essentially, they have had no right to exist.

[46] Sam Harris, *The End of Faith: Religion, Terror, and the Future of Reason* (New York: W. W. Norton & Co., 2004), p. 97. Harris notes that based on Augustine's argument, the Jews were "doomed to wander the earth bearing witness to the truth of scripture and the salvation of the gentiles. The suffering and servitude of the Jews was proof that Christ had been the messiah after all."

[47] Sadly, in history, many of the Jews themselves came to believe that they were exiled from their land because of their sins. As Stephen Wylen says, "The nations had their own reasons for oppressing the Jews, but the Jews themselves agreed that they deserved no more than to be treated as homeless exiles." Stephen M. Wylen, *Settings of Silver: An Introduction to Judaism* (Mahwah, NJ: Paulist Press, 2000), p. 167.

CHAPTER 17

# CHRISTIAN ANTI-ZIONISM

## Believers Beguiled or Just Willfully Ignorant?

During the twentieth century, much of the Christian church, which in history had either supported or condoned unrelenting attacks upon the Jewish people for over a thousand years, was duped into either endorsing, condoning, or ignoring the Third Reich and its atrocities. More recently, through the postmodern world of multiculturalism, the ancient antisemitism that eventuated in the Holocaust has found new forms for asserting itself in politically and socially acceptable forms. Sarah Cardaun explains the process by which this tragedy occurred: "Waxing and waning throughout the centuries, but never disappearing completely, in the past, antisemitism assumed religious, cultural, political, racist, and many other forms. . . . [W]hile often rearticulating familiar tropes, antisemitism also finds novel ways of expressing itself."[1]

### Arrogant Thinkers, Defying the Almighty

Since the end of the first century AD, when the Jewish apostles and disciples of Jesus were succeeded by Gentile leaders, the Christian church has often been arrogant toward and dismissive of the Jewish people. Christianity, which was founded on Hebrew block logic[2] of joyous acceptance and obedient fulfillment of God's Word, has supplanted God's instructions with Greek thought that forces everything to be logically confirmed before it can possibly be considered, much less fulfilled. Christians have, therefore, done too much thinking and not enough obeying. This is especially true of the Christian view of God's Torah and his Chosen People. The church has ignored this divine

[1] Sarah K. Cardaun, *Countering Contemporary Antisemitism in Britain: Government and Civil Society Responses between Universalism and Particularism* (Leiden, The Netherlands: Koninklijke Brill NV, 2015), p. 60.

[2] For an excellent discussion of Hebrew block logic, see Marvin R. Wilson, *Our Father Abraham: The Jewish Roots of the Christian Faith* (Grand Rapids, MI: Wm. B. Eerdmans Publishing Co., 1989), p. 150–153.

imperative that came from the mouth of Jesus: "Think not that I have come to destroy the Torah or the prophets."[3] Now, once and for all, Christians need to stop such thinking—stop rationalizing with exegetical gymnastics and circular logic in order to invent clever circumlocutions that they think will somehow negate the very words of the Master and give them an excuse to nullify the commandments of God and purge Christianity of its inherent Jewishness. Regardless as to what theologians and church leaders may think, it is impossible for anyone to make the law of God illegal!

For nearly two thousand years, Christians have manifest arrogant disdain and contempt for the Jewish people in direct defiance of this divine imperative that came from the pen of the apostle Paul: "Boast not against the [natural] branches."[4] This arrogant triumphalism toward the Jewish people was already operating in the time of Paul, for, otherwise, he would not have raised the issue. From Paul's day forward, too many Christians through the centuries have believed that Gentile inclusion demanded Jewish exclusion. Paul's argument, however, was for Gentile inclusion in God's family tree—a tree that was itself Jewish. "Has God rejected his people?" he asked. And he immediately answered his own rhetorical question by saying, "Absolutely not!"[5] The one to whom God had given the apostolate to the Gentiles concluded that even those Jews who were at that time "enemies" of the gospel were "beloved" of God "for the sake of the patriarchs"[6] when it came to God's "election" of the Chosen People.[7] The question then was "Are Gentiles to be included in God's covenant?"—not "Are Jews excluded from God's covenant?"

Despite the strongest possible warnings from both Jesus and Paul, through the ensuing years from the end of the first century to the present day, Christianity has consistently manifest varying degrees of disdain and

[3] Matthew 5:17.

[4] Romans 11:18.

[5] Romans 11:1, HCSB. The KJV translation is more graphic than "Absolutely not!" It says, "God forbid!"

[6] In making this declaration, Paul maintained continuity with the sages of Israel who had established the doctrine of *Zekhut Avot* ("Merits of the Fathers"). In this teaching, they maintained that "God visits the virtues of the fathers upon the children for His name's sake and as a mark of grace; but it would appear, on the other hand, that the principle applies only when the children continue the piety of their parents. . . . If the covenant is still kept with descendants, though they be unworthy, this is the result of God's grace." Isidore Singer, Cyrus Adler, et. al., eds., *The Jewish Encyclopedia: A Descriptive Record of the History, Religion, Literature, and Customs of the Jewish People from the Earliest Times to the Present Day* (New York: Funk and Wagnalls Co., 1907), vol. 12, p. 441. Also, Abraham P. Bloch, *The Biblical and Historical Background of Jewish Customs and Ceremonies* (Jersey City, NJ: KTAV Publishing House, 1980), p. 253.

[7] Romans 11:28. Paul said unequivocally, "As far as the gospel is concerned, they are enemies for your sake; but as far as the election is concerned, they are loved on account of the patriarchs."

contempt for Jews in its theology and practice.[8] Supersessionism, which is the church's oldest heresy, has been accompanied by triumphalism, which is perhaps the church's greatest sin, and together they have wreaked havoc on the Jewish people in the unfolding centuries since the earliest days of Christianity. All of this could have been avoided if only the Christian church, the "body of Christ," had simply listened to the instructions of the Christ himself and to those of the apostles who succeeded him and obeyed two simple imperatives: "Think not!" and "Boast not!"

## Never Learning the Lessons of Christian History

Tragically, however, this has not been the case. The church has had a painful record of being beguiled from the utter simplicity of biblical truth and ethics.[9] Again and again it has been captivated by worldly agendas that all too often have been inimical to the faith of the Scriptures. Small compromises with seemingly small evils from both the pagan and secular realms have gradually led to even greater evils. It happened when Christians killed Jewish "infidels" during the Crusades. It happened when Christians tortured and executed Jews for "poisoning" their wells during the Black Death. It happened time and again when Christians maliciously and falsely accused the Jews of deicide and sought to impose capital punishment upon them for the supposed sins of their ancestors. It happened repeatedly when Christians tormented and murdered Jews based on the Christian Blood Libel that accused Jews of murdering Christian children to obtain blood for making Passover *matzah*. It happened in continuing Inquisitions when Christian prelates and magistrates ordered Jews to be burned at the stake.

Much too much of the Christian church did not even learn the shocking lessons of twentieth century when many Christians stood in solidarity with the Nazi regime and even participated in the Holocaust. As a result, many twenty-first century Christians have followed blindly in the same path that Germany's Evangelical Free Church and Roman Catholic Church walked when to varying degrees they supported the German Reich. Blinded and deceived by Adolph Hitler's March 23, 1933, speech to the German Reichstag in which he declared, "The Government of the Reich . . . regard Christianity as the unshakable foundation of the morals and moral code of the nation,"[10] both

[8] Christians can legitimately delineate and discuss differences between their faith and Judaism; however, too often Christian apologetics and polemics have drifted beyond discussion of differences into manifestations of pure antisemitism that would certainly have met with the condemnation of both Jesus and Paul.

[9] 2 Corinthians 11:3.

[10] E. Christopher Reyes, *In His Name* (Bloomington, IN: Trafford Publishing, 2014), p. 364.

of Germany's largest Christian denominations supported the fervent nationalism and xenophobia that eventually produced the Holocaust. Obviously, these Christians were duped by the Hitler's mendacity; however, the result was the same: beguiled and willfully ignorant German Christians supported the Third Reich and were seduced to join in its unprecedented antisemitic acts.

At that time, most of Germany's 40 million Protestants were members of the Evangelical Free Church,[11] which was a federation of the Lutheran, Reformed, and United churches, representing the major theological traditions that were produced by the sixteenth-century Protestant Reformation.[12] This denomination was so grounded in historical loyalty to the German state that in the 1920s it had spawned the *Deutsche Christen* ("German Christians") movement. Then, during the time of the Nazi regime, "fully two-thirds of German Protestants joined or voted for the *Deutsche Christen* Nazi movement,"[13] an operation that was "sympathetic to the Nazi regime's goal of 'coordinating' the individual Protestant churches into a single and uniform Reich church."[14] This movement "eventually embraced much of Nazism's nationalist and racist ideology and even produced a Nazi version of Christianity."[15] The *Deutsche Christen* movement focused theologically on deemphasizing the Old Testament, removing aspects of theology deemed "too Jewish,"[16] and even replacing the New Testament with a dejudaized *Die Botschaft Gottes* ("The Message of God").[17] From this time until the end of World War II, leaders and laypersons from both the Evangelical Free Church

[11] The Evangelical Free Church of America, which was formed in 1950, is not to be confused with the German Evangelical Free Church.

[12] "The German Churches and the Nazi State," in *Holocaust Encyclopedia* (Washington, DC: United States Holocaust Memorial Museum), posted at https://www.ushmm.org/wlc/en/article.php?ModuleId=10005206. Also, David B. Barrett, George T. Kurian, and Todd M. Johnson, eds., *World Christian Encyclopedia: The World by Segments: Religions, Peoples, Languages, Cities, Topics* (Oxford, UK: Oxford University Press, 2001), p. 301.

[13] Michael R. Marrus, ed., *The Nazi Holocaust: Historical Articles on the Destruction of European Jews Part 8: Bystanders to the Holocaust* (Westport, CT: Meckler Corporation, 1989), vol. 3, p. 1376.

[14] Jackson J. Spielvogel and David Redles, *Hitler and Nazi Germany: A History* (Abingdon, UK: Routledge, 2014), p. 115.

[15] Spielvogel and Redles, p. 115.

[16] Susannah Heschel, *The Aryan Jesus: Christian Theologians and the Bible in Nazi Germany* (Princeton, NJ: Princeton University Press, 2008), pp. 70–72. Heschel noted the work of the *Bund für Deutsches Christentum* (The Organization for German Christianity) which called for "creating a judenrein [Jew-free] Christianity for a judenrein Nazi Reich." This work was focused on "a thorough de-judaizing of Christian scriptures, worship, music, theology, and anything else related to the church."

[17] Susannah Heschel, "When Jesus Was an Aryan: The Protestant Church and Antisemitic Propaganda," in *In God's Name: Genocide and Religion in the Twentieth Century*, Omer Bartov and Phyllis Mack, eds. (New York: Berghahn Books, 2001), pp. 82–88. Also Mary C. Boys, *Redeeming Our Sacred Story: The Death of Jesus and Relations Between Jews and Christians* (Mahweh, NJ: Paulist Press, 2013), p. 221, and Robert P. Ericksen and Susannah Heschel, *Betrayal: German Churches and the Holocaust* (Minneapolis, MN: Augsburg Fortress Press, 1999), p. 198.

and the Roman Catholic Church openly supported the Nazi regime. Photographic images that have survived the war even document scenes in which prelates participated in the *Sieg Heil*[18] salute to the *Führer*! While most of the leaders of the Third Reich were atheists, agnostics, occultists, or neopagans, some were at least nominal Christians. Richard Steigmann-Gall reports that Nazi propagandist Joseph Göbbels "always emphasized his continuing church membership to other party members."[19] Like Hermann Göring, Hitler's second-in-command, he also 'had his children baptized."[20] Eventually, says Robert Leverenz, ordinary German Christians actually went so far as to go "to church every Sunday" and man "the gas chambers and the ovens" through the week.[21]

During this time, "a significant number of German theologians and clergy made use of the 16th-century writings by Martin Luther on Jews and Judaism to reinforce the racial antisemitism and religious antisemitism."[22] Robert Ericksen notes that the German "intellectual and spiritual leaders enthusiastically partnered with Hitler's regime, becoming active participants in the persecutions of the Jews."[23] Gerhard Kittel, a professor at the famed University of Tübingen and one of the most prominent German Protestant theologians of the time, supported the Nazi regime enthusiastically[24] and was a self-proclaimed anti-Semite.[25] Before 1933, Kittel had "argued vehemently against attempts to amputate Christianity's Jewish roots"[26]; however, after that time, he "joined the Nazi Party" and began to identify the Jews as "the source of Germany's misfortunes."[27] Kittel became an advocate for a purified *judenrein* church and society,

---

[18] *Sieg Heil* (German for "hail" [*heil*] "victory" [*sieg*]) was the official Nazi salute, which featured the right arm extended into the air with a straightened hand. Tilman Allert, *The Hitler Salute: On the Meaning of a Gesture* (New York: Picador, 2008), p. 32.

[19] Richard Steigmann-Gall, *The Holy Reich: Nazi Conceptions of Christianity, 1919–1945* (Cambridge, UK: Cambridge University Press, 2003), p. 233.

[20] Steigmann-Gall, p. 233.

[21] Robert E. Leverenz, *There Is Nothing New under the Sun* (Eugene, OR: Wipf and Stock Publishers, 2015), p. 41. Harry James Cargas, *Shadows of Auschwitz: A Christian Response to the Holocaust* (New York: Crossroad Press, 1990), p. 1. Cargas noted that the death camps, in major part, "were conceived, built, and operated by a people who called themselves Christians."

[22] Christopher J. Probst, *Demonizing the Jews: Luther and the Protestant Church in Nazi Germany* (Bloomington, IN: Indiana University Press, 2012), cover matter.

[23] Robert P. Ericksen, *Complicity in the Holocaust: Churches and Universities in Nazi Germany* (Cambridge, UK: Cambridge University Press, 2012), p. i.

[24] Ericksen, pp. 8, 31.

[25] Robert P. Ericksen, *Theologians Under Hitler* (New Haven, CT: Yale University Press, 1985), p. 42.

[26] Suzanne Marchand, "Nazism, Orientalism and Humanism," in *Nazi Germany and the Humanities: How German Academics Embraced Nazism*, Anson Rabinbach and Wolfgang Bialas, eds. (London, UK: Oneworld Publicaitons, 2014), p. 292.

[27] Marchand, p. 292.

which he argued was God's design for the outcast Jewish people.[28] He further declared that the Jews were part of the *Unheilsgeschichte* (damnation history) rather than the *Heilsgeschicte* (redemptive history). "Let others call what we do barbarism," boasted Professor Kittel, "We know that it represents obedience to God."[29]

One major voice that was raised against the German government effort to unify all Christians into one pro-Nazi Protestant Reich Church was the Confessing Church (*Bekennende Kirche*). Among its founders were Lutheran pastor Martin Niemöller, who was imprisoned in a Nazi concentration camp and narrowly escaped execution, and Old Prussian Union Evangelical Church pastor Dietrich Bonhoeffer, who was executed by the Nazis in 1945. Both of these leaders offered strong dissent to the growing trend toward unified church support of the Nazi regime and the persecution of Jews. Another leader of the Confessing Church, Swiss Reformed theologian Karl Barth, actively opposed the Nazi establishment of a Nazi-controlled state church and wrote the Barmen Declaration, which denounced the *Deutsche Christen* movement. German Catholic theologian and philosopher Dietrich von Hildebrand was even more bold in his opposition to the Nazis' determination to co-opt the Christian church in support of their agenda than his German Protestants counterparts were.[30] In the totalitarian environment of Nazi German nationalism, however, all opposition by people of conscience was a losing battle, for by 1934, even the Confessing Church had bowed to the pressure of the Nazis and had ousted all of its pastors who were "tainted" with Jewish blood.[31]

Sadly, these examples have been lost on too many Christians who have failed to recognize the evil of the Holocaust and admit the responsibility that historical Christian leaders had for contributing to the philosophical and theological environment that led to that tragedy. Likewise, many have also failed to recognize the degree to which Christian denominations, leaders, and laypersons either supported the Third Reich or, in some cases, actively participated in the Holocaust itself. Additionally, many Christians and church organizations outside of Germany and the other European nations that were complicit in or tolerant of the Holocaust have failed to confess their responsibility for remaining silent in the face of knowledge of the enormity of what

[28] Isaac C. Rottenberg, "They Just Don't Get It." *Restore!*, Issue 10, pp. 16–18.

[29] Gerhard Kittel, quoted in Rottenberg, p. 18.

[30] Dietrich von Hildebrand, *My Battle against Hitler: Defiance in the Shadow of the Third Reich*, John H. Crosby and John F. Crosby, trs. and eds. (New York: Random House, 2014).

[31] Ericksen, *Complicity*, p. 94.

was occurring in the Nazis' systematic genocide of European Jewry. By failing to recognize that Christian triumphalism and supersessionism contributed to the atmosphere of antisemitism that eventuated in the Holocaust, too many Christians have left the door ajar to the archenemy of biblical faith who crept back into the darkness when his effort to destroy the Jewish people was exposed, and it gave room for a cunningly sanitized, cosmetically disguised, and ceremoniously reclothed form of antisemitism to creep back into the body politic of Christianity to deceive, corrupt, and befoul Christianity yet again.

## Dressed in New Garments: Repeating Old Mistakes

Franklin Littell identified the source of the new, improved version of the old Christian antisemitism: "The rage for universal truths, accompanied by abandonment of holy events and the Scriptures that record them, came to dominate university thinking following the Enlightenment. It is this style of thinking that is the most fertile single source of liberal Antisemitism—whether religious or secular."[32] David Patterson has made the historical connection that anti-Zionist Christians need to recognize but would prefer to ignore: "The diatribes of the anti-Zionist anti-Semites reek of the odor of the camps, and they reek most disgustingly in the sanctimonious denunciations of the Israelis that erupt from the mouths of well-meaning liberal Christians and not-so-well-meaning liberal intellectuals."[33] He observed that in both of these groups, "we discover that time-worn manifestations of Jew hatred turn out to be timeless. Liberal Christian anti-Zionism has implications that play into the hands of supersessionist theology. Left-wing intellectual anti-Zionism is the fashionable expression of Jew hatred traceable to what we have seen in the Enlightenment and the socialist liberalism that followed in its wake."[34]

The Roman Catholic Church has led the way for all Christians in identifying and removing many historical and theological foundations that have engendered outright Christian antisemitism.[35] With the almost prophetic fervor of Pope John XXIII for Vatican II, the Roman Catholic Church, with its enactment of *Nostra Aetate* made radical and sweeping changes in Christian thought concerning the Jews." At the same time,

[32] Franklin Littell, *The Crucifixion of the Jews: The Failure of Christians to Understand the Jewish Experience* (Macon, GA: Mercer University Press, 1986), pp. 38–39. The abandonment of Scripture by Enlightenment academia was common in Nazi and Bolshevik thinking as it is in general Western scholarship today.

[33] David Patterson, *Anti-Semitism and Its Metaphysical Origins* (Cambridge, UK: Cambridge University Press, 2015), p. 207.

[34] Patterson, p. 207.

[35] Roman Catholicism has far outpaced most Protestant denominations in acknowledging the Christian church's historical sins against the Jews, recognizing the continuing dimensions of God's relationship with Israel, and promoting repentance and restitution for evils perpetrated against the Jews by Christians.

however, it has maintained a posture toward the state of Israel that has often demonstrated a not-so-subtle anti-Zionism, a posture that can be traced to the very beginning of the Zionist movement. "When in 1903 Herzl visited Pope Pius X, the latter declared that whereas the Church could not prevent a Jewish return to Jerusalem, it could never sanction it."[36] This policy was maintained until 1993,[37] when the Vatican finally granted the state of Israel official recognition. Even then, the Vatican policy was not one of complete acceptance of the Jewish right to the whole land of Israel, including its undivided capital city, Jerusalem. In fact, when all of the old city of Jerusalem, including the Temple Mount, was wrested from Jordanian occupying forces and returned to Jewish control during the Six-Day War, "the Vatican began to issue a series of calls" for the internationalization of Jerusalem,[38] something that it had never requested "during the nineteen years that the city [had been] under Jordanian control."[39] Even during the historical deliberations of Vatican II and the development of the *Nostra Aetate* declaration—which rejected the historical Christian charge of deicide that had been lodged against the Jewish people for centuries—Muslim pressure, together with that of "Arabophile Catholic factions," succeeded in having its original draft replaced "with a watered-down version."[40] As a matter of fact, "the *dhimmi* Arab clergy considered the passage which annulled the collective accusation of deicide against the Jews as untimely and demanded its removal."[41] The Arab Catholic clergy even argued that Muslim protests "against the disculpation of the Jewish people" were made in "a perfectly authentic pursuit of the Koran," a demand "for the honor of God and of both Christ and the Virgin."[42]

Among mainstream Protestant denominations, the World Council of Churches (WCC) became a champion of Christian anti-Zionism—and, indeed, of Christian antisemitism—after Israel's Declaration of Independence. Not surprisingly, even before the WCC was founded in 1948, the mainstream Protestant denominations that formed this organization lobbied against

---

[36] Emil L. Fackenheim, *What Is Judaism?* (New York: Macmillian, 1987), pp. 231–232.

[37] Interestingly enough, even though it took 45 years for the Vatican to recognize the state of Israel, the Holy See, in a deal that was brokered by the then-future Pope Pius XII, was the first entity to give diplomatic recognition to Nazi Germany by signing the *Reichskonkordat* on July 20, 1933.

[38] One could only wonder what the reaction of the Vatican would be if any nation or other political entity called for the "internationalization" of the Vatican!

[39] Fackenheim, pp. 231–232.

[40] Bat Ye'or, *Islam and Dhimmitude: Where Civilizations Collide* (Cranbury, NJ: Associated University Presses, 2002), p. 272.

[41] Ye'or, p. 272.

[42] Ye'or, p. 272.

the formation of the Israeli state, arguing that the land of Israel (Palestine) should be nothing more than a cultural center for Jews. In a 1933 editorial, the *Christian Century*, the leading mainstream Protestant magazine, revealed the general liberal Protestant view regarding Israel and the Jews: "The Christian mind has never allowed itself to feel the same concern for Jewish suffering that it has felt for the cruelties visited upon the Armenians, the Boers, the people of India, American slaves or Congo Blacks. Christian indifference to Jewish suffering has for centuries been rationalized by the tenable belief that such sufferings were the judgment of God upon the Jewish people for their rejection of Jesus."[43] Hertzel Fishman notes that this editorial further attempted to parallel Jews in the first century with their counterparts in the twentieth century by "distinguishing between Jews as Jews and Jews as nationalists," exonerating the former and judging the latter guilty of the death of Jesus, and then arguing that present-day "Jews as Jews should not be despised by the Christian world" while Zionists, like the national Jewish leaders of the first century, should be repudiated by Christians for their nationalism.[44]

Because of its general attitude toward the Jews, Jonathan Rynhold says that "mainline Protestantism . . . focused its opposition on the Jewish national movement—Zionism."[45] Howard Sachar summed up the attitude of the mainline churches saying that "the Christian establishment seemed to be disoriented by the theological dilemma posed by Jews functioning as victorious conquerors rather than as perennial martyrs and as convenient scapegoats for Christian imperfections."[46] Mainline theologian Roy Eckhardt identified one of the main reasons for Christian ambivalence and antipathy toward the Jewish people and their nation, Israel: "The entire movement to re-establish the Jewish people in their ancient homeland . . . has been a traumatic experience from which the collective Christian psyche has never entirely recovered. How presumptuous for Israel to be 'reborn' in clear violation of Christian eschatology!"[47]

As a result of liberal Protestant press promotions, the World Council of

[43] *The Christian Century*, May 3, 1933, quoted in Hertzel Fishman, "The Apparition of Jewish Nationalism," in *Essential Papers on Judaism and Christianity in Conflict*, Jeremy Cohen, ed. (New York: New York University Press, 1990), p. 246.

[44] Fishman, in Cohen, ed., p. 246.

[45] Jonathan Rynhold, *The Arab-Israeli Conflict in American Political Culture* (Cambridge, UK: Cambridge University Press, 2015), p. 121.

[46] Howard M. Sachar, *A History of the Jews in America* (New York: Random House, 1992), p. 875.

[47] A. Roy Eckhardt, *Elder and Younger Brothers* (New York: Charles Scribner's Sons, 1967), p. 171. Eckhardt referenced Augustine's replacement theology which coopted Israel's covenantal relationship with God and replaced it with "new Israel," the church.

Churches was—and has continued to be—the leading Christian voice that regularly denounces Israel. Melanie Phillips notes that in WCC-backed publications "the critique of some Israeli sin would be severe, while Arab countries were spared any kind of condemnation in order not to jeopardize Christian missionary interests there."[48] Virtually all Christian denominations predicated their position toward the Jewish people and the land of Israel on what was in the best interest of their own financial and property holdings in Arab and Muslim countries. In 1948, "pressure from Arab Protestants and local missionaries, supersessionist theology, oil ties, dislike of Jews and the emphasis on peace and justice issues led the new World Council of Churches to be ambivalent or even hostile to the new state [Israel]."[49] Then, from its earliest days, the WCC Middle East media were "composed of people from Arab countries"[50] and did not have even one Israeli or Jewish voice. In 1948, the *Christian Century* "supported the internationalization of Jerusalem" and "blamed the creation of Israel on New York Jewish voters."[51]

Mainstream Protestantism's subtle antisemitism that has been manifest in its anti-Zionism became particularly clear after the Six-Day War "when the influential Protestant journal *Christianity and Crisis* switched from a pro-Israel position to the Palestinian camp on the grounds that nothing could 'sanctify the right of conquest in the twentieth century.'"[52] The utter asininity of the WCC's argument ignored the fact that the Six-Day War actually liberated the West Bank and East Jerusalem from the nineteen-year occupation that resulted from the Jordanian "conquest" and confiscation of that territory from Israel in 1948. British journalist Melanie Phillips states the obvious when she says, "If one wonders how it could possibly be that both the liberal churches in particular and the West in general consistently blame Israel not just for crimes it has not committed but *of which it is often the victim*, one need look no further than the WCC."[53] She also gives a withering account of the impact that the

[48] Phillips, p. 377. As Isaac Rottenberg noted, the primary concern of Christian denominations has never been for justice for Israel and the Jewish people. Their agendas have always been driven by self-interest in protecting their own properties and parishioners in Arab and Muslim nations. Isaac C. Rottenberg, personal communication.

[49] Jonathan Adelman, *The Rise of Israel: A History of a Revolutionary State* (New York: Routledge, 2008), p. 96.

[50] Melanie Phillips, *The World Turned Upside Down: The Global Battle over God, Truth, and Power* (New York: Encounter Books, 2010), p. 377.

[51] Adelman, p. 96. For a comprehensive study of the anti-Zionist posture of the World Council of Churches, see Adelman, pp. 95–99.

[52] Phillips, p. 377.

[53] Phillips, p. 378.

WCC's anti-Zionist position had upon European nations, particularly Great Britain where incipient and longstanding antisemitism within the Anglican Church found an avenue of release in anti-Zionism[54] after mainstream Protestant churches and the WCC attacked Israel.

Phillips also points to the case of Canon Andrew White, the archbishop of Canterbury's former envoy to the Middle East and later vicar of Baghdad, who charged that "replacement theology has now gone viral within the Church of England" and that "the establishment of the State of Israel would probably have had more opposition from the church had it not been for the Holocaust."[55] Now, however, Phillips agrees with White when he says that "with modern Israel being represented as behaving in an analogous fashion to the Nazis, that brake on prejudice has been removed."[56] She says that Anglican tradition concludes that "the Promised Land is where the church will be established, that Jerusalem is the heavenly city, and that it will eventually be the home of all Christians."[57] Obviously, leaders in the Anglican church believe that the Jewish people have no legitimate place in their own ancestral home. The absurdity of this position is obvious when one considers what the Anglican reaction might be if they were told that the English ancient claim to Great Britain has been superseded by the rights of Muslim claimants to that land mass and that any attempt to argue otherwise would be racist.

Mainstream Protestant anti-Israelism was developed largely on the back of the radical and heretical doctrine of liberation theology, one of the concepts that have been "drawn in large measure from the radical ideas of the World Council of Churches."[58] This posture was clearly on display in the major role that the WCC played in the 2001 United Nations Conference on Racism, Racial Discrimination, Xenophobia, and Related Intolerance, which branded Israel as a racist state.[59] Continuing WCC anti-Zionism and antisemitism have been so pervasive as to produce innumerable examples of the duplicity of double standards, wherein it denounces Israel for offenses that are minor in comparison to those of its persecutors from the Muslim

[54] Phillips, pp. 380–381.

[55] Andrew White, quoted in Phillips, p. 381.

[56] White, in Phillips, p. 381.

[57] Phillips, p. 381. While much of historical Anglicanism has been supersessionist against Israel and the Jewish people, there have been notable exceptions such as John Wesley and the leaders of the Wesleyan revival who prayed for and preached about the restoration of the Jewish people in their ancestral homeland.

[58] Phillips, p. 381.

[59] Phillips, p. 378.

world for which the WCC has little, if any, condemnation.

Amazingly, but not unexpectedly,[60] the many organizations that have taken up the assault of the Palestinian Authority's Boycott, Divest, Sanction movement on Israel include virtually all of the mainstream denominations of Protestant Christianity.[61] Most prominent among these is the Presbyterian Church USA, which voted to divest $21 million from Caterpillar, Inc. (because it is the manufacturer of the D9 Caterpillar bulldozer that the PCUSA says has been used to "destroy Palestinian homes"), Motorola, Inc. (because it manufactures surveillance equipment used in the West Bank), and Hewlett-Packard, Inc. (because it invented the technology that is employed in Israel's blockade of Gaza).[62] To one degree or another, the United Church of Christ, the Episcopal Church USA, and the United Methodist Church have followed the lead of the PCUSA.[63] Additionally, the Evangelical Lutheran Church, while not calling for total divestiture of investments, has instituted a "diversion of all denominational resources and aid to 'those who need it most,' code language for the Palestinians."[64]

Diana Appelbaum has written powerful op-ed articles in the conservative *American Thinker* "accusing Presbyterians of anti-Semitism and false allegations against Israel."[65] She has pointed out numerous absurd charges launched by Presbyterian ministers against Israel, including their claim that "[the Israelis] stripped the dead [Palestinian] body and dragged it completely around the city behind the jeep" and their canard that "[the Israeli] level of spousal and child abuse is one of the highest in the world." She also reported this description that Presbyterian minister Arthur Suggs' gave of his meetings with Palestinians: "[When invited to] sit down on these persian [*sic*] carpets

[60] Indeed, it could only be expected that the Christian denominations that have not supported the restoration of the nation of Israel, including some that have openly fought against it since before 1948, would jump on the divestiture bandwagon with both feet! Old prejudices never really die; they simply lie dormant until a fresh opportunity arises for them to flourish again.

[61] These are denominations in which historical Christian antisemitism has found a new incarnation in anti-Zionism.

[62] Sandy Tolan, *Children of the Stone: The Power of Music in a Hard Land* (New York: Bloomsbury Publishing, 2015), p. 423.

[63] C. J. Conner, *Jesus and the Culture Wars: Reclaiming the Lord's Prayer* (Mustang, OK: Tate Publishing & Enterprises, 2007), p. 157.

[64] Conner, p. 157.

[65] Diana Appelbaum, "Presbyterians Bearing False Witness," in *The American Thinker*, June 3, 2006, posted at http://www.americanthinker.com/articles/2006/06/presbyterians_bearing_false_wi.html. Also, Nathan Guttman, "Presbyterians Divest Themselves from Israel," in *Haaretz*, July 22, 2004, posted at www.haaretz.com/print-edition/features/presbyterians-divest-themselves-from-Israel-1.129171, and Maia Carter Hallward, *Transnational Activism and the Israeli-Palestinian Conflict* (New York: Palgrave Macmillan, 2013), p. 149.

. . . and talk politics . . . I was in heaven. I was talking only with muslims [*sic*]."[66] Appelbaum also noted that Rev. Clifton Kirkpatrick, Stated Clerk of the PCUSA, has portrayed "Israelis as immoral monsters" who engage in "indiscriminate shooting of children and adults on the streets . . . invasion of hospitals . . . brutal attacks on . . . women, men and children inhabitants of refugee camps." Of course, "none of this is true," she concluded.[67] No wonder another opinion piece in the *Jewish World Review* accused the Presbyterian Church of committing a sin against God.[68]

Christian complicity in the abominable attacks of Muslim extremists on Israel can also be found in yet another Christian parachurch organization, the National Coalition of Christian Organizations in Palestine (NCCOP). The Palestinian Boycott, Divestment, and Sanctions National Committee warmly welcomes a historic open letter by NCCOP which urged the WCC to "recognize Israel as an apartheid state," as well as to "support the nonviolent, Palestinian-led global BDS movement, help intensify Boycott, Divestment and Sanctions (BDS) campaigns and actively refuse Christian complicity in ongoing Israeli violations of Palestinian human rights."[69]

Another major example of the influence of Christianity in generating support for antisemitic anti-Zionism can be seen in the seven Scandinavian countries which are often viewed as "bulwark of democracy" because of the "peaceful images" that they have constructed around the theme of "a major concern for human rights."[70] All of this sounds noble; however, at the same time, Norway and Sweden have long been ranked in the Simon Wiesenthal Center's worst category for refusing "in principle to investigate, let alone prosecute, suspected Nazi war criminals because of legal (statute of limitation) or ideological restrictions."[71] Because Lutheranism dominates these nations, the ancient antisemitic legacy of Martin Luther—though it has been officially denounced in most Lutheran circles—seemingly has "mutated into anti-Israeli feelings," with some Scandinavian church

---

[66] Appelbaum, "Presbyterians."

[67] Appelbaum, "Presbyterians."

[68] Prager and Telushkin, p. 204.

[69] "BNC Welcomes Call by Christian Organizations Urging the World Council of Churches to Support the BDS Movement for Palestinian Human Rights," Palestinian Boycott, Divestment and Sanctions National Committee (BNC), *Christian Palestinians*, June 20, 2017.

[70] Manfred Gerstenfeld, ed., *Behind the Humanitarian Mask: The Nordic Countries, Israel and the Jews*, (Jerusalem, Israel: Jerusalem Center for Public Affairs and Friends of Simon Wiesenthal Center for Holocaust Studies, 2008), p. 18.

[71] Gerstenfeld, p. 18.

leaders manifesting "profound anti-Israeli bias," perhaps even joining "the anti-Israeli bandwagon mainly because of its popularity,"[72] says Manfred Gerstenfeld. Sadly, "the stereotypes of the long-existing religious and ethnonational varieties of anti-Semitism are also substantially present in these countries. In recent decades they have been reactivated and adapted to the currently prevailing *Zeitgeist*. The anti-Semitic core motif is that the Jew is the absolute evil,"[73] he notes. Obviously, medieval forms of antisemitism are still alive and well in much of Scandinavia!

## Right Passion, Wrong Target

One would think that if Christians of conscience sincerely desired to divest their resources from nations or organizations that engage in racism, terrorism, crimes against humanity, and even genocide—and from the international business organizations that facilitate such actions—their prime target would be those Muslim nations and businesses that sponsor terrorism not only against Israel and the Jewish people, but also against Christians and people of other religions. Neither Christians nor Jews are terrorists while Muslim jihadists clearly are. Virtually all terrorists in today's world have one thing in common: they are Islamists! If Christians desire to stand against oppression and human suffering, the choice of whom to challenge is very clear, and it is not Jews or Christians!

While such atrocities can be incontrovertibly ascribed to organizations like the Islamic State of Iraq and al-Sham (ISIS), Al Qaeda, and Boko Haram, they can also be leveled at Palestinian Arab organizations like Hamas and the Palestinian Authority in Israel, as well as Hezbollah in neighboring Lebanon. Certainly the nation of Israel has never ordered the murder of even one Christian or the destruction of even one Christian shrine. At the same time, the murder of Coptic Christians and the destruction of their properties, including sanctuaries, have become routine practices of the Muslim Brotherhood in Egypt. Indeed, "ancient traditions of the Christian Church—Armenia, Coptic, and Chaldean Christians—are in grave danger of extinction by mass genocide" at the hands of Muslim terrorists.[74] In fact, ISIS butchers have committed virtual genocide against the historical Chaldean Church of

[72] Gerstenfeld, p. 19.

[73] Gerstenfeld, p. 20.

[74] William F. Dopp, *Is There Hope for the Christian Faith?: Five Hundred Years After Martin Luther, the Christian Church Is Beginning a New Reformation* (Bloomington, IN: AuthorHouse, 2015), p. 124.

Babylon that has continually functioned since 1552 but increasingly faces extinction because of the systematic slaughter of its people and the confiscation or destruction of its properties. Doubtless Christian intolerance for Israel's self-defense when coupled with its tolerance for the Palestinian Muslims' aggressive terrorism is patently absurd!

## Waning Evangelical Philosemitism and Pro-Israelism

In 2014, David Brog noted that "a mere decade ago, Christian Zionism was seen as an emerging force in American politics. As if out of nowhere, a block of fifty to one hundred million friends of Israel were poised to enter the national debate and safeguard the US-Israel relationship for generations to come."[75] Marc Ellis observes the tragic results of the ongoing—and increasingly one-sided—Christian debate about Israel: "Holocaust remembrance events suffer from a loss of energy and attendance" as "more and more Christians see that the Holocaust now functions to limit dissent about Israeli policies toward Palestinians." Ellis says that "the Holocaust as a lifeline to Israel is coming to an end. So, too, the endless discussion of antisemitism is seen as a relic rather than a contemporary challenge."[76]

What Ellis describes in mainstream denominations is also beginning to take root in Evangelicalism, which was once the bastion of Christian support for the restoration of Israel. Within the past twenty years, however, a shocking and troubling trend has emerged within the larger Evangelical community. "The year 2010 was one of dramatic escalation in the efforts to drive a wedge between American evangelicals and Israel"[77] with the production of three "documentary" films: *Waiting for Armageddon*, *With God on Our Side*, and *Little Town of Bethlehem*, all of which were "focused on discrediting Christian support for Israel."[78] While the first of these was produced by secular film makers, tragically, the second was produced by a former Youth with a Mission executive, and the third was produced and funded by the chairman of Oral Roberts University's board of trustees. David Brog describes these two Christian productions succinctly and accurately as "masterpieces of deception," because "they feature compelling protagonists wandering earnestly through a Middle Eastern landscape in which all Arab violence, aggression, and rejectionism have been magically erased. . . . The

[75] David Brog,"The End of Evangelical Support for Israel?: The Jewish State's International Standing," in *Middle East Quarterly*, vol. 21, no. 2, Spring 2014.

[76] Marc H. Ellis, *Future of the Prophetic: Israel's Ancient Wisdom Re-presented* (Minneapolis, MN: Augsburg Fortress Publishers, 2014), p. 46.

[77] Brog, "The End."

[78] Brog, "The End."

Israeli security measures they encounter along the way" are "baffling persecutions, which any decent person would condemn."[79] A more recent documentary, *The Stones Cry Out*, seeks to repackage the "conflict in Palestine" as now being between Palestinian Christians and Jews rather than between Muslim Arab "Palestinians" and Jews.

These media presentations, however, represent only a small sampling of what is taking place across the landscape of Evangelicalism. Apparently a new generation of Evangelicals is emerging, leaders and laypersons who are like the Pharaoh "to whom Joseph meant nothing."[80] These Evangelicals are being infected with a subtle form of anti-Zionism that diminishes support for Israeli Jews in favor of standing with Palestinian Christians against supposed Israeli oppression and injustice. Sadly, during the Third Lausanne Congress of World Evangelization in 2010, a Pew survey of Evangelical leaders revealed that only a minority sympathized primarily with Israel.[81] Additionally, some Evangelicals, second and third generations removed from those unequivocal supporters of Israel who founded their churches, universities, and ministry organizations, have been so influenced by the secular media's antisemitic drumbeat and now empathize totally with the plight of Palestinian Christians at the expense of support for Israel that they often express blatant antisemitism in their anti-Zionist diatribes.[82] No one would have been surprised at mainstream Protestant Christianity's abandonment of support for Israel and the Jews—if it ever had any in the first place—since most of those denominations were largely antisemitic in their supersessionist teachings even before Zionism arose; however, declining Evangelical support for Israel is another matter that few would have predicted fifty, even twenty, years ago.[83]

---

[79] Brog, "The End."

[80] The waning support for Israel and the Jewish community in some Christian circles parallels the loss of celebrity that the Israelites experienced after Joseph had saved the Egyptian civilization from a protracted seven-year famine when he was Egypt's prime minister. When a later Pharaoh came to power in Egypt "to whom Joseph meant nothing," the once-celebrated Israelites rapidly found themselves enslaved (Exodus 1:8, NIV). Could history repeat itself with even Evangelical Christians turning against Israel and embracing Palestinian Muslim and Palestinian Christian propaganda? For an overview of the blindness of the religious left to the extreme violence of communist regimes, see Lloyd Billingsley, *The Generation That Knew Not Josef: A Critique of Marxism and the Religious Left* (Colorado Springs, CO: Multnomah Press, 1985).

[81] Alison Weir, "Christian Evangelicals Increasingly Support Palestinian Human Rights," in *CounterPunch*, September 29, 2014, posted at http://www.counterpunch.org/2014/09/29/christian-evangelicals-increasingly-support-palestinian-human-rights/.

[82] For a comprehensive study of this phenomenon, see Tricia Miller, *Jews and Anti-Judaism in Esther and the Church* (Cambridge, UK: James Clarke & Co., 2015), pp. 178–190. Also Brog, "The End." Both Miller and Brog name specific evangelical ministries that are becoming increasingly anti-Zionist and antisemitic.

[83] While some Evangelical groups have never supported Israel, a significant portion of Evangelicalism has stood in solidarity with the international Jewish community and the nation of Israel.

Evangelical organizations have begun to drift away from their founders' vision for unequivocal Christian support for the right of the Jewish people to live in their own nation and in their own land, Israel. Wheaton College, a former bastion of pro-Israel activity, has drifted toward anti-Israelism. This "Evangelical Harvard" that produced the likes of the late Dr. Billy Graham is also home to anti-Israel activists who have fought against such pro-Israel organizations as Christians United for Israel, even thwarting a pro-Israel event that was planned at Wheaton in 2009. Oral Roberts University, which was founded by a strong supporter of Israel and which featured some of the strongest names in Charismatic Evangelicalism and supporters of Israel on its board of trustees,[84] has now come under the control of Evangelical businessmen and Pentecostal administrators who have aligned themselves with Palestinian Christians against Israeli Jews and who support both antinomianism and supersessionism.

Most of the weakening of Evangelical support for Israel can be attributed to the widespread discrimination against Palestinian Christians—whose families had lived in Palestine for centuries—that began when the Muslim Palestinian Authority assumed control of the Palestinian Christians' ancient homeland and began to spread their anti-Zionist propaganda among them. Palestinian Christian problems are, indeed, troubling, and they deserve to be addressed in practical, balanced ways; however, unilaterally blaming Israel for their circumstances is reprehensible and undeserved. As is usually the case, most Christian denominations and power centers tend to make their political and "moral" judgments based on how those judgments affect their own assets in the Muslim world. In this respect, Evangelicals differ little from their mainstream Christian counterparts.

One needs to look at the bigger picture to see the source of the dilemma. The problem in the land of Palestine, including where Palestinian Christians live, is not a Jewish problem. Instead, it is a Muslim problem. If Muslims genuinely wanted peace, it could be achieved overnight, and the situation of both the Palestinian Christians and the Palestinian Muslims could be improve dramatically. In fact, with Israel's perspectives on religious liberty and economic opportunity, Israel could become an even greater global economic powerhouse that would elevate the quality of life for both Muslims and Christians. Sadly,

[84] For decades, the Oral Roberts University faculty has had one of the world's leading Hebrew scholars and advocates of ongoing Christian-Jewish dialogue and greater Christian understanding and support of Jews and Judaism in the person of Brad H. Young, who received his Ph.D. from Hebrew University in Jerusalem under Professor David Flusser. Young is the author of numerous books that help Christians to understand the Jewishness of Jesus and the apostles and the influence that Second-Temple Judaism had on the nascent Christian community.

such peace and prosperity escape Palestinian Christians and Arab Muslims, for the terrorist organizations that dominate the area where most Palestinian Christians live—Hamas and the Palestinian Authority—intend to maintain their power with murderous efficiency.

## The Palestinian Christian Dilemma

While Palestinian Christians who live in Israel have had the freedom of religion that the nation of Israel extends to all faiths, those who live in the West Bank and Gaza have found that virtually all of their freedoms have been restricted, if not totally denied—especially in Gaza—since the time that Israel ceded control of those areas to the Palestinian Authority and Hamas subsequently seized control of Gaza.[85] Additionally, Palestinian Christians have suffered from many inconveniences[86] that are inevitable consequences of Israel's need to exercise of control over Judea and Samaria in order to fulfill its responsibility for providing security of all of its citizens—whether they be Jews, Christians, Muslims, Druze, or Bahá'ís—in response to the unrelenting ambition of Muslims, especially Arab Muslims, to destroy the Jewish state and effect the genocide of its Jewish citizens.[87]

Nowhere is the Palestinian Christian dilemma more clearly evident than in Bethlehem, the birthplace of Jesus. In the shadow of the city of Jerusalem, the town of Bethlehem has long been "a major center for Palestinian Christianity" because "it contains one of Palestine's most significant Christian churches and because it has long constituted a major site of Christian pilgrimage."[88] Because Palestinian Christians are, indeed, Christians, they can connect their faith and experience with the earliest forays of Jewish Christian missionaries into the non-Jewish world population, beginning, as Jesus instructed them, at Jerusalem and continuing

[85] Michael Prior, "Holy Places, Unholy Domination: The Scramble for Jerusalem," in *My Jerusalem: Essays, Reminiscences, and Poems*, Salma Khadra Jayyusi and Safar Ishaq Ansari, eds. (Northampton, MA: Olive Branch Press, 2005), p. 84. Prior reports that in 2005 some 114,000 Palestinian Christians lived in Israel, while 50,352 lived in the "Occupied Territories" of the West Bank and Gaza.

[86] Prominent among these often embarrassing and demeaning inconveniences is the Israeli West Bank Barrier which, in effect, has walled off those who live in the area. While this barrier has effectively reduced the wave of suicide bombings and other terrorist attacks in Israel by 90%, the inconvenience it has imposed upon the residents of the West Bank has been considerable and has elicited much negative response, including from Palestinian Christians.

[87] Reza Aslan, *Muslims and Jews in America: Commonalities, Contentions, and Complexities* (New York: Palgrave Macmillan, 2011), p. 1. With regard to the security fence, Aslan says, "For Jewish Israelis, the separation is necessary to keep Israel's citizens safe from Palestinian terrorists. For Muslim and Christian Palestinians, the divide is merely the most physical manifestation of what they view as Israel's policy of ethnic and religious segregation."

[88] Philip Mattar, *Encyclopedia of the Palestinians* (New York: Facts on File, Inc., 2000), p. 101.

through Judea and Samaria into the "remotest part of the earth."[89] Munib Younan speaks for his own community of embattled Palestinian Christians when he says, "We believe that we represent the continuity of the Old Testament and New Testament peoples' existence on the land. This is not merely an emotional attachment, but one that has geographical, historical, traditional, cultural, and social, as well as spiritual roots. We are tied to the land as the land belongs to us."[90] Younan probably expresses the sentiments of a significant portion of the Palestinian Christian community when he says, "We will exist and coexist [with the Jews] as long as the land is also our land of milk and honey."[91] For Palestinian Christians, therefore, "the security of Israel is interdependent with the issues of justice in the land and freedom for Palestinians."[92]

Palestinian Christians do, indeed, have far more legitimate reasons for claiming a right to live in the land of Israel than Muslims do, for their lineal heritage in the land exceeds all Muslim claims by as much as eight centuries and many are likely descended from non-Arab inhabitants of the ancient Negev and Transjordan.[93] Unfortunately, in efforts to establish historical connections to the land in which they live, some within the larger community of Palestinian Christians have resorted to a revisionist approach to both Christian theology and church history that invokes elements of the heresy of supersessionism and is, therefore, inherently antisemitic.[94] A new Palestinian form of South American liberation theology—which some have called "Marxized Christianity"[95]—has revived the Christian supersessionism and triumphalism that the Holocaust and Vatican II drove underground.

---

[89] Acts 1:8.

[90] Munib Younan, *Witnessing for Peace: In Jerusalem and the World* (Minneapolis, MN: Augsburg Fortress Press, 2003), p. 64.

[91] Younan, p. 64.

[92] Younan, p. 64.

[93] Michael Kohn, *Israel & the Palestinian Territories* (Footscray, Australia: Lonely Planet Publications, 2007), p. 43. Kohn points out that while some Muslim Palestinians "argue that they arrived in Jerusalem with Caliph Omar, which would mean they have been on the land for 1400 years," at the same time, "Palestinian Christians claim to be the descendants of the first Christians—those that guided Queen Helena on her tour of the Holy Land" in the fourth century AD, which, if true, would have placed them in the land hundreds of years before any Muslims arrived. Many Gentile Christians in Palestine during and before that time were likely descended from the Nabataeans who were not Arabians and who during pre-Islamic times spoke Aramaic and Greek, not Arabic. Jane Taylor, *Petra and the Lost Kingdom of the Nabataeans* (London, UK: I. B. Tauris & Co., Ltd., 2002), p.213, and Witt Raczka, *Unholy Land: In Search of Hope in Israel/Palestine* (Lanham, MD: Rowman & Littlefield, 2016), p. 275.

[94] Salim J. Munayer, "Reconciliation as a Christian Response," in *Christians and the Middle East Conflict*, Paul S. Rowe, John H. A. Dyck, and Jens Zimmermann, eds. (New York: Routledge, 2014), p. 17. Munayer points out that within the Palestinian Christian community "attitudes towards replacement theology vary greatly"; however, such attitudes tend to be "a largely theological and non-political issue."

[95] David Horowitz, *The Professors: The 101 Most Dangerous Academics in America* (Washington, DC: Regnery Publishing, 2006), p. 143.

"Now it's back," says Melanie Phillips, "kick-started by Palestinian Christian liberation theology, which states falsely that the Palestinian Arabs were the original possessors of the land of Israel."[96]

One such effort that supports Palestinian Christian liberation theology has been organized and promoted by Bethlehem Bible College, which hosts a biennial "Christ at the Checkpoint Conference" that is designed to seek "justice" for Palestinian Christians by advancing just such revisionist ideas. The name of the college's conference, "as well as [its] logo—which depicts a church behind the security barrier built by Israel to prevent suicide bombers from targeting Israeli civilians—demonstrates the focus of these meetings," says Tricia Miller.[97] Though the college asserts its commitment "to the great truths and abiding fundamentals of the Christian faith,"[98] it simply ignores or distorts inconvenient theological truths that are set forth incontrovertibly in Holy Scripture. Amazingly, some leaders of the movement that supports this agenda boldly proclaim that "if Jesus lived in Bethlehem today, he would have to go through the checkpoints just like the Palestinians do."[99] Others even promote a Palestinian version of supersessionism in which it is said that "Palestinians replace Jews as the indigenous people of the Holy Land" and that "Jesus and the early Christians were all Palestinians."[100] Christians have, indeed, been present in the countries of the Middle East for two millennia, and they, therefore, "are not an exogenous entity intruding into a homogeneous Arab Muslim world."[101] At the same time, however, they did not replace the Jews or assume the Jewish right to the Land of Promise.

In reality, Jews predated Arab Christians in the Middle East and in the land of Israel by two millennia; therefore, Jews have been rightful residents of the land of Israel for some four thousand years. Jewish Christians also predated Arab Christians in Jerusalem and in Israel by at least ten years following the

[96] Phillips, p. 379. Phillips quotes Riah Abu El-Assal, former Anglican bishop of Jerusalem, as claiming that Palestinian Christians "are the true Israel," and then adding, "no-one can deny me the right to inherit the promises, and, after all, the promises were first given to Abraham and Abraham is never spoken of in the Bible as a Jew. . . . He is the father of the faithful."

[97] Miller, p. 198.

[98] Miller, p. 198.

[99] Miller, p. 198. The fact is that since Jesus was—and still is—a Jew, he would simply go through the checkpoints in the same manner as the Israelis do! Since Jesus was—and still is—a Jew, he would experience the life of an Israeli citizen.

[100] Miller, p. 198.

[101] Michael Curtis, *Jews, Antisemitism, and the Middle East* (New Brunswick, NJ: Transaction Publishers, 2013), p. 173. While the ministry of Jesus featured his interaction with various Gentiles (*e.g.*, the Syrophoenician woman in Matthew15:21–28, the Gadarene demoniac in Luke 8:26–39, and even the Samaritan woman in John 4), there is no scriptural evidence that they joined the community of Jesus.

death, resurrection, and ascension of Jesus, for the first Gentiles that were added to the Christian church were Romans of the household of Cornelius, the Roman centurion.[102] The Jews, therefore, were not an exogenous intrusion into either a homogeneous Arab Christian world or a homogeneous Arab Muslim world! Jews were the rightful inhabitants of the entire land of Israel at least 1500 years before there was such a thing as an Arab Christian and at least 2100 years before there was such a thing as an Arab Muslim.

Aside from being utterly fallacious and lacking both historical and scriptural support, arguments that attempt to make Jesus and his apostles Arab Christians are rife with anti-Judaism and antisemitism, both of which are inimical to the Christian faith. Whether subtle or blatant, Palestinian Christian supersessionism flies in the face of the Apostolic Scriptures which affirm that Jesus[103] and all of the apostles, including Paul, were Jews and citizens of Israel,[104] not Arabs, Canaanites, or Palestinians. It is a simple fact of history that the very earliest form of Christianity was exclusively Jewish—indeed, one of the many Judaisms or sects of Judaism that existed in the first century of the Common Era. Cecil Sherman rightly observes that because Jesus and his disciples were all Jews, "they were expected to have the loyalties, traditions, patriotism that goes with being a good Jew. That meant that when the Council (the Sanhedrin) commanded them to do something, they obeyed."[105] This statement is categorically true in light of Jesus' own instruction to his disciples: "The teachers of the law and the Pharisees sit in Moses' seat. So you must be careful to do everything they tell you."[106]

There simply were no non-Jews in the earliest community of believers who recognized Jesus as the Messiah and Lord of Israel. During the three and one-half years of his ministry, Jesus did not seek to add a single Gentile to the number of his original disciples during his ministry on earth. This is clear from the specific instructions that Jesus gave to his apostles: "Do not go in the way of the Gentiles, and do not enter any city of the Samaritans; but rather go to the lost sheep of the house of Israel."[107] It is further confirmed by the fact that Jesus initially refused to respond to a "Canaanite" woman

---

[102] Acts 10:1–48.

[103] Hebrews 7:14.

[104] Mike Liles, Jr., *Christian Faith in Contemporary Society: The Framework for Belief* (Lincoln, NE: iUniverse, 2005), p. 366. Liles notes the fact that "Jesus' apostles and the leaders of the early Christian Church were all ethnically Jewish," though he also observes correctly that "within a few centuries, indeed even decades, Jewish Christian leadership of the Christian Church all but vanished."

[105] Cecil E. Sherman, *Formations Commentary: Luke–Acts* (Macon, GA: Smyth & Helwys Publishing, 2006), p. 174.

[106] Matthew 23:2–3, NIV.

[107] Matthew 10:5, NIV.

who had petitioned him to exorcise a demon from her daughter. When his disciples questioned him for ignoring the woman, Jesus replied, "I was sent only to the lost sheep of Israel."[108] Then, he answered the woman's petition by saying, "It is not right to take the children's bread and toss it to the dogs."[109]

Coupled with his foray into Galilee of the Gentiles,[110] where he delivered a demon-possessed Gadarene,[111] the Master's ultimate response to the Canaanite woman's faith wherein he delivered her daughter, was, no doubt, predictive of the fact that the mission of his community would eventually include the non-Jews of the world. Indeed, such a mission was necessary in order for God's promise to Abraham to be fulfilled when he said, "In your offspring all the nations of the earth will be blessed."[112] It was not, however, until after his resurrection that Jesus commanded his disciples to herald the gospel of the kingdom into all the world.[113] Even when the apostle Peter was commissioned by the Holy Spirit to visit the household of Cornelius in Caesarea Maritima,[114] he would only undertake that mission after receiving divine instructions in a vision that was set in the context of Jewish kosher laws.[115] Saying that Jesus and his apostles were Arabs or Canaanites, therefore, is not only patently absurd; it is also mendacious and highly antisemitic.

Ultimately, if Palestinian Christians and their supporters in mainstream Protestant Christianity, as well as some in Evangelical circles, actually believe that the resurrected Jesus will ultimately return to earth, then they must get used to the idea that when he returns, he will not be a cosmic Christ[116] or a universal man.[117] Instead, he will

---

[108] Matthew 15:24, NIV.

[109] Matthew 15:26, NIV. Jesus used the term *dogs* that was then commonly used by Jews to describe Gentiles. See Cynthia A. Jarvis and E. Elizabeth Johnson, *Feasting on the Gospels—Mark* (Louisville, KY: Westminster John Knox Press, 2014), p. 209. This incident proves that Jesus and his disciples were not "Canaanites."

[110] Isaiah 9:1 speaks of an area "beyond Jordan, in Galilee of the Gentiles." This same term is used in Matthew 4:15, where it describes the territory east of the Jordan River, which included eight of the ten cities of the Decapolis (Greek for "Ten Cities") in what is now Jordan and Syria. (The other two cities of the Decapolis, Scythopolis [Beit-Shean] and Hippos, were in Israel.) Gadara, the town and territory where the demoniac whom Jesus delivered lived, was also included in the area of "Galilee of the Gentiles."

[111] Mark 5:1–10.

[112] Genesis 22:18.

[113] Acts 1:8.

[114] Acts 10:1–48.

[115] Acts 10:14.

[116] John R. Levison and Priscilla Pope-Levison, "The New Contextual Christologies: Liberation and Inculturation," in *Global Dictionary of Theology: A Resource for the Worldwide Church*, William A. Dyrness and Veli-Matti Kärkkäinen, eds. (Downers Grove, IL: InterVarsity Press, 2008), p. 185. The Levisons maintain that Jesus is manifest as the cosmic Christ across ethnic lines and in all of the world's major religions.

[117] Patrick Carnegie Simpson, *The Fact of Christ: A Series of Lectures* (Grand Rapids, MI: Fleming H. Revell Co. 1901), p. 51. In an effort to establish the universal appeal of Jesus, Simpson has magnanimously, but wrongly, said that Jesus "transcends all ethnic limitations and divisions."

still be the same Jew that he was when he ascended into heaven.[118] This truth was confirmed unequivocally and unambiguously in Peter's Pentecost sermon, in which he said that because "God had sworn with an oath to [King David] that he would seat one of his descendants on his throne, he looked ahead and spoke of the resurrection of the Messiah, that he was neither abandoned in Hades, nor did his flesh suffer decay."[119] Christian Scripture proves that Jesus was born to a Jewish mother,[120] lived his life as a Jew,[121] died as a Jew,[122] was resurrected as a Jew,[123] ascended into heaven as a Jew,[124] is seated at God's right hand as a Jew,[125] and will also return as a Jew.[126] Any attempt to make Jesus the cosmic Christ or universal man instead of the Jewish Jesus—or to ascribe to him any ethnicity except his inherent Jewishness—perpetuates historical Christian anti-Judaism and mirrors pre-Nazi antisemitism. As Nigel Leaves notes, when "pastors, bishops, professors of theology, religion teachers, and laity" in pre-World War II Germany advanced a "perverted scholarship, that denied the Jewishness of Jesus and falsely promoted his Aryan roots," they "laid the foundations for anti-Semitism that was a short-step away from countenancing the horrors of the concentration camp."[127]

All attempts to disconnect Jesus and his apostles from their Jewish families and the Jewish milieu in which they lived or to wrench their message from the matrix of biblical and Second Temple Judaism from which it emerged clearly diminish the credibility of any who engage in such efforts, including Palestinian Christians. The connection of many Palestinian Christians with their Arab heritage has, therefore, created a dilemma for them. Kathleen Christison says that "in a milieu so strongly perceived by the non-Arab world to be Islamic and therefore alien, Arab Christians have always been the poor relatives

[118] Acts 1:11. The two angels who witnessed Jesus' ascension assured the disciples, "This same Jesus . . . will come back in the same way you have seen him go into heaven." Jesus was a Jew, and he never changed his ethnicity. Since Jesus ascended in a glorified Judean body, he will return in the same body.

[119] Acts 2:30–31.

[120] Matthew 2:2.

[121] John 4:9.

[122] Luke 23:38.

[123] Romans 1:2–3.

[124] Acts 2:34.

[125] Hebrews 7:14–17.

[126] Acts 1:11.

[127] Nigel Leaves, "Who Do You Say that I Am? Preaching Jesus Today," in *Wisdom and Imagination: Religious Progressives and the Search for Meaning*, Rex A. E. Hunt and Gregory C. Jenks, eds. (Eugene, OR: Wipf and Stock Publishers, 2014), p. 126.

of Western Christianity. . . . Western Christians, if they know of their Arab co-religionists at all, are unsympathetic to this unique theological and national dilemma."[128] The answer to this dilemma is not a false narrative that makes Jesus and his apostles Palestinian Christians and ignoring Arab Muslim atrocities against both Jews and Christians. It is Arab and Palestinian Christians embracing their long-alienated brothers and cousins, the Jewish people, and finding a place of mutual respect in the land of the Bible.

It is a sad twist of history that the Muslim Arab intransigence that obviated the opportunity for the League of Nations Covenant and Mandate for Palestine to produce a homeland for the Jews also prevented the creation of a homeland for both Christian and Muslim Palestinians, especially the Christians. "That a 'national home' materialized for the Jewish inhabitants of Palestine is an unfortunate consequence of a mandate that had as its original aim to enable the inhabitants of the lands once ruled by the Ottoman Empire one day to 'stand by themselves.'"[129] Will Stalder observes that when the British "endeavored to establish a home for both peoples . . . the nature of that home was unsatisfactory in the eyes of the 'non-Jewish communities of Palestine' and was the cause of much opposition from the land's Arab inhabitants."[130] Benny Morris points out that a settlement of the League of Nations Covenant for Palestine and its British Mandate that would have been satisfactory to the Palestinian Arabs at the time was virtually precluded by the fact that most of the Arabs had supported the Ottoman Empire in World War I. Because these Arabs had aligned themselves against the Christian Allied powers that were led by Britain, the British were not inclined to help them. Additionally, Morris observes that at the same time, neither a "Palestinian Arab national movement nor any separate Palestinian Arab national consciousness"[131] existed. The self-identifying ethnicity preferred by Arab Palestinians of the time was that of Arabs, not Palestinians.

In reality, Palestinian Christians have been caught in a no-man's

[128] Kathleen Christison, "Dilemmas of Arab Christianity," *Journal of Palestinian Studies,* vol. 22, no. 1 (Autumn 1992), pp. 117–119.

[129] This provision was a key declaration of the original League of Nations Covenant with Palestine, Article 22. Will Stalder, *Palestinian Christians and the Old Testament History, Hermeneutics, and Ideology* (Minneapolis, MN: Augsburg Fortress Press, 2015), pp. 145–146.

[130] Stalder, p. 146.

[131] Benny Morris, *1948: A History of the First Arab-Israeli War* (New Haven, CT: Yale University Press, 2008), p. 10.

land, "squeezed by Israel's crippling military blockage of the West Bank and the rise of Muslim fundamentalism."[132] Now, "in Bethlehem, the once-prosperous hub of Palestinian Christian life, [Christians] no longer represent a majority [of the population]."[133] Tom Doyle notes that by 2000, "Palestinian Christians [were] already suffering under Hamas rule," and he noted that "if a Palestinian State becomes a reality, it will only get worse. Religious freedom will be nonexistent."[134] Finally, he observed that "this is vastly different [from] what the Palestinians have experienced with Israel's government. The Israelis have destroyed no mosques since 1948," and they have destroyed no Christian churches. In reality, Israel is the only nation in the Middle East that truly protects Christians and allows them to coexist in peace and security alongside the majority population.[135] Leaders in most Muslim nations give lip service to Christian religious freedom; however, Christians who live in these societies are always second-class citizens, for they remain vulnerable to the whims of autocratic leaders, and they periodically experience violence, rape, murder, and the destruction of their properties, including their churches and schools.[136] As a result of such atrocities, 80% of Palestinian Christians have fled territories controlled by the Palestinian Authority and Hamas.

A few Palestinian Christians have come to understand the right relationship that they should have with the Jewish people as co-heirs of God's promises to Abraham. These brave and visionary believers have begun to work toward rapprochement with the Jewish community by engaging in dialogue and striving for mutually supportive

[132] Mat Spetalnick, "War-Weary Christians Seek Escape from Holy Land," *Reuters News Service*, 12/17/2003, posted at http://www.unitedjerusalem.org/index2.asp?id=384317&Date=12/25/2003. The use of the term *fundamentalism* here is not to be confused with fundamentalist Christian denominations.

[133] Spetalnick, "War-Weary."

[134] Tom Doyle, *Two Nations Under God: Why You Should Care about Israel* (Nashville, TN: B&H Publishing Group, 2004), pp. 145–146.

[135] To affirm this statement, one only has to recall the unrelenting Muslim Brotherhood violence against Coptic Christians in Egypt, the rape, torture, enslavement, and slaughter of Iraqi Christians by ISIS, the fate of Syrian Christians caught between ISIS and Bashar al-Assad's vicious regime, and the total abuse, debasement, and violence that is constantly experienced by Christians in Pakistan.

[136] Doyle, p. 146. In fact, even after the Six-Day War wrested control of East Jerusalem from the Jordanians, Israel continued to allow Jordanian Muslims to oversee the Al-Aqsa Mosque and the Dome of the Rock that were built on the ruins of the ancient Jewish Temple complex by Caliph Abd al-Malik in the late seventh century AD. This was quite an amazing Jewish gesture for peace considering the fact that when Jordan seized control of the West Bank and much of Jerusalem in 1948, its armies looted and destroyed 58 synagogues, ransacked the Jewish cemetery on the Mount of Olives where Jews had buried their dead for more than two millennia, and then, for nineteen years, denied all Jews access to their holiest shrine, the Western Wall of the Temple Mount. The grace and mercy that the Israeli government has shown in its efforts to promote peace and religious freedom even in the face of the cynical banality of religious bigotry that has been—and is still being—directed against its citizens by the Muslim authorities has been, and continues to be, simply incredible!

relationships with Jews who love peace and want to share it and who understand human suffering and wish to help alleviate it within the Palestinian Christian community.[137] Those Palestinian Christians who have made such efforts have been roundly criticized by other Christians and have been threatened with significant violence by Muslim Arab "Palestinians." Efforts toward cooperation between these Palestinian Christians and Jews represent small beginnings, but they could well have significant long-term consequences. It would only be fitting if two parallel streams of faith in the God of Scripture, Christians and Jews, could demonstrate to the rest of the Arab and Muslim world—as well as to the antisemitic anti-Zionists—that the family of Abraham can have peace among themselves when they fully demonstrate once and for all Abraham's unequivocal faith in God and his magnanimous deference toward all, including his family and his non-Hebrew neighbors. Only time will tell.

## Never Experiencing True Biblical Repentance

It would be reasonable to think that the entire Christian church would have brought its centuries-old non-Christian attitudes and actions toward the Jewish people to a complete and irreversible halt, especially when the Holocaust finally revealed the deepest depths to which human depravity could sink. Sadly, however, this has not been the case, for the old, deep-seated hatred of Jews and things Jewish has continued to smolder in the church's corporate subconsciousness, just waiting for an excuse to vaunt itself again in a new, improved form. Tragically, the historical morphing of antisemitism "has occurred not only in the secular realm but also in the religious world."[138] In many cases, the old demons of ancient antisemitism burrowed themselves into the deepest recesses of the Christian consciousness where they eventually spawned new politically correct and even

[137] What is relatively unknown to most Western Christians, including Evangelicals, is the fact that Israeli Orthodox Rabbi Shlomo Riskin's Center for Jewish Christian Understanding and Cooperation (CJCUC) is lending both moral and material support to Palestinian Christians through its "Blessing Bethlehem" program which assists Palestinian Christians who are suffering under the restrictive control of the Arab Muslim Palestinian Authority and Hamas. CJCUC also began raising funds to aid in the construction of a $3.75 million multi-purpose facility to house the operations of Holy Land Missions after this Palestinian Christian organization was evicted from its facilities in East Jerusalem. See David Nekrutman, "A Call to Action," in *The Jerusalem Post Christian Edition*, October 2013, posted at http://jewishisrael.ning.com/page/cjcuc-s-executive-director-david-nekrutman-appeals-for-funds-to-b. Also, "Director of Rabbi Riskin's Interfaith Center Appeals for Funding to Build Church in Jerusalem," in *Jewish Israel*, October 27, 2013, posted at http://jewishisrael.ning.com/profiles/blogs/director-of-rabbi-riskin-s-interfaith-center-appeals-for-funding-.

[138] Cardaun, p. 60.

morally justifiable manifestations of Judaeophobia, anti-Judaism, and antisemitism.[139]

More than forty years ago, Alan Davies accurately predicted the emergence of just such new forms of antisemitism in the religious realm: "Anti-Zionism sooner or later reveals a distressing tendency to shade into anti-Semitism"[140] because "anti-Semitic convictions can be transposed without any difficulty into the new language of anti-Zionism."[141] While many of the Christian supporters of anti-Israelism may appear to be innocuous, their anti-Zionism is at bottom nothing more than another manifestation of antisemitism. As a matter of fact, anti-Zionism is the new antisemitism that is now in vogue in many Christian circles, where attacks on Zionist "colonialism" usually give vent to latent, but insidious, antisemitism. The seeds of this new form of antisemitism began to germinate in Christianity when the Muslim Arab and Palestinian propaganda that had been directed relentlessly against the state and people of Israel was so augmented by the antisemitic Western news media that it began to impact mainstream Christian denominations and, more recently, even some formerly pro-Israel Evangelicals.

Shockingly, Christianity has learned very little from its own abysmal history of religious, social, and political positions relative to the Jews and Judaism. In spite of the history of more than a millennium of violence against the Jewish people, an amazing number of Christians today still either have antipathy toward the Jewish people or are at best apathetic toward them. Despite gut-wrenching, Holocaust-induced efforts at repentance and reconciliation with Jews by some Christians, the virulent antisemitism that led Christians in past centuries to wreak abominable havoc and unmentionable atrocities upon the Jewish people was never fully expunged from the corporate Christian consciousness or its polities. Godly sorrow brought on by one generation's confrontation with the horrors of the Holocaust has been forgotten by succeeding generations simply because Christianity has had a non-Hebraic—and therefore non-biblical—understanding of repentance.

---

[139] Manfred Gerstenfeld, *The War of a Million Cuts: The Struggle Against the Delegitimization of Israel and the Jews, and the Growth of New Anti-Semitism* (Jerusalem, Israel: Jerusalem Center for Public Affairs, 2015), p. 12. In this comprehensive study, Gerstenfeld exposes a wide range of issues regarding the new antisemitism that is manifest today in anti-Zionism and anti-Israelism. Understanding that these circumstances are rooted not merely in political or social strife but in pure antisemitism enables students of the Middle Eastern conflict to gain a broader perspective on these issues.

[140] Alan T. Davies, "Anti-Zionism, Anti-Semitism and the Christian Mind," *The Christian Century*, August 19, 1970, p. 987.

[141] Davies, p. 987.

For centuries, the Christian concept of repentance has been influenced by the fact that the word for repentance that appears in the Greek text of both the Septuagint and the Apostolic Scriptures, *metanoia*, literally means "to change one's mind."[142] This Greek word can be contrasted with the word that Hebrew Scriptures use for repentance, *teshuvah*, which means to "turn [the whole person] around and go in the opposite direction."[143] The prophets, sages, and apostles understood that turning the whole person, not just changing the mind, was necessary for repentance. This is why John the Baptizer required the baptism of the body, not the mind, when he preached repentance to Israel.[144] The immersion of the whole body demonstrated that the whole person had turned from sin and started in the opposite direction toward obedience.[145] True *teshuvah* requires more than a change of mind: it requires recognition of the sin, confession of the sin, remorse (godly sorrow) for the sin, resolution never to repeat the sin again, and finally overcoming the temptation that originally produced the sin when that temptation reappears.

The church's repentance for antisemitism may have represented a change of mind for many; however, in many cases, it did not represent genuine Godly sorrow for the sin of antisemitism and making a 180-degree turn and going in the opposite direction with the utter resolve never again to commit that sin. Sadly, while Christianity has changed its mind, it has not completed the process of repentance.

---

[142] Louw and Nida's *Greek-English Lexicon of the New Testament* says that *metanoia* and its related verb forms *metanoeo* and *metamelomai* mean to "change one's mind, to think differently," and they expand the meaning to include "to change one's way of life as the result of a complete change of thought and attitude with regard to sin and righteousness." For a comprehensive discussion of *metanoia*, see L. Michael White, "Repentance," in *Encyclopedia of Early Christianity*, Everett Ferguson, ed. Abingdon, UK: Routledge, 1999), pp. 977–978.

[143] In reality, the Septuagint captured the Hebrew idea of *teshuvah* much better when it used the Greek word *strepho*, which means "to turn" or "to return." In contrast, the Septuagint generally used the Greek word *metanoia* to translate the Hebrew word *nacham*, which meant "to sigh" as a way of expressing regret for sorrow as in 1 Samuel 15:11, where God is said to have regretted that he anointed Saul king over Israel. Interestingly, the Greek word *metamelo*, a verbal form of *metanoia*, was used to express the danger that the Israelites "might *change their minds* and return to Egypt" (Exodus 13:17 [emphasis added]). Clearly, the Greek word *strepho* is a better translation of the Hebrew word *shuv* than *metanoia* is. For some reason, the word *metanoia* was preferred in the Koine Greek of the Apostolic Scriptures over the Septuagint's word *strepho*; therefore, the full extent of the meaning of repentance (that of "turning") is not nearly as clear in the Greek New Testament as it was in the Septuagint rendering of the Hebrew Scriptures.

[144] Mark 1:4.

[145] John's immersion rites were carried out at the south ford of the Jordan River adjacent to the Dead Sea, the very place where the Israelites had entered the Promised Land some 1500 years before that time. By leading the repentant Jews eastward into the Jordan and then having them turn again westward toward Israel, John had them demonstrating that they had left their old status in the land of their ancestors and were turning themselves, returning with a new status of righteousness in the kingdom of God.

Consequently, it has found itself constantly changing its mind—changing with the winds of doctrine, social pressure, and political expediency—vacillating between support for the Jewish people and arrogance against them.

Isaac Rottenberg has pointed out the fundamental problem with Christian repentance for the Holocaust: it has never really faced the facts of its own complicity with antisemitism during the two millennia of its history. "The pathology of a past not faced can be very subtle but still very powerful," Rottenberg observed, because "unfaced facts do not disappear; they become the underground saboteurs of human existence."[146] The problem for Christians, he said, is that "the Holocaust is isolated from Christian history."[147] The church, therefore, has failed to engage in the first step of biblical repentance: recognition of its sin. In order to underscore the importance of recognizing sin, Rottenberg paraphrased the words of Jesus thus: "You hypocrites, you are quite good at analyzing the phenomena of nature, but you refuse to face those aspects of history which disturb your complacency and call you to account."[148]

Today's Christians would do well to imitate the prophet Daniel who, though not guilty of personal transgressions, nevertheless repented for the sins of his people in this manner: "I prayed to the LORD my God and confessed and said . . . we have sinned, committed iniquity, acted wickedly and rebelled. . . . Open shame belongs to us, O LORD, to our kings, our princes and our fathers, because we have sinned against you."[149] Because most Christians have not recognized and repented for the sins of the past that their Christian ancestors perpetrated against the Jewish people, they have left themselves vulnerable to new and even more subtle temptations in the same genre. If they had been wise enough to recognize and confess the sins of their fathers as well as their own mistakes, they would have been better equipped to have overcome the new forms of the same old temptation to sin when they were challenged with them.[150]

[146] Rottenberg, p. 17.

[147] Rottenberg, p. 17.

[148] Rottenberg, p. 17, paraphrasing Luke 12:56.

[149] Daniel 9:4–8.

[150] See page 431 for a *Personal Teshuvah* document that can assist you in expressing your own remorse and repentance for the historical Judaeophobia, anti-Judaism, and antisemitism that have been perpetrated against the Jewish people and to affirm your solidarity with the Jewish people and their nation.

## New Garments: Same Old Mistakes

Today, almost no Western Christian would ever even think of joining the Crusaders in herding Jews into their synagogues and burning them alive, nor would they participate in a Spanish-Inquisition *auto de fé* by burning Jews at the stake, nor would they ever sport the *Sieg Heil* salute and work in one of the Nazi death camps. At the same time, however, a staggeringly high percentage of Western Christian denominations have compromised the faith of Jesus and the apostles by importing pagan philosophies into their doctrines and polities. They have lost their mooring in the safe harbor of the Jewish teachings of Jesus and the apostles and have found themselves adrift in a maelstrom of politically correct but biblically deplorable ideas.

Sadly, these are the denominations that have eagerly joined arm in arm with Muslim nations and others who openly seek to destroy Israel and annihilate the Jewish people. When they advocate for the destruction of the nation of Israel and openly support efforts to disenfranchise the Jewish people and do them emotional, material, and physical harm, Christians today have been duped into believing that their antisemitism is justifiable, even divinely inspired because it serves their higher cause of humanitarianism, multiculturalism, or globalism! Most mainstream Christian denominations in the West have been tricked again by the archenemy of true Christian faith and have fallen prey to the same devices that prompted Paul to chide the Corinthian church with these words: "I am afraid that just as Eve was beguiled by the serpent's cunning, your thoughts will be led astray from the simplicity that is in Christ."[151] The church that should never have been "ignorant of Satan's schemes"[152] has again been "outwitted"[153] by the enemy so that it has been swept up in a tidal wave of deception and has found itself on the wrong side of history, but, more importantly, on the wrong side of God. The old adage, "There are none so blind as those who will not see,"[154] applies to far too many Christians,[155] especially to those whose smug and sanctimonious self-righteousness clouds their own vision and renders them as little more than blind guides leading naïve blind followers into the ditch

[151] 2 Corinthians 11:3, author's translation.

[152] 2 Corinthians 2:11.

[153] 2 Corinthians 2:11, ESV.

[154] The complete adage says, "There are none so blind as those who will not see. The most deluded people are those who choose to ignore what they already know." *Random House Dictionary of Popular Proverbs and Sayings* attributes this saying to John Heywood, 1546.

[155] As a matter of fact, if Paul were writing to the church in today's world, he would likely say, "I would not have you to be ignorant of this one thing that blindness [or hardness] in part has happened to the church!" as a parallel to his observation regarding the "partial blindness of Israel" in the first century (Romans 11:25).

of prophetic oblivion in a manner shockingly similar to that of the "blind guides" whom Jesus excoriated in his day.[156]

Right when God has been sovereignly restoring his Chosen People to their land in the greatest miracle of modern times, large segments of the Christian church have taken up arms against God to challenge his right to fulfill his covenant, oath, and promises to Abraham and his lineal descendants. Armed with pompous self-righteousness, they vaunt their own ideas and standards of "justice," "human rights" and "fairness." They shake their fists in God's face and shout, "Stop! You can't do this! We won't let you!" What if God is restoring Israel by fulfilling the promise he made to Israel through the prophet Isaiah, wherein he predicted that he would produce a miracle that would be so spectacular that it would eclipse the drama of the Exodus from Egypt?[157] Indeed, what if he is bringing the Jewish people from the north, south, east, and west[158] so he can plant them again in their own land never to be removed?[159] "We know better," the critics say. "Anyway, our great German and British theologians long ago proved that all that Old Testament stuff is nothing but myth and legend,"[160] they sneer. "And besides that, we now have a new, more refined God, a universalist who would never even remotely consider letting himself be viewed as a particularist tribal god."[161]

[156] Matthew 15:14; 23:24. It is hardly comforting to know that even in Jesus' day there were "blind guides"who failed to lead God's people in paths of justice, mercy, and faith and, instead, were utterly focused on minutiae to such a degree that they "closed the doors of the kingdom in the people's faces" (Matthew 23:13).

[157] Jeremiah 16:14–15: "Therefore behold, the days are coming, declares the Lord, when they will no longer say, 'As surely the Lord lives, who brought up the sons of Israel from the land of Egypt,' but they will say, 'As surely as the Lord lives, who brought the descendants of Israel up out of the land of the north and out of all the countries where he had banished them.' Then they will live in their own land." This has been the miracle of the twentieth century, and it continues.

[158] Isaiah 43:6

[159] 1 Chronicles 17:9; Amos 9:15.

[160] The effort to "demythologize" both the Hebrew and Apostolic Scriptures began with Julius Wellhausen in the late nineteenth century and was built on the foundation of the thinking of Baruch Spinoza and other Enlightenment biblical critics. G. T. Sheppard and A. C. Thiselton, "Biblical Interpretation in Europe in the Twentieth Century," in *Dictionary of Major Biblical Interpreters*, Donald K. McKim, ed. (Downers Grove, IL: InterVarsity Press, 2007), p. 88. Also, Peter L. Berger, *The Sacred Canopy: Elements of a Sociological Theory of Religion* (New York: Random House, Inc., 1990), p. 201, n. 18., and John Rogerson, *Old Testament Criticism in the Nineteenth Century: England and Germany* (Eugene, OR: Wipf and Stock Publishers, 1984), pp. 152, 266. Rudolph Bultmann took the argument of demythologizing Scripture further by interpreting what he described as mythological elements of Scripture existentially, and by saying that "salvation history . . . must be demythologized to get to the reality of God's salvation of a human being." Yung Hoon Hyun, *Redemptive-Historical Hermeneutics and Homiletics: Debates in Holland, America and Korea from 1930 to 2012* (Eugene, OR: Wipf and Stock Publishers, 2015), p. 6. John Timbrell maintained that historical higher criticism's demythologizing efforts produced arguments that "the vast body of Old Testament prophecy relative to [the] glorious future of restored Israel is simply a 'myth," or a 'divine romance,' which somehow got mixed in [the] inextricable confusion with the whole body of Messianic prophecy." John Hamilton Timbrell, *The Last Message of Jesus Christ: or, The Apocalypse in a New Light* (New York: Eaton & Mains, 1905), p. 97.

[161] Neil Ormerod, *A Public God: Natural Theology Reconsidered* (Minneapolis, MN: Augsburg Fortress Press, 2015), pp. 150–152.

So much of this new generation of Christianity is so steeped in humanistic theories of "biblical origins as well as in an evolutionary world view" that, as Bronson Barkley says, "such literal considerations are mere poppycock when measured against the weight of their intellectual relativism and pragmatic considerations of social survival."[162] In other words, "the legitimacy of their place in the stream of history and of their institutional survival is on the line; thus there is now underway a great falling away from biblical integrity."[163]

Many Christians have indeed created a god in their own image by sanitizing the God of Scripture and freeing him from some of his more unsavory "Jewish" qualities. With its entrenched Greek rationalism, Christianity has come to fit the Pauline description: "Ever learning but unable to acknowledge the truth."[164] This is especially true when it comes to recognizing and affirming God's continuing relationship with the Jewish people and his support for their nation and land. When God sees all of this, he laughs, and then he further depletes the membership rolls of those churches that challenge his authority by leading thousands, yea millions, to abandon the hallowed—and hollow—sanctuaries of nominal, mainstream Christianity.[165]

## Shedding Misotheist Apparel, Being Arrayed in Divine Justice

The tragic barbaric brutality of the Holocaust did not bring enough individual Christians and enough Christian denominations to true biblical repentance for the church's complicity in being one of many breeding grounds that produced the nadir of human depravity. For so many, it only served to drive much of Christian antisemitism underground where it continued to seethe, awaiting an opportunity and an excuse to erupt. Like the political and religious leaders in ancient Israel whom the Hebrew prophets excoriated for their arrogant rebellion in the face of divine imperatives, many Christians have

[162] Bronson Barkley, personal communication.

[163] Barkley, personal communication.

[164] 2 Timothy 3:7.

[165] Axel R. Schäfer, *Countercultural Conservatives: American Evangelicalism from the Postwar Revival to the Christian Right* (Madison, WI: The University of Wisconsin Press, 2011), p. 17. Schäfer reports that while mainstream denominational membership grew significantly in mid-twentieth century, by the last decade of the twentieth century, despite the fact that the population of the United States had grown by 38%, the membership of Presbyterian denominations had declined by 29%, Episcopalians by 22%, Congregationalists by 27%, and United Methodist by 18%. In the thirty years since that time, membership losses have continued at alarming rates. Also, Douglas Jacobsen, *The World's Christians: Who They Are, Where They Are, and How They Got There* (Chichester, UK: John Wiley & Sons, 2011), p. 234. Jacobsen reports that in the past forty years, mainline Protestantism has lost almost 50% of its membership (adjusted for population growth). Statics are even more grim in European churches where once bustling and proud cathedrals and basilicas are have been transformed into museums and restaurants. Also, David T. Olson, *The American Church in Crisis* (Grand Rapids, MI: Zondervan Publishing, 2008).

adopted the ways of the heathen and even dare to vaunt themselves against the Lord. They give open support to "the kings of the earth and the rulers," the political leaders of society who demand acquiescence to their agendas in return for recognition, accolades, and elevated social status. Then, they join such political forces in "plotting together against the LORD and against his anointed," saying, "Let us break their chains and free ourselves from their restraints."[166]

The human heart, whether Christian, agnostic, atheist, or pagan hates YHWH, the God of the Jews, for the moral constraints that he places upon it through his commandments, and it hates his Chosen People because they represent those commandments and live by them.[167] Despite the rebellion against the absolute ethics of Holy Scripture in which those of the carnal mind engage, however, "the one enthroned in heaven laughs; the LORD ridicules them," saying, "I have installed my chosen king on the throne in Jerusalem, on my holy mountain."[168] The "rulers and authorities, the cosmic powers of the world's darkness, and the spiritual forces of evil in the heavenlies[169] think they have established the center of gravity for world order in New York or in Brussels or in Washington or in Moscow or in Beijing, but God has other plans. His kingdom will be universal, but it will be headquartered in the one piece of real estate where he chose to place his name,[170] the city of Jerusalem, the foundation of world peace.

Surely it is time, at the very least for Christians, if not for the secular, postmodern, neopagans of Western societies, to take off the blinders and see the picture that is much bigger than the propaganda of the anti-Zionist antisemites that is vaunted in the liberal media. Christians who sit in churches and listen to diatribes against Israel or read reports of such charges in denominational literature should engage in boycotts and divestiture themselves by boycotting the churches that engage in such anti-Israelism and by divesting themselves of their membership in and support for such churches and denominations. Organizations that call for the boycott of Israeli-made goods and services should themselves be boycotted

---

[166] Psalm 2:2–3, NIV, NLT.

[167] Paul establishes this truth in Romans 8:7: "The mind of the flesh is hostile toward God; for it does not subject itself to the law of God, for it is not even able to do so." It is the nature of the human mind to hate God and his restrictions. The only solution to this dilemma is this: "Do not conform to the pattern of this world, but be transformed by the renewing of your mind. Then you will be able to test and approve what God's will is."

[168] Psalm 2:4–6, NIV, NLT, HCSB.

[169] Ephesians 6:12.

[170] 2 Chronicles 6:6. The sages have suggested that God literally stamped his name in the topography of the city of Jerusalem because the valleys that circumscribe and intersect the city of Jerusalem form the Hebrew letter *shin* which universally stands for the divine name, *Shaddai* ("the Almighty").

by tithe-paying parishioners. If one claims to be a Christian, it is time to take a stand for what the Bible, the founding document of the Christian faith, says! And, much to the chagrin of many nominal Christians, the Bible just happens to be a Jewish book![171] It is time to open this Jewish book, read it, and live by it—all of it, not just a few selected passages that serve as pious platitudes for many Christian leaders who are more dedicated to political correctness than they are to divine truth.

Many Christians today desperately need a Damascus Road experience, a supernatural encounter with the living Jesus. If and when they do, they will once and for all be knocked off their high horse of triumphalistic supersessionism against the Jews. And, then, they will be so utterly stunned that they will only moan, "Who are you, Lord?" They would have to ask this question because they would never have recognized the real Jesus—the Jewish Jesus—unless he were standing before them in the flesh—Jewish flesh! Finally, they would receive a new commission that would redirect their path away from the deceptive beguilement of the enemy, reconnect them with the Hebrew truth of the Bible, and send them on a mission of loving support for the international Jewish community and the nation of Israel.

Neither Jesus nor Paul encouraged believers to learn the views of the godless societies in which they lived and syncretize their Hebraic faith with those views. In the richest of Jewish tradition, they instructed believers to read and practice Holy Scripture.[172] It is far better to be biblically correct than it is to be politically correct! At best, political correctness will gain only ephemeral recognition and evanescent validation in the constantly changing relativism of atheistic, secularist, and neopagan societies. Biblical correctness will ensure blessings that will endure in eternity.

Perhaps the majority of Christians who have either joined or tacitly support secular or religious anti-Zionist movements have done so in an honest and conscientious effort to combat what their political and denominational leaders have described as Israeli racism, discrimination, colonialism, and human suffering. It is time now for them to open their eyes and see the larger picture and to conform their thinking and actions to the purposes of God, which he has explicitly stated in his unilateral, unequivocal, irrevocable, and eternal covenant with the Jewish people.

[171] John D. Garr, *Christian Fruit—Jewish Root: Theology of Hebraic Restoration* (Atlanta, GA: Golden Key Press, 2015), pp. 35–48.

[172] John 5:39; 2 Timothy 3:15–16.

CHAPTER 18

# A CURE FOR ANTISEMITISM?

## Is Peace Possible in the Middle East?

When King David recorded the divine injunction: "Pray for the peace of Jerusalem," he also said, "May there be peace within your walls and security within your citadels."[1] The commitment to pray for peace, however, "is not facile optimism nor mere wishful thinking."[2] In reality, it is "eschatological," for when the Psalmist speaks of entering Jerusalem, he "*really does* mean to enter a new world."[3] His speaking of living for God's sake[4] and for the sake of others[5] is a call "to experience, embody, and extend the justice God intends for the world."[6] The prophets of Israel, says Paul Steinberg, "place the welfare of Israel at the epicenter of the struggle for peace. That peace is not simply geographical, but rather peace for all peoples. . . . In praying for the security of Israel, we pray, too, for morality and peace everywhere."[7]

### Jerusalem: The Foundation of Peace

The Hebrew word *Yerushalayim* (Jerusalem) probably means "people, house, or habitation of peace," with *Yeru-* being a segolate noun meaning "men or people and hence house or habitation" and *shalayim* meaning "peace." Wilhelm Gesenius also suggests that the *Yerushalyim* can mean "foundation of peace," with "the former part of this name [*Yeru-*] from the

[1] Psalm 122:6–7, NIV.

[2] J. Clinton McCann, Jr., *A Theological Introduction to the Book of Psalms: The Psalms as Torah* (Nashville, TN. Abingdon Press, 1993), p. 154.

[3] McCann, Jr., p. 154.

[4] Psalm 120:9.

[5] Psalm 120:8.

[6] McCann, Jr., p. 154.

[7] Paul Steinberg, *Celebrating the Jewish Year: The Spring and Summer Holidays: Passover, The Omer, Shavuot, Tisha b'Av*, Janet Greenstein Potter, ed. (Philadelphia, PA: The Jewish Publication Society, 2009), p. 117.

root [*yarah*], signifying foundation [and *shalayim* meaning "peace]."[8] Whatever etymological definition is used for *Yerushalayim*, however, the focal point of the name of the Holy City is *Salem*, which means peace. Indeed, this was the name of the city in Abraham's day when he visited Melchizedek the priest-king of Salem.[9] The place where God chose to place his name has always meant—and will always mean—"peace." Ironically, however, from the pages of the most ancient of recorded history to the headlines of today's newspapers, Jerusalem, the "city of peace," the "foundation of peace," has been the scene of ongoing violence as a veritable parade of princes, kings, megalomaniacs, despots, religious leaders, messianic pretenders, and zealots of different religious faiths have vied for dominance over this area. Despite the machinations of men, however, God has ordained that his city will always be the "foundation of world peace."

Perhaps this is why King David made this profound declaration regarding peace: "Shun evil and do good: seek peace and *pursue* it."[10] One rabbinic *midrash* interprets this command to mean that the believer is to seek peace in his own place and then to pursue it everywhere else.[11] It is not enough to seek peace only in one's family or community or in one's small personal sphere of influence. *Shalom bayit* ("peace in the home")[12] and peace in one's community represent only the beginning of the peace continuum. One must also *pursue* peace among all people. "Wishing for peace will not get the job done. Nor will thinking good thoughts. Judaism's call is to dedicated action, the tireless pursuit of peace."[13]

Interestingly, the only other passage in the Hebrew Scriptures that uses the imperative *pursue* is found in Deuteronomy 16:20, which says, "Justice, justice, you shall *pursue*, so that you may thrive and occupy the land that the Lord your God is giving you."[14] Sid Schwartz expands on the connection between these, the only *Tanakh* passages that employ the imperative *pursue*: "It is interesting that

[8] Wilhelm Gesenius, *Gesenius's Hebrew and Chaldee Lexicon to the Old Testament Scriptures*, tr. Samuel Prideaux Tregelles (London, England: Samuel Bagster and Sons, 1860), p. 367. Gesenius gives a comprehensive commentary on the word *Yerushalayim*.

[9] Genesis 14:18; Hebrews 7:1.

[10] Psalm 34:14, (emphasis added).

[11] *Midrash* Leviticus *Rabbah* 9:9.

[12] For an extensive discussion of *shalom bayit*, see John D. Garr, *Feminine by Design: The God-Fashioned Woman* (Atlanta, GA: Golden Key Press, 2014), pp. 306–308.

[13] Richard Alan Schwartz, *Eyewitness History: The 1990s* (New York: Infobase Publishing, 2006), p. 68.

[14] Deuteronomy 16:20, TNK (emphasis added).

the challenge, 'pursue it [peace],' added as a device to underscore the imperative ['seek peace'], is also used to emphasize the importance of pursuing justice as in 'Justice, justice shall you pursue.'"[15] From the parallel of these two passages that command Israel—and, indeed, the world—to pursue both peace and justice, it is clear that there can be no peace in the absence of justice. Because of the words of the Torah, the Jewish people remember that their rightful claim to "live in and occupy" the land that God has given them is predicated on their pursuit of justice. "When you pursue justice," God says, "you will occupy the land I am giving you." Possessing the land of peace is contingent upon pursuing justice.

This pursuit of both justice and peace characterized Abraham's life. The primary reason that God gave for choosing Abraham was this: "I know him, that he will command his children . . . *to do justice* and judgment, so that the LORD may bring upon Abraham what he has spoken about him."[16] Abraham's understanding of the dynamics of justice prompted God to say of him, "Abraham obeyed me and kept my charge, my commandments, my statutes, and my instructions."[17] Since Abraham knew that God's judgment is always tempered with mercy,[18] he also balanced his own righteous conformity to God's commandments with a strong sense of mercy and grace. Doing justice while loving mercy is what the prophet Micah described as "walking humbly with God."[19] Jewish tradition teaches that the power to balance justice and mercy is a quality of the Divine by pointing out that the most sacred name of God, the Tetragrammaton, specifically "symbolizes the attribute of Mercy, and its obverse, the attribute of Judgment."[20]

---

[15] Schwartz, p. 68.

[16] Genesis 18:19 (emphasis added).

[17] Genesis 26:5.

[18] Ronald L. Eisenberg, *What the Rabbis Said: 250 Topics from the Talmud* (Santa Barbara, CA: ABC-CLIO, 2010), p. 11. Eisenberg says, "God's strict judgment is always tempered by Divine mercy. Indeed, the Talmud relates that God prays that 'My mercy may suppress My anger,' so that when forced to punish His children (the Israelites), His mercy will make Him 'stop short of the limit of strict justice'" (*Berachot* 7a).

[19] Micah 6:8.

[20] Jacob Culi, Isaac ben Moses Magriso, Zvi Faier, Areh Kaplan, Shmuel Yerushalmi, and Eliyahu Touger, *The Torah Anthology* (Brooklyn, NY: Moznaim Publishing Co., 1987), vol. 14, p. 122. Jewish thought suggests that God's name *Elohim* identifies the divine attribute of justice because "every reference to Elohim means His attribute of justice." See Israel Konowitz, *The God Idea in Jewish Tradition* (Jerusalem, Israel: Jerusalem Publishing House, 1989), p. 8. At the same time, Jewish thought maintains that God's personal name YHWH identifies his attribute of mercy. In fact, when God revealed his name YHWH to Moses, he said of himself, "YHWH, YHWH *El*, merciful (*rachum*) and gracious (*channum*), longsuffering ('arek), and abounding in steadfast love (*chesed*) and truth (*'emet*)" (Exodus 34:6, author's translation). See Isidore Singer, Cyrus Adler, *et. al*, eds., *The Jewish Encyclopedia* (New York: Funk and Wagnalls Co., 1902), vol. 5, p. 299.

Abraham epitomized both of these virtues of justice and mercy as he obeyed God's command instructing him to "walk before me and be perfect."[21] He proved his sense of justice by his instant response to divine commands,[22] but he also demonstrated true justice tempered with mercy through the amazing deference that he demonstrated throughout his life. When conflict arose between his herdsmen and those of his nephew Lot, Abraham made peace by being content to take what was left of the Promised Land after he allowed Lot to choose the part that he preferred.[23] Likewise, at the very moment when God covenanted with Abraham that he and his wife would witness the birth of their promised son Isaac, the patriarch exclaimed incongruously, "O that Ishmael may live before you."[24] Instead of relishing the moment of the fulfillment of the hopes and prayers that had dominated his heart for decades, Abraham believed God's promise but also prayed immediately that its fulfillment "should not lead to the rejection and exclusion of Ishmael."[25] Finally, when God announced to his friend Abraham that he intended to destroy two of the most evil cities on earth, the patriarch of faith was compelled by his own sense of mercy and deference to intercede for those cities to see if peradventure God might spare them the full execution of his wrath.[26] In interceding for both Ishmael and Sodom and Gomorrah, Abraham proved his divine call as a prophetic intercessor for blessing that was based on God's covenant promise to him that "in you all the families [nations] of the earth will be blessed."[27]

Both Jews and Christians understand the prime importance of the second of the great divine commandments: "Love your neighbor as

---

[21] Genesis 17:1. The Hebrew word that is translated "perfect" in this passage is *tameem*, which means "complete," "whole," or "healthful," rather than the attainment of an apex of righteousness or holiness that some Christian perfectionists have sought to achieve. Perfection, therefore is a spirit of striving for constant improvement, not an achieved status.

[22] The Scriptures repeatedly say that when God gave a command to Abraham, he "rose up early in the morning" and proceeded to fulfill that command (Genesis 19:27; 21:14; 22:3). Immediate response to divine imperatives is evidence of Abrahamic faith.

[23] Genesis 13:8.

[24] Genesis 17:18.

[25] Melancthon W. Jacobus, *Notes, Critical and Explanatory, on the Book of Genesis* (New York: Robert Carter & Brothers, 1865), p. 290.

[26] Genesis 18:16–33. Maleah Bell, B. C. Blackwell, Misty Bourne, *et. al.*, eds., *Compass: The Study Bible for Navigating Your Life* (Nashville, TN: Thomas Nelson, Inc., 2012), p. 21. This text says, "Scripture records here an amazing exchange between the Lord and Abraham. In all of the Bible there is nothing quite like it. In these verses Abraham is negotiating with God over the fate of Sodom and its inhabitants. But this is no game. . . . Abraham has followed God long enough and knows Him well enough to stand confident as he presses and probes the extent of God's mercy."

[27] Genesis 12:3.

yourself."[28] There is, moreover, another commandment in the Torah that says, "The foreigner residing among you must be treated as your native-born. Love them as yourself, for you were foreigners in Egypt. I am the LORD your God."[29] This commandment is made all the more powerful because it concludes, just as the commandment to love one's neighbor does, with the declaration: "I am the LORD your God."[30] Taken together, both of these texts provided a foundation for the parable of the Good Samaritan in which Jesus gave a graphic answer to the classical question, "Who is my neighbor?"[31] While the word *neighbor* can be variously interpreted,[32] the term *foreigner* (*ger* in Hebrew) is unmistakable. Abraham was a *ger* in Canaan, and the Israelites were *gerim* in Egypt; therefore, the *gerim* among the Israelites were no different in God's eyes from Abraham and the Israelites. They were to be loved as the Israelites loved themselves, and they were to be treated as though they were native-born citizens of the commonwealth of Israel. Stephen Dempster is correct when he says that "a concern for resident aliens was etched into the [Israelite] legal system."[33]

Pursuing justice is seeking diligently to do what is right in God's sight and to engage in proper ethical conduct toward all people. When one loves God, one's neighbor, and the foreigner who has no connection with him or his people, that person is not only praying for peace: he is also pursuing it. Such pursuit of peace is not just wishful thinking. It is an activity of "walking faith," the kind of faith that through action works itself out in faithfulness.[34] It is the faith that is conjoined with good works—in this case the action of praying and pursuing peace—thereby bringing faith to life through positive

[28] Leviticus 19:18; Matthew 22:39. Jesus said that the commandment to "love your neighbor as yourself" is second only in importance to the commandment to "love the LORD God with all your heart, mind, and strength." The apostle John went even further by saying, "If someone says, 'I love God,' and hates his brother, he is a liar, for the one who does not love his brother whom he has seen, cannot love God whom he has not seen" (1 John 4:20).

[29] Leviticus 19:34.

[30] Exodus 20:2.

[31] Matthew 22:39.

[32] The great Rabbi Akiva said that the term *neighbor* included all humanity; however, his colleagues limited its meaning to "Israelites." Others said it applied only to one's nearest kin. Louis Finkelstein, "The Jewish Vision of Human Brotherhood," in *Religious Pluralism and World Community*, Edward Jabra Juri, ed. (Leiden, The Netherlands: E. J. Brill, 1969), pp. 87–88. Finkelstein referenced *Abot of R. Nathan* I, chap. 16, 32b and *Mekilta Mishpatim*, chap. 12, p. 290; chap. 15, p. 302.

[33] Stephen G. Dempster, "Foreigner," in *Evangelical Dictionary of Biblical Theology*, Walter A. Elwell, ed. (Grand Rapids, MI: Baker Books, 1996), p. 265.

[34] This kind of faith transcends the Greek idea of *pistis*, faith as "agreement with a premise," and moves into the arena of the Hebrew concept of *emunah*, faith as "faithfulness." Faithfulness can be described as "walking faith," faith in action.

fulfillment.[35] This attitude can even empower one with the capacity to love one's enemy,[36] hoping to rescue him from his deception, as Abraham attempted to do for the residents of Sodom and Gomorrah.

Jerusalem is also the foundation of justice.[37] Herein, therefore, lies the key for achieving peace in Jerusalem and working outward from God's "foundation of peace" into all the world. Righteous claims to the Promised Land must also be tempered by Abrahamic deference. Jesus set a high standard when he said that Abraham's children must evidence their patrimony by doing the works of Abraham.[38] Abraham's descendants include both Jews, who are lineal descendants of Abraham, and Christians, who trace their spiritual ancestry to the patriarch of faith through their Messiah Jesus.[39] Claims to the Holy Land today should be made in the context of the love which the Torah required the Israelites to have for those who, although they were foreigners and not citizens of the commonwealth of Israel,[40] still deserved God's blessing and inclusion among his native-born Chosen People.[41]

God blessed Abraham and Isaac, but he also blessed Ishmael. In the great tradition of Abraham, therefore, the Israelis are to be careful not to allow righteous nationalism to devolve into unjust exclusivity and racism. In truth, however, modern Israel already manifests an exceptional degree of respect for diversity. Israeli Jews come from a wide range of racial, ethnic, and even religious backgrounds, and Bedouins, Druze, and Arabs are also citizens of Israel. Despite living in an atmosphere that is often bellicose and violent, Israel has already established a climate for peace among its own diverse citizenry. This needs only to be expanded to be even more inclusive of the *gerim* among them and those who are in their extended neighborhood. And, indeed, the Jews do understand very well "that if they were to build their house securely," they cannot "live in a narrow nationalism or isolationism and must be good neighbors to their Arab brothers, or cousins."[42]

At the same time, the Palestinian Arabs must also learn to embrace their

[35] James 2:17.

[36] Matthew 5:44.

[37] Isaiah 2:3; Micah 4:2: "The Torah will go forth from Zion, and the word of the LORD from Jerusalem."

[38] John 8:39.

[39] Galatians 3:29.

[40] Exodus 22:21. In this passage, God commanded Israel, "The foreigner who resides with you shall be to you as the native among you, and you shall love him as yourself. . . . I am the Lord your God." This commandment parallels God's instruction in Leviticus 19:18, "You shall love your neighbor as yourself; I am the Lord." Love for one's neighbor and love for and inclusion of the foreigner are incumbent upon the Chosen People because "I am the the Lord your God," the Almighty declares.

[41] Ephesians 2:12.

[42] "Zionism," *Palestine, Volumes 1–5* (New York: American Zionist Emergency Council, 1943), p. 4.

cousins, the Jews. Among many, but not all, Arabs, "rejection of direct negotiations [for peace] is not based on a preference for some other procedure of settlement; they have rejected any procedure for terminating the conflict. They have rejected every gradual or staged settlement unless an opening is left for them to revert to their fundamental position advocating the liquidation of Israel."[43] The Muslims must find a way to respect the Jews whom Muhammad originally called the "People of the Book."[44] Perhaps Golda Meir understood the key to peace: "Peace will come when the Arabs will love their children more than they hate us."[45] She certainly evoked the profound Jewish views concerning the sanctity of all human life—which undoubtedly is central to any quest for peace—when she poignantly declared, "When peace comes, we will perhaps in time be able to forgive the Arabs for killing our sons, but it will be harder for us to forgive them for having forced us to kill their sons."[46]

## Continual Prayer for Peace

Around the world, people of virtually all faiths are praying for world peace. Ultimately, however, universal peace upon this planet is impossible until peace is achieved first in Jerusalem and in the land of Israel. Perhaps this is the reason why out of all the people in the world who pray for peace, none prays more consistently or more passionately than the Jewish people. Three times daily in synagogues around the world, observant Jews pray the *Amidah*, the Jewish prayer *par excellence*. Each time this prayer is prayed, it

[43] Yehoshafat Harkabi, *Palestinians and Israel* (Jerusalem, Israel: Israel Universities Press, 1974), p. 176. In fact, in 2002, when Israeli Prime Minister Ehud Barak offered to accept all of the PLO's demands for "peace," offering Yasser Arafat 97% of the West Bank of the original land of Israel, the Egyptian terrorist extraordinaire flatly rejected the offer, proving that his strategy for "peace" was to demand and negotiate while engaging in relentless acts of terrorism with no intention of ceasing and desisting from his violent agenda until Israel no longer existed. "Peace" for the PLO and for other terrorist organizations like Hamas and Hezbollah has long meant—and still means—the obliteration of the nation of Israel and the genocide of the Jewish people. Only then would they be able to achieve their "land-for-peace" objectives. The PLO, now the Palestinian Authority, has made it clear that their final objective is possession of all the land of Israel.

[44] Muhammad Abdel Haleem, *Understanding the Qur'an: Themes and Style* (New York: I.B. Tauris & Co., 1999), p. 75. Haleem says that "Christians and the Jews who lived among an overwhelming Muslim majority are referred to in the Qur'an by the honorific term *ahl al-kitab* (the 'People of the Book') not as 'minorities.' . . . The Qur'an does not brand the 'People of the Book' as a whole as unacceptable. It says: 'There are some among the People of the Book who are upright, who recite God's revelations during the night, who bow down in worship, who believe in God and the Last Day, who order what is right and forbid what is wrong, who are quick to do good deeds. These people are among the righteous, and they will not be denied [the reward] for whatever good deeds they do: God knows exactly who is conscious of Him" (*Qur'an* 3:113–115). While this statement was certainly not a blanket acceptance of those who were not Muslims, it did at least offer some measure of respect that could be expanded into a level of understanding that might make peaceful coexistence possible.

[45] Golda Meir during a 1957 speech, quoted in Paul Carlson, *Media Bias and the Middle East* (Bloomington, IN: XLibris Corp., 2003), p. 10.

[46] Golda Meir, *A Land of Our Own: An Oral Autobiography,* Marie Syrkin, ed. (New York: G. P. Putnam's Sons, 1973), p. 242.

concludes with these words: "He who makes peace in the Heavens, May he make peace upon us and upon all Israel." This is not, however, a vainly repeated, mindlessly chanted mantra. It is an outpouring of the heart of every Jew who prays it. But, more than that, it is a collective prayer of the whole house of Israel, including the people in the Promised Land. Dalia Gavriely-Nuri says it well: "This ethos has been an integral part of Israel's declared political culture since the beginning of the Zionist movement in the late 19th century."[47]

So Jews pray for and pursue peace. Muslims, however, often pray for and pursue *jihad*. With such intractability among the Muslim nations and the Arab peoples in relation to Israel, one could easily despair of prospects for peace in the Middle East or even resign oneself to the conclusion that peace in Israel can be achieved only in the eschatological Age to Come. While the Hebrew Scriptures doubtless point to a final denouement of the ages when the Messiah comes as the *Sar Shalom* (Prince of Peace), the Jewish and Christian ethos requires that one pray for and pursue peace in every day that will precede that event. Believers in God should not only dream of a day when peace will cover the earth; they are also expected to work assiduously for peace. In fact, Jesus made this duty clear when he said, "Blessed are the peacemakers; for they shall be called the children of God."[48] What Jesus said is in context with rabbinic tradition which teaches that "the messianic hope for a peaceful world" is "an ideological premise about the real world and not merely a sweet dream or vision of the future."[49] It is also consistent with the Jewish concept of *Tikkun Olam* ("Restoration of the World"), in which God and his children are to work together in partnership to improve the world in every generation.[50] The Psalmist echoed the vision of Messianic peace: "The Lord bless you from Zion, and may you see the prosperity of Jerusalem all

[47] Dalia Gavriely-Nuri, *Israeli Peace Discourse: A Cultural Approach to CDA* (Amsterdam, The Netherlands: John Benjamins Publishing Co. B.V., 2015), p. 4.

[48] Matthew 5:9.

[49] Joseph Isaac Lifshitz, "War and Aesthetics in Jewish Law," in *War and Peace in Jewish Tradition: From the Biblical World to the Present*, Yigal Levin and Amnon Shapira, eds. (New York: Routledge, 2012), p. 107.

[50] Blair P. Grubb, "Tikkun Olam," in *Jewish Stories from Heaven and Earth: Inspiring Tales to Nourish the Heart* (Woodstock, VT: Jewish Lights Publishing, 2008), p. 113. Grubb says that the process of *tikkun olam*, "repairing the world is accomplished by individual conscious acts of compassion, mercy, justice, and kindness." Also, Philip D. Ben-Shmuel, "*Hagshamah*: A Theology for an Alternate Messianic Jewish Zionism," in *The Land Cries Out: Theology of the Land in the Israeli-Palestinian Context*, Salim J. Munayer and Lisa Loden, eds. (Eugene, OR: Wipf and Stock Publishers, 2012), p. 154. Ben-Shmuel says, "In Jewish terms, this active pursuit of the kingdom of heaven on earth is called *tikkun 'olam*—the restoration of the *cosmos*." For this reason, he says, a truly biblical Zionism "cannot be concerned only with the redemption of Israel in their land, but rather with the redemption of all the families of the earth." He concludes by saying that "this can be referred to as 'general Zionism,' because it looks towards the establishment of New Jerusalem." Pursuit of peace is not just an eschatological expectation, it is a daily endeavor.

the days of your life. May you live to see your children's children. Peace be upon Israel."[51]

## Peace and Messianic Expectation

Rabbi Judah ben Yosi once said, "Great is peace, for God's name is peace. . . . Great is peace, for it encompasses all blessings. . . . Great is peace for when the Messiah comes, he will commence with peace, as it is said: 'How beautiful upon the mountains are the feet [footsteps] of the messenger of good tidings, who announces peace.'"[52] The Jewish Scriptures speak poignantly of such a time: "They shall hammer their swords into plowshares and their spears into pruning hooks. Nation will not lift up sword against nation, and never again will they learn war."[53] This event will occur when many people say, "Come, let us go up to the mountain of the LORD, to the house of the God of Jacob; that he may teach us concerning his ways and that we may walk in his paths. For the Torah will go forth from Zion and the word of the LORD from Jerusalem."[54] Chaim Weizmann made this very astute observation: "The prophetic vision that out of Zion comes forth the word of the LORD is not a legacy of the past but is the commandment of the present and the hope of the future."[55] The foundation and fountainhead of global peace will be Jerusalem, and its agent will be God's Torah. "Rejoice greatly, O daughter Zion! Shout aloud, O daughter Jerusalem! Behold, your king comes to you; just and endowed with salvation. . . . [T]he battle bow will be broken. He will proclaim peace to the nations. His dominion will be from sea to sea and from the River to the ends of the earth."[56] The prophet Isaiah further spoke of the profound impact of God's peace: "I will extend peace to her like a river. . . . As one whom his mother comforts, so I will comfort you; and you will be comforted in Jerusalem."[57]

Through the agency of the Holy Spirit, God is seeking righteous Gentiles who will renew the affirmation that Ruth the Gentile made, "Your people shall be my people," thereby confirming their determination to identify themselves with and among the ancient people of God. Such intercessors from among all the nations of the earth must stand shoulder-to-shoulder with the

---

[51] Psalm 128:5–6.

[52] Leviticus *Rabbah* 9:9.

[53] Isaiah 2:4; Micah 4:3.

[54] Isaiah 2:3.

[55] Chaim Weizmann, quoted in Ferdynand Zweig, *Israel: The Sword and the Harp: The Mystique of Violence and the Mystique of Redemption; Controversial Themes in Israeli Society* (Cranbury, NJ: Associated University Presses, 1969), p. 216.

[56] Zechariah 9:9–10, NIV, NRS, NASB, edited.

[57] Isaiah 66:12–13.

Jewish people, imploring the God of peace to bring peace first to Jerusalem and then to the whole world. They must join the ranks of those about whom the God of Israel spoke when he said, "I have posted watchmen on your walls, O Jerusalem; they will never be silent day or night. You who remind the LORD, give yourselves no rest, and give him no rest until he establishes and makes Jerusalem a praise in the earth."[58]

The passion that the Jewish people have for the peace of Jerusalem, of Israel, and of the whole world is an outworking of their calling as the Chosen People. It is not so much that they have chosen God and the land where the Almighty has placed his name as it is that God has chosen them, placed his name on them, and brought them to his land to be his people and his nation. David Patterson confirms this truth when he says that "the Jews do not lay claim to Jerusalem—Jerusalem lays claim to the Jews."[59] The magnet of the holy Presence that resides in the Holy City draws this people inexorably toward God and his land. Like King David, they know that the Lord is great and "greatly to be praised in the city of our God, his holy mountain."[60] Patterson concludes that "when Jews pray to the Holy One, they never refer to Jerusalem as 'our city,' but rather as *irkha*, 'Your city,' that is, God's city, invoking God as the *Boneh Yerushalyim*, the 'Builder of Jerusalem.'"[61] The God of Israel has promised to make peace, and he will not and cannot be thwarted in fulfilling his purposes. "The LORD will give strength to his people; the LORD will bless his people with peace."[62] In that day, "the LORD of hosts shall reign in Mount Zion, and in Jerusalem, and before his ancients gloriously."[63] This is God's final promise: "I will fill this house with glory . . . the latter glory of this house will be greater than the glory of the former, and in this place I will give peace, declares the LORD of hosts."[64]

## Hope in a Morass of Hopelessness

Without God, human beings are hopeless creatures for whom the banality of barbarity knows no bounds. Although the Age of Reason and the Enlightenment of the seventeenth and eighteenth centuries postulated that human beings were inherently good and were moving toward a perfect

---

[58] Isaiah 62:6–7, NIV, NRS, NASB, edited.

[59] David Patterson, *Anti-Semitism and Its Metaphysical Origins* (Cambridge, UK: Cambridge University Press, 2015), p. 204.

[60] Psalm 48:1.

[61] Patterson, p. 204.

[62] Psalm 29:11.

[63] Isaiah 24:23.

[64] Haggai 2:7–9, NASB, NIV edited.

social form,[65] and although social Darwinism of the nineteenth century fully expected the human animal to continue evolving until it reached Utopia,[66] the mass violence of the twentieth century destroyed that hope.[67] Secular postmodern nihilists thus despair not only of even the possibility of truth and secular ethics, but also of humanity's future, fearing a continued downward spiral that will inevitably lead it to self-obliteration.[68] Two violent world wars confirmed the fact that, apart from God, human beings are hopelessly violent and self-destructive. Along with the crimes against humanity perpetrated by Stalin, Mao, and Pol Pot, the Holocaust was the final nail in the coffin of modernity and its lofty expectations for human self-achievement and self-generated peace.[69] And the continuing and unrelenting violence that has taken countless innocent human lives during the past century has done nothing but add to the ominous sense of the inevitable death-spiral of the human race. All that seems to be left in today's world is the banality of hedonism and barbarism—the ultimate demonstration of humanity's destiny after its rejection of the restraints imposed on mankind by God's commands and its embrace of tolerance for every perversion that the human mind can conceive.

What is true in the macrocosm of the world is true also in the microcosm of the Middle East where competing worldviews and mindsets have created and maintained a dilemma of human suffering that seems to have no pragmatic resolution, much less a utopian conclusion. The difference between the adherents to Judaism and Christianity and those of other religions in the postmodern world—and particularly those who eschew any religious persuasion whatsoever—is at least a minimal belief in God's biblical design for humanity. This is the fundamental knowledge that the God of Scripture created theomorphic human beings and infused within them a spark of the Divine. Because humans breathe the *neshamah* ("breath") of the Eternal, they

[65] Markus Mühling, *T & T Clark Handbook of Christian Eschatology* (London, UK: Bloomsbury T & T Clark, 2015), p. 231.

[66] Dave Breese, *Seven Men Who Rule the World from the Grave* (Chicago, IL: Moody Publishers, 1990), p. 32. Breese notes that social Darwinism assumed that "the social structure is engineered and controlled by impersonal forces rather than by God," that Western society has moved and will move "through progressive states of secularization from Christianity to atheism," and that "society is moving upward from a mean past to an improving future" and will continue to do so "until perfect culture comes into being," which is Utopia.

[67] Christopher Falzon, *Philosophy Goes to the Movies: An Introduction to Philosophy* (New York: Routledge, 2007), p. 188. Falzon observes that instead of moving toward a social Darwinian utopia, the twentieth century instilled "more pessimistic, dystopian visions of the future."

[68] Nikos Kazantzakis, *Friedrich Nietzsche on the Philosophy of Right and the State* (Albany, New York: The State University of New York Press, 2006), p. 17. Kazantzakis points out that Nietzsche's "Pessimistic Nihilism" leads "to the obliteration and self-destruction of life" while his Optimistic or Dionysian Nihilism leads only to the obliteration of "the currently reigning table of values."

[69] J. Richard Middleton and Brian J. Walsh, *Truth Is Stranger Than It Used to Be: Biblical Faith in a Postmodern Age* (Downers Grove, IL: InterVarsity Press, 1995), p. 23.

have the potential to manifest the divine likeness, and, therefore, they have the capacity to join in partnership with God to bring to pass his primordial design for Planet Earth. This is possible, however, only when humans recognize the existence of manifest evil in the world and its utter rejection of the God of Scripture and his specific and uncompromisable instructions for human existence. If evil is not acknowledged for what it is, "good" becomes entirely a perspective of such subjective relativism that, in effect, concludes that there is no objective good. In this case, anything can be rationalized as good such that the ends always justify the means, no matter how heinous they may be.

In spite of all the reasons for despair, "Hope springs eternal in the human breast,"[70] as Alexander Pope said over five centuries ago. This is particularly true for believers in the God of Scripture, who know above all things that Israel's God is faithful and that he does "great and unfathomable things."[71] What has appeared to be a hopeless morass of intractable conflict that has bedeviled the Jewish people for centuries can be resolved by God in one moment of time. The same God who has restored his people to their land in this day[72] will not only build the "highway from Assyria to Egypt" that he promised the prophet[73] but also reconcile Isaac and Ishmael, the long-estranged sons of Abraham and call Egypt, Assyria, and Israel "my people."[74]

## A Reformation for Islam?

Is it possible for the seemingly incurable proclivity toward violence that has characterized so much of the Muslim Arab world to be abated? Is it possible for Islam to undergo a reformation that would move it away from its militant and violent past and toward a more peaceful future? Appeals for such a reformation have become increasingly numerous in recent times and in various places. In a speech before Al-Azhar and the Awqaf Ministry, a gathering of Islamic clerics, scholars, and leaders, Egyptian President Abdel Fattah al-Sisi boldly called for a "religious revolution" in the world of Islam, saying, "It's inconceivable that the thinking that we hold most sacred should cause the entire Islamic world to be a source of anxiety, danger, killing, and destruction for the rest of the world. Impossible!"[75] Ayaan Hirsi Ali, however,

---

[70] Alexander Pope, *An Essay on Man* (London, England: Thomas Tegg, 1811), p. 48.

[71] Job 9:10.

[72] Isaiah 11:11.

[73] Isaiah 19:23.

[74] Isaiah 19:24–25.

[75] Abdel Fattah al-Sisi, quoted in John Hayward, "Egyptian President Al-Sisi Calls for an Islamic Reformation," *Breitbart News*, 9 Jan 2015, posted at http://www.breitbart.com/national-security/2015/01/09/egyptian-president-al-sisi-calls-for-an-islamic-reformation/.

underscores the difficulty of such a revolutionary quest, noting that "neither Muslim reformers nor Western liberals have so far been able to articulate a coherent program for a Muslim Reformation." At the same time, however, she still has hope, believing that "the Muslim Reformation has begun."[76] Ali's emphasis on Muslim Reformation is similar to early nineteenth century Muslim philosopher-poet Muhammad Iqbal who boldly declared, "We need a new theology, a period similar to the Protestant Reformation."[77]

Abdeslam Maghraoui goes further, suggesting that under the name of *tajdid*,[78] a "systematic reconsideration and rationalization of Islamic doctrines, institutions, beliefs, and practices" is taking place in Islam.[79] Many other scholars like Zuhdi Jasser,[80] Asra Nomani,[81] Tawfiq Hamid,[82] Irshad Manji,[83] and Tariq Ramadan[84] have made arguments for Islamic reformation that are increasingly being heard. Timothy Winter "unequivocally rejects suicide bombing as an act of suicide as well as the killing of noncombatants as always forbidden, noting that some sources regard it as worse than murder."[85] Yusuf Qaradawi "denounces extremism [and] those who subscribe to a negative Islam."[86] He says, "Islam, the religion of tolerance, holds the human soul in high esteem, and considers the attack against innocent human beings a grave sin."[87] The Free Muslims

[76] Ayaan Hirsi Ali, quoted in Clifford D. May, "The Case for Islamic Heresy: Ayaan Hirsi Ali Risks All with Her Call for a Muslim Reformation," *The Washington Times*, April 14, 2015, posted at http://www.washingtontimes.com/news/2015/apr/14/clifford-may-ayaan-hirsi-ali-risks-life-with-call-/. Also, Ayaan Hirsi Ali, *Heretic: Why Islam Needs a Reformation Now* (New York: HarperCollins, 2015).

[77] Muhammad Iqbal, quoted in John Esposito, *The Future of Islam* (Oxford, UK: Oxford University Press, 2010), p. 91.

[78] *Tajdid* is the Arabic word for "renewal." When used in its Islamic context, it refers to a revival of Islam to bring society to greater justice.

[79] Abdeslam Maghraoui, "American Foreign Policy and Islamic Renewal," in *Conflict, Identity, and Reform in the Muslim World: Challenges for U.S. Engagement*, Daniel Brumberg and Dina Shehata, eds. (Washington, DC: United States Institute of Peace, 2009), p. 51. Maghraoui says that the systematic approach to Islamic Reformation includes efforts 1) "to reclaim the Islamic heritage from traditional clerics (associated with autocratic states), extremist Islamist groups (bent on waging holy war against the West and their own 'adulterated' societies), and radical movements (whose goal is to apply strict Sharia law once they gain power through democratic elections or through informal *da'wa*—a religious call to fellow Muslims to abide by Islamic principles), and 2) "to adapt Islamic principles, values, and institutions to the modern world while recognizing the importance of Islam as a cultural frame of reference."

[80] Zuhdi Jasser is featured regularly on major television news programs, and he contributes many articles to various newspapers and journals.

[81] Asra Quratulain Nomani, *Standing Alone in Mecca: An American Woman's Struggle for the Soul of Islam* (New York: HarperCollins Publishers, 2006).

[82] Tawfiq Hamid, *Inside Jihad: How Radical Islam Works, Why It Should Terrify Us, How to Defeat It* (Pembroke, VA: Mountain Lake Press, 2015).

[83] Irshad Manji, *The Trouble with Islam Today* (New York: St. Martin's Press, 2003).

[84] Tariq Ramadan, *Radical Reform: Islamic Ethics and Liberation* (New York: Oxford University Press, 2009).

[85] John S. Esposito, *The Future of Islam* (Oxford, UK: Oxford University Press, 2010), p. 99.

[86] Esposito, p. 100.

[87] Yusuf Qaradawi, quoted in Esposito, p. 100.

Coalition advocates "a critical examination of Islam that will eliminate aspects such as . . . the teachings of hatred, intolerance, and violent *jihad*; and the conspiracy theories blaming Jews for all Muslim problems," and "it calls on 'moderate' Muslims to break their silence and passivity and unite to defeat the forces of extremist Islam."[88]

John Esposito notes an important fact regarding the impetus for a reformation of Islam: "Most [Muslim] reformers were not traditionally trained religious scholars but rather modern educated 'laymen,' professionals who repudiated the authority of conservative ulama as the sole 'keepers of Islam,' as well as the tradition that the ulama's legal doctrines and interpretations of the past were binding."[89] These reformers have "reinterpreted Quranic verses to promote greater gender equality, to restrict polygamy and a husband's unilateral right to divorce, and to promote education for women."[90] The reformers' impact, however, "was limited by the influence of authoritarian regimes and an entrenched conservative religious establishment."[91] Like most reformed movements, the reformers are not from the mainstream of religious and political leaders. Instead, they resemble the prophets of ancient Israel, railing against entrenched, self-serving bureaucracies.

Is it possible that these lay reformers might lay foundations that will transform a religion that has been exploited for violence more than any other religion in history and transform it into a religion of peace not just in word but in deed? Perhaps long-dormant seeds in Islamic sacred literature which envision a future Muslim messianic event[92] may at least have a chance of flowering into a new Islamic focus on peace, rather than conflict. Maybe this is what Abraham had in mind when he prayed to the Almighty: "O that Ishmael might live before you!" Islam is due a reformation, and it could well come from a handful of visionaries just as the Protestant Reformation did in the sixteenth century when a few "Christian Hebraists" began to teach "*veritas Hebraica*" and launched a movement that changed the face of Christianity.

Could it also be that some Islamic reformers might also actually come to recognize and acknowledge the Jewish foundations on which many aspects of the Muslim faith were built? The bedrock absolute monotheism of Islam certainly rests on the monotheism of Judaism which preceded monotheistic

[88] Patrick Sookhdeo, *Global Jihad: The Future in the Face of Militant Islam* (McLean, VA: Isaac Publishing, 2007), p. 384.

[89] Esposito, p. 93.

[90] Esposito, p. 93.

[91] Esposito, p. 93.

[92] Though the Muslim messianic idea of the *Mahdi* was clearly expropriated from Christianity, at least it anticipates a final eschatological denouement when justice and peace will reign supreme on Planet Earth.

belief in Arabian Peninsula by over two millennia.[93] Other concepts were also borrowed, if not expropriated, from the Jews and Judaism by Muhammad and his associates.[94] Could it be that—in a fashion similar to twentieth-century Christianity's experience vis-à-vis the Jews and Judaism—Islam, which is the world's most triumphalistic and supersessionist religion,[95] might also come to acknowledge that some, if not most, of its theological foundations were established in the faith of Abraham as defined and codified by Jewish patriarchs and prophets and by the sages of Judaism?[96] Some Jewish scholars have already demonstrated distinct parallels between Judaism and Islam.[97] Could such insights prompt a reformation of restoration in Islam that would abandon its non-Abrahamic concepts[98] and return to the purity of Abrahamic faith?

## With God All Things Are Possible!

Less than a century ago, who could have imagined that nearly a millennium of overt Christian violence against the Jewish people would finally come to an abrupt end? Yet, for at least some Christians, Holocaust-shocked consciences finally exclaimed, "Never again!" Increasing numbers of Christians began to confess the long-neglected

---

[93] There was no concept of monotheism in the most ancient Arabian traditions where tribal gods dominated and polytheism was common.

[94] Acknowledgment by Muslims of Islam's Jewish roots would not be new, as Ross Brann points out when he cites eleventh-century Muslim Qadi Sa'id al-Andalusi's statement in his *Al-tarif bi-tabaqat al-umam (Exposition of the Generations of Nations)* that "their scholars [i.e., the Banu Isra'il = the Jews] were best informed in the story of creation and in knowledge of the prophets. Muslim scholars such as 'Abd Allah ibn 'Abbas, ka'b al-Ahbar, and *Wahb ibn Munabbih* acquired this knowledge from them" (author's emphasis). Ross Brann, *Power in the Portrayal: Representations of Jews and Muslims in Eleventh and Twelfth Century Islamic Spain* (Princeton, NJ: Princeton University Press, 2002), p. 31.

[95] While it has recognized Moses and Jesus as two of its own prophets, Islam has always claimed that Muhammad was the ultimate and greatest prophet and that Islam superseded both Judaism and Christianity. This is supersessionism *par excellence*. Islam has also proven its triumphalistic mindset by expanding its dominion on the edge of the sword. Islam, therefore, has achieved and maintained a level of triumphalism to which neither Judaism nor Christianity ever aspired and which neither has attained.

[96] Studies in the Jewish roots of Islam have been ongoing since the nineteenth century when Jewish scholars such as Abraham Geiger and Ignác Goldziher "stressed the Judaizing nature of early Islam." Sander Gilman, *Multiculturalism and the Jews* (Abingdon, UK: Routledge, 2006), p. 5. Susannah Heschel points out that these Jewish scholars hoped to affirm that Judaism was not a "dead religion" as German Christian scholarship maintained but was not only a living religion that had produced "children"—Christianity and Islam—but had futurity. Susannah Heschel, "Constructions of Jewish Identity," in *Faithful Narratives: Historians, Religion, and the Challenge of Objectivity*, Andrea Sterk and Nina Caputo, eds. (Ithaca, NY: Cornell University Press, 2014), pp. 169–172.

[97] J. R. Wegner, "Islamic and Talmudic Jurisprudence: The Four Roots of Islamic Law and Their Talmudic Counterparts," *American Journal of Legal History* 26 (1982), pp. 26–29. Also, Patricia Crone and Michael Cook, *Hagarism: The Making of the Islamic World* (Cambridge, UK: Cambridge University Press, 1980).

[98] Steven Bayme, *Understanding Jewish History: Text and Commentaries* (Jersey City, NJ: KTAV Publishing House, 1997), p. 128. Bayme maintains that perhaps Islam's most important departure from Jewish thought has been its "conflict over territory and territorial imperatives" which "divided the world into *dar al-Islam*, or 'territory of Islam' and *dar al-harb* or 'territory of the nations.'"

truth that Christian faith is deeply rooted in the soil of Judaism, and they began to acknowledge the Jewish people as continuing co-participants with them in the faith of Abraham. Surely, the God who produced this miracle can also work wonders in the world of Islam by making the quest for peace between the lineal descendants of Abraham far more important than other theological, sociological, or political agendas! This holy vision can be worked out practically. As Jonathan Sacks says, "We must raise a generation of young Jews, Christians, Muslims and others to know that it is not piety but sacrilege to kill in the name of the God of life, hate in the name of the God of love, wage war in the name of the God of peace, and practice cruelty in the name of the God of compassion."[99]

Astonishing changes have already begun to take place among Islamic academics. In an official letter to the US Holocaust Memorial Museum on the occasion of International Holocaust Remembrance Day, 2018, Dr. Mohammad Alissa, Secretary General of the Saudi-Arabia based Muslim World League, expressed "great sympathy with the victims of the Holocaust, an incident that shook humanity to the core, and created an event whose horrors could not be denied or underrated by any fair-minded or peace-loving person. . . . This human tragedy perpetrated by evil Nazism won't be forgotten by history, or meet the approval of anyone, except criminal Nazis or their genre. . . . Any denial of the Holocaust or minimizing of its effect [is] a crime to distort history and an insult to the dignity of those innocent souls who have perished."[100]

With God, all things are possible! With God, many things are plausible and likely. With God, what he has proclaimed and prophesied in his Holy Word is not only possible, it is also inevitable! Nothing can be taken from it or added to it, and nothing on the earth can ever prevent its ultimate accomplishment. *Yhwh Shalom*,[101] the God of peace, will surely and finally bring peace on earth to people of good will, and he will create the divine *shalom* that infinitely exceeds all human comprehension or imagination.[102]

---

[99] Jonathan Sacks, "How to Defeat Religious Violence," *The Wall Street Journal*, Oct. 2, 2015, posted at http://www.wsj.com/articles/how-to-defeat-religious-violence-1443798275.

[100] Mohammad Alissa, quoted in *Al Arabiya English* (Friday, 26 January 2018), posted at http://english.alarabiya.net/en/News/gulf/2018/01/26/Saudi-Based-Muslim-World-League-expresses-sympathy-for-Holocaust-victims.html. For background of this historic statement, see Robert Satloff, "A Historic Holocaust Awareness Awakening in Saudi Arabia, of All Places: Applaud This Significant Step from the Heart of Islam," *New York Daily News* (JAN 26, 2018), posted at http://www.nydailynews.com/opinion/holocaust-awareness-awakening-saudi-arabia-places-article-1.3780749.

[101] Judges 6:24.

[102] Philippians 4:7.

CHAPTER 19

# RESTORING PHILOSEMITISM

## CURING CHRISTIAN ANTI-ZIONIST ANTISEMITISM

Because of its theological and historical connection with Judaism, the Jewish people, and the land of Israel, support for Israel should be as natural as breathing for every Christian! As a matter of fact, philosemitism should be a part of the Christian autonomic nervous system, for the core principles of the Jewish faith are foundational to the Christian faith. Indeed, there would be no Christians if there had been no Hebrews, no Israelites, and no Jews.[1] And there would be no Christianity if there had been no biblical Judaism or Second Temple Judaism.[2] Also, since God had joined himself in an irrevocable covenant with Abraham and his descendants, the Israelites, it was utterly impossible for Jesus to have come from any people group other than the Jewish people.

Jesus was a Jew, and his religion was Judaism—and he never changed either his ethnicity or his religion. If anything, Jesus strengthened Judaism by promoting a reformation of restoration[3] in order to return the faith of his people to the original spirit of the Torah.[4] Likewise, the apostle Paul

[1] Robert A. Ashworth, quoted in Don A. Pitman, "Reflections on Religious Pluralism," in *The Theologically Formed Heart: Essays in Honor of David J. Gouwens*, Warner M. Bailey, Lee C. Barrett, and James O. Duke, eds. (Eugene, OR: Wipf and Stock Publishers, 2014), p. 22.

[2] Richard W. Rosseau, ed., *Christianity and Judaism: The Deepening Dialogue* (Montrose, PA: Ridge Row Press, 1983), vol. 3, p. 186. Also Lemuel Baker, *The Many Faces of Judaism: Jewish Studies for the Busy Person* (Bloomington, IN: Xlibris Corp., 2012), p. 92. Baker observes that if Israel had been annihilated by Antiochus Epiphanes in the time of the Maccabees, "Jesus Christ would not have come and thus Christianity as a religion or belief system would not exist." He concludes, therefore, that "without Judaism and Israel there would be no Christianity."

[3] Hebrews 9:10. The nature of Jesus' reformation as that of restoration is seen in the antitheses of the Sermon on the Mount (Matthew 5:21–48) in which he strengthened the Torah by emphasizing its original intent and giving greater emphasis to its heart issues rather than its external punctilious performance.

[4] Per Bilde, *The Originality of Jesus: A Critical Discussion and a Comparative Attempt* (Göttingen, Germany: Vandenhoeck & Ruprecht GmbH & Co., 2013), p. 145. Bilde says that "the most important feature of Jesus' relationship to the Mosaic Law is that Jesus tightened, strengthened and intensified the Law of Moses partly by referring to the more original, authentic and stricter 'law of creation.'"

followed the example of Jesus and affirmed his own continuity with the faith of his ancestors. To his dying day, he professed to be a Pharisee,[5] and he affirmed in civil legal proceedings that as a member of a Jewish sect called "The Way," he believed—and practiced—everything that was in accordance with the Torah and that was written by the prophets.[6] Evan Freed rightly says that Paul "did not even change from Judaism to Christianity because he never gave up his Jewish beliefs."[7]

Christians owe a profound debt of gratitude to the Jewish people of history—and by association, to the Jewish people of the present day—for being the source of the foundational elements of the Christian faith. The God that Christians worship is the God of the Jews,[8] the Bible that Christians read is a Jewish book,[9] the Messiah whom Christians revere and follow was and is a Jew,[10] and the salvation that Christians cherish is "from the Jews."[11] In truth, Christianity is for all intents and purposes "the other Jewish religion." Tragically though, millions of Christians have been denied access to the Hebrew foundations—the Jewish roots—of their faith by one of history's greatest aberrations—the Hellenization, Latinization, and paganization of Christian faith. For much too long, Christianity has defined itself as being "not Jewish,"[12] while Judaism, often in response, has defined itself as being "not Christian." Now, both Christianity and Judaism must fully understand that they are kindred faiths,[13] springing

[5] Acts 23:6.

[6] Acts 24:14.

[7] Edwin D. Freed, *The Apostle Paul, Christian Jew: Faithfulness and Law* (Lanham, MD: University Press of America, 1994), p. 8.

[8] Christians received the understanding of monotheism from the Jews. The God whom Jesus called "Father" is YHWH, the God of the Jews. Darrell J. Fasching, *The Jewish People in Christian Preaching* (Lewiston, NY: The Edwin Mellen Press, 1984), p. 24.

[9] The Bible is a book written by Jews for Jews in the language of the Jews about the God of the Jews. Indeed, both the Hebrew Scriptures and the Apostolic Scriptures were written, compiled, and edited by Jews. Richard Watson, *An Exposition of the Gospels of St. Matthew and St. Mark and Some Other Detached Parts of Holy Scripture* (London, UK: John Mason, 1833), p. 532.

[10] The Apostolic Scriptures ("New Testament") begin with these words: "A record of the origin of Jesus Christ, the son of David, the son of Abraham." Katherine Sonderegger, *That Jesus Christ Was Born a Jew: Karl Barth's Doctrine of Israel* (State College, PA: Pennsylvania State University Press, 1992).

[11] John 4:22. Jesus himself said that "salvation is from the Jews." Rosemary Ruether, *Faith and Fratricide: The Theological Roots of Anti-Semitism* (Eugene, OR: Wipf and Stock Publishers, 1995), p. 256. Ruether says that "the Christian messianic experience in Jesus was a Jewish experience, created out of Jewish hope."

[12] Peter Steinfels, "The Jewishness of Jesus," in *No Religion Is an Island: The Nostra Aetate Dialogues*, Edward Bristow, ed. (New York: Fordham University Press, 1998), p. 24. Steinfels says that "for most of two millennia Christianity has largely defined itself, and therefore Jesus, over against Judaism. Judaism in its own way often defined itself against Christianity."

[13] Bruce D. Chilton and Jacob Neusner, *Comparing Spiritualities: Formative Christianity and Judaism on Finding Life and Meeting Death* (Harrisburg, PA: Trinity Press International, 2000), p. x.

from the common root of biblical and Second Temple Judaism.[14]

Michael Kogan captured the essence of this historical fact very well: "In the first century of the present era a number of Jewish sects flourished, each with its own faith-based reading of the texts available to them and many with their own messianic expectations. . . . But of all these schools of thought, only two survived the Jewish revolt and Roman conquest of 64–70 C.E. The Nazarene movement and the Pharisee movement emerged and grew into Christianity and rabbinic Judaism." Then, Kogan suggested the kind of mutual respect that makes Christian support for Jews and Judaism not only possible but also essential: "Both began as sects of Judaism, and each cherished its own messianic vision. Why should they be expected to agree? One is no more legitimate than the other, but they are different. Only the ultimate messianic advent will settle the matter."[15]

## Christian Ambivalence and Vacillation

While it was surely the hand of God that regathered the Jewish people to their land, the restoration of the people to the land and the land to the people has also been supported by Gentiles from around the world, particularly from the international Christian community. The kind of massive, unequivocal Gentile support that the prophets envisioned, however, has not yet been fully realized. Many Christian denominations have at best vacillated in their stand for Jewish people's right of self-determination in the land that God himself deeded to their ancestors and their descendants in perpetuity. Even moderate support for Jewish causes in recent times has been a radical departure from the norm in many Christian circles. Christian leaders, including some Evangelicals, have learned from secularists how to mask Christianity's old forms of antisemitism as "anti-Zionism." Such actions, however, have simply been a refinement of heretical theologies and practices that have characterized historical Christianity for centuries.

How does the church get beyond the confusing mixed signals of its historical love/hate relationship with the Jews? How can Christians come to manifest unequivocal support for the Jewish community and for the nation of Israel that is based on pure, biblical motives, not on

[14] Peter J. Tomson, "The Didache, Matthew, and Barnabas," in *Jews and Christians in the First and Second Centuries: How to Write Their History*, Peter J. Tomson and Joshua J. Schwartz, eds. (Leiden, The Netherlands: Koninklijke Brill NV, 2014), p. 349.

[15] Michael S. Kogan, *Opening the Covenant: A Jewish Theology of Christianity* (New York: Oxford University Press, 2008), p. 126.

evanescent emotionalism? How can Christians arise in this time of restoration of the nation of Israel to become solidly pro-Israel,[16] thereby fulfilling in a spiritual dimension the words of the prophets that Gentiles would come to Israel's light and build up her walls?[17] First, the church around the world must be educated concerning the truth that Christianity is inherently a Jewish religion that was birthed from the matrix of Second Temple Judaism. This fact of Christian Scripture permits Christians to join the Jewish people and the nation of Israel as part of the greater family of God, sharing both the blessings and the responsibilities of biblical faith.

Then, in order to restore what has been lost, Christians must become proactive. A significant place to begin is in learning something about the language of Jesus and the apostles: biblical Hebrew. Despite the fact that most traditional historical Christian scholars do not believe Jesus was conversant in Hebrew, the truth is that he was well versed in the language of the Hebrew Scriptures. He certainly had no problem reading the *parashah* (Torah portion) and the *haftarah* (prophets portion) in the synagogue of Nazareth.[18] Paul was probably a polyglot, but his theology was taken from the Hebrew Scriptures,[19] and he did not hesitate to address Jewish audiences in the Hebrew tongue that they understood.[20] Reconnecting with the language of Jesus and the primary language of Paul, therefore, will help Christians gain a better understanding of the worldview, mindset, and practices of the earliest Christian community which cannot help but make their own Christianity more vibrant.

When Christians fully realize that their faith was and remains a branch of biblical and Second-Temple Judaism, they will gain a

---

[16] Being unequivocally pro-Israel does not mean that one must endorse and support every political, social, and military action undertaken by the government of Israel, nor does it mean that one must be anti-Arab.

[17] Isaiah 60:1–10.

[18] Luke 4:16–19; Isaiah 61:1.

[19] That Paul used the Hebrew text of Scripture for his theological arguments is proven in 1 Corinthians 15:54, where the apostle renders Isaiah 25:8 as, "Death is swallowed up *in victory*." Most versions translate Isaiah 25:8 as "Death is swallowed up *forever*." The Hebrew word translated "forever," however, is *netzach*, which usually means "perpetuity" or "forever" but also can take the rare and obscure meaning of "victory." Paul used this meaning when he translated the Hebrew *netzach* with the Greek *nikos*, "victory." It is certain that the apostle used the Hebrew *Tanakh* as his source rather than the Septuagint, for the Septuagint renders Isaiah 25:8, "Death has prevailed and swallowed *men* up." In the Hebrew text, eternity or eternal life swallows up death. In Paul's Isaiah 25:8 translation, therefore, eternal life is victorious over death; in the Septuagint, death is victorious over humans. It was easy for Paul to extrapolate his meaning from the *Tanakh*; however, it was impossible for him to have derived the same meaning from the Septuagint.

[20] Acts 21:40; 22:2.

profound sense of ownership in the vision of Jewish well-being and Israeli security. They will then be far more inclined to utter these immortal words and to mean them: "Wherever you go, I will go, and wherever you live, I will live; your people will be my people, and your God will be my God. Where you die, I will die, and there I will be buried. May YHWH punish me, and do so severely, if anything but death separates you and me."[21] These words spoken over three millennia ago by a Gentile woman named Ruth to her Jewish mother-in-law and, in effect, to all of the Jewish people of her day must echo from the heart of every Christian on the planet in this time.

Old prejudices must melt away in the loving warmth of face-to-face relationship when Christians embrace their ancient, long-abandoned Jewish family. When Christians are led out of the ignorance of their heritage, they will abandon the church's old prejudicial caricatures of Jews and Judaism, and they will unequivocally and fully embrace the faith of Abraham, who Paul declared is the father of us all.[22] Then, Christians will fully realize that the Jewish people are to be restored to their land, not because of some Christian eschatological scenario,[23] but because of Jewish entitlement to the land through God's unilateral and irrevocable covenant with their father Abraham and his posterity in perpetuity. With this biblical understanding firmly established in their hearts, Christians by the millions will come to support the Jewish people and their nation without all the self-interest-driven ecclesiastical vacillation that has produced so much Jewish suffering in the past.

## Solidarity with Israel and the Jewish People

The restoration of the nation of Israel has been an unfolding act of God's hand to fulfill his covenant with Abraham including his promise that the patriarch's descendants would inherit the land of Canaan forever.[24] As such, it portends of even greater things that the God of Israel will do as he fulfills all his promises to the Jewish community and to the world. As Abraham Joshua Heschel wisely said, "The state of Israel is not the fulfillment of the messianic promise,

[21] Ruth 1:16–17, HCSB.

[22] Romans 4:16.

[23] Isaac C. Rottenberg, "Israelic Christians," *Restore!*, Issue 52, p. 32. Rottenberg notes that eschatological scenarios tend to be apocalyptic in nature, making "Israel's role in end-time speculations key" and "Armageddon and the Rapture . . . central theological foci." These often place Jews in the position of "being treated as marionettes in an almost mechanical Christian end-time scenario."

[24] Genesis 13:15.

but it makes the messianic promise possible."[25] The miracle of Israel's rebirth confirms to a skeptical world that "the gifts and callings of God are irrevocable,"[26] and it gives hope to both Jews and Christians that the Messianic Age will yet come, bringing God's gift of universal peace and blessing. As Isaac Rottenberg so eloquently said, "The nation of Israel, blessed with the gift of Torah, can and should manifest signs of the coming reign of God. So should countries and continents where the Gospel of the Kingdom has been proclaimed. The world desperately needs such pointers to the promises of Zion. This is the best model for those who seek to pursue what might be called the 'Shalomization' of the world along the way revealed in the Jewish Torah and the Christian Kerygma."[27]

## Taking the Initiative

Christians have the greater responsibility for coming alongside the Jewish community in true fraternal relationship because the church has been the greater source of division through its overt persecution of the Jewish people for the past eighteen centuries. Christianity has been the agent of the triumphal and supersessionist claims that have sought to disenfranchise the Jewish people from God's promises by saying that Christianity replaced Judaism, that Christians replaced the Jews, and that the church replaced Israel in the purposes of God. Rottenberg said it well: "Divorced from Israel, torn from the nurturing Hebraic roots of biblical faith (Romans 11:17ff.), the church becomes *ipso facto* a wayward church adhering to a (supersessionist) theology that is sadly off course."[28] Now, it is time to right historical wrongs, for Christians to bridge the gap that their forebears created.

When Christian understanding of the church's Jewish connection becomes universal, the one people group that should always have stood alongside the Jewish people and the nation of Israel in unswerving, loving support will once again become solidly pro-Israel, just as its Jewish Lord and his Jewish disciples were two millennia ago. This means that the constituents of largest religion in the world, representing one-third of the world population or 2.3 billion people, would be faithful supporters of Israel! This support will not be a blanket endorsement of any particular political

[25] Abraham Joshua Heschel, *Israel: An Echo of Eternity* (New York: Macmillan, 1967.), p. 223.

[26] Romans 11:29.

[27] Rottenberg, p. 34.

[28] Rottenberg, p. 33.

party, agency, or action in Israel.[29] It would not be "an unnuanced loyalty to Israel that looks very much like 'blank-check solidarity.'"[30] It would, however, be an affirmation of the fundamental rights of the Jewish people to exist in the land of Israel as Jews with complete self-determination, void of any political, economic, or religious coercion, with full entitlement to establish and maintain their nation as they collectively see fit and proper.

Sigmund Freud was completely correct when he argued that Christian "hatred for Judaism is at bottom hatred for Christianity."[31] He also zeroed in on one of the real causes of such antipathy: "The peoples who now excel in the practice of anti-Semitism became Christians only in relatively recent times, sometimes forced to it by blood compulsion. One might say that they are 'badly christened' under the thin veneer of Christianity [and] they have remained . . . barbarically polytheistic."[32] Freud's maxim is true: Christian hatred for Jews is, in essence, a form of self-loathing. Christians who are ignorant of the foundations of their faith do not realize that when they hate Jews and Israel—or even are apathetic toward that people and that nation—those same emotions redound toward themselves and their own Christian faith. Rather than define themselves *in contrast to* Judaism, the Jewish community, and the nation of Israel, as Christianity has historically done, it is time for Christians to define themselves fully *in context with* Judaism, the Jewish community, and the nation of Israel just as Jesus and the apostles of original Christianity did two millennia ago.

It is profoundly difficult to hate one's own family, even when some members of that family are dysfunctional. Christians must embrace Jews as fellow members of the divine family that was birthed in Abraham,[33]

---

[29] Unequivocal support for the people and nation of Israel is not putting the biblical message "into the service of ideological interests" or allowing "propaganda to be presented as gospel truth—all in the name of relevancy and prophecy." See Rottenberg, p. 34. It is simply aligning oneself with the purposes of God as outlined in his Word.

[30] Rottenberg, p. 32.

[31] Sigmund Freud, *Moses and Monotheism* (New York: Random House, 1939), pp. 116–117.

[32] Freud's description of Christian antisemites as those with only a thin veneer of Christianity covering the barbaric polytheism of their past certainly described those German citizens who supported the Nazi regime and joined in its horrific acts of depravity against the Jews. Those "Christians" had been inoculated with just enough Christianity to make them immune to the Judaic-based conscience of true Christianity and, therefore, readily vulnerable to recidivism into their former polytheistic religion and its ethos. Many of them were outright advocates of neopaganism, and many of their Nazi leaders who professed to be Christians were actually atheistic occultists. For a discussion of neopaganism in Germany, see Abir Taha, *Nietzsche, Prophet of Nazism: The Cult of the Superman* (Bloomington, IN: AuthorHouse, 2005), p. 11ff. For an analysis of the impact of the occult on the Nazi party, see Nicholas Goodrick-Clark, *The Occult Roots of Nazism: Secret Aryan Cults and Their Influence on Nazi Ideology* (New York: New York University Press, 2004).

[33] Paul declares that "Abraham is the father of us all," both Jew and Gentile (Romans 4:16).

nurtured in the prophets and sages of Israel, and expanded by the rabbi from Nazareth and his disciples. Then, like those Jewish apostles who, at God's direction, welcomed Gentiles into the faith of God "without passing judgment on them,"[34] they will find that true familial love will overlook faults and failures of the past[35] and will anticipate joy and success in future relationships of true mutuality. As Alain Weaver has said, "collaboration and mutual support between Jews and Christians can become possible around the task of recovering exilic traditions within Christianity and Judaism, even as Jews and Christians recognize and affirm the differences that separate them and the possibility of mutual learning from and challenge to those differences."[36]

## Leading Others Out of Ignorance and Prejudice

Racists, bigots, and antisemites will always slither from under their rocks, rear their ugly heads, shout their obscenities, and spew their hateful venom, and they must always be challenged when they do so. Rather than expending excessive energies, emotions, and resources counterattacking such evil, however, Christians should commit themselves to the task of educating the church, bringing it out of the dark ages of prejudice into the light of its rightful biblical relationship with the international Jewish community. Education is the key. By self-definition, education leads those who acquire it out of ignorance, superstition, and prejudice.[37] And prejudice is nothing more than being down on something one is not up on! Could Christian Judaeophobia and antisemitism be any better defined? At the same time, knowledge is power. In this case, knowledge of Christianity's Judaic heritage is the dynamic antidote to historical Judaeophobia, anti-Judaism, antisemitism, anti-Zionism, and anti-Israelism and the prophylaxis against its recurrence.

The words of Edward Flannery bear repeating: "The over-Hellenized, over-Latinized Christian church needs a re-Judaization process in order to return it to its original ideal."[38] This process is not the conversion of Christians to Judaism. It is merely embracing the faith of

[34] Romans 14:1.

[35] 1 Peter 4:8. Peter instructed the Christians: "Above all, keep loving one another earnestly, since love covers a multitude of sins" (ESV).

[36] Alain Epp Weaver, *Mapping Exile and Return: Palestinian Dispossession and Political Theology* (Minneapolis, MN: Augsburg Fortress Press, 2014), p. 72.

[37] The word *education* is from the Latin *ex* ("from" or "out of") and *ducere* ("to lead").

[38] Edward Flannery, quoted in George Cornell, "The Church after Jesus Loses Its Jewish Context," *Fredericksburg, VA Free Lance-Star*, Friday, March 28, 1975, p. 16.

Jesus and the apostles, all of whom were observant Jews who were faithful to the teachings of the Hebrew Scriptures. In fact, it is the discovery that Christianity is established on faith in the God of the Jews as understood through the Scriptures of the Jews, and realized by faith in the Jew whom the apostles recognized as Messiah and Lord. It is making the sincere effort to go where the church has not gone in nineteen centuries—back to the "faith once delivered to the saints,"[39] the faith of Abraham, Moses, David, Isaiah, Jesus, and Paul, and to true salvation, which is from the Jews.[40]

## Following in the Footsteps of Courageous Christians

Fortunately, there *are* solid examples of faith-filled bravery in the history of Christianity in whose footsteps believers today can follow in demonstrating unequivocal support for the international Jewish community and the people and nation of Israel. Individuals and communions, academic institutions and political entities, and certainly prelates and scholars can make stands against antisemitism and its latest manifestation, anti-Israelism and anti-Zionism.

Individual Christians can establish their connection with and support for the Jewish community and the nation of Israel from the biblical Gentile believer Ruth, who famously declared, "Your people shall be my people, and your God, my God. Where you die, I will die."[41] A more recent example of faith and practice is Corrie ten Boom, who, along with her family, continually risked her life to protect individual Jews from the evils of the Nazi regime in harrowing demonstrations of faith and faithfulness to God's call on her life.[42] The stories of a considerable number of people whom the Jewish people have honored as "Righteous Gentiles" whom Christians can imitate and emulate can be found in David Gushee's book, *The Righteous Gentiles of the Holocaust*.[43]

In the spirit of the late Billy Graham who literally helped turn the tide of the evil *Yom Kippur* War of 1973 that threatened to destroy

[39] Jude 1:3.

[40] John 4:22.

[41] Ruth 1:16–17.

[42] The extraordinary dedication of the ten Boom family to saving the lives of individual Jews during the time of the Holocaust is recounted in Corrie ten Boom, Elizabeth Sherrill, and John Sherrill, *The Hiding Place* (Grand Rapids, MI: Baker Publishing Group, 1971).

[43] David P. Gushee, *The Righteous Gentiles of the Holocaust: Genocide and Moral Obligation* (St. Paul, MN: Paragon House, 2003).

the nation of Israel and its people when he personally plead with United States President Richard Nixon to airlift arms to Israel,[44] spiritual leaders of the Christian community can let their voices be heard in the halls of government in support of the cause of safety and security for the people of Israel. Christian leaders can also model their relationship with the Jewish community and the nation of Israel after the life's work of G. Douglas Young, founder of the American Institute of Holy Land Studies (now Jerusalem University College), who merged various perspectives on Evangelical thought into a clear understanding of Israel that became a model for the evangelical activism of Christian Zionists that continues to be used to day.[45]

Christian scholars today can follow in the footsteps of the great German Catholic philosopher and theologian Dietrich von Hildebrand, who Pope John Paul II said was "one of the great ethicists of the twentieth century,"[46] when he stood tall against antisemitism as a vocal and uncompromising opponent of Hitler and the Nazis, even founding and editing the anti-Nazi weekly periodical, *Der Christliche Ständestaat* ("The Christian Corporative State"), in which he excoriated the Nazi regime.[47] They can also imitate the intellectual and spiritual honesty of arguably the greatest Christian theologian of the twentieth century, Karl Barth, who famously said, "The Bible . . . is a Jewish book. It cannot be read and understood and expounded unless we are prepared to become Jews with the Jews."[48] In the United States, scholars have an outstanding model in Marvin R. Wilson whose fifty-year career in academia has produced invaluable resources, including his classic book, *Our Father Abraham: Jewish Roots of the Christian Faith*, and has established a stellar record in Christian-Jewish relations.[49]

In the political realm, Christian legislators can actively seek to support the welfare of Israel at every level of government in context of those in

---

[44] Marc H. Tanenbaum, *A Prophet for Our Time: An Anthology of the Writings of Rabbi Marc H. Tanenbaum* (New York: Fordham University Press, 2002), p. 142.

[45] Paul Charles Merkley, *Christian Attitudes Towards the State of Israel* (Kingston, Canada: McGill-Queen's University Press, 2001), pp. 163–164.

[46] John Paul II, quoted in Robert Struble, Jr., "What Is Past Is Prologue: Dietrich von Hildebrand's 'Battle,'" *Catholic Lane*, Aug 03, 2015, posted at http://www.catholiclane.com/what-is-past-is-prologue-dietrich-von-hildebrands-battle/.

[47] Scot McKnight, *The Jesus Creed: Loving God, Loving Others* (Brewster, MA: Paraclete Press, 2004), p. 281.

[48] Karl Barth, *Church Dogmatics: The Doctrine of the Word of God*, tr. Geoffrey W. Bromiley, *et. al.* (Edinburgh, Scotland: T. & T. Clark, 1956), vol. 1/2, p. 511.

[49] For testimonials to Marvin Wilson's stellar career in Christian-Jewish relations, see Steven A. Hunt, ed., *Perspectives on Our Father Abraham: Essays in Honor of Marvin R. Wilson* (Grand Rapids, MI: Wm. B. Eerdmans Publishing Co., 2010).

the legislatures of at least half of the state governments in the United States who have passed laws censuring and penalizing individuals and businesses that promote, participate in, or acquiesce to the Boycott, Divest, Sanction Movement (BDS) that has been organized to impose political, social, and economic pressures on Israel by harming the Israeli economy, in an attempt to force it to capitulate to Palestinian demands.[50]

## Turning the Tide of Anti-Israelism and Antisemitism

The state of Israel has made many mistakes in its near seventy-year history, and it has suffered considerably for them. Since it is a fact that all human beings err,[51] the Jewish people should not be held to a higher standard than everyone else, even though the prophets did tend to hold "their own people up to higher moral standards than they [did] other people . . . because the Hebrews were introduced to a moral and religious code that made certain demands on them."[52] On the stage of world politics, Jews cannot be expected to lay down their lives so their enemies can bolster their own self-worth and expand their power and resources. The murderous spirit that is determined to annihilate the Jews must not be allowed to triumph either in the church or in the world community.

Now is the time for Christians to take the lead in helping to turn the tide of lies and deceptions that has become the staple of radical Muslim propagandists and the Western media. Surely it is time to stop supporting individuals and movements which, with their distortions and outright prevarications, make it possible for people like the young Palestinians in Germany to express the views of the most extremist Muslims regarding the nation of Israel and Jews in general by saying outrageous things like, "The damned Jews should be burnt," and, "They should be slaughtered like pigs," and, "I would eradicate all Jews, shooting them into the sea and goodbye."[53] How utterly insane is it that anyone could possibly mouth such abominable statements—and do so in the name of God and religion!

[50] Jewish Virtual Library, "Anti-Semitism: State Anti-BDS Legislation," posted at http://www.jewishvirtuallibrary.org/anti-bds-legislation. Also, http://thehill.com/blogs/congress-blog/foreign-policy/346434-federal-anti-bds-legislation-common-sense-and-nobodys-happy, and https://www.jta.org/2017/10/23/news-opinion/politics/state-anti-bds-laws-are-hitting-unintended-targets-and-nobodys-happy.

[51] Romans 3:23: "All have sinned and fall short of the glory of God."

[52] Mordecai Schreiber, *The Man Who Knew God: Decoding Jeremiah* (Lanham, MD: Rowman & Littlefield Publishers, 2010), p. 141.

[53] Günther Jikeli, *European Muslim Antisemitism: Why Young Urban Males Say They Don't Like Jews* (Bloomington, IN: Indiana University Press, 2015), p. 125.

A groundswell of support for the people and the nation of Israel must arise, especially among those who seek peace on earth.[54] It is time to recognize the bountiful oasis of peace-loving Jews in Israel that is surrounded by a desiccated desert of anger, hate, violence, terror, and war. Christians everywhere must come to the understanding that "what the anti-Zionists would obliterate is precisely the voice of the Torah—and with the Torah, God and Israel as well."[55] Ultimately, any plan to annihilate the Jews is at bottom a plan to neutralize, if not destroy, the God of the Jews. The promises of God to the descendants of Abraham are, however, secure, and nothing can prevent their fulfillment. The time has come for the world to admit that the Jewish people have suffered enough.[56] Those who recognize the righteous precepts of the God of Scripture must grant the Jews the blessings of freedom and security. It is time to stop both Holocaust deniers who "deny the Jews their deaths and their past" and anti-Zionists who "deny the Jews their lives and their future."[57]

The spirit of anti-Zionism, the unholy new garments of ancient and enduring antisemitism, must be discarded. Of a truth, anti-Zionism's days are numbered, for when the Messiah comes, he will not establish his throne in New York, London, Rome, Athens, Geneva, Moscow, Tokyo, Beijing, Damascus, Istanbul, or Mecca. His universal dominion will be headquartered on Mount Zion in the city of Jerusalem, and from that foundation, he will extend peace like a river to the inhabitants of Israel and from them to all the inhabitants of the earth.[58] It is time for songs of peace to echo around the world, for "peace sown by peacemakers brings a harvest of justice."[59] This is what YHWH, the God of Israel says of his holy nation and his holy land: "I will return to Zion and will dwell in the midst of Jerusalem. . . . Old men and old women will again sit in the streets of Jerusalem . . . and the streets of the city shall be filled with boys and girls playing in its streets."[60]

---

[54] Luke 2:14.

[55] David Patterson, *Anti-Semitism and Its Metaphysical Origins* (Cambridge, UK: Cambridge University Press, 2015), pp. 100–101.

[56] This is true for some Christians whose eschatological scenarios anticipate yet another "time of Jacob's trouble" (Jeremiah 30:7) that will result in the destruction of two-thirds of the Jewish population of the "whole land." (Zechariah 13:8). Surely such prophecies have already been fulfilled enough to have been "filled full." At some point, an end must come to "restoration followed by destruction" in the prophetic pronouncements. Whatever the case, all Christians, like Father Abraham, should be interceding for mercy and against judgment!

[57] Patterson, p. 197.

[58] Isaiah 66:12.

[59] James 3:18.

[60] Zechariah 8:3–5.

CHAPTER 20

# THE ULTIMATE RESTORATION

## God's Final Solution to Antisemitism

For centuries after the destruction of the temple in AD 70, Israel—the people, the nation, and the land—hovered between life and death, often nearer to death than to life. The words of Josif Rabinovich poignantly encapsulate Israel's historical condition: "Nation of Israel! . . . In only one portion of your heart is it still possible to notice now and then a small throbbing, your limbs shudder, and the traits of your face attest that it is not yet possible to place you on the list of nations that have expired. Yes, you are still alive, the name *Israel* still flutters above you."[1] In spite of centuries of efforts to secure the genocide of the Jewish people that reached their nadir in the Nazis' "Final Solution," Israel has continued to exist as a people—indeed, as *the* Chosen People. And finally, after centuries of unrelenting hatred, persecution, violence, mayhem, and murder against them individually and corporately, the Jews came together against all odds as the People of Israel to form the Nation of Israel, and they have done so in the Land of Israel! "Israel," in fact, cannot be fully considered without each of these three elements, for Israel is not one or the other; it is an indivisible unity of all three: People, Nation, and Land.[2] It is impossible, therefore, to delegitimize one

[1] Josef Rabinovich, quoted in V. S. Soloviev, *Freedom, Faith, and Dogma: Essays by V. S. Soloviev on Christianity and Judaism* (Albany, NY: The State University of New York Press, 2008), p. 91.

[2] This is proven by the fact that from the time when the Roman Empire forcibly removed the Jewish people from their land and denied their nationhood, the corporate heart of the people—and, indeed, of every individual Jew—refused to accept the destruction of their nation and the expropriation of their land. The expectation of the full restoration of people, nation, and land continued to be central expressions of the *Amidah*, the Jewish prayer *par excellence*. Three times each weekday since that time, Jews in synagogues around the world have prayed the fourteenth of the *Amidah's* eighteen benedictions, the *Bo'ne Yerushalayim B'rakhah* ("Builder of Jerusalem Blessing"), saying, "Return in compassion to your city, Jerusalem, and rest within it as you have said. Rebuild it speedily, and in our days, a structure forever. And may you establish the throne of David within Jerusalem speedily. Blessed are you, LORD, the Builder of Jerusalem."

without, at the same time, delegitimizing the others. The legitimacy of the People of Israel, the Nation of Israel, and the Land of Israel is not, however, derived from any human institution. Though unrelenting efforts have been made in century after century to separate the people, the nation, and the land of Israel, all three are inexorably and indissolubly connected. As Aaron Klingerman has rightly argued, "the peculiar Book, the peculiar people, and the peculiar land must always be viewed together. What God has put together let no man, be he theologian or politician, put asunder."[3] The authentication of all three entities is based solely on divine decree and is validated and made certain by the only eternally enduring reality that exists in the universe and beyond: the divine faithfulness of a God who never changes and remains in covenant with his Chosen People—the worldwide community of Jews and the nation of Israel.[4]

This was *the* miracle of the twentieth century. No other event could have approached comparison with what emerged from the world chaos of this time.[5] The resurrection of Israel was without a doubt an act of God! In fact, God himself established this truth in utterly explicit fashion when he declared: "For I am YHWH—I have not changed; and you are the children of Jacob—you have not ceased to be."[6] As Jon D. Levenson says, "Israel exists only because of God's choice, and apart from God, it has no existence at all."[7] It is for this reason that "Israel has no profane history, only a sacred history, a history of redemption, of backsliding and return, punishment and restoration."[8] As William Klein rightly observes, "Israel exists as a people because of God's choice."[9] God, therefore, "proved his sovereign faithfulness to his people, preserving them in spite of their unfaithfulness."[10] Indeed, "It is by God's grace and faithfulness—not by race, language, culture or religion—that the Jews have continued

[3] Aaron Klingerman, quoted in Matthew Avery Sutton, *American Apocalypse: A History of Modern Evangelicalism* (Cambridge, MA: Harvard University Press, 2014), p. 302.

[4] James 1:17: "Every good and perfect gift descends from above, from the Father of lights with whom there is no change nor a shadow of variation" (ABPE).

[5] Yehoshua Pfeffer, *Prophecies and Providence: A Biblical Approach to Modern Jewish History* (Jerusalem, Israel: Urim Publications, 2015).

[6] Malachi 3:6, TNK.

[7] Jon D. Levenson, "The Universal Horizon of Biblical Particularism," in *Ethnicity and the Bible*, Mark G. Brett, ed. (Leiden, The Netherlands: E. J. Brill, 1996), p. 153.

[8] Levenson, p. 153.

[9] William Klein, *The New Chosen People: A Corporate View of Election* (Eugene, OR: Wipf and Stock Publishers, 1990), p. 34.

[10] Klein, p. 34.

to exist in the face of persecution and genocide."[11] Karl Barth concluded that the Jewish people cannot be "overlooked, or banished, or destroyed—for the grace of God upholds [them]."[12]

God's "covenantal faithfulness to Israel was eternal."[13] The perduration of Israel as people, nation, and land is not predicated on evanescent musings or Machiavellian stratagems of philosophers or politicians. It is guaranteed by the God "who does not change like shifting shadows."[14] This God is the one whose "plans [were] formed long ago, with perfect faithfulness."[15] Israel's greatness, therefore, has always been viewed solely in the context "of the greatness of her God."[16] This is what God had clearly predicted through the prophet Isaiah: "'No weapon that is formed against you will prosper; and every tongue that accuses you in judgment you will condemn. This is the heritage of the servants of the LORD, and their vindication is from me.'"[17] What was true in the ancient kingdoms of Babylon and Persia has continued to be true in the centuries since that time. God has always brought life from the dead to his Chosen People. Despite every effort to destroy them, *Am Yisrael Chai.*[18]

A veritable parade of tyrants has marched across the annals of history, each one seeking to solve the "Jewish problem" and impose his own "final solution" on God's Chosen People. From Pharaoh, to Nebuchadnezzar, to Haman, to Antiochus, to Titus, to Hadrian, and, finally, to Hitler, "history's worst tyrants have always reserved a special hatred for the Jewish people."[19] At the same time, however, Israel—and especially the city of Jerusalem—has long been an "unmovable rock"[20] to such megalomaniacal despots and an almost unending succession of others who have sought to dominate the Jewish people, their body politic, and their land. Without exception, however, all the nations in history that have

[11] Mark R. Lindsay, *Barth, Israel, and Jesus: Karl Barth's Theology of Israel* (Burlington, VT: Ashgate Publishing Co., 2007), p. 79.

[12] Karl Barth, *Church Dogmatics, III/3: The Creator and His Creature*, G. W. Bromley, ed. (London, UK: T & T Clark International, 2000), p. 220.

[13] Glenn Stanfield Holland, *Gods in the Desert: Religions of the Ancient Near East* (Lanham, MD: Rowman & Littlefield Publishers, 2009), p. 252.

[14] James 1:17, NIV.

[15] Isaiah 25:1.

[16] Horst Seebass, "בחר *Bachar*," in *Theological Dictionary of the Old Testament*, C. J. Botterweck and H. Ringgren, eds. (Grand Rapids, MI: Wm. B. Eerdmans Publishing Co., 1975), vol. 2, p. 84.

[17] Isaiah 54:17.

[18] *"The People of Israel Live."*

[19] George W. Bush in an April, 2001, speech, quoted in David B. MacDonald, *Thinking History, Fighting Evil: Neoconservatives and the Perils of Analogy* (Lanham, MD: Rowman & Littlefield Publishers, 2009), p. 98.

[20] Zechariah 12:3a, NIV.

meddled in the affairs of Israel have herniated themselves, broken their backs, or become paralyzed and incapacitated as a result of their attitudes and actions toward Israel.[21] And as the Prophet Zechariah spoke of what could well be a yet future attempt to destroy this people, this nation, and this land, "All who try to move [this stone] will injure themselves."[22]

Any present or future efforts by nations or peoples to align themselves against Israel will be met with the same catastrophic consequences that have afflicted the magnificent and mighty in history who have attempted to brutalize and enslave the Jewish people. They will find themselves "staggering" from the profound inebriation imposed upon them by God himself.[23] Indeed, God declared that when the all the nations of the world launch the final eschatological assault against Israel and its capital, Jerusalem, they will run headlong into the only omnipotent entity in the universe, God himself, who promised that he would personally "set about to destroy all the nations that come against Jerusalem."[24] Any person, social entity, or political system that threatens any part of the Abrahamic covenant and its land contract will be cursed by God, for the Almighty has declared incontrovertibly, "The one who curses you I will curse."[25] Likewise, any person or social entity that blesses what God has blessed by supporting, defending, and facilitating the fulfillment of the Abrahamic promise and its land contract will also be blessed by God, who has also pledged, "I will bless those who bless you."[26] And, indubitably, the Lord of heaven has categorically assured the world that he is ever on guard and alert to recognize and deal with affronts of any kind against his Chosen People and their land: "Behold, he who keeps Israel will neither slumber nor sleep."[27]

Here is a lesson that everyone should learn about God and Israel: inflicting pain on Israel also causes God to suffer. Isaiah said it well: "I was appalled that no one gave support, so my own arm achieved salvation for me. . . . So he became their Savior. In all their distress he too was distressed, and the angel of his presence saved them."[28] A rabbinic *midrash*

---

[21] Even when those nations, including Babylon and Rome, that God commissioned to bring judgment upon Israel met the same fate when they exceeded their commission and began to brutalize the Chosen People.

[22] Zechariah 12:3b, NIV.

[23] Zechariah 12:2.

[24] Zechariah 12:9.

[25] Genesis 12:3.

[26] Genesis 12:3.

[27] Psalm 121:4.

[28] Isaiah 63:5, 8–9.

on the prophetic declaration *in all their distress he too was distressed* suggests that anyone "who hates Israel is as if he hated God. . . . And he who helps Israel is as if he helped God. Whenever Israel is enslaved, the Shechinah is enslaved with them, as it says, 'In all their afflictions He was afflicted (Isa. LXIII, 9).'"[29] Robert Bleakney observes, "The Almighty cannot change with regard to his steadfast love and power, yet he can change in responsiveness to the pain of his creatures."[30] All the inhabitants of the earth would be wise not to inflict pain on God!

Sadly, "instead of accepting Israel's election with humility," the Gentile nations "rail against it, mocking the God of the Jews," says Michael Wyschogrod. "Israel's presence is a constant reminder to them that they were not chosen but that this people was, and that this people remains in their midst as a thorn in the flesh. Minute by minute, the existence of Israel mocks the pagan gods, the divine beings who rise out of the consciousness of all peoples but which are gentile gods because they are deifications of humanity and the forces of nature rather than the true, living God of Abraham."[31] In the name of their gods, the Gentile nations have repeatedly shaken their fists in the face of the God of Israel. Naftali Rothenberg rightly observes, however that "the paradox is that those people who left only monuments behind as a record of their existence have vanished with time, whereas the Jews, who left ideas, have survived."[32] Egyptians, Assyrians, Babylonians, Hittites, and Philistines "disappeared from the stage of history, leaving behind archaeological remains, but no living way of life."[33]

## Restored Israel: A Work of God

While numerous prophecies are set forth in the Hebrew Scriptures predicting the restoration of the Jewish people to their land, there is one that has a ring of finality. This is the prophecy of Amos in which he recorded this promise from God to Israel, "In that day I will restore David's fallen *sukkah*—I will repair its broken walls and

[29] Sifre to Numbers 64.4.5, in Jacob Neusner, *A Theological Commentary to the Midrash: Sifre to Numbers and Sifre to Deuteronomy*, Jacob Neusner, ed. (Lanham, MD: University Press of America, 2001), pp. 21–22. Also Paul M. van Buren, *A Theology of the Jewish-Christian Reality: A Christian Theology of the People of Israel* (Lanham, MD: University Press of America, 1995), p. 166.

[30] Robert W. Bleakney, personal communication.

[31] Michael Wyschogrod, *Abraham's Promise: Judaism and Jewish-Christian Relations*, P. Kendall Soulen, ed. (Grand Rapids, MI: Wm. B. Eerdmans Publishing Co., 2004), p. 182.

[32] Max I. Dimont, *Jews, God, and History* (New York: Penguin Books, 2004), cover.

[33] Naftali Rothenberg and Eliezer Schweid, eds., *Jewish Identity in Modern Israel: Proceedings on Secular Judaism and Democracy* (Jerusalem, Israel: Urim Publications, 2002), p. 69.

restore its ruins—and will rebuild it as it used to be."[34] The restoration that YHWH promised was to be accompanied by agricultural wonders: "Behold, days are coming, declares the LORD, when the plowman will overtake the reaper and the treader of grapes him who sows seed; when the mountains will drip sweet wine."[35] In that day, the restored people of Israel are to enjoy the richness of the land: "They will plant vineyards and drink their wine; they will make gardens and eat their fruit."[36] Most importantly, God established perhaps the most important prophetic promise about this restoration that had ever been made when he said, "I will plant Israel in their own land, *never again to be uprooted from the land I have given them*, says the LORD your God."[37] While other prophecies promised restoration to the land, an abundance of miracles in the land, and abiding peace in the land, through Amos, the Almighty declared that his ultimate plan for Israel would feature this promise: *Israel will never again be uprooted from its land!* Once and for all time, the people who have been dislodged from their land again and again by violence will be restored to the land with the promise that they will never be uprooted from it.

Yet another miracle that God promised to Israel through Amos is the final reconciliation of the non-Jewish nations to the Chosen People. Here is what God predicted: "[Israel will] possess the remnant of Edom and all the nations that bear my name, declares the LORD, who will do these things."[38] The culmination of the "never-to-be-uprooted" promise includes the full application of Israel's Abrahamic blessing to the nations, the expansion of God's particularity into his universality by extending to the nations the unilateral covenant of inclusion. This was the mystery[39] to which Paul alluded when he discussed Gentile inclusion in God's family tree[40] and their adoption as naturalized citizens of the commonwealth of Israel.[41] Amos' Gentile inclusion in Israel's blessing was echoed by Isaiah's divine message to Israel: "Arise, shine; for your light has come. . . . Nations will come to your light. . . . [T]he flocks of Kedar [and] the rams of Nebaioth will minister

---

[34] Amos 9:11, NIV.

[35] Amos 9:13.

[36] Amos 9:14.

[37] Amos 9:15 (emphasis added).

[38] Amos 9:12, NIV.

[39] Ephesians 3:4–9.

[40] Romans 11:11.

[41] Ephesians 2:12–19.

to you. They will go up with acceptance on my altar. . . . Foreigners will build up your walls, and their kings will minister to you."[42] God had already promised Isaiah that foreigners (Gentiles) would be added to his Chosen People: "Many peoples will come and say, 'Come, let us go up the mountain of the LORD, to the temple of the God of Jacob. He will teach us his ways, so that we may walk in his paths.'" The prophet said that this prediction would be possible because "the Torah will go forth from Zion and the word of the LORD from Jerusalem."[43] Then God even predicted that the Gentiles who would lay hold on his Torah would be given a name "better than that of sons and daughters . . . which will not be cut off."[44]

Jacob Neusner discusses Jewish thought on the manner in which this Gentile inclusion in Israel can take place: "Israel is Israel by reason of accepting the Torah . . . that conviction . . . represents the final solution to the gentile-problem: how the gentile overcomes his alienation from God and becomes Israel. His condition is not beyond remediation but readily corrected. And when the gentile becomes Israel, then he or she joins Israel without differentiation as to origin or status."[45] Within the general mystery of God's sovereign dealings with all the people of the earth, another Jewish rabbi, the apostle Paul proclaimed this solution: "If you belong to the Messiah, then you are Abraham's offspring, heirs according to the promise,"[46] and he also predicted that a "full number of the Gentiles" would be included in the Abrahamic covenant in the same time frame in which "all Israel will be saved."[47] This all-inclusive work of divine sovereignty is intrinsically connected with the full restoration of David's *sukkah*, the tabernacle of Israel, to its glory. God's word to the prophet Haggai best describes this miraculous event: "The latter glory of this house will be greater than the former . . . and in this place I will give peace, declares the LORD of hosts."[48]

The return of the Jewish people who have made *aliyah* from

---

[42] Isaiah 60:1, 3, 7, 10. Here, Kedar and Nabaioth, the first two of Ishmael's twelve sons, represent the Gentiles.

[43] Isaiah 2:3, NIV.

[44] Isaiah 56:5.

[45] Jacob Neusner, *A Theological Commentary to the Midrash: Ruth Rabbah and Esther Rabbah I* (Lanham, MD: University Press of America, 2001), p. 46.

[46] Galatians 3:29.

[47] Romans 11:25–26.

[48] Haggai 2:9.

the four corners of the earth has certainly set the stage for the final fulfillment of God's prophetic promise to Amos. Both Jews and Christians surely hope and pray for the complete and final restoration of Israel—the people, the nation, and the land—that has taken place in the modern era will transcend the post-exilic restoration in the days of Ezra, Nehemiah, Zerubbabel, and Joshua and will have the permanency that God promised to Amos. Prayerfully, it will be the final restoration, the one that will firmly and securely place the Jewish people in their land so that they will never be removed again. Given the extraordinary miracle that occurred in 1948 and the continuing miracles of preservation that have taken place since that time, may all people of biblical faith affirm God's words of final truth by saying, Amen![49]

## God's Final Word for Israel

God can no more forsake his land promise to Abraham's progeny than he can decide not to send the Messiah to earth. If God can forsake Israel, he can forsake the whole world, withdraw himself into the heavenlies, and nullify the promise of the resurrection. But, if he did any of these things, he would not be God, for God "cannot lie."[50] For this reason, God has given his personal assurance: "The LORD will not abandon his people on account of his great name, because the LORD has been pleased to make you a people for himself."[51] David Klinghoffer asks, "We are confronted here with the choice between the instrumentalist theory of faith, and the truth theory. Is religion about man, or is it about God?"[52] Marvin Wilson says that Klinghoffer's question is a reminder that "the religion and calling of Israel have their origin either in the eternal counsel of God or in the changeable theories of man. If the permanence of Israel's election is in doubt, the trustworthiness of God's Word is likewise in doubt."[53]

Ultimately, therefore, God will bring an end to the litany of Gentile "final solutions" to the "Jewish problem" when he initiates his own

[49] Daniel 2:44; 4:3; 7:14, 18, 27.

[50] Numbers 23:19; Titus 1:2.

[51] 1 Samuel 12:22, NIV.

[52] David Klinghoffer, "God Is Not a Pluralist," in *The Role of Religion in Politics and Society*, Arthur A. Cohen and Paul Mendes-Flohr, eds. (New York: Free Press, 1987), p. 152.

[53] Marvin R. Wilson, *Exploring Our Hebraic Heritage: A Christian Theology of Roots and Renewal* (Grand Rapids, MI: Wm. B. Eerdmans Publishing Co., 2014), p. 250. In support of his statement, Wilson references Genesis 17:7; Deuteronomy 7:7–9; 2 Samuel 7:24; and Jeremiah 31:35–36.

"final solution" to the "Gentile problem" by reversing the Gentile trend of engaging in downward spirals of condemnation, caricature, and violence against his Chosen People. This he will do when he reestablishes the faith of the Jewish people on the new covenant of the Torah written on their hearts.[54] In fact, then the nations will understand that resurrected Israel *is*, as Jacob Neusner describes it, "God's final solution to the human problem."[55]

In the final analysis, God will have the last word regarding Israel. Based on the principle of divine immutability which establishes the truth that God is utterly faithful to fulfill his covenants and promises, it can be asserted that God's ultimate word for his Chosen People will be the same as the final word in his own ancient blessing for Israel. When God composed this everlasting benediction for Israel and dictated it to Moses, he instructed the prophet to make sure that the following words would be continually spoken over the children of Israel in all their generations:

יְבָרֶכְךָ יהוה וְיִשְׁמְרֶךָ׃
יָאֵר יהוה פָּנָיו אֵלֶיךָ וִיחֻנֶּךָּ׃
יִשָּׂא יהוה פָּנָיו אֵלֶיךָ וְיָשֵׂם לְךָ שָׁלוֹם׃

May the Lord bless you, and keep you;
May the Lord cause his face to shine upon you
and be gracious unto you;
May the Lord turn his face toward you
and give you *shalom*.

The final Hebrew word of this divine benediction is *shalom*. The word *shalom* is a self-contained blessing that means far more than peace in the sense of an absence of conflict. Trevor Bechtel describes the word *shalom* in this manner: "The most common meaning of shalom is material well-being and prosperity. This means our physical health, our access to food and care and shelter . . . an integrated state of well-being or health."[56] In contemporary use in Israel, *shalom* is also viewed as a sense of justice, "the restoration or creation of right

---

[54] Jeremiah 31:31.

[55] Jacob Neusner, *The Native Category-Formations of the Aggadah: The Earlier Midrash-Compilations* (Lanham, MD: University Press of America, 2000), p. 150.

[56] Trevor George Bechtel, *The Gift of Ethics: A Story for Discovering Lasting Significance in Your Daily Work* (Eugene, OR: Wipf and Stock Publishers, 2014), p. 38.

relationships between individuals or groups."[57] Yet another use of *shalom* connects with "personal integrity and honesty." Since true *shalom* does involve "physical well-being, justice, and integrity," it essentially means that "everything is exactly as it should be."[58]

This, then, is God's final word for Israel: "The LORD turn his face toward you and give you *shalom* [health, justice, and integrity]," thereby making "everything precisely as it should be" in the individual and corporate lives of his Chosen People. No matter what anyone else may have to say to the Jewish people, the nation of Israel, and the Promised Land, God's final word to Israel is *Shalom*! Is it any wonder, then, that God said to Jerusalem, "I will extend peace to her like a river," and that he promised his people, "No weapon that is formed against you will prosper."[59] Ultimately, God will have the final word in the conflict with humanity, and he has already spoken, he still speaks, and, through the terms of his eternal covenant, he will continue to speak his everlasting *shalom* to the people, the nation, and the land of Israel.

May the entire earth join in joyous expectation of the fulfillment of what Paul envisioned as God's final solution for the Jewish people: "All Israel shall be saved."[60] Those who do will also be able to share in the apostle's doxology by exclaiming with him, "Oh, the depth of the riches both of the wisdom and knowledge of God! How unsearchable are his judgments and unfathomable his ways! . . . For from him and through him and to him are all things. To him be the glory forever. Amen."[61]

---

[57] Bechtel, p. 38.

[58] Bechtel, p. 38.

[59] Isaiah 66:12; 54:17.

[60] Romans 11:26.

[61] Romans 11:33, 36.

# BIBLIOGRAPHY


Abadeer, Adel Az. *Norms and Gender Discrimination in the Arab World*. New York: Palgrave Macmillan, 2015.

Abasciano, Brian J. *Paul's Use of the Old Testament in Romans 9.1–18: An Intertextual and Theological Exegesis*. New York: T & T Clark International, 2011.

Abbas, Mahmoud. *The Other Side: The Secret Relationship Between Nazism and Zionism*. Amman, Jordan: Dar Ibn Rushd lil-Nashr wal-Tawzi', 1984.

Aberbach, Moshe. *Jewish Education and History: Continuity, Crisis and Change*. Abingdon, UK: Routledge, 2009.

Abu-Sahlieh, Sami Awad Aldeeb. *Male & Female Circumcision: Among Jews, Christians and Muslims*. Ithaca, NY: Shangri La Publications, Ltd., 2001.

Abulof, Uriel. *The Mortality and Morality of Nations*. Cambridge, UK: Cambridge University Press, 2015.

Adam, Thomas, ed. *Germany and the Americas: Culture, Politics, and History*. Santa Barbara, CA: ABC-CLIO, Inc., 2005.

Adel, Farid. *The Champions of the True Faith*. Bloomington, IN: Xlibris Corp., 2016.

Adelman, Jonathan. *The Rise of Israel: A History of a Revolutionary State*. New York: Routledge, 2008.

Ådna, Gerd Marie. "The Reception of Islamic Prophet Stories within Muslim Communities," in *Islamic Myths and Memories: Mediators of Globalization*, Itzchak Weismann, Mark Sedgwick, and Ulrika Mårtensson, eds. Abingdon, UK: Routledge, 2014.

Adelman, Penina. *Praise Her Works: Conversations with Biblical Women*. Philadelphia, PA: Jewish Publication Society, 2005.

Ahamkaari, Ahamkaari. *Will I Be Killed? (for writing the following contents. . .)*. Lincoln, NE: iUniverse, 2003.

Ahlström, Gösta W. *History of Ancient Palestine*. Sheffield, UK: Sheffield Academic Press, 1993.

Ahmed, Akbar S. *Islam Today: A Short Introduction to the Muslim World*. London, UK: I. B. Tauris & Co., 1999.

Ajaj, Azar, Duane A. Miller, and Philp Sumpter. *Arab Evangelicals in Israel*. Eugene, OR: Wipf and Stock Publishers, 2016.

Akbari, Daniel, and Paul Tetreault. *Honor Killing: A Professional's Guide to Sexual Relations and Ghayra Violence from the Islamic Sources*. Bloomington, IN: AuthorHouse, 2014.

Akhtar, Shabbir. *Islam as Political Religion: The Future of an Imperial Faith*. Abingdon, UK: Routledge, 2011.

Akinwale, Anthony. "Reconciliation," in *The Oxford Handbook of Sacramental Theology*, Hans Boersma and Matthew Levering, eds. Oxford, UK: Oxford University Press, 2015.

Alexander, Philip S. "Madame Eglentyne, Geoffrey Chaucer and the Problem of Medieval Anti-Semitism." *Bulletin of the John Rylands Library* 74 (1992), 119–120.

Ali-Karamali, Sumbul. *Growing Up Muslim: Understanding the Beliefs and Practices of Islam*. New York: Random House, 2012.

Allen, S. J., and Emilie Amt, eds. *The Crusades: A Reader*. Toronto, Canada: The University of Toronto Press, 2014.

Allert, Tilman. *The Hitler Salute: On the Meaning of a Gesture*. New York: Picador, 2008.

Allport, Gordon W. *The Nature of Prejudice*. New York: Perseus Books Publishing, 1954.

Almog, Shmuel. *Zionism and History: The Rise of a New Jewish Consciousness*. New York: St. Martin's Press, 1987.

Alon, Mati. *Holocaust and Redemption*. Victoria, Canada: Trafford Publishing, 2003.

Alter, Robert. *Genesis: Translation and Commentary*. New York: W. W. Norton, 1996.

Adamec, Ludwig W. *Historical Dictionary of Islam*. Lanham, MD: Rowman & Littlefield Publishing Group, 2009.

Amstutz, Mark R. *Evangelicals and American Foreign Policy*. Oxford, UK: Oxford University Press, 2014.

Anbar, Michael. *Israel and Its Future: Analysis and Suggestions*. Lincoln, NE: iUniverse, Inc., 2004.

Andersen, Hans Christian. *Fairy Tales from Hans Christian Andersen*. London, UK: J. M. Dent & Co., 1906.

Aouragh, Miriyam. "Revolutionary Manoeuvrings," in *Media and Political Contestation in the Contemporary Arab World: A Decade of Change*, Lena Jayyusi and Anne Sofie Roald, eds. New York: Palgrave Macmillan, 2016.

Apple, Raymond. *Let's Ask the Rabbi*. Milton Keynes, UK: AuthorHouse UK, Ltd., 2011.

Applebaum, Anne. *Gulag: A History*. New York: Doubleday, 2003.

Appelbaum, Diana. "Presbyterians Bearing False Witness." *The American Thinker* (June 3, 2006).

Applewhite, Ashton, William R. Evans III, and Andrew Frothingham, eds. *And I Quote: The Definitive Collection of Quotes, Sayings, and Jokes for the Contemporary Speech-Maker*. New York: Macmillan, 1992.

## ANTI-ISRAELISM


Arad, Yitzhak. *Belzec, Sobidor, Treblinka: The Operation Reinhard Death Camps*. Bloomington, IN: Indiana University Press, 1987.

Arden, Stuart. *Sense and Nonsense: Everything You Need to Know About the Arab-Israeli Conflict*. Jerusalem, Israel: Gefen Publishing House, 2013.

Arendt, Hannah. *The Origins of Totalitarianism*. Orlando, FL: Harcourt-Brace, Inc., 1968.

Armstrong, Karen. *Islam: A Short History*. New York: Random House, 2000.

_______*Jerusalem: One City, Three Faiths*. New York: Random House, 2005.

_______*The Spiral Staircase: My Climb Out of Darkness*. New York: Random House, 2004.

Arnal, William. "The Cipher 'Judaism' in Contemporary Historical Jesus Scholarship," *Apocalypticism, Anti-Semitism and the Historical Jesus: Subtexts in Criticism*, John S. Kloppenborg and John Marshall, eds. New York: T&T Clark International, 2005.

Aron, Raymond. *De Gaulle, Israel and the Jews*, tr. John Sturrock. New Brunswick, NJ: Transaction Publishers, 2009.

Aronson, Ran. "Settlement in Eretz Israel—A Colonialist Enterprise? 'Critical' Scholarship and Historical Geography." *Israel Studies*, Indiana University Press, vol. 2, no. 2, (1997), 214–229.

Aryeetey-Attoh, Samuel. *Geography of Sub-Saharan Africa*. New York: Prentice Hall, 2003.

Ashton, John, and David Down. *Unwrapping the Pharaohs: How Egyptian Archaeology Confirms the Biblical Timeline*. Forest Green, AR: New Leaf Publishing Group, 2006.

Aslan, Reza. *Muslims and Jews in America: Commonalities, Contentions, and Complexities*. New York: Palgrave Macmillan, 2011.

Aslanian, Sebouh David. *From the Indian Ocean to the Mediterranean: The Global Trade Networks of Armenian Merchants from New Julfa*. Berkeley, CA: The University of California Press, 2011.

Ateek, Naim S. "Foreword," in *Zionism through Christian Lenses: Ecumenical Perspectives on the Promised Land*, Carole Monica Burnett, ed. Eugene, OR: Wipf and Stock Publishers, 2013.

Auerbach, Jerold S. *Jewish State, Pariah Nation: Israel and the Dilemmas of Legitimacy*. New Orleans, LA: Quid Pro Books, 2014.

Aven, Tricia, and Tricia Miller. *Jews and Anti-Judaism in Esther and the Church*. Cambridge, UK: James Clark & Co., 2015.

Awwad, Nariman. *Beleaguered Word: Documentation of Israeli Aggression Against the Palestinian Media*. Baghdad, Iraq: Ittihad al-Suhufiyin al-'Arab Press, 2000.

Azous, Paul. *In The Plains of the Wilderness*. Jerusalem, Israel: Mazo Publishers, 2006.

Babbin, Jed L., and Herbert I. London. *The BDS War Against Israel: The Orwellian Campaign to Destroy Israel*. New York: The London Center for Policy Research, 2014.

Bahat, Dan, ed. *Twenty Centuries of Jewish Life in the Holy Land*. Jerusalem: *The Israel Economist*, 1976.

Baker, Alan, ed. *Israel's Rights as a Nation-State in International Diplomacy*. Jerusalem, Israel: Jerusalem Center for Public Affairs, 2011.

Baker, Lemuel. *The Many Faces of Judaism: Jewish Studies for the Busy Person*. Bloomington, IN: Xlibris Corp., 2012.

Baker, Todd D. *Matthew 27:25: "His Blood Be on Us.": Are the Jewish People Racially Condemned for the Death of Christ?* Bloomington, IN: iUniverse, 2008.

Bakhos, Carol. *Ishmael on the Border: Rabbinic Portrayals of the First Arab*. Albany, NY: The State University of New York Press, 2006.

Baldwin, Neil. *Henry Ford and the Jews: The Mass Production of Hate*. New York: PublicAffairs, 2001.

Bank, Richard D. *The Everything Jewish History and Heritage Book*. Avon, MA: F+W Publications, 2003.

Banks, Diane. *Writing the History of Israel*. London, UK: T & T Clark International, 2006.

Banks, William C., Renée de Neveres, and Mitchel B. Wallerstein. *Combating Terrorism: Strategies and Approaches*. Washington, DC: CQ Press, 2008.

Bar-Am, Micha. *Jews in Arab Lands Today*. Tel Aviv, Israel: Beit Hatfutsot, The Nahum Goldmann Museum of the Jewish Diaspora, 1996.

Barclay, William. *The Gospel of John*. Edinburgh, UK: Saint Andrew Press, 1975.

Bard, Michael. *The Complete Idiot's Guide to the Middle East Conflict*. New York: Penguin Books, 2008.

_______, and Moshe Schwartz. *One Thousand and One Facts Everyone Should Know about Israel*. Lanham, MD: Rowman & Littlefield Publishers, 2005.

Barghouti, Omar. *BDS: Boycott, Divestment, Sanctions: The Global Struggle for Palestinian Rights* (Chicago, IL: Haymarket Books, 2011.

Barkan, Elazar, Elizabeth A. Cole, and Kai Struve. *Shared History, Divided Memory: Jews and Others in Soviet-Occupied Poland 1939–1941*. Leipzig, Germany: Erscheint im Leipziger Universitätsverlag GmbH, 2007.

Baron, Salo W. *A Social and Religious History of the Jews*. New York: Columbia University Press, 1937.

Barrett, David B., George T. Kurian, and Todd M. Johnson, eds. *World Christian Encyclopedia: The World by Segments: Religions, Peoples, Languages, Cities, Topics*. Oxford, UK: Oxford University Press, 2001.

## BIBLIOGRAPHY


Bartal, Shaul. *Jihad in Palestine: Political Islam and the Israeli-Palestinian Conflict*. Abingdon, UK: Routledge, 2016.

Barth, Karl. *Against the Stream: Shorter Post-War Writings, 1946–1952*, Ronald Gregor Smith, ed. London, UK: SCM Press, 1954.

_______*Church Dogmatics: The Doctrine of the Word of God*, tr. Geoffrey W. Bromiley, et. al. Edinburgh, Scotland: T. & T. Clark, 1956.

_______*Church Dogmatics, II/2: The Election of God; the Command of God*. New York: Bloomsbury Academic, 2004.

_______*Church Dogmatics, III/3: The Creator and His Creature*, G. W. Bromley, ed. London, UK: T & T Clark International, 2000.

Bartlett, Steven J. *The Pathology of Man: A Study of Human Evil*. Springfield, IL: Charles C. Thomas Publisher, 2005.

Baskin, Judith R. *The Cambridge Dictionary of Judaism and Jewish Culture*. Cambridge, UK: Cambridge University Press, 2001.

Bateman, Steve. *Brothers, Stand Firm: Seven Things Every Man Should Know, Practice, and Invest in the Next Generation*. Eugene, OR: Wipf & Stock, 2014.

_______*Islam and Dhimmitude: Where Civilizations Collide*. Cranbury, NJ: Associated University Presses, 2002.

Bauckham, Richard. *The Bible in Politics: How to Read the Bible Politically*. London, UK: Society for Promoting Christian Knowledge, 1989.

Bauer, Yehuda. *The Jews: A Contrary People*. Zürich, Switzerland: Lit Verlag GmbH & Co., 2014.

Baum, Steven K. *Antisemitism Explained*. Lanham, MD: University Press of America, 2012.

Bayefsky, Anne. "Human Rights Watch Coverup." *The Jerusalem Post* (April 13, 2004).

Bayme, Steven. *Understanding Jewish History: Text and Commentaries*. Jersey City, NJ: KTAV Publishing House, 1997.

Bechtel, Trevor George. *The Gift of Ethics: A Story for Discovering Lasting Significance in Your Daily Work*. Eugene, OR: Wipf and Stock Publishers, 2014.

Bein, Alex. *The Jewish Question: Biography of a World Problem*. Madison, NJ: Fairleigh Dickinson University Press, 1990.

Beir, Robert L. *Roosevelt and the Holocaust: How FDR Saved the Jews and Brought Hope to a Nation*. New York: Skyhorse Publishing, 2006.

Beker, Avi. *Jewish Communities of the World*. Minneapolis, MN: Lerner Publishing Group, 1998.

_______*The Chosen: The History of an Idea, and the Anatomy of an Obsession*. New York: Palgrave Macmillan, 2008.

Bell, Dean Phillip. "Host Desecration," in *Antisemitism: A Historical Encyclopedia of Prejudice and Persecution*, Richard S. Levy, ed. Santa Barbara, CA: ABC-CLIO, Inc., 2005.

_______*Jews in the Early Modern World*. Lanham, MD: Rowman & Littlefield Publishers, 2008.

Bell, Maleah, B. C. Blackwell, Misty Bourne, *et. al.*, eds. *Compass: The Study Bible for Navigating Your Life*. Nashville, TN: Thomas Nelson, Inc., 2012.

Bell, Richard. *The Irrevocable Call of God: An Inquiry into Paul's Theology of Israel*. Tübingen, Germany: Mohr Siebeck Verlag, 2005.

Beller, Steven. *Vienna and the Jews, 1867–1938: A Cultural History*. Cambridge, UK: Cambridge University Press, 1989.

Ben-Itto, Hadassa. *The Lie That Wouldn't Die: The Protocols of the Elders of Zion*. Estree, UK: Vallentine Mitchell Publishers, 2005.

Ben-Sasson, Haim Hillel. *A History of the Jewish People*. Cambridge, MA: Harvard University Press, 1976.

Ben-Shmuel, Philip D. "*Hagshamah*: A Theology for an Alternate Messianic Jewish Zionism," in *The Land Cries Out: Theology of the Land in the Israeli-Palestinian Context*, Salim J. Munayer and Lisa Loden, eds. Eugene, OR: Wipf and Stock Publishers, 2012.

Ben-Yehuda, Eliezer. *Fulfillment of Prophecy: The Life Story of Eliezer Ben-Yehuda*. Charleston, SC: BookSurge Publishing, 2009.

Ben-Yehudi, Nachman. *Masada Myth: Collective Memory and Mythmaking in Israel*. Madison, WI: The University of Wisconsin Press, 1995.

Bender, Sara. *The Jews of Białystok during World War II and the Holocaust*, Yaffa Murciano, tr. Boston, MA: Brandeis University Press, 2008.

Benedictow, Ole J. "The Black Death: The Greatest Catastrophe Ever." *History Today*, Vol. 55, Issue 3 (March 2005).

Benin, Joel. "North American Colleges and Universities and BDS," in *The Case for Sanctions Against Israel*, Audrea Lim, ed. London, UK: Verso Books, 2012.

Bennett, Clinton. *In Search of Muhammad*. London, UK: Wellington House, 1998.

Berenbaum, Michael. *Not Your Father's Antisemitism: Hatred of the Jews in the 21st Century*. St. Paul, MN: Paragon House, 2008.

_______, and Arnold Kramer. *The World Must Know*. Washington, DC: United States Holocaust Memorial

Museum, 1993.
Berent, Irwin M. *Norfolk, Virginia: A Jewish History of the 20th Century*. Norfolk, VA: United Jewish Federation of Tidewater, 2001.
Berg, Philip S. *The Power of You: Kabbalistic Wisdom to Create the Movie of Your Life*. New York: Research Centre of Kabbalah, 2004.
Bergen, Jeremy M. *Ecclesial Repentance: The Churches Confront Their Sinful Pasts*. New York: T & T Clark International, 2011.
Berger, Alan L., and David Patterson. *Jewish-Christian Dialogue: Drawing Honey from the Rock*. St. Paul, MN: Paragon House, 2008.
Berger, Peter L. *The Sacred Canopy: Elements of a Sociological Theory of Religion*. New York: Random House, Inc., 1990.
Bergmann, Werner, and Rainer Erb. *Anti-Semitism in Germany: The Post-Nazi Epoch From 1945 to 1995*, tr. Belinda Cooper and Allison Brown. New Brunswick, NJ: Transaction Publishers, 1997.
Berkovits, Eliezer. "European and American Responses during and following the War," in *Wrestling with God: Jewish Theological Responses during and after the Holocaust*, Steven T. Katz, Shlomo Biderman, and Gershon Greenberg, eds. Oxford, UK: Oxford University Press, 2007.
______*Faith After the Holocaust*. New York: KTAV Publishing House, 1973.
______*With God in Hell: Judaism in the Ghettos and Deathcamps*. Brooklyn, NY: Hebrew Publishing Co., 1969.
Berkowitz, Michael. *The Crime of My Very Existence: Nazism and the Myth of Jewish Criminality*. Berkeley, CA: The University of California Press, 2007.
Berlin, Adele, ed. *The Oxford Dictionary of the Jewish Religion*. Oxford, UK: Oxford University Press, 2011.
Beverley, James A. *Christ & Islam: Understanding the Faith of the Muslims*. Joplin, MO: College Press Publishing Co., 1997.
______*Islam: An Introduction to Religion, Culture, and History*. Nashville, TN: Thomas Nelson, 2011.
Bhutto, Zulfikar Ali. *A South Asian View: A Collection of Speeches and Excerpts*. Information Division, Embassy of Pakistan, 1964.
Biale, David. *Power & Powerlessness in Jewish History*. New York: Schocken Books, 1986.
Bickerman, Elias Joseph. *Four Strange Books of the Bible: Jonah, Daniel, Koheleth, Esther*. New York: Schocken Books, 1984.
Bickerton, Ian J., and Carla L. Klausner. *A History of the Arab-Israeli Conflict*. Abingdon, UK: Routledge, 2016.
Bilde, Per. *The Originality of Jesus: A Critical Discussion and a Comparative Attempt*. Göttingen, Germany: Vandenhoeck & Ruprecht GmbH & Co., 2013.
Bilefsky, Dan. "Fear on Rise, Jews in France Weigh an Exit." *The New York Times* (Jan. 12, 2015).
Billingsley, Lloyd. *The Generation That Knew Not Josef: A Critique of Marxism and the Religious Left*. Colorado Springs, CO: Multnomah Press, 1985.
Bishop, Jordan. "Aquinas on Torture." *New Blackfriars*, Vol. 87, Issue 1009 (May 2006), 229.
Bisk, Tsvi. "The War on Islamism," in *Lone Actors—An Emerging Security Threat*, Aaron Richman and Yair Sharan, eds. Amsterdam, The Netherlands: IOS Press, 2015.
Black, Edwin. *Banking on Baghdad: Inside Iraq's 7,000-Year History of War, Profit, and Conflict*. Hoboken, NJ: John Wiley & Sons, Inc., 2004.
______ "How British and American Aid Subsidises Palestinian Terrorism," *The Guardian* (11 November 2013).
Blackstone, William E. "May the United States Intercede for the Jews?" *Our Day* VIII, (October, 1891), 46.
Bleakney, Robert W. "Hitler's Mindset for Mass Murder: A Review of Books by Steven F. Sage and Richard Weikart." *Restore!*, vol. 17, no. 4, Issue 62.
Blech, Arthur. *The Causes of Anti-Semitism: A Critique of the Bible*. Amherst, NY: Prometheus Books, 2006.
Blech, Benjamin. *Understanding Judaism: The Basics of Deed and Creed*. Northvale, NJ: Jason Aronson, 1991.
Bloch, Abraham P. *The Biblical and Historical Background of Jewish Customs and Ceremonies*. Jersey City, NJ: KTAV Publishing House, 1980.
Bloom, Jack. *Out of Step: Life-Story of a Politician: Politics and Religion in a World at War*. Bloomington, IN: The Indiana University Press, 2005.
Blum, Yehuda Z. *For Zion's Sake*. New York: Herzl Press, 1987.
Blumenthal, David. "Antisemitism," in *A Dictionary of the Jewish-Christian Dialogue*, Leon Klenicki and Geoffrey Wigoder, eds. Mahwah, NJ: Paulist Press, 1984.
Boehling, Rebecca, and Uta Larkey. *Life and Loss in the Shadow of the Holocaust: A Jewish Family's Untold Story*. Cambridge, UK: Cambridge University Press, 2011.
Boersma, Gerald P. *Augustine's Early Theology of Image: A Study in the Development of Pro-Nicene Theology*. Oxford, UK: Oxford University Press, 2016.
Bok, Francis. *Escape from Slavery: The True Story of My Ten Years in Captivity and My Journey to Freedom in America*. New York: St. Martin's Press, 2003.
Bolaffi, Guido. *Dictionary of Race, Ethnicity, and Culture*. Thousand Oaks, CA: SAGE Publications, 2003.

Booker, Richard. *Radical Islam's War against Israel, Christianity, and the West*. Shippensburg, PA: Destiny Image Publishing, 2008.
Bornkamm, Heinrich *Luther and the Old Testament*, tr. E. W. Gritsch and R. C. Gritsch. Philadelphia, PA: Fortress Press, 1969.
Borowitz, Eugene B. *Reform Judaism Today*. Springfield, NJ: Behrman House, Inc., 1983.
Bostom, Andrew G. *The Legacy of Islamic Antisemitism: From Sacred Texts to Solemn History*. Amherst, NY: Prometheus Books, 2008.
Bower, Bruce. *While Europe Slept: How Radical Islam Is Destroying the West from Within*. New York: Broadway Books, 2006.
Boyarin, Daniel. *Border Lines: Partition of Judaeo-Christianity*. Philadelphia, PA: The University of Pennsylvania Press, 2004.
Boyer, Paul. *When Time Shall Be No More: Prophecy Belief in Modern American Culture*. Cambridge, MA: Harvard University Press, 1992.
Boys, Mary C. *Redeeming Our Sacred Story: The Death of Jesus and Relations between Jews and Christians*. Mahwah, NJ: Paulist Press, 2013.
Branick, Vincent P. *Understanding the New Testament and Its Message: An Introduction*. Mahwah, NJ: Paulist Press, 1998.
Brann, Ross. *Power in the Portrayal: Representations of Jews and Muslims in Eleventh and Twelfth Century Islamic Spain*. Princeton, NJ: Princeton University Press, 2002.
Breese, Dave. *Seven Men Who Rule the World from the Grave*. Chicago, IL: Moody Publishers, 1990.
Brenner, Reve Robert. *The Faith and Doubt of the Holocaust Survivors*. Abingdon, UK: Routledge, 2017.
Breitman, Richard, and Allan J. Lichtman. *FDR and the Jews*. Cambridge, MA: Belknap Press, 2013.
Bremmer, Jan N. *Greek Religion and Culture, the Bible, and the Ancient Near East*. Leiden, The Netherlands: Koninklijke Brill NV, 2008.
Brennan, Terry. *The Sacred Cipher*. Grand Rapids, MI: Kregel Publications, 2009.
Breslauer, S. Daniel. *The Seductiveness of Jewish Myth: Challenge or Response?* Albany, NY: The State University of New York Press, 1997.
Brog, David. "The End of Evangelical Support for Israel?: The Jewish State's International Standing." *Middle East Quarterly*, vol. 21, no. 2 (Spring 2014).
Brown, David. *The Restoration of the Jews*. Charleston, SC: BiblioLife, 2008.
Brown, Michael L. *What Do Jewish People Think about Jesus? And Other Questions Christians Ask about Jewish Beliefs, Practices, and History*. Grand Rapids, MI: Baker Publishing Group, 2007.
Brown, Peter. *A Companion to Medieval English Literature and Culture*. Chichester, UK: Wiley Blackwell Publishing, 2009.
Browning, Christopher R. "The German Bureaucracy and the Holocaust," in *Genocide, Critical Issues of the Holocaust: A Companion Volume to the Film "Genocide,"* Alex Grobman and Daniel Landes, eds. West Orange, NJ: Behrman House, 1983.
_______*The Origins of the Final Solution: The Evolution of Nazi Jewish Policy, September 1939–March 1942*. Lincoln, NE: The University of Nebraska Press, 2007.
Brustein, William. "European Antisemitism before the Holocaust and the Roots of Nazism," in *The Routledge History of the Holocaust*, Jonathan C. Friedman, ed. Abingdon, UK: Routledge, 2011.
Bulka, Reuven P. *Jewish Marriage: A Halakhic Ethic*. New York: KTAV Publishing House, 1986.
Bullock, Alan. *Hitler and Stalin: Parallel Lives*. New York: Random House, 1991.
Burg, Avraham. *The Holocaust Is Over; We Must Rise from Its Ashes*. New York: Palgrave Macmillan, 2008.
Burnett, Carole Monica. "Eastern Orthodox Perspectives on Zionism and Christian Zionism," in *Zionism and the Quest for Justice in the Holy Land*, Donald E. Wagner and Walter T. Davis, eds. Cambridge, UK: The Lutterworth Press, 2014.
Burrell, David James. *The Religions of the World: An Outline of the Great Religious Systems*. Philadelphia, PA: Presbyterian Board of Publication and Sabbath-School Work, 1888.
Byrne, Joseph P. *The Black Death*. Westport, CT: Greenwood Publishing, 2004.
Byron, John. *Cain and Abel in Text and Tradition: Jewish and Christian Interpretations of the First Sibling Rivalry*. Leiden, The Netherlands: Koninklijke Brill NV, 2011.
Callimachi, Rukmini. "ISIS Enshrines a Theology of Rape: Claiming the Quran's Support, the Islamic State Codifies Sex Slavery in Conquered Regions of Iraq and Syria and Uses the Practice as a Recruiting Tool." *The New York Times*, August 13, 2015.
Calvin, John. *The Acts of the Apostles*, tr. Oliver and Boyd, Ltd. Grand Rapids, MI: Wm. B. Eerdmans Publishing Co., 1965.
Campo, Juan Eduardo. *Encyclopedia of Islam*. New York: Infobase Publishing, 2009.
Cardaun, Sarah K. *Countering Contemporary Antisemitism in Britain: Government and Civil Society Responses between Universalism and Particularism*. Leiden, The Netherlands: Koninklijke Brill NV, 2015.
Cargas, Harry J. *Holocaust Scholars Write to the Vatican*. Westport, CT: Greenwood Press, 1998.

______*Shadows of Auschwitz: A Christian Response to the Holocaust*. New York: Crossroad Press, 1990.
Carlson, Paul. *Media Bias and the Middle East*. Bloomington, IN: XLibris Corp., 2003.
Carol, Steven. *Understanding the Volatile and Dangerous Middle East: A Comprehensive Analysis*. Bloomington, IN: iUniverse, 2015.
Carter, Jimmy. *Palestine: Peace Not Apartheid*. New York: Simon & Schuster, 2006.
Celli, Carol. "Comedy and the Holocaust in Roberto Benigni's *Life Is Beautiful / la vita è bella*," in *The Changing Face of Evil in Film and Television: At the Interface, Probing the Boundaries*, Martin F. Norden, ed. Amsterdam, The Netherlands: Rodopi B. V., 2007.
Chamy, Israel W. *Fighting Suicide Bombing: A Worldwide Campaign for Life*. Westport, CT: Greenwood Publishing, 2007.
Chanes, Jerome A. *Antisemitism: A Reference Handbook*. Santa Barbara, CA: ABC-CLIO, Inc., 2004.
Charles River Editors. *Decoding the Conflict Between Israel and the Palestinians: The History and Terms of the Middle East Peace Process*. Cambridge, MA: Create Space, 2013.
Charlesworth, James H. *The Historical Jesus: An Essential Guide*. Nashville, TN: Abingdon Press, 2008.
Charny, Israel W. *Fighting Suicide Bombing: A Worldwide Campaign for Life*. Westport, CT: Greenwood Publishing, 2007.
Chase, Anthony Tirado. "Nongovernmental Organizations: Arab NGOs," in *Encyclopedia of Human Rights*, David P. Forsythe, ed. Oxford, UK: Oxford University Press, 2009.
Chaucer, Geoffrey. *The Prioress's Tale*, Beverly Boyd, ed. Norman, OK: The University of Oklahoma Press, 1987.
Chazan, Robert, ed. *Church, State, and Jew in the Middle Ages*. New York: Behrman House, 1980.
______*European Jewry and the First Crusade: Hebrew Chronicles of the First and Second Crusades*. Berkeley, CA: University of California Press, 1996.
______*In the Year 1096: The First Crusade and the Jews*. New York: The Jewish Publication Society of America, 1996.
Cheerma, Amar. *The Crimson Chinar: The Kashmir Conflict: A Politico Military Perspective*. New Dehli, India: Lancer Publishers, 2014.
Chemotsky, Harry I., and Heidi H. Hobbs. *Crossing Borders: International Studies for the 21st Century*. Thousand Oaks, CA: SAGE Publications, Inc., 2016.
Chesler, Phyllis. *Living History: On the Front Lines for Israel and the Jews 2003–2015*. Jerusalem, Israel: Gefen Publishing House, 2015.
______*The New Antisemitism: The Current Crisis and What We Must Do About It*. San Francisco, CA: Jossey-Bass Publishers, 2003.
Childs, Brevard S. *Introduction to the Old Testament as Scripture*. Philadelphia, PA: Fortress Press, 1979.
Chilton, Bruce D., and Jacob Neusner. *Comparing Spiritualities: Formative Christianity and Judaism on Finding Life and Meeting Death*. Harrisburg, PA: Trinity Press International, 2000.
Chirot, Daniel. "Comparing World War II Memories," in *Confronting Memories of World War II: European and Asian Legacies*, Daniel Chirot, Gi-Wook Shin, and Daniel Sneider, eds. Seattle, WA: The University of Washington Press, 2014.
Chaouat, Bruno. *Is Theory Good for the Jews: French Thought*. Liverpool, UK: Liverpool University Press, 2016.
Chowdhury, Chipamong. "Identity and Representation: Marma People in the Chittagong Hill Tracts, Bangladesh," in *Nationalism and Intra-State Conflicts in the Postcolonial World*, Fonkem Achankeng, ed. Lanham, MD: Lexington Books, 2015.
Christison, Kathleen. "Dilemmas of Arab Christianity." *Journal of Palestinian Studies*, vol. 22, no. 1 (Autumn 1992), 117–119.
Chu, Chin-ning. *Asian Mind Game*. New York: Rawson Associates Scribner, 1991.
Ciment, James, and John Radzilowski, eds. *American Immigration: An Encyclopedia of Political, Social, and Cultural Change*. New York: Routledge, 2014.
______"Anti-Semitism in France," in *Social Issues in America: An Encyclopedia*, James Ciment, ed. Abingdon, UK: Routledge, 2015.
______*World Terrorism: An Encyclopedia of Political Violence from Ancient Times to the Post-9/11 Era*. Armonk, NY: M. E. Sharpe Publishing, 2011.
Çitak, Zana, Aykan Erdemir, and Tugba Tanyeri-Erdemir. "Differential, Disguised and Deterritorialized: State Funding of Religion in Turkey," in *Public Funding of Religions in Europe*, Francis Messner, ed. Abingdon, UK: Routledge, 2016.
Citron, Sabina. *The Indictment*. Jerusalem: Gefen Publishing House, 2006.
Clark, E. J., and Brooks A. Agnew. *The Ark of Millions of Years: Book of Updates*. Bloomington, IN: AuthorHouse, 2011.
Cline, Eric H. *Jerusalem Besieged: From Ancient Canaan to Modern Israel*. Ann Arbor, MI: The University of Michigan Press, 2004.
Cohen, Jack J. *Democratizing Judaism*. Brighton, MA: Academic Studies Press, 2010.

______*Jewish Education in Democratic Society*. Tyler, TX: Reconstruction Press, 1964.
Cohen, Jeffrey M. *Prayer and Penitence: A Commentary on the High Holy Day Machzor*. Northvale, NJ: Jason Aronson, 1994.
Cohen, Mark R. "Islam and the Jews: Myth, Counter-Myth, History," in *Jews among Muslims: Communities in the Precolonial Middle East*, Shlomo Deshen and Walter P. Zenner, eds. London, UK: Macmillan Press, 1996.
______"Medieval Jewry in the World of Islam," in *The Oxford Handbook of Jewish Studies*, Martin Goodman, Jeremy Cohen, and David Jan Sorkin, eds. Oxford, UK: Oxford University Press, 2002.
______"Muslim Anti-Semitism: Old or New?" in *A History of Jewish-Muslim Relations: From the Origins to the Present Day*, Abdelwahab Meddeb and Benjamin Stora, eds. Princeton, NJ: Princeton University Press, 2013.
______"The Neo-Lachrymose Conception of Jewish-Arab History." *Tikkun* 6.3 (1991), 58.
______*Under Crescent and Cross: The Jews in the Middle Ages*. Princeton, NJ: Princeton University Press, 1994.
Cohen, Michael J. "Zionism and British Imperialism II: Imperial Financing in Palestine." *Journal of Israeli History: Politics, Society, Culture*, vol. 30, no. 2 (2011), 115–139.
Cohen, Rich. *Israel Is Real: An Obsessive Quest to Understand the Jewish Nation and Its History*. New York: Farrar, Straus and Giroux, 2009.
Cohen, Richard A. "The Holocaust Is a Christian Issue: Christology Revisited," in *The Philosopher as Witness: Fackenheim and Responses to the Holocaust*, Michael L. Morgan, and Benjamin Pollock, eds. Albany, NY: State University of New York Press, 2008.
Cohen, Richard M. "With Israel, the World Is Blaming the Victims." *The Washington Post*, July 28, 2014.
______*Israel: Is It Good for the Jews?* New York: Simon & Schuster, 2014.
Cohen, Robin. *The Cambridge Survey of World Migration*. Cambridge, UK: Cambridge University Press, 1995.
Cohen, Shaul Ephraim. *The Politics of Planting: Israeli-Palestinian Competition for Control of Land in the Jerusalem Periphery*. Chicago, IL: The University of Chicago Press, 1993.
Cohen, Susan Sarah. *Antisemitism: An Annotated Bibliography*. München, Germany: Walter de Gruyter, 2007.
Cohen, Tamara. "More British Jews Considering Move Abroad as Anti-Semitism Fears Grow," *Sky News*, Sunday, 20 August, 2017.
Cohen, Yehuda. *The Spanish: Shadows of Embarrassment*. Eastbourne, UK: Sussex Academic Press, 2012.
Cohn-Sherbok, Dan. *Judaism: History, Belief and Practice*. Abingdon, UK: Routledge, 2017.
Cole, Julie, Sarah Snyder, and Teresa Garlake. *Making Peace: Teaching About Conflict and Reconciliation*, Teresa Garlake and Rose Welshman, eds. Oxford, UK: Oxfam, 2002.
Collier, Martin, Bill Marriott, and Rosemary Rees. *Colonisation and Conflict 1750–1990*. Oxford, UK: Heinemann Educational Publishers, 2002.
Collins, John J. *Between Athens and Jerusalem: Jewish Identity in the Hellenistic Diaspora*. Grand Rapids, MI: Wm. B. Eerdmans Publishing Co., 2000.
Conquest, Robert. *The Great Terror: Stalinist Purge of the Thirties*. Oxford, UK: Oxford University Press, 1990.
______*The Harvest of Sorrow: Soviet Collectivization and the Terror-famine*. Oxford, UK: Oxford University Press, 1986.
Conner, C. J. *Jesus and the Culture Wars: Reclaiming the Lord's Prayer*. Mustang, OK: Tate Publishing & Enterprises, 2007.
Constantelos, Demetrios J. "The Jews in the Works of the Church Fathers," in *Early Christianity and Judaism*, Everett Ferguson, ed. New York: Garland Publishing, Inc., 1993.
Coogan, Michael D., Marc Z. Brettler, Carol A. Newsom, and Pheme Perkins, eds. *The New Oxford Annotated Bible with Apocrypha: New Revised Standard Edition*. Oxford, UK: Oxford University Press, 2010.
Cook, Jonathan. *Blood and Religion: The Unmasking of the Jewish and Democratic State*. London, UK: Pluto Press, 2006.
Cook, William A. *The Plight of the Palestinians: A Long History of Destruction*. New York: Palgrave Macmillan, 2010.
Cornell, George. "The Church after Jesus Loses Its Jewish Context." *Fredericksburg, VA Free Lance-Star*, (March 28, 1975), 16.
Correale, Robert M. *Sources and Analogues of the Canterbury Tales*. Cambridge, UK: D. S. Brewer, 2005.
Cotte, Suzette. *Criminological Theories: Bridging the Past to the Future*. Thousand Oaks, CA: Sage Publications, 2002.
Coughlin, Kathryn M., ed. *Muslim Cultures Today: A Reference Guide*. Westport, CT: Greenwood Press, 2006.
Coulibaly, Shalem. "Equations in Contemporary Anti-Zionism," in *Global Antisemitism: A Crisis of Modernity*, Charles Asher Small, ed. New York: Institute for the Study of Global Antisemitism and Policy [ISGAP], 2014.
Coxe, A. Cleveland, James Donaldson, and Alexander Roberts, eds. *The Ante-Nicene Fathers*. Peabody, MA: Hendrickson Publishers, 1994.

## ANTI-ISRAELISM


Creyer, F. H. "On the Recently Discovered 'House of David' Inscription," *Scandinavian Journal of the Old Testament* 8 (1994), 14–15.

Crone, Patricia, and Michael Cook. *Hagarism: The Making of the Islamic World*. Cambridge, UK: Cambridge University Press, 1980.

Culi, Jacob, Isaac ben Moses Magriso, Zvi Faier, Areh Kaplan, Shmuel Yerushalmi, and Eliyahu Touger. *The Torah Anthology*. Brooklyn, NY: Moznaim Publishing Co., 1987.

Curry, Andrew. "Here Are the Ancient Sites ISIS Has Damaged and Destroyed." *National Geographic* (September 2015).

Curta, Florin, and Andrew Holt, eds. *Great Events in Religion: An Encyclopedia of Pivotal Events in Religious History, Volume 1: Prehistory to AD 60*. Santa Barbara, CA: ABC-CLIO, LLC, 2017.

Curtis, Michael. *Jews, Antisemitism, and the Middle East*. New Brunswick, NJ: Transaction Publishers, 2013.

Dalacoura, Katerina. *Islamist Terrorism and Democracy in the Middle East*. Cambridge, UK: Cambridge University Press, 2011.

Dalin, David G. *The Myth of Hitler's Pope: Pope Pius XII and His Secret War Against Nazi Germany*. Washington, DC: Regnery Publishing, Inc., 2005.

Danon, Danny. *Israel: The Will to Prevail*. New York: Macmillan, 2013.

Darwish, Nonie. *The Devil We Don't Know: The Dark Side of Revolutions in the Middle East*. Hoboken, NJ: John Wiley & Sons, 2012.

_______*Wholly Different: Why I Chose Biblical Values over Islamic Values*. Washington, DC: Regnery Publishing, 2017.

Davids, A. "Cyril of Alexandria's First Episcopal Years." *The Impact of Scripture in Early Christianity*, Jan den Boeft and M. L. van Poll-van de Lisdonk, eds. Leiden, The Netherlands: Koninklijke Brill NV, 1999.

Davies, Alan T. "Anti-Zionism, Anti-Semitism and the Christian Mind." *The Christian Century* (August 19, 1970), 987.

_______, and Marilyn F. Nefsky. *How Silent Were the Churches?: Canadian Protestantism and the Jewish Plight during the Nazi Era*. Waterloo, Canada: Wilfrid Laurier University Press, 1997.

Davies, Philip R. "'House of David' Built on Sand." *Biblical Archaeology Review* (July/August, 1994).

_______*In Search of Ancient Israel*. Sheffield, UK: Sheffield Academic Press, 1992.

Davies, Thomas Witton. *Ezra, Nehemiah, and Esther*. Charleston, SC: Nabu Press, 2010.

Davis, Gregory M. *Religion of Peace? Islam's War Against the World*. Los Angeles, CA: World Ahead Publishing, Inc., 2006.

Davis, Leonard J. *Myths and Facts: A Concise Record of the Arab-Israeli Conflict*, Eric Rozenman and Jeff Rubin, eds. Washington, DC: Near East Report, 1989.

Davis, Uri. *Apartheid Israel: Possibilities for the Struggle Within*. London, UK: Zed Books, 2003.

_______*Israel: An Apartheid State*. London, UK: Zed Books, 1987.

Dawidowicz, Lucy S. *The War against the Jews: 1935–1945*. New York: Holt, Rinehart and Winston, 1975.

Dawson, Ashley, and Bill V. Mullen. *Against Apartheid: The Case for Boycotting Israeli Universities*. Chicago, IL: Haymarket Books, 2015.

Delanty, Gerard. *Routledge Handbook of Cosmopolitanism Studies*. Abingdon, UK: Routledge, 2012.

Del Sarto, Raffaella A. *Israel under Siege: The Politics of Insecurity and the Rise of the Israeli Neo-Revisionist Right*. Washington, DC: Georgetown University Press, 2017.

de Lubac, Henri. *Theological Fragments*, tr. Rebecca Howell Balinski. San Francisco, CA: Ignatius Press, 1989.

Dempster, Stephen G. "Foreigner," in *Evangelical Dictionary of Biblical Theology*, Walter A. Elwell, ed. Grand Rapids, MI: Baker Books, 1996.

Denny, Frederick M. *Islam and the Muslim Community*. Long Grove, IL: Waveland Press, 1987.

Dershowitz, Alan M. *Chutzpah*. New York: Simon & Schuster, 1991.

_______"Countering Challenges to Israel's Legitimacy," in *Israel's Rights as a Nation-State in International Diplomacy*, Alan Baker, ed. Jerusalem, Israel: Jerusalem Center for Public Affairs, 2011.

_______*Rights from Wrongs: A Secular Theory of the Origins of Rights*. New York: Basic Books, 2004.

_______*The Case Against Israel's Enemies: Exposing Jimmy Carter and Others Who Stand in the Way of Peace*. Hoboken, NJ: John Wiley & Sons, Inc., 2008.

_______*The Case Against the Iran Deal: How Can We Now Stop Iran from Getting Nukes?* New York: Rosetta Books, 2015.

_______*The Vanishing American Jew: In Search of Jewish Identity for the Next Century*. New York: Touchstone, 1997.

Dew, James K. *Science and Theology: An Assessment of Alister McGrath's Critical Realist Perspective*. Eugene, OR: Wipf and Stock Publishers, 2011.

Dimont, Max I. *Jews, God, and History*. New York: Penguin Books, 2004.

Dinstein, Yoram, and Mala Tabory, eds. *Israel Yearbook on Human Rights 1987*. Dordrecht, The Netherlands: Kluwer Academic Publishers Group, 1988.

Djebali, Taoufik, and Lee Whitfield. "The Ethnic Mosaic in the Maghreb: Cultures in Crisis," in *North African*

*Mosaic: A Cultural Reappraisal of Ethnic and Religious Minorities*. Newcastle, UK: Cambridge Scholars Publishing, 2007.

Dobroszycki, Lucjan. "Captured Nazi Documents on the Destruction of Jews in the Soviet Union," in *The Holocaust in the Soviet Union: Studies and Sources on the Destruction of the Jews in the Nazi-Occupied Territories of the USSR, 1941–1945*, Lucjan Dobroszycki and Jeffery S. Gurock, eds. Abingdon, UK: Routledge, 1993.

Dopp, William F. *Is There Hope for the Christian Faith?: Five Hundred Years After Martin Luther, the Christian Church Is Beginning a New Reformation*. Bloomington, IN: AuthorHouse, 2015.

Dosick, Wayne. "Anti-Semitism," in *An Introductory Dictionary of Theology and Religious Studies*, Orlando O. Espin and James B. Nickoloff, eds. Collegeville, MN: Liturgical Press, 2007.

Doyle, Tom. *Two Nations Under God: Why You Should Care about Israel*. Nashville, TN: B&H Publishing Group, 2004.

Driver, Samuel R. *The Book of Genesis*. London, England: Methurn & Co., Ltd., 1916.

Drummond, Robert B. *Erasmus, His Life and Character*. London, England: Smith, Elder & Co., 1873.

Drummond, Susan G. *Unthinkable Thoughts: Academic Freedom and the One-State Model for Israel*. Vancouver, Canada: The University of British Columbia Press, 2013.

Duffey, John M. *Science and Religion: A Contemporary Perspective*. Eugene, OR: Wipf and Stock Publishers, 2013.

Duiker, William, and Jackson J. Spielvogel. *The Essential World History, Seventh Edition*.Boston, MA: Wadsworth Cengage Learning, 2012.

Dundes, Alan. *The Blood Libel Legend: A Casebook in Anti-Semitic Folklore*. Madison, WI: The University of Wisconsin Press, 1991.

Dylan, Bob. *Blowin' in the Wind*. Burbank, CA: Warner Bros, Inc: 1963.

Eaglestone, Robert. *Postmodernism and Holocaust Denial*. London, UK: Icon Books, 2001.

Eakin, Frank E. *What Price Prejudice?: Christian Antisemitism in America*. Mahwah, NJ: Paulist Press, 1998.

_______*Heritage: Civilization and the Jews*. New York: Simon & Schuster, 1984.

Eckardt, Alice L. and A. Roy Eckardt. *Long Night's Journey into Day: A Revised Retrospective on the Holocaust*. Detroit, MI: Wayne State University Press, 1982.

Eckhardt, A. Roy. *Elder and Younger Brothers*. New York: Charles Scribner's Sons, 1967.

Edersheim, Alfred. *The Life and Times of Jesus the Messiah*. Longmans, Green, and Co., 1899.

Ehle, Jr., Carl F. "Prolegomena to Christian Zionism in America: The Views of Increase Mather and William E. Blackstone Concerning the Doctrine of the Restoration of Israel," Ph.D. Dissertation for New York University, 1977.

Ehrlich, Mark Avrum. *Encyclopedia of the Jewish Diaspora: Origins, Experiences, and Culture*. Santa Barbara, CA: ABC–CLIO, LLC, 2009.

Eidelberg, Paul. *An American Political Scientist in Israel: From Athens to Jerusalem*. Lanham, MD: Rowman and Littlefield Publishers, Inc., 2010.

Eidelberg, Shlomo. *The Jews and the Crusaders: The Hebrew Chronicles of the First and Second Crusades*. Jersey City, NJ: KTAV Publishing, 1996.

Einhorn, Stefan. *A Concealed God: Religion, Science and the Search for Truth*. Radnor, PA: Templeton Foundation Press, 1998.

Eisenberg, Ronald L. *What the Rabbis Said: 250 Topics from the Talmud*. Santa Barbara, CA: ABC-CLIO, 2010.

Eisenstat, Stuart E. *The Future of the Jews: How Global Forces Are Impacting the Jewish People, Israel, and Its Relationship with the United States*. Lanham, MD: Rowman & Littlefield Publishers, 2012.

El-Haj, Nadi Abu. *Facts on the Ground: Archaeological Practice and Territorial Self-Fashioning in Israeli Society*. Chicago, IL: The University of Chicago Press, 2001.

Elass, Marteen. *Understanding the Koran: A Quick Christian Guide to the Muslim Holy Book*. Grand Rapids, MI: Zondervan Publishing, 2004.

Eldemann, Richard. "Ahasuerus, the Wandering Jew: Origin and Background," in *The Wandering Jew: Essays in the Interpretation of a Christian Legend*, G. Hasan-Roken and A. Dundes, eds. Bloomington, IN: Indiana University Press, 1986.

Eliade, Mircea, and Charles J. Adams. *The Encyclopedia of Religion*. London: UK: Macmillan Library Reference, 1987.

Ellis, Marc H. *Future of the Prophetic: Israel's Ancient Wisdom Re-presented*. Minneapolis, MN: Augsburg Fortress Publishers, 2014.

Elman, R. Amy. "The EU's Responses to Contemporary Antisemitism," in *Deciphering the New Antisemitism*, Alvin H. Rosenfeld, ed. Bloomington, IN: The Indiana University Press, 2015.

Elukin, Jonathan. "Post-Biblical Jewish History Through Christian Eyes: Josephus and the Miracle of Jewish History in English Protestantism," in *The Jew as Legitimation: Jewish-Gentile Relations beyond Antisemitism and Philosemitism*, David J. Wertheim, ed. Cham, Switzerland: Palgrave Macmillan, 2017.

Elwell, Walter A., ed. *Evangelical Dictionary of Theology*. Grand Rapids, MI: Baker Academic, 2011.

_______, and Philip W. Comfort. *Tyndale Bible Dictionary*. Wheaton, IL: Tyndale House Publishers, 2001.

## ANTI-ISRAELISM


Ember, Melvin, Carol R. Ember, and Ian Skoggard, eds. *Encyclopedia of Diasporas: Immigrant and Refugee Cultures around the World.* New York: Springer Science+Media, 2005.

Engberg, Katarina. *The EU and Military Operations: A Comparative Analysis.* New York: Routledge, 2014.

Engel, David. *Zionism.* New York: Routledge, 2013.

Engineer, Asghar Ali. *Islam in Contemporary World.* Elgin, IL: New Dawn Press Group, 2007.

Enns, Paul P. *The Moody Handbook of Theology.* Chicago, IL: Moody Publishers, 1989.

Epstein, Lawrence J. "The Moral Case of Zionism: If Both Jews and Palestinian Arabs Start Their Historical Narrative with Beginning of Zionism, Jews Have Deeper Moral Claim to the Land of Israel." *Israel Opinion* (April 17, 2014), 1.

Epstein, Lawrence Jeffrey. *A Treasury of Jewish Anecdotes.* Northvale, NJ: Jason Aronson, Inc., 1989.

_______*A Treasury of Jewish Inspirational Stories.* Northvale, NJ: Jason Aronson, 1993.

Erez, Edna. "Protracted War, Terrorism and Mass Victimization: Exploring Victimological/Criminological Concepts and Theories to Address Victimization in Israel," in *Large-Scale Victimisation as a Potential Source of Terrorist Activities.* U. Ewald and K. Turkoviç, eds. Amsterdam, The Netherlands: IOS Press, 2006.

Ericksen, Robert P., and Susannah Heschel. *Betrayal: German Churches and the Holocaust.* Minneapolis, MN: Augsburg Fortress Publishers, 1999.

Ericksen, Robert P. *Complicity in the Holocaust: Churches and Universities in Nazi Germany.* Cambridge, UK: Cambridge University Press, 2012.

_______*Theologians Under Hitler.* New Haven, CT: Yale University Press, 1985.

Esposito, John S. *The Future of Islam.* Oxford, UK: Oxford University Press, 2010.

Etzioni-Halevy, Eva. *The Divided People: Can Israel's Breakup Be Stopped?* Lanham, MD: Lexington Books, 2002.

Evans, Craig A. *Jesus and His Contemporaries: Comparative Studies.* Leiden, The Netherlands: E. J. Brill, 1995.

Evans, Richard. *In Hitler's Shadow: West German Historians and the Attempt to Escape from the Nazi Past.* New York: Pantheon Books, 1989.

Eyerly, Dean R. *Between Heaven and Hell: The Historical Jesus.* Mustang, OK: Tate Publishing, 2006.

Fackenheim, Emil L. "Post-Holocaust Anti-Jewishness, Jewish Identity and the Centrality of Israel," in *World Jewry and the State of Israel,* Moshe Davis, ed. New York: Arno Press, 1977.

_______*The Jewish Bible after the Holocaust: A Re-reading.* Bloomington, IN: Indiana University Press, 1991.

_______*To Mend the World: Foundations of Post-Holocaust Jewish Thought.* Bloomington, IN: Indiana University Press, 1982.

_______*What Is Judaism?* New York: Macmillian, 1987.

Fagan, Bryan. *The Little Ice Age: How Climate Made History.* New York: Basic Books, 2000.

Fairbairn, Patrick. *The Imperial Bible-Dictionary: Historical, Biographical, Geographical, and Doctrinal.* London, England: Blackie and Son, 1866.

Falk, Avner. *Anti-semitism: A History and Psychoanalysis of Contemporary Hatred.* Westport, CT: Greenwood Publishing Group, 2008.

Falk, Gerhard. *The Restoration of Israel: Christian Zionism in Religion, Literature, and Politics.* New York: Peter Lang Publishing, 2006.

Falzon, Christopher. *Philosophy Goes to the Movies: An Introduction to Philosophy.* New York: Routledge, 2007.

Farber, Daniel, and Suzanna Sherry. *Beyond All Reason: The Radical Assault on Truth in American Law.* Oxford, UK: Oxford University Press, 1997.

Farmer, Brian R. *Understanding Radical Islam: Medieval Ideology in the Twenty-First Century.* New York: Peter Lang Publishing, 2007.

Fasching, Darrell J. *The Jewish People in Christian Preaching.* Lewiston, NY: The Edwin Mellen Press, 1984.

Federbusch, Simon. *World Jewry Today.* New York: Thomas Yoseloff, 1959.

Federow, Stuart. *Judaism and Christianity: A Contrast.* Bloomington, IN: iUniverse, 2012.

Fein, Helen, ed. *The Persisting Question: Sociological Perspectives and Social Contexts of Modern Antisemitism.* Berlin, Germany: Walter de Gruyter & Co, 1987.

Fenby, Jonathan. *Modern China: The Fall and Rise of a Great Power, 1850 to the Present.* New York: Ecco Press, 2008.

Fernandez-Morera. Dario. *The Myth of the Andalusian Paradise: Muslims, Christians and Jews under Islamic Rule in Medieval Spain.* Wilmington, DE: Intercollegiate Studies Institute, 2016.

Ferrari, Silvio, and Andrea Benzo. *Between Cultural Diversity and Common Heritage: Legal and Religious Perspectives on the Sacred Places of the Mediterranean.* Abingdon, UK: Routledge, 2014.

Fiedler, Seymour. *The Orphans Among God's Children: The History of Anti-Semitism.* Bloomington, IN: AuthorHouse, 2003.

Finan, Thomas. *Scriptural Interpretations in the Fathers: Letter and Spirit.* Dublin, Ireland: Four Courts Press, 1995.

Finkelstein, Israel, and Amihai Mazar. *The Quest for the Historical Israel: Debating Archaeology and the*

*History of Early Israel*. Atlanta, GA: The Society of Biblical Literature Press, 2007.
_______, and Neil Asher Silberman. *David and Solomon: In Search of the Bible's Sacred Kings and the Roots of the Western Tradition*. New York: Simon & Schuster, 2006.
_______, and Neil Asher Silberman, *The Bible Unearthed: Archaeology's New Vision of Ancient Israel and the Origin of Its Sacred Texts*. New York: Simon & Schuster, 2001.
Finkelstein, Louis. "The Jewish Vision of Human Brotherhood," in *Religious Pluralism and World Community*, Edward Jabra Juri, ed. Leiden, The Netherlands: E. J. Brill, 1969.
Firestone, Reuven. *An Introduction to Islam for Jews*. Philadelphia, PA: The Jewish Publication Society, 2008.
_______*Holy War in Judaism: The Fall and Rise of a Controversial Idea*. Oxford, UK: Oxford University Press, 2012.
Fisher, Eugene J., and Dennis D. McManus. "Good Friday Prayer for the Perfidious Jews," in *A Dictionary of Jewish-Christian Relations*, Edward Kessler and Neil Wenborn, eds. Cambridge, UK: Cambridge University Press, 2005.
Fishman, Hertzel. "The Apparition of Jewish Nationalism," in *Essential Papers on Judaism and Christianity in Conflict*, Jeremy Cohen, ed. New York: New York University Press, 1990.
Flannery, Edward. *The Anguish of the Jews: Twenty-Three Centuries of Antisemitism*. Mahwah, NJ: Paulist Press, 2004.
Fleischner, Eva. *Judaism in German Christian Theology Since 1945*. Lanham, MD: Scarecrow Press, 1975.
Flinn, Frank K. *Encyclopedia of Catholicism*. New York: Facts On File, Inc., 2007.
Forbes, Christopher. *Prophecy and Inspired Speech in Early Christianity and Its Hellenistic Environment*. Tübingen, Germany: J.C.B. Mohr, Siebeck, 1995.
Fox, Michael V. *Character and Ideology in the Book of Esther*. Eugene, OR: Wipf and Stock Publishers, 1991.
Francis, Matthew H. G. "Blessed is the One Who Reads Aloud. . .": The Book of Revelation in Orthodox Lectionary Traditions," in *Exegesis and Hermeneutics in the Churches of the East*, Vahan S. Hovhanessian, ed. New York: Peter Lang Publishing, 2009.
Franks, Robert. *A History of the Doctrine of the Work of Christ*. Nashville, TN: Thomas Nelson and Sons, 1962.
Franck, Thomas M. *Nation Against Nation: What Happened to the U.N. Dream and What the U.S. Can Do About It*. Oxford, UK: Oxford University Press, 1985.
Frazier, T. L. *A Second Look at the Second Coming: Sorting Through the Speculations*. Ben Lomond, CA: Conciliar Press, 1999.
Fredricksen, Paula. *From Jesus to Christ: The Origins of the New Testament Images of Christ*. New Haven, CT: Yale University Press, 1988.
Fredrickson, George M. *Diverse Nations: Explorations in the History of Racial and Ethnic Pluralism*. Abingdon, UK: Routledge, 2016.
Freed, Edwin D. *The Apostle Paul, Christian Jew: Faithfulness and Law*. Lanham, MD: University Press of America, 1994.
Freedland, Jonathan. "Is Anti-Zionism Antisemitism?" in *A New Antisemitism? Debating Judeophobia in 21st-Century Britain*, Paul Iganski and Barry Kosmin, eds. London, UK: Profile Books, 2003.
Freedman, Robert O. *Contemporary Israel: Domestic Politics, Foreign Policy, and Security Challenges*. Bolder, CO: Westview Press, 2009.
Freshman, Clark. "Whatever Happened to Anti-Semitism? How Social Science Theories Identify Discrimination and Promote Coalitions between Different Minorities." *Cornell Law Review* 85, 313–442.
Freud, Sigmund. *Moses and Monotheism*. New York: Random House, 1939.
Friedländer, Saul. *History and Psychoanalysis: An Inquiry into the Possibilities and Limits of Psychohistory*, tr. Susan Suleiman. London, UK: Holmes & Meier Publishers, 1978.
Friedman, Jonathan. *The Lion and the Star: Gentile-Jewish Relations in Three Hessian Towns, 1919–1945*. Lexington, KY: The University of Kentucky Press, 1998.
Friedmann, Robert R. *A Diary of Four Years of Terrorism and Anti-Semitism: 2000–2004*. Lincoln, NE: iUniverse, 2005.
Gabriel, Brigitte. *Because They Hate: A Survivor of Islamic Terror Warns America*. New York: St. Martin's Press, 2006.
Gabriel, Mark A. *Islam and the Jews: The Unfinished Battle*. Lake Mary, FL: Charisma House Book Group.
_______ *Islam and Terrorism*. Lake Mary, FL: Charisma Media, 2003.
Gabriel, Richard A. *Muhammad: Islam's First Great General*. Norman, OK: The University of Oklahoma Press, 2007.
Gabriel, Theodore, and Rabiha Hannan. *Islam and the Veil: Theoretical and Regional Contexts*. London, UK: Continuum International Publishing Group, 2011.
Gager, John G. *The Origins of Anti-Semitism: Attitudes toward Judaism in Pagan and Christian Antiquity*. Oxford, UK: Oxford University Press, 1983.
Gal, Allon. *Envisioning Israel: The Changing Ideals and Images of North American Jews*. Jerusalem: The Magnes Press, 1996.

## ANTI-ISRAELISM

Gans, Chaim. *A Just Zionism: On the Morality of the Jewish State*. Oxford, UK: Oxford University Press, 2008.
Garaev, Polina. "Anti-Semitism on the Rise in Germany, But No Anti-Semites to be Found." *i24 News* (12/30/2016).
Garr, John D. *Christian Fruit, Jewish Root: Theology of Hebraic Restoration*. Atlanta, GA: Golden Key Press, 2016.
______*Coequal and Counterbalanced: God's Blueprint for Women and Men*. Atlanta, GA: Golden Key Press, 2014.
______*Feminine by Design: The God-Fashioned Woman*. Atlanta, GA: Golden Key Press, 2014.
______*God and Israel: Chosen People, Holy Nation, Promised Land*. Atlanta, GA: Golden Key Press, 2016.
______*Life from the Dead: The Dynamic Saga of the Chosen People*. Atlanta, GA: Golden Key Press, 2014.
Garrard, Eve. "Anti-Judaism, Anti-Zionism, Antisemitism." *Fathom* (Winter, 2015).
Gauss, James F. *Islam & Christianity: A Revealing Contrast*. Alachua, FL: Bridge-Logos Publishing, 2009.
Gavriely-Nuri, Dalia. *Israeli Peace Discourse: A Cultural Approach to CDA*. Amsterdam, The Netherlands: John Benjamins Publishing Co. B.V., 2015.
Gavron, Daniel. *Holy Land Mosaic: Stories of Cooperation and Coexistence between Israelis and Palestinians*. Lanham, MD: Rowman & Littlefield Publishers, 2008.
Geldart, Anne. *Judaism, Second Edition*. Portsmouth, NH: Heinemann Library, 2001.
Gelvin, James. *The Israel-Palestine Conflict: One Hundred Years of War*. Cambridge, UK: Cambridge University Press, 2007.
Gensicke, Klaus. *The Mufti of Jerusalem and the Berlin Years*, tr. Alexander Gunn. Middlesex, UK: Middlesex House, 2011.
George, David Lloyd. *Memoirs of the Peace Conference*. New Haven, CT: Yale University Press, 1939.
Gerber, David A., ed. *Anti-Semitism in American History*. Urbana, IL: The University of Illinois Press, 1986.
Gerstenfeld, Manfred, ed. *Behind the Humanitarian Mask: The Nordic Countries, Israel and the Jews*. Jerusalem, Israel: Jerusalem Center for Public Affairs and Friends of Simon Wiesenthal Center for Holocaust Studies, 2008.
Gerstenfeld, Manfred. *The War of a Million Cuts: The Struggle Against the Delegitimization of Israel and the Jews, and the Growth of New Anti-Semitism*. New York: RVP Press, 2015.
Gesenius, Wilhelm. *Gesenius's Hebrew and Chaldee Lexicon to the Old Testament Scriptures*, tr. Samuel Prideaux Tregelles. London, England: Samuel Bagster and Sons, 1860.
Ghanim, David. *Gender and Violence in the Middle East*. Westport, CT: Praeger Publishers, 2009.
Gilbert, Martin. *Kristallnacht: Prelude to Destruction*. New York: Harper Collins, 2006.
Gilman, Sander L. *Multiculturalism and the Jews*. Abingdon, UK: Routledge, 2006.
______"Karl Marx and the Secret Language of Jews," in *Karl Marx's Social and Political Thought: Critical Assessments*, Bob Jessop and Russell Wheatley, eds. London, UK: Routledge, 1999.
Glick, Caroline B. *The Israeli Solution: A One-State Plan for Peace in the Middle East*. New York: Crown Forum, 2014.
Glickman, Elaine Rose. *Haman and the Jews: A Portrait from Rabbinic Literature*. New York: Jason Aronson, 1999.
Glickman, Mark S. *Sacred Treasure—The Cairo Genizah: The Amazing Discoveries of Forgotten Jewish History in an Egyptian Synagogue Attic*. Woodstock, VT: Jewish Lights Publishing, 2012.
Gold, Dore. "Defending Israel's Legal Rights to Jerusalem," in *Israel's Rights as a Nation-State in International Diplomacy*, Alan Baker, ed. Jerusalem, Israel: Jerusalem Center for Public Affairs, 2011.
______*The Fight for Jerusalem: Radical Islam, the West, and the Future of the Holy City*. Washington, DC: Regnery Publishing, Inc., 2009.
Goldberg, Jeffrey. "Is It Time for the Jews to Leave Europe?" *The Atlantic* (April 2015).
Goldhagen, Daniel J. *Hitler's Willing Executioners: Ordinary Germans and the Holocaust*. New York: Random House, 1996.
______*The Devil That Never Dies: The Rise and Threat of Global Antisemitism*. New York: Little, Brown, and Co., 2013.
______*The Rise and Threat of Global Antisemitism*. New York: Little, Brown and Company, 2013.
Goldman, Shalom. *Zeal for Zion: Christians, Jews, & the Idea of the Promised Land*. Chapel Hill, NC: The University of North Carolina Press, 2009.
Goldstein, David. *Jewish Panorama*. Boston, MA: Catholic Campaigners for Christ, 1940.
Golson, Richard J. "Antisemitism in Modern France" in *Antisemitism: A History*, Albert S. Lindemann and Richard S. Levy, eds. Oxford, UK: Oxford University Press, 2010
Goode, Erich. *Deviant Behavior*. Abingdon, UK: Routledge, 2016.
Goodrick-Clark, Nicholas. *The Occult Roots of Nazism: Secret Aryan Cults and Their Influence on Nazi Ideology*. New York: New York University Press, 2004.
Gordis, Daniel. *The Promise of Israel: Why Its Seemingly Greatest Weakness Is Actually Its Greatest Strength*. Hoboken, NJ: John Wiley & Sons, 2012.

Gordon, Evelyn. "Israeli Apartheid? To Arabs, It's a Model Democracy." *Commentary* (05.09.2014).
Gordon, Sarah Ann. *Hitler, Germans, and the "Jewish Question."* Princeton, NJ: Princeton University Press, 1984.
Gottheil, Richard, and Meyer Kayserling. "Granada," in *The Jewish Encyclopedia*. New York: Funk & Wagnalls, 1906.
Gray, Michael. *Teaching the Holocaust: Practical Approaches for Ages 11–18*. Abingdon, UK: Routledge, 2015.
Green, Roberta. *Blind Spot: When Journalists Don't Get Religion*. Oxford, UK: Oxford University Press, 2009.
Greenberg, Gershon. "Ultra-Orthodox Jewish Thought about the Holocaust since World War II," in *The Impact of the Holocaust on Jewish Theology*, Steven T. Katz, ed. New York: New York University Press, 2005.
Greenberger, Robert. *Suicide Bombers*. New York: The Rosen Publishing Group, 2007.
Greenspan, Stephen. *Annals of Gullibility: Why We Get Duped and How to Avoid It*. Westport, CT: ABC–CLIO, 2009.
Greenstein, Howard, Kendra G. Hotz, and John Kaltner. *What Do Our Neighbors Believe?: Questions and Answers on Judaism, Christianity, and Islam*. Louisville, KY: Westminster John Knox Press, 2007.
Grentz, Stanley J. *The Millennial Maze*. Downers Grove, IL: InterVarsity Press, 1992.
Grief, Howard. *The Legal Foundation and Borders of Israel Under International Law: A Treatise on Jewish Sovereignty over the Land of Israel*. Jerusalem, Israel: Mazo Publishers, 2008.
Grishaver, Joel Lurie. *Talmud with Training Wheels*. Los Angeles, CA: Torah Aura Productions, 2005.
Grubb, Blair P. "Tikkun Olam," in *Jewish Stories from Heaven and Earth: Inspiring Tales to Nourish the Heart*. Woodstock, VT: Jewish Lights Publishing, 2008.
Gruber, Ruth. *Virtually Jewish: Reinventing Jewish Culture in Europe*. Berkeley, CA: The University of California Press, 2002.
Guigui, A. "Jewish Morality with Respect to Medicine and Biotechnology," in *The Human Rights, Ethical and Moral Dimensions of Health Care*. Strasbourg, France: Council of Europe Publishing, 1998.
Guillaume, Alfred. *Islam*. London, UK: Penguin Books, 1956.
Gunkel, Herman, and Mark E. Biddle. *Commentary on Genesis*. Macon, GA: Mercer University Press, 1997.
Gunner, Goran, and Robert O. Smith. *Comprehending Christian Zionism: Perspectives in Comparison*. Minneapolis, MN: Augsburg Fortress Press, 2014.
Gunning, Jeroen. "Social Movement Theory and the Study of Terrorism," in *Critical Terrorism Studies: A New Research Agenda*, Richard Jackson, Marie Breen Smyth, and Jeroen Gunning, eds. Abingdon, UK: Routledge, 2009.
Gupta, Akhil, and James Ferguson. "Beyond 'Culture': Space, Identity, and the Politics of Difference." *Cultural Anthropology*, vol. 7, no. 7 (1992).
Gura, Nicholas. *Divine Wisdom and Warning: Decoded Messages from God*. Lanham, MD: Rowman & Littlefield, 2011.
Gurfinkiel, Michel. "France, Antisemitism, and the Prognosis for European Jewry," in *Anti-Judaism, Antisemitism, and Delegitimizing Israel*, Robert S. Wistrich, ed. Lincoln, NE: The University of Nebraska Press, 2016.
Gushee, David P. *The Righteous Gentiles of the Holocaust: Genocide and Moral Obligation*. St. Paul, MN: Paragon House, 2003.
Guttman, Nathan. "Presbyterians Divest Themselves from Israel." *Haaretz* (July 22, 2004).
Hachlili, Rachel. *Ancient Jewish Art and Archaeology in the Land of Israel*. Leiden, The Netherlands: E. J. Brill, 1988.
Haddad, William W., and Mary M. Hardy. "Jordan's Alliance with Israel and its Effects on Jordanian-Arab Relations" in *Israel, the Hashemites, and the Palestinians: The Fateful Triangle*, Efraim Karsh and P. R. Kumaraswam, eds. London, UK: Frank Cass Publishers, 2003.
Haeri, Shahla. *Law of Desire: Temporary Marriage in Shi'i Iran*. Syracuse, NY: Syracuse University Press, 1989.
Halberstan, Itta, and Judith Leventhal. *Small Miracles of the Holocaust: Extraordinary Coincidences of Faith, Hope, and Survival*. Guilford, CT: The Globe Pequot Press, 2010.
Haleem, Irm. *The Essence of Islamist Extremism: Recognition through Violence, Freedom through Death*. London, UK: Routledge, 2012.
Haleem, Muhammad Abdel. *Understanding the Qur'an: Themes and Style*. New York: I.B. Tauris & Co., 1999.
Halkin, Hillel. *Yehuda Halevi*. New York: Random House, 2010.
Hallam, Elizabeth, ed. *Chronicles of the Crusades: Nine Crusades and Two Hundred Years of Bitter Conflict for the Holy Land*. New York: Weidenfeld and Nicolson, 1989.
Hallward, Maia Carter. *Transnational Activism and the Israeli-Palestinian Conflict*. New York: Palgrave Macmillan, 2013.
Halpern, Baruch. "Erasing History: The Minimalist Assault on Ancient Israel," in V. Phillips Long, ed., *Israel's Past in Present Research: Essays on Ancient Israelite Historiography*. Winona Lake, IN: Eisenbrauns, Inc., 1999.
Hamerow, Theodore S. *Why We Watched: Europe, America, and the Holocaust*. New York: W. W.

Norton & Co., 2008.
Hamid, Tawfiq. *Inside Jihad: How Radical Islam Works, Why It Should Terrify Us, How to Defeat It*. Pembroke, VA: Mountain Lake Press, 2015.
Hammack, Phillip L. *Narrative and the Politics of Identity: The Cultural Psychology of Israeli and Palestinian Youth*. Oxford, UK: Oxford University Press, 2011.
Hardtmann, Getrud, ed., *Spuren der Verfolgung: Seelische Auswirkungen des Holocaust auf die Opfer und ihre Kinder*. Stuttgart, Germany: Bleicher, 1992.
Harees, Lukman. *The Mirage of Dignity on the Highways of Human 'Progress': The Bystanders' Perspective*. Bloomington, IN: AuthorHouse, 2012.
Harkabi, Yehoshafat. *Arab Attitudes to Israel*. Jerusalem, Israel: Keter Publishing House, 1972.
Harris, David A. *In the Trenches: Selected Speeches and Writings of an American Jewish Activist*. Jersey City, NJ: KTAV Publishing House, 2004.
Harris, Ellen Francis. *Guarding the Secrets: Palestinian Terrorism and a Father's Murder of His Too-American Daughter*. New York: Charles Scribner's Sons, 2005.
Harris, Sam. *The End of Faith: Religion, Terror, and the Future of Reason*. New York: W. W. Norton & Co., 2004.
Harrison, Bernard. "Anti-Zionism, Antisemitism, and the Rhetorical Manipulation of Reality," in *Resurgent Antisemitism: Global Perspectives*, Alvin H. Rosenfeld, ed. Bloomington, IN: Indiana University Press, 2013.
_______*The Resurgence of Anti-Semitism: Jews, Israel, and Liberal Opinion*. Lanham, MD: Rowman & Littlefield Publishers, 2006.
Hartmann, Betsy, and James K. Boyce. *A Quiet Violence: View from a Bangladesh Village*. London, UK: Zed Books Ltd., 1983.
Hassan, Riaz. *Islam and Society: Sociological Explorations*. Melbourne, Australia: Melbourne University Publishing, 2014.
Hassner, Ron E. *War on Sacred Grounds*. Ithaca, NY: Cornell University Press, 2009.
Havardi, Jeremy. *Refuting the Anti-Israel Narrative: A Case for the Historical, Legal and Moral Legitimacy of the Jewish State*. Jefferson, NC: McFarland & Company, Publishers, 2016.
Haynes, Stephen R. *Reluctant Witnesses: Jews and the Christian Imagination*. Louisville, KY: Westminster/John Knox Press, 1995.
Hayward, John. "Egyptian President Al-Sisi Calls for an Islamic Reformation." *Breitbart News* (9 Jan 2015).
Haywood, John. *Medieval Europe*. Chicago, IL: Reed Elsevier, Inc., 2008.
Hazleton, Lesley. *After the Prophet: The Epic Story of the Shia-Sunni Split in Islam*. New York: Knopf Doubleday Publishing Group, 2009.
Hazony, Yoram, *God and Politics in Esther*. Cambridge, UK: Cambridge University Press, 2016.
Hearden, Patrick J. *Architects of Globalism: Building a New World Order During World War Two*. Fayetteville, AR: The University of Arkansas Press, 2002.
Heller, Max. *Ethnic Stratification and Economic Inequality around the World*. Abingdon, UK: Routledge, 2016.
Hen-Tov, Jacob. *Communism and Zionism in Palestine: The Comintern and the Political Unrest*. Cambridge, MA: Schenkman Publishing Co., 1974.
Herb, Guntram H., and David H. Kaplan. *Nations and Nationalism: A Global Historical Overview*. Santa Barbara, CA: ABC-CLIO, Inc., 2008.
Herf, Jeffrey. *Nazi Propaganda for the Arab World*. New Haven, CT: Yale University Press, 2009.
_______"Nazi Propaganda to the Arab World during World War II and the Holocaust: and Its Aftereffects," in *Antisemitism before and since the Holocaust: Altered Contexts and Recent Perspectives*, Anthony McElligott and Jeffrey Herf, eds. Cham, Switzerland: Palgrave Macmillan, 2017.
Herman, Chaya. *Prophets and Profits: Managerialism and the Restructuring of Jewish Schools*. Cape Town, South Africa, HSRC Press, 2006.
Herodotus. *Herodotus: Thalia. Melpomene. Terpsicore.*, tr. William Beloe. London, England: Henry Colburn and Richard Bentley, 1830.
Hertzberg, Arthur. *The French Enlightenment and the Jews: The Origins of Modern Anti-Semitism*. New York: Columbia University Press, 1990.
Heschel, Abraham Joshua. *Israel: An Echo of Eternity*. New York: Farrar, Straus and Giroux, 1969.
Heschel, Susannah. "Constructions of Jewish Identity," in *Faithful Narratives: Historians, Religion, and the Challenge of Objectivity*, Andrea Sterk and Nina Caputo, eds. Ithaca, NY: Cornell University Press, 2014.
_______*The Aryan Jesus: Christian Theologians and the Bible in Nazi Germany*. Princeton, NJ: Princeton University Press, 2008.
_______"When Jesus Was an Aryan: The Protestant Church and Antisemitic Propaganda," in *In God's Name: Genocide and Religion in the Twentieth Century*, Omer Bartov and Phyllis Mack, eds. New York: Berghahn Books, 2001.
Heyboer, Marvin W. *Journeys into the Heart and Heartland of Islam*. Pittsburgh, PA: Dorrance Publishing

Co., 2009.
Higgs, Johanna. "It Still Exists: Slavery Drags on in Mauritania Despite Being Illegal." *PassBlue* (February 15, 2017).
Hilberg, Raul. *The Destruction of the European Jews*. New Haven, CT: Yale University Press, 1961.
Hillerbrand, Hans J. *Encyclopedia of Protestantism*. Abingdon, UK: Routledge, 2004.
Hippolytus, Romanus. *Treatise on Christ and the Anti-Christ* Sn. 54, tr. Philip Schaff, in *The Ante-Nicene Fathers*, A. Cleveland Coxe, James Donaldson, and Alexander Roberts, eds. Edinburgh, Scotland: T & T Clark, 1885.
Hirszowicz, Lukasz. *The Third Reich and the Arab East*. London, UK: Routledge & Kegan Paul, 1966.
Hitler, Adolf. *Mein Kampf*, tr. Ralph Manheim. Boston: Houghton Mifflin, 1971.
Hoare, Liam. "The Scandal of Scandinavia: Despite their image of moral innocence and best intentions, the lands of the north have become home to a scary, new form of anti-Semitism." *The Tower Magazine* (April 2013).
Hodge, Bodie. *The Tower of Babel: The Cultural History of Our Ancestors*. Green Forest, AR: Master Books, 2014.
Hoffmeier, James K. *Israel in Egypt: The Evidence for the Authenticity of the Exodus Tradition*. Oxford, UK: Oxford University Press,1999.
_______*Israel in Sinai: The Evidence for the Authenticity of the Wilderness Tradition*. Oxford, UK: Oxford University Press, 2005.
Holland, Glenn Stanfield. *Gods in the Desert: Religions of the Ancient Near East*. Lanham, MD: Rowman & Littlefield Publishers, 2009.
Holland, Tom. "When I Questioned the History of Muhammad." *The Wall Street Journal* (January 9, 2015).
Hood, John Y. B. *Aquinas and the Jew*. Philadelphia, PA: The University of Pennsylvania Press, 1995.
Horak, Stephan M., and Richard Blanke. *Eastern European National Minorities, 1919–1980: A Handbook*. Santa Barbara, CA: Libraries Unlimited, 1985.
Horowitz, David. *The Professors: The 101 Most Dangerous Academics in America*. Washington, DC: Regnery Publishing, 2006.
Horrox, Rosemary. *The Black Death*. Manchester, UK: Manchester University Press, 1994.
Hughes, Judith M. *The Holocaust and the Revival of Psychological History*. Cambridge, UK: Cambridge University Press, 2015.
Hughes, Paul. *Finishing History Well*. Maitland, FL: Xulon Press, 2012.
Hughes, Thomas Patrick. *Dictionary of Islam: Being a Cyclopaedia of the Doctrines, Rites, and Ceremonies, and Customs, Together with the Technical and Theological Terms, of the Muhammadan Religion*. London, England: W. H. Allen & Co., 1885.
Hunt, Elgin F., and David C. Colander. *Social Science: An Introduction to the Study of Society*. Boston, MA: Pearson, 2006.
Hunt, Steven A., ed., *Perspectives on Our Father Abraham: Essays in Honor of Marvin R. Wilson*. Grand Rapids, MI: Wm. B. Eerdmans Publishing Co., 2010.
Huttenbach, Henry R. "In Memoriam: Harry James Cargas." *Journal of Genocide Research*, 1 (3), 311.
Hyamson, A. M. "Jews in Islam," in *Encyclopaedia of Religion and Ethics*, James Hastings, ed. New York: Charles Scribner's Sons, 1915.
Hyun, Yung Hoon. *Redemptive-Historical Hermeneutics and Homiletics: Debates in Holland, America and Korea from 1930 to 2012*. Eugene, OR: Wipf and Stock Publishers, 2015.
IBP, Inc. *Middle East and Arabic Countries' Environmental Law Handbook*. Washington, DC: International Business Publications, 2015.
Ibrahim, Raymond, ed. *The Al Qaeda Reader*, Raymond Ibrahim, tr. New York: Doubleday, 2007.
Idinopulos, Thomas A. "Zionism and Racism." *Christian Attitudes on Jews and Judaism*, Issues 40–54. New York: Institute of Jewish Affairs, 1975.
Isaacson, Jason F., and Colin L. Rubenstein. *Islam in Asia: Changing Political Realities*. New Brunswick, NJ: Transaction Publishers, 2002.
Isaacson, Marshall D. *Children of the Covenant: What Christians Should Know about Jews*. Bountiful, UT: Horizon Publishers, 1998.
Ishaq, Ibn. *The Life of Muhammad*, tr. Alfred Guillame. Karachi, Pakistan: Oxford University Press, 2004.
Israeli, Raphael. *Blood Libel and Its Derivatives: The Scourge of Antisemitism*. New Brunswick, NJ: Transaction Publishers, 2012.
_______*Fundamentalist Islam and Israel: Essays in Interpretation*. Lanham, MD: University Press of America, Inc., 1993.
_______*Islamikaze: Manifestations of Islamic Martyrology*. London: UK: Frank Cass Publishers, 2003.
_______*The Islamic Challenge in Europe*. Abingdon, UK: Routledge, 2008.
'Izzati, Abu al-Fazl. *The Spread of Islam: The Contributing Factors*. London, UK: Islamic College for Advanced Studies Press, 2002.
Jacobs, Daniel. *The Rough Guide to Jerusalem*. New Delhi, India: Rough Guides, Ltd., 2009.

Jacobsen, Douglas. *The World's Christians: Who They Are, Where They Are, and How They Got There*. Chichester, UK: John Wiley & Sons, 2011.
Jacobus, Melancthon W. *Notes, Critical and Explanatory, on the Book of Genesis*. New York: Robert Carter & Brothers, 1865.
Jaher, Frederic C. *A Scapegoat in the New Wilderness: The Origins and Rise of Antisemitism in America*. Cambridge, MA: Harvard University Press, 1994.
Janin, Hunt. *Four Paths to Jerusalem: Jewish, Christian, Muslim, and Secular Pilgrimages*. Jefferson, NC: McFarland & Company Publishers, 2002.
Jarvis, Cynthia A., and E. Elizabeth Johnson. *Feasting on the Gospels—Mark*. Louisville, KY: Westminster John Knox Press, 2014.
Jaspal, Rusi. *Antisemitism and Anti-Zionism: Representation, Cognition and Everyday Talk*. Farnham, UK: Ashgate Publishing Limited, 2014.
Jasser, Zuhdi. *A Battle for the Soul of Islam: An American Muslim Patriot's Fight to Save His Faith*. New York: Simon and Schuster, 2012.
Jikeli, Günther. *European Muslim Antisemitism: Why Young Urban Males Say They Don't Like Jews*. Bloomington, IN: Indiana University Press, 2015.
Johnson, Hannah. *Blood Libel: The Ritual Murder Accusation at the Limit of Jewish History*. Ann Arbor, MI: The University of Michigan Press, 2012.
_______, and Heather Burton, *The Critics and the Prioress: Antisemitism, Criticism, and Chaucer's Prioress's Tale*. Ann Arbor, MI: The University of Michigan Press, 2017.
Johnson, Irving Chan. *The Buddha on Mecca's Verandah: Encounters, Mobilities, and Histories Along the Malaysian-Thai Border*. Seattle, WA: The University of Washington Press, 2012.
Johnson, Paul. *A History of the Jews*. London, UK: Orion Press, 1993.
_______"The Anti-Semitic Disease." *Commentary* (1 June 2005), 34.
Josephus, Flavius. *Against Apion*, in Steve Mason, ed., *Flavius Josephus: Against Apion,* tr. John M. G. Barclay. The Netherlands: Koninklijke Brill NV, 2007.
Judis, John B. *Genesis: Truman, American Jews, and the Origins of the Arab/Israeli Conflict*. New York: Macmillan, 2014.
Julius, Anthony. *Trials of the Diaspora: A History of Anti-Semitism in England*. Oxford, UK: Oxford University Press, 2010.
_______*T. S. Eliot, Anti-Semitism, and Literary Form*. Cambridge, UK: Cambridge University Press, 1995.
Jurkiewicz, Carole L. *The Foundations of Organizational Evil*. Abingdon, UK: Routledge, 2015.
Juster, Daniel C. "Anti-Semitism Again." *Jewish Voice Today Magazine* (July/August/September 2015), 7.
Kahn-Harris, Keith, and Ben Gidley. *Turbulent Times: The British Jewish Community Today*. London, UK: Continuum International Publishing Group, 2010.
Kalman, Aaron. "Abbas Condemns Hamas Head's Statements." *The Times of Israel* (December, 2012).
Kaltner, John. *Ishmael Instructs Isaac: An Introduction to the Qur'an for Bible Readers*. Collegeville, MN: The Liturgical Press, 1999.
Kamen, Henry. *The Spanish Inquisition: A Historical Revision*. New Haven, CT: Yale University Press, 1998.
Kamp, Marianne. "Femicide as Terrorism: The Case of Uzbekistan's Unveiling Murders," in *Sexual Violence in Conflict Zones: From the Ancient World to the Era of Human Rights*, Elizabeth D. Heineman, ed. Philadelphia, PA: The University of Pennsylvania Press, 2011.
Kant, Immanuel. *Grounding for the Metaphysics of Morals*. New Haven, CT: Yale University Press, 2002.
Kantor, Máttis. *Codex Judaica: Chronological Index of Jewish History*. New York: Zichron Press, 2005.
Kaplan, Shmuel. *Beneath the Sheltering Wings*. Bloomington, IN: ExLibris Press, 2011.
Karesh, Sara E., and Michael M. Hurvitz, *Encyclopedia of Judaism*. New York: Infobase Publishing, 2006.
Karsh, Efraim, ed., *Israel: The First Hundred Years, Volume I: Israel's Transition from Community to State*. London, UK: Frank Cass Publishers, 2000.
_______"The Middle East's Real Apartheid." *The Jerusalem Post* (03/05/2012).
Katanacho, Yohanna. *The Land of Christ: A Palestinian Cry*. Eugene, OR: Wipf and Stock Publishers, 2013.
Katz, David S. *Philo-Semitism and the Readmission of the Jews to England 1603–1655*. Oxford, UK: Clarendon Press, 1982.
Katz, Mordechai. *Understanding Judaism: A Basic Guide to Jewish Faith, History, and Practice*. Brooklyn, NY: Mesorah Publications, 2000.
Katz, Morris. *The Journey: A Trip to Eternity*. Victoria, Canada: Trafford Publishing, 2004.
Katz, Samuel. *Battleground—Fact and Fantasy in Palestine*. New York: Bantam Books, 1977.
Katz, Steven T. *The Impact of the Holocaust on Jewish Theology*. New York: New York University Press, 2005.
_______"The Issue of Confirmation and Disconfirmation in Jewish Thought after the Shoah," in *The Impact of the Holocaust on Jewish Theology*, Steven T. Katz, ed. New York: New York University Press, 2005.
Katzner, Kenneth. *The Languages of the World*. New York: Taylor & Francis Group, 2002.
Kaufman, Menahem. *An Ambiguous Partnership: Non-Zionists and Zionists in America 1939–1948*. Jerusalem,

Israel: Magnes Press, 1991.
Kazantzakis, Nikos. *Friedrich Nietzsche on the Philosophy of Right and the State*. Albany, New York: The State University of New York Press, 2006.
Keaney, Heather N. "Caliph," in *Encyclopedia of Islam*, Juan Eduardo Campo, ed. New York: Infobase Publishing, 2009.
Keithly, David M. *The USA and the World*. Lanham, MD: Rowman & Littlefield Publishers, 2007.
Keller, Tait. *Apostles of the Alps: Mountaineering and Nation Building in Germany and Austria, 1860–1939*. Chapel Hill, NC: The University of North Carolina Press, 2016.
Kenen, Isaiah L. *Near East Report—Volumes 18–20*. Washington, DC: Near East Report, 1974.
Kent, Simon. "'This Place Is Lost': Barcelona Chief Rabbi Tells Spain's Jews to Head for Israel." *Breitbart News* (20 Aug 2017).
Kessler, Edward, and Neil Wenborn, eds. *A Dictionary of Jewish-Christian Relations*. Cambridge, UK: Cambridge University Press, 2005.
Kilzer, Louis C. *Hitler's Traitor: Martin Bormann and the Defeat of the Reich*. New York: Presidio Press, 2000.
Khader, Jamal. "Opportunities and Threats for Religions in Conflict and Violence: How (Not) to Use the Name of God," in *Postcolonial Europe in the Crucible of Cultures: Reckoning with God in a World of Conflicts*, Jacques Haers, Norbert Hintersteiner, and Georges De Schrijver, eds. Amsterdam, The Netherlands: Editions Rodopi B.V., 2007.
Khalidi, Rashid. *Palestinian Identity: The Construction of Modern National Consciousness*. New York: Columbia University Press, 1997.
Khamenei, Seyyed Ali, reported in Vincent Funaro, "Iran's Supreme Leader Ayatollah Ali Khamenei Pens Book with Plan to Destroy Israel." *Christian Post* (August 5, 2015).
______*Palestine*, reported in "Iran's Khamenei Reportedly Publishes Book on How to Destroy Israel." *Haaretz* (Aug. 02, 2015).
"Khamenei: Israel Is a Cancerous Tumor." *Jerusalem World News* (February 3, 2011).
Khan, M. A. *Islamic Jihad: A Legacy of Forced Conversion, Imperialism, and Slavery*. Bloomington, IN: iUniverse, 2009.
Kheirabadi, Masoud. *Islam*. Philadelphia, PA: Chelsea House Publishers, 2004.
Kilpatrick, William. *Christianity, Islam, and Atheism: The Struggle for the Soul of the West*. San Francisco, CA: Ignatius Press, 2012.
Kimmerling, Baruch. "Academic History Caught in the Cross-Fire," in *Postzionism: A Reader*, Laurence Jay Silberstein, ed. New Brunswick, NJ: Rutgers, the State University Press, 2008.
________*The Invention and Decline of Israeliness: State, Society, and the Military*. Berkeley, CA: The University of California Press, 2001.
King, Margaret L. *Western Civilization: A Social and Cultural History*. Upper Saddle River, NJ: Prentice Hall, 2000.
Kiracofe, Clifford A. *Dark Crusade: Christian Zionism and US Foreign Policy*. New York: I. B. Tauris & Co., 2009.
Kirn, Hans-Martin. "Traces of Targum Reception in the Work of Martin Luther," in *A Jewish Targum in a Christian World*, Alberdina Houtman, E. van Staalduine-Sulman, and Hans-Martin Kirn, eds. Leiden, The Netherlands: Koninklijke Brill NV, 2014.
Kistanal, Tamás. "The Holocaust as a Paradigm for Ethical Thinking and Representation," in *Comparative Central European Holocaust Studies*, Louise O. Vasvári and Steven Tötösy de Zepetnek, eds. West Lafayette, IN: Purdue University Press, 2009.
Kittrie, Orde F. *Lawfare: Law as a Weapon of War*. Oxford, UK: Oxford University Press, 2016.
Klein, Aaron. "UNESCO Recognizes Hebron's Tomb of the Patriarchs—Judaism's Second Holiest Place—as Palestinian Heritage Site." *Breitbart News* (7 Jul 2017).
Klein, William. *The New Chosen People: A Corporate View of Election*. Eugene, OR: Wipf and Stock Publishers, 1990.
Klinghoffer, David. "God Is Not a Pluralist," in *The Role of Religion in Politics and Society*, Arthur A. Cohen and Paul Mendes-Flohr, eds. New York: Free Press, 1987.
Klug, Brian. *Being Jewish and Doing Justice*. London, UK: Vallentine Mitchell, 2011.
_______"Interrogating 'New Anti-Semitism,'" in *Radicalization and Religion: Race, Culture and Difference in the Study of Antisemitism and Islamophobia*, Nasar Meer, ed. Abingdon, UK: Routledge, 2014.
Knapp, Bettina Liebowitz, *Céline, Man of Hate*. Tuscaloosa, AL: The University of Alabama Press, 1974.
Knittel, Susanne C. *The Historical Uncanny: Disability, Ethnicity, and the Politics of Holocaust*. Bronx, NY: Fordham University Press, 2015.
Knowles, Andrew. *The Bible Guide: An All-in-One Introduction to the Book of Books*. Oxford, UK: Lion Publishing, 2001.
Knysh, Alexander D., Yaron Eliav, and Ralph Williams. *Judaism, Christianity, and Islam: A Source Book*. Atlanta, GA: Kendall Hunt Publishing Co., 2007.

Kogan, Barry S. *A Time to Be Born and a Time to Die: The Ethics of Choice*. Hawthorne, NY: Aldine De Gruyter, Inc., 1991.
Kohn, Michael. *Israel & the Palestinian Territories*. Footscray, Australia: Lonely Planet Publications, 2007.
Kohn, Murray J. *Is the Holocaust Vanishing?: A Survivor's Reflections on the Academic Waning of Memory and Jewish Identity in the Post-Auschwitz Era*. Lanham, MD: Hamilton Books, 2005.
Kolig, Erich. "Conclusion," in *Muslim Integration: Pluralism and Multiculturalism in New Zealand*, Erich Kolig and Malcom Voyce, eds. Lanham, MD: Rowman & Littlefield, Inc., 2016.
Konowitz, Israel. *The God Idea in Jewish Tradition*. Jerusalem, Israel: Jerusalem Publishing House, 1989.
Kooman, Willem. *Veiled Threat*. Bloomington, IN: AuthorHouse, 2011.
Korn, Eugene. *The Jewish Connection to Israel, the Promised Land: A Brief Introduction for Christians*. Woodstock, VT: Jewish Lights Publishing, 2008.
Kort, Michael. *The Handbook of the New Eastern Europe*. Brookfield, CT: Twenty-First Century Books, 2001.
Kovel, Joel. *Overcoming Zionism*. London, UK: Pluto Press, 2007.
Kraut, Alan M., and Richard D. Breitman. "Anti-Semitism in the State Department, 1933–44: Four Case Studies," in *Anti-Semitism in American History*, David A. Gerber, ed. Urbana, IL: The University of Illinois Press, 1986.
Kressel, Neil J. *The Sons of Pigs and Apes: Muslim Antisemitism and the Conspiracy of Silence*. Washington, DC: Potomac Books, Inc., 2012.
Krinov, E. L. *Principles of Meteoritics: International Series of Monographs on Earth Sciences*. New York: Pergamon Press, Inc., 1960.
Krondorfer, Björn. *Remembrance and Reconciliation: Encounters between Young Jews and Germans*. New Haven, CT: Yale University Press, 1995.
Krosney, Herbert. "The PLO's Moscow Connection." *New York Magazine* (Sep 24, 1979), 64–72.
Krämer, Gudrun, and Graham Harman. *A History of Palestine: From the Ottoman Conquest to the Founding of the State of Israel*. Princeton, NJ: Princeton University Press, 2008.
Kuperwasser, Yossi. "Incentivizing Terrorism: Palestinian Authority Allocations to Terrorists and their Families." *Jerusalem Center for Public Affairs*.
Kwiet, Konrad, and Jürgen Matthaus. *Contemporary Responses to the Holocaust*. Westport, CT: Greenwood Publishing Group, 2004.
Köstenberger, Andreas J. *John: Baker Exegetical Commentary on the New Testament*. Grand Rapids, MI: Baker Academic, 2004.
Lachs, Samuel Tobias. *Humanism in Talmud and Midrash*. Cranbury, NJ: Associated University Press, 1993.
La Guardia, Anton. *War Without End: Israelis, Palestinians, and the Struggle for a Promised Land*. New York: St. Martin's Press, 2001.
Lander, Janis. *Spiritual Art and Art Education*. Abingdon, UK: Routledge, 2014.
Langmuir, Gavin I. "Continuities, Discontinuities and Contingencies of the Holocaust," in *Studies in Contemporary Jewry: Volume XIII: The Fate of the European Jews*, Jonathan Frankel, ed. Oxford, UK: Oxford University Press, 1997.
Lanzmann, Claude. "The Obscenity of Understanding: An Evening with Claude Lanzmann." *American Imago*, vol. 48, no. 4 (Winter 1991), 473–495.
Laor, Emmett. *The Invention of the "Palestinians": 27 Theses They Won't Let You Hear*. Bloomington, IN: Xlibris Corp., 2012.
Lapid, Yair. "Gaza Conflict: Hamas Chooses to Let Children Die for Its Own Crazy Ends." *The Telegraph* (July 23, 2014).
Lapidus, Ira M. *A History of Islamic Societies*. Cambridge, UK: Cambridge University Press, 1988.
Laqueur, Walter. *The Changing Face of Anti-Semitism: From Ancient Times to the Present Day*. Oxford, UK: Oxford University Press, 2006.
_______*The New Terrorism: Fanaticism and the Arms of Mass Destruction*. Oxford, UK: Oxford University Press, 1999.
Lardner, Nathaniel. *The Works of Nathaniel Lardner*, Andrew Kippis, ed. Whitefish, MT: Kessinger Publishing, 2010.
Latourette, Kenneth Scott. *A History of Christianity*. New York: Harper & Brothers, 1953.
Laurenzi, Elsa. *Jewish Catacombs: The Jews of Rome: Funeral Rites and Customs*. Rome, Italy: Gangemi Editore Spa, 2013.
Laub,Thomas J. *After the Fall: Germany Policy in Occupied France, 1940–1944*. Oxford, UK: Oxford University Press, 2010.
Lavezzo, Kathy. *The Accommodated Jew: English Antisemitism from Bede to Milton*. Ithaca, NY: Cornell University Press, 2016.
Lazara, Bernard. *Antisemitism, Its History and Causes*. New York: The International Library Publishing Co., 1903.
Lazaroff, Tovah. "UN in New York Votes on Ignoring Jewish Ties to Temple Mount." *The Jerusalem Post* (November 8, 2016).

Leaman, Oliver. *Controversies in Contemporary Islam*. Abingdon, UK: Routledge, 2014.

Leaves, Nigel. "Who Do You Say that I Am? Preaching Jesus Today," in *Wisdom and Imagination: Religious Progressives and the Search for Meaning*, Rex A. E. Hunt and Gregory C. Jenks, eds. Eugene, OR: Wipf and Stock Publishers, 2014.

Lee, George R. *Holocaust, Grades 5–8*. Quincy, IL: Mark Twain Media, 1998.

Leeming, H., and K. Leeming, eds. *Josephus' Jewish War and Its Slavonic Version: A Synoptic Comparison (Arbeiten Zur Geschichte Des Antiken Judentums Und Des Urchristentums)*. Leiden, The Netherlands: Koninklijke Brill NV, 2003.

Lefkovitz, Lori Hope. *In Scripture: The First Stories of Jewish Sexual Identities*. Lanham, MD: Rowman & Littlefield Publishers, 2010.

Leinwand, Gerald. *Pageant World History*. Upper Saddle River, NJ: Prentice-Hall, 1990.

Lemche, Niels Peter. *The Israelites in History and Tradition*. Louisville, KY: Westminster John Knox Press, 1998.

Lenarz, Julie. "How Can the Palestinian Authority Defend Paying Lifetime Salaries to Terrorists Convicted of Murder?" *International Business Times* (July 27, 2017).

Lentz, Rex. *An Abridged History of World Religions*. Lincoln, NE: iUniverse, Inc., 2002.

Lerner, Michael. *The Socialism of Fools: Anti-Semitism on the Left*. Berkeley, CA: Tikkun Books, 1992.

Lerner, Robert E. "Millennialism," in *The Encyclopedia of Apocalypticism*, John J. Collins, Bernard McGinn, and Stephen J. Stein, eds. New York: Continuum Press, 2000.

Levack, Brian P. *The Witch-Hunt in Early Modern Europe*. Abingdon, UK: Routledge, 2006.

Levene, Mark. *Genocide in the Age of the Nation State, Volume 2: The Rise of the West and the Coming of Genocide*. New York: I.B. Tauris & Co., 2005.

Levenson, Jon D. *The Death and Resurrection of the Beloved Son: The Transformation of Child Sacrifice in Judaism and Christianity*. New Haven, CT: Yale University Press, 1993.

_______"The Universal Horizon of Biblical Particularism," in *Ethnicity and the Bible*, Mark G. Brett, ed. Leiden, The Netherlands: E. J. Brill, 1996.

Leverenz, Robert E. *There Is Nothing New under the Sun*. Eugene, OR: Wipf and Stock Publishers, 2015.

Levin, Daniel. "Denial on the Temple Mount." *Forward* (Oct. 14, 2009).

Levin, Kenneth. *The Oslo Syndrome: Delusions of a People Under Siege*. Hanover, NH: Smith and Kraus Publishers, 2005.

Levine, Aaron. *Moral Issues of the Marketplace in Jewish Law*. New York: Yashar Books, 2005.

Levison, John R., and Priscilla Pope-Levison. "The New Contextual Christologies: Liberation and Inculturation," in *Global Dictionary of Theology: A Resource for the Worldwide Church*, William A. Dyrness and Veli-Matti Kärkkäinen, eds. Downers Grove, IL: InterVarsity Press, 2008.

Levy, Reuben. "The Social Structure of Islam," in *Orientalism: Early Sources, vol. XII*. London: Routledge, 1957.

Levy, Richard S. *Antisemitism: A Historical Encyclopedia of Prejudice and Persecution, Volume 1*. Santa Barbara, CA: ABC-CLIO, Inc., 2005.

Lewis, Bernard. *The Jews of Islam*. Princeton, NJ: Princeton University Press, 1984.

Lewis, Damien, and Halima Bashir. *Tears of the Desert: A Memoir of Survival in Darfur*. New York: Random House, 2009.

Lewis, Jonathan, ed. *World Mission: An Analysis of the World Christian Movement*. Pasadena CA: William Carey Library, 1987.

Lewis, Tyson, and Richard Kahn. "The Reptoid Hypothesis: Utopian and Dystopian Representational Motifs in David Icke's Alien Conspiracy Theory." *Utopian Studies*, vol. 16, no 1 (Winter, 2005), 45–70.

Libermann, Oren. "Israel Suspends Ties with UNESCO in Spat over Jerusalem Holy Site." *CNN News* (October 14, 2016).

_______"Au Revoir and Shalom: Jews Leave France in Record Numbers." *CNN News* (January 25, 2016).

Liessin, Abraham. *Di Tsukunft*. (January 1920), 1.

Lifshitz, Joseph Isaac. "War and Aesthetics in Jewish Law," in *War and Peace in Jewish Tradition: From the Biblical World to the Present*, Yigal Levin and Amnon Shapira, eds. New York: Routledge, 2012.

Liles, Mike Jr. *Christian Faith in Contemporary Society: The Framework for Belief*. Lincoln, NE: iUniverse, 2005.

Lilienblum, Moshe L. "Antisemitism as an Incurable European Disease," in *Glorious, Accursed Europe: An Essay on Jewish Ambivalence*, Jehuda Reinharz and Yaacov Shavit, eds. Waltham, MA: Brandeis University Press, 2010.

Lim, Audrea. *The Case for Sanctions Against Israel*. London, UK: Verso, 2012.

Lindemann, Albert S., and Richard S. Levy, *Antisemitism: A History*. Oxford, UK: Oxford University Press, 2010.

Lindsay, James E. *Daily Life in the Medieval Islamic World*. Indianapolis, IN: Hackett Publishing Co., 2005.

Lindsay, Mark R. *Barth, Israel, and Jesus: Karl Barth's Theology of Israel*. Burlington, VT: Ashgate Publishing Co., 2007.

Lipstadt, Deborah E. *Denying the Holocaust: The Growing Assault on Truth and Memory*. New York: Simon & Schuster, 1993.

Littell, Franklin H. *The Crucifixion of the Jews*. Macon, GA: Mercer University Press, 1986.
Little, Lester K. "Life and Afterlife of the First Plague Pandemic," in *Plague and the End of Antiquity: The Pandemic of 541–750*, Lester K. Little, ed. Cambridge, UK: Cambridge University Press, 2007.
Litvak, Meir. *Palestinian Collective Memory and National Identity*. New York: Palgrave Macmillan, 2009.
_______"The Islamic Republic of Iran and the Holocaust: Anti-Semitism and Anti-Zionism," in *Anti-Semitism and Anti-Zionism in Historical Perspective: Convergence and Divergence*, Jeffrey Herf, ed. Cambridge, UK: Routledge, 2007.
Lock, Stephen, John M. Last, and George Dunea, eds. *The Oxford Illustrated Companion to Medicine*. Oxford, UK: Oxford University Press, 2001.
Locke, Hubert G. *Learning from History: A Black Christian's Perspective on the Holocaust*. Westport, CT: Greenwood Press, 2000.
Loewenberg, Frank M. *From Charity to Social Justice*. New Brunswick, NJ: Transaction Publishers, 2001.
Loewenstein, David. *Treacherous Faith: The Specter of Heresy in Early Modern English Literature*. Oxford, UK: Oxford University Press, 2013.
Loimeier, Roman. *Between Social Skills and Marketable Skills: The Politics of Islamic Education in 20th Century Zanzibar*. Leiden, The Netherlands: Koninklijke Brill NV, 2009.
Lourie, Arthur. "Palestine Under the British Mandate (1918–1948)" in *A History of Israel and the Holy Land*, Michael Avi-Yonan, ed. New York: The Continuum International Publishing Group, 2003.
Lovat, Terence, and Robert Crotty. *Reconciling Islam, Christianity and Judaism: Islam's Special Role in Restoring Convivencia*. New York: Springer, 2015.
Luel, Steven A. and Paul Marcus, eds. *Psychoanalytic Reflections on the Holocaust: Selected Essays*. Denver, CO: Holocaust Awareness Institute, 1984.
Lupovici, Amir. *The Power of Deterrence*. Cambridge, UK: Cambridge University Press, 2016.
Lust, Ellen. *The Middle East, 13th Edition*. Thousand Oaks, CA: SAGE Publications, 2014.
Luther, Martin. *On the Jews and Their Lies*, in *Luther's Works*, tr. Martin H. Bertram. Philadelphia: Fortress Press, 1971.
_______*Table Talk XXIV*, in William Hazlitt, *Table-Talk; or Original Essays*. London, England: John Warren, 1821.
Lévinas, Emmanuel. *Difficult Freedom: Essays on Judaism*, tr. Sean Hand. Baltimore, MD: Johns Hopkins University Press, 1990.
_______*Nine Talmudic Readings*, tr. Annette Aronowicz. Bloomington, IN: Indiana University Press, 1990.
Maccoby, Hyam. *Antisemitism and Modernity: Innovation and Continuity*. Abingdon, UK: Routledge, 2006.
MacIntyre, Alasdair C. *Whose Justice? Which Rationality?* South Bend, IN: The University of Notre Dame Press, 1989.
Madigan, Kevin J., and Jon D. Levenson. *Resurrection: The Power of God for Christians and Jews*. New Haven, CT: Yale University Press, 2009.
Maghraoui, Abdeslam. "American Foreign Policy and Islamic Renewal," in *Conflict, Identity, and Reform in the Muslim World: Challenges for U.S. Engagement*, Daniel Brumberg and Dina Shehata, eds. Washington, DC: United States Institute of Peace, 2009.
Magill, Frank N. *The Middle Ages: Dictionary of World Biography*. New York: Routledge, 1998.
Mallmann, Klaus-Michael, and Martin Cüppers. *Nazi Palestine: The Plans for the Extermination of the Jews in Palestine*, tr. Krista Smith. New York: Enigma Books, 2010.
Mangano, Mark. *The College Press NIV Commentary: Esther & Daniel*. Goshen, IN: College Press Publishing Co., 2001.
Manji, Irshad. *The Trouble with Islam Today*. New York: St. Martin's Press, 2003.
Mann, Cuthbert Carson. *Hitler's Three Struggles: The Neo-Pagan Revenge*. Chicago, IL: Chicago Spectrum Press, 1995.
Mann, John. *Antisemitism: The Oldest Hatred*. London, UK: Bloomsbury Publishing, 2015.
Mannes, Aaron. *Profiles in Terror: The Guide to Middle East Terrorist Organizations*. Lanham, MD: Rowman & Littlefield Publishers, 2004.
Maoz, Zeev. *Defending the Holy Land*. Ann Arbor, MI: The University of Michigan Press, 2009.
March, Wallace Eugene. *Israel and the Politics of Land: A Theological Case Study*. Louisville, KY: Westminster/John Knox Press, 1994.
Marchand, Suzanne. "Nazism, Orientalism and Humanism," in *Nazi Germany and the Humanities: How German Academics Embraced Nazism*, Anson Rabinbach and Wolfgang Bialas, eds. London, UK: Oneworld Publications, 2014.
Marcus, Ivan G. "A Jewish-Christian Symbiosis," in *Cultures of the Jews: A New History*, David Biale, ed. New York: Schocken Books, 2002.
Marcus, Jacob Rader, *The Jew in the Medieval World: A Source Book*, 315–1791. Cincinnati, OH: Hebrew Union College Press, 1938.
Marcus, Kenneth L., & Ilan Troen. "Anti-Jewish Boycotts in History," in *Dreams Deferred: A Concise Guide*

*to the Israeli-Palestinian Conflict & the Movement to Boycott Israel*, Cary Nelson, ed. Bloomington, IN: Indiana University Press, 2016.

______*The Definition of Anti-Semitism*. Oxford, UK: Oxford University Press, 2015.

Marone, Antonio M. "The African Migratory Factor in Libyan Transition," in *North African Societies after the Arab Spring: Between Democracy and Islamic Awakening*, Leila El Houssi, Alessia Melcangi, Stefano Torelli, and Massimiliano Cricco, eds. Newcastle upon Tyne, UK: Cambridge Scholars Publishing, 2016.

Marrus, Michael R., ed. *The Nazi Holocaust: Historical Articles on the Destruction of European Jews Part 8: Bystanders to the Holocaust*. Westport, CT: Meckler Corporation, 1989.

Marshall, Edgar S. *Israel: Current Issues and Historical Background*. Hauppauge, NY: Nova Science Publishers, 2002.

Marshall, Randall. "Learning from 9/11: Implications for Disaster Research and Public Health," in *9/11: Mental Health in the Wake of Terrorist Attacks*, Yuval Neria, Raz Gross, and Randall Marshall, eds. Cambridge, UK: Cambridge University Press, 2012.

Marx, Karl, and Friedrich Engels. *The Communist Manifesto*. Portland, OR: The Floating Press, 2008.

MacDonald, David B. *Thinking History, Fighting Evil: Neoconservatives and the Perils of Analogy*. Lanham, MD: Rowman & Littlefield Publishers, 2009.

Massaquoi, Hans J. *Destined to Witness: Growing Up Black in Nazi Germany*. New York: William Morrow and Company, 2001.

Massey, Irving. *Philo-Semitism in Nineteenth-Century German Literature*. Tübingen, Germany: Max Niemeyer Verlag GmbH, 2000.

Matas, David. *Aftershock: Anti-Zionism & Anti-Semitism*. Toronto, Canada: Dundurn Press, 2005.

Mattar, Philip. *Encyclopedia of the Palestinians*. New York: Facts on File, Inc., 2000.

May, Clifford D. "The Case for Islamic Heresy: Ayaan Hirsi Ali Risks All with Her Call for a Muslim Reformation." *The Washington Times* (April 14, 2015).

Mazur, Yosef. *Zionism, Post-Zionism & the Arab Problem: A Compendium of Opinions About the Jewish State*, Mike Cohen, ed. Bloomington, IN: WestBow Press, 2012.

Mazza, Roberto. *Jerusalem: From the Ottomans to the British*. New York: I.B. Tauris & Co., 2009.

Ma'oz, Moshe, ed. *The Meeting of Civilizations: Muslim, Christian, and Jewish*. Eastbourne, UK: Sussex Academic Press, 2009.

McCann, J. Clinton, Jr. *A Theological Introduction to the Book of Psalms: The Psalms as Torah*. Nashville, TN. Abingdon Press, 1993.

McCoy, Terrence. "Why Hamas Stores Its Weapons Inside Hospitals, Mosques and Schools." *The Washington Post* (July 31, 2014).

McCulloch, John Ramsay. *A Dictionary, Geographical, Statistical, and Historical*. London, England: Longman, Orme, Brown, Green, and Longmans, 1841.

McDaniels, Aaron. *Truth Between the Lies*. Bloomington, IN: Ex Libris 2016.

McGahern, Una. *Palestinian Christians in Israel: State Attitudes towards Non-Muslims in a Jewish State*. Abingdon, UK: Routledge, 2011.

McGonagle, Joseph. *Representing Ethnicity in Contemporary French Visual Culture*. Oxford, UK: Oxford University Press, 2017.

McKnight, Scot. *The Jesus Creed: Loving God, Loving Others*. Brewster, MA: Paraclete Press, 2004.

MacShane, Denis. *Globalising Hatred: The New Antisemitism*. London, UK: Weidenfeld & Nicolson, 2008.

Medoff, Rafael. *FDR & the Holocaust: A Breach of Faith*. Washington DC: The David S. Wyman Institute for Holocaust Studies, 2013.

Medved, Michael. "Does Israel Have a Right to Exist? Does the U.S.?" *Townhall* (July 26, 2006).

Medzini, Meron. *Israel's Foreign Relations: Selected Documents*. Jerusalem, Israel: Israel Ministry for Foreign Affairs, 1988.

Meir, Golda. *A Land of Our Own: An Oral Autobiography,* Marie Syrkin, ed. New York: G. P. Putnam's Sons, 1973.

Melville, Herman. *Clarel: A Poem and Pilgrimage in the Holy Land*. Evanston, IL: Northwestern University Press, 1991.

Mendels, Doron. *The Rise and Fall of Jewish Nationalism*. Grand Rapids, MI: Wm. B. Eerdmans Publishing Co., 1992.

Menocal, María Rosa. *The Ornament of the World: How Muslims, Jews, and Christians Created a Culture of Tolerance in Medieval Spain*. New York: Little, Brown and Co., 2002.

Merkley, Paul C. *Christian Attitudes Towards the State of Israel*. Kingston, Canada: McGill-Queen's University Press, 2001.

______*The Politics of Christian Zionism 1891–1948*. New York: Routledge, 1998.

Merrill, Eugene H., Mark F. Rooker, and Michael A. Grisanti. *The World and the Word: An Introduction to the Old Testament*. Nashville, TN: B &H Academic, 2011.

Merriman, Scott A. *Religion and the Law in America: An Encyclopedia of Personal Belief and Public Policy*.

Santa Barbara, CA: ABC–CLIO, Inc., 2007.
Meuschen, J. G., ed. *Hermanni Gygantis, ordinis fratrum minorum, Flores Temporum seu Chronicon Universale ab Orbe condito ad annum* Christi MCCCXLIX. Leiden, The Netherlands, 1750.
Michael, Robert, and Philip Rose. *Dictionary of Antisemitism from the Earliest Times to the Present*. Lanham, MD: Roman & Littlefield Publishing, 2007.
_______*Holy Hatred: Christianity, Antisemitism, and the Holocaust*. New York: Palgrave Macmillan, 2006.
Middleton, J. Richard, and Brian J. Walsh. *Truth Is Stranger Than It Used to Be: Biblical Faith in a Postmodern Age*. Downers Grove, IL: InterVarsity Press, 1995.
Mikaberidze, Alexander. *Atrocities, Massacres, and War Crimes: An Encyclopedia*. Santa Barbara, CA: ABC-CLIO, 2013.
Mill, John Stuart. *Considerations on Representative Government*. Chicago, IL: Gateway Publishing, 1962.
Miller, Charles E. *Fight or Surrender: A Reef of Political Essays*. Bloomington, IN: Trafford Publishing, 2013.
Miller, Clyde R. "Prejudice Can Be Prevented." *The Jewish Veteran*, vol. XIII, no. 4 (December, 1943), 7.
Miller, Fergus. *A Study of Cassius Dio*. Oxford, UK: Oxford University Press, 1964.
Miller, Tricia. *Jews and Anti-Judaism in Esther and the Church*. Cambridge, UK: James Clarke & Co., 2015.
Milton-Edwards, Beverley. *The Israeli-Palestinian Conflict: A People's War*. New York: Routledge, 2009.
Montefiore, Claude. *Judaism and St. Paul: Two Essays*. New York: Arno Press, 1973.
Moffett, Samuel H. *A History of Christianity in Asia: Beginnings to 1500*. San Francisco: HarperSanFrancisco, 1992.
Moll, Sebastian. *The Arch-Heretic Marcion*. Tübingen, Germany: Mohr Siebeck Verlag, 2010.
Moore, Johnnie. *Defying ISIS: Preserving Christianity in the Place of Its Birth and in Your Own Backyard*. Nashville, TN: Thomas Nelson, Inc., 2015.
Moore, Megan Bishop, and Brad E. Kelle. *Biblical History and Israel's Past: The Changing Study of the Bible and History*. Grand Rapids, MI: Wm. B. Eerdmans Publishing Co., 2011.
Moore, R. I. "Anti-Semitism and the Birth of Europe," in *Christianity and Judaism*, Diana Wood, ed. Oxford, UK: Ecclesiastical History Society, 1992.
Morgan, Michael L., ed. *A Holocaust Reader: Responses to the Nazi Extermination*. Oxford, UK: Oxford University Press, 2000.
_______*The Jewish Thought of Emil Fackenheim: A Reader*. Detroit, MI: Wayne State University Press, 1987.
Morris, Benny. *1948: A History of the First Arab-Israeli War*. New Haven, CT: Yale University Press, 2008.
_______*The Road to Jerusalem: Glubb Pasha, Palestine and the Jews*. London, UK: I. B. Tauris & Co, 2002.
Mosse, George L. "Racism and Nationalism," in *Nationalism: Critical Concepts in Political Science*, John Hutchinson and Anthony D. Smith, eds. New York: Routledge, 2000.
_______*Nazi Culture: A Documentary History*. New York: Random House, 1966.
Motzkin, Gabriel. "The Memory of Crime and the Formation of Identity," in *The Lesser Evil: Moral Approaches to Genocide Practices (Totalitarianism Movements and Political Religions)*, Helmut Dubiel and Gabriel Motzkin, eds. Abingdon, UK: Routledge, 2004.
Moubayed, Sami. *Under the Black Flag: At the Frontier of the New Jihad*. London, UK: I. B. Tauris & Co., 2015.
Mounce, Robert H. *The Book of Revelation*. Grand Rapids, MI: Wm. B. Eerdmans Publishing Co., 1977.
Msoka, Gabriel Andrew. *Basic Human Rights and the Humanitarian Crises in Sub-Saharan Africa*. Eugene, OR: Wipf & Stock, 2007.
Mühling, Markus. *T & T Clark Handbook of Christian Eschatology*. London, UK: Bloomsbury T & T Clark, 2015.
Muir, William. *The Life of Mahomet and History of Islam*. London, England: Smith, Elder, and Co., 1858.
Müller, Margret. *The World According to Israeli Newspapers: Representations of International Involvement in the Israel-Palestinian Conflict*. Berlin, Germany: Herstellung durch Frank & Timme GmbH, 2017.
Munayer, Salim J. "Reconciliation as a Christian Response," in *Christians and the Middle East Conflict*, Paul S. Rowe, John H. A. Dyck, and Jens Zimmermann, eds. New York: Routledge, 2014.
Murphy, Gannon, ed. *American Theological Inquiry*, Vol. 7, Issue 1, 50.
Murray, Iain. *The Puritan Hope*. Edinburgh, Scotland: Banner of Truth Publishers, 1971.
Muthuswamy, Moorthy S. *Defeating Political Islam: The New Cold War*. Amherst, NY: Prometheus Books, 2009.
Nagel, Merav. *Addiction Is an Illness We All Share*. Bloomington, IN: XLibris Corporation, 2013.
Nance, Penny Young. *Feisty and Feminine: A Rallying Cry for Conservative Women*. Grand Rapids, MI: Zondervan Publishing, 2016.
Nanos, Mark D. *The Mystery of Romans: The Jewish Context of Paul's Letters*. Minneapolis, MN: Augsburg Fortress Press, 1996.
Naor, Moshe. *Social Mobilization in the Arab/Israeli War of 1948: On the Israeli Home Front*. Abingdon, UK: Routledge, 2013.
Nekrutman, David. "A Call to Action." *The Jerusalem Post Christian Edition* (October 2013).
Nelson, Cary, and Gabriel Brahm. *The Case Against Academic Boycotts of Israel*. New York: MLA Members for Scholar's Rights, 2014.
_______"Divestment Campaigns," in *Dreams Deferred: A Concise Guide to the Israeli-Palestinian Conflict and*

*the Movement to Boycott Israel*, Cary Nelson, ed. New York: MLA Members for Scholars' Rights, 2016.
Nelson, Michael. *Guide to the Presidency*. New York: Routledge, 2015.
Nelson, Todd D. *Handbook of Prejudice, Stereotyping, and Discrimination.* New York: Psychology Press, 2009.
Neusner, Jacob. *Comparing Religions Through Law: Judaism and Islam*. Routledge, 1999.
_______*A Theological Commentary to the Midrash: Lamentations Rabbah*. Lanham, MD: University Press of America, 2011.
_______*A Theological Commentary to the Midrash: Ruth Rabbah and Esther Rabbah I*. Lanham, MD: University Press of America, 2001.
_______*A Theological Commentary to the Midrash: Sifre to Numbers and Sifre to Deuteronomy*, Jacob Neusner, ed. Lanham, MD: University Press of America, 2001.
_______*The Native Category-Formations of the Aggadah: The Earlier Midrash-Compilations*. Lanham, MD: University Press of America, 2000.
_______*The Theology of the Halakhah*. Leiden, The Netherlands: Koninklijke Brill NV, 2001.
Newman, Carey C. *Jesus & the Restoration of Israel: A Critical Assessment of N. T. Wright's* Jesus and the Victory of God. Downers Grove, IL: InterVarsity Press, 1999.
Nichols, Joel A. "Multi-Tiered Marriage: Reconsidering the Boundaries of Civil Law and Religion," in *Marriage and Divorce in a Multi-Cultural Context: Multi-Tiered Marriage and the Boundaries of Civil Law and Religion*, Joel A. Nichols, ed. Cambridge, UK: Cambridge University Press, 2012.
Nietzsche, Friedrich. *The Birth of Tragedy and the Genealogy of Morals*. Garden City, NY: Doubleday, 1956.
Niewyk, Donald L. "The Holocaust: Jews, Gypsies, and the Handicapped," in *Centuries of Genocide: Essays and Eyewitness Accounts*, Samuel Totten and William S. Parsons, eds. Abingdon, UK: Routledge, 2013.
Nirenberg, David. *Anti-Judaism: The Western Tradition*. New York: W. W. Norton & Co., 2013.
_______"The Rhineland Massacres of Jews in the First Crusade, Memories Medieval and Modern," in *Medieval Concepts of the Past: Ritual, Memory, and Historiography*, Gerd Althoff, Johannes Fried, and Patrick J. Geary, eds. Cambridge, UK: Cambridge University Press, 2002.
Nirenstein, Fiamma. "How I Became an 'Unconscious Fascist'," in *Those Who Forget the Past: The Question of Antisemitism*, Ron Rosenbaum, ed. New York: Random House Publishing, 2004.
Noll, K. L. *Canaan and Israel in Antiquity: An Introduction*. New York: Sheffield Academic Press, 2001.
Nomani, Asra Quratulain. *Standing Alone in Mecca: An American Woman's Struggle for the Soul of Islam*. New York: HarperCollins Publishers, 2006.
Nordlinger, Jay. *Peace, They Say: A History of the Nobel Peace Prize, the Most Famous and Controversial Prize in the World*. New York: Encounter Books, 2012.
Novak David. *Zionism and Judaism*. Cambridge, UK: Cambridge University Press, 2015.
Oberman, Heiko. *The Origins of Anti-Semitism in the Age of Renaissance and Reformation*, tr. James I. Porter. Philadelphia, PA: Fortress Press, 1984.
Ochs, Peter. *Another Reformation: Postliberal Christianity and the Jews*. Grand Rapids, MI: Baker Academic, 2011.
Oeste, Gordon K. *Legitimacy, Illegitimacy, and the Right to Rule: Windows on Abimelech's Rise and Demise in Judges 9*. London, UK: T & T Clark International, 2011.
Ohana, David. *The Origins of Israeli Mythology: Neither Canaanites Nor Crusaders*. Cambridge, UK: The Cambridge University Press, 2012.
Okeowo, Alexis. "Freedom Fighter: A Slaving Society and an Abolitionist's Crusade." *The New Yorker* (September 8, 2014).
Oliphant, Laurence. *Haifa: Life in Modern Palestine*. London, England: William Blackwood, 1887.
Olson, David T. *The American Church in Crisis*. Grand Rapids, MI: Zondervan Publishing, 2008.
Olson, Roger E. *The Mosaic of Christian Belief: Twenty Centuries of Unity & Diversity.* Downers Grove, IL: InterVarsity Press, 2002.
Origen. "Commentary on the Epistle to the Romans," in *Ancient Christian Commentary on Scripture: New Testament VI: Romans*, Gerald Bray, ed. Downers Grove, IL: InterVarsity Press, 1998.
_______*The Song of Songs*, in *Ancient Christian Writers*, J. Quasten and J. C. Plumpe, eds. Westminster, MD: Newman Press, 1957.
Ormerod, Neil. *A Public God: Natural Theology Reconsidered*. Minneapolis, MN: Augsburg Fortress Press, 2015.
Ostow, Mortimer. *Myth and Madness: The Psychodynamics of Antisemitism*. New Brunswick, NJ: Transaction Publishing, 1995.
O'Daly, Gerard. *Augustine's City of God: A Reader's Guide*. Oxford, UK: Oxford University Press, 1999.
O'Hare, Padraic. *The Enduring Covenant: The Education of Christians and the End of Antisemitism*. Valley Forge, PA: Trinity Press International, 1997.
O'Shea, Paul. *A Cross Too Heavy: Pope Pius XII and the Jews of Europe*. New York: Palgrave Macmillan, 2011.
Pacepa, Ion Mihai. "The *KGB's* Man." *The Wall Street Journal*, September 22, 2003.
______, and Ronald Rychlak. *Disinformation: Former Spy Chief Reveals Secret Strategies for Undermining Freedom, Attacking Religion, and Promoting Terrorism*. Washington, DC, WND Books, Inc., 2013.

Paldiel, Mordecai. *Churches and the Holocaust: Unholy Teaching, Good Samaritans and Reconciliation.* Jersey City, NJ: KTAV Publishing House, 2006.
Panchyk, Richard. *World War II for Kids.* Chicago, IL: Chicago Review Press, 2002.
Pappé, Ilan. *The Forgotten Palestinians: A History of the Palestinians in Israel.* New Haven, CT: Yale University Press, 2011.
Parfitt, Tudor. *The Jews of Africa and Asia: Contemporary Anti-Semitism and Other Pressures.* Budapest, Hungary: Minority Rights Group, 1987.
Pasachoff, Naomi E., and Robert Littman. *A Concise History of the Jewish People.* Lanham, MD: Rowman & Littlefield Publishers, 1995.
______*Great Jewish Thinkers: Their Lives and Work.* Springfield, NJ: Behrman House, 1992.
Patai, Raphael, and Jennifer Patai. *The Myth of the Jewish Race* (Detroit, MI: The Wayne State University Press, 1975.
Patterson, David. *Anti-Semitism and Its Metaphysical Origins.* Cambridge, UK: Cambridge University Press, 2015.
______*Emil L. Fackenheim: A Jewish Philosopher's Response to the Holocaust.* Syracuse, NY: Syracuse University Press, 2008.
______*Open Wounds: The Crisis of Jewish Thought in the Aftermath of the Holocaust.* Seattle, WA: The University of Washington Press, 2006.
Pauley, Bruce F. *From Prejudice to Persecution: A History of Austrian Anti-Semitism.* Chapel Hill, NC: The University of North Carolina Press, 1992.
Peck, Jeffrey M. "Afterword," in *The New German Jewry and the European Context: The Return of the European Jewish Diaspora*, Y. Michal Bodemann, ed. Basingstoke, UK: Palgrave Macmillan, 2008.
Peleg, Ilan, and Dov Waxman. *Israel's Palestinians: The Conflict Within.* Cambridge, UK: Cambridge University Press, 2011.
Penny, Ralph J. *Variation and Change in Spanish.* Cambridge, UK: Cambridge University Press, 2000.
Pentiuc, Eugen J. *The Old Testament in Eastern Orthodox Tradition.* Oxford, UK: Oxford University Press, 2014.
Perry, Marvin, and Frederick M. Schweitzer. *Antisemitism: Myth and Hate from Antiquity to the Present.* New York: Palgrave Macmillan, 2002.
______, and Howard E. Negrin, eds. *The Theory and Practice of Islamic Terrorism: An Anthology.* New York: Palgrave Macmillan, 2008.
Peters, Joan. *From Time Immemorial: The Origins of the Arab-Jewish Conflict Over Palestine.* London, UK: Michael Joseph Publishers, 1985.
Petersen, Hans-Christian. *Antisemitism in Eastern Europe: History and Present in Comparison.* New York: Peter Lang Publishing, 2010.
Peterson, Erik. *Die Kirche aus Juden und Heiden.* Salzburg, Germany: Anton Pustet Verlag, 1933.
Petronoti, Marina. "Disguising the Sense of Insecurity in 'Multicultural' Greece," in *Dangerous Others, Insecure Societies: Fear and Social Division,* Michalis Lianos, ed. Abingdon, UK: Routledge, 2016.
Pew Research, "Muslim Americans: Middle Class and Mostly Mainstream," *Pew Research* (May 22, 2007) 97.
Pfeffer, Yehoshua. *Prophecies and Providence: A Biblical Approach to Modern Jewish History.* Jerusalem, Israel: Urim Publications, 2015.
Pfeiffer, Alex. "Drexel Professor Has a History of Hating White People and Wishing for Their Genocide," *The Daily Caller* (12/25/2016).
Phayer, Michael. *The Catholic Church and the Holocaust, 1930–1965.* Bloomington, IN: Indiana University Press, 2000.
Phillips, Melanie. *The World Turned Upside Down: The Global Battle over God, Truth, and Power.* New York: Encounter Books, 2010.
______"Remember This? Palestinian Arab Propaganda Stages Fake Israeli 'Attacks' for Media." *The Muslim Issue* (September 28, 2012).
Pisani, Elizabeth. *Indonesia, Etc.: Exploring the Improbable Nation.* New York: W. W. Norton & Company, 2014.
Pitman, Don A. "Reflections on Religious Pluralism," in *The Theologically Formed Heart: Essays in Honor of David J. Gouwens*, Warner M. Bailey, Lee C. Barrett, and James O. Duke, eds. Eugene, OR: Wipf and Stock Publishers, 2014.
Pogrund, Benjamin. *Drawing Fire: Investigating the Accusations of Apartheid in Israel.* Lanham, MD: Rowman & Littlefield, 2014.
Poliakov, Léon. *The History of Anti-Semitism, Volume 1: From the Time of Christ to the Court Jews*, tr. Richard Howard. Philadelphia, PA: The University of Pennsylvania Press, 2003.
______*The History of Anti-Semitism, Volume 3: From Voltaire to Wagner.* Philadelphia, PA: The University of Pennsylvania Press, 2003.
Pope, Alexander. *An Essay on Man.* London, England: Thomas Tegg, 1811.
Prager, Dennis, and Joseph Telushkin. *Why the Jews?: The Reason for Antisemitism.* New York: Simon and

Schuster, 1983.
Prah, K. K., ed. *Reflections on Arab-Led Slavery of Africans*. Cape Town, South Africa: Centre for Advanced Studies of African Society, 2005.
Prescott, Andrew, and Elizabeth M. Hallam, eds. *The British Inheritance: A Treasury of Historic Documents*. Berkeley, CA: The University of California Press, 1999.
Prescott, Deborah Lee. *Imagery from Genesis in Holocaust Memoirs: A Critical Study*. Jefferson, NC: McFarland & Company, Publishers, 2010.
Pressfield, Steven. *The Lion's Gate: On the Front Lines of the Six Day War*. New York: Penguin Group, 2014.
Pressman, Jacob. *Dear Friends: A Prophetic Journey through Great Events of the 20th Century*. Jersey City, NJ: KTAV Publishing House, 2002.
Price, Randall. *Fast Facts on the Middle East Conflict*. Eugene, OR: Harvest House Publishers, 2003.
Primoratz, Igor, and David W. Lovell. *Protecting Civilians during Violent Conflict: Theoretical and Practical Issues for the 21st Century*. Abingdon, UK: Routledge, 2012.
Prior, Michael. "Holy Places, Unholy Domination: The Scramble for Jerusalem," in *My Jerusalem: Essays, Reminiscences, and Poems*, Salma Khadra Jayyusi and Safar Ishaq Ansari, eds. Northampton, MA: Olive Branch Press, 2005.
Probst, Christopher J. *Demonizing the Jews: Luther and the Protestant Church in Nazi Germany*. Bloomington, IN: Indiana University Press, 2012.
Provost, René, and Payam Akhavan, eds. *Confronting Genocide*. Dordrecht, The Netherlands: Springer Science+Business Media B.V., 2011.
Rabinowitz, Aaron. *Judaism and Psychology: Meeting Points*. New York: Jason Aronson, 1999.
Rajan, V. G. Julie. *Al Qaeda's Global Crisis: The Islamic State, Takfir and the Genocide of Muslims*. Abingdon, UK: Routledge, 2015.
Rakeffet-Rothkoff, Aaron, and Joseph Epstein. *The Rav: The Word of Rabbi Joseph B. Soloveitchik*. Hoboken, NJ: KTAV Publishing House, 1999.
Ramadan, Tariq. *Radical Reform: Islamic Ethics and Liberation*. New York: Oxford University Press, 2009.
Rancour-Laferriere, Daniel. *The Sign of the Cross: From Golgotha to Genocide*. Piscataway, NJ: Transaction Publishers, 2011.
Raphael, Frederic. *Anti-Semitism*. London, UK: Biteback Publishing, Ltd., 2015.
Rappaport, Ernest. *Anti-Judaism: A Psychohistory*. Chicago, IL: Perspective Press: 1975.
Rasheed, Adil. ISIS: Race to Armageddon. Dehli, India: Vij Books India Pvt. Ltd., 2015.
Rausch, David. *Legacy of Hatred: Why Christians Must Not Forget the Holocaust*. Grand Rapids, MI: Baker Publishing Group, 1990.
Raczka, Witt. *Unholy Land: In Search of Hope in Israel/Palestine*. Lanham, MD: Rowman & Littlefield, 2016).
Redden, Elizabeth. "Backing the Israel Boycott." *Inside Higher Education* (17 December, 2013).
Reiter, Yitzhak. *Contested Holy Places in Israel—Palestine: Sharing and Conflict Resolution*. Abingdon, UK: Routledge, 2017.
Reitsma, Bernard. *The God of My Enemy: The Middle East and the Nature of God*. Eugene, OR: Wipf and Stock Publishers, 2014.
Reitter, Paul. *The Anti-Journalist: Karl Kraus and Jewish Self-Fashioning in Fin-de-Siècle Europe*. Chicago, IL: The University of Chicago Press, 2008.
Rejwan, Nissim. *Israel's Place in the Middle East: A Pluralist Perspective*. Gainesville, FL: The University of Florida Press, 1998.
________*The Last Jews in Baghdad: Remembering a Lost Homeland*. Austin, TX: The University of Texas Press, 2004.
Resnicoff, Steven H. "Ends and Means in Jewish Law," in *The Jewish Law Annual*, Berachyahu Lifshitz, ed. London, UK: Routledge, 2004.
Reuchlin, Johannes. *Recommendation Whether to Confiscate, Destroy, and Burn All Jewish Books*, Peter Wortsman, tr. and ed. Mahwah, NJ: Paulist Press, 2000.
Reyes, E. Christopher. *In His Name*. Bloomington, IN: Trafford Publishing, 2014.
Rich, Dave. "Book Review: Some of My Best Friends: A Journey Through Twenty-First Century Anti-Semitism." *Fathom* (Autumn/2014).
Ridderbos, Herman N. "The Future of Israel," in *Prophecy in the Making: Messages Prepared for Jerusalem Conference on Biblical Prophecy*, Carl F. H. Henry, ed. Carol Stream, IL: Creation House, 1971.
Rimare, Christopher. *Blinded by Paradise: The Rise and Fall of Hadrian*. Bloomington, IN: iUniverse, 2010.
Riskin, Shlomo. "Covenant and Conversion: The United Mission to Redeem the World," in *Covenant and Hope: Christian and Jewish Reflections*, Robert W. Jenson and Eugene B. Korn, eds. (Grand Rapids, MI: Wm. B. Eerdmans Publishing Co., 2012.
Roald, Anne Sofie. *Women in Islam: The Western Experience*. London, UK: Routledge, 2001.
Roberts, Jo. *Contested Land, Contested Memory: Israel's Jews and Arabs and the Ghosts of Catastrophe*. Toronto, Canada: Dundurn Press, 2013.

Robertson, David. *The Routledge Dictionary of Politics*. Abingdon, UK: Routledge, 2004.
Robertson, Ritchie. "Varieties of Anti-Semitism," in *Encyclopedia of the Jewish Diaspora: Origins, Experiences, and Culture*, Mark Avrum Ehrlich, ed. Santa Barbara, CA: ABC-CLIO, LLC, 2009.
Robinson, Henry Wheeler. *The Old Testament: Its Making and Meaning*. London, UK: University of London Press, 1966.
Rodman, David. *Sword and Shield of Zion: The Israel Air Force in the Arab-Israeli Conflict*. Eastbourne, UK: Sussex Academic Press, 2014.
Rodriguez, Jarbel. *Muslim and Christian Contact in the Middle Ages: A Reader*. Toronto, Canada: Toronto University Press, 2015.
Rogan, Eugene. *The Arabs: A History*. New York: Basic Books, 2009.
Rogerson, John. *Old Testament Criticism in the Nineteenth Century: England and Germany*. Eugene, OR: Wipf and Stock Publishers, 1984.
Rohl, David M. *Exodus: Myth or History*. Minneapolis, MN: Thinking Man Media, 2015.
______*From Eden to Exile: The Five-Thousand-Year History of the Bible*. Lebanon, TN: Greenleaf Press, 2002.
______*Pharaohs and Kings: A Biblical Quest*. New York: Crown Publishers, 1995.
Rose, John. *The Myths of Zionism*. London, UK: Pluto Press, 2004.
Rose, Paul Lawrence. *Revolutionary Antisemitism in Germany from Kant to Wagner*. Princeton, NJ: Princeton University Press, 1990.
Rosefielde, Steven. *Trump's Populist America*. Hackensack, NJ: World Scientific Publishing Co., 2017.
Rosenberg, Stuart E. *The Christian Problem: A Jewish View*. New York: Hippocrene Books, 1986.
Rosenfeld, Alvin H. *Anti-Zionism in Great Britain and Beyond: A 'Respectable' Anti-Semitism?* New York: American Jewish Committee, 2004.
Rosenthal, Gilbert S. *A Jubilee for All Time: The Copernican Revolution in Jewish-Christian Relations*. Eugene, OR: Wipf and Stock Publishers, 2014.
Roshandel, Jalil, and Sharon Chadha. *Jihad and International Security*. New York: Palgrave Macmillan, 2006.
Rosner, Fred, and Robert Schulman. *Medicine and Jewish Law*. Brooklyn, NY: Yashar Book, 2005.
Ross, Jeffrey Ian. *Religion and Violence: An Encyclopedia of Faith and Conflict from Antiquity to the Present*. Abingdon, UK: Routledge, 2011.
Rosseau, Richard W., ed. *Christianity and Judaism: The Deepening Dialogue*. Montrose, PA: Ridge Row Press, 1983.
Rossman, Vadim Joseph. *Russian Intellectual Antisemitism in the Post-Communist Era*. Lincoln, NE: The University of Nebraska Press, 2002.
Roth, Cecil. "Was Hebrew Ever a Dead Language?" in *Personalities and Events in Jewish History*, Cecil Roth, ed. Philadelphia, PA: Jewish Publication Society of America, 1953.
Roth, Daniel J., and Eytan Halon, "Border Police Officer Killed in Jerusalem Terror Attack." *The Jerusalem Post* (June 17, 2017).
Roth, John K. *Holocaust Politics*. Eugene, OR: Wipf and Stock Publishers, 2001.
Rothenberg, Naftali, and Eliezer Schweid, eds. *Jewish Identity in Modern Israel: Proceedings on Secular Judaism and Democracy*. Jerusalem, Israel: Urim Publications, 2002.
Rothmann, John F. *Icon of Evil: Hitler's Mufti and the Rise of Radical Islam*. New Brunswick, NJ: Transaction Books, 2009.
Rottenberg, Isaac C. "Israelic Christians." *Restore!*, Issue 52, 34.
______*Judaism, Christianity, Paganism: A Judeo-Christian Worldview and Its Cultural Implications*. Atlanta, GA: Hebraic Heritage Press, 2007.
______"They Just Don't Get It." *Restore!*, Issue 10, 16–18.
Rozenblit, Marsha L. "European Jewry: 1800–1933," in *The Cambridge Guide to Jewish History, Religion, and Culture*, Judith R. Baskin and Kenneth Seeskin, eds. Cambridge, UK: Cambridge University Press, 2010.
Rozett, Robert, and Shmuel Spector, eds. *Encyclopedia of the Holocaust*. Jerusalem, Israel: The Jerusalem Publishing House, 2000.
Rubenstein, Richard L. *After Auschwitz: History, Theology and Contemporary Judaism*. Baltimore, MD: Johns Hopkins University Press, 1992.
______, and John K. Roth. *Approaches to Auschwitz: The Holocaust and Its Legacy*. Louisville, KY: Westminster John Knox Press, 2003.
______*Wrestling with God: Jewish Theological Responses during and after the Holocaust*. Oxford, UK: Oxford University Press, 2007.
Rubin, Barry M. *Revolution Until Victory? The Politics and History of the PLO*. Cambridge, MA: Harvard University Press, 1994.
Rubin, Jordan. *The Great Physician's Rx for Health and Wellness*. Nashville, TN: Thomas Nelson, Inc., 2005.
Rubin, Theodore Isaac. *Anti-Semitism: A Disease of the Mind*. New York: Skyhorse Publishing, Inc. 2009.
Rubin, Uri. "The Assassination of Ka'b b. al-Ashraf." *Oriens: Journal of Philosophy, Theology and Science*

*in Islamic Societies*, vol. 32 (1990) 65–71.
Rudin, Arnold James. *Christians & Jews Faith to Faith: Tragic History, Promising Present, Fragile Future.* Woodstock, VT: Jewish Lights Publishing, 2011.
Ruether, Rosemary Radford. *Faith and Fratricide: The Theological Roots of Anti-Semitism.* Eugene, OR: Wipf and Stock Publishers, 1995.
_______"The Quest for Peace with Justice in the Middle East: Christian Zionist and Palestinian Theologies," in *Theologies of Liberation in Palestine-Israel: Indigenous, Contextual, and Postscolonial Perspectives*, Nur Masalha and Lisa Isherwood, eds. Eugene, OR: Wipf and Stock Publishers, 2014.
_______, and Herman J. Ruether. *The Wrath of Jonah: The Crisis of Religious Nationalism in the Israeli-Palestinian Conflict.* Minneapolis, MN: Augsburg Fortress Press, 2002.
Rufin, Jean-Christophe. "Chantier sur la lutte contre le racisme et l'antisémitisme." *La Monde* (October 19, 2004).
Runes, Dagobert D. *The War against the Jew.* New York: Philosophical Library, 1968.
Ruska, Anna. "Kashmir," in *Atrocities, Massacres, and War Crimes: An Encyclopedia*, Alexander Mikaberidze, ed. Santa Barbara, CA: ABC–CLIO, LLC, 2013.
Russell, Letty M. *Hagar, Sarah, and Their Children.* Louisville, KY: Westminster John Knox Press, 2006.
Russell, Malcolm. *The Middle East and South Asia 2015–2016.* Lanham, MD: Rowman & Littlefield, 2015.
Ruud, Jay. "Dante and the Jews," in *Jews in Medieval Christendom: Slay Them Not*, Kristine T. Utterback and Merrall L. Price, eds. Leiden, The Netherlands: Koninklijke Brill NV, 2013.
Ryback, Timothy W. "The First Killings of the Holocaust." *The New York Times* (Jan. 3, 2012).
Rynhold, Jonathan. *The Arab-Israeli Conflict in American Political Culture.* Cambridge, UK: Cambridge University Press, 2015.
Sachar, Howard Morley. *A History of the Jews in America.* New York: Random House, 1992.
Sacks, Jonathan. *Future Tense: Jews, Judaism, and Israel in the Twenty-first Century.* New York: Schocken Books, 2009.
________"How to Defeat Religious Violence." *The Wall Street Journal* (Oct. 2, 2105).
Safrai, Samuel. "The Lands of the Diaspora," in *A History of the Jewish People*, Haim Hillel Ben-Sasson, ed. Cambridge, MA: Harvard University Press, 1985.
Sage, Steven F. *Ibsen and Hitler: The Plagiarist, the Poet, and the Plot for the Third Reich.* New York: Carroll & Graf Publishers, 2006.
Sailhamer, John H. *Biblical Archaeology.* Grand Rapids, MI: Zondervan Publishing, 1998.
_______*Old Testament History.* Grand Rapids, MI: Zondervan Publishing, 1998.
Samuelson, Norbert M. *An Introduction to Modern Jewish Philosophy.* Albany, NY: State University of New York Press, 1989.
Sanasarian, Eliz. "The Comparative Dimension of the Baha'i Case and Prospects for Change in the Future," in *Bahá'ís of Iran: Socio-Historical Studies*, Dominic P. Brookshaw and Seena B. Fazel, eds. Abingdon, UK: Routledge, 2008.
Sand, Shlomo. *The Invention of the Jewish People*, tr. Yale Lotan. London, UK: Verso Books, 2009.
________*The Invention of the Land of Israel: From Holy Land to Homeland*, tr. Jeremy Forman. London, UK: Verso Books, 2012.
Sang, Lucia I. Suarez. "California Imam Calls on Allah to Annihilate Jews." *Fox News U.S.* (July 26, 2017).
Santayana, George. *Reason in Common Sense: The Life of Reason Volume 1.* Mineola, NY: Dover Press, 1980.
Saraiva, António José, Herman P. Salomon, and Isaac S. D. Sasson, trs. and eds. *The Marano Factory: The Portuguese Inquisition and Its New Christians, 1536–1765.* Leiden, The Netherlands: Koninklijke Brill NV, 2001.
Robert Satloff, "A Historic Holocaust Awareness Awakening in Saudi Arabia, of All Places: Applaud This Significant Step from the Heart of Islam." *New York Daily News* (JAN 26, 2018).
_______*Among the Righteous: Lost Stories from the Holocaust's Long Reach Into Arab Lands.* Philadelphia, PA: Perseus Books Group, 2006.
Sazgjn, Yüksei. *Human Rights under State-Enforced Religious Family Laws in Israel, Egypt and India.* Cambridge, UK: Cambridge University Press, 2013.
Schäfer, Axel R. *Countercultural Conservatives: American Evangelicalism from the Postwar Revival to the Christian Right.* Madison, WI: The University of Wisconsin Press, 2011.
Schäfer, Peter. *Judeophobia: Attitudes toward the Jews in the Ancient World.* Cambridge, MA: Harvard University Press, 1998.
Schechtman, Joseph B. *The Mufti and the Fuehrer: The Rise and Fall of Hajj Amin el-Husseini.* New York: Thomas Youseloff, 1965.
Schecter, Solomon. *Some Aspects of Rabbinic Theology.* New York: The Macmillan Company, 1910.
Schein, Sylvia. *Gateway to the Heavenly City: Crusader Jerusalem and the Catholic West (1099–1187).* Burlington, VT: Ashgate Publishing Co., 2005.
Schiffman, Lawrence. *Reclaiming the Dead Sea Scrolls.* New Haven, CT: Yale University Press, 1995.

Schleifer, Ron, and Jessica Snapper. *Advocating Propaganda—Viewpoints from Israel: Social Media, Public Diplomacy, Foreign Affairs, Military Psychology, and Religious Persuasion Perspectives*. Eastbourne, UK: Sussex Academic Press, 2015.

Schloss, Chaim. *2000 Years of Jewish History: From the Destruction of the Second Bais HaMikdash until the Twentieth Century*. Jerusalem, Israel: Feldheim Publishers, 2002.

Schmidt, Imanuel Clemens. "Revealing the Absurdity of Jewish Hopes: From Polemical Ethnography to Basnage's *L'Histoire des Juifs*," in *Revealing the Secrets of the Jews: Johannes Pfefferkorn and Christian Writings about Jewish Life and Literature in Early Modern Europe*, Jonathan Adams and Cordelia Heß, eds. Berlin, Germany: Walter de Gruyter, 2017.

Schniedewind, William M. *A Social History of Hebrew: Its Origins through the Rabbinic Period*. New Haven, CT: Yale University Press, 2013.

Scholem, Gershom G., and R. J. Zwi Werblowsky. *Sabbatai Sevi: The Mystical Messiah, 1626–1676*. Princeton, NJ: Princeton University Press, 1976.

Schreiber, Mordecai. *The Man Who Knew God: Decoding Jeremiah*. Lanham, MD: Rowman & Littlefield Publishers, 2010.

Schwanitz, Wolfang G., and Barry Rubin. *Nazis, Islamists, and the Making of the Modern Middle East*. New Haven, CT: Yale University Press, 2014.

Schwartz, Richard Alan. *Eyewitness History: The 1990s*. New York: Infobase Publishing, 2006.

Schweid, Eliezer. "Is the *Shoah* a Unique Event?" in *Wrestling with God: Jewish Theological Responses during and after the Holocaust*, Steven T. Katz, Shlomo Biderman, and Gershon Greenberg, eds. Oxford, UK: Oxford University Press, 2007.

_______*The Land of Israel: National Home or Land of Destiny*. Cranbury, NJ: Associated University Presses, 1985.

Seebass, Horst. "בחר *Bachar*," in *Theological Dictionary of the Old Testament*, C. J. Botterweck and H. Ringgren, eds. Grand Rapids, MI: Wm. B. Eerdmans Publishing Co., 1975.

Segal, Ronald. *Islam's Black Slaves: The Other Black Diaspora*. New York: Farrar, Straus & Giroux, 2002.

Segev, Tom. *1967: Israel, the War, and the Year that Transformed the Middle East*. New York: Metropolitan Books, 2005.

_______*The Seventh Million: The Israelis and the Holocaust*. New York: Hill and Wang, 1993.

Seizer, Michael. *"Kike!" A Documentary History of Anti-Semitism in America*. New York: World Publishing, 1972.

Selengut, Charles. *Sacred Fury: Understanding Religious Violence*. Lanham, MD: Rowman & Littlefield Publishing Group, 2017.

Service, Robert. Lenin: *A Political Life: Volume 3: The Iron Ring*. Blasingstoke, UK: MacMillan Press Ltd., 1995.

Sevenster, Jan Nicholaas. *The Roots of Pagan Anti-Semitism in the Ancient World*. Leiden, The Netherlands: E. J. Brill, 1975.

Sezgin, Yüksel. *Human Rights under State-Enforced Religious Family Laws in Israel, Egypt and India*. Cambridge, UK: Cambridge University Press, 2013.

Shafiq, Muhammad, and Mohammed Abu-Nimer. *Interfaith Dialogue: A Guide for Muslims*. Herndon, VA: The International Institute of Islamic Thought, 2011.

Shahar, Ido. "A Contextual Analysis of a Legal Circular," in *Law, Custom, and Statute in the Muslim World: Studies in Honor of Ahron Layish*, Ron Shaham, ed. Leiden, The Netherlands: Koninklijke Brill NV, 2007.

Shahrani, M. Nazif. "State Building and Social Fragmentation in Afghanistan: A Historical Perspective," in *The State, Religion, and Ethnic Politics: Afghanistan, Iran, and Pakistan*, Ali Banuazizi and Myron Weiner, eds. Syracuse, NY: Syracuse University Press, 1986.

Shandler, Jeffrey. *While America Watches: Televising the Holocaust*. Oxford, UK: Oxford University Press, 1999.

Shapira, Anita. *Israel: A History*, tr. Anthony Berris. London, UK: Weidenfeld and Nicolson, 2014.

Sharan, Shlomo, and Dawid Bûqay, *Crossovers: Anti-Zionism and Anti-Semitism*. Piscataway, NJ: Transaction Publishers, 2010.

Sharif, Regina. *Non-Jewish Zionism: Its Roots in Western History*. London, UK: Zed Books, 1983.

Sharpe, Victor. *Politicide: The Relentless Attempts by the Arab and Muslim World to Destroy the State of Israel*. Raleigh, NC: Lulu Press, Inc., 2011.

Shavit, Michal. *Media Strategy and Military Operations in the 21st Century: Mediatizing the Israel Defense Forces*. Abingdon, UK: Routledge, 2017.

Shemer, Ze'ev. *Israel and the Palestinian Nightmare*. Bloomington, IN: iUniverse, 2010.

Shenk, David W. *Journeys of the Muslim Nation and the Christian Church: Exploring the Mission of Two Communities*. Nairobi, Kenya: Uzima Publishing House, 2006.

Shenker, Israel, and Mary Shenker, eds. *As Good as Golda: The Warmth and Wisdom of Israel's Prime Minister*. New York: McCall Publishing Co., 1970.

Sheppard, G. T., and A. C. Thiselton. "Biblical Interpretation in Europe in the Twentieth Century," in *Dictionary of Major Biblical Interpreters*, Donald K. McKim, ed. Downers Grove, IL: InterVarsity Press, 2007.

Sherman, Cecil E. *Formations Commentary: Luke–Acts*. Macon, GA: Smyth & Helwys Publishing, 2006.

Shermer, Michael, and Alex Grobman. *Denying History: Who Says the Holocaust Never Happened and Why Do They Say It?* Berkeley, CA: The University of California Press, 2000.

Sherwin, Byron L. *Faith Finding Meaning: A Theology of Judaism*. Oxford, UK: Oxford University Press, 2009.

Shimoni, Gideon. *The Zionist Ideology*. Boston, MA: Brandeis University Press, 1995.

Sider, Sandra. *Handbook to Life in Renaissance Europe*. Oxford, UK: Oxford University Press, 2005.

Siegel, Bill. *The Control Faction: Our Struggle to See the True Threat*. Lanham, MD: Hamilton Books, 2012.

Siker, Jeffrey S. *Disinheriting the Jews: Abraham in Early Christian Controversy*. Louisville, KY: Westminster John Knox Press, 1991.

Silberman, Neil Asher, and Israel Finkelstein. *The Bible Unearthed: Archaeology's New Vision of Ancient Israel and the Origin of Its Sacred Texts*. New York: Touchstone, 2001.

Simpson, Patrick Carnegie. *The Fact of Christ: A Series of Lectures*. Grand Rapids, MI: Fleming H. Revell Co., 1901.

Sina, Ali. *Understanding Muhammad: A Psychobiography of Allah's Prophet*. LaVergne, TN: Felibri Publications, 2008.

Singer, David, and Lawrence Grossman. *American Jewish Yearbook 2005*. Atlanta, GA: American Jewish Committee, 2006.

Singer, Isidore, Cyrus Adler, *et. al.*, eds. *The Jewish Encyclopedia: A Descriptive Record of the History, Religion, Literature, and Customs of the Jewish People from the Earliest Times to the Present Day*. New York: Funk and Wagnalls Co., 1907.

_______"The Basel Program," in *The Jewish Encyclopedia*. New York: Funk and Wagnalls Company, 1906.

Sizer, Stephen. *Christian Zionism: Road Map to Armageddon*. Downers Grove, IL: InterVarsity Press, 2004.

Skarsaune, Oskar. *In the Shadow of the Temple: Jewish Influences on Early Christianity*. Downers Grove, IL: InterVarsity Press, 2002.

Slatin, Pasha, and Rudolf Von Slatin. "Slavery," in *Historical Dictionary of the Sudan,* Robert S. Kramer, Richard A. Lobban, Jr., and Carolyn Fluehr-Lobban, eds. Lanham, MD: Rowman & Littlefield Publishing Group, 2013.

Slavicek, Louise Chipley. *The Black Death*. New York: Infobase Publishing, 2008.

Smith, Helmut W. *The Holocaust and Other Genocides: History, Representation, Ethics*. Nashville, TN, Vanderbilt University Press, 2002.

Snyder, Howard A., and Joel Scandrett. *Salvation Means Creation Healed: The Ecology of Sin and Grace: Overcoming the Divorce between Earth and Heaven*. Eugene, OR: Wipf and Stock Publishers, 2011.

Solberg, Mary M., tr. *A Church Undone: Documents from the German Christian Faith Movement 1932–1940*. Minneapolis, MN: Fortress Press, 2015.

Solomon, Lawrence. "Playing Make-Believe over Gaza." *The Financial Post* (August 7, 2014).

Soloviev, V. S. *Freedom, Faith, and Dogma: Essays by V. S. Soloviev on Christianity and Judaism*. Albany, NY: The State University of New York Press, 2008.

Somerville, Robert. *The Councils of Urban II: Decreta Claromontensia*. Amsterdam, The Netherlands: Adolf M. Hakkert Publishing, 1972.

Sonderegger, Katherine. *That Jesus Christ Was Born a Jew: Karl Barth's Doctrine of Israel*. State College, PA: Pennsylvania State University Press, 1992.

Sookhdeo, Patrick. *Global Jihad: The Future in the Face of Militant Islam*. McLean, VA: Isaac Publishing, 2007.

Sparks, Kenton L. *Ethnicity and Identity in Ancient Israel: Prolegomena to the Study of Ethnic Sentiments and Their Expression in the Hebrew Bible*. Winona Lake, IN: Eisenbrauns, Inc., 1998.

Spector, Stephen. *Evangelicals and Israel: The Story of American Christian Zionism*. Oxford, UK: Oxford University Press, 2009.

Spencer, Philip, and Sara Valentina Di Palma. "Antisemitism and the Politics of Holocaust Memorial Day in the UK and Italy," in *Perceptions of the Holocaust in Europe and Muslim Communities: Sources, Comparisons, and Educational Challenges*, Günther Jikeli and Joëll Alouche-Benayoun, eds. Dordrecht, The Netherlands: Springer Science+Business Media, 2013.

Spencer, Robert. *The Complete Infidel's Guide to ISIS*. Washington, DC: Regnery Publishing, 2015.

_______*The Myth of Islamic Tolerance: How Islamic Law Treats Non-Muslims*. Amherst, New York: Prometheus Books, 2005.

_______*The Politically Incorrect Guide to Islam (and the Crusades)*. Washington, DC: Regnery Publishing, Inc., 2005.

_______*The Truth about Muhammad: Founder of the World's Most Intolerant Religion*. Washington, DC: Regnery Publishing, Inc., 2006.

Spetalnick, Mat. "War-Weary Christians Seek Escape from Holy Land." *Reuters News Service* (12/17/2003).

Spielvogel, Jackson J., and David Redles. *Hitler and Nazi Germany: A History*. Abingdon, UK: Routledge, 2014.

_______*Western Civilization: Alternate Volume: Since 1300*. Boston, MA: Wadsworth, Cengage Learning, 2006.

Spilly, Alphonse P., ed. *Selected Works of Joseph Cardinal Bernardin*. Collegeville, MN: The Liturgical Press, 2000.
Springer, A. J. "Proof of Identification: Patristic and Rabbinic Exegesis of the Cain and Abel Narrative," in *Papers Presented at the Fourteenth International Conference on Patristic Studies*, Frances Margaret Young, Mark J. Edwards, and Paul M. Parvis, eds. Louvain, Belgium: Peeters Publishers, 2006.
St. John, Robert. *Tongue of the Prophets: The Fascinating Biography of Eliezer Ben-Yehuda, the Father of Modern Hebrew*. Beverly Hills, CA: Wilshire Book Co., 1972.
Stakelbeck, Erick. *ISIS Exposed: Beheadings, Slavery, and the Hellish Reality of Radical Islam*. Washington DC: Regnery Publishing, 2015.
Stalder, Will. *Palestinian Christians and the Old Testament History, Hermeneutics, and Ideology*. Minneapolis, MN: Augsburg Fortress Press, 2015.
Stanley, Christopher D. *The Hebrew Bible: A Comparative Approach*. Minneapolis, MN: Fortress Press, 2010.
Stark, Rodney. *One True God: Historical Consequences of Monotheism*. Princeton, NJ: Princeton University Press, 2001.
Stavans, Anat. "Challenges Faced by a Medium-Sized Language Community in the 21st Century: The Case of Hebrew," in *Survival and Development of Language Communities: Prospects and Challenges*, F. Xavier Vila, ed. Bristol, UK: Multilingual Matters, 2013.
Steiman, Lionel B. *Paths to Genocide: Antisemitism in Western History*. New York: Palgrave Macmillan, 1998.
Steigmann-Gall, Richard. *The Holy Reich: Nazi Conceptions of Christianity, 1919–1945*. Cambridge, UK: Cambridge University Press, 2003.
Steinberg, Paul. *Celebrating the Jewish Year: The Spring and Summer Holidays: Passover, The Omer, Shavuot, Tisha b'Av*, Janet Greenstein Potter, ed. Philadelphia, PA: The Jewish Publication Society, 2009.
Steinfels, Peter. "The Jewishness of Jesus," in *No Religion Is an Island: The Nostra Aetate Dialogues*, Edward Bristow, ed. New York: Fordham University Press, 1998.
Stemplowski, Ryszard. *Transnational Terrorism in the World System Perspective*. Warsaw, Poland: Polish Institute of International Affairs, 2002.
Stephens, Barbara D. "Noah," in *Learn Torah with . . . , 1994–1995 Torah Annual: A Collection of the Year's Best Torah*, Joel L. Grishaver and Stuart Kelman, eds. Los Angeles, CA: Aleph Design Group, 1996.
Stephenson, Hunter W. *Forecasting Opportunity: Kairos, Production, and Writing*. Lanham, MD: University Press of America, 2005.
Stern, Kenneth S. "Proposal for a Redefinition of Antisemitism," in *Antisemitism Worldwide 2003/2004*. Tel Aviv, Israel: The Stephen Roth Institute, 2005.
Stillman, Norman A. "Dhima" in *Medieval Islamic Civilization: A–K, Index*, Josef W. Meri and Jere L. Bacharach, eds. Abingdon, UK: Routledge, 2006.
Stoff, Sheldon, and Barbara Smith Stoff. *Conscious Evolution: The Dance of Intuition and Intellect*. Bloomington, IN: iUniverse, 2010.
Straub, Ervin. *The Roots of Evil: The Origins of Genocide and Other Group Violence*. Cambridge, UK: Cambridge University Press, 1989.
Strauss, Leo. *Studies in Platonic Political Philosophy*. Chicago, IL: The University of Chicago Press, 2003.
_______*The Rebirth of Classical Political Rationalism: An Introduction to the Thought of Leo Strauss*. Chicago, IL: The University of Chicago Press, 1989.
Struble, Jr., Robert. "What Is Past Is Prologue: Dietrich von Hildebrand's 'Battle.'" *Catholic Lane* (Aug 03, 2015).
Sullivan, Bob. *Escape the Global Storm*. Maitland, FL: Xulon Press, 2008.
Sundquist, Eric J. *Strangers in the Land: Blacks, Jews, Post-Holocaust America*. Cambridge, MA: Harvard University Press, 2005.
Sutcliffe, Adam. *Judaism and Enlightenment*. Cambridge, UK: Cambridge University Press, 2003.
Sutton, Matthew Avery. *American Apocalypse: A History of Modern Evangelicalism*. Cambridge, MA: Harvard University Press, 2014.
Suzuki, Norio. "The Problem of Peace and World Order in an Islamic Context: The Case of Modern Japan," in *Peace Movements and Pacifism after September 11*, Shin Chiba and Thomas J. Schoenbaum, eds. Cheltenham, UK: Edward Elgar Publishing, 2008.
Svonkin, Stuart. *Jews against Prejudice: American Jews and the Fight for Civil Liberties*. New York: Columbia University Press, 1997.
Swanson, R. N., ed. *The Routledge History of Medieval Christianity: 1050–1500*. Abingdon, UK: Routledge, 2015.
Swedenburg, Ted. *Memories of Revolt: The 1936–1939 Rebellion and the Palestinian National Past*. Fayetteville, AR: The University of Arkansas Press, 2003.
Sylla, Ibrahima. "Mauritania's Parliament Passes Law Banning Slavery." *Reuters World News* (August 9, 2007).
Taban, Alfred. "Activist Says Child Slavery Exists in Sudan." *Reuters* (July 19, 1997).
Taha, Abir. *Nietzsche, Prophet of Nazism: The Cult of the Superman*. Bloomington, IN: AuthorHouse, 2005.
Tal, Alon. "Combating Desertification: Evolving Perceptions and Strategies," in *Between Ruin and Restoration: An Environmental History of Israel*, Daniel E. Orenstein, Alon Tal, and Char Miller, eds. Pittsburgh, PA: The University of Pittsburgh Press, 2013.

______*Pollution in a Promised Land: An Environmental History of Israe*l. Berkeley, CA: The University of California Press, 2002.

Taylor, Jane. *Petra and the Lost Kingdom of the Nabataeans*. London, UK: I. B. Tauris & Co., Ltd., 2002.

Tanenbaum, Marc H. *A Prophet for Our Time: An Anthology of the Writings of Rabbi Marc H. Tanenbaum*. New York: Fordham University Press, 2002.

Taylor, Bayard. *The Lands of the Saracen*. Alexandria, Egypt: The Library of Alexandria, 1854.

Telushkin, Joseph. *A Code of Jewish Ethics: Love Your Neighbor as Yourself*. New York: Bell Tower, 2009.

______*Jewish Literacy: The Most Important Things to Know about the Jewish Religion*. San Francisco: HarperCollins Publishers, 2001.

______*The Book of Jewish Values*. New York: Bell Tower Publishing, 2000.

Temporal, Paul. *Islamic Branding and Marketing: Creating A Global Islamic Business*. Hoboken, NJ: John Wiley & Sons, 2011.

ten Boom, Corrie, Elizabeth Sherrill, and John Sherrill. *The Hiding Place*. Grand Rapids, MI: Baker Publishing Group, 1971.

Tenen, Stan. *The Alphabet that Changed the World: How Genesis Preserves a Science of Consciousness in Geometry and Gesture*. Berkeley, CA: North Atlantic Books, 2011.

Teplinsky, Sandra. *Why Care about Israel? How the Jewish Nation Is Key to Unleashing God's Blessings in the 21st Century*. Grand Rapids, MI: Baker Publishing Group, 2004.

Tepper, Aryeh. "Christians in the Holy Land: Don't Call Us Arabs." *The Tower*, Issue 22 (January 2015).

Tessler, Mark A. *A History of the Israeli-Palestinian Conflict*. Bloomington, IN: Indiana University Press, 1994.

Thirgood, J. V. *Man and the Mediterranean Forest*. London, UK: Academic Publishers, 1981.

Thomas, W. H. Griffith. "The Lord's Coming and the Supreme Theme of the Bible." *The Christian Workers Magazine*, vol. XX, no. 1 (September, 1919), 96.

Thompson, Deanna A. *Crossing the Divide: Luther, Feminism, and the Cross*. Minneapolis, MN: Augsburg Fortress Press, 2004.

Thompson,Thomas L. *Early History of the Israelite People*. Leiden, The Netherlands: Koninklijke Brill NV, 1992.

______*The Historicity of the Patriarchal Narratives*. London: T & T Clark, 2002.

______*The Mythic Past: Biblical Archaeology and the Myth of Israel*. New York: Basic Books, 1999.

Thurston, Herbert. "History of Toleration," in *The Catholic Encyclopedia*. New York: Robert Appleton Company, 1913.

Tierney, Patrick. *The Highest Altar: The Story of Human Sacrifice*. New York: Viking Press, 1989.

Tilley, Virginia. *The One-State Solution: A Breakthrough for Peace in the Israeli-Palestinian Deadlock*. Ann Arbor, MI: The University of Michigan Press, 2005.

Timbrell, John Hamilton. *The Last Message of Jesus Christ: or, The Apocalypse in a New Light*. New York: Eaton & Mains, 1905.

Times of Israel Staff. "Palestinians Paid Terrorists $1b in Past 4 Years, Knesset Panel Hears." *The Times of Israel* (May 29, 2017).

______"Nasrallah, in Vicious Public Address, Calls for the Destruction of Israel." *The Times of Israel* (August 2, 2015).

Tingle, Donald S. *Islam & Christianity*. Downers Grove, IL: InterVarsity Press, 1985.

Tobin, Gary A., and Dennis R. Ybarra. *The Trouble with Textbooks: Distorting History and Religion*. Lanham, MD: Rowman & Littlefield Publishers, 2008.

______, Aryeh Kaufmann Weinberg, and Jenna Ferer. *The UnCivil University: Intolerance on College Campuses*. Lanham, MD: Rowman & Littlefield Publishers, 2009.

Tobin, Jonathan S. "Why Gaza Doesn't Have Bomb Shelters." *Commentary* (07.12.2014).

Todd, Emmanuel. *Who Is Charlie? Xenophobia and the New Middle Class*. Cambridge, UK: Plity Press, 2015.

Tolan, Sandy. *Children of the Stone: The Power of Music in a Hard Land*. New York: Bloomsbury Publishing, 2015.

Tomson, Peter J. "The Didache, Matthew, and Barnabas," in *Jews and Christians in the First and Second Centuries: How to Write Their History*, Peter J. Tomson and Joshua J. Schwartz, eds. Leiden, The Netherlands: Koninklijke Brill NV, 2014.

Topper, David R. *Idolatry and Infinity: Of Art, Math, and God*. Boca Raton, FL: Universal Publishers, 2014.

Torrance, Thomas Forsyth, *The Mediation of Christ*. Grand Rapids, MI: Wm. B. Eerdmans Publishing Co., 1984.

Totten, Samuel, and Stephen Feinberg. "Teaching and Studying the Holocaust: Curricular Issues, Teaching Strategies, and Learning Activities," in *Essentials of Holocaust Education: Fundamental Issues and Approaches*, Samuel Totten and Stephen Feinberg, eds. Abingdon, UK: Routledge, 2016.

______*Teaching about Genocide: Issues, Approaches and Resources*. Charlotte, NC: Information Age Publishing, Inc., 2004.

Towner, W. Sibley. "Exodus 20:1–17, Exegetical Perspective," in *Feasting on the Word: Lent through Eastertide*, David Lyon Bartlett and Barbara Brown Taylor, eds. Louisville, KY: Westminster John Knox Press, 2008.

Trachtenberg, Joshua. *The Devil and the Jews: The Medieval Conception of the Jew and Its Relation to Modern Antisemitism*. Philadelphia, PA: Jewish Publication Society, 1983.

Trepp, Leo. *Judaism: Development and Life*. Belmont, CA: Dickenson Publishing Co., 1966.
Troy, Gil. *Moynihan's Moment: America's Fight against Zionism as Racism*. Oxford, UK: Oxford University Press, 2013.
______*The Key to the Middle East: Discovering the Future of Israel in Biblical Prophecy*. Bloomington, MN: Chosen Books, 1982.
Turner, David. "From Anti-Judaism to Antisemitism: The Enlightenment." *The Jerusalem Post* (11/08/2012).
Tutu, Desmond. "Apartheid in the Holy Land." *The Guardian (*April 28, 2002).
Twain, Mark. *The Innocents Abroad: The New Pilgrims' Progress*. Hartford, CT: The American Publishing Co., 1869.
Twerski, Abraham J. *The Enemy Within: Confronting Your Challenges in the 21st Century*. Brooklyn, NY: Shaar Press, 2002.
Tyerman, Christopher. *God's War: A New History of the Crusades*. Cambridge, UK: Belknap Press, 2006.
Umen, Samuel. *Jewish Concepts and Reflections*. New York: Philosophical Library, 1962.
Uschan, Michael V. *Terrorism in Today's World: Suicide Bombings in Israel and Palestinian Terrorism*. Milwaukee, WI: World Almanac Library, 2006.
van Buren, Paul M. *A Theology of the Jewish-Christian Reality: A Christian Theology of the People of Israel*. Lanham, MD: University Press of America, 1995.
van der Horst, Peter Willem, *Philo's Flaccus: The First Pogrom (Philo of Alexandria Commentary Series)*. Leiden, The Netherlands: Koninklijke Brill NV, 2003.
van Loon, Hans. *The Dyophysite Christology of Cyril of Alexandria*. Leiden, The Netherlands: Koninklijke Brill NV, 2009.
van Pelt, Robert Jan. *The Case for Auschwitz: Evidence from the Irving Trial*. Bloomington, IN: Indiana University Press, 2002.
Van Seters, John. *Abraham in History and Tradition*. Brattleboro, VT: Echo Point Books & Media, 2014.
______*Prologue to History*. New Haven, CT: The Yale University Press, 1992.
Verete, Mayir. "The Restoration of the Jews in English Protestant Thought, 1790–1840." *Middle Eastern Studies*, vol. 8, no. 1 (1972), 14.
Vermeulen, Pieter. "The Novel Form and the Timing of the Nation," in *See Under: Shoah: Imagining the Holocaust with David Grossman*, Marc De Kesel, Bettine Giertsmea, and Katarzyna Szurmiak, eds. Leiden, The Netherlands: Koninklijke Brill NV, 2014.
Verlin, Jerome R. and Lee S. Bender. *Pressing Israel: Media Bias Exposed from A–Z*. Philadelphia, PA: Pavilion Press, 2012.
Vlach, Michael J. *Has the Church Replaced Israel? A Theological Evaluation*. Nashville, TN: B & H Publishing Group, 2010.
______"Israel in Church History," in *The People, the Land, and the Future of Israel: Israel and the Jewish People*, Darrell L. Bock and Mitch Glaser, eds. Grand Rapids, MI: Kregel Publications, 2014.
von Hildebrand, Dietrich. *My Battle against Hitler: Defiance in the Shadow of the Third Reich*, John H. Crosby and John F. Crosby, trs. and eds. New York: Random House, 2014.
Vulliamy, Elsa, "6 in 10 French People Think Jews Are Responsible for Anti-Semitism, Survey Finds." *The Independent* (3 February 2016).
Waagenaar, Sam. *The Pope's Jews*. Chicago, IL: Open Court Pub. Co., 1974.
Wagner, Matthew. "Israel's Only Crematorium To Re-open." *The Jerusalem Post* (10/28/2007).
Waithe, Mary Ellen, ed. *Ancient Women Philosophers: 600 B.C.–500 A.D.* Dordrecht, The Netherlands: Martinus Nijhoff Publishers, 1987.
Wallace, Cynthia D. *Foundations of the International Legal Rights of the Jewish People and the State of Israel and Implications for the Proposed Palestinian State*. Lake Mary, FL: Creation House, 2012.
Wangila, Mary Nyangwesto. *Female Circumcision: The Interplay of Religion, Culture and Gender in Kenya*. Maryknoll, NY: Orbis Books, 2007.
Ware, Kallistos. "'In the Image and Likeness': The Uniqueness of the Human Person," in *Personhood: Orthodox Christianity and the Connection between Body, Mind, and Soul*, John T. Chirban, ed. Westport, CT: Bergin & Garvey, 1996.
Warraq, Ibn. *The Origins of the Koran: Classic Essays on Islam's Holy Book*. Amherst, NY: Prometheus Books, 1998.
______*Why I Am Not a Muslim*. Amherst, NY: Prometheus Books, 2003.
Watson, Richard. *An Exposition of the Gospels of St. Matthew and St. Mark and Some Other Detached Parts of Holy Scripture*. London, UK: John Mason, 1833.
Weaver, Alain Epp. *Mapping Exile and Return: Palestinian Dispossession and Political Theology*. Minneapolis, MN: Augsburg Fortress Press, 2014.
Webb, Matthew J. *Kashmir's Right to Secede: A Critical Examination of Contemporary Theories of Secession*. Abingdon, UK: Routledge, 2012.
Wegner, J. R. "Islamic and Talmudic Jurisprudence: The Four Roots of Islamic Law and Their Talmudic Counterparts." *American Journal of Legal History* 26 (1982), 26–29.
Wei, James. *Great Inventions that Changed the World*. Hoboken, NJ: John Wiley & Sons, 2012.

Weikart, Richard. *From Darwin to Hitler: Evolutionary Ethics, Eugenics, and Racism in Germany*. New York: Palgrave Macmillan, 2004.

______*Hitler's Ethic: The Nazi Pursuit of Evolutionary Progress*. New York: Palgrave Macmillan, 2009.

Wein, Berel. *Patterns in Jewish History: Insights into the Past, Present, and Future of the Eternal People*. Jerusalem, Israel: Koren Publishers, 2011.

Weinthal, Benjamin. "Why Europe Blames Israel for the Holocaust: Post-1945 Anti-Semitism." *The Jerusalem Post* (01/28/2014).

Weir, Alison. "Christian Evangelicals Increasingly Support Palestinian Human Rights." *CounterPunch* (September 29, 2014).

Weizmann, Chaim. *Trial and Error: The Autobiography of Chaim Weizmann*. Westport, CT: Greenwood Publishing Group, 1972.

Wellman, Christopher Heath. *Liberal Rights and Responsibilities: Essays on Citizenship and Sovereignty*. Oxford, UK: Oxford University Press, 2014.

Wenkel, David. "Palestinians, Jebusites, and Evangelicals." *Middle East Quarterly* (Summer 2007), 49–56.

West, Diana. *American Betrayal: The Secret Assault on Our Nation's Character*. New York: St Martin's Press, 2013.

Westermann, Claus. *Genesis 12–36: Continental Commentary*. Minneapolis, MN: Fortress Press, 1995.

Wheatcroft, Andrew. *Infidels: A History of the Conflict between Christendom and Islam*. New York: Random House, 2005.

White, Ben. *Israeli Apartheid: A Beginners Guide*. London, UK: Pluto Press, 2009.

White, L. Michael. "Repentance," in *Encyclopedia of Early Christianity*, Everett Ferguson, ed. Abingdon, UK: Routledge, 1999.

Whitelam, Keith. *The Invention of Ancient Israel*. Abingdon, UK: Routledge, 1996.

Wiedmer, Caroline Alice. *The Claims of Memory: Representations of the Holocaust in Contemporary Germany and France*. Ithaca, NY: Cornell University Press, 1999.

Wiesenthal, Simon. *Sails of Hope: The Secret Mission of Christopher Columbus*, Richard Winston and Clara Winston, trs. New York: MacMillan Publishing Co., 1979.

Wiesel, Elie. *Messengers of God: Biblical Portraits and Legends*, tr. Marion Wiesel. New York: Simon & Schuster, 2005.

______"Trivializing the Holocaust: Semi-Fact and Semi-Fiction." *The New York Times* (April 16, 1978), § 2, 29.

______ *Twilight: A Novel*, tr. Marion Wiesel. New York: Summit Books, 1998.

Wilber, Ken. *The Eye of Spirit: An Integral Vision for a World Gone Slightly Mad*. Boston, MA: Shambhala Publications, Inc., 2001.

Wilcox, Howard D. *Divine Providence*. Bloomington, IN: Life Way Publishers, 2011.

Wilensky, Gabriel. *Six Million Crucifixions: How Christian Teachings about Jews Paved the Road to the Holocaust*. San Diego, CA: Qwerty Publishers, 2010.

Wiley, Tatha. *Original Sin: Origins, Developments, Contemporary Meanings*. Mahwah, NJ: Paulist Press, 2002.

Wilken, Robert L. "Christian Pilgrimage to the Holy Land," in *City of the Great King: Jerusalem from David to the Present*, Nitza Rosovsky, ed. Cambridge, MA: Harvard University Press, 1996.

Wilkinson, Robert J. *Tetragrammaton: Western Christians and the Hebrew Name of God*. Leiden, The Netherlands: Koninklijke Brill NV, 2015.

Williams, Paul R. "The Spirit of Amalek." *Restore!*, Issue 25, 16–18.

Williamson, Clark M. *A Guest in the House of Israel: Post-Holocaust Church Theology*. Louisville, KY: Westminster John Knox Press, 1993.

Willis, Ellen. *Beginning to See the Light: Sex, Hope, and Rock-and-Roll*. Minneapolis, MN: The University of Minnesota Press, 2013.

Wilson, Arthur. *Diderot*. Oxford, UK: Oxford University Press, 1972.

Wilson, Dwight. *Armageddon Now: The Premillenarian Response to Russia and Israel since 1917*. Grand Rapids, MI: Baker Book House, 1977.

Wilson, Marvin R. *Exploring Our Hebraic Heritage: A Christian Theology of Roots and Renewal*. Grand Rapids, MI: Wm. B. Eerdmans Publishing Co., 2014.

______*Our Father Abraham: Jewish Roots of the Christian Faith*. Grand Rapids, MI: Wm. B. Eerdmans Publishing Co., 1989.

Wilson, Mary Christian. *King Abdullah, Britain and the Making of Jordan*. Cambridge, UK: Cambridge University Press, 1987.

Wise, Stephen S., in *Momentous Century: Personal and Eyewitness Accounts of the Rise of the Jewish Homeland and State 1875–1878*, Levi Soshuk and Azriel Louis Eisenberg, eds. Cranbury, NJ: Cornwall Books, 1984.

Wine, Sherwin T. *A Provocative People: A Secular History of the Jews*. Farmington Hills, MI: International Institute for Secular Humanistic Judaism, 2012.

Wistrich, Robert S. *A Lethal Obsession: Anti-Semitism from Antiquity to the Global Jihad*. New York:

Random House, 2010.
______*Anti-Zionism and Antisemitism in the Contemporary World*. Basingstoke, UK: Macmillan Press, Ltd., 1990.
______*From Ambivalence to Betrayal: The Left, the Jews, and Israel*. Lincoln, NE: The University of Nebraska Press, 2012.
______"Gaza, Hamas, and the Return of Antisemitism." *The Israel Journal of Foreign Affairs*, VIII:3 (July, 2014), 38.
______, ed. *Holocaust Denial: The Politics of Perfidy*. Berlin, Germany: Walter de Gruyter GmbH & Co., 2012.
Wolf, Alex. *The Arab-Israeli War since 1948*. Chicago, IL: Capstone Global Library, 2012.
Wolfe, Robert. *From Habiru to Hebrews and Other Essays*. Minneapolis, MN: Mill City Press, Inc., 2011.
Wood, Leon J. *A Survey of Israel's History*. Grand Rapids, MI: Zondervan Publishing House, 1970.
Wylen, Stephen M. *Settings of Silver: An Introduction to Judaism*. Mahwah, NJ: Paulist Press, 2000.
Wyman, David S. *The Abandonment of the Jews: America and the Holocaust, 1941–1945*. New York: The New Press, 1998.
Wynbrandt, James. *A Brief History of Saudi Arabia*. New York: Infobase Publishing, 2004.
Wyschogrod, Michael. *Abraham's Promise: Judaism and Jewish-Christian Relations*. Grand Rapids, MI: Wm. B. Eerdmans Publishing Co., 2004.
______"Faith and the Holocaust," *Judaism* 20 (1971), 286–294.
Yakira, Elhanan. "Antisemitism and Anti-Zionism as a Moral Question," in *Resurgent Antisemitism: Global Perspectives*, Alvin H. Rosenfeld, ed. Bloomington, IN: Indiana University Press, 2013.
______"Five Reflections on Holocaust Denial, Old and New Forms of Hatred of Jews and the Deligitimation of Israel," in *Antisemitism before and since the Holocaust*, Anthony McElligott and Jeffrey Herf, eds. New York: Palgrave Macmillan, 2017.
Yardeni, Myriam. "New Concepts of Post-Commonwealth Jewish History in the Early Enlightenment: Bayle and Basnage." *European Studies Review* 7.3 (1977), no. 90, 251.
Yehuda, Zvi. "*Ve-Khof Et Yitzrenu Le-Hishtabed Lakh*—Direct Our Impulses [*Yetzer*]," in *Yom Kippur Readings: Inspiration, Information, Contemplation*, Dov Peretz Elkins, ed. Woodstock, VT: Jewish Lights Publishing, 2005.
Ye'or, Bat. *The Dhimmi: Jews and Christians under Islam*. Madison, NJ: Fairleigh Dickinson University Press, 1985.
Younan, Munib. *Witnessing for Peace: In Jerusalem and the World*. Minneapolis, MN: Augsburg Fortress Press, 2003.
Young, Brad H. *Paul the Jewish Theologian*. Peabody, MA: Hendrickson Publishing, 1997.
Young-Bruehl, Elisabeth. *The Anatomy of Prejudices*. Cambridge, MA: Harvard University Press, 1996.
Zahler, Diane. *The Black Death*. Minneapolis, MN: Lerner Publishing Group, 2009.
Zakim, Leonard P. *Confronting Anti-Semitism: A Practical Guide*. Hoboken, NJ: KTAV Publishing House, 2000.
Zander, Walter. *Israel and the Holy Places of Christendom*. London: Weidenfeld & Nicolson, 1991.
Zaslow, David. *Jesus: First-Century Rabbi*. Brewster, MA: Paraclete Press, 2014.
Zeitlin, Irving M. *The Historical Muhammad*. Cambridge, UK: Polity Press, 2007.
Zephyr, Alexander. *State of Israel: Its Friends and Enemies: Prophetic Future*. Bloomington, IN: iUniverse, 2013.
Zick, Andreas. "Anti-Semitism," in *Encyclopedia of Group Processes and Intergroup Relations*, John M. Levine and Michael A. Hogg, eds. Thousand Oaks, CA: SAGE Publications, Inc., 2010.
Zimmermann, Moshe. *Wilhelm Marr: The Patriarch of Anti-Semitism*. Oxford, UK: Oxford University Press, 1986.
Zolfagharifard, Ellie. *The Daily Mail*. (1 October 2013).
Zuckerman, Bruce, and Zev Garber. *The Impact of the Holocaust in America*. West Lafayette, IN: Purdue University Press, 2008.
Zweig, Ferdynand. *Israel: The Sword and the Harp: The Mystique of Violence and the Mystique of Redemption; Controversial Themes in Israeli Society*. Cranbury, NJ: Associated University Presses, 1969.

# INDEX

## S



## T



## U



## V



## W



## X



## Y



## Z

*Featuring the Informative, Inspiring Books of*
## Dr. John D. Garr

***God and Israel: Chosen People, Holy Nation, Promised Land*** is a comprehensive study of the continuing fulfillment of God's four-thousand-year-old immutable and irrevocable covenant with Abraham which empowered his descendants to inherit the land of Israel centuries ago and has produced the miracle of the restored people, nation, and land of Israel today.
432 pages, ISBN 978-1-940685-27-4.

***Life from the Dead: The Dynamic Saga of the Chosen People*** examines the sweep of history to discover the amazing divine protection that has been upon the children of Abraham in order to preserve them through constant threat of extinction and to establish them as the people of God. This volume demonstrates unequivocally the resurrection power of God in everyday life.
380 pages, ISBN 978-1-940685-20-5.

***Christian Fruit: Jewish Root: Theology of Hebraic Restoration*** is an in-depth study of the foundational principles of Christian faith which reveals the Jewish roots of each principle from the Hebrew Scriptures and from the teachings of Second Temple Judaism. This volume provides solid academic insight into the biblically Hebraic foundations of the Christian faith.
416 pages, ISBN 978-1-940685-27-4.

***Blessings for Family and Friends*** provides you with solid information about God's blessing system and with demonstrations and examples of blessings that you can pronounce over your family and friends for all occasions. This is a spectacular gift book that you will want to keep for yourself. Amazing blessings await you in this inspiring and beautiful volume.
160 pages, ISBN 978-0-9794514-3-0.

***Tehillim: The Psalms of King David*** is a stunningly beautiful leather-bound edition that features insightful Hebrew-English study of the most inspirational of the 150 Psalms of David. This volume helps believers understand and claim the blessings that God has provided for them. Your faith will be expanded, and your life will be enriched as you use this book.
110 pages, ISBN 978-0-9996-264716.

*God and Women: Woman in God's Image and Likeness* is a comprehensive, scholarly examination of the way in which God created woman in order to mirror the divine image and likeness. This book will take you back to the beginning of the Genesis narrative when God created humanity male and female and then made them one: coequal, consubstantial, and complementary.
320 pages, ISBN 978-0-9794514-4-7.

*Coequal and Counterbalanced: God's Blueprint for Women and Men* is an in-depth analysis of God's creation of humanity with a focus on the coequality of male and female that makes it possible for men and women to live counterbalanced and complementary lives of loving mutuality and respect. These pages will give you new insight about female and male relationships.
368 pages, ISBN 978-0-9794514-9-2.

*Feminine by Design: The God-Fashioned Woman* is an exhaustive study of the manner in which God designed woman in the beginning of time with all the unique qualities, characteristics, and preferences that have made all women uniquely feminine and equipped with the means by which they can achieve self-fulfillment in family, society, and church.
368 pages, ISBN 978-0-9794514-5-4.

*Our Lost Legacy: Restoring Christianity's Hebrew Foundations* is a provocative, inspiring primer on the Jewish roots of the Christian faith. This volume presents selected essays in which Dr. John D. Garr urges the church to recover its Hebrew heritage. These pages call Christians back to the Bible, to the roots of their faith, and to the understanding of their Hebrew Lord.
240 pages, ISBN 0-96782797-2-2.

*Generosity: The Righteous Path to Divine Blessing* is a study of the Hebraic foundations of biblical giving with a view to understanding why believers should tithe and give of their means. It is only through the Hebraic model of generosity that people can find the amazing blessings that God has promised to those who obey him and his precepts for living.
304 pages, ISBN 978-1-940685-20-5.

*God's Lamp, Man's Light: Mysteries of the Menorah* is a masterful analysis of the menorah, the only biblical symbol that has the distinction of being designed by God himself. As you read this book, you will be amazed at the wealth of insight that has been hidden from the historical church because of its separation from Judaism and things Jewish.
160 pages, ISBN 0-9678279-4-9.

*Family Worship: Making Your Home a House of God* is a provocative look at the modern home that offers clear answers for families in crisis and for those who want to restore their families to biblical foundations. Reading this book will be a life-changing experience for you and for your family as you learn to adopt a biblical family lifestyle by doing what Bible teaches about family.
240 pages, ISBN 978-0-9794514-7-8.

*Bless You! Restoring the Power of Biblical Blessing* is a systematic, comprehensive study of the biblically Hebraic concept of blessing and the impact that it has had in the lives of believers from ancient times until today. This powerful dynamic of biblical faith can now be experienced in every Christian home. As you read this, you will recover a key part of the faith of Jesus and the apostles.
160 pages, ISBN 096782797-7-3.

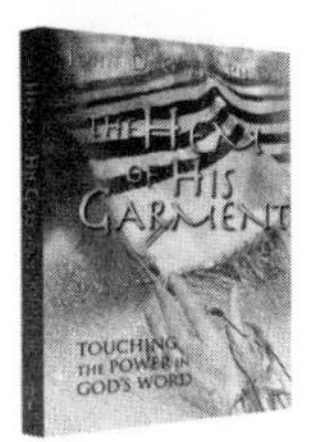


*The Hem of His Garment: Touching the Power in God's Word* discusses the context of the woman who was healed when she touched the hem of Jesus' garment. You will simply be amazed at the great impact that the ancient Jewish tradition of attaching fringes to the four corners of their mantles had upon the lives of biblical people, including this woman.
160 pages, ISBN 0-96782797-0-6.

*Living Emblems: Ancient Symbols of Faith* will help you understand the biblical symbols that were designed by God and by his people Israel. Each emblem is full of rich insight that points to the person and work of the Messiah, Jesus. Recognizing these spiritual truths is a profound means of underscoring the truth of Christianity's Jewish connection.
160 pages, ISBN 096782797-1-4.

*Passover: The Festival of Redemption* helps Christians understand the biblical festival that is part of their heritage, celebrating the Exodus and Calvary. With this exciting resource, you can celebrate Passover just as Jesus and the disciples did at the Last Supper. And you can remember the Lord's death as he commanded at the time when he died.
160 pages, ISBN 978-0-9794514-6-1.

# Christian *Teshuvah*

## Repentance for Antisemitism

WHEREAS I recognize that for centuries the Christian church has been characterized by antisemitism that has been manifest in word, through caricatures and vilifications of the Jewish people, and in deed, through systematic and unrelenting acts of violence and murder against individual Jewish men, women, and children and against the corporate Jewish community, and

WHEREAS I recognize my connection with the historical church either literally through the traditional doctrine of the communion of saints or figuratively by association through the collective consciousness of the Jewish people, and

WHEREAS in true repentance, I wish to acknowledge, confess, renounce, and turn from these sins against the Jewish people,

NOW, THEREFORE, in the spirit of Ezra and Daniel, who repented on behalf of all of their people, I hereby acknowledge, confess, and renounce the individual and corporate sins of the Christian church against the Jewish people, sins that have been manifest in (1) Judaeophobia—the fear of Jews and things Jewish that has been ingrained into the corporate consciousness of the church, (2) anti-Judaism—the church's sin of supersessionism in teaching that God rejected Judaism and Israel and replaced them with Christianity and the church, (3) antisemitism—attempts to degrade, debase, dehumanize, and destroy the Jewish people and their faith, and (4) silence and absence of protest against others who have so abused the Jewish people and their faith.

I ACKNOWLEDGE, confess, renounce, and turn from any conscious or subconscious sins of Judaeophobia, anti-Judaism, and antisemitism, or silent neglect on my own part. I personally resolve to support in word and in deed the right of all the Jewish people to exist as Jews with complete self-determination, free from political, economic, social, or religious coercion, intimidation, or persecution, and I hereby profess my determination to stand with the international Jewish community against any threat, whether individual or corporate.

I HEREBY ATTEST that I have been adopted into the family of Abraham by virtue of my personal faith in Jesus Christ, the son of David, the son of Abraham, who caused Israel's light to come to the nations, and I also affirm my identity with the corporate body of the international Jewish community by virtue of my personal faith in the God of Israel and by being grafted into Israel, God's Family Tree.

In witness whereof, I have set my seal to execute this document on this ____________________day of ________________________, ____________.

Signed________________________________________

Hebraic Christian Global Community
P. O. Box 421218
Atlanta, GA 30342